JEWS AND MUSLIMS IN THE ISLAMIC WORLD

JEWS AND MUSLIMS IN THE ISLAMIC WORLD

edited by
Bernard Dov Cooperman and Zvi Zohar

University Press of Maryland
Bethesda, Maryland
2013

LIBRARY OF CONGRESS CATALOGING-IN-PUBLICATION DATA

Jews and Muslims in the Islamic world / edited by Zvi Zohar and Bernard Dov Cooperman.
p. cm.
Includes bibliographical references.
ISBN 978-1-934309-32-2 (alk. paper)
1. Judaism—Relations—Islam. 2. Islam—Relations—Judaism. I. Zohar, Zvi.

BP173.J8J485 2012
296.3'97091767—dc23 2012020589

ISBN 9781934309322

Studies and Texts
in
Jewish History and Culture

The Joseph and Rebecca Meyerhoff Center
for Jewish Studies
University of Maryland

UNIVERSITY OF MARYLAND 1856

XXI

General Editor: Bernard D. Cooperman

and

The Dahan Center, Bar-Ilan University

אוניברסיטת בר-אילן
מרכז דהאן
המרכז לחברה, תרבות וחינוך במורשת יהדות ספרד
ע"ש אהרן ורחל דהאן

UNIVERSITY PRESS OF MARYLAND

Contents

Preface

In August 2007 a major conference was held at the University of Maryland, jointly sponsored by two Academic Centers: The Dahan Center of Bar Ilan University and the Meyerhoff Center of the University of Maryland. The Aharon and Rachel Dahan Center for Culture, Society and Education in the Sephardic Heritage was established with the aim of promoting and preserving Jewish heritage by encouraging awareness of the cultural riches of the Jewish Sephardic communities. The Center conducts an extensive program of activities in the academic and educational spheres, as well as for the general public: seminars and international conferences, research and publication of academic papers, university courses, tours, exhibitions, cultural evenings, in-service training courses and workshops for teachers, projects for high schools students, etc.

The Joseph and Rebecca Meyerhoff Center for Jewish Studies is devoted to the research and study of Judaism and the Jewish people in all periods and places. The Center is home to a multi-disciplinary faculty with expertise drawn from a broad range of humanistic and social scientific disciplines. The Center offers undergraduate programs for majors and minors in Jewish Studies, Israel Studies, and Religious Studies. The Center also offers Master's candidates a wide range of programs aimed at both academic and pedagogic careers.

The joint conference was convened under the title "Jews and Muslims in the World of Islam," and was co-chaired by Prof. Bernard Cooperman of the University of Maryland and Prof. Michael M. Laskier of Bar Ilan University.[1] Over the course of three days, 37 scholars from six countries presented papers on a wide variety of topics. Of the 20 articles in the current volume, 15 are based on lectures given at that conference, and the others are contributions by scholars who were unable to attend in person (Abourabia, Bar-Asher, Bornstein-Makovetsky, Charvit and Mualem). All articles are original

---

1 For personal reasons, Prof. Laskier was unable to participate in editing this volume, and Prof. Zvi Zohar agreed to assume that task in his stead.

works of scholarship and all were accepted for publication only after rigorous peer review.

Geographically, the articles range from Yemen in the south-east (Mualem) to France in the north-west (Hershco), encompassing the Middle East, including Israel (Abourabia, Bornstein-Makovetsky, Charvit, Harel, Reiter, Seroussi, Shemesh, Shtober), North Africa, with special emphasis on Morocco (Amzallag, Bar-Asher, Bin-Nun, Charvit, Hassine, Kenbib, Simon) and Spain (Ray, Tobi). Chronologically, articles begin with late antiquity (Cassuto), through medieval Spain (Ray, Tobi), the sixteenth to the eighteenth centuries (Bornstein-Makovetsky, Pomeroy, Seroussi, Shemesh, Shtober), the nineteenth and twentieth centuries (Amzallag, Bar-Asher, Bin-Nun, Harel, Hassine, Kenbib, Simon), and up to the present: the late twentieth and early twenty-first centuries (Abourabia, Charvit, Hershco, Mualem, Reiter). Note that while the title of each article reflects its major theme, many articles relate to more than one issue. By way of example, Seroussi's article relates not only to music but also to links between Jewish and Muslim mystical traditions, Shemesh's article is significant not only with regard to medicine but also with regard to the development of Jewish Law (*halakha*) about desecration of the Sabbath, and Simon's article reflects not only attitudes of Libyan Jews to Muslims but also their view of Italian and British rule.

Now that the volume is ready for publication the editors would like to extend their thanks and appreciation to Dr. Shimon Ohayon of the Dahan Center and Prof. Hayim Lapin, then Director of the Meyerhoff Center, for their support and encouragement over the years. Above all we must thank Ms. Ora Kobelkowsky, who on an almost daily basis over more than four years ably and painstakingly oversaw editing the articles, sometimes having to deal with overly occupied and not overly responsive authors.

We are gratified and somewhat relieved to have (finally) reached this point and hope that the contents of the volume will be of interest to both scholars and laypersons who care about Jewish life in Muslim lands and about Jewish-Muslim relations and interactions throughout the ages.

Bernard D. Cooperman, Maryland
Zvi Zohar, Israel

Conversion to and from Islam

KHALIL ABOURABIA

The Prophet Muhammad (born at Mecca in 570) was the last of the prophets. He began his prophecy in order to spread the Islamic religion. The Qur'ān was revealed in stages over a period of 23 years (610–632), and not as a complete book in one single act of revelation. In Islam, the other prophets and religions are mentioned, and a great deal of emphasis is placed on spreading Islam. It is important to mention that the five pillars of Islam (*arkan al-Islam*) are five duties incumbent upon every Muslim. These duties are *shahada*, the basic creed of Islam: "I testify that there is no god (deity) but Allah, and I testify that Muhammad is fully submitted and messenger of Allah." The second pillar of Islam is the *salat*, the requirement to pray five times a day at fixed times. The third pillar is *zakat*, alms-giving. The fourth pillar is *sawm*, fasting during the month of Ramadan from dawn to sunset. The fifth pillar is the *hajj*, pilgrimage; every able-bodied Muslim is obliged to make the pilgrimage to the holy city of Mecca once in his lifetime if he can afford it.

Non-Muslims wishing to convert to Islam are required to recite the *shahada* in front of at least two adult Muslim witnesses. It is recommended that the converted adopt a Muslim name, take a basic course on Islam, and keep in the company of other Muslims. A man converting to Islam should have his head shaved either before or after taking the formal *shahada*. A boy who has not attained puberty must be circumcised when he converts to Islam. Circumcision is optional for a man above the age of puberty. The converted adopts a Muslim name for the sake of identification as a Muslim, because when Muslim enter Mecca and Medina to perform pilgrimage, the pilgrim must produce a document proving that he or she is a Muslim, since non-Muslims are forbidden to enter these cities.

Islam, from its emergence in the Arabian Peninsula in the seventh century to its current expansion, won converts and was adopted by entire ethnic groups in Asia and Africa,[1] and was considered to be an indigenous religion. Conversion to Islam has continued for the last fourteen centuries in the East

1 Nehemiah Levtzion, ed., *Conversion to Islam* (New York & London: Holmes & Meier Publications, Inc., 1979), 1.

and in the West.[2] It is worth noting that diversity has not destroyed the unity of Islam, and the many local forms and cultures should be considered as variations of one universal religion.[3]

Reviewed Literature

The process of conversion to Islam has its own internal dynamic. Lofland and Skonovd proposed a descriptive system for the study of religious conversion.[4] They identified six conversion motifs. Each motif is characterized by the degree of social pressure involved, temporal duration, and level of affective arousal, affective content, and the sequence of belief, participation. The six motifs are (1) "intellectual," which involves reading and other investigations of alternative theodicy. This motif is normally brief, entailing self-conversion with little social pressure; affective arousal is medium and the content illuminative; (2) "mystical," a situation that is an effectively intense, brief, ineffable experience and often occurs when a person is alone. Social pressure is low; affective content involves awe, love, or fear; (3) "experimental," in which the convert adopts a "show me and I'll try it" posture, with participation followed by belief; social pressure and affective arousal are low; (4) "affection," in which personal attachments or strong liking play a central role. Social pressure is medium, functioning as a support and an attraction; usually the process is relatively long, with participation preceding belief; (5) "revivalist," which is managed ecstatic arousal in a group context. Duration is brief, social pressure is high, and belief follows participation; (6) "coercive," in which compulsion, confession of guilt, and acceptance of the ideological system are central. Social pressure is high and belief follows participation. The process may be prolonged. The primary affect is fear, and love is secondary.

Lewis R. Rambo distinguished between religious groups that are affirmative of the wider world and those that reject or are suspicious of the world.[5] The latter are more likely to be considered "deviant," maintaining boundaries and exercising rigid control over communication beyond the group.

---

2 Ali Kose and Kate Miriam Loewenthal, "Conversion Motifs Among British Converts to Islam," *International Journal for the Psychology of Religion*, 10 (2000): 101–10; L. Poston, *Islamic Da'wah in the West* (New York: Oxford University Press, 1992).

3 Levtzion, *Conversion to Islam*, 1.

4 J. Lofland and N. Skonovd, "Conversion Motifs," *Journal for the Scientific Study of Religion*, 20 (1981): 373–85. The literature on conversion basically deals with new religious movements in the United States (Bruce 1999); Aldridge 2000) and does not include conversion to Islam. Although the spread of Islam in historical perspective has received attention (Richard Bulliet, "Conversion to Islam and the Emergence of a Muslim Society in Iran," in *Conversion to Islam*, ed. Levtzion, pp. 30–51; Dutton 1999), conversions in present-day Western countries are not widely covered.

5 Lewis R. Rambo, *Understanding Religious Conversion* (New Haven, Ct.: Yale University Press, 1993), 104–15.

World-affirming religious groups are open to seekers and employ loose encapsulation and low social pressure. Converts would be likely to report intellectual, experimental, and sometimes mystical motifs, reflecting the new converts' active search for new possibilities and the group's encouragement of the free pursuit of spiritual goals. A study carried out by Kose and Loewenthal dealing with conversion motifs among British converts to Islam reveals that the intellectual, experimental, and affection motifs were frequently present in the conversion biographies studied.[6] This means that the most frequent features of the religious biographies of those interviewed were searching for a meaning or a path in life by reading and discussion (intellectual); experimentation with Muslim religious requirements (such as prayer, diet, dress, and social relationships; experimental); and liking or esteem for Muslims or friendship, marriage, or both with a Muslim (affection). One way of looking at these findings sees two broad groups of converts to Islam. Members of the first group were more likely to be men, non-Sufi, not married to a Muslim at the time of conversion, and reporting intellectual and experimental motifs and a generally world-affirming conversion history. Among those interviewed, this is the normative conversion to Islam. Members of the second group were more likely to be women, Sufi, or both; married to a Muslim at the time of conversion; and reporting affection and mystical motifs and a more world-rejecting conversion history. Another study carried out by Kose finds that since Islam is an encompassing religious worldview and does not compartmentalize religion, choosing Islam enables the converts to connect their daily life to their beliefs.[7]

Luckmann presents a general background to the discussion of conversion to Islam in Europe by restating an outline of what is known about the social form of religion in contemporary Europe.[8] The main courses leading to the prevalence of this social form of religion are structural differentiation and a modern form of pluralism. The main consequences with respect to conversion are a changed frame both of subjective and social plausibility for the change from one optional way of life to another.

According to Allievi and Hofmann, the religious discourse of converts on the attraction of Islam over Christianity converges at certain points, for instance, the encompassing ritual praxis and the direct accessibility of God without mediators make Islam seem a rational and undeniable truth.[9]

Crossing religious and ethnic boundaries generally disturbs conventions and can engender hostility. Female conversion to Islam summons up partic-

---

6 Kose and Miriam, "Conversion Motifs," 101–10.

7 Ali Kose, "The Journey from the Secular to the Sacred: Experiences of Native British Converts to Islam," *Social Compass,* 46 (1999):301–12.

8 Thomas Luckmann, "The Religious Situation in Europe: The Background to Contemporary Conversions," *Social Compass*, 46 (1999): 251–58.

9 Allievi 1998 and Hofmann 1997.

ularly fierce battles because gender issues have been pivotal in the construction of Otherness between "Islam" and the "West." Female converts are thus regularly treated with hostility. Western female converts to Islam outnumber their male counterparts by an estimated ratio of 4:1.[10] Some academic research indicates, however, that maybe not four-fifths, but still two-thirds, of converts to Islam are female.[11] It is worth noting that for most western countries no statistics are available or the statistics do not distinguish between second-generation-born Muslims and native converts.

Allievi developed a useful typology of conversion itineraries to Islam.[12] He distinguishes relational from rational conversions. Relational conversions are further subdivided into instrumental and non-instrumental forms. Non-instrumental relational conversions are induced by relationships with Muslims either by way of marriage, family, meeting immigrants, or traveling. Instrumental conversions are usually related to marriage of a European male with a Muslim woman and do not necessarily entail a religious transformation. The rational conversions, in contrast, are not induced by personal contacts but rather by an intellectual search. This form is, therefore, more specifically Islamic in its discourse and rationalizations. Needless to say, that the rational conversion includes intellectual, political, or mystically oriented paths.

It is worth noting that ideas of religion as a commodity on the expanding market of religious goods, picked and chosen by religious agents, are particularly applied to new religious movements.[13] Yet ideas of the religious market and rational choice can be applied also to Islam.[14] Islam has become one of the players on the religious market in the West, and its message makes sense to individual converts.

McCloud understands the conversion of African Americans to Islam as a response to American racism.[15] Islam promises a new identity, a feeling of "somebodiness," denied by the dominant culture. Conversion brought liberation from Christian domination, perceived as the root of their oppression for its glorification of suffering and promise of redemption in the hereafter.

Muslims are obligated to proselytize. Moreover, under Islamic law, one who renounces Islam (*murtadd*) is subject to death. In the religious sense, the *da'wa* is the invitation, addressed to men by God and the prophets, to believe in the true religion, Islam (Qur'ān: XIV, 46). Muhammad's mission was to repeat the call and invitation.

---

10 Allievi 1998, 241; Nieuwkerk 2006.

11 Monika Wohlrab-Sahr, "Conversion to Islam: Between Syncretism and Symbolic Battle," *Social Compass* 46 (1999): 351–62; Haleem 2000.

12 Allievi 1998, 283–300.

13 Bruce 1999; Finke and Stark 2000.

14 Wohlrab-Sahr 2006.

15 Aminah McCloud, *African American Islam* (New York: Routledge, 1995).

Moreover, one who renounces Islam (*murtadd*) is subject to death. Apostasy is called *ridda*; it may be committed verbally by denying a principle of belief or by an action, such as treating a copy of the Qur'ān with disrespect. The Prophet is said to have permitted the blood to be shed *of murtadd* "he who abandons his religion and separates himself from the community."[16] According to the Islamic jurisprudence (*fiqh*) there is unanimity that a male apostate must be put to death, but only if he is an adult (*baligh*) and *compos mentis* (*'aqil*) and has not acted under compulsion.[17]

The *Shari'a* recognizes the existence of a non-Muslim population within the Muslim state. Intermarriages occurred between Muslim men and non-Muslim wives, and the children reared as Muslims. A Muslim man is permitted to marry any unmarried woman, provided she observes one of the religions of the Book, called *ketabiyya* (that is, Judaism or Christianity), with the implied hope that she will eventually convert to Islam. The husband of such a woman is considered to be doing a great deed by causing his wife to convert to Islam. Until her conversion, a non-Muslim wife has limited rights: she cannot inherit the property of her husband, and she cannot rear children in her own religion–they are automatically considered Muslims.

There are many reasons for non-Muslim men and women to convert to Islam. In eleventh-century Iran, conversion to Islam was undergone in order to be exempted from the poll tax and to retain governmental positions.[18] Conversion to Islam was advantageous, since social and political statuses were recorded in most regions under Muslim rule, for example, as with fief holders in the Ottoman Empire and *zamindaris* in Mughal India.[19]

Nomads carried the burden of the militant extension of Islam, and traders served as vehicles for the propagation of Islam beyond the boundaries of the military expansion. They carried Islam across the steppes to central Asia, as far as China, through the desert to sub-Saharan Africa, and over the ocean to Indonesia and East Africa. Trade and trade routes were important as lines of communication between remote Muslim communities and the centers of Islam.[20] Religious status, such as pilgrim (*hajj*), is important for trade at levels other than merely that of the new convert who is starting to trade, as it described by Last in Hausaland (Nigeria).[21] Conversion myths

---

16 Al-Bukhari, *Diyat, bab* 6; Muslim, *Qasama*, tr. 25, 26; al-Nasa'i, *Tahrim al-dam, bab* 5, 14.

17 W. Heffening, "Murtadd," in *Encyclopedia of Islam* (1999).

18 Bulliet (1979):30–51.

19 V. L. Menage, "The Islamization of Anatolia," in *Conversion to Islam*, ed. Levtzion, pp. 52–67; and *zamindaris* in Mughal India (P. Hardy, "Modern European and Muslim Explanations of Conversion to Islam in South Asia: A preliminary Survey of the Literature," in Levtzion, ed., *Conversion to Islam*, pp. 68–99).

20 Levtzion, ed., *Conversion to Islam*, pp. 15–16.

21 Murray Last, "Some Economic Aspects of Conversion in Hausaland-Nigeria," in Levtzion, ed., *Conversion to Islam*, pp. 236–46.

from Indonesia describe the arrival of Muslims by sea from the Arabian Peninsula via southern India; on board these ships there were saints, men of religion.[22] Islamization of each principality becomes the work of saints gifted with magical powers, if not of the Prophet himself. It is worth noting that saints and visits to holy saints are important feature of social life among people of Cyrenaica[23] and Morocco,[24] as well as elsewhere in the Muslim world.[25] The Bedouin make their pilgrimages to saints on the basis of three ties: those between the tribal members, those between the tribes of southern Sinai, and those between the tribal members and all of Islamic *Umma*.[26]

In eastern Sudan, the *fuqara'*,[27]as those divines are known there, were responsible for the southern thrust of the Islamic frontier between the fourteenth and the sixteenth centuries. As more *fuqara'* settled there, Islamic influence on the sultanate of Dar Fur increased.[28] Mystics of different sorts (Sufi Orders) played an important role in promoting conversion to Islam and furnished Islam's philosophical contact with different cultural and ethnic groups in the East, as well as in the West.[29]

Research Population

Today, there are more than seven million people living in Israel, 1.5 million of which are Arabs, constituting 20 percent of the overall population of the

22 Russell Jones, "Ten Conversion Myths from Indonesia," in Levtzion, ed., *Conversion to Islam*, pp.129–58.

23 E.E. Evans-Pritchard, *The Sanusi of Cyrenaica* (Oxford: Clarendon Press, 1949), 66–67; Emrys L. Peters, *The Bedouin of Cyrenaica* (Cambridge: Cambridge University Press, 1990), 107–8.

24 Ernest Gellner, *Saints of the Atlas* (London: Weidenfeld & Nicholson, 1969), 114–30; idem, *Muslim Society* (Cambridge: Cambridge University Press, 1983), 207–20.

25 Ignaz Goldziher, "Veneration of Saints in Islam," in *Muslim Studies*, vol. 2 (London: George Allen & Unwin Ltd., 1971), 268–78.

26 Emanuel Marx, "Bedouin Pilgrimages to Holy Tombs in Southern Sinai," *Notes on the Bedouin*, 8 (1977) 14–22.

27 According to some commentators the word *fuqara'* refers to the *ahl al-Suffa* who lived in the mosque of the Prophet and devoted all their time to prayers and meditation. In mystic terminology *faqir* means a person who "lives for the Lord alone"; he does not rest content with anything except God. Total rejection of private property and resignation to the will of God (*tawakkul*) were considered essential for a *faqir* who aspired for gnosis.

28 R.S. O'Fahey, "Islam, State, and Society in Dar Fur," in Levtzion, ed., *Conversion to Islam*, pp.18–206.

29 El-Sayed el-Aswad, "Spiritual Genealogy: Sufism and Saintly Places in the Nile Delta," *International Journal of Middle East Studies* 38 2006):501–18; Hardy, "Modern European," pp. 68–99; Meir Hatina, "Where East Meets West: Sufism, Cultural Rapprochement, and Politics," *International Journal of Middle East Studies* 39 (2007): 389–409; Menage, "The Islamization of Anatolia," 52–67.

country. Approximately 82 percent of Arabs in Israel are Sunni Muslims, the rest (200,000) are divided equally between Christians and Druze. All 1.5 million Arabs in Israel are citizens of Israel.

In Israel, matters of personal status are distinguished from those pertaining to other branches of the law in two main respects at least: the choice of jurisdiction and the choice of law. Matters concerning marriage and divorce are in the exclusive jurisdiction of the religious courts.[30] The religious courts in Israel are: the Muslim religious courts;[31] those of the recognized Christian communities;[32] the rabbinical courts;[33] and the Druze religious courts.[34] Application of the criterion of religious affiliation is likely to create situations in which a person may be deemed to be "without religion" or of "dual religion." This occurs when no religious group in Israel claims the individual as an adherent or when two religions each claim his exclusive adherence, as in the case of a child born of a Jewish mother and a Muslim father,[35] or in the case of a person who has changed his religion but is claimed by both faiths, the one that he abandoned and the one that he has newly adopted. According to Israeli legal authority, any person whose religious affiliation is claimed by two faiths cannot be considered a member of one particular religious community, but must be referred to as a person of "dual religion."[36]

My own experience has allowed me to examine the subject in depth, having performed years of research on the *Mahkama shar'iyya* in Beer-Sheva. A sampling of case studies from the *Mahkama shar'iyya* demonstrates the importance of this issue for the field of family law in Israel.

Case Study 1

In 1978, a Muslim man from Hebron with a Palestinian identity card married a Jewish woman of Romanian origin with an Israeli identity card. He applied to the *Shari'a* court to formalize the marriage and to have it approved, so that he could receive legal validation of the marriage in order to change his personal status from "bachelor" to "married" and in order to be eligible to receive an Israeli identity card. In the Ministry of Religion and

30 Menashe Shava, "Legal Aspects of Change of Religious Community in Israel," *Israel Yearbook on Human Rights*, 3 (1973): 256–69. See also Palestine Order-in-Council Art. 52.

31 Palestine Order-in-Council Art.52.

32 Art.54.

33 The Rabbinical Courts Jurisdiction, marriage and divorce-Law, 1953.

34 The Druze Religious Courts Law, 1962.

35 According to Jewish religious law, which is the personal law of the mother, the child is a Jew; according to Muslim religious law (*Shari'a*), which is the personal law of the father, the child is a Muslim.

36 Shava, "Legal Aspects," pp. 170–84.

the Ministry of Internal Affairs, the process of making these changes is lengthy and includes a number of stages. First, the wife must convert to Islam before she can request a Muslim marriage certificate from the *Shari'a* court. Conversion, according to Islamic religious law, is carried out in a very simple manner: the person requesting to convert must apply to the *Shari'a* court, where he or she will explain his/her motives for converting to Islam and abandoning his/her original religion. He or she then makes a declaration (*al-shahadatain*) that "God is one, there is no other, and Mohammed is the Prophet of Islam," and states that he or she renounces his or her former faith and takes upon himself the religion of Islam. This declaration takes place in the presence of two witnesses and before a Muslim religious judge (*qadi*).

In the case under discussion, as soon as this declaration was made, the wife received a certificate of conversion to Islam and became a Muslim according to Muslim religious law. She then changed her attire, to dress like the Palestinian women. From the moment she became a Muslim, she was eligible to marry in a *Shari'a* court. According to Israeli civil law, however, the woman was not yet a Muslim–she remained a Jew until the Muslim Department of the Ministry of Religion investigated her individual case in her presence. Only following this investigation could the Ministry of Religion grant the woman a certificate of religious conversion. The Ministry of the Interior is obligated to act in accordance with this certificate and not according to the certificate of conversion or marriage certificate provided by the *Shari'a* court.

In this particular case, the woman married and became pregnant. Following the birth of her son, Ramzi, the family moved to Hebron. The woman was operating under the assumption that she had officially become a Muslim. The process of officially changing her religious status took over two years, and eventually she had other children. Eighteen years later, Ramzi received a letter (sent to his mother's family in the south of Israel) informing him that he was absent without leave from the army. His parents asked me to intervene. When I contacted the draft board and explained that Ramzi was a Muslim Arab who was not required by law to serve in the military, I was told that this was not true and that Ramzi was Jewish. Despite all of my efforts I was unable to convince them that he was, in fact, from Hebron.

As it turned out, when Ramzi was born, his mother was still registered as Jewish. According to Jewish religious law, a child born to a Jewish mother is a Jew. This is in contrast to Muslim religious law, which states that a child born to a Muslim father is a Muslim. In this case, the legal system considered Jewish religious law as binding, and used its authority to draft the young man into the military without taking into account the dangerous and complex realities involved. There was no choice but to bring Ramzi to the *Shari'a* court in Beer-Sheva and to have him convert to Islam, despite the fact that he was considered by that court to be a Muslim in any case. The fact that Ramzi was born, lived, and studied in Muslim Hebron made it very difficult to convince the *Shari'a* court to accept his conversion, which was, in essence, contrary to Muslim religious law. In spite of the many hurdles along the way, we succeeded within a few months to arrive at a situation whereby the State of Israel would accept Ramzi's status as a Muslim, and by doing so, to cancel his draft notice.

Case Study 2

Mahmoud converted to Judaism from Islam so he could marry his Jewish fiancé. His name was changed to Harel. In order to marry this woman, he divorced his first wife, leaving her their house and the custody of their children. After he married the Jewish woman according to Jewish law, a daughter was born, and the couple began to suffer from problems stemming from the cultural differences between them. Eventually they divorced in the rabbinical court. The daughter was considered Jewish, and she remained in the custody of her mother, who received child support payments in accordance with Israeli law and retained ownership of the family home.

When Mahmoud decided to remarry, this time to a Muslim woman, he did not succeed in finding a wife in his own area in the south, so he went seeking a wife in the north of the country. He presented himself as "Mahmoud" rather than "Harel." Eventually he remarried.

Case Study 3

A Muslim woman from Morocco had been born to a Muslim father and a Jewish mother. She married a Muslim man who was originally from Sudan, but who was now living in Morocco. They had several children. The couple and their children moved to Israel, the wife using her status as a Jewish woman for this purpose. The family lived in Israel as a Jewish family and the children attended Jewish schools. When the time came, the children were inducted into the military, as Israeli law requires. After several years, the couple decided to divorce. The husband gave up custody of the children and the family home, and demanded nothing from his wife. The future fate of the children is unknown, since both parents see their children as Muslims according to Islamic law. The wife prefers that Israeli law, rather than Islamic law, be applied to the children, since Israeli law will provide them with more rights.

Case Study 4

In the 1970s, a Palestinian man from the Gaza Strip came to work in Israel. He met a Jewish woman of North African origin and they decided to marry. He asked her to convert to Islam. But she refused, asking him to convert to Judaism so that he would be accepted into her family, qualify for an Israeli identity card and Israeli citizenship, and could raise a family together. He agreed to convert to Judaism (*murtadd*), and the couple was married according to Jewish law. They had children, and when the children were teenagers, the couple began to have problems that eventually led to divorce in the rabbinical court. The father left the house, the children remained in the wife's custody, and the house remained hers.

After a number of years, he decided to remarry, this time to a Palestinian woman introduced to him by his family. They were married in a *Shari'a* court in the Gaza Strip. Neither the Palestinian woman nor anyone else there was aware that he was a Muslim who had converted to Judaism. From the perspective of Islamic law, such a marriage is invalid. An Ottoman family law from 1917 states: "The marriage of a Muslim to a non-Muslim is invalid and forbidden." According to this law, the husband was required to have his marriage approved in an Israeli *Shari'a* court so that the marriage would be legally valid. The husband applied to one of the *Shari'a* courts in Israel for recognition and validation of his marriage to the woman from Gaza. Of course, he did not mention the fact of his conversion to Judaism in Israel, and the court did not pursue this matter. Eventually the *Shari'a* court in Israel decided to recognize his marriage, viewing him as a Muslim for all intents and purposes. It should be noted that the same man applied to the Ministry of the Interior in order to register his marriage in accordance with the decision of the *Shari'a* court, but after an investigation the Ministry refused to register him as married until such time as he provided a decision from the *Shari'a* court stating that he was a Muslim. This is despite the fact that he had kept his being Jewish a secret, since he had to change his marital status so he could be united with his wife and children. What is perhaps most interesting is that it was the Ministry of the Interior that took legal responsibility for this matter, and not the *Shari'a* court, whose job it was to do so. Even if the man involved denied being Jewish, it was that court's duty to ask him to provide a summary of his personal information from the Ministry of the Interior and then to decide whether to approve the marriage agreement between him and his Palestinian wife from the Gaza Strip. As a convert from Islam to Judaism, he is considered a *murtadd*, and must be sentenced to death according to Islamic law. As a Jew, he could have brought his Palestinian wife to Israel as a new immigrant, with all the rights that any new immigrant receives.

Discussion

It should be noted that cases such as these have become commonplace, particularly following the large wave of immigration from the former Soviet Union to Israel in the 1990s. In all these cases, the children became the victims and marital love often faded once the children were born. Lack of awareness of the legal issues involved in mixed marriages and the future implications on the lives of the children and the couples if these marriages are not successful may damage families and children irreparably.

Historical, anthropological, sociological, psychological, and religious studies have attempted to construct a profile of the typical convert to Islam. However, many of these studies conclude that it is difficult to do so; Muslim converts form a far too heterogeneous group. Kose's study of native British Muslims applies several psychological and religious theories to his sample of converts. He critically assesses "crises" theories with regard to the pre-conversion life histories. He finds that commonly held ideas on conversion as being induced by moral and religious crises of adolescence or failed socialization do not apply in the case of Islam. Rambo analyzed diverse routes to conversion, trying to describe typologies of converts. In addition, Allievi develops a useful typology of conversion itineraries to Islam. He distinguishes relational from rational conversions.

Conversion takes place in several stages and is usually experienced as a substantial transformation of religious, social, and cultural aspects of daily life: praying, fasting, and eating certain foods; changing one's name and appearance, including *hijab* (veil); or changing social and cultural practices, particularly those related to contacts with the opposite sex. Some of these transformations create problems with the family of origin.

Islam offers structured activities, such as prayers and lessons, and an alternative social space within the confinement of prison. The new Islamic identity also signals a fresh start. Islam is perceived by converts as clear, simple, and rational. It has sources that anyone can consult without mediators. And for the mystically inclined there is the Sufi tradition.

Wohlrab-Sahr defined three types of conversion as the symbolic transformation of crisis experiences. The first type of conversion is a related to sexuality and gender. Converts report previously experiencing feelings of personal devaluation with regard to sexuality and gender norms. The second type of conversion is related to social mobility. Upon experiencing a failed attempt at upward social mobility, conversion to Islam can provide an alternative career. Third, conversion may be a response to problems related to nationality and ethnicity, a lack of "belonging." Islam, then, offers converts an opportunity to transform experiences of devaluation, degradation, or disintegration. Conversion is a multi-layered, continuous process in which new identities and discourses are produced and reproduced.

Conversions to Islam in Israel
(from the protocols of the *Shari'a* courts)

1979–2000	80
2000	24
2001	31
2002	16
2003	15
up to July 2004	7

Cases of conversion from Islam studied by Khalil and Bilici reveal intellectual motivations, theoretical and ideological concerns, and experimental /social motivations that concern personal experience and historical examples of social behaviors exhibited by individuals or groups belonging to a particular belief system.[37]

Summary and Conclusion

Islamic discourse can appeal to individuals for various reasons, and can address manifold aspects of their identities. It is should be noted that various aspects of a person's identity inform discourses, and discourses appeal to different aspects of identities. Islam offers various religious discourses, such as on race and gender, that appeal to different ethnic groups. Converts remake and negotiate discourses and these, in turn, inform the process of identity construction.

It is important to bear in mind that there is no single, definite explanation for women converting to Islam, but rather a complex contextual picture of identities and discourses exists. It will sensitize us to the many ways in which these converted women make sensible choices, choices that can change over time.

In many western cases, conversion serves the multiple ends of spiritual fulfillment, community belonging, the desire for a husband and family, and a new sense of self-assurance. Of course, conversion to or from Islam (or any religion, for that matter) is not always black and white; there are always individuals who either are unsure of their new commitment or oscillate back and forth.

Bibliography of Laws and Decisions

1. The Ottoman Family Law Act of 1917 (articles 234, 235, 236).
2. The King's Article 52 of His Commission on The Land of Israel 1922–1947.
3. Decisions of the *Shari'a* Courts.
4. Protocols of the *Shari'a* Courts.
5. Article 3A of the Family Law Act (Alimony and Child Support), 1950.
6. Article 3A of the Women's Equal Rights Act, 1951.
7. Article 14, The Capacity and Guardianship Act, 1962.
8. Civil Appeal 86/63 El-Safadi v. N. Benyamin, 1410.
9. Miron, "Muslim Legal and Judicial Jurisdiction in Israeli Inheritance Laws," *Hapraklit* 1971. 12.
10. Decision 56/61 of the Israeli Supreme Court, Abu-Angela v. The Registration Clerk of the Resident's Registration Office of Tel Aviv-Yaffo. (1) 380.

[37] Mohammad Khalil and Mucahit Bilici 2007. "Conversion out of Islam: A Study of Conversion Narratives of Former Muslims, *The Muslim World*, 97 (2007):111–24.

The Ghrnati Modal System in Moroccan Jewish Music

AVI EILAM AMZALLAG

In Europe and in the Arab-speaking countries, such as Iraq and Morocco, the Jews excelled in the world of music and were considered to be leaders in the field.[1] In Morocco, the Jews integrated into the local music scene, adopting its rules and creating their own music, one whose style overlapped with those of the Arabs of the Maghreb. The Moroccan Jews produced their own frameworks, forms, and styles,[2] which include Classical Andalusian, Milhun,[3] Sha'abi, Berber, and Ghrnati. Much of the sung religious poesy (*piyyutim*) of Moroccan Jews today is based on the Ghrnati modal system.[4] The classical Andalusian musical style of Algeria serves as a basis for the daily sung poesy of Moroccan Jewry. It is worth noting that even though the achievements of Andalusian music are great, it has remained without notation and thus undergoes constant change.

Using both older and more recent recordings,[5] our research is based on a comparison of selections from each of the modes belonging to the Ghrnati.[6] The performing artists are Jews from Israel, Canada, Morocco, and France. I shall examine two important elements that characterize the modal system of the Ghrnati: (1) the sources of the repertoire of the Ghrnati modal system, its scope, and the melodic significance of its modes; and (2) the new

---

1 Mahmoud Guetat has published several books on North-African music, but has ignored the Jewish role in this music. See Guettat Mahmud, *La musique Classique du Maghreb* (Paris, 1980); *La musique arabo-andaluse L' empreinte du Maghreb* (El-Ouns, Paris-Montreal, 2000); *Musique du monde Arabo-Musulman* (guide bibliographic et discographic Approche analitique et critique; Dardanelles al-unsaddle, Paris, 2004).

2 This is a common attitude throughout the Jewish Diaspora. The "Daqaqat" and female ensembles in Irak and Persia, the famous "Tshalghi Bagdad" Jewish ensemble and the unique Jewish ensembles in Morocco. See A. Shiloah, *Music in the World of Islam: A Socio-cultural Study* (London, 1995), 23.

3 Or Qassida, based on combining classical Andalusian styles with local ones.

4 Derived from "Granada," the last Moorish town in Spain.

5 Recordings were classified on CDs according to appropriate modes for seminars I conducted for the Department of Music, Haifa University.

6 For a detailed discussion, see Abraham Eileenam-Amzallag, *Modal Aspects of the Singing of Supplications ("Baqqashot") among Moroccan Jews* (Thesis submitted to the Senate of the Hebrew University in Jerusalem, 1986), 42–61 [Hebrew].

Western influences that occurred in the Ghrnati modal system in the twentieth century as a result of the contact with French popular music as representative of the West.

Andalusian Music

The Andalusian musical tradition in the North African countries exists in three styles: the Tunisian, the Algerian, and a style common to Morocco. The Moroccan music retains more of its original flavor, since it escaped the Turkish musical influence, which affected the Tunisian and Algerian music. The Ghrnati style, known to the Jewish musicians as the "Djiri" style, apparently reached Morocco via migrant Jewish families that arrived from Algeria and settled in Ujda and Rabat at the end of the nineteenth and the beginning of the twentieth century.

This was a stormy period in the history of Algerian Jewry. There were pogroms (1897–98), mainly in Algiers (1898) and in Wehran (1897). In 1934 there were serious riots in the city of Constantine, which resulted in twenty Jews killed and fifty injured. The Vichy government worsened the situation of the Jews when it cancelled the Cremieu Decree of 1870. These events were clear signals for both internal and external Jewish migration to Morocco.

The Ghrnati style has a pivotal role in the common sung poesy, particularly in the Singing of Supplications (*Shirat Habaqqashot*). The tunes of *Shirat Habaqqashot* have been adopted from the well-known musical styles of Morocco, including Moroccan Andalusian music, music in the Ghrnati style, and the Milhun. The sung poesy of *Shirat Habaqqashot* is organized into series and frameworks known as Trkan (sing. *tarik* "way," "continuity"). The Trik is a continuity of poesy generally formed around one single mode. In this mode, a Mawal ("vocalization") is sung, followed by several other songs in the same mode, arranged from slow to fast. The Jewish Moroccan song, in the main, uses the modal Ghrnati system within the Trik framework.

The Ghrnati Modal System

The Ghrnati mode, an open style, is mainly common to western Algeria: Tlemsen and Wehran, as well as the Moroccan towns of Ujda and Rabat. As a result of the "from the village to the city" internal migration of Jewish communities in Morocco, the Ghrnati is shared by most Jewish communities. Since the beginning of the twentieth century, Moroccan Jewish composers have used the Ghrnati modal system. And although they rarely borrow melodies from Algerian Ghrnati classical music, Arab Algerian popular melodies are regularly adapted as part of the Jewish repertoire. Moroccan Jewish singers and musicians are familiar with each mode's name and are aware of the melodic rules and significance.

THE REPERTOIRE OF THE GHRNATI MODAL SYSTEM

Seroussi and Karsenti have noted in their pioneering article "The Study of Liturgical Music of Algerian Jewry" four Jewish musical traditions in Algeria,[7] one of which is the Wehran-Tlemsan tradition. The Ghrnati modal system common within the Moroccan Jewish communities is related to this tradition.

This modal system of the Ghrnati consists of rhythmic and melodic modes, both of which are used almost exclusively by Jews. The rhythmic modes are unnamed, whereas each of the melodic modes bears a unique name. Several melodic modes bear names known from other modal systems, although the actual musical content completely differs.[8]

Salvador Daniel lists the eight modes common in Algeria,[9] only a few of which are identical to the common modes within of the Moroccan Jewish Ghranti:[10]

1. Irak - on D, corresponds to Dorian
2. Mazmum - on E, corresponds to Phrygian
3. Dhil - on F, corresponds to Lydian
4. Zarka - on G, corresponds to Mixolydian
5. Hsin - on A, corresponds to Hypodoryan [Aeolian]
6. Sika - on B, corresponds to Hypophrygian
7. Maya - on C, corresponds to Hypolydian [Ionian]
8. Rasd-Aadhil - on D, corresponds to Hypomixolydian

Leaning on Greek philosophers, a natural, non-musical character is ascribed to each mode. The following is a list of seven the Ghrnati modes common to the Moroccan Jewish community:

1. Ramal-Maya is known by Moroccan Jewish musicians as *Ramal-Maya Djiri*. The addition of the term "Djiri" is to distinguish this Ramal-Maya from that of the Classical Andalusian modal system. Both modes are based on D and correspond to the Dorian mode. The improvisation on the Ghrnati starts with the 5th note (A) and goes down to the D.

[7] E. Seroussi and E. Karsenti, "The Study of Liturgical Music of Algerian Jewry," *Pe'amim* 91 (2002): 35.

[8] Similarities in modal names can be confusing, e.g., a mode named Ramal-Maya exists both in Classical Andalusian music and in the Ghrnati style.

[9] Salvador Daniel, "La musiqe arabe: ses rapports avec la musique grecque et le chant gregorien," *Revue African* (Algiers, 1863; reprint 1879): 55–65.

[10] I have made an analogy of the Algerian and the Church modes. In his explanation of

2. Sika corresponds to Phrygian, with the possibility of raising the 3rd. This mode is constructed upon on the 5th of the Minor scale. This mode is used in Flamenco music with its varied styles. It is assumed that this mode was created as a result of the combination of Gypsy and Arab music.[11] The improvisation in this mode opens mainly with the 5th note, moves to the fourth, and descends to the tonic.
3. Irak corresponds to Phrygian and its tonic is generally G. The improvisation opens mainly with the 3rd.
4. Zraka corresponds to Mixolydian, i.e., Ionian with minor seventh. Improvisation opens mainly with the 3rd.[12]
5. Hijaz and Zidan. This mode is known in the Middle East as Hijaz and in its classical Andalusian Moroccan version as Al Hijaz Al Kabir.[13] The Zidan is constructed on E with an augmented 3rd and minor 2nd between the 2nd and 3rd notes. This mode is known in Eastern European Jewish music as Steiger *Ahava Rabba*. The Zidan differs in its musical contents from those of the Hizaj, be it from the Middle East or from Classical Andalusian music. The improvisation opens generally with the 7th note of the mode. The following are the notes of *She'hi Lael*, a chant from *Shirat Habaqqashot* that is sung in the Zidan mode.

the Jewish Steiger (Eastern Jews' modal system) Idelsohn makes a similar analogy. See A.Z. Idelsohn, *Jewish Music in Its Historical Developmen* (New York: Schoken Books, 1967), 143 and A. Chottin *Tableau de la musiqe marocain* (Paris: Paul Geuthner, 1939), 122.

11 R. De Zayas, "Musicology and the Cultural Heritage of the Spanish Moors," in *Musical Repercussions of 1492*, ed. Carol E. Robertson (London: The British library, 1992), 129. After the 1492 expulsion, Arabs and Jews could convert to Christianity or stay in Spain as slaves.

12 "Bllarz" (Arabic name for the stork) is a very well-known female's song in this mode. This is a love song in which a young girl asks the stork to see where her love is... She identifies herself by her bracelets.

13 Another mode with the "Hijaz" prefix is the "Hijaz al Mashriki," one of the twenty-four modes of the Classical Nauba. This Hijaz al Mashriqi is actually a major scale without the augmented 2nd. On the other hand, the most characteristic feature of the Ghranti Hijaz is its raised 6th.

This is Hijaz on E. The 6th note C is raised to C#.[14] "Normal" Hijaz is less common, occurring in melodies that combine Ghrnati rhythms with the known Hijaz:

6. Mazmum, which, with a minor melodic variant, is called Istekhbar Mazmum. This mode is parallel to the Lydian (Major with the fourth note raised a half tone). The improvisation opens with the 3rd and concludes with the tonic. Three versions of this mode exist:
   a. The original Ghrnati Mazmum (Lydian).
   b. Major Mazmum Ionian, that is, simple Major.
   c. Istekhbar Mazmum, regular Ionian with a stressed descent to the 4th.[15]
7. Sahli. This mode is unattested in the literature and, to the best of our knowledge, is noted here for the first time. This is a new mode, probably created as a result of contact with French music. This is the Minor scale that contains elements known to us from the Western Minor scale: Natural, Harmonic, and Melodic Minor. This mode, as it will be clarified in the following stages, bears clear harmonic connotations.

---

[14] This melody is very rich and it contains 10 of the 12 notes. The notes Bb and Db are missing.

[15] This phenomenon of a unique nickname to denote an exclusive melodic pattern clearly clarifies the nature of the modal world as leaning mainly on melodic conception.

Musical and Historical Characteristics of the Ghrnati Modes and the Distinction between Central Mode and Secondary Modes

1. RAMAL MAYA GHRNATI

This mode when constructed on D, generally opens with the descending tetrachord A-E, temporarily stands on E, and finally gets back to D. Ramal-Maya always brings the minor 7th, that is, the C, and never the leading tone. This mode is characterized in its final melodic pattern by the notes E-C-D.[16] The Moroccan musicians know this mode in two versions: the classical Andalusian and the Ghrnati. The first example is a transcription of a melody from the classical Andalusian music (the chant *Dodi Yarad Legano*); the second is Ramal-Maya in its Ghrnati style (the chant *Biti al Tifkhadi*). The following is first strophe of *Dodi Yarad Legano*[17] in the classical Andalusian style.

Ex. 4

[16] On the other hand, this mode in its classical Andalusian style ends differently: the ending melodic pattern uses C-B (natural)-C-D.

[17] ("My Love Descends to His Garden"), a symbolic poem describing the love between God and the Nation of Israel (lyricist: Hayim Cohen) and is sung every Shabbat at the beginning of the *Baqqashot*. This Kabbalist poet lived in the sixteenth century and was a disciple of Rabbi Hayim Vital, who studied with Ha'ari. The melody's source lies in Mukta'at of the Basit (part of the classical Andalusian Music). The Mukta'at are simple melodies used in the classical Nauba. This poem begins all the poems and "sets the tone," the mode, for the following poems.

Remarks:

- The central note D serves as the opening and closing pattern.
- The improvisation opens with an embellishment around the A, the 5th note of the mode. In my collection, most improvisations in this mode open in a similar manner.
- No leading tone in Ramal-Maya.
- The opening pattern generally opens with the A, momentarily rests on this note but ends on the D note. This process is repeated twice till the thirteenth bar.
- After the central note affirms itself, there is a series of new secondary central notes: Bb, G, and C.
- After the new three secondary central notes, the opening structure repeats itself.

In addition to this chant, eleven other additional chants in this mode were checked and the findings are similar.

2. SIKA, OR SIKA ESPAGNOL

This mode occurs in Flamenco music. De Zayas raises the possibility that the popular music of southern Spain known as Flamenco in its varied forms contains traceable Andalusian musical elements. The music of this mode is very close to Flamenco. An analysis of the transcription of the Sika improvisation as it is presented here indicates that:

- The central note of this mode is E.
- The improvisation opens with the B in order to embellish the A and so creates the descending Tetrachord A-E.
- Within the Tetrachord we observe the G sharp and G natural.
- Before arriving at the central tone of the mode, there is a rest on F. This note serves two roles: On one hand it emphasizes the minor 2nd above the central note, and on the other hand it brings out the typical augmented fourth, created with opening B.

Central mode and secondary modes:

The issue of central notes appears again in this Sika Espagnole improvisation: What is the significance of the secondary notes B, G and C here?

Let's examine the source of the melodic patterns used in the secondary central notes. Isolating the musical essence of the secondary patterns reminds us of known patterns. The source of those patterns is hidden in an interesting musical reality: the melodic patterns of the secondary central notes sound familiar because each individual pattern uses one of the other modes as a central pattern! In other words: The central melodic patterns of the Ghrnati modes are unique and characteristically form its identity. Those patterns start the improvisation of the specific mode and at the end they conclude the improvisation. Those opening patterns repeat a few times to determine and reinforce the unique character of each mode and are repeated at the end to create a full circle and to keep a permanent tonality. The internal melodic patterns based on secondary notes are all borrowed from the other modes within the modal repertoire of the Ghrnati.

Thus, the Ghrnati modal frame has its own character, while the internal patterns are borrowed from central patterns of other modes, serving here as secondary patterns, enriching and filling the space between the repetitions of the central pattern. Each mode of the Ghrnati recalls other modes. Most performing artists of this style are familiar with this phenomenon and insist on a particular order to the secondary patterns. The internal material of those borrowed patterns consists of melodic passages, quasi-scales, which incorporate clear components of other Ghrnati modes. These patterns are not known patterns from the other modes, but rather scale melodic passages that bring whatever is required to establish other Ghrnati modes. These Ghrnati modes are always "relative" modes that belong to the principal mode.

Is there a fixed order to the internal modes and, if so, are the performers aware of it? Do they keep bringing "right" order to the internal modal melodic patterns?

As to the order of the internal patterns it seems that at some time in the past there was a "logical" order to those internal passages. However, with the passage of time, immigration, and, most significantly, the dispersion of the Moroccan Jewish community this order was forgotten.[18] Today's musicians no longer know the original order, resulting in some internal melodic patterns being left out. Today, few internal modal melodic patterns can be considered as being close to the main mode and most of my recordings prove that. The mode Hijaz, for example, is used as "fill" for the Mazmum and Irak modes. A. Ramal-Maya (natural minor on d: D-Bb-D) as principal mode includes internal passages:

[18] Most of the Jewish Moroccan community relocated to Israel, but some live in France and Canada.

1. On Bb, which stresses augmented 4th (Bb-E) (Lydian-)Internal mode: Ghrnati Mazmum.[19]
2. On C stressing Minor seventh (C-Bb - Mixolydian) the internal mode is Zarka.
3. On G (Turning Bb to b natural) - Mazmum (Major) the internal mode is the Ionian Mazmum.

B. Sika on E (E-E) - Phrygian alternating G-G#:

1. On B-F (Diminished 5th) - Ghrnati Mazmum.
2. On G (Mixolydian G-G with natural F) - Zarka.
3. On C (C Major) Ionian Mazmum

3. IRAK

Daniel mentions this mode as being built on D and based on church mode Dorian. Irak exists in Tunisian and Algerian music, as well. In its North-African Jewish style this mode is built on G with Ab parallel to Phrygian church mode.[20] Sometimes, during the improvisation, the musicians alternate between A natural and Ab. The improvisation in this mode generally starts with the 3rd note of the mode and descends to the tonic. Secondary modes used in Irak are Zidan and Mazmum. Musicians in Israel who are acquainted with Middle-Eastern music incorporate Eastern melodic patterns into the Ghrnati modal system. They convert this mode into Bayat and Bayat into Irak, considering the Bayat to be Irak with an Eastern character. This mode may be described as Minor with lowered 2nd.

[19] Ghrnati Mazmum is parallel to the Lydian church mode; Mazmum is parallel to the Ionian church mode.

[20] A Middle-Eastern mode parallel to Phrygian, known as Curd; see D. Muallem, *The Scale and the Maqam in the Arabic Musical System* (Kfar-Saba: Or-Tav, 2007), 154–73. Variations of the Curd are, Hijaz-car, Lami, and Traz nawin. One should always keep in mind that modes with the same scale structure have different musical content and conception in different musical cultures.

4. ZARKA

This mode, like Irak, is built on G but the scale is Mixolydian, in other words, Major with F natural. Like the mode Irak, improvisation on this mode starts always with a 3rd[21] and even the melodic development is identical to that of this mode, just without the Bb. An Improvisation on melodic patters on Zarka while adding the Bb and Ab will turn the improvisation into Irak.

The next example is a melody from *Shirat Habaqqashot*, in the mode Zarka:

Nura bi 'Amram

Natan Jeyn

The melody of Bllarz is found in Jewish "female" music and is considered by some musicians to be a unique mode. Actually, there is no such mode. Bllarz is a very beautiful melody, known throughout the Moroccan Jewish community in such degree that it is the best representative of Zarka.[22] The beauty of Bllarz attracted many singers to adapt other texts to this melody.

---

21 Several times performers start by embellishing the 3rd.

22 This "method" of naming a mode using the name of famous song is common in women's songs. Another disappearing mode is 'Arobi or 'Arubai, which is a collection of women's songs using the same musical "scale" of Phrygian, but its musical content is completely independent. These "songs," 'Arobi and Bllarz, are actually "frame songs" where the female singer can create her own text according to the specific ceremony, company, celebration, etc. The best-known song in 'Arobi is: *rfed dac l'ezin ya mqmulat azin* (lift up that dough, you perfect beauty). This 'Arobi mode is used also

Bllarz

Ya'akov Azerad

5. HIJAZ AND ZIDAN

Hijaz and *Zidan* parallel the Hijaz mode, common in many non-European musical cultures. Raising the 6th note adds a unique character and "light" to this mode, a light that one may call "Andalusian light." The opening note, in most cases, is the 7th note of the mode.

Hijaz

as an improvisation before singing the qassida (A.E. Amzallag, "The Qassida in *Shire Yedidot*: Sources, Texts and Music," *Pe'amim*, 19 [1984]: 101) and is commonly attached to the Qassida on Joseph, which tells of Joseph son of Ya'aqov, who became second only to the king of Egypt.

6. 'AROBI

'Arobi probably doesn't belong to the modal repertoire of the Ghrnati. On few occasions is 'Arobi attached to Ghrnati modes.

7. MAZMUM AND SAHLI

The Mazmum is major with a raised 4th note, parallel to the church mode Lydian. This I call "Ghrnati Mazmum" or "original Mazmum." Another Mazmum is a simple Major, which we can refer to as "Majorian Mazmum." The 3rd Mazmum is Istekhbar Mazmum: a simple Major opening with a distinct descent to the 4th note and an ascent back to the tonic. Sahli acts like a Western minor scale.

Adaptation of Major and Minor Scales to the Ghrnati System

It is unnatural for an orally transmitted, living culture not to be influenced by its surroundings. Adaptation of foreign melodies to the repertoire of Jewish music is common. The Moroccan Jewish musicians could not ignore the presence of the French and the sound of their language, a new language in Morocco and North Africa. The new interesting melodies the children brought from the schools of Alliance Israélite Universelle had an immense influence. The presence of the French culture left strong musical traces in the musical culture of Algeria and Morocco.

We can assume that in the first phase of this influence the French popular melodies easily found their way into the Moroccan Jewish music. A large number of French Major and Minor melodies demanded some theoretical adjustment. The Jewish Moroccan musician readily understood these melodies as being of two types, classified in the West as major and minor scales. Major and Minor didn't stand alone–the musician assimilated them into his music. They were no longer independent "scales." They had to be adjusted to his music and they had to "work" as a part of the Ghrnati modal repertoire.

The Major Scale in Moroccan Jewish Music

The Mazmum, or Dhil, is a mode that has some "major" character with the raised 4th. The central note of the Ghrnati Mazmum on C is always the note C. The difference between Mazmum and the Major is very small; all one needs is to take away that F#. Now, the musician can enjoy two "Mazmums," one with raised 4th and the other with natural 4th.

But then something very interesting happened to the melody: the Major chord. Non-Western music, like the music of Palestrina, generally prefers steps to jumps. The Major chord includes two jumps.

The popular tune *Wajini Wajini* ("Come to Me") is familiar to the Jewish community. Here we have a major chord and after a few bars, which we may consider as major, the major scale becomes clear. One should observe the broken chord of C in contrast to the diatonic continuation of the tune. This melody is composed of two musical components: jumps (Major chord) and steps, the common technique in Moroccan music.

Ah Ah Ah Wajini Wajini

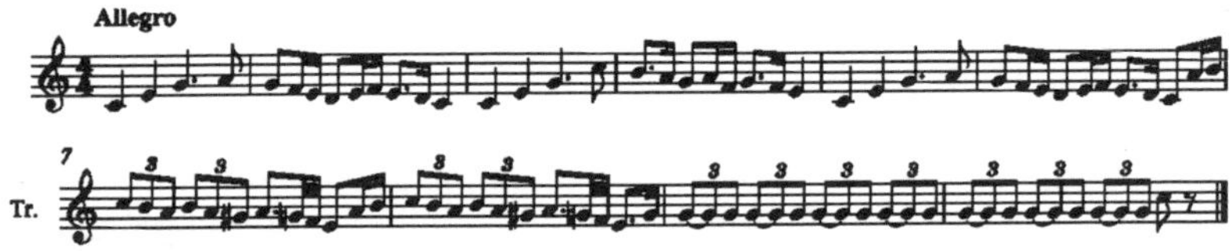

Another Major melody known as Algerian but used by the Moroccan Jewish community is *'Et Dodim*. This melody was composed by *Lili al 'Abassi*,[23] the Algerian Jewish composer. The original melody was composed to the Arabic text, *Gululi 'alash ghdbana Gululi 'alash w'alash frana*.[24] Singers of the Moroccan Jewish community adapted this melody to the poem *'Et dodim kala*.[25] Again we meet the major chord, this time with strong connotations of Tonic-Dominant.

Et Dodim Kala

---

[23] I am indebted to David Nidam, who sings this song in his concerts, for this information.

[24] "Let me know why she is sad and why she is happy."

[25] This poem was written following the style of *Shir Hashirim* (The Song of Songs). The Mode in Mazmum and the Metrum 3/4 + 6/8. To facilitate the notation it was written in 3/4 but one can easily feel the alternating 3/4 and 6/8.

Istekhbar Mazmum is a unique name for Major with a special melodic change: an interval emphasizing the 4th under the tonic immediately after the start. *En dei baer* is a chant from *Shirat Habaqqashot* (*Parashat Vaye'hi Ya'aqov*).

The next two melodies bring more than a chord and major scale; here we again see French popular melodic flavor. Both are sung in *Shirat Habaqqashot* (The singing of Supplications) and their mode is Mazmum with an emphasis on the 4th, which categorizes them as Istekhbar Mazmum.[26]

En de Baer

Lenin tam tsur lama

[26] We could not find the French source of these melodies, but one cannot dismiss the possibility that these are, indeed, French.

By adapting new melodies to his repertoire, the Jewish musician was not yet satisfied; he needed professional confirmation, some kind of "*hekhsher*" ("approval"). He needed to integrate the newly adapted Western melodies into his modal system. He needed to locate them somewhere; order was essential. The new melodies were understood as being close to the Mazmum. New melodies were composed with this new Mazmum and in some of them the major broken chord is included. The Dominant broken chord is never in use.

Summary of the Incorporation of the Major Scale into the Ghrnati Style

The original Mazmum is parallel to the Lidyan, the church mode. This original Mazmum generally is performed as an introduction to songs in Western Mazmum. Nevertheless, *Shirat Habaqqashot* includes many beautiful Mazmum melodies with this pure Mazmum. The augmented 4th sounds natural and smooth. The Western Major here also is called Mazmum, but is distinguished by musicians from the Ghrnati original. Mode Istekhbar Mazmum, with its 4th down, may imply that Tonic-Dominant is used many times as an introduction to songs in Western Major Mazmum.

In addition to composed Mazmum melodies, many melodies in Major scale were incorporated into the Moroccan Jewish repertoire. Some of these melodies are Western and not necessarily French. Yet, I still believe that the only way for these melodies to have assimilated into the Jewish repertoire was through the French educational system, to which many Jewish families sent their children. How else can one explain the melody of *Auld Lang Syne* being used for *Yigdal Elohim Khay*?[27] Another melody, this time in Minor scale, is *La neige tombe,*[28] which describes the Moroccan Jewish pupil, who actually studied in two schools: in the morning he studied at the Alliance School, where he learned the French language, history, mathematics, and so forth, while in the afternoon he studied at the synagogue.

La neige tombe

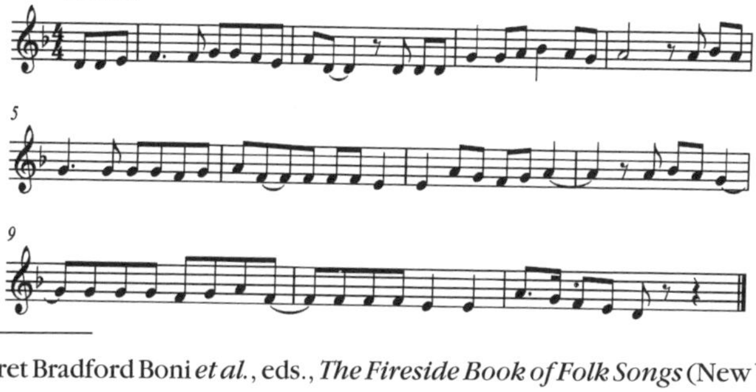

[27] Margaret Bradford Boni *et al.*, eds., *The Fireside Book of Folk Songs* (New York, 1949), 76.

[28] French, "The snow is falling and there remain the children of Israel despite the end of the day" (free translation of the first phrase).

It is not surprising that other songs and French melodies found their way into the musical life and the prayer-book of the Moroccan Jew. One Zionist song is *Sur le pont de Haifa il y a le drapeau Juif*[29] ("On Haifa's bridge there is the Jewish flag").

Sur le pont de Haifa il y a le drapeau juif

History, ethnicity, and geography created a situation in which Western influence on Moroccan Jewish music went beyond just an adaptation of Western melodies.

The Minor Scale in Moroccan Jewish Music

Did French influence exceed the mere adaptation of melodies and actually "invade" other inner musical components and, if so, can we locate these influences? Did the Tonic-Dominant affect Moroccan Jewish music? In other words, did the Major and Minor scales in Moroccan Jewish music constitute some portion, even a small one, of the Western harmonic functionality?

Here we need to clarify that there is no way to talk about functional harmonic accompaniment that is common in Western music. Major and Minor scales on their unique harmonic function remain solely in the monophonic melody. This step of adding harmonic accompaniment did not occur in Moroccan music.[30]

The Western minor scale exists in the Moroccan Jewish music in its three types: natural, harmonic, and melodic. The mode Sahli bears its source in its name: Sahli = Shore.[31] Thus, this mode joins that small group of modes named after a person or a location, such as Huseyni, Hijaz, and Ispahan.

---

29 I transcribed this melody from the singing of the poet Doudou Eli'az.

30 In Israel, I found a cassette of Rabbi Haym Look, the famous *paytan*, accompanied by a full Western Orchestra with Western arrangements.

31 This Mode was considered as coming from the north, from the shore.

THE MODE SAHLI

The Western Minor scale in its three variations, natural, harmonic and melodic is concentrated in the Ghrnati "mode" Sahli. This mode is new and unknown to the research literature.

This mode has a minor and major 6th and a leading tone and the improvisation opens always with a minor broken chord on the tonic. In this improvisation we meet many Western harmonic representatives, such as leading tone, strong dominant, and soon. Actually, in Sahli one can feel the western harmony hidden in the monophonic melody, not to mention the broken chord at the end. Below is a possible transcription of Sahli:

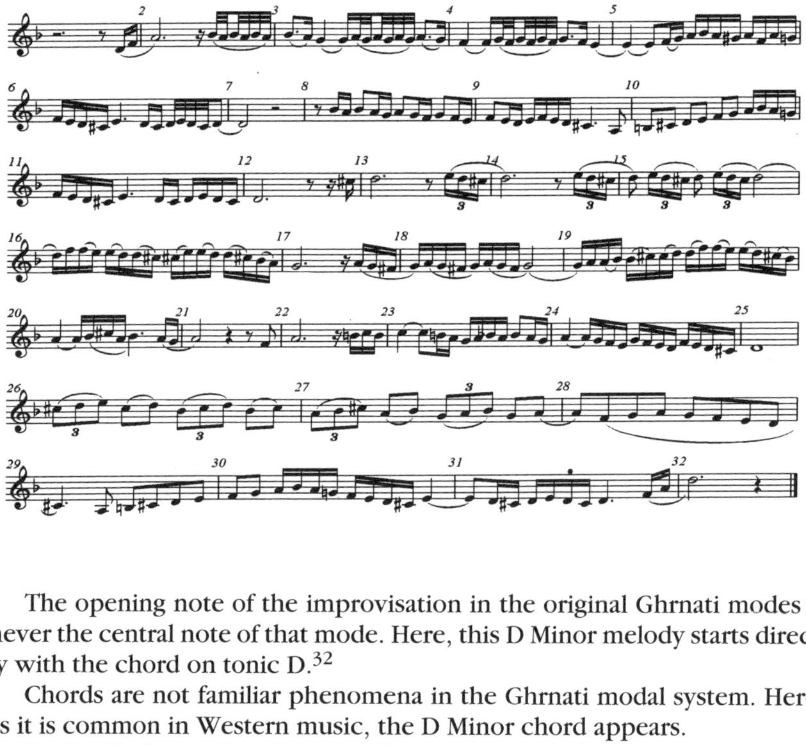

The opening note of the improvisation in the original Ghrnati modes is never the central note of that mode. Here, this D Minor melody starts directly with the chord on tonic D.[32]

Chords are not familiar phenomena in the Ghrnati modal system. Here, as it is common in Western music, the D Minor chord appears.

In this Mode we found for the first time, a melody that starts and ends with a jump.

Let us examine the first sentence.

[32] Ramal Maya Ghrnati always starts on the 5th note; The Mode Sika starts on the 5th note; Zarka and Irak start on the 3rd note.

Stripping away the embellishments we have:

The Western harmonic connotations are now clearer; one can easily feel the tonic, the subdominant, the dominant, and finally, with help of the leading tone, we are back to our tonic.

The next melody is a well-known chant that exemplifies strong Western qualities: a broken minor chord and tonic-dominant-tonic.

Ahalel El

Here again, it is amazing to see that only the tonic appears as a broken chord, whereas all the rest of the melody is diatonic.

Later, American influence came to Morocco: In November 1943, the Allies under Eisenhower initiated the "Torch" operation in North Africa with the landing of British and American troops in Morocco and Algeria. The Moroccans were deeply impressed by the Americans as expressed in this song:

> The Americans are here and people are delighted.
> Married females became younger, disappearing from their husbands.
> Their beautiful blue eyes brought goodness.
> They gave us candies, chewing gum, cigarettes, and even a dollar.

> All one can hear is: okay, okay, come on, buy, buy.
> Give me a dollar!

Many other songs echo the presence of Americans in Morocco. This is a unique Jewish repertoire, which includes love songs depicting the courting of local females by American soldiers.

Conclusion

The Jewish Ghrnati modal system is a hybrid product of that vast field we call Andalusian North African music. This modal system, based on the classical Algerian version of the Andalusian music that migrated to Morocco, was adapted by the Moroccan Jewish community and became popular in daily use. This new modal system ignored its original classical source and started a new life, creating a unique repertoire that served the Jewish music in Morocco in its Andalusian conception.

The music created in the Ghrnati modal system, sometimes still called "Djiri," encompasses all the important kinds of Moroccan Jewish music, be it religious or secular, Hebrew or Arabic, sung by women or men.

A musical by-product of the French occupation of Algeria and Morocco and the French educational systems in those two countries was the adoption of the major and minor western scales. The modes Istekhbar Mazmum and Sahli were adopted and introduced into the Ghrnati modal system.

The new modes functioned within the Ghrnati in the North African conventional way, and accepted the unique Ghrnati technique of being used as "fill" for other modes. The major and minor scales were assimilated into the Ghrnati, recognized and accepted by all Jewish musicians and performers as a part of this modal system. Each mode starts with its unique melodic patterns and uses passages of other modes, as secondary central patterns. One can assume that before the mass immigration to Israel, there was an obligatory order to the internal patterns, which was eventually lost. Nevertheless, strong family connections between the modes dictate the order of the internal patterns.

One must always bear in mind that the Moroccan Jewish musician didn't go too far and didn't use harmony. Western harmony does not stand alone; it is an integral part of the melody. They support and build upon each other. We can assume that the students of the Alliance Israélite Universelle brought home French melodies but not Western classical music.

Today, the Ghrnati modal system plays an important role in the musical life of Jewish communities in Israel and in the Diaspora, being highly valued by composers, performers, and listeners. Numerous activities utilizing the Ghrnati are still taking place throughout the North-African Jewish world. Singers continually adapt new melodies of the Western style to sacred Hebrew poems; composers are still creating Hebrew and Arabic "hits" using the modes of the Ghrnati, and the new Ghrnati melodies are finding their way into the synagogue.

The Emancipation of North-African Jewish Women
The Alliance Israélite Universelle

SHALOM BAR-ASHER

The Arrival of Spanish Jews to North Africa (1391–1492)

Perhaps the phenomenon that most characterized this period in the Maghreb was the Christian invasion, mainly of Italian merchants, but also of some mercenaries and missionaries. None of these attempts achieved a permanent result until the capture of Ceuta by the Portuguese. At the end of the fifteenth century, the Maghreb appears as a territory completely Islamized, except for the relatively few Jewish communities, and thoroughly Arabized in spite of the presence of compact Berber-speaking groups.[1] Jews lived in Libya, Tunisia, Algeria, and Morocco, mainly in the major cities of Tripoli, Tunis and Djerba, Tlemcen, Fes, and Marrakesh. There was the large influence of thousands of immigrants who had left Spain as refugees in 1391, after the atrocities committed against them throughout Spain. They came mainly to Algiers, the capital of Algeria. That was the first stage in this area.[2]

From the arrival of the Spanish Jews to North Africa until the end of the eighteenth century, an essential change in the status of Jews and their organization occurred. Rabbis such as Itshaq Ben-Sheshet Perfet (=Rivash, 1326–1408), Shim'on ben Tsemah Duran (=Rashbatz, 1361–1444), and his son Shelomo (=Rashbash, 1400–1461) attempted to define the laws for these new communities. The issuing of *taqqanot* [ordinances] was one of the means by which rabbis and community leaders became involved in the society, while still relying on precedents from elsewhere. This community of leaders was perceived as if it were the Grand Rabbinic Tribunal in Jerusalem, which had the authority to issue *taqqanot* affecting all facets of society. Already by the geonic period (seventh to tenth centuries) its authority was considered equal to that of the Torah, and this was accepted also in the Maghreb.[3]

---

1 P.M. Holt and Ors, eds., *The Cambridge History of Islam* (Cambridge: Cambridge University Press, 1978), 211–37.

2 Haim Zeev Hirschberg, *A History of the Jews in North Africa, vol. 1: From Antiquity to the Sixteenth Century* (Leiden, 1974).

3 For more on the *taqqanot*, see Menachem Elon, *Hamishpat Haivry: Toldotav, Meqorotav, Eqronotav* [*Jewish Law: History, Sources, Principles*], 2 vols., (Jerusalem, 1978), 558–654; Shalom Bar-Asher, "Qave Yesod le-Toldot ha-Yehude ha-Magh-

From the end of the fifteenth through the entire sixteenth century, the Jews of North Africa continued to abide by the *taqqanot* that had been issued in Spain, though, on occasion, with modification, for the purpose of maintaining economic harmony within the community.[4] For example, according to the *taqqana* of Castile, at the death of the wife, her estate–that is, *her* assets only–was to be divided between her family and her husband. Now, however, according to the *taqqanot* of Fes, the assets to be divided included those of the husband, a decision that reflected the concept of spousal joint assets and respect for the status of the wife.

This tendency to elevate the wife's status can be discerned in a *taqqana* from 1540. It was customary that when a husband died without having any children, one third of the *ketubba* monies was given to his heirs. A local *taqqana*, however, stated that if the man had married a second wife, in addition to "the wife of his youth," even if the second wife had bore children, nothing was to be deducted from the first wife's *ketubba*.[5]

Another example. A royal decree had overridden the accepted custom of monogamy. However, influential Jews, "viewers of the face of king," managed to procure the *Bet Din* the right to maintain the custom of monogamy, thus prohibiting bigamy except in the case of the first wife's infertility during the first decade of marriage, as was the custom of the sages. If the couple had children, however, any deviation was regarded only as a means to "satisfy the husband's passions." This approach was intended to ensure tranquility between husband and wife and monogamy prevailed in most North-African families.

---

reb ve-Aliyyat ha-Merkaz be-Algir, 5151–5252" [Basic Trends in the History of the Jews of the Maghreb and the Rise of the Center in Algiers, 1391–1492], *Pe'amim: Studies in the Cultural Heritage of Oriental Jewry*, 31 (1987): 22–39, [Hebrew]. On The *taqqanot* of Fes, see *Spanish and Portuguese Jews in Morocco, Sefer Ha-Taqqanot* (Jerusalem, 1990).

4 Bar-Asher, "Qave Yesod le-Toldot," 49–53.

5 Avraham Hayyim Freimann, *Seder Qiddushin ve-Nisu'in* [The Order of Betrothal and Marriage], (Jerusalem, 1965) [North Africa, 24–25, 83–92, 111, 272–73], [Hebrew]. Yom-Tov Assis, "Herem de-Rabeinu Guershom ve-Kefel Nashim be-Sefarad" [The Ex-Communication of Rabbi Gershom and Bigamy in Spain], *Zion: A Quarterly for Research in Jewish History*, 81 (1997): 277–51. The sages of the Talmud condemned a husband who deserted the wife of his youth, including her sons and daughters, in favor of another woman.

This *taqqana* reflected the reality of a custom at the time "that some of the residents of the land found a more beautiful [woman]." See Shalom Bar-Asher, *Sefer HaTaqqanot*, 69–70.

Morocco

The Activities of International Organizations

The deterioration of security during the rein of Sultan Mulai Abd al-Rahman (1822–1859) caused the Jews of Morocco to seek help from the European powers in order to improve their political and social situation. During the early nineteenth century the situation of the Moroccan Jews varied. Those who lived in the cities in which the sultan's rule was effective were protected and enjoyed economic opportunity. The situation, however, was not as benign for most other Jews in the kingdom, as the attitude of the Muslim community toward the Jewish minority became quite negative. Security was the most urgent problem faced by the Jewish leaders at the end of the nineteenth century.

Documents published by Eliezer Bashan in his book *Jewish Women in Morocco: Seen through Letters from 1733–1905*[6] relate horrific incidents directed at Jews, such as the raping of women or the killing of peddlers on the highway. Similar incidents had been documented since the fifteenth century, occurring each time security had deteriorated, especially in the outlying areas. The weakness of the Jewish community caused it to be an easy target of the baser elements in Muslim society from the mid-nineteenth century onward.

External changes, mainly in Western Europe, were to affect the North African Jewish communities. These changes entered North Africa with missionaries and settlers from Europe, including hundreds of Jews from Europe and the United States. They offered the Eastern Jews the opportunity to change or adapt the legal system. The new educated class, graduates of European institutions of higher learning, identified with the new approaches, and Morocco was fertile ground for their ideas. International institutions and especially Jewish individuals and organizations were the first to help the Jews of Morocco in the nineteenth century. Among those at the forefront in the quest for rights were Jewish women from affluent families in Mogador who owned property and were involved in commerce, such as Ramo Abitbol, Esther Halfon, and Esther Anahori. They fearlessly demanded their rights. Note, for example, the case of Hola Ben Susan, a woman from Tangiers who, according to an 1888 letter, had inherited sheep, oxen, and seeds from her father. As part of the Arabic protection ceremony 'Ar, customarily performed by both Jews and Muslims in Morocco, Ben Susan slaughtered a sheep in front of the British consulate in Mazagan.[7] Performance of this public ceremony was intended to "obligate" the British gov-

6 *Nashim Yehudiyyot be-Marocco, Seen through Letters from 1733–1905* (Ramat-Gan: Bar-Ilan University, 2005) [Hebrew].

7 Eliezer Bashan, *Jewish Women of Valor in Morocco, from the Time of the Exile from Spain until the Twentieth Century* (Tel-Aviv, 2003), 61–73 [Hebrew].

ernment to help her claim her inherited property from the agent representing her father's estate, who had been imprisoned in order to prevent Ben Susan from getting her inheritance.

Other documents include personal petitions, such as the granting of British citizenship to Stella Corcos (New York 1858 - Casablanca 1948). She was the principal of the Jewish girls school in the city, which had been founded in order to discourage Jewish girls from studying in the missionary schools.[8] Stella's students were taught to demand their rights in the Muslim kingdom.[9]

Stella Corcos' efforts were, by and large, directed at the violence committed against Jewish women during the second half of the nineteenth century. Jews living in the inland Moroccan communities continually suffered violence and other abuses. The murder of Jews, including women and children, was not uncommon. Documents tell of Jewish women being captured, raped, and lashed. In some cases the women were forced to convert to Islam. Stella became involved in the plight of the Jews of Demnat, who frequently were the victims of robbery and other hardships. Demnat was quite unlike her native Mogador on the Atlantic shore, which Stella viewed as almost an English colony, where the rights of Jews holding English citizenship were preserved. Around Demnat Jewish woman were being abducted and sold by tribes. "They would rob the men and kill some of them, and sell the women and children for 25-30 dollars each!" reported Cantor David Azulai in 1894.[10] Such atrocities occurred not only in Demnat in the remote Dar'a Valley between the High Atlas mountains, but also in other cities. The helplessness of the central government and the rejection of the testimony of a Jew according to Islamic law made it difficult to prevent such criminal activity. Moreover, although, according to Islam, religion should not be forced on the "People of the Book," the governor of Marrakesh was infamous for forcing Jewish women who had married Muslim husbands to convert to Islam. Special delegations petitioned the king in Marrakesh to spare Jewish widows of Muslim husbands from being forcibly converted.[11] These were not the affluent women who often received the protection of the European powers. These were the women from the lower classes, which formed most of the population that lived in poverty in the Jewish neighborhoods that were separate from the Muslim city, the Mellahs.

---

8 Bashan, *Jewish Women in Morocco*, 82-93.

9 Note the case of Costa Assor, who had embraced Christianity due to the influence of a Jewish missionary activist whom she married. Stella Corcos tried to separate Costa from her husband, but was unsuccessful due to the girl's dedication to the conversion act (Bashan, *Jewish Women in Morocco*, 74-81).

10 Ibid., 206-21.

11 Ibid., 194-205; 232-36.

Jewish women were victims in all sorts of circumstances. For example, Yehuda Levy-Yuli, who worked in the British consulate in Mogador, but received only minor punishment for violence against a Jewish servant due to his being a British subject. Most of these acts were perpetrated by Moroccan soldiers and officials, such as the soldier who, mounted on a mule, crushed the leg of Jewish woman, necessitating the amputation of her toe. Although the soldier was punished and the lady compensated, such penalties did not prevent on-going abuse. The governor of Demnat commanded that a Jewish woman who had refused to sew his clothes on the Sabbath day be lashed.[12] The British consul seduced three Jewish girls, one of which bore a child by him. An elderly man complained to the governor of Tangiers about the murder of his son and rape of his seven-year-old granddaughter by the nephew of the governor. An act of revenge took place.[13]

The punishment for murder committed during a robbery (against either Jew or Muslim) was quite severe, but the punishment for other crimes against Jews usually involved only a fine or compensation, and only in severe cases life in prison. In some instances foreign diplomats were able to alleviate the suffering being endured by those in the Jewish communities, thanks to representatives of these communities lobbying London and the Alliance in Paris.

Of Stella Corcos we read: "Stella was a unique figure in the fields of educational and public activity in Morocco from the 1880s and on."[14] As the first principal of the girl's school in Mogador, she viewed her job as a trust to provide knowledge and to be a leader. In 1894 she fended for the Jews of Demnat after they had been raided once more. The Jews were robbed, women and children sold like livestock, and Torah scrolls looted. Due to Stella's intervention everything was restored to the Jews of Demnat, but for one woman who remained with the Gentiles. Stella Corcos was but one of many exemplary Jewish women who were active in seeking relief and justice for their people.[15]

The Alliance Israélite Universelle

A major step toward the elevation of the status of North-African women was taken by the French *Alliance Israélite Universelle* in the nineteenth and twentieth centuries. Among the most important research written on the emancipation of women is that of Frances Malino on the activity of the *Alli-*

[12] Ibid., 101–20.

[13] Ibid., 121–36 and see also 137–94 for more data on the torturing Jewish women during the years 1880–1892.

[14] Ibid., 82.

[15] Ibid., 99–106.

ance in Morocco.[16] Malino writes of three sisters from Tetuan in Northern Morocco whose family was Benchimol, a famous name in Fes since the end of the seventeenth century. Malino quotes 24-year-old Hassiba, one of the three Benchimol sisters, in her impassioned letter to the president of the *Alliance Israélite Universelle*, in the fall of 1900:

> A year ago, when I accepted the post [at the school] at Fes, I knew I was taking responsibility for a very difficult mission. My purpose was already becoming clear and I admit that the undertaking frightened me. Nevertheless, I was firm in my resolve and I answered the words of discouragement that were addressed to me with a staunch hope of success. My goal became suddenly more serious. I was to restore dignity to the women of Fes, to give them a place in society, to develop their hearts and minds. Such seemed to me to be the duties I was to fulfill.[17]

Malino describes the harsh conditions facing the young teachers in the *Alliance* and in the eastern countries in general, noting that they

> confronted in their hard work, loneliness and the sense of being abandoned....We disembark in a city of the Orient or of Africa that is unknown to us. In effect, according to the laudable and prudent–but not agreeable–traditions of the Central Committee [of the *Alliance*], those who come from Haifa are sent to Smyrna while the Tunisians are sent to Egypt. It is necessary to install oneself, look for a room, a pension; neither mother, nor older sister guides us; besides, not having earned our first trimester salary, we have no funds....We are isolated and miserable, with no relations and no friends ....Interrogate my colleagues, ask them if exhausted by the first weeks of teaching, not yet broken into a profession that taxes the brain no less than the lungs, they have not cried secretly in the evening, alone in their room furnished with the four traditional pieces of furniture (two chairs, one bed, a table, a lamp) bequeathed by the teacher whom they have just replaced.[18]

Malino relates more details about the other two sisters.

> [An] absolutely brilliant student in Paris, Claire Benchimol returned to her home town of Tetuan (Northern Morocco), believed fervently in her mission, [and] she was nominated as a teacher in the girls' school. As one who had appropriated as her own the education and mores of Western Europe she asked, 'Who are we to demand a change?"

Another sister, Alégrina, would ask the *Alliance*, "Why do we think our ways are better?" At just 21 years of age Alégrina had been promoted to director of the Tripoli school. In addition to her more than 200 students, she supervised the education of her younger sisters and became the main

16 In particular, note Frances Malino, "Cross-Cultural Encounters: Jewish Sisters in Muslim Lands," (2004, accepted online 11/15/2008), 1.

17 Ibid.

18 Ibid.

financial support for her sisters, her mother, and her invalid father. They and their mother never failed to provide for each other. "If I did not have my mother with me..." became Hassiba's constant refrain as she and her mother shared the struggles of founding two schools (Fes and Larache), and nursed each other when an epidemic destroyed half of the Jewish population of Fes. When Claire died in childbirth in 1905, Alégrina remained in Tripoli to care for Claire's children. Four years later, Claire's husband Maïr asked Alégrina to marry him. "I thought a great deal about this," she wrote, revealing that her own love for Maïr was not the consideration. "I concluded that it was a sacred duty, in memory of my poor adored sister who had so loved me."[19]

Like Joy Land's criticism on the patronizing attitude of the *Alliance* toward the "native" Tunisian Jews, so Frances Malino described

> the dissonance between Paris-nurtured dreams and the realities they confronted on a daily basis, and by the exhaustion of trying to satisfy an organization whose presumptuous goals and autocratic methods they often questioned, Claire and her sisters would be demoralized and frustrated by similar paternalistic policy.

and yet, writes Malino:

> in spite of epidemics, war, and an increasingly anti-Semitic environment, these three sisters successfully mediated the demands of the *Alliance* and the expectations they held for themselves and the young girls in their charge....In spite of this very real dependence, however, reinforced by gender relations in France and the *Alliance*'s view of "Orientals," Claire and her sisters matured into ferociously independent women both in mind and spirit.[20]

Bashan, too, tells of the terrible situation in Tetuan:

> On April 19, 1893, during the month of Ramadan, a young Jewish boy of ten was accidentally trampled to death by an Arab on a horse. Hoping to obtain justice from the governor of Tetuan as he passed in procession, the bereaved parents presented him with the corpse. Annoyed rather than solicitous, the governor quickly retreated to his palace, leaving a hostile crowd throwing stones and brandishing knives as they shouted "Get the Jews!"[21]

Describing the events of fall 1893 in Northern Morocco, Claire, in her letter to Jacques Bigart, *secrétaire général* of the *Alliance*. Bigart tried to calm Claire's fears from his more secure position in Paris. But she reacted with her feminist pride:

---

[19] Ibid.

[20] Ibid.

[21] Ibid.

> I can say, without flattering myself too much, that in this situation, I have been and I still am braver than many of the men....You have made an abstraction of me and have forgotten what I accomplished in Tetuan to make it the school it has become today," she angrily wrote when she found herself transferred, or as she described it, "exiled" to Tripoli.[22]

Both Claire and Hassiba sought to eradicate the custom of child marriage. In Tetuan the practice existed only among the poorer members of the community, whereas in Fes child marriages were the domain of the wealthy. Claire writes (1894):

> [Miriam Choiron (Chokron[23])] has left the school today. In spite of her youth, her parents are going to marry her off in three months. The poor child does not want to separate herself either from her classmates or from the teachers, and the day that she said goodbye to us, she cried warm tears, so much did she regret leaving. Claire sought out Miriam's mother. "Why," she asked her, "was she so pressed to marry off her daughter?" "What else can I do?" she explained. "Today someone came requesting my daughter without demanding a dowry or trousseau; we are poor and I can not afford to wait only to find that I myself must then search for a husband." "How can one respond to such reasoning?" Claire asked herself. "Civilization alone will be able to make this disappear but we will have to wait so very long. Everything goes slowly, but this will go at the speed of a tortoise."

A much less patient Hassiba pointed to the "degradation" of the women of Fes as the reason for their early marriages.

> A woman is a slave who owes passive obedience to her lord and master. If you entered any home in Fes you would have trouble distinguishing the servant from her mistress. They both perform the same household tasks; they both eat in the kitchen. Only his sons are allowed to sit at the master's table. The daughters necessarily share their mother's lot. From the moment of her birth, a woman in Fes feels the weight of her inferiority. Whereas there are cries of joy and endless celebration upon the birth of a son, it is cries of mourning that welcome into the world the young girl, whose only sin is to have been born....Daughters are so loved by their father that as soon as they begin to walk and to talk, a husband is sought for them, a convenient way to get rid of them. This explains the deplorable practice of child marriage.

Hassiba found herself refusing re-admission to girls of eight and nine who had left to be married. "I did not want to accept any married girls," she explained to the *Alliance*.[24]

---

22 Ibid.

23 It could be that Malino had copied this name incorrectly, resulting in a French name instead of the popular Moroccan name to which I corrected it.

24 Ibid., 5–6; see also, Aron Rodrigue, *Images of Sephardi and Eastern Jewries in Transition* (Seattle: University of Washington Press, 1993), 80–91. To understand the reasons behind child-marriage, I cite from an interview with Rachelle Abitbol-Shriqi,

More pleasing is Malino's chapter on solidarity among the Jews of the world. The Benchimol girls

> spontaneously thought almost exclusively in terms of Jews of different countries, languages, and cultures. And, indeed, this global solidarity became an important goal not only for global purposes but for the teachers as well. Claire, Alégrina and Hassiba, for example, often explained the events in Eastern Europe to their young charges and, despite their own poverty, collected small sums from them earmarked for those Jews suffering pogroms and massacres. But solidarity was not merely connecting the Sephardic world to the Ashkenazic one, or coming to the aid of beleaguered coreligionists in distant countries. One needed to build solidarity, Alégrina argued, within individual communities as well."[25]

Alégrina's work in Libya is described with one more personal insight:

> Post-occupation Tripoli presented problems as well as new opportunities both of which Alégrina astutely analyzed and communicated to Paris. Describing the anti-Semitism that had erupted after the Italian conquest, she suggested that paradoxically it might serve a useful purpose...If the call for solidarity within the disparate and diverse Jewish communities might be seen as an expansion of the *Alliance*'s initial mandate, the solidarity that bound Alégrina, Claire and Hassiba and that permeated the lives of the women teachers, had neither been anticipated nor espoused by the founders of the *Alliance*. Yet, it was often this solidarity, touchingly expressed by Alégrina in her portrait of the Tripolitaine woman, which inspired the teachers and redefined their mission.[26]

The Benchimol sisters convinced their leaders in Paris to incorporate chapters on Jewish religion, Jewish history, and Hebrew language into the *Alliance* curriculum. This would affect not only the Libyan Jews, who at that time numbered no more than two dozen communities–most of them but a few hundred Jews each–but also the Moroccan Jews, whose communities numbered in the hundreds, or the Tunisian and the Algerian Jews, where each community numbered three or four times those in Libya.

---

who was born in Mogador about seventy years ago. She was married at the age of twenty-one, while her mother had been married at fourteen. She learned at the *AIU* elementary school and then at the French high school. "In my mother's time girls didn't go to school, so they got married." This custom survived in the rural areas until the 1930s. Rivka Mor-yoseph from Ntifa village was married at the age of 13 and was a mother to two boys by age 15. Another possible reason for such early marriage is the fear that girls would be kidnapped and converted by Muslims, mainly in times of chaos, which were very frequent in Morocco, but also in the other North-African countries. (The two interviews took place in Jerusalem: the former on 12/10/2008 and the latter on 12/8/2008.)

25 Malino, "Cross-Cultural Encounters," 7–8.

26 Ibid.

Thanks to the prodding of the Benchimol sisters, the *Alliance* opened both the Maghreb and Europe, for the first time, for the common people.[27]

> For failing in their attempts to assimilate [among the Italian settlers], the wealthy notables of the Jewish community might finally turn to the Jews in their midst, building a "new, solid, serious and sacred tie" between themselves and their less fortunate coreligionists.[28]

Malino summarized his research on the three sisters with the following sentences:

> Significantly, they appropriated the *Alliance*'s institutions to implement goals that they deemed essential for their female students–for example, earning one's living, finding dignity in life, preparing for an "independent future," avoiding early marriage. At times this meant advocating a more radical model of Westernization than that of the *Alliance*. Paradoxically it always required a sensitivity to and pride in local culture and tradition. Not surprisingly, the cross-cultural encounters of the teachers led to an increasingly fragmented identity. They were simultaneously colonizers and colonized, ethnographers and spokeswomen for the young girls among whom they lived and with whom they often identified, despite differences of class and language...But what the teachers were not, however, they were not citizens in the countries in which they had been born and in which they worked.[29]

This last statement is significant, since the North African Jews remained *dhimmi*, a tolerated minority in Muslim countries. They lacked equal status with the Arab majority nor had they French citizenship, as did the Algerian Jews.[30]

---

27 Frances Malino, "Prophets in Their Own Land? Mothers and Daughters of the *AIU*," *Nashim* 3 (2000): 56–73.

28 Ibid.

29 Ibid.

30 Another woman of importance and courage deserving note is Helen Qazes Ben-Attar, an attorney, the representative of the American Jewish Joint Distribution Committee, and an activist in the Zionist Federation of Casablanca. She contested the "pro-Nazi Government" in Morocco by establishing in July 1940 a relief organization for the Jewish refugees from Europe who had come to Morocco. Qazes Ben-Attar was born in Tangiers in 1898 and at the age of twenty transferred to Casablanca. During a period in which thousands of Jewish refugees fled from Hitler, a little while after the surrender of France to Nazi Germany, she founded the Moroccan branch of the Joint and served as its first president. The relief activities took place underground, and Qazes Ben-Attar was not deterred, even when the Vichy government in Morocco declared her activity to be criminal. Thousands of Jewish refugees from Europe worked in the labor camp of Wad-Zem near Casablanca. For most of them it was a temporary asylum until they could find a final destination. In the meantime they worked in the camp or in six other camps around Morocco, awaiting visas to the United States or South America. President Roosevelt met with her in Marrakesh on the 24th of January, 1943 to express his appreciation of her efforts. Qazes Ben-Attar also acknowledged those in

The Taqqanot *of the Rabbinical Council in Morocco*

In the twentieth century the Moroccan Rabbis Council continued to issue *taqqanot* as a way to halakhically address issues concerning women raised by modernity.

Inheritance *taqqanot* were again a major thrust of their legislation. Since husbands now were stipulating large sums on behalf of their wives in the *ketubbah*, the council in 1949 legislated that all assets should be divided equally between the wife and up to at least four children.

In 1952 the Moroccan rabbis decided not to force a woman to marry her brother-in-law in the case of her husband dying without issue - Levirate marriage. This was a bold step, since this custom was based on Mosaic Law and had been observed seemingly forever in the Maghreb.

In talmudic and medieval times, marriage without preliminary betrothal was frowned upon in Jewish practice. Only the couple's parents were involved, and the groom and the bride saw each other for the first time at their wedding. An amendment in this custom was carried out in 1947, enabling the couple to meet for a mutual recognition before marriage, for a period of only six months.[31]

Finally, according to talmudic law, a husband is obligated to provide sustenance, clothing, and housing for his wife (*Shulhan Arukh*, *Even Haezer* 69, 1-3). In Morocco, the custom had developed for young married couples to reside with their parents. In the new *taqqanot* it was decided "that there is no such living with parents anymore."[32] The reason for this change was the realization that new couples needed privacy, and that there should be no friction, mainly between the mother-in-law and the young wife, that might jeopardize this new marriage.

Aliyah

It was common to stipulate in Jewish marriage contracts that husbands were prohibited from changing the family place of residence, even to just another city, without the wife's consent. The renown Fes rabbi Ya'acov

---

the French and Spanish governments who had helped her. In 1945 she was nominated to be a delegate to the Jewish Joint Distribution Committee in Algeria, Tunisia, and Libya. (Bar-Asher, "Jewish Refugees from Nazi Europe in North Africa: A Document from the Archive of Qazes Ben-Attar," *Pe'amim: Studies in the Cultural Heritage of Oriental Jewry* 114-115 (2008): 257-62).

31 Moshe Ammar, ed., *Sefer haTaqqanot: haMishpat haIvri beQihillot Maroqo* [*Book of Ordinances: Jewish Law in Moroccan Communities*] vol. 1, (Jerusalem: 1980), 219.

32 Shalom Bar-Asher, "The Jews of North Africa and the Land of Israel in the Eighteenth and Nineteenth Centuries: The Reversal in Attitude toward *Aliyah* [Immigration to the Land] from 1770 to 1860," in *The Land of Israel: Jewish Perspectives*, ed. Lawrence A. Hoffman (Notre Dame, Ind.: University of Notre Dame Press, 1986), 305.

Aben-Tsur (1678–1753) had not granted the Land of Israel a special exemption from this prohibition. Historically, rabbis had sided with wives who refused to emigrate to Palestine with their husbands, most often due to the dangers of the journey or the hardships of living there. But, since the close of the eighteenth century, there were rabbis who decreed that since the routes to the Land of Israel had become safe—mainly due to the defeat of the Algerian corsairs—there was no longer such a restriction.[33]

Tunisia

The Alliance Israélite Universelle

Historiography is based primarily on statistics. According to some numbers given by Norman Stillman and Aaron Rodrigue, from the mid-nineteenth century onward, the *AIU* established a network of schools in the Ottoman Empire, in Iran, and in its Arab provinces, the Levant and North Africa. By the turn of the twentieth century there were more than one hundred schools with over 26,000 students. The first *AIU* School was founded in Tetuan, Morocco, in 1862 and served as a model for other schools throughout the Middle East and North Africa.[34] By 1878 a school for boys opened in Tunisia and another one for girls followed soon after in 1882.[35] Joy Land notes that

> the establishment of the School for Girls in Tunis (near ancient Carthage) occurred in tumultuous times: the French occupied Tunisia in 1881 and established a Protectorate there in 1883. The women teachers of Tunis were also multi-ethnic and multi-religious: European and North African, Jewish and non-Jewish. During its first decade of operation, the non-Jewish teaching staff of the *AIU* School for Girls included two Protestants and one Catholic. No men taught on its staff at that time.[36]

Land emphasizes the social function of the women educators.

> With the introduction of Jewish women educators in the region they too assumed the role of intermediaries between cultures. Their venture, however, lay between bridging the modernized culture of French Jewry and the traditional life of the *hāra* (Cl. Ar. *harāt al-Yahūd*, the Jewish quarter), in Tunisia or elsewhere. The women teachers were exhorted to be exem-

---

33 Bar-Asher, "The Jews of North Africa," 297–315.

34 Norman A. Stillman, *The Jews of Arab Lands in Modern Times* (Philadelphia: Jewish Publication Society, 1991), 23–25; Aron Rodrigue, *Jews and Muslims: Images of Sephardi and Eastern Jewries in Modern Times* (Seattle: University of Washington Press: 1993), 12–21.

35 Rodrigue, *Jews and Muslims*, 19–20.

36 Joy Land, "Corresponding Lives: Women Educators of the *Alliance Israélite Universelle* [*AIU*] School for Girls in the city of Tunis, 1882–1914" (Ph.D. diss., University of California, Los Angeles, 2006), 1–3.

> plars of moral rectitude for an impressionable group of youngsters. However, the theme of woman as intermediary who then becomes empowered and/or limited in her new role, serves as a central argument for research on women educators of the *AIU* in Tunis.[37]

Another area of successful change brought by the French to the North African countries was its modern culture and its assets.

> Language and literacy emerge as another arena for Tunisian young girls and women to take responsibility for their lives. According to Tunisian (and Libyan) mothers, French language proves an asset on the marriage market; according to *Alliance directrices* in Tunis and administrators in Paris, an education raises the age of marriage and eliminates child marriages. It provides increased employment opportunities in the *Alliance* school itself. Learning a trade is also a measure for theoretically ensuring a livelihood. Thus, alterations in attitudes and expectations occurred for the *directrices*, their students, and the families of the students. In addition, the *directrices* reached out to local female elites, engaging them in the formation of voluntary associations, a sign of an emerging modernity.[38]

Here, Land should question why these French agents of social change did not consider teaching the rich heritage of the Tunisian girls. The two Jewish communities in the Djerba Island in the south of Tunisia refused to have an *Alliance* school, but they still had an impressive communal and cultural life.[39] In the Jewish quarter of Tunis there were voices that spoke for a return to their own culture, rather than emulation of a foreign import. It happened in just one generation. The first schoolgirls of the 1880s received French first names to replace the Arabic ones used at home—but if the girls had Hebrew first names, they continued to use them. Also, the schoolgirls wore European clothes in school, although they changed into traditional clothing at home. By 1900 the *Alliance* was facing opposition to its policy of assimilation to French culture.[40]

ALGERIA

Yossef Charvit posits that "historical-sociological research works present the Jewish woman as the central force pushing for modernization."[41] He attributes the same level of importance to the woman in the framework of

---

[37] Ibid., 4–5.

[38] Ibid., 266.

[39] See Lucette Valensi, "*Le Fait Divers, Temoin des Tensions Sociales* [=Miscellaneous, A Witness of Social Tensions [French], Djerba, 1892," *Annales Economies, Sociétés, Civilisations* 7–8 (1983): 884–910.

[40] Land, "Corresponding Lives," 267–68.

[41] Joseph Charvit, "The Jewish Woman in Algeria in the Modern Era as Portrayed in Research Studies and Rabbinic Literature: Contradictions and Complements," in *The*

the Jewish family in Algeria. The woman, who was the most familiar with modernity due to her intensive contacts with French and European society in Algeria, was the moving force behind the family's push toward modernity. Conversely, the father remained the pillar of tradition. The children acted vis-à-vis the parents as a "Trojan horse," since they were under the influence of the French school. They felt somewhat embarrassed by the traditions at home and in the Jewish educational institutions.

Charvit's observations raise a basic question: Was the wife the prime mover in the modernization of the Jewish family, or did she serve as a mediator between the old traditions and the new developments that the French conquerors and settlers introduced to the new colony in the Maghreb? And if the mother did serve as mediator between tradition and modernity, why then did the children feel embarrassment toward her? After all, she would have been the representative of modernity!

Charvit's assumption of the central influence of the Jewish woman in Algeria on the modernization process is similar to that of Joy Land on the emancipation process in Tunisia, for there, too, female teachers in the *Alliance* had a strong influence on the belief in civil liberty and the development of independent women. In Tunisia, as in Algeria, the women were the ones who introduced manifestations of modernity: French life-style, French language, and French dress code. At the French school girls studied the language and culture of the conquerors, falling under the sway of nineteenth-century French society.[42] Girls in Morocco were accepted into the ranks of Jewish community educators in the mid-twentieth century after the First World War. It was thanks to *Em Habanim* [The Children's Mother], a local enterprise of rabbis that was supported by Jewish Orthodox institutions and individuals in Western Europe and the Unite States. They had not studied Hebrew and Judaism until this time.[43]

Jewish women in Algeria had frequent social contact with colonial society through their employment as household maids, seamstresses, and clerks. Traditional aspects of the Jewish family in Algeria began to disappear. Jewish cuisine retreated in favor of French cuisine during the late years of French rule in Algeria, which should be regarded as a rebellion of the woman against the status of a "Jewish housewife."[44] Traditional garb was replaced by European-style dress. In particular, during periods of heightened anti-Semitic activity, the Jewish woman dressed her children in

Jewish Woman in Algeria by Yossef Charvit (in press). I thank Yossef Charvit for kindly allowing me to read this article before it is publication.

42 Ibid.

43 David Ovadia, *Qehillat Sefrou* [*The Community of Sefrou*], vol. 3, (Jerusalem: 1975–1976), 220–21, [Hebrew].

44 Charvit, "The Jewish Woman in Algeria."

European clothes, even if she herself continued to wear the traditional garb. Children were often called by names given by the woman and a connection could be discerned between the Jewish-Arab name and the French name: Fortuna instead of Mas'uda, Mary instead of Miriam, Moris instead of Moshe, Raymond instead of Rahamim, Alfred instead of Faradj, or George instead of Yahya. Although the actual Hebrew name was given by the father at the synagogue, it did not appear on the identity card.

The observance of religious law became relegated to private life: "Be a Jew at your home and a French citizen any place." Children attended school on the Sabbath day, and the parents did not demand an exemption. Dietary laws were kept at home but not in the public sphere. A true cultural syncretism was established in Algeria. Bathing in the ritual bath was losing status with the advance of sanitation. The terms for ritual purity got mixed up with hygiene, such as *mikvah* (ritual) and *hamam* (bath). Some adopted the custom of bathing in the *mikvah* only prior to the wedding night and never thereafter.[45]

Charvit sums up this development by asserting that this path–stemming from the lenient Sephardic tradition, which was liberal and pluralistic–served the Jews through the tests and challenges of modernity. Here, he concludes, despite this assimilation, at least in the public sphere the women pushed toward modernity in the style of Algeria, in which tradition and modernity, a French signature and a Jewish signature, went hand-in-hand. A sociological study conducted with women who grew up during the early twentieth century shows evidence of nostalgia for the warmth of the Jewish holidays, for their extravagance, culinary abundance, together with an abundance of customs, melodies and richness of color.[46] Holidays maintained the sense of family, tribalism, solidarity, and brotherhood, in which the woman filled the central role of organizer, consultant, and assistant.

But if, as Charvit posits, the Jewish woman found the balance between the traditional past and the modern present, why did she still hope for better days in the Land of Israel? And why did she think that the situation in the Holy Land at the end of the nineteenth century would be any better than that in Algeria? Also, did all the Algerian communities react to modernity in similar manner? Was there not a difference between the Constantine community in the East or Telmcen in the West, which had strong traditional elements, as opposed to the community of Algiers, which was the capital city and center of French activity? The M'zab communities and primarily Gardayya maintained a conservative nature for many generations.

The main part of Charvit's article focuses on the response of the rabbis of Algeria to modernization, especially under the influence of the rabbis of

45 Ibid.

46 Ibid.

the Land of Israel. On the one hand, there is the halakhic rule called "*Dina DeMalchuta Dina*," which says that Jews are to keep the laws of the country in which they reside. On the other hand, there was the duty of the Jew to abide by Jewish law, *halakhah*. The rabbis of Algeria treated modernity as an objective and a universal process, which it was. They were forced to walk a "tightrope" by not automatically ruling out manifestations of modernity, as did their counterparts in European Jewry, but rather by tackling the issues practically and individually as each arose.[47] Charvit cites the words of the Great Rabbi:

> The number of those who transgress publicly has increased and they [the rabbis] cannot provide salvation. This is due to the fact that political liberty caused the destruction of all religions and any person does what is right in his mind.[48] The Gentiles [Christians] do not observe their own religion; some of them work on their holidays. This is due to the fact that political liberty ruined all religions.[49]

The response of some rabbis to this liberalization of society was a harsher interpretation of rabbinic law as, for instance, that of Rabbi Ben-Zion Alqal'ai, who stated that all divorces that took place according to French law in 1884 were voided and the women were to be considered to be *agunot* (women whose husbands are absent and therefore cannot remarry), and Rabbi Avraham Anqawa of Maskara, who ruled that a husband may not divorce a wife who was sexually faithful.[50] Rabbi Yoseph Nissim Burla, noting the trend toward promiscuity within Jewish society, attacked the unconscionable ease with which a husband could disparage his wife and thus, on the sheer basis of innuendo, have his marriage dissolved.

Fairly open social relations took place, even with Gentiles, and the unity of the Jewish family suffered. This openness included the appearance of the *nouveaux riches*, who seemingly had lost their sense of morality and were willing to divorce their wives without sufficient reason, at least as defined in the *Shulhan Arukh*: "A man should not divorce his first wife unless he discovered sexually improper conduct" (*Even ha-Ezer* 119). Charvit sums up the situation:

> The fight against the weakening of the family in Algeria is persistent—the woman appears repeatedly as the weak element that is exposed to the problems of [a] complicated double court system. The intention of the rabbis of the community was to reduce the injury as a result of the legal duality.

---

47 Ibid.

48 Ibid.

49 Ibid.

50 Ibid.

Charvit discusses the case of two rabbis in Algiers, Eliyahu Hazzan and Rahamim Franco, who jointly served on a tribunal in a case involving conversion.[51] The woman was a Gentile, a French woman married to a Jew with whom she had children. The issue involved was whether, once the children had been converted to Judaism, the religion of their father, it would be permissible to convert the mother. Rabbi Hazzan took into consideration the effect a Christian mother would have on the other members of the family. If husband and wife eventually separated, the children would probably remain with their mother, which was the natural tendency. And, since the mother had remained Christian, the children then would be drawn into the Christian world, even though they had once been converted.

Rabbi Hazzan held that, if it is clear to the *Bet Din* that it was impossible to separate the couple, two negative outcomes might occur: the Jewish spouse might move toward the position of the Gentile spouse to the point that he or she would leave Judaism or the Jewish party would not convert but continue to live with the Gentile spouse. Either of these possibilities, Rabbi Hazzan determined, was a severe transgression of *halakhah*. The rabbi was convinced that since the mother is the major influence in the education and rearing of the children, it would ensure the Jewish future of the children were she converted, even if only for family reasons, rather than for spiritual ones. Therefore, he ruled, it was preferable for the *Bet Din* to convert the Gentile spouse:[52]

> I told them that permitting her conversion is a matter of high priority because of the welfare of the children to whom she already has given birth and who are dependent on her. The future children to whom she may give birth would be conceived and be born with holiness.[53]

As this case illustrates, the effects of modernity had pervaded Jewish life to such a degree that it had become necessary for rabbinic *halakhah* to adjust and address it directly, and, in this instance, to utilize conversion as a means to ameliorate its seemingly deleterious effects upon the Jewish family.

In Conclusion

Yossef Charvit, in summarizing the relationship between women and modernity in Algeria, paints a picture valid for women throughout all North Africa:

> The instability of the early nineteenth century is replaced during the late nineteenth and early twentieth centuries, toward a new family and community stability. In this context the woman appears as an island of stability on

---

[51] Ibid.

[52] Ibid.

[53] Ibid.

> the one hand, and a dynamic vector on the other hand. The woman also creates a pattern of "leadership behind the scenes," although she sometimes appears as soft and fragile. The woman fights for the future identity and serves as the seismograph of the society and the time of the "earthquake of modernity." In this sense the woman plays an ambivalent role toward tradition. Surely she treats modernity in a favorable way, as the modern world is perceived as the tomorrow, however, she does not reject the traditional world.[54]

Of course, there were pockets in the peripheries, as well as among traditional communities in the big cities, where the female population guarded its traditions zealously, such as at Djerba in Tunisia and Sefrou in Morocco.[55]

There seems to be general agreement on a special link between women and modernity. Historical-sociological research and its secular sources view this link as positive. French narrative obligates the assimilation approach, according to which the woman was deeply involved in the general society and, in her own way, was able to adapt Jewish society to the majority society. Rabbinic literature, however, views it as problematic. The halakhic-rabbinic narrative in Algeria, for example, while not denying that modernity is a universal phenomenon, rejects its assimilationist aspects, which they saw as weakening Jewish identity and the unity of the Jewish family.

Nevertheless, the women in North African communities fulfilled a significant and historic role in maintaining Jewish identity for the family without rejecting the process of modernization and the benefits it offered.

---

[54] Ibid.

[55] Ovadia, *Qehillat Sefrou*, 252–55.

The Disputes regarding the Jewish Emigration from Morocco 1956–1961

YIGAL BIN-NUN

The subject of Jewish emigration from Morocco or, as it has been coined by both parties, the right to freedom of movement troubled the leaders of the Jewish community regarding difficulties the authorities were creating for Jews seeking to obtain passports. This issue was no less troubling for the leaders of the World Jewish Congress, the government of the State of Israel, the Jewish Agency, and the agents of the Misgeret who worked secretly on behalf of the Mossad in Morocco.[1] Liberal circles within the Moroccan leadership rejected the idea of Jewish emigration, because, with the advent of Moroccan independence, they wished to create the appearance of a progressive country in which all its citizens, regardless of religion, enjoyed equal rights so that none would have any desire to leave. Liberals also opposed emigration because of the concern that if Jews left the country, the economy would suffer. Pan-Arabists in the conservative wing of the Istiqlal,[2] for their part, were unhappy that wealthy Jews from Morocco would emigrate to Israel, thus strengthening the Zionist forces there against Arab nations.

The history of the Jewish community during the early years of Moroccan independence is one of continuous worry regarding an unclear future and the possibility of impending disaster. During that period, the Jewish community was forced to address several critical questions that would ultimately determine the future of Moroccan Jewry, as well as the future of individual Jews in the community. While the struggle for independence had been waged without much involvement on the part of the Jewish community, the withdrawal from colonialism presented each Moroccan Jew with fateful options: whether to seek personal and communal success within a democratic progressive country or to escape from the country out of fear of possible disaster.

---

1 The Mossad had established a network in Morocco, which it called Misgeret (Framework). The network dealt with the subject of Jewish self-defense and, later on, the issue of illegal emigration.

2 The Istiqlal Party—the word means "independence"—was established after the publication of the proclamation of independence in Fès. Its 58 signatories made up a group of young people who had already in 1934 formed a group called Action du Peuple, which demanded reforms from the colonial administration. Allal Al Fassi and Ahmed Balafrej headed the party.

The Moroccan monarchy also had to choose between continuing its connection to France, the democratic West and its culture and language, or aligning Morocco with the countries of the Middle East, which had pan-Arabist policies and negative relations with their own Jews. At the time, the future of the country's government and the fate of the Jews' legal status in Morocco were not at all clear. The Jewish community as a whole had a decision to make. It could, on the one hand, demand the rights of an ethnic minority and receive the isolation that went along with such a status. This would mean experiencing life as a state within a state, while preserving their separate ethnic identity. Alternatively, it could permit itself to be absorbed by the new society, its culture and its language, to the point of total assimilation, as was the case of the Jewish communities of Western Europe. The first option was not very popular, because its potential backers simply preferred to go to Israel. The second option was preferable for only a relatively short period of time among the educated Jewish class. This group was soon forced to deal with an unpleasant truth, as it quickly became clear that what was true for the Jews of France after the French Revolution and, subsequently, for all of Western Europe's Jews, did not apply in the reality of a new Arab-Muslim state in the twentieth century, even one that had just emerged from a period of French colonial control that had lasted for little over forty years. Most of Moroccan Jewry chose a path that was midway between a search for complete community autonomy and an attempt at cultural assimilation. This "golden mean" was most strongly supported by the community's official leader of that period, David Amar.

Despite many public declarations that they were being fully integrated into Moroccan politics, society, and, to a certain degree, its culture (which was itself in the middle of being formulated) most of the community's leaders chose to preserve the clearly ethnic public institutions that went beyond any religious function and were more connected to the social, educational, and cultural spheres. These were the kind of institutions that give a community an ethnic identity different from that of the general population. The Jews of Morocco thus had a triple set of loyalties, their first being formal loyalty to the Moroccan homeland, the country in which their fathers had lived even before the advent of Islam, along with faithfulness to its language, society, and royal house. At the same time, the Jews preserved their Jewish identity, not just in religious terms, but with regard to ethnicity and culture as well, and this brought along with it a hidden emotional connection to the State of Israel and a certain pride in its successes. Along with these two national and ethnic loyalties, the Jews of Morocco continued to develop their connection to French cultural, educational, and linguistic values, all of which were a guarantee of social advancement.

Three principles guided the leadership of the State of Israel in their relations with the Jewish community in Morocco, and they determined the basic guidelines of the Zionist understanding of the situation: first, anti-

Semitism is timeless and universal; second, the ingathering of all Diaspora Jewry in Israel must eventually be accomplished in order to defeat this eternal anti-Semitism; and third, Israel must take the responsibility for having the Jews brought to Israel preemptively in order to overcome the demographic fear stemming from the regional situation and to strengthen the Jewish base within it. After the Holocaust in Europe, the Jews of North Africa and especially the community in Morocco became the most important Jewish bloc in the world for American Jewry, which wished to mark the tradition of maintaining Jewish existence in the face of the danger of assimilation. They were also an important group for the Jews in Israel, who were interested in this area as a source of emigration and as a potential supplier of human resources for the strengthening in Israel of the economy, and for its industry, agriculture, and defense.

The Jewish Population of Morocco and Emigration after 1948

In the two years following Israel's declaration of independence a total of 22,900 Jews left Morocco for Israel. Between 1948 to the independence of Morocco, 108,243 Jews emigrated to the young state at an average rate of 3,000 Jews per month. During all the years in which the Jewish Agency's Qadima[3] organization functioned in Morocco, approximately 110,000 Jews left the country and about another 120,000 had left by 1961. Altogether, almost 237,813 Jews came to Israel from Morocco in the years 1948 to 1967.

A census held in November of 1957 showed that the Moroccan Jewish community as a whole numbered 164,216, which made up 1.8% of the general population, and that seventy-five percent of it lived in twelve cities or villages. The remaining Jews (a group that numbered at varying times approximately 80,000 people in total) lived in smaller groupings in over 150 communities. In 1956, most of the Moroccan Jewish community lived in cities, with only 40,000 Jews living in 145 small villages. Families were large, and the population was relatively young–the average Jewish family had six family members and children under the age of 16 made up 50.7% of the Jewish population. Only 10.6% of the community was elderly. The Jews lived mainly in the cities of Casablanca, Fès, Marrakech, Meknès, Rabat, Tanger, Sefrou, Qenitra, Oujda, Tétouan, Midelt, and Erfoud.

The situation three years later was not much different, although the size of the Jewish community had already begun to shrink. In July of 1960, the official Moroccan Ministry of the Interior's first census was completed, and the Jewish population was given at 160,032, making up only 1.4% of the general population. 71,175 Jews lived in Casablanca alone, where the gen-

3 Qadima (1949–1956) was the Jewish Agency's organization in Morocco. It was also the name of the transit camp run by the Jewish Agency near Al Jadida, which housed Jews emigrating to Israel.

eral population numbered 965,000. Half of the Jews were under the age of 20 and most of the Jewish population was urban. The Jews made up only 2% of the population, but constituted 8% of the country's industrial workers and artisans, 10% percent of all merchants, and 5% of the members of the free professions and of those employed in managerial positions. Thirty percent of the general Moroccan population worked in modern industries, while 99% of Jews were employed in such fields. By June 30, 1963, 60,017 Jews had come to Israel from Morocco, which is why it is assumed that 110,000 Jews remained in Morocco as of that date.

Between 1957 and November of 1961, when the government began to permit Jews to leave under collective passports, 29,472 Jews left legally or through various paths of illegal emigration organized by the Israeli security services. If those leaving in 1957 are discounted–a year in which most Jews left the country with legal passports–it appears that the number who left in the context of Misgeret, the Israeli Secret Service's illegal immigration program, came to a little less than 10,200 Jews. From November of 1961 through the end of 1963, more than 72,500 Jews left Morocco legally. By 1964, when the Yakhin campaign ended, a total of 83,707 Jews had left. In 1965, 55,000 Jews remained in Morocco, but by 1972 no more than 30,000 were living there. By 2003 the community numbered under 5000. Because of the limitations created by Israel's policy adopted in 1953 of allowing only "selected" Moroccan Jews to immigrate, there was a negative balance in terms of immigration to Israel during the year of the policy's adoption: the number of Jews who returned from Israel to Morocco was greater than the number who emigrated to Israel.

The disputes regarding emigration caused divisions not only between the Moroccan government and the Israeli emissaries and the World Jewish Congress, but they arose also between World Jewish Congress on the one side and the leadership of the Mossad and the Israeli government on the other. Although the WJC acknowledged that Zionism and the State of Israel were the life-blood of the Jewish people, they nevertheless argued that the Jews who still lived in the Diaspora should not be forgotten and that their welfare should continue to be a cause of concern. The WJC leaders saw their primary goal as being the preservation of the spiritual lives of the Diaspora Jews, since, no matter what, Israel would not be able to absorb all of Diaspora Jewry. The WJC leadership, therefore, decided to establish cultural and other activities within North African Jewish communities. They set for themselves the goal of "increasing the Jewish presence" by exerting pressure on the community's leadership and by responding to every attack on the community's special rights that might emanate from government sources. To strengthen its position, the WJC maintained continuous contact with governmental authorities, even providing them with certain services. Even if the WJC representatives were not always optimistic regarding the outcomes of their activities, they continued to meet with government ministers and senior officials frequently, so as to maintain an unbroken connection with the authorities. They complained that Israel did not help them with their work, even though they saw themselves as Israel's unofficial ambassadors in places where the state did not have diplomatic contacts.[4] This was the reason for their harsh criticism of Misgeret's underground work involving clandestine emigration. They claimed that not only was such activity insufficient to solve the problem of restrictions on emigration, it would also damage the WJC's diplomatic efforts and their chances for reaching an agreed arrangement with the government leadership.

From the perspective of the Jewish Agency's representatives, the activities of the WJC leaders had both positive and negative aspects. The WJC leadership saw itself as working to achieve peace and quiet for the North African Jews by ensuring relief from occasionally renewed anti-Jewish regulations. The World Zionist Organization and the government of Israel had a different perspective. They rejected the very possibility of peaceful life in the Diaspora and saw a need for radical action in order to change the situation. According to Baruch Duvdevani, who ran the Immigration Department of the Jewish Agency in Europe:

> Our perspective was a Zionist one. We did not avoid difficult and dangerous decisions, because we were persuaded that there was no future for Jews in Morocco and that their only hope was in emigration to Israel. And we felt the pressure of time very clearly. The WJC felt differently–they worked to achieve temporary solutions and an easing of the situation on the spot [...] Nevertheless, it should be said to their credit, that their friendly connections with many government officials was what prevented bloodshed on the Jewish street during the times when control of the government was transferred from one group to another. These connections also contributed to the easing of the situation in the transit camp next to Casablanca.[5]

Isser Harel, the director of the Mossad at the time, also understood that the Jewish side was divided schematically into two separate camps. In one camp were those who supported mass emigration, which was to be minimally funded, and in the other were those who supported the path of quiet diplomacy, of lobbying and adopting a patient approach with respect to the Moroccan authorities. This second camp minimized the importance of Harel's organization's work in getting Jews out of Morocco. According to him, the first camp included Prime Minister Ben-Gurion, Foreign Minister Golda Meir, and S. Z. Shragay, while the leader of the other camp was Nahum

---

4 Levinsky, addressing Mossad activists in Paris, November 7, 1958 (Israel National Archives, Foreign Ministry, 4317/10/1).

5 Testimony of varuch Duvdevani, *The Organization of Underground Activists in North Africa*, vol. 4 (Tel Aviv, 1994). The reference is to the Qadima transit camp for emigrants.

Goldmann, the President of the World Jewish Congress.[6] In reality, the division was more complicated and many other elements were also involved, elements that related not only to emigration and Israel's ability to absorb immigrants, but also to the estimated degree of danger that the Jews could expect in Morocco and the two sides' respective views regarding the proper way to persuade the Moroccan authorities to allow the Jews to leave.

On the Moroccan side, the leadership's various arguments against Jewish emigration reflect the differences in political culture that existed among the factions making up that leadership. Thus, there were several different reasons for their opposition:

- The paternalistic-traditional approach, which characterized the king's attitude, saw the Jews of the community as having been placed under the personal protection of the ruler. The monarchy saw itself as being obligated to "protect its Jewish sons" as it had done for generations. This approach involved a certain degree of sentimentality, which was devoid of any *realpolitik*.
- Another argument against emigration flowed from the view that the Jews' exit from the country immediately upon its attaining independence from France would destabilize the country in terms of its public administration, commerce, and economy. This argument was based on the realization that the Moroccan Jews as a group played an important economic and administrative role in the country. Another version of this argument was one that emphasized that such a mass exodus of Jews would certainly be covered in the international media and would create the impression that the young state was collapsing economically. Furthermore, those putting forth this argument feared that such coverage would portray Morocco as a country governed by intolerant rulers.[7]
- Others argued that allowing the Jews to leave *en masse* would expose Morocco to world public opinion as an undemocratic, non-progressive country whose government was unable to provide its non-Muslim citizens with the conditions necessary for proper integration into Moroccan society.
- An additional reason given for opposing Jewish emigration was that most of the Jews would emigrate to Israel, and their departure from Morocco would, therefore, impact on Morocco's relations with the other Arab countries, which it needed for the sake of stabilizing its

---

6 Testimony of I. Harel, *The Organization of Underground Activists in North Africa*, vol. 4 (Tel Aviv, 1994).

7 Report submitted by Hayim Yahil, Deputy Director-General, Israel Foreign Ministry, regarding his conversation with Marcel Stein, who had returned from talks in Morocco, November 8, 1957 (Israel National Archives, Foreign Ministry II 4317/10).

political condition as its struggle against colonial France came to an end.

- Finally, the argument was made that the massive emigration of young Jews to Israel would strengthen the Israeli Defense Forces in its war with Morocco's fellow Arab countries.

Whatever the reasoning, Morocco was united from one corner of the political spectrum to the other in its opposition to the idea of allowing the Jews to leave the country. Israel's representatives and the heads of the international Jewish organizations tried to answer these claims with opposing arguments. They pointed out that the financial factor was not that important since approximately 60,000 Jews (out of 160,000 in 1960) were being sustained by aid from the American Joint Distribution Committee.[8] In their conversations with the authorities, the Israeli representatives also pointed out that the emigration of Jewish professionals from the country would create many job opportunities for educated Muslims. As for concerns regarding the response of Middle Eastern Arab countries, the Israeli emissaries responded that even Arab League countries–even those that were in a state of war with Israel–were permitting their Jews to leave for Israel, and that these young immigrants were also serving in the Israel Defense Forces. They were, in fact, referring to the experience of the Jews of Egypt, Iraq, Yemen, Libya, Tunisia, and even Syria and Lebanon. According to Alexander Easterman, while Nasser was actually encouraging Jews to leave Egypt and even expelled them after the Sinai Campaign in 1957 as part of his struggle for national unity, Morocco was discouraging Jews from leaving as part of a policy of encouraging the maintenance of national ethnic variety.[9] The Israelis also pointed to Tunis' liberal policy as a positive example, a policy that had been shaped by Habib Bourguiba. Despite his having allowed the Jews of his country to leave freely, the Jews had not stormed the exit gates.[10]

In the eyes of the Moroccan leadership, the Jews' economic situation was similar to that of the French colonialists. Despite the difference between the two groups in terms of actual statistics, the Jews constituted a

---

8 Victor Malka points to a census that was held in 1960 in which 160,000 Jews were counted in the country, compared to 230,000 in 1950. V. Malka, "La situation des communautés juives en Tunisie et au Maroc. L'exemple marocain," L'Arche, no. 62, March 1962.

9 A. Easterman, speaking at the Fourth General Assembly of the World Jewish Congress Political Department at Stockholm, report for August 1959; M. Laskier, "The Emigration of the Jews of Morocco, the Government's Policy and the Positions of the World Jewish Organizations, 1949–56," *Shorashim ba mizrah, Research of the Zionist and Pioneering Movement in the Sephardic and Islamic Communities*, vol. 2, 354 [Hebrew].

10 M. Gazit, of the Israeli embassy in Washington, to Y. Maroz at the Israeli Foreign Ministry in Jerusalem, February 22, 1961 (Israel National Archives, Foreign Ministry, 941/8).

considerable consumers' market and a source of skilled manpower for management positions. According to historian Daniel Rivet, "it would not be an exaggeration to state that the exodus of this community would, from a human perspective, impoverish Morocco more than would the return of all Europeans to the northern coast of the Mediterranean."[11] But the Jews, from their perspective, were concerned about what might happen once the country overcame the difficulties of adjusting to political and economic independence. Ironically, however, for most Moroccan Jews, the calls by Moroccan and world Jewish leadership for freedom of movement and for the granting of passports were irrelevant. At most, the freedom to leave the country with individual passports would have served the needs of only merchants and businessmen who could leave for Europe because of their businesses or for vacations or visits. Positive responses to the demands for passports and freedom of movement would still not have solved the problems of the many village-dwelling Jews or of the lower-class urban Jewish communities. These groups needed more than just the technicality of obtaining passports to leave; they required the assistance of an organization that could arrange their departure, take care of shipping their goods, and deal with their absorption into a new country. Nevertheless, on a practical level, it was better for the Jewish organizations to mention just the two essential demands, for freedom of movement and the issuance of passports. They realized that it would be much harder to go further and ask that a foreign country be expressly granted permission to organize—on Moroccan territory—a framework for the departure of Moroccan Jews *en masse* for Israel.

Indeed, with time, the Moroccan authorities were forced to give up their goal of hermetically sealing the country's borders against departing Jews. They eventually adopted a policy of more or less ignoring the fact that Jews were leaving, so long as the departures were discrete and not visible to the opposition parties. Since political opposition to emigration had served for so long as a political weapon in the hands of the various parties in their attacks against each other and in their opposition to various royal policies, neither side dared to officially proclaim its agreement to allow the Jews to leave. However, in private conversations, several politicians did not oppose such emigration and did not do anything to block it. Gradually, the king was forced to make peace with reality and to give up his wish to hold the Jews against their will. It was difficult to put up an artificial obstacle to effectively stem the growing desire on the part of the Jews to leave their homeland and to seek their future in new geo-cultural horizons. This change in the king's attitude had more than one cause. Alongside the pressure of Jewish and non-Jewish world public opinion was the gradual development of a more pragmatic perspective among Morocco's rulers.

---

[11] D. Rivet, *Le Maroc de Lyautey à Mohammed V, Le double visage du protectorat, Denoël*, 418.

The World Jewish Congress and the Moroccan Nationalist Movement

The relationship between the leadership of the Moroccan Nationalist Movement and the representatives of the international Jewish organizations began long before the country achieved independence. In June of 1952, the leaders of the World Jewish Congress had already held their organization's first North-African conference, the intention of which was to prepare the local Jewish leadership for the changes expected in light of the probability that the countries of the region would soon be achieving independence.

The goal was to enable the North African communities to avoid the experience of their sister communities in Middle Eastern countries, where there had been considerable anti-Jewish oppression and even violence. According to the World Jewish Congress' leaders, they were surprised to discover that the region's community leaders had an unreasonable sense of security and could not imagine the political changes that would, sooner or later, change their way of life.[12] At this time, in 1952, Nahum Goldmann invited a group of young members of the Zionist youth movements in Morocco to a meeting in order to convince them to support the nationalist movement in their country. Meyer Toledano, Salomon Azoulay, and their colleagues travelled to Geneva and heard Goldmann tell them of his forecast for the future in Morocco after it achieved independence. The French authorities were convinced that they would remain in North Africa for a long time. Goldmann was able to persuade the group of young Moroccan Jews, however, and upon their return to Morocco, they contacted activists within the nationalist movement and collected funds for them from the Jewish merchants in Casablanca.[13]

Also beginning in 1952, the leaders of the WJC made a series of visits to Morocco and noticed that the situation there was more serious than that in Tunisia. Attacks carried out by the nationalist movement against the colonial authorities caused considerable unease and fear among many groups within the Jewish community, which, in turn, created pressure for increased emigration. The WJC leaders reached the conclusion that the Moroccan Jewish community had two options in order to prevent a disaster: to emigrate or to negotiate with the nationalist movement.

During the summer months, the WJC Coordinating Committee met to establish a policy regarding the community's fate. The goal was to establish the necessary conditions for a harmonious transfer from one historical period to another. At the time, it was not at all clear that the transfer would necessarily take place without violence and bloodshed. Nevertheless, the World Jewish Congress was the only organization that could envision a

---

12 G. Riegner, *Ne jamais désespérer* (Paris: Éditions du Cerf , 1998), 529–33.

13 Personal testimony in a conversation with th author, S. Azoulay, Paris, June 11, 2001.

future for the Jews in Morocco. The rest of the Jewish organizations, in the United States, France, and Israel, were indebted in various ways to the French authorities and, therefore, supported its policies in North Africa. Despite this unique perspective, the World Jewish Congress' leadership insisted that the French authorities should be notified of the direct contacts with the Moroccan nationalist movement before they took place. With this purpose in mind, Nahum Goldmann met with the French foreign minister, Mendes-France, and notified him and those of his ministers who were dealing with Moroccan and Tunisian affairs–among them Christian Fouché, Pierre July, and Alain Savary–about his organization's wish to establish contacts with representatives of the Moroccan nationalist movements. The World Jewish Congress' goal in doing this was to ensure the safety of the Jews, as well as to secure their status and emigration rights, without having the meeting with the nationalists interpreted as reflecting any anti-French feeling. Mendes-France assured him that the rights of the Jews and of all national minorities would be taken into consideration in any future negotiations. The French Foreign Ministry encouraged the representatives of the WJC to maintain contact with the nationalists and promised to update them regarding developments.[14]

In November of 1954, the Moroccan prime-minister designate, Mbark Bekkay, met with the representatives of the American Jewish Committee and indicated to them that he shared the position taken by writer André Chouraqui regarding the future status of the Jews in the as-yet-to-be-created independent state. This status was to be based on brotherly relations among the various groups within the country's population.[15] Bekkay's declaration earned him considerable respect among the various Jewish organizations. Two months later, in January of 1955, the World Jewish Congress' Action Committee met in the UNESCO building in Paris. After the French newspaper "Combat" published the WJC's leadership's declaration–which noted that while the Tunisian authorities treated their country's Jews with respect, the Moroccans, in contrast, had refused to make any statements regarding the status of Moroccan Jewry–the leaders of Istiqlal and the PDI (Parti Démocratique pour l'Indépendance) asked to meet with them. They complained that the Moroccan Jewish community had never supported their demands for independence. They stressed the democratic nature of

[14] G. Riegner, *Ne jamais désespérer*, 535–43. Armand Kaplan, WJC representative to N. Goldmann, in M. Laskier, "The State of Israel and the Jews of Morocco in the Mix of Moroccan Politics," *Mikhael* 14 (1994): 252 [Hebrew].

[15] Chouraqui was especially familiar with the Jewish community as a separate ethnic community with a legal status different from that of the general Muslim population. This was in contrast to the status of Jews as individuals in the West European countries, in which religion alone separated the Jews from others in the society of which they were a full and equal part.

their movement, which was based on the idea of granting freedom and equality to all citizens regardless of religion or ethnic origin. Although no decisions were made at the first official meeting between the Moroccan nationalist leaders and the WJC, it did lead to a series of personal meetings in Paris, all of which were held at the initiative of the nationalist movement.

Thus, thanks to Jo Golan's contacts, Mbark Bekkay held a luncheon meeting at the beginning of February at a Paris restaurant with the participation of leaders of the WJC, Istiqlal, and the PDI, in order to discuss the issue of Moroccan Jewry. Jo Golan of Paris attended,[16] as did Gerhart Riegner of Geneva,[17] the WJC's legal counsel, Morris Perlzweig of New York,[18] Alexander Easterman of London, and Armand Kaplan of Paris. The participating Moroccans were Abderahim Bouabid, Mehdi Ben Barka, Mohammed Bouceta, Abdelqader Benjelloun, and Ahmed Ben Souda. The WJC leaders asked the nationalist movement leaders to see to it that the commanders of the Liberation Army's field units refrained from injuring innocent Jews. At the recommendation of Bouabid, a promise was given and the armed forces were

16 Jo Golan (Joseph Guldin, 1922–2003) was born in Alexandria and grew up in Damascus. He spoke Arabic in addition to English and French. Because he knew the Arab countries so well, he was drafted in 1940 to work for the Hagana's intelligence agency and for the Jewish underground organization in Cairo. Upon the establishment of the State of Israel, he joined Israeli intelligence and was slated to be appointed as Isser Harel's deputy. (The appointment was never actually carried out.) He studied law and political science in Paris from 1949 until 1953 and was chosen there to be the Director-General of the "Students Against Colonialism" organization. At the recommendation of Moshe Sharret, he was appointed to serve as Nahum Goldmann's political secretary from 1954–1971. After Golda Meir confiscated his Israeli passport in retribution for his having disobeyed orders by warning Algerian Jewish leaders of an impending attack by the Algerian Liberation Organization in the city of Constantine, he served for several years as an economic adviser to several African states, and received Senegalese citizenship. Six months after the confiscation, his passport was restored, and he lived in Europe for the rest of his life. He died in the summer of 2003 while visiting Morocco; the authorities there arranged to have his body flown to Israel.

17 Gerhart Riegner (1911–2001) was born in Germany. He was the World Jewish Congress' representative in Geneva during World War II. In August of 1942, he provided the deputy American consul in that city with information that he had received from a German industrialist regarding the Nazis' plan to exterminate millions of Jews. The message was transmitted to the United States and to England, but the authorities in those countries did not act upon it. After the war, Riegner directed the World Jewish Congress' liaison office and was eventually named as the WJC's Secretary General. He contributed to the strengthening of the relationship between the Vatican and the State of Israel. He wrote a memoir, *Ne jamais désespérer, Soixante années au service du peuple juif et des droits de l'homme*, published by Editions du Cerf, Paris 1998.

18 Dr. Morris Perlzweig was the director of the World Jewish Congress' International Department in New York.

sent explicit instructions to respect the Jewish population. On this same occasion, the Moroccan nationalist leaders announced their intention to appoint a Jew as a minister in the future government.[19] Upon his return to Geneva, Riegner met PDI leader Mohammed Hassan Ouazzani and discussed with him the legal status of the Jews in a future independent Morocco.[20]

On May 1, 1955, economist Felix Nataf called a secret meeting that was held in the home of Mohammed Dadi, one of the leaders of the "Amitiés Marocaines" movement. At the meeting, Nataf introduced a group of young Jews to Mehdi Ben Barka, one of the young leaders of Istiqlal. Participants included Meyer Toledano, Jacques Perez,[21] and Salomon Azoulay.[22] During the negotiations with the French regarding Moroccan independence, the leaders of Istiqlal asked the representatives of the World Jewish Congress to use their contacts in the United States Congress to persuade President Eisenhower to put pressure on the French concerning their demands for independence. Easterman reported these conversations to Israeli Prime Minister Moshe Sharet on May 4, 1955. Sharet supported the maintenance of these contacts, but conditioned Israeli assistance on the granting of freedom of emigration and equal rights for Jews in the future independent Moroccan state.[23]

On the 15th of August, Easterman met secretly with Ahmed Balafrej, the director of Istiqlal's public relations and documentation office in New York. After this meeting, Balafrej published an announcement according to which there was no Jewish "problem" regarding Morocco at all:

> The Jews need have no concern that they will suffer from any form of discrimination in an independent Morocco. The Jews of Morocco, like its Muslims, are both *de jure* and *de facto* citizens. They will enjoy the same rights and will be subject to the same obligations. Their religious faith will not be affected. The positive development that they will see will be their release from the burden of colonial control that exploited them as well. Morocco is their independent country and whoever helps the Jews of Morocco helps Moroccan independence as well.[24]

---

19 Riegner, *Ne jamais désespérer*, 535–43.

20 I.M.H. Ouazzani, *Entretiens avec mon père* (Fes: Fondation MHO, 1989), 213–18.

21 Jacques Perez was deputy Secretary-General of the Conseil des Communautés Juives and one of the six Jewish representatives in the Government Council that the French colonial authority established after the Second World War in Morocco.

22 F. Nataf, *L'indépndence du Maroc, témoignages d'actions 1950–1956* (Paris: Plon, 1975), 208–12. Personal testimony in a conversation with the author, S. Azoulay, Paris, June 11, 2001.

23 S. Segev, *Operation Yakhin* (Tel Aviv, 1984), 87. [Hebrew].

24 Phil Baum and Herbert Foster, "Memorandum Regarding Morocco, International Council of the World Jewish Congress," January 30, 1961 (Israel National Archives, Foreign Ministry, 4318/4/III).

Morocco's "Conseil des Communautés Juives" (Council of Jewish Communities) took part in talks held with the French government in Aix-les-Bains on the 20th of August–conversations in which representatives of the nationalist movement also took part–for the purpose of finding solutions to the "crisis in Morocco." In conformance with the French policy of separating the Jewish and Muslim populations of Morocco, the Jewish delegation took part in these talks separately. The Jewish delegation even met separately with the French delegation. The French "Résidence" (The French government in Morocco) had approved the composition of the Jewish delegation, which included the president of the Jewish community, Jacques Dahan, and his deputy, Sam Nahon, the treasurer, Joseph Berdugo, and his deputy, Albert Levi, and Georges Benabou. The commission agreed to add Dr. Léon Benzaquen to these representatives on a "personal" basis, as well as Attorney Meyer Toledano, also to be included as participating "privately," with Easterman and Pierre Dreyfus-Schmidt taking part on behalf of the World Jewish Congress. The official Jewish delegation was not especially well supported by the nationalist movement. At the same time, the French authorities encouraged the Moroccan delegation to establish contacts with the World Jewish Congress. French Prime Minister Edgar Faure, who wished to consult with the delegation regarding Morocco's future, received the Jewish delegation from Morocco. At the end of the meeting, the delegation still did not see fit to express clear support for the claims of the Moroccan nationalists and preferred to use evasive language. After mentioning the community's ancient roots in the country, the Jewish delegation added the following to their official public statement:

> We hope that our country is able to escape from the serious crisis in which it now finds itself and that all political movements in Morocco are able to find a place for themselves to live in peace and in unity.[25]

The heads of the community continued to give cautious support to the colonial government, but the World Jewish Congress delegation, in contrast, evoked positive responses from the Moroccans, because it did not oppose their avowed intentions to achieve independence. Because of this supportive position, René Cassin invited Easterman and Riegner and asked them to explain their position. The two did not see fit to announce to the president of the "Alliance Israélite Universelle" that the French government knew of their contacts with the Moroccans. According to Riegner, Cassin's deputy, Jules Brunshvig, admitted to him years later that the World Jewish Congress' leaders' views were more correct in those days than were those of the Alliance's leaders.[26]

---

25 Assaraf, *Mohammed V*, 218; Y. Tsur to N. Goldmann, September 19, 1959 (Israel National Archives, Foreign Ministry, 2525/9).

26 Riegner, *Ne jamais désespérer*, 542. As a leading France-based international Jewish

On September 2, Golan and Easterman organized a meeting between the leaders of the nationalist movement and the members of the Conseil des Communautés Juives in order to bring about a change in the Jewish communities' leaders' position of not supporting the nationalists. The independence fighters accused the Jewish community leaders of lining up behind the French political authorities and supporting its traditional imperialistic policy of using the "divide and conquer" method to control the general population in its colonies. The president of the community, Jacques Dahan, denied the accusations and argued that the community had never made any statement against the Moroccan claims for independence. The Jews responded to the accusation that they had never joined in the struggle, by pointing out that the restrictive Vichy laws had forced them to be extra cautious and to refrain from making any public statements regarding the issue. In response to comments published in the "Jewish Chronicle," the leaders of the PDI agreed to cancel all existing legal restrictions imposed on the Jews after the country obtained independence, but the Istiqlal leadership did not get involved.[27]

The secret agreement between the PDI and the leadership of the Jewish community led to a turning point in the relations between the community's leaders and the colonial authorities. The Moroccan Jewish leaders began, in accordance with Meyer Toledano's suggestion, to support the concept of a parliamentary monarchy in which the king would not actually conduct the affairs of state. In an article that Toledano published in "Le Monde" and republished in the "Jewish Chronicle," the writer spoke of his vision of an independent state in which the religious element would no longer be a determining factor and which would be governed by a liberal democratic constitutional system, rather than by religious law. The state would provide the same services to Muslims, Christians, and Jews.[28]

As was the norm in his meetings with representatives of the Moroccan nationalist movements, Easterman was impressed by the high level of the representatives of the nationalist movement at the conference, by their perseverance, and by the righteousness of their struggle. He appreciated the fact that the French government had invited them to talks and did not relate to them as primitive hotheads. According to him, even though the Jews had not taken part in the Moroccan nationalist struggle in the past, they had not supported either side and, although they had not objected to French influ-

organization, the Alliance took a pro-French anti-nationalist position with regard to Morocco.

27 G. Ollivier, *L'Alliance Israélite Universelle 1860–1960, AIU, Documents et temoignages* (Paris, 1959), 225–28.

28 Assaraf, *Mohammed V*, 21.

ence, they felt completely Moroccan. Easterman called on the Moroccan leadership to look out for Jewish interests in the new Morocco.[29]

In anticipation of the king's return from exile in Madagascar, the "Coordinating Committee of the Jewish Organizations in Morocco" met in Paris on the 19th of September. This committee included the Moroccan branch of the "Alliance Israélite Universelle," the organization of "Alliance" graduates, and the council of Moroccan Jewish communities. The World Jewish Congress representatives announced at this meeting that the Jewish question had been raised in talks that were held in Madagascar between Sultan Sidi Mohammed Ben Youssef and the prime minister designate, Mbark Bekkay, and Abdelqader Benjelloun. The sultan informed them that the new government would grant Jews rights equal to those of Muslim citizens, that there would be no restrictions on emigration rights and that any citizen would be able to leave the country if he wished to do so. Benjelloun reported to Easterman regarding these talks with the sultan, and noted that the monarch had stressed that he would regret the emigration of every single Jew, but that he would not prevent anyone from leaving, as he would be taking into consideration the freedom of the individuals involved.[30]

The heads of the World Jewish Congress–Golan, Easterman, Riegner, and Jacques Lazarus–reached Morocco on October 13. During their twelve-day stay there, they attempted to persuade the official Jewish organizations to adopt the claims of the nationalist movement, in anticipation of the expected independence. Their intention was to draft a charter to be signed by all the Jewish bodies, within the framework of the "Coordination and Research Committee," which Dahan had initiated. The charter would include all the demands regarding the subject of the community's future status. Despite the efforts of the World Jewish Congress representatives, the language of the charter reflected the many doubts the community leaders had regarding the future that they anticipated for Morocco. This resulted from the position taken by the leaders of the "Alliance" in Europe and especially from that adopted by its president René Cassin. Nevertheless, the fast pace at which political developments began to unfold, along with the sultan's return, led to the charter quickly becoming outdated.[31]

While bloody attacks shook the general Moroccan society during the process in which it obtained independence and afterward, the Jewish community was hardly affected. The liberation armies, *Jish attahrir* in the vari-

---

29 Ouazzani, *Entretiens avec mon père*, 213–18. Easterman's comments in London during a BBC broadcast, August 30, 1955, 9:15 PM.

30 Assaraf, *Mohammed V*, 219–20. Assaraf calls the PDI's Secretary-General Ahmed, not Abdelqader. However, it could be that he is not referring to Abdelqader Benjelloun, the future Finance Minister, but to Abdelkrim Benjelloun, the first Minister of Justice.

31 Ibid., 220.

ous regions of Morocco and the various types of the *Munaddama siriyya* and the *Hilal al-aswad* (Black Storm) terrorist organizations, were careful not to hurt Jews who had collaborated with the French colonial commission. They refrained from "punishing" such Jews, even though they executed Muslims who were suspected of similar collaboration. Paradoxically, even though the Jews generally preferred to refrain from supporting the struggle for national liberation and even though their formal organizations even coordinated their positions with the policies of the French Commission, the returning sultan and the heads of the political parties did not hold a grudge against them. At every opportunity, the monarch declared that the newly independent Morocco needed the Jews' talents in order to develop as a progressive state. It was not only the royal house that treated them in this fashion. A similar stance was taken by the leadership of the state, which opened its arms to the Jewish community with warmth, even to those who had collaborated with the occupying authorities. Thus began a period that lasted several years in which the Jews enjoyed a clear preference in obtaining government positions. Jewish doctors and lawyers were able to obtain preferred clients. This period of understanding, which marked the golden age of Muslim-Jewish relations in Morocco, became weaker as the political struggle between the palace and the parties strengthened, as Jewish emigration came to serve as a tool in the ensuing political infighting.

The turnaround in the relationship of the community leadership with the future leadership of independent Morocco began only during the last days of the French presence. On October 30, 1955, the day after the French sultan Ben-Arafa gave up his throne and escaped to Tanger, the leaders of the "Conseil des Communautés Juives" met in Rabat and made a sharp change in their declarations. Their first announcement expressed great joy at the return of His Excellency Sidi Mohammed Ben Youssef and of his exalted family members. The Jewish population was called upon to join their Muslim brothers in celebrating his return to the throne. For his part, the reinstated sultan made significant efforts to allay the Jewish community's concerns. After meeting with the heads of the Istiqlal and the PDI upon his arrival at Saint Germain en Laye, the king received several Jewish delegations. Prince Hassan served as a translator during the king's talks with the Jewish groups. Mohammed V declared to Easterman, Golan and Riegner of the World Jewish Congress:

> I have always seen my Jewish subjects as completely free citizens, and as Moroccans who are completely equal to my Muslim subjects. This is the policy that I will take in the future. All of my subjects will benefit from equal rights and share equal obligations, without regard to their religious beliefs. You can be certain that my intentions will be fully carried out in practice upon my return to Morocco.[32]

[32] Baum and Foster, "Memorandum regarding Morocco"; Riegner, *Ne jamais désespérer*, 535–43.

The Golan-Laghzaoui Agreement regarding the Vacating of the Qadima Camp

Because of the changes expected with the coming of independence, the Israeli leadership had been concerned since autumn 1955 about the fate of the activities of the Jewish Agency and the functioning of the Qadima transit camp. After the independence, approximately 2,000 Jews, most of them from remote villages, had left their homes and were living in the camp, awaiting departure for Israel. Living conditions were crowded and sanitary facilities were limited. At an earlier point, the camp had served as housing for people awaiting emigration in only a few days, during the period in which medical examinations and final administrative arrangements regarding registration and preparation of documentation were carried out.

The Jewish Agency emissaries had acted on the assumption that when the negotiations were initiated with the new administration regarding the camp's fate, the government would have to allow all its residents to leave the country. They, therefore, thought it was important to bring as many Jews as possible into the camp during this interim period in advance of the final arrangement, and to fill it up with more people as soon as any group of residents left.[33] Consequently, the Jewish Agency leadership sent their emissaries to every population center in which there were potential candidates for emigration and secretly moved the families into the camp. By the time the authorities gave their approval for emptying the camp, the number of its residents had gradually reached more than 7000, although it had been planned for holding only approximately 1,500 people in ordinary times.[34]

In this situation, the leaders of Qadima could not maintain minimal living conditions in the camp because of overcrowding. Many illnesses began to spread, and the camp was faced with the threat of an epidemic. Duvdevani describes the situation in the camp when families were told that the authorities were not allowing their departure for Israel:

> What happened during those hours in the beleaguered camp is hard to describe. Women wailed, children cried, old people tore their clothes and the shouts and the cries reached the heavens [...] A rebellious air covered those who were assembled in the camp.

---

33 Testimony of Y. Dominitz. *The Organization of Underground Activists in North Africa*, vol. 4 (Tel Aviv ,1994).

34 HIAS report mentioned in T. Szulc, *The Secret Alliance: The Extraordinary Story of the Rescue of the Jews Since World War II*, 234–35; Riegner, *Ne jamais désespérer*, 542. Testimony of Baruch Duvdevani, E. S,hoshani, Comments of Colleagues (Tel Aviv: Mossad and Jewish Agency publication, 1964), "Top secret" [Hebrew]. According to Duvdevani, there were 9000 residents in the camp; Riegner states that there were 8000; and the HIAS report gives their number at 7000. E. Temime and N. Deguigné, *Le Camp du Grand Arenas, Marseille, 1944–1966*, Ed. Autrement (Paris, 2001), 79.

The families argued that they would not leave the spot because they no longer had any place to which they could return.

The authorities in Morocco tried, on their part, to convince the camp's residents to return to their homes, but these attempts were unsuccessful and there is no record of anyone leaving the camp to return to his former place of residence. When the head of the new country's security forces, Mohammed Laghzaoui, asked those responsible for the camp to post guards at the entrance, his request was refused.[35] For some time, mounted police were posted outside the camp, but Laghzaoui was eventually deterred by the thought that it would look to outsiders as if he had locked the Jews into a concentration camp against their will, and he was forced to remove his police. The lack of police allowed the Jewish Agency emissaries to bring new families into the camp without being discovered.[36]

At this point, Israeli Prime Minister David Ben Gurion turned to Nahum Goldmann and asked him to have the World Jewish Congress representatives lobby the king on behalf of the families waiting in the camp. The World Jewish Congress representatives responded immediately and were able to resolve the situation. Jo Golan, Alexander Easterman of London, Gerhart Riegner of Geneva, and André Jabès of Paris took part in the discussions with the government. The Jewish Agency emissaries were not enthusiastic about the involvement of the World Jewish Congress leadership. They knew of Golan's and Easterman's contacts with the leaders of the nationalist movement, but they disagreed with them about their interpretation of the intentions of the leadership of the Istiqlal and their practical evaluation of the promises made by that leadership. According to Duvdevani, their declarations were calming and mixed with support for the Zionist movement as well, but these statements contributed significantly to calming public opinion among Moroccan Jewry, as well as in Israel and throughout the Jewish world. The Jewish Agency emissaries even blamed the World Jewish Congress for causing the "Tragedy of Moroccan Jewry" that took place after

35 Mohammed Laghzaoui of Fès joined Istiqlal in 1940. After he had worked as a petty merchant in the textile market, he established, together with a Jewish merchant, a successful moving company that enriched its owners. He made his capital and his assets available to the party, but he never served as a member of its executive committee. He financed its activities and its offices in Paris, New York, and at the United Nations, where he also had contacts with Easterman. At the end of his term as the head of the Moroccan security forces, he was appointed on July 1, 1960 to direct the National Phosphates Authority. In July of 1962, he was appointed to be the minister in charge of nationalized enterprises and in June of 1965 he was named the Minister of Industry and Tourism, serving until July 1967. He died in 1998.

36 HIAS report mentioned in T. Szulc, *The Secret Alliance: The Extraordinary Story of the rescue of the Jews Since World War II* (New York: Farrar, Straus and Giroux, 1991), 234–35. Testimony of Duvdevani and Shoshani, "Comments of Colleagues"; testimony of Judith Friedman, ibid.

independence was obtained, because their "calming" statements regarding the situation effectively quieted public opinion about the potential danger that the Moroccan Jews were facing.[37]

For this reason, the Jewish Agency leadership asked to attach an Israeli to the World Jewish Congress delegations in order to ensure that they were directly involved in the negotiations with the Moroccan authorities. Although the WJC's Joe Golan was Israeli, the Jewish Agency did not trust him. Yehuda Dominitz of the Agency's Immigration Department recommended that Akiva Levinsky be attached to the delegation as one who had considerable experience with clandestine emigration.[38] Dominitz assumed that because of his Swiss passport, the Moroccan authorities would allow Levinsky to enter Morocco, even if they knew of his close connection to Israeli authorities.[39]

On May 24, 1956, after consulting with Shragay and with Yaaqov Tsur[40] (who was at the time the Israeli ambassador to France), Easterman arrived in Morocco. He stayed there almost continuously until September, and spent most of his time in Rabat and Casablanca. His first meeting was with Morocco's new (and Jewish) postmaster general, Léon Benzaquen, as preparation for his meetings with the government's leadership. Easterman informed the Jewish cabinet minister that, since 1953, he had been talking to the heads of the nationalist movement about Jewish emigration from an independent Moroccan state and that his interlocutors had always expressed their understanding regarding his demands.

---

37 Testimony of Duvdevani, Shoshani, "Comments of Colleagues."

38 Yehuda Dominitz was appointed in 1956 as the deputy to the Jewish Agency's Director-General Duvdevani and as an aide to the chairman, S. Z. Shragay. Beginning in 1978 he served as the director-general of the department. He also served as a liaison between the Jewish Agency and the Mossad and visited Morocco at the end of 1961, at the beginning of Operation Yakhin.

39 Akiva Levinsky, a native of Geneva, was active in the work of the Aliyya Bet institution. Afterward, he maintained contact with the Mossad. He was sent to Morocco in anticipation of the closing of the Qadima camp and returned to Morocco in July and November of 1958, together with several WJC delegates, to conduct negotiations with the Moroccan leadership. Levinsky had already gone to Morocco during May of 1956 with Easterman and Golan during the negotiations with the Moroccan authorities regarding the evacuation of the Qadima camp. He served as the Israeli supervisor of the World Jewish Congress' activities.

40 Yaakov Tsur served as Israel's ambassador to France from 1953 until 1959. From the time he took up his position, he was interested in what was happening in Morocco and recommended to Moshe Sharet that he stir up Jewish public opinion in the United States in favor of France's colonial policy in North Africa so that France would repay Israel with support on political matters. Upon his return to Israel he served for a short time as the director-general of the Foreign Ministry and in 1960 he was made chairman of the Zionist Executive Committee.

The Moroccan nationalist movement had even accepted as fact that such emigration was not only a natural impulse, but also a democratic right. The nationalist leaders had further promised that the state that would be established would adopt the principle of freedom of emigration in accordance with the provisions of the International Declaration of Civil and Political Rights. If Morocco were to deny these rights, Easterman argued, its name would be blackened in the eyes of the Western governments and in terms of Western public opinion. It could also hurt its own political and economic interests and impact on its application for membership in the United Nations.[41] In his talks with Easterman, Benzaquen made the argument that the Jews of Morocco were an important economic factor within the country and that mass emigration would not be good for Morocco. Easterman responded by noting that the Jews who wished to leave for Israel were poor and destitute and had no economic importance for Morocco. By contrast, the middle class did not wish to leave the country and would do so only if their situation was to deteriorate.[42]

After this conversation, Easterman sent a note to Prime Minister Bekkay, dated May 31, in which he expressed his distress that his organization was being forced to struggle against administrative decrees that limited or even prevented Jewish emigration. He responded to the economic arguments raised by Benzaquen and reminded Bekkay of his previous contacts with the nationalist movement, and of the World Jewish Congress' aims regarding the struggle against limitations on emigration. Within Bekkay's administration, the conservative elements, including the secretary-general of the Istiqlal and Foreign Minister Balafrej, tended to oppose allowing the Jews to leave the transit camp, although the prime minister, Finance Minister Bouabid, Ben Barka, and the PDI ministers tended to approve of allowing the camp's residents to leave the country, even though they opposed Jewish emigration from Morocco in principle.[43]

During the ten days following the sending of his letter, Easterman tried to meet with the prime minister, but, despite their previous friendship, he did not succeed in scheduling a meeting. Because he had arrived at this

---

41 Morocco was accepted as a member of the United Nations three months later, on August 8, 1956.

42 N. Kropsof, Easterman's secretary, note (classified top secret) to M. Sharet (several days before the latter resigned from the Foreign Ministry) and to N. Goldmann, on May 29, 1956 (Israel National Archives, Foreign Ministry, 2398/IB).

43 In the eyes of the Mossad's representatives, Balafrej appeared to be pro-Egypt, Ben Barka seemed to be concerned with Morocco's international image, and Bouabid was viewed as a pro-Western liberal opposed to the Nasserite influence in Morocco (Letter of S.Z. Shragay, August 6, 1958. Central Zionist Archive, Shragay folder, S59).

dead end, Goldmann sent his political adviser Jo Golan to Morocco and asked him to join Easterman in Casablanca.

While a student in Paris, Jo Golan had known some of the people who later on became part of the independent country's leadership. These people included Prime Minister Bekkay, Foreign Minister Balafrej, Finance Minister Bouabid, Finance Minister Abdelqader Benjelloun, and the chairman of the Advisory Council, Ben Barka. Golan and his wife Esther entered Morocco as the guests of the Istiqlal, with Israeli passports that were stamped with two of the earliest visas issued by the newly independent country–in fact, they bore the numbers 3 and 4.[44] From the moment they entered the country, the Moroccan security forces followed Golan's movements in Morocco and gave instructions to the security forces to allow him to enter and to leave the country despite his being an Israeli citizen.[45]

Mohammed Laghzaoui had known Golan in New York. Easterman and Golan had helped him to make contacts at the United Nations General Assembly regarding the issue of Moroccan independence. However, the first conversation between them in Rabat was disappointing. Despite the friendly atmosphere, the two sides were forced to conduct long discussions before they came to a conclusion, one that allowed for the camps to be vacated. On the third of June, Laghzaoui clarified to his interlocutors that the government faced a dilemma with regard to Jewish emigration. According to him, Qadima was a foreign organization that served to organize Moroccan citizens on behalf of a foreign country. From his perspective, the situation was even more problematic because the Moroccan citizens with whom Qadima worked were members of a group that had in the past collaborated with the French colonial authorities and were now working to strengthen the Israeli army in its struggle against Middle Eastern countries with which Morocco had both religious and ethnic ties.

The Arab countries were pressuring Morocco to prevent the strengthening of Israel's military forces. Moreover, Laghzaoui claimed, Morocco could not allow itself to give up its Jewish citizens, who constituted a skilled foundation within the population and were an essential part of its economy, especially in light of the difficulties that the new country was facing. Furthermore, since Morocco had given the Jews full equal rights, it was natural that it would expect them to display civic loyalty and assistance while its new society was being shaped at the conclusion of the colonial era.[46]

44 Segev, *Operation Yakhin*, 99.

45 Moroccan Security Forces, Circular DGSN/RG, July 29, 1956 (Israel National Archives, Foreign Ministry, 4318/1/I).

46 M. Laskier, "The Jews in Independent Morocco: Government Policy and the Role of the Jewish International Organizations (1956–1976)," *Shorashim ba mizrah*, Research of the Zionist and Pioneering Movement in the Sephardic and Islamic Communities, vol. 3, 167. [Hebrew].

Because of the difficulties that arose during the conversations with Laghzaoui, Easterman decided, despite some ambivalence, to turn to Interior Minister Driss Mhamdi, who was in charge of the security forces, and ask him to intervene. After making inquiries, the minister called Laghzaoui and asked him to present his position. Laghzaoui spoke with much vehemence. He began by recalling the principle that the Moroccan government did not oppose the idea of the Jews leaving the country.

In the past, he further acknowledged, a promise had been given to the World Jewish Congress that the right to freely emigrate would be preserved for all Moroccan citizens, regardless of their religion. However, he added, he strongly opposed the actions of a foreign country within the borders of Morocco in carrying out propaganda activity to encourage emigration and to establish a type of state-within-a-state. The Moroccan government could not tolerate this situation, the source of which he saw as being the foreign French government. He attacked the Qadima organization sharply and announced that he would no longer agree to the presence of Israeli emissaries. He added that collective exit visas would no longer be issued, as had been the case in the past. At the same time, he took care to point out that any person interested in leaving the country could submit an application and the Ministry of the Interior would deal with it on an individual basis.

After a lengthy argument, the Minister of the Interior agreed to the following two points:

- The Qadima office and the emissaries associated with it would be allowed to continue their activities for a period of three months. During that time, previous procedures would continue to be in force and the security forces would handle visas in accordance with the Jewish Agency's proposals.
- At the end of that time, the Qadima office would be permanently closed and new procedures more appropriate for the needs of the new government would be established. The intention was to transform the matter of leaving Morocco into an individual issue, and to oppose the maintenance of an Israeli emigration center within Moroccan territory.[47]

On June 9, 1956, Goldmann, Tsur, and Shragay met to hear Easterman, who had just landed in Paris, report on his conversations in Morocco. (Golan was at the time still in Morocco, continuing the talks with Laghzaoui.) The WJC representative described the agreement he had reached with Laghzaoui and Driss Mhamdi. Those attending received the impression that although the WJC representatives had succeeded in putting off the final decree for three months, the threat that emigration would be permanently stopped remained. In the meantime, the goal was to strive for the maximum

[47] Ibid.

number of emigrants possible during the period of time allowed and to try to lengthen that period of time as well.

Shragay proposed that a new tactic be used for the continuation of the contacts with the authorities. Instead of demanding that the interim period in which emigration would be allowed be extended beyond three months, it would be more worthwhile to fix a number–62,000 emigrants–who should be allowed to leave during the permitted period of time and thus "sew up" the problem of the Jews leaving the country. This number would include the 48,000 Jews who had already undergone the various examinations and had been found to be fit for emigration, and to whom would be added 14,000 Jews who had submitted applications for emigration and had not yet undergone the required examinations. In the years prior to independence, more than 1500 Jews had left Morocco each month. Goldmann and Tsur feared that the high numbers that Shragay had picked were likely to deter the Moroccan government, from granting the request. Therefore, they agreed that the new tactic would be chosen in the future in accordance with the relations that would develop with the security forces. If it turned out that the Moroccan government agreed to the departure of such large numbers and was not putting up obstacles, an effort would be made to continue with the arrangement that had already been reached but to ask that the deadline be extended. However, if the authorities appeared to actually be trying to put a stop to emigration, in an effort not to anger world public opinion, the Israeli representatives would present the problem of the numbers openly and put maximum pressure on the authorities.[48]

Meanwhile, back in Morocco, Golan and Laghzaoui had concluded a week of meetings by formulating a summarizing document (dated June 11, 1956) regarding the subject of emigration. According to this document, Israel accepted that emigration of the type that had until then been carried out in an organized fashion by its representatives would cease within three months. The Qadima camp would close during the month of October and by then all the families with legal visas would have been removed and their emigration would be allowed, in an orderly fashion, within three months. However, the number of Jews who would leave under this framework was not fixed. In order not to arouse the anger of the Arab countries, it was agreed that the Jews from the Qadima camp would leave only at night from sea and airports, after work hours. After the closure of the transit camp, the collective exit permits, which had been customarily issued during the French colonial era, would be cancelled and the Ministry of the Interior would issue individual passports only. Later on, the Israeli emissaries received a letter signed by Laghzaoui informing them that the visitors' per-

48 Ibid.

mits they held had expired on the first of July 1956 and that their visas would not be renewed.[49]

Notwithstanding the agreement, the government quickly decided to take immediate measures to close the camp and place severe restrictions on emigration. On June 12, 1956, only one day after the agreement was signed, and three months after the country obtained independence, the authorities sent an official letter to Amos Rable, ordering him to close the Qadima offices in Casablanca, Fès, Marrakech, and the transit camp near Al Jadida (Mazagan) within 8 days, by June 20. The government even pointed out that the travel permits and passports that had been issued until then were cancelled, as well as the exit visas to France, and would no longer be honored by the border police, who would receive instructions to hold up the departure of any Jew.[50]

On the same day, Easterman left for Paris in order to receive Tsur's and Shragay's approval of the agreement that had been reached. Shragay, who had informed Goldmann of the details of the agreement, understood to his regret that the agreement's most important clause had been Israel's consent to cease its group emigration activities within Moroccan territory at the end of three months. Effectively, the agreement's meaning for the Israelis involved in emigration activities was that the emigration gates had been closed and that further difficulties were to be expected. He, therefore, proposed to conduct a widespread public relations campaign against the Moroccan government and to stir up public opinion against it in order to force it to allow Israel to take the Jews out of the country. He also recommended to the president of the World Jewish Congress that he "ensure the continuation of emigration from any place and in every manner."[51]

On the first of July, Easterman and Golan were forced to return to Morocco to save the achievements of the agreement that had been signed the previous month. This time they met with Foreign Minister Balafrej, who suggested to them that they meet with one of the Istiqlal's original leaders, Allal Alfassi. The two were the guests in Fès of Haj Ahmed Mekouar, known as "the conscience of the Istiqlal," and lunched with Allal Alfassi.[52]

In the past, Alfassi had led a struggle against Jewish emigration to Israel and was suspected of anti-Jewish sentiment because of his having lived for so long in Cairo and because of his expertise in the Islamic religion. Alfassi, however, refuted these charges in his talks with Easterman and Golan, and

49 Y. Tsur to M. Sharret, June 11, 1956 (Israel National Archives, Foreign Ministry, 2525/9).

50 Ibid.

51 S.Z. Shragay to N. Goldmann, June 10, 1956 (Israel National Archives, Foreign Ministry 2525/9).

52 Personal testimony in conversation with the author, Joe Golan, Jerusalem, November 23, 1997 and January 2, 1999.

sought to demonstrate his neutrality by acknowledging the positive contribution Fès Jewry had made to Moroccan culture. Like his colleague Balafrej, he mentioned to his guests the pressures that were being placed on the Moroccan government by the Arab countries bordering on Israel. In the end, Alfassi left his guests with the impression that if the subject were raised at a cabinet meeting, his party would not reject the agreement that had been signed by Laghzaoui.

At the end of the meeting with Alfassi in Fès, Easterman and Golan returned to Rabat and met with Prime Minister Bekkay. When the prime minister heard of the agreement reached with Alfassi, he promised the two that the government would soon ratify the Laghzaoui agreement. On July 7, less than a month after the agreement had been signed, Easterman wrote to the prime minister and described the various stages of the negotiations that had been held with the head of the security forces, regarding the eventual closing of the Qadima camp. Due to later disputes that arose in the course of the implementation of the agreement, Golan, Easterman, and Riegner were forced to return to Rabat on the 9th of August, and to again meet with Laghzaoui. By that time, the head of the security forces had received a long list of those applying to leave, but had approved the departure of only 6300 of the camp's residents.

Prime Minister Bekkay informed the World Jewish Congress representatives that an inter-ministerial committee had met under his direction and had approved the camp's being closed under the following conditions:

- Every person leaving the camp would have to prove that he had not left behind any financial debts and that he did not have a criminal background.
- Every person leaving would have to announce his wish to either retain or waive his Moroccan citizenship.
- The emigration would be carried out without any publicity.

Even though these conditions were likely to cause delays in the process of leaving, Easterman and Riegner approved the new arrangement. After the World Jewish Congress representatives gave a guarantee for those Jews who might possibly be leaving the country without paying their debts, Laghzaoui was prepared to allow all the Jews in the camp to leave the country between August and the beginning of December.[53]

The leaders of the World Jewish Congress discovered, meanwhile, that their agreement was likely to lead to the cancellation of the planned departure of a group of emigrants on July 12. Golan immediately wrote to his friend Bouabid, the Moroccan ambassador in Paris, on the day before the

53 S.Z. Shragay to Zalman Shazar, August 14, 1956, and S.Z. Shragay to N. Goldmann, August 27, 1956 (Israel National Archives, Foreign Ministry 2398/IB); Segev, *Operation Yakhin*, 104.

group's planned departure and asked him to quickly appeal to the government ministers before they left to accompany the king on a trip to the northern part of the country.[54] After the government's efforts to persuade the camp's residents to return to their homes had proved to be a failure, Baruch Duvdevani received approval for the camp to be closed and its residents to leave the country. The approval came on the 15th of September, on Yom Kippur. He was asked to give Laghzaoui's office a list of those leaving by 4:00 in the afternoon of that day. Despite the holiness of the day, Duvdevani, who was a religiously observant Jew, did not hesitate to bring the list at the time he was asked to do so, because of the possible danger to those involved. He left for Rabat immediately with a list that had been prepared in advance.[55]

As stated above, according to the Golan-Laghzaoui agreement, 6,300 people were to leave the country. In practice, during the months of September and October of 1956, more than twice that number had actually left the camp. The moment the authorities notified the Jewish Agency's representatives that they could evacuate the camp's residents and move them to Marseilles in boats operated by the "Compagnie Paquet," Mendel Vilner stood at the ramp of the boat and counted the number of those boarding. Instead of the one hundred persons who were supposed to receive an entry permit, three or four times as many boarded the ship.[56] The members of the Misgeret organized a day-night watch and, when it was dark, they helped new families to come in through holes in the camp fence, in the place of families that had already boarded the ship for Marseilles. Thus the camp was filled with replacements. Instead of becoming smaller after each ship's departure, the number of the camp's residents only grew.

The head of the security services was not unaware of what was happening. He called Golan in for a meeting and protested to him regarding the activities of the Jewish Agency workers who had doubled the number of the camp's residents in violation of the arrangement that had been agreed to in writing back in June. In the presence of Laghzaoui, Golan called Duvdevani, who explained that the situation was a result of Jews streaming to Casablanca from the surrounding small villages. According to Duvdevani, these Jews were coming into Aljadida and the police at the camp gates were allowing new families to take the places of those who had left. Duvdevani, therefore, asked that these Jews also be allowed to leave along with those whose

54 Joseph Guldin to Abderahim Bouabid in Paris, July 10, 1956 (Israel National Archives, Foreign Ministry 2525/9).

55 Testimony of Solomon (Zouzou) Azoulay, Paris, June 11, 2001.

56 According to Friedman, the Moroccan officials knew about Vilner's activities, but they didn't do anything to put a stop to the matter. "Methods and Manners of Operation for Illegal Emigration" testimony of Y. Nessiyahu (Friedman), *The Organization of Underground Activists in North Africa*, vol. 4 (Tel Aviv, 1994).

departure had been officially approved.[57] Laghzaoui agreed to this and 13,000 Jews were able to leave through group visas and sailed for Marseille,[58] and from there to Israel.

At the end of the three months that had been set for the emptying of the transit camp, on the 27th of September 1956, Laghzaoui gave in to pressures from the pan-Arabists in his party, and he sent Circular Number 424 to all regional governors. The circular, which was issued in his name and in the name of the Minister of the Interior, stated as that "it is absolutely forbidden for Jewish emigrants to return to Morocco, as it is forbidden for Jewish citizens to leave their homeland and emigrate to Israel." The authorities understood that even if the Jews were to apply for passports in order to leave the country only for a short period, there was nothing to prevent them from using them later on for the purpose of emigrating to Israel. In effect, the issuance of passports to Jews already had been almost completely stopped by June 30. The few who were able to receive them at this stage were merchants who traveled abroad for business purposes and students who had left to study in Paris, of which only a few had gone on to Israel. At the same time, the authorities continued to tell the rest of the world that nothing had changed and that there were no restrictions on the Jews' ability to leave the country.[59] After the issuance of Circular 424, Easterman felt that he had concluded his mission and he left Morocco, after having been there for five months.

David Ben-Gurion, who meantime had been returned to the premiership in Israel, understood that the Moroccan kingdom was facing a dilemma, that it was caught between its desire, on the one hand, to obtain support from the West because of its need for capital investment and, on the other, its obligations to the Arab world, which had helped it in its struggle for independence. He gave instructions that the subject of Jewish emigration be strictly censored in the Israeli media in order to save the Moroccan administration from embarrassment. He also asked Goldmann to continue to maintain contacts in the name of the World Jewish Congress. However, at the same time, Israel distributed announcements to the world press (instigated by the head of the Mossad) regarding torture and arrests that were being carried out among the Jewish community in Morocco, and of anti-Jewish terror in the country. The shocking descriptions were intended to raise concern throughout the world regarding the fate of North African Jewry in general.[60]

57 Segev, *Operation Yakhin*, 104.

58 Testimony of Yehudit Friedman and Moshé Arnon, Shoshani, Comments of Colleagues; S. Yehezqeli, "Memoirs," Chapter 10 A (Private archives of Y. Yehezqeli).

59 Assaraf, *Mohammed V*, 242

60 Ibid.

Since Israel did not believe that the government of Morocco would fulfill the agreement, Foreign Minister Moshe Sharet in June of 1956–a week before his resignation[61]–called Philip Klutznik of the World Jewish Congress executive and asked him to intervene with the Rabat authorities. Klutznik met with Bekkay, who promised him that the agreement with Laghzaoui would be honored. On June 26, Ambassador Tsur went to the Comte de Paris, to General George Catroux, and the former governor of Morocco, Gilbert Grandval, and asked them to lobby the sultan–their personal friend–on behalf of the Jews.

After a conversation with the prime minister, the Comte de Paris transmitted Bekkay's response to Ambassador Tsur on September 18. In his letter, Bekkay stressed the sultan's firm opposition to the Jews' abandonment of his country and accused France and Zionist propaganda of creating an atmosphere that encouraged escape:

> The question before us now is not whether the Jews have the right to enjoy freedom of movement. This is a natural right, which is granted to every citizen on the basis of the Universal Declaration of Human Rights. Morocco, like other democratic countries, recognizes this declaration but does not waive its right to arrange emigration in the context of its laws and its sovereignty.[62]

The World Jewish Congress' Delegations to Morocco in the Late 1950s

Against the background of the Middle Atlas rebellion and the struggles between the various power centers in the country, and while the Mossad was already smuggling Jews out, Alexander Easterman and André Jabès came to Morocco on June 27, 1957 in order to meet with Prime Minister Bekkay, with Minister of the Interior Driss Mhamdi, and again with the head of the security services, Mohammed Laghzaoui. This was the first time that Easterman had returned to Morocco after the previous year's five-month stay, when the subject had been the treatment of the Qadima transit camp.

Because of the socio-political situation in the country, and despite their many efforts, the World Jewish Congress representatives were unable to schedule the meetings for which they had hoped. An American Jewish Committee delegation, headed by Zacharia Schuster, also came to Morocco at this time, arriving on July 2 for a trip that lasted only 36 hours. Unfortunately for both delegations, an "unexpected bombshell"–as Easterman termed it–exploded just at that time. On the 30th of June, the Misgeret organized a group of 500 Jews to be smuggled out of the country illegally.[63] Those intending to escape were caught by the police in the city of Tanger

---

61 Sharet was forced to resign from his position as Ben-Gurion's Foreign Minister on June 17, 1956, and was replaced by Golda Meir.

62 S.Z. Shragay to N. Goldmann, June 10, 1956 (Israel National Archives, Foreign Ministry 2525/9).

63 Baum and Foster, "Memorandum Regarding Morocco."

on their way to Sebta (Ceuta) and British Gibraltar. The communities of Tanger and Tétouan had organized temporary shelter for the families that had already left their homes and sold their property. Approximately 70 people returned to their homes and the others stayed in the area to await trial.[64]

It was obvious that in such an atmosphere, the delegations would have trouble convincing the authorities to grant passports to Jews on the basis of promises that had been given to the World Jewish Congress representatives a year before. Easterman was angered by the "unorthodox activities" carried out by the Mossad, which he saw as serving only to enrage the authorities and undermine the various diplomatic efforts being made on behalf of the Jews' emigration rights. According to Easterman, activities of this type had increased over the course of the previous year and the Moroccan authorities were aware that they were going on. He was convinced that the country's leaders would not believe that he had not taken part in these "unorthodox activities" and would reject his proposals for an agreement for the legal emigration of Moroccan Jews. He also felt helpless in terms of his ability to help the Jewish arrestees in Tanger. Despairing of the situation, he wrote an angry letter to Goldmann and told him that he had not choice but to leave the area quietly.[65]

However, Israel's ambassador to France, Yaaqov Tsur, did not agree with Easterman and argued that the concentration of emigrants in Tanger need not interfere with the World Jewish Congress' representative, since the government of Morocco had itself failed to keep its promises and, therefore, Israel was under no obligation toward the Moroccans.[66] In the end, Easterman did not leave and on July 2 met with Ben Barka, Minister Bouabid, Minister Benzaquen, and Bensalem Guessous.

Because of the political tension and economic difficulties, Easterman noted that, during the second year of Moroccan independence, the pressures regarding the Jewish issue had disappeared and it was even possible to sense an atmosphere of less emotionalism, less demagoguery, and less aggression. He appreciated the position taken by the authorities because, despite the unemployment and the increase in the cost of living, the government did not attempt to distract the attention of the population from domestic problems through reference to foreign issues, such as the Israeli-Egyptian war. The traditional leader of the Istiqlal, a pan-Arabist, even spoke moderately regarding Morocco's relations with France. But the matter that surprised Easterman particularly was the objective reporting on the radio

64 Report of Dr. Wolfgang Bertholz from Berne, June 22, 1958 (Israel National Archives, Foreign Ministry, 4317/10/II).

65 A. Easterman to N. Goldmann at the King David Hotel in Jerusalem, July 1, 1957 (Israel National Archives, Foreign Ministry, 2525/9).

66 Y. Tsur, July 26, 1957 (Israel National Archives, Foreign Ministry, 4317/10/II).

and in the newspapers regarding the Israeli-Arab dispute. Despite the caution with which the Moroccans handled their relations with Egypt, the government and the palace both ridiculed President Nasser's intentions of ruling the Arab world.[67]

In the presence of Easterman and Jabès, Postmaster-General Léon Benzaquen spoke bitterly about the government's policy regarding the granting of passports, which he saw as constituting government discrimination. He told his interlocutors about two Jewish students who had applied for passports. He had personally lobbied on behalf of one of them, who was granted a passport. However, the friend was denied, which bothered the minister. Easterman strengthened his sense of insult at the discrimination practiced against the Jews and the minister promised to raise the subject with the cabinet and with the king.[68] When Easterman and Jabès met with Abderahim Bouabid, the Minister of Finance promised to bring to the attention of Minister of the Interior Driss Mhamdi the claims of the two Jewish representatives. On the one hand, he opposed discrimination against the Jews with respect to the granting of passports, while, on the other, he condemned the illegal emigration.

Bensalem Guessous was one of the Istiqlal leaders in Fès, the chairman of the economic committee of the advisory council and close to the liberal minister, Reda Guedira. He told the World Jewish Congress representatives that on the basis of an earlier conversation with André Jabès and with the heads of the Jewish community in Fès, he had had a difficult conversation with Ben Barka and had criticized him sharply, telling Ben Barka that he could not "change Morocco into a prison for its citizens." During this conversation, Ben Barka did not deny that the Jews had been prevented from receiving passports, but he added that the issue was sensitive and complicated. Guessous responded to Ben Barka that preventing emigration was a negative move that would cause damage to the country, primarily in terms of foreign affairs. Ben Barka then promised to raise the subject with the executive board of his party. The Istiqlal did, indeed, hold a long discussion about the subject, and authorized Minister Bouabid to bring up the subject for discussion within the cabinet.[69]

The president of the Moroccan national Advisory Council, Mehdi Ben Barka, on his part, repeated to Easterman and Jabès, without enthusiasm, the well-known three reasons for the authorities' objection to illegal emigration: the fear that Jewish capital would be leaving the country, the country's need for the Jewish contribution to its economy, and the objection to the

67 Report of A. Easterman from Casablanca, July 4, 1957 (Israel National Archives, Foreign Ministry, 3113/9).

68 Ibid.

69 Ibid.

departure of skilled manpower from Morocco to Israel–a country that was involved in a military conflict with the Arab countries. He advised his interlocutors to stop the illegal emigrants, about whom the authorities were aware anyway, and promised that the Jews' exodus from the country would resume upon the conclusion of the Arab-Israeli conflict. He asked the two of them to wait in Morocco for an additional, longer meeting with him to be held on July 8, by which time he would study the subject more intensively and review additional information given to him by the World Jewish Congress representatives. Because of the rivalry that existed between the World Jewish Congress leaders and the representatives of the American Jewish Committee, the latter group avoided meeting with Easterman despite his efforts to contact them in their hotel, and they did not report to him about their meetings.[70]

Ironically, in contrast to Easterman, whose contacts with the Moroccan leadership were well known, the American Jewish Committee delegation succeeded in meeting with the prime minister and even discussed with him the "bombshell" of the Jews who had been stopped in Tanger and the subject of illegal emigration in general. Without mentioning Israel, they argued that such phenomena were taking place precisely because the Jews' freedom of movement was being restricted. The prime minister used the opportunity to ask for their help in encouraging capital investment on the part of private American interests. The delegation met also with Finance Minister Bouabid and with Ben Barka. The two told the delegation that they would honor the Jews' freedom of movement in accordance with national economic interest, and stressed their sensitivity to American public opinion.[71]

Easterman returned to Morocco for yet another round of talks in January of 1958. Easterman's delegation was going to collide with Zacharia Schuster's American Jewish Committee delegation yet again, but Shragay succeeded in preventing Schuster from departing so that he could not damage Easterman's mission. As an alternative to the meeting, the Committee's representatives submitted a memorandum to Foreign Minister Balafrej. At Easterman's meeting with Balafrej and Laghzaoui, the head of the security services differentiated between two types of passports the issuance of which would be handled in the capital city: regular passports and emigration passports. The second type would be issued only upon instructions from the government.[72] Minister of Finance Bouabid, as was his custom, was more

70 Ibid. Summary of report of A. Easterman, July 3, 1957 (Israel National Archives, Foreign Ministry, 2525/9). A. Easterman's report regarding his visit to Morocco from June 27 through July 4, 1957 (Central Zionist Archives, Z6/1763).

71 Conversation between Assael of the Jewish Agency Immigration Department in Paris and Z. Schuster, July 11, 1957 (Israel National Archives, Foreign Ministry, II 4317/10).

72 Cable from Y. Tsur, February 27, 1957 (Israel National Archives, Foreign Ministry, II 4317/10).

generous and supported the principle of issuing up to about 500 to 600 passports a month under the express condition that no centralized activity would be carried out to encourage mass emigration.[73] The prime minister agreed to this proposal and promised to raise the issue with the cabinet quickly and to discuss the issue of the quota. The Istiqlal also supported a positive decision regarding this subject. The Israeli embassy in Paris had already agreed to an additional visit by Easterman in Morocco, which took place on the 7th of March.[74]

One can follow the frequent visits made by Easterman to Morocco from May until September of 1956, and see that those in the Israeli embassy in Paris who had sent him did not let up, asking him to continue to pressure the Moroccans, to meet the same people frequently, and to make new claims in his discussions with them. The Israelis believed that it was important that the pressure not let up, even if there was no chance at arriving at an agreement. After his visit on the 26th of June in 1957, the wandering ambassador was in Morocco around the 5th of September on a visit that was described as a failure, since he was not able to raise the issue of the recognition of the Jewish organization that was supposed to deal with emigration from within Morocco. Around the 7th of November, Easterman met again with Ben Barka and Bouabid. In anticipation of his meeting with Mohammed V in the United States, Easterman held another meeting close to the 26th of November, a meeting that was also seen as a failure after a conversation with Ben Barka. On January 10, 1958, Easterman returned to Morocco to apply for a fixed emigration quota and succeeded in reaching an agreement in principle. During April, in the middle of a government crisis, he returned to Morocco to have the promise carried out, at which time he met with Laghzaoui, but returned without obtaining any results.[75]

At the end of the Balafrej government's term of office, in October of 1958, more than two years after independence and after several hesitations, Morocco was prepared to join the Arab League, and afterward, the office of the Arab boycott. The Balafrej government had concluded its term of office prematurely, after only six months. A short time before the 7th of November 1958, Golan and Riegner came to Morocco for a round of talks. The two joined a representative of the Israeli Foreign Ministry, one of the founders of the intelligence community, Akiva Levinsky, who had arrived in Morocco on his Swiss passport. Easterman did not join the delegation because of a lengthy illness. Jo Golan, as was his custom, had entered Morocco on his

73 Cable from M. Shneurson after a conversation with Easterman, January 19, 1958 (Israel National Archives, Foreign Ministry, II 4317/10).

74 Cable from Y. Tsur, February 27, 1957 (Israel National Archives, Foreign Ministry, II 4317/10).

75 Various cables; Israel National Archives, Foreign Ministry, II 4317/10.

Israeli passport. Apparently, this was the only case in which an Israeli was allowed to enter Morocco at that time, despite the fact that the authorities refused to allow Jews to return to Morocco after they had visited Israel, and even though Morocco had just joined the Arab League. Upon Golan's intervention, his entry visas were stamped on the passports, and not on separate pages, as they had earlier been told would be done. Levinsky was impressed by Golan's contacts with the Moroccan leadership and was also surprised that their movements were not followed at all while they were in Morocco.

The members of the delegation again strove to have the promise made in January regarding a quota of personal passports of approximately 600 Jews per month put into effect. They also wished to determine whether Morocco's policy had changed after it had joined the Arab League and how the crisis of the Balafrej government–a sharp clash between conservatives and the leftist party–had impacted on the Jewish community. The delegation met with Jewish activists in the progressive branch of the Istiqlal–including Meyer Toledano, Marc Sabbah, and David Benazeraf–as well as with the Secretary General of the "Conseil des Communautés," David Amar. They also met with Léo Toledano of the Finance Ministry, with Jacques Sabbah–the Director-General of the Postal Authority, and with the director of the Joint Distribution Committee in Morocco, Henry Kirsh. The latter had been accused more than once by Israeli sources of "cozying up" to the authorities.[76] According to Riegner, even though the struggle inside the Jewish leadership had calmed down and most of the supporters of radical integration had modified their positions and become more practical, the political climate in the country was not conducive for negotiations regarding the Jews. Nevertheless, Riegner did not foresee any danger whatsoever for the Jewish community in Morocco. This conclusion led to a disagreement between the World Jewish Congress and the representatives of the Israeli Foreign Ministry.[77]

At the time that the Golan-Riegner delegation had met with Ben Barka and Bouabid in November 1958, there was significant tension between Balafrej and Allal Alfassi, on the one hand, who were accused of being too conservative, and the younger leftists led by Bouabid and Ben Barka, on the other. The latter two informed the World Jewish Congress representatives that this was not the ideal time to resolve the Jewish problem, because of the crisis in the Balafrej government. However, according to them, Morocco's membership in the Arab League would not change anything in terms of the authorities' treatment of the fundamental rights of Moroccan Jews. The proof was that Meyer Toledano had been sent to Egypt to conduct negotia-

---

76 A. Levinsky at a meeting of Mossad agents in Paris, November 7, 1958 (Israel National Archives, Foreign Ministry, II 4317/10).

77 G. Riegner to N. Goldmann, November 12, 1958 (Central Zionist Archives, Z6/1485).

tions. Ben Barka's principles had not changed; every citizen must be granted the freedom to emigrate. But there was a concern that the Jews' emigration would lead to their capital being taken out of the country, which would in turn weaken the country's economy and have a negative impact on public administration. Even though the party representatives with whom they spoke insisted that they all wished to distinguish between the treatment of the Jewish community in Morocco and the general Arab policy regarding the Middle East conflict, the WJC delegation was not convinced that a change could be expected in the policy regarding the issuance of passports for Jews.

As expected, Golan and Riegner, this time joined by Levinsky, met with Laghzaoui as well in order to discuss his promise to issue passports to 500 Jews each month. This time, the head of the security services had more pleasant things to say. He pointed out that times had changed since the incident of the evacuation of the Qadima camp and that he could now act differently. He could now agree to certain matters that two years earlier he had absolutely ruled out. He justified this by saying that, at that time, the government was still new and not in full control of the situation and, therefore, could not accept the activities of the Qadima organization. The matter was likely to have led to complications. The special problem that required an urgent resolution was the fate of the 100 arrested Jews in Tanger, who were awaiting a decision regarding their future; the problem of the Jews seeking to return to Morocco was also an issue. According to Laghzaoui, it was not a simple matter to prohibit the return to Morocco of anyone who had been in Israel. Complicated family issues would have to be resolved and, in effect, he no longer saw a visit to Israel as constituting a crime.

To the surprise of his interlocutors, Laghzaoui had prepared a file for them regarding the subject of the selection of the Jewish emigrants and accused Israel of bringing in Moroccan Jews to serve as canon fodder. According to him, Morocco would not support this trend and would not allow young Moroccans to be drafted into foreign armies. Nevertheless, he assured the two that any Jew who submitted an application for a passport and paid 1,600 francs would be allowed to leave the country:

> We will not hold up anyone [...] you must understand that I am interested in only one thing: that there should not be any noise [about the emigration] and that there shouldn't be any problems [...] I have therefore opened the stream somewhat and I am closing my eyes [regarding the numbers of the emigrants]. But everything has to be done in moderation.

He promised to personally resolve any passport problems brought to his attention and instructed the border police not to detain anyone holding a passport. He told Golan, Riegner, and Levinsky that he had charged those serving under him in the police to handle all Moroccans in an equal manner and not to distinguish between Jews and Muslims. He also told them that he did not wish to encourage profiteering in passports or to cause anyone to suffer, although according to him, there were those who had made money this way during the days of Qadima.[78]

Levinsky was impressed by the director's intellect and insight, but, in his view, there was no substantial difference between the positions held by the two Istiqlal factions regarding emigration. It could be that the leftist leaders were more hostile due to the rise of their more conservative colleagues. Levinsky told his fellow Mossad agents in Paris that after Laghzaoui had announced to them that every Jew seeking a passport was entitled to receive it, the wind was taken out of the delegation's sails. Riegner also acknowledged that he did not dare to bring up the issue of an organization that would work on emigration from within Morocco, a subject that was their undeclared goal, out of a concern that he would thus ruin the atmosphere that prevailed during their conversation. Levinsky added:

> I was especially shocked by the fact that after we had questioned tens of Jews, we could not find any incidents in which passports had been denied. No one would actually point to such incidents. We didn't receive any information regarding the subject. The representatives of the various communities always spoke about passport problems, but when they were asked, they were not willing to point to actual facts.[79]

Approximately 10 days after his meeting with Laghzaoui, Easterman sent him a letter summarizing the talks held with his colleagues, and promised him that he would soon return to Morocco.[80]

In January of 1959, all groups dealing with the subject of emigration met in Jerusalem and in New York in order to encourage Easterman to again leave for Morocco. The aim was still to clear up the problem of the Jews who were collected in Tanger, which had turned into a miniature Qadima camp and used as a means of pressure against the authorities who were trying to minimize its importance. The emigrants were living in a garage and in three small hotels, under difficult and crowded conditions.[81] A consultation was held in New York on the 19th of January in which Goldmann, Easterman, Perlzweig, and Riegner, along with various Israeli embassy personnel–Avraham Harman and Shimshon Arad–participated. Those present asked Easterman to make his visit to Morocco on the first of February, in accordance with a message that had been given to the Moroccans by Golan and Riegner. The

---

78 A. Levinsky at a meeting of Mossad agents meeting in Paris, November 7, 1958 (Israel National Archives, Foreign Ministry, II 4317/10); G. Riegner to N. Goldmann, November 12, 1958 (Central Zionist Archives, Z6/1485).

79 A. Levinsky at a meeting of Mossad agents meeting in Paris, November 7, 1958 (Israel National Archives, Foreign Ministry, II 4317/10).

80 A. Easterman to Mohammed Laghzaoui, November 26, 1958 (Israel National Archives, Foreign Ministry, II 4318/10).

81 Baum and Foster, "Memorandum Regarding Morocco."

purpose of the visit was to "conduct negotiations regarding legal departures from Morocco" and the establishment of a permanent WJC legation in the country. Goldmann and Riegner preferred that Golan and Levinsky join Easterman in Morocco, but Easterman opposed this and asked that only André Jabès assist him in his meetings with the Jewish community.[82]

Jews who had received passports were evidence that the Moroccan authorities were indeed complying with the principle of freedom of emigration. As Riegner observed, "The Moroccan authorities never denied the principle of freedom of emigration, but they opposed organized collective emigration. The difficulties were created at the lower levels."[83] It should be noted that the Moroccans' success in convincing their listeners that every Jew who wished to leave Morocco could do so forced the representatives of the World Jewish Congress to change the language of its appeals and to drop hints regarding collective departures as opposed to individual emigration, which did not solve the problem of the lower classes, the main group that would be emigrating. Groups involved with emigration stopped citing the principle of freedom of movement and the basic right to leave the country with a passport. Gradually they began to hint at an external body that would organize emigration in Morocco in a collective fashion in accordance with agreed emigration quotas. Very delicately, they suggested to the authorities that such a body must be established in order to deal with the poor and uneducated Jews who wished to emigrate in a spontaneous fashion.[84] The representatives of the Jewish Agency also changed their language and began to talk about "assisted individual emigration" as an interim measure. Those conducting the negotiations quickly understood that passports could solve the problems of merchants and students at most, but this was not their goal. In order to take out the village dwellers in significant numbers it would be necessary to operate a system that would deal with them collectively. This the authorities were not likely to approve, for reasons that were understood.[85]

Without the Israeli embassy or France's knowledge, a meeting was to be held with the crown prince on July 29, 1959, with Golan, Easterman, and Jabès in attendance. These three intended to broach subjects with the prince that dealt with continued Jewish life in the country, as well as the approval of the by-laws of the "Conseil des Communautés" and the re-open-

---

82 S. Arad to M. Gazit in Jerusalem, January 21, 1959 (Israel National Archives, Foreign Ministry, 4318/1/II).

83 Riegner, *Ne jamais désespérer*, 542.

84 H. Lehrman, "L'El Wifak chez les Juifs marocains, entente cordiale ou collaboration," L'Arche, no. 20, 21 (August-September 1958).

85 G. Riegner from Geneva to N. Goldmann, November 12, 1958 (Central Zionist Archives, Z6/1485).

ing of the World Jewish Congress' office in Morocco. According to Goldmann, the crown prince refused to receive Easterman and Riegner, on the grounds that he did not know them. He asked why Golan did not join them and when Easterman responded that Golan was ill, the prince asked the two of them to wait until Golan recovered, at which time he would receive them. Easterman and Jabès were forced to return from Morocco without having an audience with the prince. They were angry that the ambassador had not approved Golan's departure, and as a result they refused to report to him regarding their visit to Morocco.[86]

Easterman's Conversation with the Crown Prince

Two weeks after his previous meeting with the prince, on August 11, 1960, Alexander Easterman finally held serious talks with the Moroccan crown prince, which were reported by David Amar.[87] The prince had agreed to have the meeting and knew in advance the issues to be discussed, but he conditioned the continuation of such meetings on having the talks conducted in secrecy. He thus hinted that it was not his intention to have only a one-time meeting with the Israeli emissaries. The meeting was held late at night, outside of Rabat, in the private home of one of the prince's friends.[88] It was a long meeting; the talks covered several subjects and were conducted in a friendly atmosphere, which encouraged Easterman to speak relatively freely.

The prince began by noting his wish that the Jews would remain loyal to their homeland and expressed his satisfaction with the "religious revival among the Jews of Morocco." According to him, the Muslims in Morocco respected all believers. A religious person was able to respect other religious people. This was the reason, he argued, that Allal Al Fassi, unlike those aligned with the left, respected Jews. However, the prince's distinction was not really justified in light of the reality of that period, when the secularization of Morocco's young Jews was at its peak. The fact that the

86 Cable from Z. Shakh to H. Yahil, Director-General of the Foreign Ministry, August 11, 1960 (Israel National Archives, Foreign Ministry, 941/6); L. Castel to Y. Meroz, September 5, 1960 (Israel National Archives, Foreign Ministry, 941/6; another copy is located in file 4318/4/I). Easterman had his second meeting with the crown prince on the same day.

87 A. Easterman to Golda Meir, September 6, 1960 (Israel National Archives, Foreign Ministry, 4318/4 I; another copy is also located in Central Zionist Archives, Z6/1757.

88 Laskier, "The State of Israel and the Jews of Morocco"; Y. Tsur, "The Prince, the Diplomat, and the Deal," Haaretz [Hebrew], November 18, 1994. Tsur writes that the meeting was held in Sam Benazeraf's home in Rabat, but Benazeraf lived in Casablanca. Golan, in conversations held with the author in January of 1999, expressed doubts that the meeting between Easterman and the crown prince was held at all, or that it was held in a private house.

prince raised the issue was indicative of his fears and concerns regarding the communist-leftist groups among the opponents of the monarchy.

The source of this fear was the Istiqlal young guard, which saw the king and the palace as conservative elements that relied for support mainly on clerics and the feudalistic notions of the peasantry. He stressed that he was referring to the Jewish intellectual elite: "We will not accept Communism and we will not approve young Jews who are engaging in Communist activity. Communism is the greatest menace. How can a Jew be a Communist or be allied with Communists" But the crown prince's concern regarding the Jews' relationship to the monarchy was baseless. Even those who preferred emigration from Morocco were loyal to the royal family, except for a relatively small group of Jewish Communists and leftists.

It is possible to infer from Prince Hassan's language that he understood the concerns of Moroccan Jewry for their future in his kingdom. On the one hand, he was concerned that if the gates to emigration were opened, massive numbers of Jews would leave and a difficult economic climate would develop. And even if only a few left, those who did leave would constitute *une force grégaire*, and be an example to others.[89] The prince understood that since in the past the Jews had been more economically productive than the Muslims and their standard of living had been higher than that of their Muslim neighbors, they had served as a model for others. Surprisingly, he offered a new argument that had not been set forth until then from any of the Moroccan leaders, either conservatives or leftists: "Let us be realistic," the prince said to the World Jewish Congress leaders, "experience has proved that in the evolution of countries under-developed and dissatisfied turn first against foreigners and then against religious minorities."[90] Indeed, the prince's words were surprising in terms of their sharpness. In effect, he had acknowledged to his interlocutors that he despaired of the chances for integration of the Jews into the life of the independent state. He saw them now as potential candidates for emigration since, as a religious minority, they did not have a future within a society that had only now obtained its independence.

This declaration rendered irrelevant and even absurd the position taken by those within both the Jewish and Muslim communities who favored the integration of the Jews into Moroccan society. Thus, in the prince's estima-

---

[89] In his report in English, Easterman quotes the French phrase "*force grégaire,*" which may mean a snowball effect.

[90] The head of the Mossad made the same argument at a meeting with the Foreign Minister more than a year earlier. Summary of a meeting in Jerusalem on the subject of Morocco, November 9, 1959, led by the Foreign Minister and with the participation of N. Goldmann, Shragay, Harel, Morris Fisher (Foreign Ministry) Duvdevani, Moshe Rivlin and Y. Dominitz (the last 3 from the Jewish Agency), Shlomo Havilio and Aryeh Levontin (of the Mossad) (Central Zionist Archives, Z6/1474).

tion, since there was no possibility of effectively defending the Jews, they were likely to constitute a nuisance and not an asset for his country, even though he personally valued and admired them.

Beyond the interest of the Jews themselves, Prince Hassan discerned the advantages he could produce from collaborating with the State of Israel. Such collaboration could serve, he thought, as a means of acquiring American and European support, which was needed for the country's economic development. It seems that it was with this purpose in mind that he agreed to meet with Easterman in the first place. He qualified his own remarks somewhat when he mentioned his father the king. Mulay Hassan noted that his father had a different position regarding the country's Jews, one that was an emotional response, In accordance with the patriarchal tradition of the sultans who had preceded him, he saw the Jews as a "protected people" and the possibility of their leaving as something intolerable, along the lines of a father abandoning his children. He, therefore, felt obligated to protect them even from themselves, since he knew better than they did what was good for them. To Easterman, the prince added the remark that "he is not like you and me. We are Occidentals and, unlike us, he does not consider matters in a purely rational way (*esprit cartésien*)." It should be noted that these remarks attributed to Mohammed the Fifth are the exact words that Jo Golan had heard in his palace four years before, in July of 1956.[91]

The crown prince also repeated the positions of the leader of the opposition, who claimed that Jews leaving during such a difficult period would injure the country's economy. It may have been the case that in doing so he was hinting at the possibility that he wished to receive financial compensation for this potential injury.

The prince's attitude toward Israel was no less surprising. According to him, the Arab countries in the Middle East and in the Maghreb had to make a show of unity. His country, he added, could not ignore its Arab brethren. He claimed that if he were to declare his views regarding the Jews openly, the anti-monarchy opposition would not hesitate to attack him as a friend of Israel, thus putting the palace in a problematic position. He did refrain from making the argument that the emigration of Moroccan Jewry to Israel would strengthen the Israeli army, which was fighting his Arab brethren, but he added:

> The State of Israel is a fact—a reality. No one can deny the factual existence of Israel. Besides, that country is far away from us and does not directly concern Morocco. But the Arab States of the Middle East are our brothers and we cannot ignore them. I am obliged to act accordingly. If matters depended only on Morocco's opinion, I would suggest that the State of Israel should join the Arab League. But the Arab States of the Middle East feel them-

91 C. Enderlin, *Paix ou Guerre: Les secrets des négociations Israélo-arabes 1917–1990*, 190–96. Jo Golan, "La longue marche," manuscrit.

> selves threatened and are in a state of hostility (with respect to Israel) which we cannot ignore.

It is highly doubtful that an Israeli statesman would have thought of the State of Israel joining the Arab League in which the region's various countries were members. Nevertheless, most of them would naturally see that Israel, located in Western Asia, would join organizations made up of European countries. At any rate, Prince Hassan had, in this meeting, certainly established that his political thinking was unusual compared to that of other leaders of the same period.

When the prince returned to the subject of emigration, which is what had interested Easterman, he emphasized the economic loss that his country could suffer from the Jews' exodus. He said that the matter would be discussed in future meetings with the Israeli representative: "Give me time and the right conditions and we will find a way to resolve the problem to our mutual satisfaction."[92] The prince appointed Sam Benazeraf[93] to be the contact person for continued contacts and for coordinating future meetings, and added that Benazeraf would in the meantime receive any specific requests for permission to emigrate that would be submitted to him by Israel's representatives. Moulay Hassan informed Easterman that he was interested in continuing to discuss the subjects that were raised during their conversation and hinted that he was interested in holding the following meetings directly with Israeli representatives. Furthermore, in anticipation of his visit to the United States as the head of the Moroccan delegation to the Unit-

92 In noting that the economy would be the focus of his coming conversations with the Israeli emissaries, the prince hinted that he was prepared to deal with the subject of the financial compensation that Morocco sought to receive for the economic damage that would be caused by the mass exodus of Jews from his country.

93 Sam Benazeraf was a businessman, the son of a tea and sugar importer from Spanish Morocco, who had come to live in Casablanca. His uncles, Raphael and David Benazeraf, worked with the Mossad. Sam himself was a member of the Democratic Party for Independence (PDI) and served as the head of Abdelqader Ben-Jelloun's office when he was Finance Minister in independent Morocco's first government. The Israeli authorities valued his talents greatly and hoped that he would take the place of Leon Benzaquen, whom they did not like. Benazeraf died in 1963, having visited Israel in 1962. During a talk with Easterman in August of 1960, the prince mentioned Benazeraf as his contact person with the Israeli representatives, to whom all applications for emigration were to be sent until the negotiations were concluded. Several days afterward, during consultations within the Israeli Foreign Ministry, it was decided to open secret talks with Prince Hassan to be brokered by Benazeraf. All those involved agreed that Benazeraf was the best candidate for this delicate assignment, since he served as the prince's black market business manager and because of his position at the "Conseil des Communautés Juives"—but most importantly because of his strong intellectual abilities, which the prince valued very highly.

ed Nations, the prince asked his interlocutor to see to it that American Jewish organizations not organize hostile demonstrations against him.

The preliminary instructions that Easterman received in anticipation of his meeting with Moulay Hassan and the sending of his report of the meeting to the foreign minister in Jerusalem–and not just to Goldmann–show that, in this case as in earlier instances, the World Jewish Congress representatives operated as Israel's unofficial but direct ambassadors. They were thus required to cooperate with both the Mossad and the Jewish Agency. Easterman's connection with Israeli authorities was not hidden from the crown prince. This was acknowledged during the prince's meeting with the World Jewish Congress representative, when the prince challenged Easterman with regard to what Israel would and would not allow him to offer:

> You say that you would like to help me. But I am enough of a realist to know that you cannot do so. You can only help me so long as I do not need you, but if I need something from you, you will not be able to do anything. For example, if I ask you to help me in my relations with France, Israel will say to you 'Stop'–and you'll have to stop.

Thus, the prince well understood the relationship that existed between the World Jewish Congress and the Foreign Ministry and knew that he was, in effect, negotiating with a representative of the State of Israel.[94]

The head of the Immigration Department of the Jewish Agency, Shragay, did not ignore Easterman's report and in September he, Goldmann, and Easterman agreed to request a meeting with the king himself. Shragay's proposal to the Foreign Ministry exemplifies the Israeli representatives' lack of respect for the Jewish Moroccan leadership. In his view,

> Since no Jewish community representatives are to be found in Morocco, especially since the authorities do not like Toledano and David Amar and since Benzaquen has left political life, the prince should be offered André Jabès from the World Jewish Congress as a contact person between the Jews of Morocco and the Moroccan authorities.[95]

Despite David Amar's previous concerns regarding Easterman's reticence, a change took place as a result of his meeting with the crown prince. There was a significant increase in the number of those receiving passports; the atmosphere improved; and there was a more supportive attitude on the part of the police and the regional governors. The Israelis estimated that the change for the better flowed from instructions that had come from above.

Yaël Vered form the Israeli embassy in Paris deduced from this that it would be possible to advance the contacts to a more practical level

---

[94] A. Easterman to Golda Meir, September 6, 1960 (Israel National Archives, Foreign Ministry, 4318/4/I. A copy is also located in the Central Zionist Archives, Z6/1757).

[95] S.Z. Shragay to the Foreign Ministry in Jerusalem, September 11, 1960 (Israel National Archives, Foreign Ministry, 4324/5/II).

> This is a good time for clarifying whether it is possible to increase the emigration from North Africa through a financial-organizational arrangement with the prince, similar to the arrangement that was made at the time with regard to the Jews of Iraq.[96] Such an arrangement is worthwhile only if it will enable the emigration of thousands. The arrangement can be carried out through the establishment of a joint ship company for the purpose of transporting the emigrants from a port to be chosen by the Prince, or through the establishment of an airline. However, it could be that the Prince, if he is prepared to enter into such an arrangement, will make his own proposal.

If he did, Vered recommended that the Israelis should refrain from taking any drastic action or from attacking the administration in the United States press, as such actions and attacks would harden the attitude of the authorities toward the Jews. These comments indicate that at some point after the initial meetings with the prince, the negotiations regarding the Jews' departure from Morocco reached a more practical level.[97]

Toward the end of August, Benazeraf had a long conversation with Easterman. He spoke to the World Jewish Congress representative regarding a change for the better in the instructions concerning the issuance of passports to Jews and noted that this was being felt mainly in Casablanca, where city-governor Colonel Mohammed Madbouh and his deputy Sharaf were freely granting passports to anyone who applied. Those in charge of issuing passports were given new instructions according to which clear answers were to be given to applicants. If there was opposition to granting the passport, it was to be stated clearly. If there was no legal impediment or formal instruction preventing it, a passport should be issued to every applicant. In Benazeraf's estimation, the Minister of the Interior, Mbark Bekkay, who had issued these instructions, was certainly acting under instructions from the prince as it was not reasonable to believe that Bekkay would act on his own initiative regarding this sensitive subject. Easterman felt satisfied with the results of his activities and stated, "If this was so, it can be assumed that my meeting with Moulay Hassan was fruitful."[98]

Despite the lack of information on the responses to the report that Easterman submitted to the Israeli government, it can be assumed that whoev-

---

96 This comparison with the arrangement that was made with the Iraqi authorities regarding the collective departure of that country's Jews was mentioned at a meeting in Tel Aviv that was held on February 2, 1960 with the participation of the Mossad, the Jewish Agency and the Foreign Ministry. Israel National Archives, Foreign Ministry, 4319/4/D.

97 Y. Vered to Y. Meroz, September 14, 1960 (Israel National Archives, Foreign Ministry, 941/6).

98 A. Easterman to N. Goldmann, September 19, 1960 (Central Zionist Archives, Z6/1757). Y. Vered to Y. Meroz, September 14, 1960 (Israel National Archives, Foreign Ministry, 941/6).

er was interested in hearing Moulay Hassan's comments would have come to the conclusion that the subject of Jewish emigration from Morocco was about to reach a significant turning point, and would certainly have understood that the Jews' security was not being threatened. But matters did not proceed this way. The concept that guided the Israeli government, the Jewish Agency, and the heads of the Mossad was that Moroccan Jewry was still in danger and that the efforts to evacuate them had to be increased immediately.

The head of the Israeli security services did not seem to be pleased with the contacts that were likely to eliminate the system he had set up in North Africa. Thus, instead of stopping the efforts to smuggle out Jews or at least restricting them until the negotiations ended, the Mossad emissaries increased their activities and even engaged in activities that endangered the continuation of the talks as well as risking the lives of the very people whom their organization had come to "save." The Mossad leaders repeatedly expressed suspicion regarding the hidden intentions of the Moroccan authorities and in September 1960 they purchased the *Egoz* ship (Pisces) with which they intended to increase the number of families being smuggled out of the country. At the same time, the diplomatic efforts to make an arrangement with Moulay Hassan for collective emigration continued.

Thus, in the fall of 1960 there was a variety of groups that were running back and forth between the palace and the opposition in order to obtain advantages and improvements for the Jews of Morocco and approval for their departure from the country. At the same time, efforts were being made by the Israelis to distance the young country from the pan-Arabist bloc. Several brokers took part in these contacts, including André Chouraqui, Sam Benazeraf, Isaac Cohen-Olivar, Marcel Franco, and David Amar. In August of 1961, these people succeeded in realizing their goal in two areas: the Jews were allowed to leave on a collective basis and the State of Israel retained a channel of direct communication for cooperation with the head of the Moroccan government in the areas of security and intelligence, which continued to develop with time until they were formally recognized in the 1970s.

The Catastrophe that Didn't Happen

The history of the three-way relationship among Israel, the Moroccan government, and Moroccan Jewry could be entitled the "catastrophe that didn't happen." Carlos de Nesry put it well:

> The Jews of this country bring to mind the person who was saved from an explosion and is afterwards surprised to discover that he is healthy and whole. During the days of the protectorate, it seemed to them that independence would be a dramatic revolution with unpredictable results. In the end, they saw it as a sort of apocalypse in which the peace and quiet, which they knew under the French government, could be destroyed forever. The

severity of the omens justified this fatalistic fear. When independence was achieved, they learned that it was not all that terrible.[99]

One anti-Jewish incident that, more than any other, left its mark on the Jewish community took place on June 7, 1948, three weeks after the establishment of the state of Israel and the beginning of its war with the neighboring Arab states. A few days after the declaration of Israel's establishment, on May 23, Sultan Mohammed Ben Youssef understood what the results might be of a Jewish-Arab war in the Middle East for his country and he appealed to the country with a reminder of his undertaking to protect his Jewish subject. He addressed the Jewish community as well with a plea that they not engage in displays of Zionist solidarity with the new Jewish state. Despite the messages to the Moroccan people from the sultan, anti-Jewish riots broke out the eastern city of Oujda and in the neighboring town (located 46 kilometers away) of Jerrada.

These riots remained strongly etched in the general memory of the population for many years, and they were especially significant since, in those days, Oujda served as a transit station for Jews who left Morocco on their way to Israel through nearby Algeria. Since these events took place in 1948, while the Moroccan revolt against the French occupation was taking place, the Muslims had attacked the French authority's Jewish "partners" as revenge for Israel's war against the Arabs. Four Jews were killed in Oujda and a Muslim who attempted to protect them was killed as well. In Jerrada, 36 Jews were murdered, among them the community's rabbi, Moshe Cohen. In May already, the head of Oujda's Jewish community, Ovadia, had notified the French authorities of agitation against the Jews in the city, but the regional colonial governor of the city had left the place one day before. This fact gives rise to a suspicion that the French authorities were involved in planning the attacks on the Jews in order to create friction between different groups within the population. In this aspect as well, the motivation for the attack was connected to Israel and the general Middle East situation and not to local factors.[100]

---

99 C. de Nesry, *Les Israélites marocains à l'heure du choix* (Tanger, 1958), 18.

100 H. Saadon, "The Palestinian Element in Islamic Countries," *Peamim* 63 [Hebrew]. Saadon stresses the connection between the Oujda and Jerrada incident and the topic of the Middle East, the establishment of the State of Israel, and the emigration from Morocco to Israel via Oujda. A. Ben-Haim, "The Eretz Israel Mission to North-Africa: First Period, 1943–49," *The Organization of Underground Activists in North Africa*, vol. 1 (Tel Aviv 1994). p. 13. In his book, Yaakov Caroz notes that the number of those killed was 39 and not 36–of whom 10 were children–and that there were 25 wounded. Caroz, *The Man With Two Hats* [Hebrew], 66. See also Prosper Cohen, *La grande aventure*, p. 54.

Another anti-Jewish incident took place on August 3, 1954 in the town of Sidi Qassem (Petit Jean), in which six Jewish merchants from Meknès were killed. This incident had no connection to the Arab-Israeli conflict. No more than approximately fifty Jews lived in the town, though Jews from nearby Meknès came there to trade. The reason for the massacre was connected to the demand by the Nationalist Moroccan Movement to close stores on Fridays, and the opposing pressure from the French authorities, who wished to keep the stores open despite the threats. Moroccan demonstrators affixed pictures of the exiled king to the front windows of stores, including those of Jewish businesses. A French policeman who tried to remove the pictures was saved without being hurt but the mob vented its rage on Jewish merchants who were nearby and who were accused of breaking the strike. The bodies of the six Jews who were killed (after having been cruelly tortured) during the riots were burned by the mob. Afterward, Prosper Cohen, the secretary-general of the Zionist Federation, was called in by the representatives of the professional unions in Morocco to intervene on behalf of those who had been arrested.

This tragic event was not mentioned in contemporary Israeli newspapers, even though the Foreign Ministry had received pictures and a report from the field.[101] However, the political instability and uncertainty regarding the future and the administration's declarations of Arabization reminded many of the two events and pushed them toward leaving the country, which could offer them no guarantees of security.

A conviction that disaster was coming after the French left Morocco and independence was obtained was what fed the policies adopted by Israeli leaders and the activities of its emissaries. Also many Jews in Morocco had a fear of an apocalypse that would damage the Jews' status and their future in the country. Although the disaster never happened, fear of it took its toll. Those who foresaw only the negative were convinced that the disaster had only been delayed for a limited time and that it would undoubtedly still take place were forced to acknowledge that independence had not hurt the Jews but had only opened a new era for them that reminded some of the golden age in the relations between Jews and Muslims. Among the educated classes, the euphoria was predominant. The mistakes made by the Israeli government and its emissaries burst this bubble and ended the social-political-economic flowering from which all the Jews were beginning to benefit. The Jewish community of Morocco was comforted by the fact that even though Israel had unintentionally upset their social advancement in the short run, it gave them a sense of security in the long term and a clearer sense of their future.

101 Y. Tsur, *A Torn Community* [Hebrew], 394–96.

There are many answers to the critical question as to why the Jews of Morocco left. Some of the reasons were substantive and were based on matters of fundamental importance. Others were circumstantial, resulting form the specific time at which the Jews left, during the early 1960s. The Jewish community, the international Jewish organizations and the State of Israel were all concerned because, despite all the calming declarations put out by the Moroccan authorities, it was impossible to deny the basic fact that the independent Moroccan state was defined by its constitution as an Islamic state. But the problem was not connected to legal definitions alone. Post-colonial Moroccan society was characterized by a lifestyle in which religion played an important role and all of its culture was based on the Muslim experience. This socio-cultural situation did not leave any room for those who were not Muslims or for those who were secular in the style of many West European societies since the French Revolution.

With this as a starting point, any attempt to overcome the problem of the existence of a Jewish community within a Muslim society was doomed. It is true that some of the Jewish intelligentsia tried to ignore the problem for a time while the initial excitement generated by independence continued, but they were forced to face reality only soon enough. It was true that the leadership of the independent state had for some time been torn between its wish to adopt the progressive principles of the democratic West, on the one hand, and, on the other, its sense of kinship with the flag-bearers of the pan-Arabist ideology then sweeping the area and Morocco as well. Despite the leadership's early wavering, it became obvious that the pan-Arabists had won the day shortly after independence was achieved.

Morocco joined the Arab League, cut off its postal ties with Israel, and began a process of Moroccanization and Arabization of the government administration, all of which, together, tipped the scales for the Jews and eliminated the possibility that the status of the country's Jews would be similar to that of the Jews in the secular democratic countries of Western Europe.

The Arab-Israeli conflict only aggravated a problem that would have existed anyway. The fear of a loss of the advantages given them by their education as a result of the Arabization process put the Jews in a state of chronic discomfort and uncertainty, which only increased with time. Since Morocco could not offer any guarantee that the future would be better for its Jewish citizens in an Arab-Muslim state, the Jews had no choice but to leave.

It is true that the Middle East conflict, which was one of the reasons for the urge to emigrate, was an important element in the deterioration of relations between Jews and Muslims. The conflict raised concerns on both an emotional and a religious level. But sooner or later the conflicts between the Jewish and Muslim communities within Morocco would have become much more critical and the Jews' status within society would have been seriously weakened. The experience of Jews in other Arab countries did not encourage the development of good neighborly relations between Jews and Muslims in Morocco.

Along with the intrusion of the Middle Eastern conflict into the Jewish-Muslim relationship in Morocco, another concern arose regarding the loss of the advantages that the Jews had enjoyed in the past, relative to the Muslim public. The ending of these advantages was due to the country's adoption of the Arabization process, which was to cause the Jews to lose the preferences they had previously enjoyed in terms of obtaining management positions, preferences derived from their having benefited from French education. Financial shocks that flowed from the departure of the French also impacted on the Jewish merchants and artisans. Fear grew among the Jewish bourgeoisie and among the free professionals that they would indeed have to choose between French language and culture, to which they had been so open in the past, and the process of expected Arabization, which would bring along with it Muslim cultural baggage in which the Jews would be at a disadvantage. Many of Morocco's Jews understood that it would not be possible to hold onto France and the artificial imposition of its culture in the post-colonial independent state. The formal Jewish leadership remained relatively weak because of its dual loyalty to both France and Morocco. David Amar, for example, was forced to say one thing and then the opposite so as to avoid conflict with the authorities while still following his true wishes as a Jewish leader. The Hebrew-Israeli option was not ideal from this perspective, but it was still better than a Jewish future in an Arab-Muslim state that was attempting to determine its future character.

It is important to note that the Jews' departure from Morocco was also part of a social process that had begun long before Moroccan independence. This historical trend toward migration was an integral part of a natural demographic process that had been going on for a long time within the Moroccan population, in general, and even more within the country's Jewish community. The strength of this movement among the Jews was due to the socio-economic status they enjoyed. The process existed in the eighteenth and nineteenth centuries and was accelerated even more during the period of French control. This demographic change was basically a trend that began with the abandonment of villages in the direction of a nearby town, and then progressed to the move from towns to the medium-sized cities and the largest cities. With the transformation of Casablanca into a most important economic center, villagers began to migrate directly from their distant and remote homes to this new center. It should be recalled that the villagers numbered more than 30,000 people out of a total population of 250,000 Jews. Along with the exodus from the villages and the small cities to Casablanca, there was also a movement of Jews out of Morocco, even before the establishment of the State of Israel. The Jews of Morocco moved not only to France and Spain but also to Brazil, Venezuela, British Gibraltar, Great Britain, the United States, and Canada.

Departure from Morocco to more attractive locations that promised, in the long run, an improved quality of life was thus a part of an eternal demographic process that grew in strength with the passage of time. The migration to Israel, France, Canada, and South America should thus be seen in this historical demographic perspective, which itself took place as part of the process of educational and cultural development that France had brought to the Jews of Morocco. Within a relatively short time, the Jewish community had so absorbed the advantages of French civilization that a large gap between them and their Arab-Muslim geo-social environment was created, a fact that motivated them to continue the migration process in the direction of new horizons. The relative backwardness of Moroccan society would sooner or later have pushed the Jews out of independent Morocco. It was an inevitable process for the country's Jews, who sought to improve their social status and were concerned for their children's cultural future.

The assistance offered by the emissaries of the Mossad to the Jewish community should not be discounted either. This led to a sense of obligation, which the emissaries succeeded in creating among part of the community's leadership. An entire generation of young Jews who had experienced the DEJJ (Département Éducatif de la Jeunesse Juive of Charles Netter Association), youth movements, the Jewish scouts, the Alliance schools and the Israeli youth movements absorbed a great affection for the young State of Israel. The young Jewish state aroused their imagination through its victories, its scientific achievements, and the almost magical sense with which terms like *qibbutz*, *moshav*, TSAHAL, *halutzim* (pioneers), "Jerusalem" and others fired up their imaginations. On this foundation, a few sentences from the Jewish prayers and from Scripture were mixed with abstract mystical longing for the Holy Land. Thus, fertile ground was laid for a departure to a foreign land, even if the push for such a departure was somewhat mixed with the longing for a homeland in which generations of ancestors had been buried.

Regarding the circumstances of the departure that took place in the period between November 1961 (in the wake of the "Compromise Agreement" that was reached with the Moroccan authorities in august 1961) and the Six-Day War, it should be noted that the conditions of the departure themselves created a strong sense of having been abandoned, a sensation felt by many Jews.

Paradoxically, the very same Moroccan authorities that had sought to prevent it created the departure psychosis. The more they made the Jews' emigration difficult and tried to seduce them into staying, the greater was the Jews' desire to leave before it became impossible to go. Since independence, the Jews were concerned whether Morocco could, in the long run, be tolerant of their presence. Even though no actual injury was done to them, doubts for the future were sufficient to ignite the push to depart. The doubt, the fear, and the panic transformed faithful citizens into emigrants, primarily as a result of the obstacles the government had placed in the way of their departure.

Since the Jews of Morocco were not able to receive French citizenship as the Algerian Jews had, Israel was one of the significant destinations to which Jews turned. The heroic image of the Israeli sabra society that had developed in the Jewish state, its victories over the Arab armies, worked a charm on the Jews of Morocco and was a major attraction for the younger generation. Israel thus provided an available and appealing alternative to other possible destinations, despite the economic difficulties that those who arrived there could expect. The thought of a new life and a source of hope in Israel became the antithesis of a fear of an uncertain future in Morocco.

As to the basic question as to why the Jews left Morocco, there is a short answer: a psychosis of abandonment had been created. Since, during this period, emigration took place in an atmosphere of secrecy, no one in the community knew what the levels of emigration actually were. As a matter of course, no one was interested in publicizing statistics regarding this subject, so that everyone was informed only by what he saw and what he feared in his heart. In the minds of the Jews, the rate of emigration had reached proportions that caused everyone to feel that all his relatives and acquaintances had left and only he remained behind. Even those who had not left knew that sooner or later they would leave. Thus, paradoxically, the psychosis of departure was created not only by Israel's agents, who wished to instigate it, but also by the Moroccan government, which wished to stop it.

Were it not for this emigration psychosis, the Jews might have taken full advantage of their preferred status and used it for economic and social purposes. This process would no doubt have weakened when educated Muslims completed their studies and began to seek positions in the country's administration, commerce, and economy. Friction might have developed between the long-time Jewish bureaucrats and Muslims who wished to take for themselves various public positions. But this would have happened gradually, and only after a period in which the Jews would have been able to exploit the advantages given to them by their relatively high level of education. Had it not been for the overly rapid acceleration of emigration, it could be that the Jews of Morocco would have arrived in Israel with their economic-educational status much improved. At the same time, the state of Israel would have been better prepared to absorb them. The departure from Morocco could have been spread over a longer period of time. Had that happened, it might have been possible to avoid the social crises that developed in Israel and that were expressed in the riots in Wadi Salib and in those led by the "Israeli Black Panthers," among whom there were so many Moroccan immigrants.

Non-Urban Social Encounters between Jews and Muslims in the Ottoman Empire during the 16th through 18th Centuries

Characteristics and Consequences

LEAH BORNSTEIN-MAKOVETSKY

We have relatively little information about the social interaction of Jews and Muslims in the Ottoman Empire from the sixteenth to eighteenth centuries compared to the extensive information available on political and economic interaction. What we do know is based mainly on Jewish sources (particularly the Responsa literature), including letters and travel records. Some further information can be gleaned from Ottoman archives (particularly Muslim court archives), European archives, reports by ambassadors and consuls, and European travel journals.[1] Muslim chroniclers have also provided some information. Yaron Harel observes that Muslim writers hardly recognized the existence of non-Muslim testimonials, probably due to Muslim dis-

---

[1] Much research exists on this topic, in particular, emphasizing the economic relationships between Jews and non-Jews in the Ottoman Empire. See Halil Inalcik, "Jews in the Ottoman Economy and Finance 1450–1500," in *The Islamic World from Classical to Modern Times: Essays in Honor of Bernard Lewis*, eds. Clifford Edmond Bosworth, Charles Issawi, R. Savoy, and Abraham L. Udovitch (Princeton, N.J.: Darwin Press, 1989), 513–50; Benjamin Braude and Bernard Lewis, eds., *Christians and Jews in the Ottoman Empire*, 2 vols. (New York: Holmes & Meier, 1982); Mark Alan Epstein, *The Ottoman Jewish Communities and Their Role in the Fifteenth and Sixteenth Centuries* (Freiburg: Schwarz, 1980), 26ff.; Bruce Masters, *Christians and Jews in the Ottoman Arab World: The Roots of Sectarianism,* (Cambridge: Cambridge University Press, 2001); Minna Rozen, *A History of the Jewish Community in Istanbul: The Formative Years, 1453–1565* (Leiden-Boston: Brill, 2002); Haim Gerber, "Jewish Tax Farmers in the Ottoman Empire in the 16th and 17th Centuries," *Journal of Turkish Studies* 10 (1986): 143–54; idem, "Jews and Money Lending in the Ottoman Empire," *JQR* ns 71 (1981):100–11; Ariye Shmuelevitz, *The Jews of the Ottoman Empire in the Late Fifteenth and Sixteenth Centuries: Administrative, Economic. Legal and Social Relations as Reflected in the Responsa* (Leiden: Brill, 1984); Haim Gerber, *Yehudei ha-Imperia ha-Otmanit ba-Me'ot ha-Shesh-Esre ve-ha-Sheva-Esre, Chevra ve-Kalkala* (Jerusalem: Merkaz Zalman Shazar, 1983); idem, "Ha-Yehudim u-Mosad ha-Hekdesh ha-Muslemi (Waqf) ba-Imperia ha-Otmanit," *Sefunot,* 17 (1983): 105–34; idem, "Yozma u-Mischar Bein Leumi ba-Pe'ilot ha-Kalkalit Shel Yehudei ha-Imperia ha-'Otmanit ba-Me'ot ha-Shesh Esre - Sheva-Esre," *Zion* 43 (1978): 37–68; idem, "Yehudim be-Chayei ha-Kalkala Shel ha-Ir ha-Anatolit Bursa ba-Me'ah ha-Sheva Esre," *Sefunot* 16 (1980): 233–72; Amnon Cohen, *Jewish Life under Islam, Jerusalem in the Sixteenth Century* (Cambridge: Harvard University Press, 1984); Eliezer Bashan, "Chayei ha-Kalkala" in *Toledot Yehudei Mitzraim ba-Tequfa ha-Otmanit (1517–1914)*, ed. Jacob M. Landau (Jerusalem: Misgav Yerushalayim, 1984), 36–128; idem, "Eduyot Shel Tayarim Erope'im Kemakor le-Toledot ha-Kalkala Shel Yehudei ha-

interest in Jewish society, since Jews were not suspected of striving for political independence and had not rebelled against the Sultan for centuries.[2]

In the Ottoman Empire, social interaction between religions was based, first and foremost, on family and religious affiliation. The various religious denominations were socially compartmentalized, with separate residential arrangements in most cities. However, there were social encounters, albeit fairly infrequent, between members of the various religions at holy sites, medicinal sites, and on the occasion of medical visits. Jewish women, in particular, were socially isolated from non-Jewish society. Since only a few were involved in economic activities, Jewish women, for the most part, remained within the designated Jewish Quarters.[3] Thus, this study deals mainly with encounters between men of the two religions.

In the nineteenth century, Jews and Muslims throughout the Ottoman Empire developed closer associations due to the Tanzimat (reforms) that afforded equal rights and the possibility of more significant inter-religious

---

Mizrach ha-Tichon ba-Tequfa ha-Otmanit," in *Moreshet Yehudei Sefarad ve-ha-Mizrach*, ed. Yssachar Ben Ami (Jerusalem: Magnes, 1982), 35–80; Michael Winter, "Yachasei ha-Yehudim Im ha-Shiltonot ve-ha-Chevra ha-Lo Yehudit," in Landau, *op cit.*, 371–420. For the relationship in political and society areas, see Bernard Lewis, *Ha-Yehudim be-Olam ha-Islam* (Jerusalem: Merkaz Zalman Shazar, 1996); Leah Bornstein-Makovetsky, "Jewish Lay Leadership and Ottoman Authorities during the Sixteenth and Seventeenth Centuries," in *Ottoman and Turkish Jewry, Community and Leadership, Studies in Jewish History in the Ottoman Empire*, ed. Aron Rodrigue (Bloomington, Ind.: Indiana University Press, 1992), 87–121; idem, "Yachasim Chevrati'im Bein Yehudim ve-Nochrim be-Arei ha-Imperia ha-'Otmanit ba-Me'ot ha-Shesh Esre ve-ha-Sheva Esre," *Meqedem U-Me-Yam* 6 (1995): 13–34; idem, "Mumarim Le Islam ve-Le Nazrut ba-Imperia ha-Otmanit ba-Me'ot Ha 16–18," in *Hevra ve-Tarbut, Yehudei Sefarad le-Achar ha-Gerush*, eds. Michael Abitboul, Galit Hazan-Rokem, and Yom Tov Assis (Jerusalem: Misgav Yerushalayim, 1997), 3–30; idem, "Blood Money and Retaliation in Criminal Law in the Ottoman Empire in the Sixteenth and Seventeenth Centuries as Found in Jewish Society," in *Jewish Law Studies XVIII (The Bar-Ilan 2006 Conference Volume)*, ed. Joseph Fleishman (The Jewish Law Association, 2008), 16–36. An extended Hebrew version of this article was published in *Moreshet Israel, A Journal for the Study of Judaism, Zionism and Eretz-Israel*, 5 (September 2008): 62–88.

2 Yaron Harel, *Be-Sefinot Shel Esh La-Ma'arav, Temurot be-Yahadut Surya be-Tequfat Ha Reformot ha-Otmaniot, 1840–1880* (Jerusalem: Merkaz Zalman Shazar, 2003), 196–97. For information on Jews in Muslim chronicles, see Winter, "Yachasei ha-Yehudim."

3 Ruth Lamdan, *A Separate People: Jewish Women in Palestine, Syria, and Egypt in the Sixteenth Century* (Leiden: Brill, 2000); Margalit Shilo, *Princess or Prisoner?: Jewish Women in Jerusalem, 1840–1914* (trans. David Louvish) (Waltham: Brandeis University Press, 2005); Leah Bornstein-Makovetsky, "Ha'isha ha-Yehudiya be-Halab ve-Muskamot ha-Tzeniot ba-Tequfa ha-Otmanit," in *Isha ba-Mizrach – Isha mi-Mizrach*, eds. Tova Cohen and Shaul Regv (Ramat Gan: Bar-Ilan University, 2005), 55–68.

social and political encounters. However, it should be noted that social segregation in most Ottoman cities endured throughout the nineteenth and early twentieth centuries.[4] Most Jewish-Muslim encounters occurred in cities, where almost all the Jews of the empire resided. In the Arab areas of the empire, Jews, who all spoke Arabic, were influenced by their neighbors in various facets of their daily life, such as dress, music, and food. However, in the European parts of the empire and in Anatolia, Muslims had less of an influence on Jewish life, since most Jews there spoke Espaniol (Judeo-Spanish) and maintained the Judeo-Spanish culture. Jewish-Muslim commercial encounters also took place at the empire's large fairs, which may have led to occasional social relationships.

This study is an investigation into the nature and consequences of Jewish-Muslim social encounters outside the cities: on the roads, in convoys, in khans and other inns, in the homes of villagers, at shared Jewish-Muslim holy sites, and at medicinal sites, cafes, and public bath-houses.

Although these wayside encounters sometimes ended tragically, with the murder of Jews by Muslims, Jews and Muslims usually formed relationships characteristic of travel partners, and these encounters often led to business collaboration and mutual support. We can understand the nature and consequences of such encounters from information provided in Responsa literature. However, the available information is very concise and we must read between the lines of Jewish and Muslim testimonies in order to reach conclusions. The significance accorded by Jewish law to Muslim oral statements given to Jews reinforces the authenticity of information gleaned from the responsa.

Most of the sources mention Jewish encounters with traveling Muslim merchants and with Muslim villagers, whose religious zealotry often was manifested in the taunting and abuse of Jews, albeit illegal. Reports of Jewish murders on the roads and the desecration of the bodies by Muslims confirms that fanatic Muslims took advantage of their distant travels to express their hatred of the Jews. Jewish legal sources mentioning the murder of Jews normally do not state the reason for the killing, since these motives are unrelated or irrelevant to the legal discussion, usually aimed at freeing the wives of those murdered so that they can remarry.

---

4 Many researches deal with the influence of the reforms on the Jewish minority in the Ottoman Empire. See Harel, *Be Sefinot,* index; Minna Rozen, *The Last Ottoman Century and Beyond: The Jews in Turkey and the Balkans 1808–1945*, 1 (Tel-Aviv: Tel-Aviv University Diaspora Research Institute, 2005), 53–130. For the Ottoman Reforms, see Roderic H. Davison, *Reform in the Ottoman Empire 1856–1876* (New York: Gordian Press, 1973); Carter V Findley, *Bureaucratic Reform in the Ottoman Empire: The Sublime Porte, 1789–1922* (Princeton: Princeton University Press, 1980); Halil Inalcik, "Application of the Tanzimat and Social Effect," *Archivum Ottomanicum,* 5 (1973): 97–128; Bernard Lewis, *The Emergence of Modern Turkey* (London: Royal Institute of International Affairs, 1962).

In most cases of homicide, the murderers were not caught and tried. We do not hear of any decrease in the number of murders resulting from the punishment of murderers or the imposition of compensation payments. The impression is that Ottoman authorities were not very successful in preventing murder, and that security on the roads was fairly poor in many areas of the empire.[5]

However, the situation was not completely dire. In quite a few cases, Muslim-Jewish social encounters, consisting mainly of joint travels, lodging at khans and at the homes of Gentiles, common bathing, and drinking, led to friendships and close relationships. Our sources, especially the responsa literature, show no substantial fluctuations in Jewish-Muslim relationships during the sixteenth to eighteenth centuries.

Traveling in Non-Jewish Convoys and Sailing with Gentiles

Many Jews traveled in convoys, both large and small, throughout the Ottoman Empire, mainly for their extensive commercial enterprises. Fairs were often the convoys' ultimate destination. Convoys provided Jews with fairly good protection and were preferred over solitary travel, which was considered dangerous. There are stories of Jews who did not wait for convoys, set out on their own, and were subsequently murdered.[6] When Jews traveled in large convoys consisting of both Jews and Gentiles they did their best to keep the Sabbath and were accompanied by a Muslim who would walk before the convoy and thus avoid desecrating the Sabbath.[7] When convoys traveled in desert areas or in dangerous conditions Jews were compelled to remain with the convoy during the Sabbath as permitted by Jewish law. Although convoys provided protection, sometimes one or two Jews struck out on their own, evidently for business purposes or in order to keep the Sabbath, and were murdered for their money by Muslim or Christian villagers or by robbers who roamed the roads.

There is an interesting dialogue between members of a convoy and Jewish travelers who had stopped at a distant dangerous place in order to keep the Sabbath without requesting guards.[8] Members of the convoy said to the Jews:

---

5 Leah Bornstein-Makovetsky, "Blood Money and Retaliation."

6 Rabbi Shlomo Amarlliio, *Kerem Shlomo Responsa* (Salonica: Talmud Torah, 1719), no. 105. For convoy plunder, see Suraya Faroqhi, *Towns and Townsmen of Ottoman Anatolia, 1520–1650* (London-New York: Cambridge University Press, 1984), 49–75; idem, *Pilgrims and Sultans, the Hajj under the Ottomans, 1517–1683* (New York: St. Martin's, 1994), 32–75.

7 See Abraham Yaari, *Masot Eretz Israel Shel Olim Yehudi'im* (Jerusalem: Masada, 1977), 322–23.

8 Rabbi Moshe Mitrani, *Mabit Responsa* (Venice: Yoani Kalioni, 1629), no. 100. See also Rabbi David Ibn Avi Zimra, *Radbaz Responsa* (Livorno: Mildola, 1652), no. 81 (1152);

> Why didn't you explain the matter to us, and we would have given you two or three guards, as the place where you chose to sleep is very dangerous.... If the Arabs had killed you what would we have told the minister (the Pasha or Sancakbey)....No, it seems that your forefathers have special rights and your God saved you on their behalf.[9]

Jews often walked alone or in couples or threesomes and they were easy targets for murderers. For this reason, Jews often wore Muslim dress when walking alone, but nonetheless were on occasion identified as Jews and murdered.[10] Gentiles who traveled in the convoys normally did not harm the Jews.[11] Some Jews were wary of Muslim convoys. In 1604 a Jewish passerby from the city of Pilibe was traveling alone to Sofya and encountered a convoy of Turks. Fearing them, he pretended to be a Turk and so he accompanied them safely to Sofya.[12] Entire convoys, of course, could meet a tragic end. For example, in the seventeenth century all members of a small convoy consisting of several Jews, a Qadi, a Sipahi, and a Turkish woman, were murdered.[13] In another incident in the sixteenth century, when a Jew traveling in a convoy transporting goods died unexpectedly, members of the convoy were concerned that they would be falsely accused of his death.[14] In general, Jews who traveled in convoys were safe from physical harm and murder, as convoy leaders understood that any harm to Jewish travelers would result in an investigation by the Ottoman authorities, as well as demands for "blood ransom" by the deceased's relatives.[15]

Rabbi Moshe Galante, *Ramag Responsa* (Venice: Juan Zagara, 1608), no. 110; Rabbi Yosef Ibn Lev, *Maharival Responsa*, 2 (Frankfurt and Amsterdam, 1726), no. 53; Bashan, "Eduyot Shel Tayarim Erope'im," 41–43. A testimony from 1617 mentions a Jew who had left the convoy from Nikopol to Dolya fair and found lodging in a village on the Sabbath. Subsequently he was murdered on his way to Sofya. (Rabbi Haim Shabbetai, *Torat Haim Responsa* [Salonica: Kanpilias, 1722], no. 48).

9 Yaari, *Masot,* 238; See also the eighteenth-century testimony of Rabbi Yosef Haim David Azulai about the Sabbath guarding the Jews in the convoy in Egypt (Yaari, *Masot,* 372–73).

10 In 1687 two Jews were murdered on their way from Belgrade to Salonica. (Rabbi Titazhaq Ibn Sanji, *Beerot Yitzhaq Responsa* [Salonica: Kalai and Nachman, 1755], Even Ha-Ezer, no. 19).

11 A Jew from Larissa in the eighteenth century joined a convoy and was murdered. See Rabbi Yosef Nachmoli, *Ashdot ha-Pisga Responsa* (Salonica: Nachman, 1790), Even Ha-Ezer, no. 2. Three Jews who traveled in a convoy in Egypt in the seventeenth century were murdered. (Eliav Shochetman [ed.], *Rabbi Meir Gavizon Responsa*, 1 [Jerusalem: Jerusalem Institute, 1985], no. 14).

12 *Torat Haim Responsa*, 4, no. 34.

13 Rabbi Shlomo Ibn Hasson and Rabbi Shmuel Gaon, *Mishpatim Yesharim Responsa* (Salonica: Kanpilias, Falcon and Angels, 1733), no. 48.

14 *Mabit Responsa*, 3 (Jerusalem 1990), no. 162.

15 Bornstein-Makovetsky, "Blood Money."

Jews and Muslims often sailed together and there are not infrequent reports of Jews drowning.[16] Occasionally the bodies of the Jews who had drowned were buried by Muslims. Although we have no information on the interactions between Jewish and Muslim travelers on board ships, we can assume that they were similar to those in convoys and at inns.

Shared Lodgings

Jews, Muslims, and Christians often stayed at roadside inns. These were usually large and small khans (in Turkish: *han*, *kervansaray*, and in English: khan, caravanserrai) throughout the Ottoman empire. Most of them provided rooms and other services to travelers, and some provided only security.[17] At fairs, as well, travelers used the services of khans, hotels, and inns, also called *tabhane*, which fulfilled the prevalent need for lodgings.[18] Some Jews did business at the khan, as here they could meet merchants from all over the world. The Egyptian chronicler Alayani relates a serious incident that occurred in 1728 in Alexandria, in which a Jew killed a Muslim. The Janissaries (soldiers) brought him before a court of law, and when the Qadi ruled that the Muslims were jealous of this Jew the Muslims stoned the

[16] For examples: testimonies from the sixteenth century: Rabbi Joseph Caro, *Beit Yosef Responsa* (Jerusalem: Tiferet Hatorah, 1960), Mayim She'ein Lahem Sof, no. 1; *Mabit Responsa,* 1, nos. 60, 186, 188; Rabbi Shmuel de Medina, *Rashsam Responsa* (Lavov: Balaban, 1862), Even Ha-Ezer, no. 51; Rabbi Aharon Sasson, *Torat Emet Responsa* (Venice: Kaliaoni, 1626), no. 15; A testimony from 1791: Rabbi Ezra Bazri, ed., *Rabbi Gabriel Ashkenazi Responsa*, 1 (Jerusalem: Ketav Institute, 1985), no. 3. A Jew was assassinated in a boat in Egypt in the second half of the seventeenth century. (Rabbi Avraham Halevi, *Ginat Veradim Responsa*, 1 [Istanbul: Yona of Zlazitz, 1715], Even Ha-Ezer, Kelal 3 no. 10).

[17] For khans, see Dror Zeevi, *An Ottoman Century: The District of Jerusalem in the 1600s* (Albany, N.Y.: State University of New York Press, 1996), index; N. Elisséff, "Kha," *Encyclopedia of Islam,* 2nd ed., 4, E. Van Donzel, B. Lewis, Ch. Pallat and C.E. Bosworth, eds. (Leiden: Brill, 1978), 1015–17; Yaari, *Masot*, 235–36, 250, 310, 312, 320–22, 376; Stanford J. Shaw, *History of the Ottoman Empire and Modern Turkey, I. 1280–1808* (Cambridge: Cambridge University Press, 1976), 16, 28.

[18] A khan and a few hotels existed in the Eski Jama'a Fair, which was active from the eighteenth century onward. (Zvi Keren, *Qehilat Yehudei Roschuk, 1788–1878* [Jerusalem: Ben Zvi Institute, 2005], 126). For the case of a Jew who died at the beginning of the sixteenth century in a khan and was buried by Gentiles, see Rabbi Binyamin b. Mattatya, *Binyamin Zeev Responsa* (Venice: Daniel Bomberg, 1539), no. 20. For Jews who stayed in khans, see *Radbaz Responsa,* 2, no. 638; *Radbza Responsa*, 7 (Warsaw: Zetzer and Shriptgisser, 1882), no. 19. For the suspicion that a Kara-Hisar khan-keeper murdered Jews, see *Radbaz Responsa*, 7, no. 20. In one case during the sixteenth century, the owner of a hotel in Egypt stole the merchandise of a Jew. Rabbi Yosef Caro, *Avkat Rochel Responsa* (Jerusalem: Monzon, 1960), nos. 139–40. False marriage testimony was given in a khan in the village of Trianda, which accommodated Jews who traveled in a convoy from Tire to Izmir. (Rabbi Yom Tov Zahalon, *Maharitaz Hadashot Responsa* [Jerusalem: Jerusalem Institute, 1980], no. 25).

Qadi, grabbed the Jew, killed him, burned his body, and looted his home as well as the khan at which he and other Jews had been staying.[19] Violent incidents sometimes occurred at the khans as well, as in the case of a Jew who stabbed his friend at a merchants' khan in Roschuk in 1810.[20] Sometimes Jewish travelers passed away at khans.[21] These inns usually gave their guests a feeling of security and Jews were almost never murdered there. This fact led the adjudicator R. Yaakov Castro from Egypt to accept as reliable testimony on the murder of a Jew at a khan and to state that murders do not normally occur at khans.[22]

Encounters at hotels, where Jews and Gentiles sometimes smoked together, led to conversations, usually in Turkish or Arabic, wherein Muslims attested incidentally or purposefully to the death of Jews and the discovery of Jewish bodies. This information was conveyed immediately to Jewish courts and formed a very important component of rulings aimed at enabling the remarriage of women whose husbands had disappeared and finding the remains of murdered Jews and burying them in accordance with Jewish law. At times, these testimonies led to the punishment of the murderers or the payment of compensation by murderers or by villages where the bodies were discovered.[23]

The Responsa literature contains important information about the manner in which these Gentiles casually conversed on such matters. (This seems to refer to Christians and not Muslims; Christians are usually designated as *Akum* and Muslims as *Tugarmim* or *Yishmaelim*.) One example, from the second half of the eighteenth century, is the testimony of Ovadia Avraham Noah Hacohen before three witnesses:

> I was sitting among the Arabs at a place that receives guests, close to the Al Shayur market. Gentiles sat and related tales and they said to me: "Abdallah the sailor came into some money, he took with him three Jews from Basra, and God sentenced them to drown."

---

19 Winter, "Yachasei ha-Yehudim," 403.

20 Keren, *Qehilat Yehudei Roschuk,* 62.

21 For example, Moshe Halevi, a glasses-seller from Istanbul, died in 1776 in a hotel in Serres, Greece. Another guest in the hotel, Mordechai Hacohen, sent Halevi's money to his widow. (Rabbi Yom Tov Elnekave, *Shevitat Yom Tov Responsa* [Salonica: Israelija and Nachman, 1788], Even Ha-Ezer, no. 2). For Refael Nachmias from Roschuk, who traveled for business to Edirne and died in a khan, see Keren, *Qehilat Yehudei Roschuk*, 94.

22 Rabbi Yaacov Castro, *Ohalei Yaakov* Responsa (Livorno: Castilo and Saadon, 1783), no. 19. For the rumor that two Jews were murdered on their way from Tripoli to Beirut c. 1600, see Rabbi Yosef Mitrani, *Maharit Responsa*, 1 (Istanbul: Franco and Gabai, 1642), no. 52. In another case, in 1553 Yehuda Naki testified in Damascus that he had heard a rumor about the death of Yaacov Lori in the inn of Alfaskoya and that Lori had been thrown into the sea. (Castro, *Ohalei Yaacov Responsa,* no. 19).

23 Bornstein-Makovetsky, "Blood Money."

He testified that several days later Abdallah discovered the bodies floating on the water and took the Jews' clothes and money.[24] In another case, in 1779, a court in Bitola, (Monastir), heard witnesses testify to the murder of a member of the community, Yekutiel Grasiano, who was returning from the fair at Istruga and disappeared between the villages of Pitrino and Rishna. According to one of the witnesses, a gentile tanner came to the khan and told him that Yekutiel was caught by robbers upon returning from the fair and killed by one of them.[25]

Staying at a Hekdesh (Hospice)

Jews and Muslims often stayed at Imarets. These hospices existed in various cities throughout the empire, designated as soup kitchens and guest houses for poor passers-by of all religions. A resident of Salonica attested that when visiting Alexandria he stayed at the Rhodes hospice together with North-African Jews and Arabs. These Arabs conversed daily with a Jew named Yitzhak who stayed at the hospice and drowned when his ship broke down.[26] In a case from 1604, Shlomo Primo of Salonica, traveling from Philibi to Sofya, arrived at Sofya very ill. He had disguised himself as a Muslim and a convoy of Muslims that he met on the way brought him to town. He then met a Jew named Yehuda Ashkenazi, to whom he revealed that he was Jewish and what had happened to him on the way. At the advice of a sage, Ashkenazi brought him to the local hospice, where he passed away during the night. The Turks who brought him to town wouldn't let the Jews bury him, claiming that he was Muslim, and the Jews were afraid that they would be accused of burying a Muslim in a Jewish cemetery. So they did not object to his being buried in a Muslim cemetery.[27]

---

[24] *Rabbi Gabriel Ashkenazi Responsa*, 1, no. 3.

[25] Rabbi Mordechai Halevi, *Darchei No'am Responsa* (Venice: Bragdin, 1697), Even Ha-Ezer, no. 63; Haim Blanc, "Arabit Yehudit Mizrit," *Sefunot* 18 (1985): 212–14.

[26] Eliav Shochetman, ed., *Rabbi Meir Gavizon Responsa*, 2 (Jerusalem: Jerusalem Institute, 1985), no. 46. Apparently the hospice in Rhodes is the imaret founded by Sultan Suleyman the Magnificent and catered to the local trade. (Faroqhi, *Towns and Townsmen,* 117). Such hospices existed throughout the empire and accepted Jews. For example, such an imaret and a hotel were active in Kara Bonar village and in Sisi Köy village. (Yaari, *Masot,* 263–64). For the imarets in the Ottoman Empire, see Amy Singer, "Serving up Charity: The Ottoman Public Kitchen," *Journal of Interdisciplinary History* 35, 3 (2004): 481–500; Oded Peri, "Waqf and the Ottoman Welfare Policy," *Journal of the Economic and Social History of the Orient* 35, 2 (1992): 167–86; Robert Barnes, *An Introduction to Religious Foundations in the Ottoman Empire* (Leiden: Brill, 1986); William J. Griswold, "A Sixteenth-Century Ottoman Pious Foundation," *Journal of the Economic and Social History of the Orient* 27, 2 (1984): 175–98; Ronald C. Jennings, "Pious Foundations in the Society and Economy of Ottoman Trabzon, 1565–1640," *Journal of the Economic and Social History of the Orient* 33, 3 (1990): 271–336.

[27] *Torat Haim Responsa*, 4, no. 34.

Jews may have used the local hospice to house sick Jews when necessary, mainly foreigners who had contracted a dangerous illness.[28]

Lodgings in Villages and at Non-Jewish Homes

Sometimes, due to lack of space at lodgings close to the cities and for lack of close lodgings, Jews would stay at non-Jewish homes in the villages.[29] These Jews traveled to the villages to buy various agricultural products, peddle their wares, or work as artisans. Only in certain areas, such as villages in the Galilee or Kurdistan, where many Jews lived in rural areas, could Jewish passers-by stay at the homes of their fellow religionists and feel physically safe.[30] In most parts of the Ottoman Empire Jews stayed at the homes of Muslim villagers and sometimes even in Christian villages. Jews had regular Gentile hosts, usually from poor homes.[31] For example, the renown Rabbi Haim Yosef David Azulai ("Hida") stated in 1753 that he and other convoy travelers stayed at the home of a sheikh at the village a-Duima (literally, a cattle shed), while in the villages of Palestine it was customary to establish a

---

28 Some Jewish communities built hospices for Jewish wayfarers. In Salonica this institute was founded before 1560. See Yitzhaq Refael Molcho and Abraham Amarillio, "Yalkut Haskamot Saloniki be-Ladino," *Sefunot* 2 (1958), nos. 33–34, 40, 43. For other communities, see Eliezer Bashan, *Mimizrach Shemesh ad Mevo'o* (Lod: Orot Yahadut Ha-Maghreb, 1996), 67–68. During the sixteenth and seventeenth centuries the Jews of Jerusalem had a Jewish hospital. (Zohar Amar, *Peri Megadim le-Rabbi David Di Silva, Rofe mi-Yerushalayim* (Jerusalem: Yad Ben Zvi, 2004), 8.

29 See, for example, a case from the sixteenth century: *Beit Yosef Responsa*, Goy Mesiah Lefi Tomo, no, 6. In areas without khans and inns the wayfarers might spend the night in the home of a dervish or in a *Zaviye* (monastery), which provided a measure of security from robbers, though there were at times attacks upon these houses and monasteries. (Faroqhi, *Towns*, 62). There are no Jewish sources about their staying in such places, but it is reasonable to think that Jews, especially those who traveled in convoys, must have done so.

30 For Jews in the seventeenth century who were put up in a Jewish home in the village, see Rabbi Abraham Shabettai Lifshitz, ed., *Shut Rabbi Moshe Ibn Haviv Hadashot* (Jerusalem: Chochmat Shlomo Institute, 2000), Even Ha-Ezer, no.144.

31 Some cases from the sixteenth century: Jews stayed in Turkish homes in the village of Tresnik. (*Beit Yosef Responsa,* Goy Mesiah Lefi Tomo, no. 1); A Jew lodged in the house of a Gentile named Arki. (*Mahaival Responsa*, 3, no. 18); Jewish traders lodged in the inn of a Turk in Ranyasa, Greece. (Rabbi Shmuel Kalai, *Mishpetei Shmuel Responsa* [Venice: Zanity, 1599, no. 27]); a Jew stayed in the village of Gorlo. (*Rabbi Moshe Alsheich Responsa* [Venice: Di Gara, 1605], no. 42). For this phenomenon in the seventeenth century, see Rabbi Yosef Halevi Nazir, *Mate Yosef Responsa,* 1 (Istanbul: Ben Yaakov, 1717), nos. 6, 8; for the eighteenth century, see Di Boton, *Machaze Avraham Responsa,* no. 18. There were some Jews who lodged an entire month in Muslim or Christian villages. In 1828 a peddler on his way from the village of Apolaja was robbed and murdered by three Christians in Rhodes. (Rabbi Michael Yaacov Israel, *Yad Yamin Responsa* [Izmir: Roditti, 1859], Even Ha-Ezer, no. 7).

special house named "menzel" used for guests, usually adjacent to the home of the village head. The villagers did not ask for payment in return for housing and food and Christian travelers and pilgrims praise the local hospitality and generosity.[32] Jews probably paid for housing in other parts of the empire, and many often returned to the same house and formed good relationships with the hosts. A Jewish traveler in the seventeenth century relates that the villagers of Einav welcomed each convoy and took the travelers to their homes "because they have houses for guests, as this village has no designated hostel, this is their custom, and they gave us food as well as straw, feed, and barley for the horses. We gave them gifts too according to their status and the length of our stay."[33]

Staying at non-Jewish homes often led to conversations between guests and hosts in which information was revealed about the death of Jews.[34] Gentile hosts often warned Jewish guests against traveling certain roads where Jews had been murdered. Thus, when a Jew who was a regular guest of a Gentile in the Syrian village of Dimdar wished to go to the village of al-Jedida, the host warned her guest not to take a certain road where a Jew's body had been discovered.[35] Another Gentile woman told of two Jewish goldsmiths from Damascus who were regular guests at her home, where they performed their work. She said that after giving them food she had warned them "not to go anywhere because there are robbers and murderers about, but they left and did not listen to her." She added that her husband told her that he saw the bodies of these Jews thrown into a field with the bodies of three Muslims.[36] Such warnings indicate concern for Jewish

---

32 Yaari, *Masot,* 371. For the menzel, see Zeevi, *An Ottoman Century,* index. Only a few guests visited the villagers, spending their time with the villagers and the *muchtars*, with whom they would drink coffee and trade stories. All the people in the village financed the manzel and every family helped care for the lodgers. These houses were managed by sheikhs and *muchtars*. See Adel Mana. "Yshuv ve-Chevra," in *Ha-Historya Shel Eretz Israel*, 8, eds. Yehoshua Ben Arye and Yisrael Bartal (Jerusalem: Keter and Yad Ben Zvi, 1990), 173.

33 Yaari, Masot, 262–63.

34 For example, there is the case of Jews in the area of Damascus (at the end of the seventeenth century) who heard from their Gentile host about the corpse of a Jew that he had found. (*Mate Yosef Responsa*, no. 6). Two Gentile women from the Greek village of Istoriplis informed a Jew about the death of his brother.(*Rashdam Responsa*, Even Ha-Ezer, no. 75).

35 Rabbi Yizhaq Abualafia, *Penei Yizhaq Responsa*. 2 (Jerusalem: Hamaor, 1988), no. 2.

36 *Alsheich Responsa,* no. 43. For Turkish villagers who warned their Jewish lodgers, see *Maharival Responsa*, 1, no. 60; 2, no.15. In the sixteenth century, a woman warned the Jew who was lodging in her house in the village and told him about a murdered Jew. (Rabbi Moshe Alashkar, *Alashkar Responsa* [Jerusalem: Shtizberg, 1959], nos. 112–13; *Radbaz Responsa*, 7, no. 26).

guests.[37] In another case from the eighteenth century, David al 'Ajimi testified that while at his shop in one of the villages he said that he wished to go to a distant market. A Muslim friend who was present with some other Jews warned him not to go because the road was dangerous and a Jewish goldsmith from Alexandria whom he knew had been murdered there.[38]

Overnight stays at villages were normally not dangerous, but there were cases in which guests were killed by their hosts. The latter were obviously suspected and they had to bribe the investigators intent on revealing the identity of the murderers. One instant of the murder of Jews by their Gentile hosts was occurred in 1549, as testified by Yitzhak Siralo:

> One day I was walking in the village of Andrusa and I stopped at one house and the man and woman told me: "Cursed are the people who kill the innocent and do not have mercy on them, as they killed Shabbetay and Moshe and brought us their clothes to dye and they also killed Avraham Bendito and his son."[39]

In another case in the sixteenth century a Gentile from the village of Deridov in Walachia murdered his Jewish guest to whom he owed money.[40]

Villagers were less guarded in their conversations with fellow religionists, and thus information was often provided in incidental conversations about the security situation on the roads, when hosts were unaware that their guests, disguised as Muslims, were Jewish. In 1565 Jews from the district of Ipsula spent the night at the home of a Turk in Dükyan Köy. The next morning the driver of their wagon told them that the landlord mistook them for Turks due to their white turbans and wanted to invite them to eat, but that the driver told him that they were Jews. The landlord replied, "These Jews do well to wear white turbans so they will not be killed like the poor Jew Kilak Itzhak, who was killed last month."[41] Some villagers told Jews directly of the murder of other Jews for burial purposes.[42]

Jews seem to have known of the destitute financial situation of many villagers, exploited by Ottoman authorities and soldiers, and knew that many lived poorly, ate little, and performed most of the work necessary for their

---

37 For example, a case from 1610. (*Gavizon Responsa*, 1. no. 18; see also *Maharitaz Hachadashot Responsa*, no. 191).

38 Rabbi Yom Tov Crespin, *Bigdei Yom Tov Responsa* (Izmir: Di Segora, 1973), Even Ha-Ezer, no. 4.

39 *Maharival Responsa*, 1, no. 8. This information was provided by a Turkish villager to a Jew who was staying in the nearby village of Miligana.

40 *Beit Yosef Responsa*, Goy Mesiah Lefi Tomo, no. 12.

41 *Mabit Responsa*, 2, no. 104; Rabbi Yehoshua Zunzin, *Nachala le-Yehoshua Responsa* (Istanbul: Yona Ben Yaakov, 1731), no. 18.

42 For example, in the sixteenth century a Gentile from the village of Corlu, in the area of Edirne, testified about the death of a Jew. (*Alsheich Responsa,* no. 42).

existence.[43] Many Jews who came to the villages were peddlers or artisans who performed work required by the farmers. They were forced to wander among distant villages, since they could not make a living in their cities of origin. Many of them seem to have formed social contacts with the villagers and felt secure at their homes.

Staying at Muslim Homes in the Cities

Jews did not often stay at the homes of Muslims in the cities. Thus in the 1570s we hear about two Jews from the city of Yanina (Ioannina, Yanya) who ate non-kosher food and drank non-kosher wine at the home of a Muslim who sold wine and spent time with Turks.[44] We have similar information from 1830 about a Jewish Sarraf who was in a convoy that entered the home of the local Sarraf in the city of Latakya "and ate and drank and became drunk." Eventually he became so inebriated that he did not join his convoy in time and drowned in the river.[45] Gentiles knew that there were some Jews who were willing to eat with them, although others did not partake of their food. Thus, a Jew named Rachamim Shariki told of a Gentile he met who told him (in Arabic) that not all Jews were the same

> As so and so partake of our food and of our meat, buy [products] in the market and bring them to us. And we cook for them and eat together. However long Aslan from your town, may he rest in peace, that Jew strictly maintained his religion and would not eat of our food and taste of our cooking, and faithfully negotiated with truth and integrity.[46]

The famous traveler Eveliya Celeby in the seventeenth century indicates that most Jews would not sit down to eat with Gentiles or be served drinks by them, although there were exceptions to this rule.[47]

Gentiles Hosted by Jews

At times, although apparently quite seldom, villagers were hosted by Jewish acquaintances in the cities. Jews may have repaid rural hosts in such a manner and sometimes Jews were even forced to entertain soldiers at their homes. This is confirmed by a story related by a Jew of two Jews who took a

---

43 For the villagers of Rumelia, Anatolia, and the Arab provinces, see Hamilton A. R. Gibb and Harold Bowen, *Islamic Society and the West* (Oxford: Oxford University Press, 1950), 235–75. For the low intelligence of the people, see Suraiya Faroqhi, *Subjects of the Sultan, Culture and Daily Life in the Ottoman Empire* (London: I.B. Tauris, 2000), 186–88.

44 *Divrei Rivot Responsa*, no. 330; *Rashdam Responsa*, Even Ha-Ezer, no. 220.

45 Rabbi Mordechai Levton, *Nochach ha-Shulchan Responsa* (Izmir: Di Segora 1868), Even Ha-Ezer, no. 14c

46 Aslan and his partner drowned. (*Darchei No'am Responsa*, Even Ha-Ezer, no. 63).

47 Alexander Pallis, *In the Days of the Janissaries* (London: Hutchinson and Corporation, 1951), 57–58.

significant sum of money belonging to a Janissary who stayed with them and had died in their home.[48]

However, it was rare for Jews to invite Gentiles for a meal. Thus, in the 1540s, Rabbi Yaakov Beirav told R. Yosef Karo in Safed

> that he heard a tale of a Jew who had invited Ishmaelites for a meal and the Jewish host asked another Jew present: "Did you hear what happened to such and such?" And the Ishmaelites replied: "We know who killed them." And they allowed the wives [of the people killed] to remarry based on this testimony.[49]

There were also cases of Turks who drank wine in Jewish homes.[50]

Markets, Shops, and on the Roads, in Medicinal Sites and Holy Sites

Sometimes close relationships formed between Jews and Gentiles upon meeting in markets, shops, fairs, and other places.[51] In the sixteenth century, an elderly man testified to meeting a Turkish acquaintance (*ahuv* - a word used in Responsa literature to express friendship) from the Greek city of Preveza at the market and after exchanging greetings in Turkish, the Turk told him about three Jews who had been murdered.[52] In another incident in the sixteenth century a Muslim man came to the shop of Avraham Albilda, a resident of Galibolu, and mentioned in passing the death of Yosef Shealtiel.[53] In another case, some Jews related that a Gentile was introduced to them at the market and told them that he had known Yitzchak Almaridi, who was murdered with another Jew on their way from Safed to Alma, and said that "he was my beloved [friend]."[54] In another incident, when Angilo Cohen came to Durazzo (Albania), he asked his friends the Turks of a Jew who had left his ship there.[55]

---

48 Maharshch Responsa, 4, no. 10.

49 *Beit Yosef Responsa,* Dinei Goy Mesiach Lefi Tomo, no. 3.

50 Rabbi Yosef Molcho, *Ohel Yosef Responsa* (Salonica: Askenazi orphans, 1755), Yore De'ah, no. 32.

51 In 1551 several Turks met a Jew in his shop located in the fair and told him about the death of a few Jews. (*Radbaz Responsa*, 1, no. 211). In the middle of the eighteenth century a Gentile appeared in the shop of a Jew and told him about the murder of Avraham Valdan from Bitola. (Rabbi Moshe Amarillio, *Devar Moshe Responsa,* 3 [Salonica: Bezalel Ashkenazi, 1750], Even Ha-Ezer, no. 4).

52 *Mishpetei Shmuel Responsa,* no. 27.

53 *Maharival Responsa,* 1, no. 5.

54 *Ramag Responsa*, no. 52; *Mahatitaz Responsa*, no. 144; *Maharitaz Hachadashot Responsa*, no. 236.

55 *Responsa Maharival,* 1, no. 3.

A significant number of sources mention Muslims or Christians who spoke of their close relationships with Jews and sometimes deplored their murder on the road.[56]

Encounters between Jews and Muslims probably occurred in medicinal sites as well, where they exchanged information on medicine and physicians. We know that Jews and Muslims prayed at certain holy sites simultaneously, but we do not know whether these prayers led to closer relationships. Sometimes we hear that Jewish prayers aroused negative reactions among local villagers. Thus, a resident of Beit Iksa, which is near the grave of Shmuel the Prophet, complained to the Qadi of Jerusalem that when Jews from Jerusalem visit the grave they bring their animals as well as many implements and belongings, remain for a long period of time, and cause much damage to the locals.[57]

Drinking Coffee at Non-Jewish Homes, Visiting Cafes and Social Encounters at Taverns

As early as the sixteenth century, Rabbi David Ibn Avi Zimra ("Radnaz"), religious leader of the Cairo Jewish community, forbade Jews from taking part in non-Jewish parties and drinking coffee with Gentiles, for fear of Muslim influence. Other rabbis also viewed drinking coffee at non-Jewish homes as a problematic meeting point with Gentiles, for reasons of kashrut, as non-Jewish cooking is involved, and for concern for the pernicious influence of non-Jewish society.[58]

However, in practice, when Jewish artisans and peddlers came to the villages they often drank coffee with their hosts and other Gentiles. Jews also frequented cafes at some of the khans and cities around 1564.[59] The cafes offered varied social entertainment and served as a major meeting place. Men drank coffee and smoked tobacco there at all hours, to accompaniment of music. Jews drank coffee at the cafes apparently on Sabbath as well, and R. Chaim Benveniste from Izmir, in the seventeenth century, and Rabbi Yitzchak Molcho from Salonica, in the nineteenth century, both warned

---

56 For example, a case from 1694. (Rabbi Aharon Hacohen Perahya, *Parach Mate Aharon Responsa,* 3 [Amsterdam: Mendes Kotinyo, 1703], no. 89).

57 Amnon Cohen, *Yehudim be-veit ha-Mishpat ha-Muslemi, ha-Me'ah ha-Shesh Esre* (Jerusalem: Yad Nen-Zvi, 1993, 114).

58 Michael Litman, *Yahadut Mitzrayim ba-Me'ot ha-tet Zain-Yod Zain Al Pi Sifrei ha-Shut Shel Hachmei Hazeman* (Ph.D. dissertation, Bar-Ilan University, Ramat Gan 1978), 315; Elliot Horowitz, "Coffee, Coffeehouses, and the Nocturnal Rituals of Early Modern Jewry," *AJS* 14 (1989): 17–46.

59 See Ralph S. Hattox, *Coffee and Coffeehouses: The Origins of a Social Beverage in the Medieval Near East* (Seattle and London: University of Washington Press, 1985); K. N. Chaudhuri, "Kahwa," *Encyclopedia of Islam*, 2nd ed., vol. 4, 455–49.

against this state of affairs.[60] At the cafes Jews met Muslims of all social classes, professions and religions, and they afforded opportunities for conversation.

Jews and Christians residing in the Ottoman Empire were permitted to sell wine to members of their own religion but not to Muslims. The sultans occasionally completely forbade the sale of wine. It seems that Jews and Muslims did not meet at taverns (*meyhane*) during the sixteenth to eighteenth centuries.[61] Taverns were alternately opened and closed during the reign of the different sultans from the sixteenth century on and, as a rule, Jews seem to have stayed away from them.[62]

Public Bath-houses

All citizens of the empire visited the *hamam* regularly.[63] Muslim jealousy of Jews for religious and economic reasons tended to emerge during public bathing, as occurred in Jerusalem in the sixteenth century, when an attendant discriminated against rural and Jewish bathers in favor of Muslim city dwellers. Moreover, a degrading regulation required Jews to wear a bell around their necks to warn of their entrance to the bath-house, though this did not prevent Jews from bathing regularly.[64] An unsuccessful attempt at

60 Rabbi Haim Benveniste, *Sheyarei Keneset Hagedolah,* Orah Haim (Jerusalem: Ketav Institute, 1995), Tur no. 325 no. 1; Rabbi Yitzhaq Molcho, *Orchot Yosher* (Tel Aviv 1975), 35, 117–18. In the nineteenth century, according to Rabbi Yosef Alfandari from Istanbul, Jewish scholars would spend time in the coffee-houses. (Rabbi Yosef Alfandari, *Porat Yosef Responsa* (Izmir: Roditti, 1868), Hoshen Mishpat no. 4. For Jews visiting coffee-houses in the khans, see Yaari, *Masot,* 236,240, 321; for Jews in the nineteenth century who visited cafes, see Harel, *Be-Sefinot,* 201.

61 See Faroqhi, *Towns,* 70. For Muslims who drank wine in Jewish homes, see the eighteenth-century source: *Ohel Yosef Responsa,* Yore De'ah, no. 32. A responsa from the eighteenth century tells of a Jew and a converted Jew to Islam who met in a tavern of another Jew in Istanbul. (Rabbi Yizhaq Ibn Sanji, *Be'erot Hamayim Responsa* [Salonica: Kalai and Nachman, 1755), Even Ha-Ezer, no. 29. Omaric prohibitions prohibited the drinking or selling of wine and other alcoholic beverages. After the Tanzimat some taverns were opened in the Jewish and Christian quarters of Damascus. However, they disturbed the normal life of the habitants, and thus there were efforts to prevent public wine-selling by both Jews and Christians. (Harel, *Be-Sefinot,* 133–38).

62 Faroqhi, *Subjects of the Sultan,* 219–20. The only source noting Jews being entertained in a tavern is from the seventeenth century (*Maharitaz Hadashot Responsa,* no. 202). However, it seems likely that this incident occurred in Italy and not in the Ottoman Empire.

63 A. Lewis, "Hamam"' *Encyclopedia of Islam*, 2nd ed., 3 (Leiden-London: Brill, 1971), 139–46.

64 Cohen, *Jews Under Islam*, index; idem (together with Simon Pikali and Ovadia Salama), *Yehudim be-Veit Hamishpat Hamuslemi, Chevra, Kalkala ve–Irgun Qehilati be-Yerushalayim ba-Me'ah ha-Shesh-Esre* (Jerusalem: Yad Ben Zvi Institute, 1993),144, 148, 172; idem, *Yehudim be-Veit Hamishpat Hamuslemi, Chevra,*

implementing a similar regulation was made in Egypt in 1723.[65] Such incidents are the exception and do not indicate the general state of affairs. At the bath-house, Jewish bathers often conversed with the attendants, and these conversations sometimes revealed information about Jews who had died. Thus, one Jew heard of the death of another while talking to an attendant at the Izmit bath-house in 1668.[66] In another incident, on Sabbath eve two Jewish bathers listened to a conversation between Gentiles about several Jews who had been murdered and they later testified on the matter at the city of Dubnica in Bulgaria.[67]

Conversations between Jews and Muslims

We can assume that similar exchanges to those detailed by Constantine Volney between Muslim and Christian citizens of the empire, in describing his impressions from Egypt and Syria in the late eighteenth century, were also characteristic of Muslims and Jews who met purposefully or incidentally throughout the Ottoman Empire. Volney states that even the most lowly Muslim would not greet a Christian or reply to his greeting of "*Salam Alek*" and that the only acceptable greeting was "Good morning" or "Good evening," to which it was customary to add the derogatory term "*kafr*," "dog," i.e., unbeliever, used to designate Christians. In order to annoy Christians, Muslims would perform religious rites in their presence, and when talking to them frequently interrupted the conversation with the statement of faith: "*There is no god but Allah, and Muhammad is his prophet.*" They would often mention their religion and present themselves as the only people faithful to God.[68]

This afforded an important insight: Muslims spoke about their religion to members of other religions, but were probably not attentive to the opposite party. Thus, instead of holding a conversation, they engaged in preaching and took advantage of interactions to voice their own opinions and not for the purpose of theological dialogue.

Kalkala ve–Irgun Qehilati be-Yerushalayim ba-Me'ah ha-Shemone-Esre (Jerusalem: Yad Ben Zvi Institute, 1996),111–13; Minna Rozen, *Ha-Qehila ha-Yehudit be-Yerushalayim ba-Me'ah ha-Yod Za'in* (Tel Aviv: Tel Aviv University and the Ministry of Defence, 1985), 64, 259. Gedalia of Simyatiz, who lived in Jerusalem from 1700 to 1705, writes that Jews could use the magnificent *hamam* in the city, but he himself had visited it only once, since the attendant plotted against him (Yaari, *Masot*, 359–60).

65 Winter, "Yachasei ha-Yehudim," 393–94.

66 Rabbi Moshe Benveniste, *Penei Moshe Responsa*. 2 (Jerusalem 1988). no. 52.

67 *Be'erot ha-Mayim Responsa*, Even Ha-Ezer, no. 20.

68 Constantin Francis Volney, *Travels through Syria and Egypt in the Years 1783, 1784, and 1785: On the Manners, Customs and Government of the Turks and Arabs* (Westmead: Gregg, 1972).

We can assume that Jews and Gentiles tended to discuss current matters related to shared economic activities. Regretfully, we have no records of these conversations, but we may assume that since rural Muslims received a very poor education, these encounters did not involve cultural issues. During this period a majority of the population was uneducated, and any education they had was usually limited to reading the Qur'ān, a little writing, and simple arithmetic. Ignorance was a problem that encompassed most of the population, in rural as well as urban areas.[69]

Jewish-Muslim encounters seem to have created a convenient atmosphere for small-scale theological arguments. Jews, no doubt, avoided these arguments in order to refrain from violating the Covenant of Omar, but they probably took place occasionally nonetheless. We have the testimony of the traveler Aubry de La Motraye, from 1697, who stayed in Ramle at the home of Haj Muhammad, who was proficient in French and medicine, and who used to humiliate the Jews by holding debates, such as on the biblical looting of Egypt by the Israelites. However, the Jews never expressed to him any offense that they may have taken.[70]

Summary and Conclusions

The social encounters described above often led to basic friendships and diminished the derogatory attitude of Ottoman Muslims toward the Jews. Social encounters with Muslim colleagues on the road, consisting mainly of urban merchants, probably included elements of economic tension and jealousy, as well as religious zealotry. In contrast, there was almost no economic tension involved in encounters with less well-off Muslims, since Jewish peddlers and artisans who sought accommodation in the villages were themselves poor. However these encounters were not devoid of religious passions.

Close relationships with Jews often resulted in warnings of rampant murderers, providing information about the death of Jews, shared drinking and recreation, and reciprocal visits. Conversations between Jews and Muslims seem to have been limited in scope, mostly involving the one-sided voicing of Muslim opinions. Jews seem to have been concerned with becoming involved in arguments and tried to avoid arousing Muslim anger, particularly since Muslim cultural education was poor, specifically in the rural areas, and were, therefore, usually considered to be ignorant. Thus, there was no cultural dimension to these encounters, since Jews and Muslims lived in closed religious societies. Our sources do not mention, for example, that Jews sang and danced with their Muslim hosts, although such incidents assuredly occurred when people met in convoys, khans, or

69 See, for example, Volney, *Travels*.

70 See Michel Ish Shalom, ed., *Masey Notzrim le-Eretz Israel* (Jerusalem: Am Over and Devir, 1966), 378–80.

homes. In many cases friendships seemed to have formed between Jewish guests and Muslim hosts, and the latter were concerned for the lives of their guests due to the risk of robbery and murder on the roads, and tended to warn them. On the other hand, in some cases Jewish guests were murdered by their hosts, and it is indicative of a Jewish lack of trust of the Gentiles that some Jews would disguise themselves as Muslims when staying in the villages.

In extreme cases we hear of friendships between Jews and Muslims manifested in shared meals or more often spending time together at cafes in the khans and cities and drinking coffee at the homes of rural Muslims. Jews of all classes and professions seem not to have objected to this pastime and they justified it from Jewish legal and moral perspectives.

Cases of Muslim religious zealousness toward Jews in public bath-houses were an exception, and Jews usually felt safe and held conversations with the attendants and with Muslim bathers. In convoys and public places, such as khans and soup kitchens, where they were usually in the presence of other Jews, they felt relatively safe and protected from physical harm, and it seems that there they were able to hold less restricted conversations with Muslims than in private homes.

We have no proof that these social encounters caused many Jews to convert to Islam. However, it is possible that the small percentage of Jews who did convert to Islam were influenced by these social encounters.[71]

The information presented in this study does not indicate growing tensions between Jews and Muslims in specific periods throughout the sixteenth to eighteenth centuries, and no changes are noted in the various dimensions of these encounters throughout the three centuries discussed.

---

71 For the reasons that caused Jews to convert to Islam, see Leah Bornstein-Makovetsky, "Jewish Converts to Islam and Christianity in the Ottoman Empire in the Nineteenth Century," in *The Last Ottoman Century and Beyond, The Jews in Turkey and the Balkans 1808–1945*, 2, ed. Minna Rozen (Tel Aviv: Tel Aviv University, The Goldstein-Goren Diaspora Research Center, 200), 83–128.

Jewish and Muslim Houses of Prayer
Mutual Influences

DAVID CASSUTO

Judaism and Islam, if we ignore the tense moments between them, are siblings that have long lived in close proximity. Leaving aside the natural friction between different but similar faiths, there has been no shortage of opportunities for them to influence each other, both theologically and especially in the arts.

First Encounter

We know quite a bit about the earliest synagogues in Eretz Israel and their influence on sacred architecture in the pre-Mishnaic age, but especially during the Tannaitic and Amoraic periods.[1]

- Islam began building its own houses of prayer more than 400 years after the origin and first flowering of the synagogue, mainly in the Near East. Islam is the third monotheistic religion, after Judaism and Christianity, and there is no doubt that its basic tenets build to a large extent on its two predecessors. When it comes to its houses of prayer, too, Islam seems to have been influenced by what its believers saw and experienced in its older siblings.
- Several phenomena characteristic of Jewish and Christian houses of prayer penetrated Islam:[2]
    1. An unroofed court, encircled by pillars, attached to the façade of the building
    2. A direction wall that worshipers face during prayers
    3. A prayer niche in the direction wall
    4. A pulpit from which sermons are delivered
    5. A tower for calling the faithful to prayer (only in Christianity and Islam)

---

[1] I. L. Levine, *The Ancient Synagogue* (London, 1999), 291–356.

[2] E. Lambert, "La synagogue de Doura-Europos et les origines de la mosquée," *Semitica* 3 (1950): 5–18; G. Marçais, "L'église et la mosquée," in *L'Islam et l'occident*, Les Cahiers du Sud (Paris, 1947), 174–84.

Now I will discuss these points in detail:

1. An unroofed court enclosed by pillars attached to the façade can be found, to mention only a few instances, at Capernaum (fig. 1), at Susiya in the southern Hebron Hills (fig. 2),[3] at Aleppo in Syria (figs. 3 and 4),[4] and at Sardis in Asia Minor, as well as in Tunisia (fig. 5) and, most emphatically, in Dura Europos (figs. 6–8).[5] The talmudic sages,

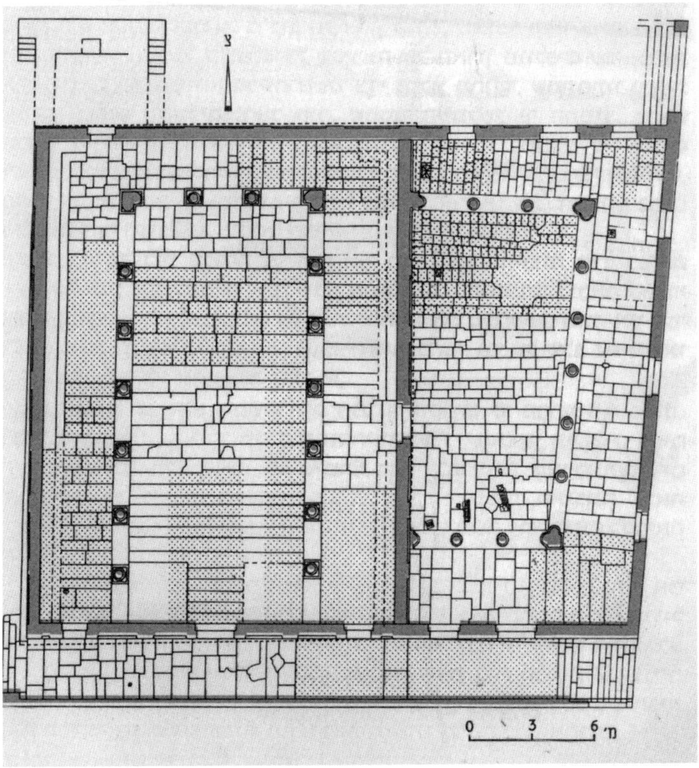

Fig. 1. Plan of the late-fourth-century synagogue in Capernaum (courtesy *Ha-Entsiklopedia Ha-Hadasha la-Hafirot Archeologiyot be-Erets Yisrael*, ed., Ephraim Stern [Jerusalem: 1992])

---

[3] E. Stern, ed., *The New Encyclopedia of Archaeological Excavation in the Holy Land* (Jerusalem, 1992), s.v. Kefar Nahum, Korazim, Samua, and Susiya, 822–26, 1098–1101 [Hebrew].

[4] M. Sobernheim and E. E. Mitwoch, "Hebräische Inschriften in der Synagogen von Aleppo," in *Festschrift zum siebzigsten Geburtstage Jakob Guttmanns* (Leipzig, 1915), 273–83; D. M. Cassuto, "Beit-ha-keneset he-atik shel Haleb ve-toledotav," *Pe'amim* 17 (Jerusalem, 1979) [Hebrew].

[5] E. L. Sukenik, *The Synagogue of Dura-Europos and Its Frescoes* (Jerusalem, 1947), 35–46.

Fig. 2. Reconstruction of the façade of the synagogue in Capernaum
(courtesy *Ha-Entsiklopedia Ha-Hadasha la-Hafirot Archeologiyot be-Erets Yisrael*, ed., Ephraim Stern [Jerusalem: 1992])

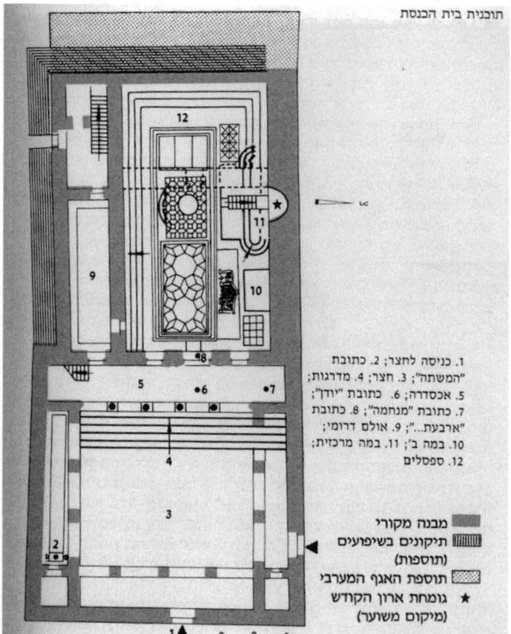

Fig. 3. Plan of the late-third-century synagogue in Susiya
(courtesy *Ha-Entsiklopedia Ha-Hadasha la-Hafirot Archeologiyot be-Erets Yisrael*, ed., Ephraim Stern [Jerusalem: 1992])

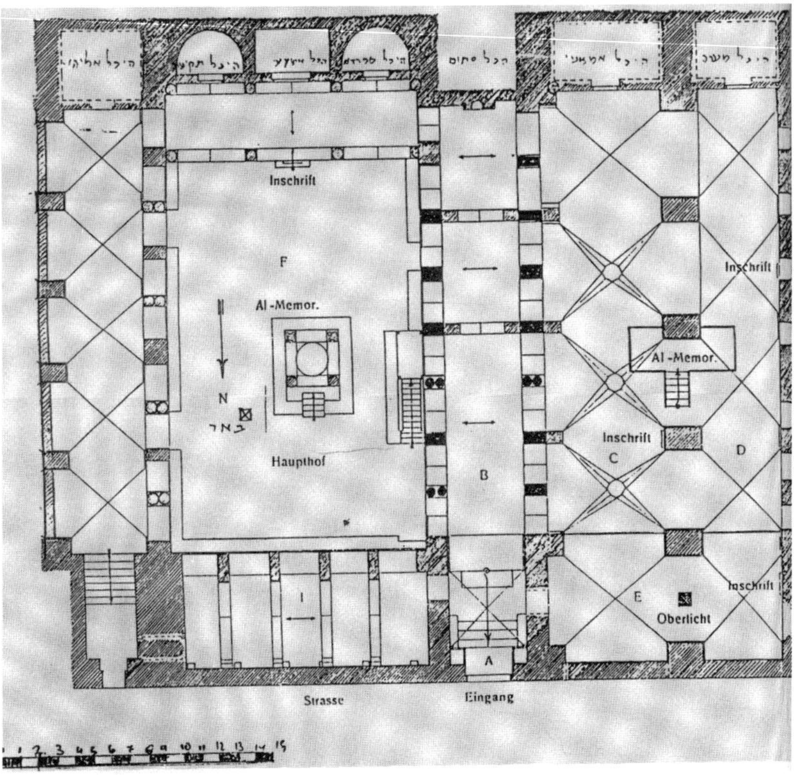

Fig. 4. Plan of the synagogue (a-Safra) in Aleppo, Syria (eighth century?)

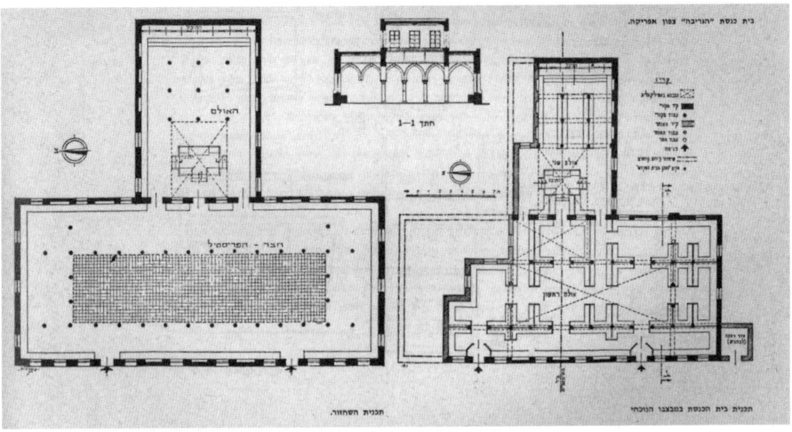

Fig. 5. Plan of the Ghriba Synagogue in Jerba, current state and possible reconstruction of original structure, according to Yaakov Pink.erfeld

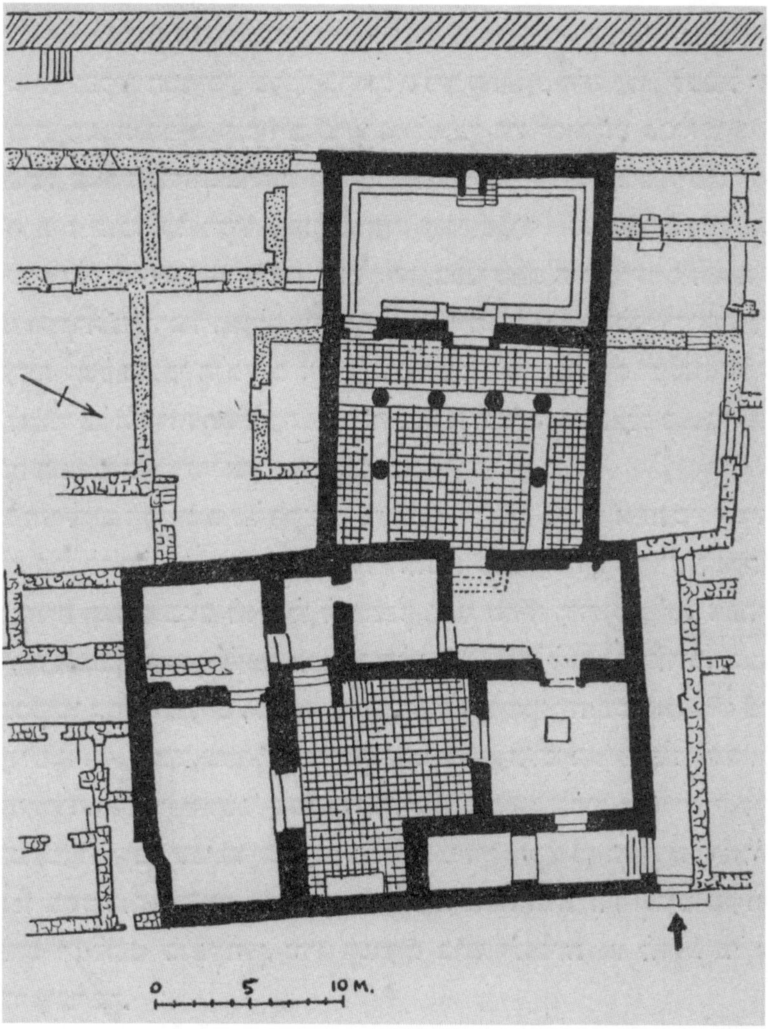

Fig. 6. Plan of the synagogue (second phase) in Dura Europos, third century (according to E. L. Sukenik, *The Synagogue of Dura-Europos and Its Frescoes* [Jerusalem, 1947])

Fig. 7. Ark façade and cantor's steps in the Dura Europos synagogue

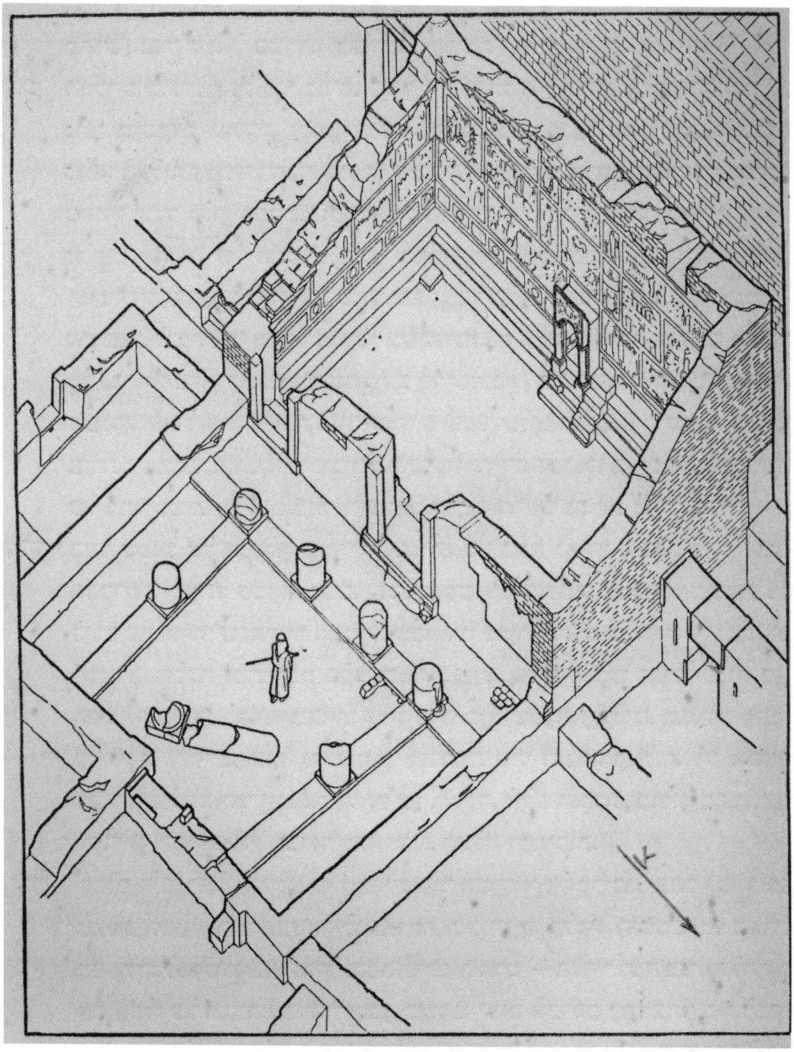

Fig. 8. Bird's-eye exonometric view of the current state of the Dura Europos synagogue

too, allude to these courtyards, which were used not only for study but also for prayer. My opinion is that the daylight that poured into them made it possible to study all through the day, as opposed to the gloom that prevailed in closed buildings. The Talmud reports that, even though there were thirteen synagogues in Tiberias, R. Ammi and R. Assi preferred to pray "between the columns" (I believe this means in the peristyle that fronted or was adjacent to the synagogue [figs. 1 and 2]), where they spent the day studying and teaching.[6]

2. The direction wall that worshipers faced during prayers is a feature of both synagogues (fig. 7) and the earliest churches (fig. 9). In the latter, the wall took on an aspect of devotion and mystery and was made more impressive.[7] In early synagogues, the holy wall was pierced by a tall opening facing Zion, flanked by lateral entrances for the congregation.[8] Later the entrances were relocated to the opposite wall and a niche was cut into the holy wall so that the congregation would face the proper direction for prayer.

3. This niche indicated the sacred direction. In mosques this niche, the *miḥrab,* is cut into the *qibla* or direction wall (fig. 10). The *qibla* in the mosque alongside the Prophet's house in Medina faced north, toward Jerusalem. It was only when Muhammad despaired of attracting the Jews to his new creed (622) that he relocated the *qibla* to face south, toward Mecca, so that the mosque had two *qiblas.*[9] In 707 the Umayyad caliph al-Walid (who also erected the Great Mosque in Damascus [figs. 11–13]) employed Coptic Christian masons to enlarge the Medina mosque; apparently they were responsible for incorporating into the *qibla* the first *miḥrab,* modeled on those in Coptic churches. This sparked a great debate, with many condemning the innovation as heretical. Eventually this element of mosque architecture achieved full legitimacy—not as something holy, but merely as an indication of the direction of Mecca.[10] This was when it received the name *miḥrab.* In synagogues, the corresponding feature is known chiefly from the Near East in the third

---

[6] B Berakhot 8a; see also Levine, *The Ancient Synagogue*, 317 n. 119.

[7] A. Ovadia, "Ha-kenesia ha-bizantit be-eretz yisrael," in *Qadmoniyot* 9/1 (1976): 6–15; J. Wilkinson, "Christian Liturgy in the Byzantine Period," *Qadmoniyot* 9/1 (1976): 3–5.

[8] M. J. Chiat, "Synagogue and Church Architecture in Antiquity," in *Proceedings of the 8th World Congress of Jewish Studies*, vol. 4 (Jerusalem, 1982–84); E. M. Goldman, *The Sacred Portal: A Primary Symbol in Ancient Judaic Art* (Detroit, 1966); Levine, *The Ancient Synagogue*, 311–13.

[9] J. Dickie, "Allah and Eternity: Mosques, Madrasas and Tombs," in *Architecture of the Islamic World*, ed. O. Grabar (London, 1978), 15–16, 33–34.

[10] Dickie, "Allah and Eternity," 34.

Fig. 9. Perspective view of the holy wall of a church in the Byzantine era (courtesy John Wilkinson, *Qadmoniyot* IX:1 [1976], p. 33)

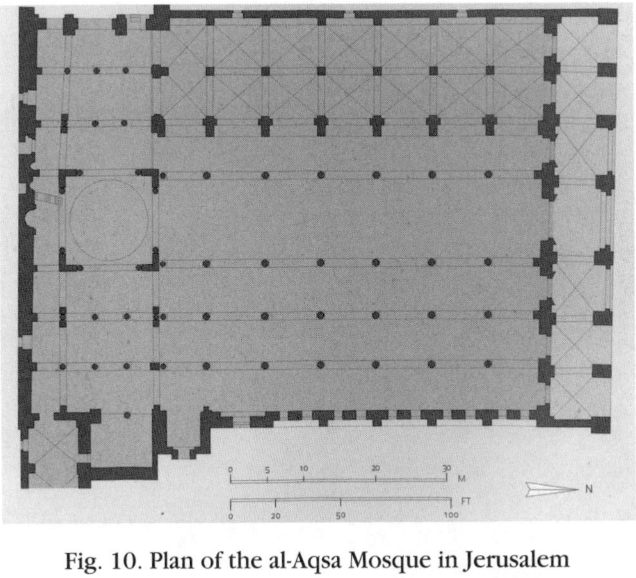

Fig. 10. Plan of the al-Aqsa Mosque in Jerusalem (courtesy Henri Stierling, *Islam*[China, 1996])

Fig. 11. View of the Great Mosque in Damascus (ibid.)

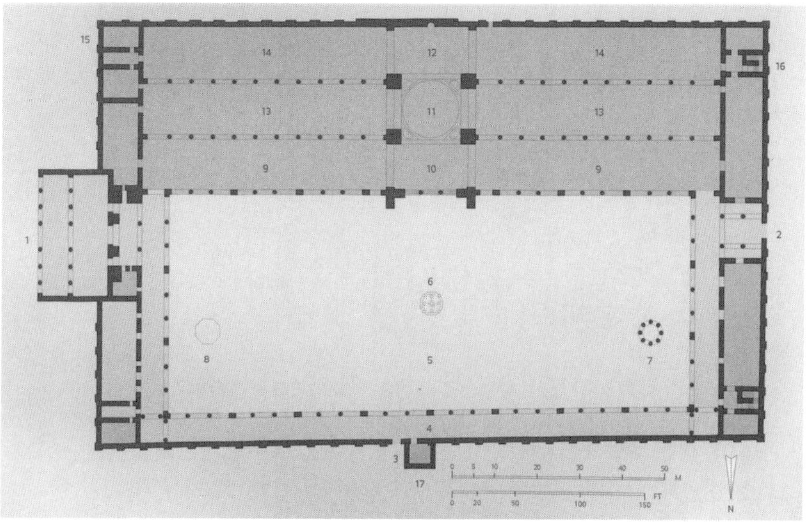

Fig. 12. Plan of the Great Mosque in Damascus (ibid.)

Fig. 13. Looking out from the courtyard of the Great Mosque in Damascus (ibid.)

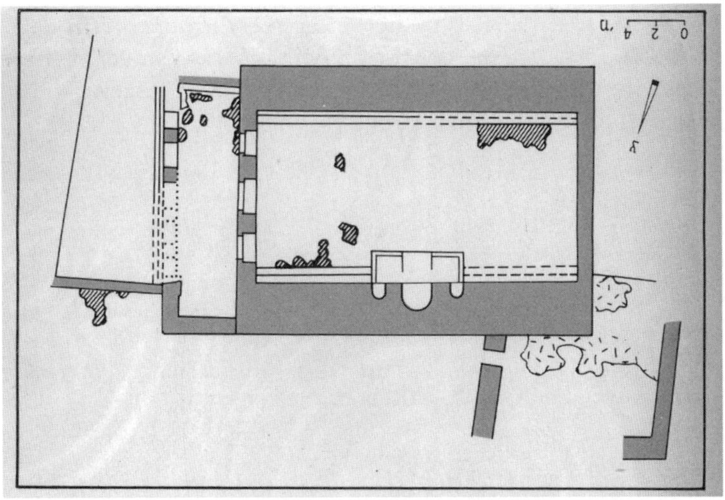

Fig. 14. Plan of the synagogue in Eshtamoa (fourth century)

and fourth centuries: for example, the fourth-century synagogue in Eshtamoa/Samua (fig. 14),[11] in the southern Judean Hills, with a niche facing north; and the synagogue in nearby Susiya (fig. 2),[12] also from the early fourth century, which has one niche facing north toward Jerusalem and, alongside it, a raised platform, evidently for the *ḥazzan hakeneset.*[13] The synagogue in Aleppo has seven niches along its "Zion wall."[14] One of them, for reasons unknown, has been filled in; it may have directed Jews toward Jerusalem or, as some conjecture, Muslims toward Mecca when the building was converted (if it was) into a mosque.[15] In Islam the phenomenon appears with the development of the mosque in the eighth century.

4. The pulpit, according to the Mishnah and Talmud, was made of wood and set in the middle of the prayer space (as in the *diopelostion* synagogue of Alexandria).[16] In churches, the ambon was near and facing the iconostasis.[17] In synagogues it was usually in the center of the room, generally made of wood but occasionally of more durable materials (stone and mortar), in which case it was located near or beside the Holy Ark or the prayer niche. This is the situation at Sardis in Asia Minor,[18] at Susiya, at Korazim,[19] at Aleppo,[20] and, of course, at Dura Europos. Here we should ask who sat on the raised platform at the head of the flight of stairs.[21] The obvious answer is the Torah reader or preacher. Another possibility, however, is that it was the official who supervised the service and had to keep his eye on what was going on in the synagogue: the *ḥazzan* (from Hebrew *ḥazoh* 'look, observe'), whose function was parallel to that of the bishop (Greek *episkopos* 'one who watches from above' [i.e., "overseer"]) on his episcopal throne.

---

11 Stern, *The New Encyclopedia*, 108–12.

12 Ibid., 1098–1101.

13 *B Sukkah* 51a.

14 Cassuto, "Beit-ha-keneset he-atiq," 86–91.

15 D. M. Cassuto, "Synagogues in Syria in the 18th–19th Centuries," in *The Jews of Syria: History, Identity, and Tradition* (Ramat Gan, in press).

16 *B Sukkah* 51b.

17 Wilkinson, "Christian Liturgy," 3.

18 Levine, *The Ancient Synagogue*, 242–49.

19 Stern, *The New Encyclopedia*, 774–79, 1098–1101.

20 Sobernheim and Mitwoch, "Hebräische Inschriften."

21 Lambert, "La synagogue de Doura-Europos," 69.

The proximity of the functionary's seat to the prayer niche in the direction wall is extremely common in Islam. In Judaism, however, it is found only at Dura Europos, some four centuries before the advent of Islam. Is this evidence of the Jewish roots of the Muslim *qibla*?

5. Because a tower for calling the faithful to prayer (bell tower or minaret) is almost never a feature of synagogues (if we ignore the *biraniyot* mentioned by Rabbenu Tam)[22] but only of churches and mosques, I will not discuss it here.

Although the holy wall in the Dura Europos synagogue is the only one of its type that has been uncovered, making it difficult to infer that it was the general case, the dissemination of this model in Islam (figs. 15a–b), some four or five centuries later, may suggest that something similar was found in other synagogues in the Near East.

The Zion wall in the Dura Europos synagogue is strikingly similar to the later *qibla* in mosques, with the *miḥrab* and *mimbar,* and may indicate the inspiration for it. Eventually, some hold, those same elements "returned" to the synagogue and proceeded from North Africa to Spain and Provence, and thence to Germany and the rest of central and eastern Europe. This transmission follows from the fact that in eastern Europe the *bima* is known also as the *almemar.* Kutscher[23] asserts that the word is a corruption of the Arabic *al-mimbar* and that the feature was adopted by synagogues all over the world in the Middle Ages.[24]

Fig. 15a. Interior of the west wall of the Dura Europos synagogue

[22] R. Meir of Rothenburg (Kahana ed.), vol. 1, §121, 164.

[23] Y. Kutscher, *Millim ve-toledotehen* (Jerusalem, 1965), 10–13.

[24] *B Sukkah* 51b. Rashi glosses *bimah* as "like our *almimbra.*"

Fig. 15b. Typical mihrab and mimbar, in the Ibn Toutun Mosque
(courtesy Stierling, *Islam*)

Second Encounter

Another way in which Islam influenced Judaism can be found in much later periods as well. Because both Judaism and Islam are fiercely opposed to the veneration of images, we do not find works of art–neither painting nor sculpture–in their houses of prayer. Consequently the architecture itself becomes the ultimate art form, especially in Islam. In addition to the formal composition, it also focuses attention on the decorative element (which has ignited the Western imagination over the generations). Judaism was influenced by this capacity for ornamentation, which is both extremely abstract and draws attention to the ornamental potential of the technics and the materials.

We cannot avoid being impressed by the influence of the *Mudéjar* style of ornamentation, common in Islam, on the medieval synagogues of Spain.

We find this at Toledo, in Santa Maria la Blanca (figs. 16a–19) (which dates to the end of Muslim period or beginning of the Reconquista there [1085?]), and El Transito (1357; see figs. 20–22), as well as at Cordoba, in the synagogue of Isaac Mehab (1315). These synagogues are in the Nasrid style,[25] which emerged after the "airier" Mudéjar style and was marked by much more massive and denser elements and the floral and calligraphic ornamentation borrowed from the dominant local Arabesque culture.

The eleventh-century "forest" of columns in Santa Maria la Blanca also has mosque-like features (compare the Madinat al-Zahara Mosque[26] and the Grand Mosque of Cordoba [figs. 23–25]). It is possible, in fact, that Santa Maria la Blanca was originally built as a mosque and was transferred to Jewish control after the Reconquista, as also happened in Seville[27] and in Palermo and Mazara del Vallo in Sicily.[28]

Open-roofed synagogues, like those in Baghdad (fig. 26),[29] could not have originated without the influence of roofless mosques. As noted above, some scholars would pray in the peristyle that fronted the synagogue, where they also studied, rather than in the interior of the building, which by mid-afternoon became too dark to see in.

Another interesting phenomenon, also mentioned previously, is the reuse of mosques as synagogues in districts from which the Muslims had been expelled by Christian kings. This is known, as noted before, from Seville, as well as from Palermo (fig. 27) and Mazara in Sicily. Emperor Frederick II, an enlightened and industrious ruler who nevertheless banished the Muslims from his realms (in the early thirteenth century), granted the abandoned mosques to Jews newly arrived from North Africa, who then converted the structures into synagogues.[30]

We know also of the inverse phenomenon, though in a much earlier era, when abandoned synagogues were reconsecrated as mosques. This happened in Susiya and Samua in Palestine in the sixth and seventh centuries, to name only two cases.[31] There is no doubt that, in either direction, the simi-

---

25 M. Rosen-Ayalon, "Artistic Interaction in Late Medieval Spain: Synagogal Decoration," in *Revue des Etudes Islamiques* 54 (1986): 271–82.

26 B. Pavón Maldonado, "Madinat al Zahara Mosque" in *Arte Toledano: Islámico y Mudéjar* (Madrid, 1973), 80 [Spanish].

27 H. L. Ecker, "The Conversion of Mosques to Synagogues in Seville: The Case of the Mesquita de la Judería," *Gesta* 36/2 (1997).

28 D. M. Cassuto, "La Meschita di Palermo," in *Architettura giudaica in Italia: Ebraismo, sito, memoria dei luoghi* (Palermo, 1994), 29–39.

29 D. M. Cassuto, "Adrikhalut batei ha-keneset be-merḥav ha-yam ha-tikhon uve-asia," in *Mahanayim* (Jerusalem, 1995), 204–219 [Hebrew].

30 Cassuto, "La Meschita."

31 Stern, *The New Encyclopedia*, 108–12; 1098–1101.

lar functional scheme of mosques and synagogues facilitated such a conversion, especially where synagogue and mosque were oriented in the same direction. But because the direction of prayer for Jews and Muslims was different, in many cases the new owners of the structure had to add a new niche/*miḥrab.* The case of Palermo, however, demonstrates that Jews, especially, were not always meticulous on this point.[32]

Fig. 16a. Interior of the former synagogue, now Santa Maria la Blanca
(courtesy of J. L. Lacave, *Sefarad Sefard* [Spain, 1992])

[32] D. M. Cassuto and N. Buccaria, "The Synagogues and Ritual Baths of Palermo according to Documents and Archaeological Findings," in *Festschrift to R. Bonfil* (in press) [Hebrew]. See also N. Bucaria and D. M. Cassuto, "La sinagoga e i miqveh di Palermo," in *Archivio storico siciliano,* Serie IV, vol. XXXI (Palermo, 2005). In Palermo the Jews were given possession of the mosque after the Muslims had been expelled from it. The Jews did not modify the internal arrangements and faced south during prayer, instead of east. Obviously in countries north of Jerusalem (such as Syria and Turkey) a structure that had served as a synagogue could be converted into a mosque, and vice versa.

Fig. 16b. Interior of the former synagogue, now Santa Maria la Blanca
(courtesy of J. L. Lacave, *Sefarad Sefard* [Spain, 1992])

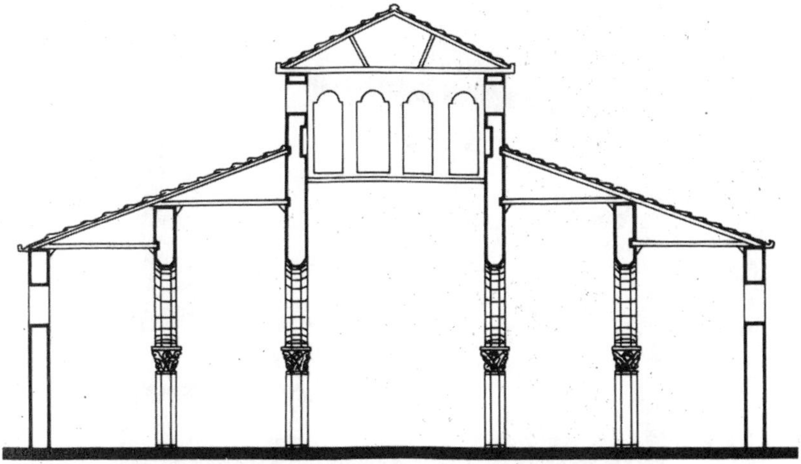

Fig. 17. Cross-section of Santa Maria la Blanca
(courtesy Meir Ben-Dov, *Bate Kneset bi-Sfarad* [Tel Aviv: 1989])

Fig. 18. View facing east from the Santa Maria la Blanca
(courtesy of J. L. Lacave, *Sefarad Sefard* [Spain, 1992])

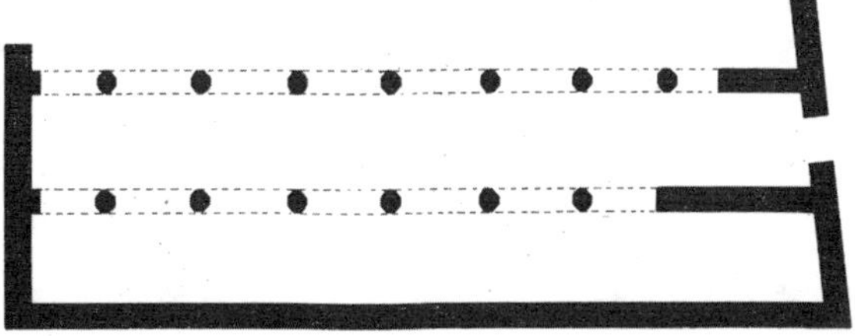

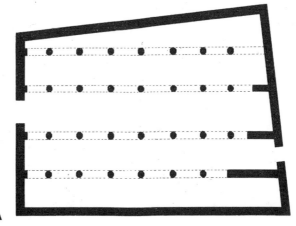

Fig. 19. Plan of the former synagogue, now Santa Maria la Blanca
(courtesy Meir Ben-Dov, *Bate Kneset bi-Sfarad* [Tel Aviv: 1989])

Fig. 20. El Transito Synagogue, Toledo
(courtesy of J. L. Lacave, *Sefarad Sefard* [Spain, 1992])

Fig. 21. El Transito Synagogue, Toledo, looking north (ibid.)

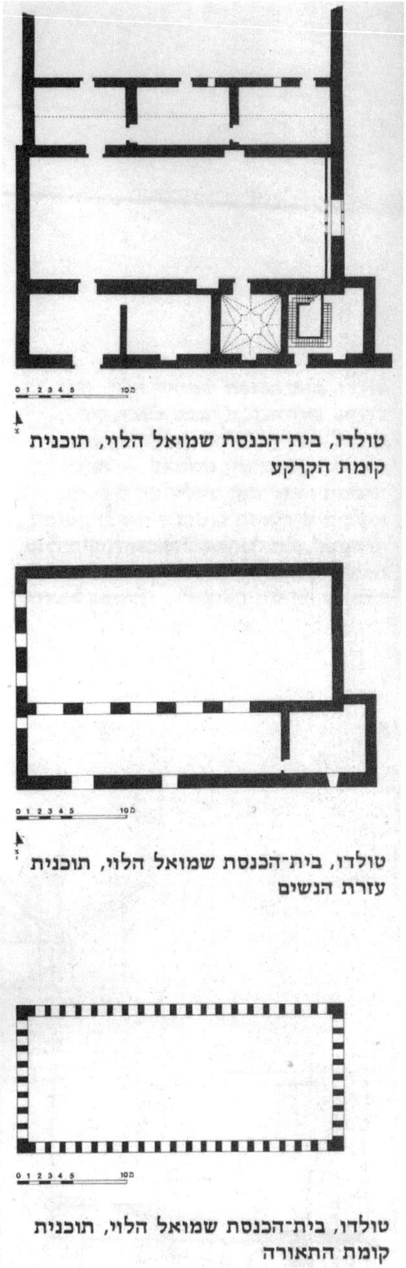

Fig. 22. El Transito Synagogue, Toledo
(1) plan of the ground floor; (2) women's gallery; (3) attic
(courtesy Meir Ben-Dov, *Bate Kneset bi-Sfarad* [Tel Aviv: 1989])

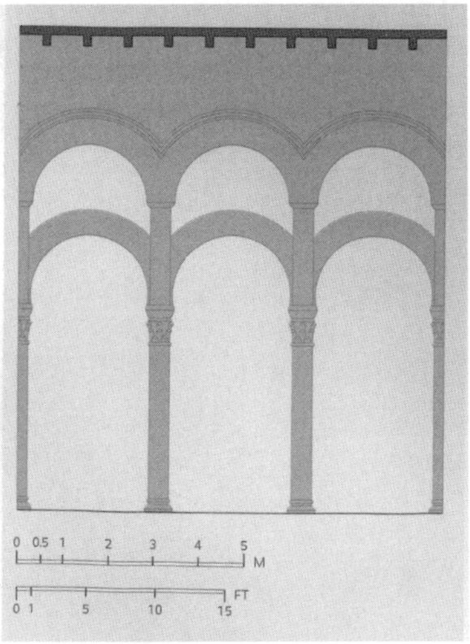

Fig. 23. Elevation of three arcades of two levels of the Grand Mosque of Cordoba (courtesy of Stierling, *Islam*)

Fig. 24. View towards the forest of columns, Grand Mosque of Cordoba (ibid.)

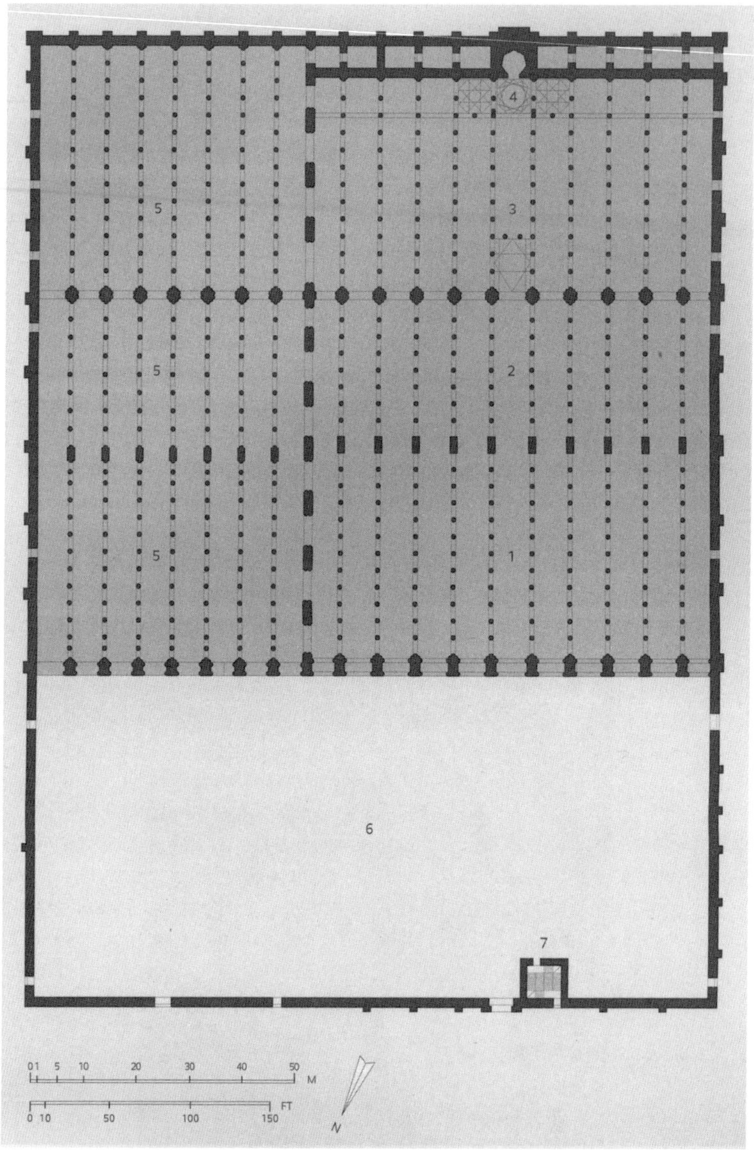

Fig 25. Plan of the Grand Mosque of Cordoba (ibid.)

Fig. 26. Ancient unroofed synagogue in Baghdad

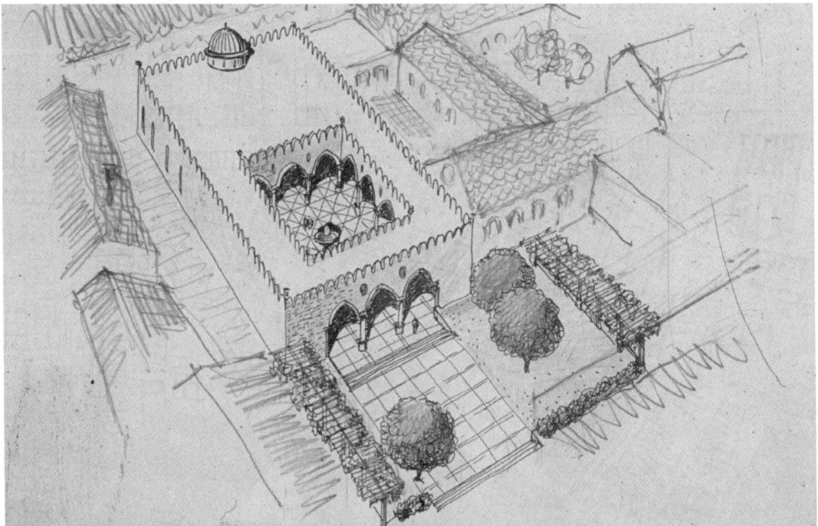

Fig. 27. Bird's-eye view of the Moghrabi Synagogue in Palermo

Third Encounter

Finally, I want to look at modern synagogues, mainly in Europe. In a number of cases, new synagogues were built along Byzantine lines, in a style transmitted chiefly by Muslim Ottoman culture. Notable examples are the synagogue in Florence (Fig. 28),[33] which dates from 1883, several synagogues in Hungary (such as that in Kecskemét), a number in Germany (destroyed on Kristallnacht), and others throughout the world.

Fig. 28. Great Synagogue in Florence (1883)

[33] A. Boralevi, "La costruzione della sinagoga di Firenze," in *Il centenario del tempio israelitico di Firenze* (Firenze, 1982), 50–74; D. M. Cassuto, "Le Caratteristiche del Tempio Italiano durante i secoli," in *Il centenario del tempio israelitico di Firenze* (Firenze, 1982), 16–25.

The echo of the Muslim–or, more precisely, the oriental–world is also evident in the Moorish ornamentation, which recalls the synagogues of Spain. This is the case also in North Africa, especially in those parts that were under Spanish control. Some of them are quite old;[34] others date from the time of the Emancipation in Europe. This period was marked by a search for a style that would express the concept of "Judaism."

As the modern world overtook Jewish society, the synagogue increasingly became a monument to a vanishing phenomenon. Such a monument has to have "Jewish" features. Because Moorish and "Egyptian" decoration and Byzantine architecture invoke the mystique of the East, they were chosen to represent Judaism and are still employed today for this purpose.

34 Y. Zack, *The Synagogues of Morocco: An Architectural Presentation Survey* (New York, 1993).

The Moral Problem in Islam and Its Resolution according to the Philosophy of Rabbi Yéhouda Léon Askénazi (Manitou)

YOSSEF CHARVIT

The philosophy of Rabbi Yéhouda Léon Askénazi (1922–1996), familiarly known as Manitou,[1] exhibits an overtly historio-centric approach, touching on the universal-human, national, and individual historic ethos alike. *Mishnat Hatoladot*,[2] the leitmotif of his outlook, sketches a cultural portrait of all identities comprising the human race, focusing on the family of nations and particularly on the family of Abraham, from which originated not only the identity of Israel but also its rival identities of Edom and Ishmael, i.e., Christian and Muslim cultures. Islam and Christianity occupy a prominent place in R. Askénazi's philosophy because of their competition with Judaism as a religion and the struggle of cultural identities for primacy.[3]

This research was facilitated by a grant from the IHEL Foundation.

1 For his life story, see: Y. Charvit, "The Algerian Jewish Community and the State of Israel - 5708–5758" in *Testimony: Testimony to Israel, Exile, Immigration, Absorption, Contribution and Integration*, eds. A. Mizrahi, A. and A. Ben-David, A. (Netanya: The Association for the Development of Society and Culture, Documentation and Research, 2001), 78–83 [Hebrew]; idem, "Identity and History: The Cultural Heritage of Rabbi Yéhouda Léon Askénazi," *Peamim Oriental Community Research Quarterly*, 91 (2002): 105–8 [Hebrew].

2 Charvit, "Identity and History," pp. 105–22 [Hebrew].

3 R. Askénazi indicates that the author of the *Torah Temimah*, Rabbi Baruch Halevi Epstein, in explaining the verse "And he said: The Lord came from Sinai, and rose from Seir unto them; He shined forth from Mount Paran, and He came from the myriads holy ..." [Deut 33:2], notes that Aramaic, Latin, and Arabic competed with the Holy Tongue as the vehicle bearing the sanctity of prophecy: "Perhaps he so reasoned because the word *veata* [and He came] is essentially Aramaic rather than Hebrew. On this foundation, the *Sifri* posited that when God revealed Himself to give the Torah to Israel, His revelation took place in not one but four languages: '*And he said: The Lord came from Sinai*' - Hebrew; '*and rose from Seir unto them*' - Latin; '*He shined forth from Mount Paran*' - Arabic and '*He came from the myriads holy*' - Aramaic." Among the seventy nations, the Christians and Muslims did not cease struggling against Israel for primacy. Most world nations recognized the authority of Israel to be "the High Priest of Mankind" (as R. Elie Benamozeg of Livorno noted), *but the incitement emanating from Ishmael, Esau and Aram interfered with Israel's bearing leadership of the sanctity of the human race* (emphasis mine - YC; from a lecture by Rabbi Askénazi on the weekly Torah reading *Balak* [Num 22:2 - 25:9]).

R. Askénazi considered interfaith dialogue essential and significant, as it reinforces common monotheistic features, i.e., belief in one God and revelation. He maintained that monotheism is based upon the assumption that Jewish history may not be separated from general human history. He conducted a thorough examination of reciprocal relations among religions, concentrating on the effects of interaction and the Jewish People's sense of responsibility and mission towards humanity.[4] Islam and Christianity occupy a prominent place in R. Askénazi's philosophy because of the competition they pose for Judaism as a religion and the Jewish People as a nation.

This study examines the reciprocal relations between Islam and Israel during periods of Jewish exile and redemption, as reflected in R. Askénazi's theory. R. Askénazi clarifies repeatedly that the conflict that was so clear and consistent throughout the years of exile may well be solved and settled some time in the future. As an educator and intellectual involved in the Israeli ethos, he sought to explain the essence of the tension, rivalry and hostility between the State of Israel, the Jewish People, Europe, and the United States on the one hand and Islamic states on the other, seeking to uncover their cultural and theological roots. He claimed that political struggles, arguments, delegitimization of Israel, Arab-Israeli wars, and conflicts and ambivalent diplomacy all reflect the basic and fundamental views of those respective cultures. This study examines and analyzes R. Askénazi's historiosophic approach.

A. Chronicles: Islam and the Moral Problem

> My teacher Jacob Gordin told us something that surprised me greatly at the time. Eventually, however, I began to realize how right he was: The rivalry between Ishmael and Israel is more intense than the one between Christianity and Judaism, as Christian Antisemitism prevailed in the Jewish Diaspora, whereas Muslim hatred accompanied the return of Israel to Zion, a far more serious development.[5]

---

4 In July 1990, R. Askénazi was invited to represent the Jewish faith on the establishment of the Temple de l'Universel in Paris, founded by the head of the Sufi order. Representatives of all world religions attended: Hindus, Buddhists, Zoroastrians, Christians, Muslims, and Jews. He composed this prayer: "Our Father, Existence of all existence, Creator of the universe, Master of the world, builder of our homes on the land in which Thy Presence was revealed in the past, Thy children have built this Universal Temple in fulfillment of the commandment '*And let them make Me a sanctuary, that I may dwell among them*' [Exod 25:8]. Heaven and earth are filled with Thy voice, yet from the beginning, the echo of Thy glory has distanced itself to accord time and purpose to existence. Return! May Thy absence cease! May it by Thy will that our unity augment Thy truth, as the Prophet Isaiah declared: '*for My house shall be called a house of prayer for all peoples*' [Isa 56:7]." [this and all succeeding translations from French mine - YC]. L. Y. Askénazi, *La parole et l'écrit, II: Penser la tradition juive d'aujourd'hui* (Paris: Albin Michel, 2005; edited by Marcel Goldman), 608–9.

5 Lecture from the CD series *Le drame de l'exil* (Jerusalem: Fondation Manitou, 2003).

These remarks open R. Askénazi's lecture entitled "The Drama of Exile: The Edomite and Ishmaelite Exiles." He suggests that Gordin's claim originates in the book *Shaarei Ora*, whose author, Spanish kabbalist R. Yosef Gikatilla (1248–1325), (a disciple of R. Avraham Aboulafia) maintains that the conflict with Ishmael is incorporated within the Edomite exile.[6]

1. *Retroactively Emerging Identity*

Biblical history, claims R. Askénazi, is the beacon of human history, the inspiration for all times. This perspective is his historiosophic explanation of the history of nations and the history of the Jewish People. It leads us on a journey to all manifestations of human culture throughout all generations, as a thorough assessment of Hebrew history demands comprehensive knowledge of all universal cultural creations. R. Askénazi was highly familiar with human cultures and what they produced in the West, the East, and even the Far East. This knowledge did not render him a member of said cultures but was rather instrumental in achieving a more intensive explanation of Hebrew identity based on Hebrew and Jewish sources.[7]

We proceed to examine R. Askénazi's position regarding Islam, the biblical Ishmael, son of Abram–not Abraham, he emphasizes–and Hagar. R. Askénazi recounts the annals of Islam in the context of its rivalry with Israel, a rivalry that bears an ethical character, contrasting with the theological confrontation between Judaism and Christianity.

---

6 This theory conforms with the Maharal's claim that Ishmael is not included among the Four Kingdoms (Babylonia, Persia, Greece, and Edom) (*Nezah Israel*, 21, p. 108; *Ner Mizva*, p. 18). "According to the Talmud, Tractate *Avoda Zara* 2b, when the Fourth Kingdom faces final judgment, two voices will be heard: that of Edom/Rome ('We introduced many markets, many bathhouses, much silver and gold') and that of Persia/Islam ('We built many bridges, we conquered many cities, we fought many wars'). Ishmael's universalism accords it character appropriate to the Four Kingdoms. Islam perceives itself as a fundamental restoration of the world's religions from the time of Abraham to Muhammad, the Seal of Prophecy" (L. Y. Askénazi, lecture); "The thaw in relations between the Jews and Islam was enabled by Christian theologians, as Islam's anti-Jewish stance ultimately originates in Christianity" (Askénazi, *La parole et l'écrit*, p. 602).

7 R. Askénazi was inspired by the *Annales* School, founded in 1920 by Lucien Febvre and Marc Bloch, which rejected event-oriented historiography, focusing instead on research concerning social and human phenomena. Manitou studied philosophy at the Sorbonne and ethnology and anthropology at the Ecole d'ethnologie et d'anthropologie du Musée de L'Homme, at which two of his most significant teachers were the well-known ethnologists and anthropologists Claude Lévi-Strauss (1908–2009) and Marcel Jousse (1886–1961). R. Askénazi's varied sources included personal contacts. Even in Algeria, he conducted dialogue with Muslims. He had connections with Muslim mystics in Paris and was a member of the "Brotherhood of the Sons of Abraham." As indicated, he was present at the dedication of the Temple de l'Universel in Paris, founded by the head of the Sufi order.

On departing Ur of the Chaldees, Abram, a descendant of the family of Eber, returns to the land of the Hebrews in fulfillment of a divine command. Abram and Sarai are refugees of the "Ur Holocaust"; Nimrod is the "Hitler" of the Ancient East, who attempts unsuccessfully to cast Abram into the fire (ancient Hebrew: *ur*). The family of the Hebrews survives the Mesopotamian exile but fears it may not be able to maintain its Hebrew identity, the identity of Israel that is destined to take shape in years to come. As Sarai was barren, she adopts a strategy that R. Askénazi suggests is typical of Diaspora Jewry: fructification of the prevailing culture, realizing what a pity it would be to see "Hebrew society" nipped in the bud. Her kindness is boundless, but her self-confidence concomitantly weak. God, indeed, promised issue to Abram, but fulfillment is slow in coming. Perceived reality ultimately triumphs over faith in promises and Sarai asks Abram to fructify the dominant culture of that time, represented by the character of Hagar, daughter of the pharaoh of ancient Egypt. Sarai is attempting to force the hand of reality: she and Abram lacked the patience to await fulfillment of the promise, resulting in the birth of Ishmael. In retrospect, this development gave rise to fierce rivalry with Israel, as manifested in the image of Isaac, son of Abraham and Sarah, who had been born in the meantime.

2. *The Roots of Rivalry between Israel and Ishmael*

The rivalry between Isaac and Ishmael is rooted in the [Hebrew] name of each.[8] Ishmael is described as "making sport" [laughing] and, from the moment Sarah sees him doing so, all history changes its appearance:

> And Sarah saw the son of Hagar the Egyptian, whom she had borne unto Abraham, making sport. Wherefore she said unto Abraham: "Cast out this bondwoman and her son; for the son of this bondwoman shall not be heir with my son, even with Isaac" [Gen 21:9–10].

What is it that Sarah saw that made her react so severely? R. Askénazi relies on the *Tosefta* on Tractate *Sotah*, chapter 6, mishna 3, to explain the depth of Ishmael's immoral approach: R. Akiva explains Ishmael's laugh as the laugh of idolatry; R. Eliezer as the laugh of fornication; and R. Ishmael as the laugh of bloodshed. R. Shimon Bar Yohai, a disciple of the former three sages, cites his teachers in this *Tosefta* but differs with them in his analysis of the biblical Ishmael's laugh. Before considering R. Shimon Bar Yohai's views, R. Askénazi emphasizes that Ishmael is a blatantly immoral personality, as idolatry is a sin between man and God, fornication a matter of human honor (between man and himself), and bloodshed a sin between man and man. "He who laughs at present cannot inherit him who will laugh [Hebrew: *Itzhak* (Isaac)]," says R. Askénazi, explaining Ishmael's immoral

---

8 L.Y. Askénazi, "La neuvième épreuve d'Abraham: le 'transfert' d'Agar et d'Ichmaël, in *Ki Mitsion I, Notes sur la paracha* (Jerusalem: Fondation Manitou & Editions Eliner, 1997), 59–64.

attitude: One who laughs in the present is expressing satisfaction with the current situation and refraining from measures that could rectify its aberrations. "He who laughs last laughs best" is an aphorism suiting the character of Isaac,[9] as he is destined to apply himself to repairing the flaws of this world. Satisfaction may come only after exerting the necessary moral efforts entailed by such endeavors. There is nothing more immoral than to enjoy this world to the fullest:

> Laughter is legitimate for the son of Abraham, for Isaac as well as for Ishmael, as Abraham's primary testimony is that the world has a Creator and therefore all creation has purpose and hope. Laughter in the present, however, is different, as it expresses satisfaction with a world in which evil and good are intermingled. One should reserve total laughter for the world to come, when good shall triumph. Sarah saw that Ishmael's "making sport" embodied a religion detached from morality, one that contents itself with the present condition of the world. By contrast, Isaac manifests a religion absolutely identified with morality. This is the messianic message of the prophets of Israel, as taught by the mentors of Rabbi Shimon Bar Yohai.[10]

---

9 This idea is elucidated by R. Askénazi with biblical verses, quotations from the Talmud and kabbalistic traditions: *When the Lord brought back those that returned to Zion, we were like unto them that dream. Then was our mouth filled with laughter* ... [Ps 126:1–2]; "R. Yohanan said on behalf of R. Shimon Bar Yohai: It is forbidden for one to fill his mouth with laughter in this world, as it is written "*Then was our mouth filled with laughter* ..." [Babylonian Talmud, Tractate *Berakhot* 31a]; "R. Yona said in R. Zeira's name: Anyone who goes seven days without dreaming is called wicked, as it is written "*... and he that hath it shall abide satisfied, he shall not be visited with evil*" [Prov 19:23]. This means that one whose conscience does not disturb him for seven days is evil [the Hebrew roots for "satisfied" and "seven" are orthographically identical but pronounced differently]" [Babylonian Talmud, Tractate *Berakhot* 14a]; "Abraham's family had four sons [cf. the Passover Haggadah]: The wise son is Isaac, who was prepared for any sacrifice to realize his purpose; the wicked son is Esau, who makes no effort at all to keep his birthright; the simple son is Jacob, '*...and Jacob was a quiet man, dwelling in tents*' [Gen 25:27] and the one who knows not how to ask is Ishmael, who is identified in the Bible by his consistent silence. All speak in the Bible, even the snake, but Ishmael is silent, perhaps because of his shame over the appellation '*the son of this bondwoman*' [Gen 21:10] or perhaps because of his inability to express himself orally (L.Y. Askénazi, lecture: L'être père et l'être fils, Dialogue et compréhension [Jerusalem: Fondation Manitou, 2005]).

10 Askénazi, "La neuvième épreuve d'Abraham," p. 62. See also:L.Y. Askénazi, "L'Histoire des Engendrements," in *La parole et l'écrit, I. Penser la tradition juive aujourd'hui* (Paris: Albin Michel, 1999), 356–57; idem, "La descendance d'Abraham: Isaac-Ismaël," in *La parole et l'écrit, II. Penser la tradition juive aujourd'hui* (Paris: Albin Michel, 2005) 201–6; Les autres Monothéismes: Convergence et Divergences, pp. 409–83; Lorsque le roi est present le serviteur n'est pas libre, pp. 411–19; idem, "Rencontre judéo-musulmane" in *La parole et l'écrit, II,* pp. 603–9; M. Koginski, *Un Hébreu d'origine juive: Hommage au rav Yéhouda Léon Askénazi* (Editions Ormaya; Jerusalem: 1998), 218–19.

In the above-cited *Tosefta* of Tractate *Sotah*, Rabbi Shimon Bar Yohai is puzzled that Ishmael is "making sport...in the home of the righteous man Abraham," leading R. Askénazi to interpret the history of Islam as follows: Until Muhammad, Ishmael was outside the "House of Abraham"; this was the period that Islam calls *Jahiliya* (ignorance). In Muhammad's time, Ishmael returned to the House of Abraham with no theological problems aroused by Islam. Ishmael's return to the God of Abraham thus takes place in the intra-Islamic moral sphere.

From here on, the words of Rabbi Shimon Bar Yohai help us to understand the extra-Islamic, political sphere that underscores the intensity of rivalry between Ishmael and Israel: "Sarah's response that 'the son of this bondwoman shall not be heir with my son' shows that Ishmael would quarrel with Isaac over the inheritance, claiming 'I am the firstborn and I take a double share.'"[11] This is the heart of the dispute over the Land of Israel, intensified by the Muslim practice of circumcision, that accords its adherents a foothold in the Land of Israel according to the Zohar:[12]

> It is no wonder that Islam has taken hold in the Land of Israel from the seventh century to the twentieth. When the British, who are uncircumcised, seized the Land of Israel, we knew that the struggle against them would be brief.[13]

3. *The Uniqueness of Rivalry with Islam*

Judaism's rivalry with Islam differs from its rivalry with Christianity. There is no theological conflict with Islam. The conflict is a moral one: "The Muslim mind finds it difficult to think in terms of moral responsibility. Why? God decides everything. To think that man is free is profanation of the sacred."

---

11 See Rashi's commentary on the biblical verse.

12 "Come and see: Four hundred years stood the [angel] responsible for the sons of Ishmael, beseeching the Holy One, Blessed be He. He said to Him: 'Does not he who is circumcised have a share in Thy name? He [God] said to him: 'Yes.' 'And Ishmael, who is circumcised, why does not he have a share as does Isaac?' He said to him: 'One is circumcised appropriately and properly and one is not. Moreover, these adhere unto Me appropriately for eight days and those are distant from me for several days.' He [the angel] said: 'And with all this, will he not have some reward for being circumcised? That is, for the time that Ishmael was born into this world and circumcised, what did the Holy One, Blessed be He do [regarding the claim of the angel responsible for Ishmael]? He distanced the sons of Ishmael from adherence to the Supreme One, gave them a share below in the Holy Land because of their circumcision and the sons of Ishmael are destined to rule the Holy Land for a long time, when it is empty of all, just as their circumcision is empty, incomplete. And they will delay the Children of Israel from returning to their place until the credit of the Sons of Ishmael has been repaid" [Zohar, Exodus, Weekly Torah Reading *Vaera* [Exod 6:2 - 9:35], 32a, Paragraph 201, translated from Aramaic [into Hebrew] by the author of the *Sulam* commentary, Rabbi Yehuda Lev Ashlag).

13 Askénazi, *Le drame de l'exil*.

> When an intelligent Muslim is influenced by the West, he indeed identifies the moral issue and immediately feels discomfort and certain difficulties with his religion. I was born in a Muslim country and I am very familiar with this problem. To be free is as if to challenge the sovereignty of God. To be Muslim is to be subjugated to absolute Divine will - maktoub [it is [all] written], as they say.[14]

In Islamic lands, social status, economic class, and the power of the authorities are most important of all:

> Although Christianity stole the heavens of Israel [spiritual metaphysics, ethics] from us and Islam the soil of Israel [materialism, the respect inherent in property, in territory[15] and in class[16]], we remained on the horizon for a long time. Now, we are again becoming Hebrews, again becoming Israel, in our own land and under our own heavens.[17]

B. From Jewish Identity in Islamic Lands to Hebrew Identity on the Return to Zion
The Correlation between Identity and Culture[18]

When exile in Christian and Islamic lands came to an end and the components of Hebrew identity, which could be revealed only under such "challenging" conditions, became clear, it again became possible to return to Zion and rebuild a pure and refined Hebrew identity:

> Ishmael dwells alongside Isaac and Jewish and Islamic theology are indeed parallel. There are no substantive theological conflicts between them... According to the biblical narrative, Ishmael quarrels with Isaac over the Promised Land, the Land of Israel. Contemporary history displays this more clearly; Ishmael does not deny that the Jews are Israel. That conflict is unique to the Christians. Ishmael simply denies the existence of the Jewish People in the Land of Israel, thereby determining the nature of coexistence of Ishma-

---

14 Askénazi, "La descendance d'Abraham," p. 204; R. Askénazi tended to differentiate between official Islam and the Sufi order, which he found to be more intense. He complained that French settlers in Algeria belittled Muslim theological terms, expressing their views of concepts such as *maktoub* in a blunt and superficial manner. Sunni Islam indeed decided that there is no free choice–that was a theological decision –but Shiites thought differently.

15 See M. Schwartz, "War, Peace and Territory as Viewed by Islam," *Mahanayim*, 1 (On Judaism and Islam), (1992): 212-15 [Hebrew].

16 This is elucidated by the humiliating *dhimmi* status that Jews and Christians bore in Islamic lands.

17 So he would say in numerous lectures.

18 I have already addressed this issue in my article "Identity and History," pp. 115-17; but I would like to include certain additional aspects concerning Christian and Islamic cultures; J. Garb, "The Chosen Will Become Herds," *Studies in Twentieth Century Kabbalah* (Carmel: Shalom Hartman Institute, 2005) 16, 41-42, 58, 61, 97-98 [Hebrew].

> elites and Israelites over the generations, with the vicissitudes that one suffered in the lands conquered by the other....Indeed, the Jews were persecuted and humiliated severely in Arab lands, contrary to the myth, disseminated as an act of good will, declaring that they lived a secure and tranquil life there....In other words, the quarrel between Israel and the Ishmaelites did not rise heavenward but rather remained on earth...whereas Esau and Jacob are competing for substantive identity; this competition does concern heaven....In Jerusalem, various disputes determined the nature of the Jews' argument with Islam and with Christianity–Ashkenazim, in their struggle with the Christians and, on an entirely different level, Sephardim in their contest with the Islamic nations. This is the origin and deeply rooted source of the difference between the two extremes in the core and spiritual structure of the two tribes. In any event, I would like to clarify that Jacob can celebrate his victory over Ishmael only to the extent that he is truly the son of Isaac. Isaac does assume responsibility for Esau; After all, he is his father. In fact, it is only in Sephardic tradition that Judaism is able to declare its victory over Christian heresy.[19]

Moreover, Jewish identity in Christian and Islamic countries took shape differentially because the challenges differed:

> Sephardim who remain loyal to themselves achieve more clarity in organizing thought and ritual itself because they encountered no fundamental opposition to their identity. However paradoxical it may seem, the converso phenomenon is more typical of the Ashkenazi world, as it involves a Jewish soul cast in a landscape of Christian opposition, whether religious or secular ....The life of the Ashkenazi Jew is more "tragic" in the Greek sense of the term....Indeed, Jewish suffering is common to both [Sephardim and Ashkenazim], but the Ashkenazi variety bears a gloomier hue....Throughout the development of Hebrew culture by Ashkenazim and Sephardim, the true theology remained with the latter. It was as if the Ashkenazi world related to theology as a forbidden zone temporarily allocated to the Christian faith, whereas no such ban existed in a Muslim environment. Effectively, all of us, Ashkenazim and Sephardim alike, understand what we believe in only by virtue of the Sephardic theologians of the Golden Age: Maimonides, Ibn Gvirol and particularly Rabbi Yehuda Halevi, author of the Kuzari ....Yehuda Halevi charted the course to be followed subsequently by the Maharal of Prague and, in our own time, by Rabbi A. I. Kook of Jerusalem, "High Priest" of the revitalized land of the Jews....Differences in ritual and mentality thus...originate in basic relations with Ishmael on the one hand and with Esau on the other. Jacob's prayer before Esau is not identical to that of Isaac before Ishmael because the specific problems they had to solve do not face the same direction.[20]

---

19 L.Y. Askénazi, "Israel in the Exile of Islam and Christianity," *Shevet Va'Am*, second series, A(6), (Jerusalem, 1971), 89 [Hebrew].

20 Ibid. pp. 89–90; *cf.* L.Y. Askénazi lecture: "Ishmael, art et musique, Fondation Manitou," (Jerusalem, 2005);idem, *Bi-Fnei mi ata omed, Introduction to Prayer,* audio CD (Fondation Manitou, 2005) [Hebrew] "The name Ishmael [Hebrew: God will hear]

C. "AND IT CAME TO PASS IN THE END OF DAYS" THE MONOTHEISTIC FAITHS AT THE END OF THE EXILE OF ISRAEL

1. The Essence of Conflict Resolution

Based on an analysis of contemporary events, R. Askénazi believed that all signs attest to the eventual termination of the historic dispute among Israel, Ishmael, and Edom, as the Creator, through Israel, has already bestowed the plan for its resolution upon humankind. Similarly, the human race is likely to realize its common "Abrahamic features," that rise on the foundations of the former conflict:

> Judaism is the root of the positivistic religions, i.e., those based on revelation. Its outlook cannot be rooted in a "founder of the religion" but rather in the essence of the Creator's revelation, that discloses the basic truths of the world, of mankind and of its history. The unmediated divine guidance that the Jews call Torah does not come from just any divinity but rather originates with the Creator of the universe Himself and therefore only biblical prophecy can attest to the immanent truth therein and the consequent historical truth. This is the way that Jewish tradition understood its monotheism. The same God who created the universe is the judge of its history, who reveals himself before Israel to disclose the ethical laws of all humanity. This ethical code was not intended to hinder human beings from achieving their historical goals but rather to assist in attaining them. The ethical conception applies to history as a whole and most of all to human history that strives for the ultimate purpose, a quest that characterizes the spiritual world of the Hebrew mind.[21]

---

bears a feature according Islam knows how to pray. A Sephardic Jew feels comfortable with Ishmael's prayers but not with the prayer of the Christians; the Sephardic synagogue is built differently from the Ashkenazi one because it seeks to avoid resembling a Christian church (Askénazi, *Le drame*); R. Askénazi clarifies this through word play [based on the concluding words of Exod 24:7] "All that the Lord hath spoken will we do and listen." While Esau perceives of himself as complete [the Hebrew word for "done" is an anagram of his name], Ashkenazic Jews say "We will do," whereas Ishmael feels unmediated proximity to God and Sephardic Jews say "We will listen." When a Muslim prays, it is clear that he is praying to one god. Consequently, the Jews feel more in harmony with his prayer, which they consider impeccable. Its melody, spiritual status, simplicity, and non-ceremonial and non-ritualized approach when compared with Christianity impart a sense of comfort to Jews. The Islamic concept of "prayer," however, does not parallel the Jewish one. In Islam, prayer is not a request but an act of praise and acceptance of authority. R. Askénazi noted that the different prayer positions of the respective religions reflect their theological conceptions: Christians kneel, as do kings and high priests, thereby expressing pretension and pride that the Messiah, they claim, has already appeared (they rest on Sunday, the "eighth day"); Muslims prostrate themselves and thus express their total submission to God and the lack of free choice (they rest on Friday); finally, the Jews stand as they pray, because they face the Heavenly Tribunal (they rest on the seventh day, the Sabbath). (L.Y. Askénazi *Sod ha-Ivri*, eds. G. Ben Shmuel and I. Pivko [Jerusalem, 2005] [Hebrew], The story of my life, p. 22, pp. 81–83).

21 L.Y. Askénazi, "Le judaïsme et le monde moderne," in *La parole et l'écrit, I*, 487–88.

Moreover, upon the Return to Zion, an authentic Hebrew identity will emerge, the identity of Israel and all imitations thereof will pale forthwith. Christianity will then have to concede the title of "the true Israel," having assumed certain metaphysical aspects of Hebrew identity, as did Islam, emulating the mother religion that they largely sought to supplant. It is incumbent upon the Jewish spiritual leadership to inform its Christian and Muslim counterparts of the full meaning of Hebrew identity and the nature of the people who embody it.[22]

2. *Islam, the God of Abraham, and the God of Isaac*

R. Askénazi, who was born in an Islamic country, Algeria, was highly familiar with the Islamic faith and aware of the Arab-Israeli conflict whose solution, he claimed, would be achieved once the conflict's ideological and spiritual roots are uncovered. After focusing on the bone of contention–the Land of Israel–R. Askénazi sought common features likely to facilitate dialogue, which was not an easy task by any means: The silence of Ishmael in the Bible is most evident, as is "the silence of contemporary Islam and its unwillingness to talk to the State of Israel."[23]

> The identity of Ishmael originates in blurred Hebrew identity "Isr[a]-El - Ishma-El"; the existential brother is Ishmael; the substantive brother is Esau; Jew and Muslim are close in religiosity, especially in their prayers, but there is a vast abyss between Jew and Christian in terms of their religiosity–but not their moral conscience. When there is peace, the world will be surprised at how close we are to the way of Abraham.[24]

On the basis of this ideological infrastructure, one may achieve resolution of the conflicts:

> When universal cultures–Islam and Christianity–are honest with themselves, they recognize the authenticity of Israel as a sacred kingdom and a divine creation.[25]

Focusing more sharply on Islam, R. Askénazi believes that the solution to the conflict may be found in the Bible. The Book of Genesis (25:8–18) describes the death of Abraham and Ishmael, in which R. Askénazi per-

---

[22] At a "This is Your Life" celebration in his honor at Binyenei Ha'Ooma in Jerusalem, R. Askénazi was asked by moderator Emanuel Halperin to explain his participation in interfaith conferences. Jokingly, he responded that he did so as an act of "Christian charity," noting that he believes the Jews are particularly obligated to explain the mystery of Israel's identity in the Era of Redemption to the Christians. "We Jews are bidden to help Christians find their positive place because their frustration is excessive and the consequences thereof are fraught with danger."

[23] Askénazi, lecture: "Ishmaël, art et musique."

[24] Askénazi, *Le drame de l'exil.*

[25] L.Y. Askénazi, "Rencontre judéo-musulmane," *La parole et l'écrit, II*, pp. 603–9.

ceives Ishmael's acknowledgment not only of the God of Abraham but also of the God of Isaac.[26] In the future, Islam will admit to the ascription of the Land of Israel to the People of Israel and thus also to the purpose of Israel. The events occur in Hebron:

> "And Abraham expired, and died in a good old age, an old man, and full of years; and was gathered to his people And Isaac and Ishmael his sons buried him in the cave of Machpelah, in the field of Ephron the son of Zohar the Hittite, which is before Mamre" [Gen 25:8–9].

> "Now these are the generations of Ishmael, Abraham's son, whom Hagar the Egyptian, Sarah's handmaid, bore unto Abraham ... And these are the years of the life of Ishmael, a hundred and thirty and seven years; and he expired and died; and was gathered unto his people" [Gen 25:12, 17].

Rashi clarifies something that R. Askénazi underscores in his explanation:

> Verse 12 notes that Ishmael is Abraham's son, not Abram's. A simplistic explanation would state that in the meantime, Abram became Abraham, so the biblical text uses only the more recent name. But why did the text stipulate "whom Hagar the Egyptian, Sarah's handmaid, bore unto Abraham"? Moreover, how could Abraham have died "in a good old age" [i.e. happy] if his sons were locked in so fierce a confrontation? In this regard, we cite Rashi's remarks on Verse 9, particularly with reference to Isaac and Ishmael: "Hence Ishmael repented and led Isaac before him. This is the 'good old age' attributed to Abraham." We note that it takes place in Hebron. Ishmael returns from Egypt to participate in the funeral of Abraham in Hebron and admits that Isaac is in his own land, in Hebron. Here, we find the point of reconciliation between Ishmael and Isaac. For this reason, the Bible says that Ishmael "expired," a term referring only to the righteous (Rashi). The Bible emphasizes that Ishmael will be considered the son of Abraham and a righteous man when he repents regarding his attitude toward Isaac, in Hebron. This is recorded in the Torah so that we might realize it and take it into account over the generations, according to the principle that Nahmanides taught us: "The deeds of the fathers are a sign for the sons."[27]

---

26 Here as well, R. Askénazi clarifies the concept with a clever Hebrew play on words: "Ishmael – '...his hand shall be against every man, and every man's hand against him ...' (Hebrew: *yado bakol veyad kol bo*) [Gen 16:12]. Abraham is represented by the word *bakol* (cf. Gen 24:1), Isaac by *mikol* (Gen 27:33) and Jacob by *kol* (Gen 33:11). Ishmael has a hand in the God of Abraham (*bakol*) but the hand of Jacob, son of Isaac (*kol*) is against Ishmael (lecture on the Book of Genesis).

27 Y.L. Askénazi, "La fin du conflit Ichmaël-Isaac," in *Ki MiTsion I*, pp. 69–73; idem, "La descendance d'Abraham," pp. 201–6; 409–83.

D. Conclusion: Jewish Humanism in Harmony with Universal Humanism

R. Askénazi's philosophy is manifestly historio-centric and humanistic, even if anchored in the basic assumption that the Jews were chosen as the theological and moral leaders of all humankind:[28] The family of earth that was created in God's image must settle all conflicts originating in each culture's aspiration to assume a position of primacy and leadership. R. Askénazi explained that throughout history, as Christianity and later Islam struggled to assume the mantle of the true religion, they plagiarized elements from the mother religion, Judaism. Each culture bore the standard of the value it lacked and applied itself to its development: Christianity nominally strove for grace and love–the religion of love–and Islam for justice: "Muhammad's Law is by the sword." At the End of Days, when the Exile of Israel is ended, each culture must return these "stolen goods" and return to its authentic self. Moral cooperation is indeed feasible under Heaven in the eyes of the Creator of humankind:

If Christianity will only learn to be the Diaspora of Israel,[29] it will resolve its own identity crisis;[30] and if Islam will admit to the Land of Israel, as did its ancestor Ishmael, it will thus rectify the moral flaw inherent in the religion of Islam regarding the extra-Islamic layer, as morality is the embodiment of respect for others. If Islam corrects its moral flaw at the intra-Islamic level, toward others who are near, when Ishmael returns to the God of Abraham, it is likely to correct its extra-Islamic moral flaw, toward more distant others, when it returns to the God of Isaac. In other words, Islam's recognition of Isaac is the completion of its repentance.[31]

---

28 L.Y. Askénazi, *Misped La-Messiah*, Tome I, eds. E. Simsovic, I. Askénazi, I. Pivko (Fondation Manitou, 2006) [Hebrew]; idem, *Sod ha-Ivri*, eds. G. Ben Shmuel and I. Pivko (Jerusalem, 2005) [Hebrew]; idem, *Sod Lashon Ha-Qodesh*, Tome I, eds. S. Ben Naim, I. Askénazi, I. Pivko (Fondation Manitou, 2007) [Hebrew].

29 Jean Vassal, *Les Eglises, diaspora d'Israël?*, Albin Michel, collections "Présences du judaïsme," 1993; Charvit Yossef, "From Monologues to Possible Dialogue, Judaism's Attitude towards Christianity According to the Philosophy of R. Yéhouda Léon Askénazi (Manitou)", in *Interaction between Judaism and Christianity in History, Religion, Art, and Literature, Jewish and Christian Perspectives Series, Volume 17*, eds. D. Golinkin, M. Poorthuis, J. Schwartz, F. van der Steen (Leiden–Boston: Brill, 2008), 319–36.

30 Askénazi, L. Y., Que dites-vous que je suis. *La parole et l'écrit, II*, pp. 589–94.

31 Some efforts in this direction may be attributed to Imam Abdul Hadi Palazzi of Italy, who declares that the Cave of Machpelah and the Land of Israel belong to the Jewish People. He belongs to the Sufi order of Islam and even explains that because he is in Europe, he can allow himself to issue such declarations. Sheikh Abdel-Salaam Manasra, Head of the Qadiri Sufi order in Israel (the oldest Sufi order in the world), is also active in promoting interfaith understanding. The order was founded by Qadiri Sheikh Abdul Qadir Jilani (1128), who instituted a way of life that emphasizes introspection, love of knowledge and science and sharing knowledge with adherents of other religions ("the

At the same time, each culture must refrain from devoting itself to the development of one exclusive value, as such efforts would be doomed to failure; instead, each must allow Israel to return to the principle of moral unity:[32]

> What Israeli-Hebrew identity strives for is success of the Divine Plan and all the values it embodies. This is the principle of unity. It did not succeed in instituting any kind of humanism. Each humanistic school launched a sole value and this is its resounding failure....Hebrew identity must accompany all moral revolutions and it must know when to dissociate itself from them and carry out the independent Hebrew revolution that entails dissemination of unity among all values....Unity of moral values should be accorded priority. Selection of one value that reigns supreme and at times even vitiates other values is one of the long-standing characteristics of idolatry that is manifested today as ideology. Through the unity of Creation, man reaches unity of his values and moral virtues. Moral unity is what we call *qedushah* (holiness) in Hebrew.[33]

---

path of Abraham"). This is undoubtedly a moderate and tolerant approach that emphasizes the essentiality of interfaith dialogue.

32 L.Y. Askénazi, "Révolution," in *La parole et l'écrit, I*, p. 150.

33 L.Y. Askénazi, "La notion de sainteté dans la pensée du Rav Kook," in *La parole et l'écrit, I*, pp. 109–25; Koginski, *Un Hébreu d'origine juive*, pp. 257–58.

The Rabbi and the Mufti against the Priest

The Missionary Activity in Gaza at the Beginning of the Twentieth Century

YARON HAREL

One of the phenomena worthy of note in the realm of relations between Jews and Christians in the Middle East during the second half of the nineteenth century is the penetration of Protestant missionaries into the region and the clear distinction the Jews made between the Catholics and the Protestants. The former had been the sworn enemy for generations, whereas the latter were a new element that had begun to feel their way, searching for cracks and weak points through which they might enter the region and entrench their influence and their religious faith.

The foundation of Protestant activity among Middle Eastern Jews was the belief that the Messiah would make his appearance only after the Jews had returned to their land and converted to Christianity. In the course of the nineteenth century, the perception that the time for the return of the Jewish people to its homeland was imminent gained support among the Millenarianist groups in the English Evangelical movement. These groups and their supporters sought to act in various ways to accelerate the coming of the end of days. The methods they adopted in pursuit of this goal included founding evangelical societies and dispatching missionaries to various places in the world to spread the Christian gospel. Such societies were set up in England, Scotland, Ireland, the United States, and elsewhere. In this matter, special attention was focused upon Jews, especially the Jews in the Middle East. The other method of hastening the second coming was the planning of practical steps to resettle the Jews in their land, some of which were actually implemented.[1]

The missionary activity in the various communities encountered various degrees of resistance. For example, in Jerusalem, the opposition was vigorous. The presence of many Jews of European-Ashkenazi origin in Jerusalem intensified the fear of an attempt to convert Jews to Christianity.[2] This fear

---

1 See, for example, Menachem Kedem, "Mid-Nineteenth-Century Anglican Eschatology on the Redemption of Israel" [Hebrew], *Cathedra* 19 (1981): 55–71; Mayir Vereté, "The Restoration of the Jews in English Protestant Thought, 1790–1840," *Middle Eastern Studies* 8 (1972): 3-50. On the second method see, for example, Yaron Harel, "Latakia: A Forgotten Colony of the First Aliyah" [Hebrew], *Cathedra* 74 (1994): 62-85.

2 See, for example, M. Eliav, *Eretz-Israel and Its Settlement in the Nineteenth Century* (Hebrew; Jerusalem, 1978), 61–65; A. Yaffe, *The American Protestant Mission and its Activities in the Levant and in the Holy Land between the Years 1810–1914*

was rooted in the perception that Jewish existence in Europe needed defending. The temptation to convert there was great, since by giving up his faith, a European Jew could improve his social and economic status. In the Middle East this temptation did not exist. There, a Jew who gave up his religion in favor of Christianity did not advance himself either socially or economically, since in the Ottoman Empire the status of both Jews and Christians was equal, as second-class subjects compared with the Muslim majority. That being the case, the response in Middle Eastern communities other than Jerusalem was less enthusiastic and more rationalistic–instrumental.[3] Missionary institutions could provide the youth with a broad education and especially teach them the languages, such as English and French, needed to engage in commerce, and more than a few Jews sent their sons to such institutions. In the absence of Jewish educational institutions for girls, the Protestant educational institutions were an acceptable substitute, and hundreds of Jewish girls throughout the Middle East were sent to be educated in the missionary schools without any fear of their being influenced by the Christian faith. Even great rabbis such as Rabbi Eliahou Behor Hazan, the Chief Rabbi of the Alexandria community, did not hesitate to send his son to a non-Jewish school when he was not satisfied with the teachers at the Alliance Israélite Universelle school in his city.[4]

This is not to say that rabbis throughout the Middle East were not opposed to the missionary activity, but rather that the timing and intensity of the opposition were usually dependent upon the degree of success of the missionaries. If it seemed that many members of the community were inclined to connect with the Protestant emissaries, then the rabbis were aroused to opposing action, usually by means of a ban forbidding contact with the missionaries. In the Baghdad community, for example, Protestant missionary activity, during the 1840s, encountered the strong opposition of the local rabbis, and excommunication and curse were imposed on anyone who dared participate in the religious activity initiated there by the emissary of the "London Society for Promoting Christianity Amongst the Jews." Because of this opposition and despite attempts of the missionaries to recruit help from the heads of the society in London, the British ambassador in Istanbul, and from authorities of the Ottoman regime, the missionary activity in Baghdad failed to expand.[5]

(Hebrew; Jerusalem, 2001); Y. Perry, *British Mission to the Jews in Nineteenth Century Palestine* (Tel Aviv, 2001); R. Yitzhaki-Harel, "The Scottish Mission in Safed Until the First World War and the Reaction of the Jewish Community to Missionary Activity," *Cathedra* 123 (2007): 67–92.

3 See Y. Harel, "Fighting Conversion to Christianity: The Syrian Case," *Jewish Studies Quarterly,* 17 (2010): 29–43.

4 See J.M. Landau, *Jews in Nineteenth Century Egypt* (Jerusalem, 1967), 241.

5 See R.S. Simon, "The Case of the Curse: The London Society for Promoting Christianity

In Aleppo Syria the opposition was minor, and we even find a missionary who was allowed to preach the Christian gospel in the great synagogue of the Jewish community. When the Chief Rabbi learned of this, he did not respond aggressively but instead politely explained to the missionary that his proselytizing mission in the Jewish community would not succeed. In Damascus, as well, missionaries were warmly received during the 1840s in the home of the Chief Rabbi, Haim Maimon Tobi. Apparently the rabbi had not discerned the intentions of the missionaries to win converts to Christianity from among the Jewish community. That was because the missionaries had not openly declared their intentions, presenting their activity as solely concerned with the sacred texts, and also because the rabbi was happy for the presence of Christians in Damascus who were "lovers of Jews" where previously only Catholic Christians who hated the Jews had lived. In later meetings, the rabbi did indeed argue with the missionaries on theological subjects, but, according to their testimony, the debate was calm and without a trace of rancor. Various testimonies show that the Chief Rabbi was not the only one who adopted a friendly stance toward the missionaries. A similar attitude was evinced by other Torah scholars. The Protestant missionaries preached about the gospel to a Jewish rabbi in the synagogue of Jobar near Damascus and in the homes of the head of the Jewish Damascus community and among influential families.[6]

In other communities throughout the Ottoman Empire, such as Istanbul, Salonika, and Izmir, struggle against missionary activity began only when a concrete danger of Jews actually converting to Christianity became evident. It should be noted that, during the second half of the nineteenth century, the leadership of these communities suffered from crises and weakness and had difficulty coping with the missionary influence. Still, when it seemed that the Protestant emissaries had achieved a certain measure of success, the heads of the Jewish community would initiate proceedings of excommunication against any who turned to the missionaries and cooperated with them.[7]

---

amongst the Jews and the Jews of Baghdad," in *Altruism and Imperialism: The Western Religious and Cultural Missionary Enterprise in the Middle East*, eds. Eleanor H. Tejirian and Reeva S. Simon (New York: Middle East Institute Columbia University - Occasional Papers 4, 2002), 45-65.

6 On the reactions in Aleppo and Damascus, see Harel, "Fighting..."

7 See, for example, L. Bornstein-Makovetsky, "Activities of the American Mission among the Jews of Istanbul, Izmir and Salonika during the Nineteenth Century," in *The Days of the Crescent: Chapters in the History of the Jews in the Ottoman Empire*, ed. M. Rozen (Tel Aviv, 1996), 273-310; L. Bornstein-Makovetsky, "Jewish Converts to Islam and Christianity in the Ottoman Empire in the Nineteenth Century," in *The Last Ottoman Century and Beyond, The Jews in Turkey and the Balkans 1808-1945*, ed. M. Rozen (Tel Aviv, 2002), 83-128.

To sum up matters thus far, during the second half of the nineteenth century there was extensive missionary activity in Jewish communities throughout the Middle East. The response of the rabbis was sometimes vigorous and sometimes subdued, depending upon the success the missionaries seemed to be having. An important point to make here is that except for one instance, that of the sage Rabbi Raphael Kassin from Aleppo, who travelled around the world and published books of anti-Christian polemic in the middle of the nineteenth century, we find no other ideological-theological anti-Christian reaction from that period.[8]

This article describes the exceptional cooperation that arose in Gaza between Rabbi Nissim Ohana and the Mufti ʿAbd Allah al-ʿAlami, in the struggle against Protestant missionary activity among the city's residents.

Missionary Convert

The Jewish community in Gaza was revived in 1881, when four families arrived in the city from Russia.[9] They sought to operate a flour mill using steam. An obstacle appeared in the form of an order from the governor of Gaza prohibiting operation of the mill before the arrival of a permit from the authorities in Istanbul. It was precisely a missionary who came to their aid, a converted Jew named Shapira, who, as a British subject, was exempt from the orders of the Ottoman governor and he allowed them to set up the mill in a structure in his yard. Shapira, too, was born in Russia and had been baptized as a Christian by British missionaries in Safed. He was sent by the mission to Gaza to try to convert Muslims to Protestant Christianity. Such activity could take place only under the new spirit of equality and freedom of religion in the wake of the Ottoman reforms. There were no Jews in Gaza at the time he settled there; clearly, the purpose of his mission was not to convince Jews to convert to Christianity, but rather Muslims.[10] Shapira attract-

---

8 Y. Harel, "An Anti-Missionary Tract in Ladino: Raffael Kassin's *Likutei Amarim en Ladino* (Izmir 1855)," in *Languages and Literatures of Sephardic and Oriental Jews*, ed. D. M. Bunis (Jerusalem, 2009), 106–19 [Hebrew]; L. Bornstein-Makovetsky, "The Attitude of Jewish Scholars to Jewish Conversion to Islam and Christianity during the Last Century of the Ottoman Empire," in *Studies in Mediaeval Halakha in Honor of Stephen M. Passamaneck*, eds. B. Jackson and A. Gray (Jewish Law Association Studies XVII; 2007), 31–47.

9 On the previously existing Jewish community in Gaza, see Joseph Breslau (Breslov), *From the Gaza Strip to the Red Sea* (Tel Aviv, 1957), 56–68; S. Rubinstein (Rubenshtain*), A View of the Jewish Community in Gaza (1870–1929)* (Jerusalem, 1995); Issachar Goldrath, *Jewish Settlement in Gaza during the Past 500 Years* (Ramat Gan, 1999). See also "Collected Papers from the Conference *Gaza and Its Satellites*" (Hebrew; Tel Aviv, 1972).

10 Shapira himself declared in the presence of Zalman David Levontin that the objective of his settling in Gaza was to spread Christianity among the Arabs and not among the Jews. See A. Yaari, *Memories of Eretz-Israel, A.* (Ramat Gan, 1974), 417.

ed the city's inhabitants thanks to a local Christian doctor whom he employed to treat them without charge and also by means of a small school he established to teach children the fundamentals of Christianity. Shapira's wife, also a converted Jew, taught Muslim girls sewing in her home, using the opportunity to preach to them about the principles of Christianity. The couple had only meager success. Contemporary testimony reports that the local Muslims exploited Shapira's assistance while belittling his efforts and those of his wife to convert them.[11] Undoubtedly, when the Jews later arrived in Gaza, the fact that the missionary and his wife were converted Jews, originally from Russia, speaking a common language, along with the assistance they extended to the newcomers, all helped to create a bond between them.[12]

Jews, Catholics, and Protestants

In 1886, with the encouragement of the Hovevei Zion Society, young Jews from Jaffa organized to settle in Gaza. That development was part of a much broader program to create blocs of Jewish settlement within Arab cities such as Lod, Nablus, Nazareth, Bethlehem, and Ashkelon. The idea was that the Jaffa youths, familiar with the language and customs of the Arabs, would pave the way for the settlement of tens of thousands of Jews from Eastern Europe in these cities.[13] Near the end of 1887 there were already thirty Jewish families in Gaza. Most were from North Africa with French, Spanish, or British citizenship. Over the years the settlement grew gradually, and in 1896 there were already more than fifty Jewish families in Gaza. These were families from Jerusalem and Hebron but also from Gibraltar. Hope of the arrival of more families from Russia proved unrealistic. One of the demands of the Russian Jews who reached Eretz Israel was the establishment of a special Jewish neighborhood in Gaza, since they could not imagine leasing homes in the Arab neighborhoods with whose residents they had no common language.[14]

While most of the Gazan population were Muslims, a veteran Catholic minority also lived there in a separate neighborhood. In 1881 Catholic

11 See Y. Berlovich (ed.), *Wandering in the Land* (Tel Aviv, 1992), 37 [Hebrew].

12 See Y. Brill, *Yesod Hama'alah* (Magenza; Mainz, 1883), 200. Eventually the settlers sold the mill and left Gaza. One of them travelled abroad collecting money from Jews to found a new settlement in Gaza called "Zera Yisrael" (Seed of Israel). Eliezer Ben Yehuda spoke of this traveler as being a swindler who apparently pocketed the contributions for himself. See *Hazvi* 3 (7 Heshvan, 1885), 11 [Hebrew]. See also the report of Rabbi Salman Mani, "Journey to Gaza," *Hazvi* 7 (5 Kislev, 1885), 27 [Hebrew].

13 See K.Z. Wisotzky (Vysotsky), collection of letters sent to well-known persons concerning settlement of Eretz-Israel (Warsaw, 1898), 156.

14 M. Elkayam, *Forty Years of Jewish Settlement in Gaza, Beersheva, and the Establishment of the Ruhama Farms* (Ramat Gan, 1994), 95.

monks began to build their monastery in what long before had been a Jewish synagogue. As happened elsewhere, the Catholic-Christian population developed a hostile attitude toward the Jews, both because of the ancient rivalry between Christianity and Judaism and because of their desire to redirect the enmity of the Muslims in the direction of the Jews.[15] Perhaps that was the reason the Jews were more friendly with the British Protestant missionaries, who were ostensibly acting for the good of the Jews and were devoid of the enmity characterizing the attitude of the local Catholics. Yet, it is worth mentioning that the Catholic monks and priests who were living in Gaza made no effort whatsoever to bring the Jews closer to Christianity, but rather were content to limit their activity to the local Christian community.[16]

In 1908, Protestant missionaries, with the encouragement and support of the British government, set up a clinic and a co-educational school. In this school, the Arabic and English languages were taught. In order to persuade Jews to send their children to the missionary institution, its founders engaged Rena Al-Rawwas, a local Jewish woman, as a teacher. Those Jews who were aware of the need for a modern education sent their children to this school primarily to learn English, but they stipulated that their children would not participate in classes where religion was taught. The school also attracted Muslim children whose parents wished them to have a modern education. But the missionary success stemmed mainly from operation of the clinic. The sanitary situation in Gaza was terrible, and the number of those needing treatment and medicine was enormous.[17] Within the clinic walls, the patients of various religious persuasions were present during prayers and sermons about Jesus and the New Testament. Participants received free copies of the New Testament and polemic literature through which the missionaries sought to prove to Gaza Muslims that the Koran was not an original book of prophesy of Muhammad but rather a syncratic collection from the Torah, Prophets, and talmudic legends.[18]

Rabbi Nissim Ohana

Rabbi Nissim Ohana was born in Algeria in 1882. As a child he moved with his parents to Jerusalem, where he was educated and ordained to the rabbinate by Rabbis Yaakov Shaul Elyashar, Haim Elyashar, and Shmuel Salant. He also trained himself in ritual slaughter, as a *mohel* (ritual circumcision), a biblical scribe, and a cantor, which made it possible for him to serve as com-

---

[15] Elkayam, 102–3.

[16] See testimony of Eliezer Zeldes in "Collected Papers ...," 180.

[17] For data on the number of patients treated in the missionary clinic in 1910, see "Collected Papers ...," 180.

[18] N.B. Ohana, *How to Respond to a Non-Believer* (Jerusalem, 1959), author's foreword.

munity rabbi. He was the son-in-law of Rabbi Nahman Batito, who would later be appointed to the position of Hacham Bashi (Chief Rabbi) in Jerusalem.[19] He recounts that in 1905 he was sent by the Hacham Bashi Yaakov Shaul Elyashar to serve as rabbi of the Gaza community.[20]

Rabbi Ohana supported the Zionist project, especially rebirth of the Hebrew language and Hebrew education in Eretz Israel. Therefore, immediately upon his arrival, he undertook a reorganization of the Talmud Torah school, where, in addition to the sacred subjects, the children studied Hebrew grammar.[21] With the support of heads of the Gaza community, Rabbi Ohana sought to accelerate establishment of a Hebrew school for the children of Gaza, to provide an alternative to the Protestant educational institute. The rabbi pronounced the presence of Jewish children in the missionary institution as desecration of God, and he demanded that from the moment the Hebrew school opened members of the community stop sending their children to the Protestant school. Rabbi Ohana's pronouncement was not only a matter of principle: he also deemed it of little use to study English in a land where the government and its institutions conducted matters in Turkish. This call encountered various responses. Some obeyed it, but others, especially those with foreign citizenship, disagreed with the rabbi. With the support of Eliezer Ben Yehuda the school was opened, and it also received the support of the Ottoman regime. In this way, all the Jewish children were removed from the missionary institution and transferred to the Hebrew school, operated by Rabbi Ohana.[22]

Between Muslims and Christians

Relations between Muslims and the Catholic Christians had their ups and downs. There usually were anti-Christian outbursts during the month of Ramadan, because the Christians ignored the Muslim fast, continuing to eat and smoke in public. Muslims also saw the Christian processions in which wooden crosses were carried in public as another provocation, and they referred to the Christians as "Abu al-Khashaba," believers in the wooden

---

19 On Rabbi Batito, see M.D. Gaon, *Eastern Jews in Eretz-Israel, Past and Present*, *B* (Jerusalem, 1938), 141–42.

20 On Rabbi Elyashar, see M.D. Gaon, 62–68. Rabbi Ohana died on 24 Adar Bet, 1962. For extensive biographical material, see A.R. Ohana-Ronen, *Book of the Family – The Family of Rabbi Nissim Binyamin Ohana* (Jerusalem, 2001). There are various versions regarding the date of Rabbi Ohana's arrival in Gaza. I regard as reliable the testimony found in the author's foreword in *How to Respond ...*

21 Elkayam, 126. At the end of 1908 there was still no Hebrew school, synagogue, or Jewish cemetery in Gaza. See *Hazvi* 28.12.1908 2 [Hebrew]. On Jewish settlement and its institutions in Gaza on the eve of the First World War, see also Aref al-Aref, *History of Gaza* (Arabic; Jaffa, 1943), 42–43.

22 On the establishment of the school and its administration, see Elkayam, 152–57.

statue. Yet another factor that sharpened the differences between the Muslims and the Christians was the latter's demand that crusader churches that had been converted to mosques by the Muslims be restored as churches. On the other hand, Muslim relations with the Jews were very good, and there were more than a few instances of commercial partnership and personal friendship between Jews and Muslims.[23]

It would seem that the Protestant missionaries were directing most of their efforts toward the Muslim community. Rabbi Ohana reports:

> In Gaza the missionaries set up a clinic that accepted all patients, and, as mentioned, they arranged a place for prayer and sermons on Jesus and the New Testament for those gathered there and even distributed copies of the gospel on the coming of the Messiah...and in particular the book *Devar Emet* [A True Thing] which set out to prove that the Koran was made up of selections from the Torah, Prophets, and Talmudic legends and not, as is alleged, prophesies of the prophet Muhammad.[24]

The success of the Protestant missionaries in attracting Muslims, enabling them to preach to a wide Muslim public, moved the Mufti of Gaza, Sheikh 'Abd Allah al-'Alami, to initiate an opposing theological polemic. His idea was to confound the missionaries with their own weapons. He used the fact that matters dealt with in the Koran are mentioned in the Torah and the Talmud as irrefutable proof of the truth of the Koran. On the other hand, Sheikh al-'Alami argued, those verses in the New Testament that were taken from the Torah and were regarded by the Christians as proof that Jesus was the son of God were nothing of the kind inasmuch as they had been removed from their actual context. To prove this, Sheikh al-'Alami needed the help of the rabbi of the Gaza community, Rabbi Nissim Binyamin Ohana.[25]

Joint Studies

As recounted by members of the Ohana family, the reasons for the first meeting between Rabbi Nissim Ohana and the Mufti were dismal. The rabbi, who was accused of attacking a Muslim in an inn between Jaffa and Jerusalem, was tried before the Mufti. The Mufti allowed the rabbi to tell him his version behind closed doors, where the rabbi explained that the same Muslim had rudely attacked his wife so that the rabbi had no choice but to hit him. The exchange between the two spilled over to religious matters,

[23] Elkayam, 100–1. Aref al-Aref speaks highly of the way the Jews and Muslims in Gaza lived alongside one another in peace and harmony until Zionist demands on Eretz-Israel aroused Arab hostility. Jews abandoned Gaza during the 1929 riots and never returned. See Aref, 44.

[24] Ohana, the author's introduction in *How to Respond ....*

[25] For a biography of Sheikh al-'Alami see A. Manna, *A'lam Filastin fi Awakhir al-'Ahd al-'Uthmani 1800–1918* (Jerusalem, 1986), 285–86.

including the closeness of Judaism and Islam and their common hostility to Christianity. In the course of the discussion, the Mufti, who was preoccupied with the question of how to combat the Protestant missionaries who were proselytizing among members of his community, initiated the joint activity against the missionaries.[26] Rabbi Ohana reports:

> The Mufti of Gaza, Sheikh 'Abd Allah al-'Alami, wanted to prove to the missionaries that the Koran is ultimately authentic since its words are found in the Torah, Prophets, and the Talmud, which is not the case with the New Testament, and to cite the Jewish sources as evidence of the truth of Jesus as the Messiah is to use them inappropriately, and they are not at all a prophesy regarding Jesus.[27]

In essence the sheikh was breaking through an open door, because Rabbi Ohana, too, was looking for various ways to struggle against the missionary problem. The sheikh's request to the rabbi was that in order to prove that the Koran was based on the truth whereas the New Testament was fundamentally false, the two would systematically read through the New Testament together and the rabbi would show him how to refute the use the Christians had made of verses from the Torah to prove the authenticity of Jesus' mission. The rabbi and the sheikh met regularly twice each week in the rabbi's home, with the mufti diligently recording Rabbi Ohana's words. The sheikh then made use of the spirit and principles of the rabbi's words in his Friday sermons in the main mosque in Gaza. For his part, based upon these meetings, Rabbi Nissim wrote his book *How to Respond to a Non-Believer*, so that Jews entering an argument with the missionaries would also have the ability to respond effectively.[28]

Conclusion

Altogether, the missionaries in Gaza, at least in regard to the Jewish public, had virtually no success. True that a few children, especially girls, continued to go to their school, and Jewish patients turned to the Protestant clinic, which continued to operate, but the struggle against the mission continued. In 1911 the situation was described thus:

> Preparations for the Passover holiday included a new source of confrontation. The head doctor of the mission went away on his travels for several months, and his replacement was a Jewish missioner – a Jew who eats kosher food and keeps the Sabbath, and also visits the Jewish house of prayer and knows considerable Hebrew. Of Jews he demands only that they, like him, believe in the "Messiah." Out of boredom, the Gazans do not refrain from verbally sparring with him. And some had successfully transformed a defen-

---

26 See extensively Ohana-Ronen, 63–64.

27 Ohana, the author's introduction in *How to Respond ...* .

28 Ohana, the author's introduction in *How to Respond ...* .

> sive confrontation into one of physical scuffles.[29] ...lately, the Gazans had tired of hearing his nonsensical utterings, and had stopped talking to him. From that response the troublemaker concluded that he had won the battle with the Jews, and, filled with the hope that soon all the Jews, husbands with their wives and children, would come to shelter under the wings of the "Messiah," he left Gaza.[30]

The failure of this missionary was nothing exceptional. In other communities throughout the Middle East successes of the missionaries were meager compared with the extensive resources that had been invested in converting the Jews to Christianity. But the close cooperation at the beginning of the twentieth century between the Jewish rabbi and the Muslim mufti in Gaza in the ideological-theological-polemical realm against the Protestant missionaries was surely unique.

[29] Collected Papers..., 180.

[30] Collected Papers..., 186.

The Relations between Judaism and Islam as Reflected in the Variant Texts of the Manuscripts about Sol Hachuel of Morocco

JULIETTE HASSINE

The aim of this study is to examine the nature of the relationship between Judaism and Islam in Morocco in the period between 1840 and 1880. The nature of the relationship can be deduced from the various versions of the Arabo-Judaic manuscripts describing the martyrdom of Sol Hachuel,[1] who was beheaded after being convicted by a Muslim court in Fez in 1834. She was accused of the crime of *ridda* (apostasy).[2]

An examination of the minor variants between previously unknown manuscripts, within the framework of research about Jewish writing dealing with Sol Hachuel, is highly relevant to an examination of a topic such as the social and cultural relations between Jews and Muslims in nineteenth-century Morocco.[3]

---

1 As regards the surname, we have adopted the form used by the author, Eugenio Maria Romero, in his play "El Martirio de la Joven Hachuel," which was published in Gibraltar in 1837, three years after Sol's execution.

2 The Jewish community of Fez has retained its official documentation of the execution of Sol Hachuel, and it is to be found in "Yahas Fez," a collection of sources on the history of the Jews of Fez. In 1879 Avner Israel Ha-Tzarfati, the head of the Jewish religious court, sent the material to Isidore Loeb, one of the heads of the Alliance israélite universelle. The documents may be found in David Ovadiah's book: *Fez we-Khahameha* (Fez and Its Sages, 2 vols. Jerusalem: 1979). Sol is referred to in vol. 1, 157. I would point out that two poems about Sol were published in *Qol Ya'aqov* by Ya'aqov Berdugo, which appeared in London in 1844. However, the official community documents were sent to Isidore Loeb only in 1879.

3 This work is part of my wider research on Moroccan Jewry in the first half of the nineteenth century, which has occupied me for more than eight years. The research deals with the *Ridda* and with the relations between Jews and Muslims during that period, for which see my articles on Sol Hachuel: "Le-Itzuv Demuta shel Giborat Tarbut lefi Teqstim" (The Formulation of a Popular Heroine Reflected in Texts), in *Isha be-Mizrah, Isha mi-Mizrah* (Woman of the Orient, Woman from the Orient) edited by Tova Cohen and Shaul Regev (Ramat-Gan: Bar-Ilan University Press, 2005), 35–54, esp. the bibliography; "Diyyun be-Gilgula shel Genre ha-qassida be-Shira ha-Ivrit ha-Modernit ube-Ketivato shel Erez Biton" in *Sha'arei Lashon,* vol. 3 (Studies Presented to Moshe Bar-Asher, edited by A. Marmon, S.E. Fassber, Y. Breuer), 334 (in Hebrew); "Kle Hamas Mekhorotehem: 'al Kle Inui ve-Hereg be-Ketavim ha-Yehudiim 'al Sol Hachuel" in *Mesorot,* vol. 15; "Le Renouveau du Genre de la qassida dans la poésie d' Erez Bitton" in *Yod (Revue d'études hébraiques et juives)* no. 24 (Paris, 1987), 83–90; "The Martyrdom of Sol Hachuel: The Ridda in Morocco in 1834" in *Proceedings of the Conference*

This discussion, which draws from the study of hermeneutics and culture, is founded on linguistic issues in Judeo-Arabic in Morocco and on studies in poetics and folklore.

Our discussion is based upon an examination of the variants in the *qesā* composed by Yosef Elbaz, which was published by Heinrich Fleischer in 1864 in his article, "Jüdisch-Arabisches aus Magreb," which appeared in *Zeitschrift der Deutschen Morgenlandischen Gesellschaft*, 18, 329–40.

The *qesā*[4] on Sol Hachuel opens with the sentence: אביאד אלי חדר פי מות אצביייא "Happy is he who was a witness to the death of the girl." Fleischer reproduces the text of the *qesā* in Judeo-Arabic in Hebrew letters accompanied by a translation into German with a critical apparatus in the footnotes (pp. 329–33). This is followed by a linguistic discussion (pp. 333–40). In this version, the name of the author Yosef Elbaz appears at the end of the poem. This is not the case in the other manuscripts. A version with substantial differences was published in Algeria[5] in 1892 as part of a collection of liturgical *qesot* on the destruction of the Temple, which were to be read on the fast of the Ninth of Av (which commemorates the destruction of the Temple) and on Shabbat Hazon (which is the first of three sabbaths within the period of mourning that precede the fast). The collection was entitled: *Qesot ha-Arash* ("*Qesot* to be declaimed").[6]

This rare collection includes the dirge on Hannah and Her Seven Sons (pp. 1–9), a dirge on Job (pp. 10–19), and a dirge on the Ten Martyrs (pp. 19–29), as well as the dirge on Sol Hachuel (pp. 29–32). The dirges had been handed down orally and were eventually published by Shalom Bakash, who, on the title page, describes himself as a "printer and bookseller." One may also assume that he was in charge of editing and preparing the *qesot* for

---

Between Judaism and Islam" (held at Bar-Ilan University in December 2006; edited by Michael M. Laskier; in press).

4 Qesā (or *kissa*) means "story" in Arabic and may designate a literary genre that is based on the art of story-telling. In the case of the *qesot* about Sol Hachuel in Judeo-Arabic, we are discussing a popular production that is trying to achieve two aims: (1) the telling of a story, the describing of events and (2) the maintenance of a poetical framework that retains a uniform style with a division into verses and a regular meter together with rhymes. For additional material about this genre, see Haim Zafrani, "La kissa judéo-arabe et judéo-berbère" in *Encyclopaedia of Islam,* vol. V. (Leiden, 1986), 206–7; *Littératures dialectales et populaires juives en Occident musulman: l'écrit et l'oral* (Paris, 1982).

5 For biographical details about Rabbi Shalom Bakash from Algiers, see Avraham Hattal, "Sifre Rabbi Shalom Bakash – Ish Haskalah, Madpis, u-Mokher Sefarim be-Algier" in *Ale Sefer,* Issue 2, January 1967.

6 The phrase *Areshet Sefataim* (literally: "request of his lips") originates in Psalm 21:3 and means "prayers"; *Qesot ha-Arash* (where *ha-Arash* is an abbreviation for *ha-Areshet*) may be rendered as *Qesot Tefilla u-Tehina* ("*qesot* of prayers and entreaties").

publication. Apparently he had access to the various manuscripts and oral traditions, for his *Qesāt Hanna Solika di blād Fass* was collated from different versions, with variant readings, including Fleischer's version. We treat the Fleischer version as the original on which the other manuscripts were based, including the version of *Qesot ha-Arash.*

The poetic changes that resulted from different popular versions of the story of the righteous Sol reflect the social and political changes in Jewish life. This is especially true with reference to the variants connected with idioms and images that are relevant to the differences between Jews and Muslims within the context of their beliefs. Sol claims that her connection to her religion is extremely strong and one should not suspect that her faith is "jerry-built" *(din belkhyut maqbud)*, since her religion is the true religion as opposed to Islam, which is characterized in the other versions as the "corrupt religion" *(adin almafsud)*. We will examine the phenomenon of the variant readings and their influence on the *qesā* genre. We will use the example of the *din belkhyut maqbud* and consider its semiotic weight within the context of the Jewish experience in Morocco, including daily life. In conclusion, we will use it as a metonymy to explain the transformation in the genre in the later versions of Yosef Elbaz's *qesā.* These transformations are the consequence of the social and cultural changes in the relationship between Jews and Muslims in North West Africa that occurred prior to the beginning of the twentieth century.

I. *The Variants of the Text Relating to Religion and Faith*

a. *adin almafsud*

Our study of the variants in the manuscripts of the *qesot* about Sol Hachuel and their influence on the content, form, and characteristics of the *qesā* is based on both the studies of scholars of Judeo-Arabic and the studies of literary genre. In a previous article,[7] we have already discussed the changes and developments in the phrase: *bsif al-mahnud* in the *Qesā Abiad di hdar fi mut assbiya* in the Fleischer edition (see above). We endeavoured to prove that the variants were necessary to rectify a rhetorical mistake made by the author, Yosef Elbaz, a change that rebuffs the Arab Moslem substratum and strengthens the Jewish experience. However, there are additional variants of a linguistic nature that fulfill the same rôle in different ways, for example, the introduction of a Latin substratum into the Arabo-Jewish *qesā*. These changes are the subject of the present article. The two types of variants have a socio-cultural aspect that concentrates on the denunciation of

[7] See my article "Kle Hamas Mekhorotehem" (above n. 3), which discusses the significance of the phrase *bsif al-mahnud* as used in the *qesā* by Yosef Elbaz, where I examine both content and form. In this *qesā,* Sol begs her executioners to stop trying to persuade her to live as a Muslim and that they should immediately take *bsif al-mahnud* (a sharp sword of Indian steel) in order to execute her.

the judges who condemned Sol to death and also on the construction of a barrier between the Jews and Muslim society. In the Fleischer (1864) *qesā*, Sol says to the Muslims who try to tempt her:

מה תגווינ׳ בקנטר ולא במייא
מה תטלעסי מני הארא למקסוד

You cannot tempt me be the bribe small or large;
you are wasting your time.

Below we show the parallel verse with the variants as it appears in *Qesāt Hanna Solika di blād Fass* taken from the collection *Qesot ha-Arash:*

משיין עלייא מה תגיוני לא בקנטר ואל במייא
מה תנציוו מני האגאג יא האד אדין למפסוד

Go away! You cannot tempt me, be the bribe small or large;
you will not succeed in taking anything from me,
representatives of a corrupt religion.

To clarify our point, it is important to reproduce an additional variant from the *Qesā di Solikha a-tzdikā*, which is part of a collection of manuscript *qesot* and *piyyutim* in the possession of Bar-Ilan University, their no. 582.

קאלתלהום מא נג׳ווא לא בלקנאטר ולא בלמייאה
מה תעטלוסי בהאד לקונסיל למפסוד

She said to them, "I will not be tempted either by a small bribe
or by a large bribe. You will not succeed in this failed counsel."

This would seem to be an appropriate opportunity to discuss the use of the Latin term *qonsil* (*consilium*) in an Arabo-Jewish *qesā.* At issue are the conditions under which such a term can be used without compromising the linguistic and stylistic structure of the text of the *qesā*; the extent to which such a phenomenon is legitimate and acceptable; and whether the variants can be traced to a specific area in North Africa, in general, and in Morocco, in particular.

Moshe Ben Asher's research into the dialect of the *Tafilalet* reveals the presence of a Latin substratum in the dialect spoken by the Jews of the area.[8] He claims that the traces of Latin date to the period when the Romans were to be found in the area of the Berbers and survived solely in the Jewish dialect due to the tendency of the Jewish speakers to be far more conservative than their Muslim neighbors. Furthermore, the Latin substratum was preserved in Jewish dialects in the periphery to a greater extent than in the

8 Moshe Bar-Asher, "Darkhe haqtana be-Lahage ha-aravit ha-Yehudit be-Tafilalet" (The Diminutive in the Judeo-Arabic Dialects in Tafelalet) in *Mesorot u-Leshonot shel Yehude Zefon Africa* (Jerusalem, 1998), 133–46. For a discussion of the Latin substratum in the dialect, see pp. 141–44.

dialects spoken in the major cities. However, there is also a possibility that the phrase *leqonsil lemafsud* may be present in the Jewish dialects of central and northern Morocco, in cities such as Fez and Meknes and their hinterlands where Jews of Spanish origin were to be found. These exiles from Spain still retained Spanish words in their vocabulary. Rabbi Ya'akov ibn Tsur, for example, composed poetry in Spanish.[9] According to Jeffrey Heath, the exiles who reached Morocco from Toledo and its hinterland and had not lived under Muslim rule in Spain spoke Spanish.[10] This explains the existence of a Spanish substratum in the dialect of the congregations of Fez and Meknes. The effects of the Latin substratum are apparent in the basic phonology of their speech. The phenomenon has been examined by Joseph Chetrit[11] and Simon Levi.[12] The strong resemblance between the Latin substratum and the Spanish substratum (since Spanish belongs to the Romance language group) militates against the identification of the source of manuscript no. 582 from Bar-Ilan University, which includes the phrase *leqonsil lemafsud.* The compiler could have been either from Tafilalet (an area where the Latin substratum had been preserved) or from the Fez/Meknes area (where the Spanish substratum had been preserved). In northern Morocco, the Jews spoke Judeo-Arabic and Haketiya (a local dialect). In the light of the researches of David Bunis,[13] we can claim that the change from *had lmaqsud* to *leqonsil lmafsud,* using the Latin substratum, implies a statement by the Jews against the Muslims. In addition to the philological phenomenon, Bunis is of the opinion that the introduction of a such a textual change has sociological implications. In his opinion, it is an attempt to mark the cultural divide between Islam and Judaism. In this context, we point out that the word *lmafsud* also served the Jews in Morocco as a nickname for the prophet Muhammad, and this had been inspired by Maimonides' *Igeret ha-Shemad.*[14] The Jewish writing about Sol, both in Hebrew and in the Arabo-Jewish dialects, is strongly influenced by Maimonides' approach to Jewish-Islamic relations. In other *qesot* about Sol, the

9 See B. Bar-Tikva, *Piyyute Rabbi Ya'akov ibn Tsur* (Jerusalem, 1988), 69.

10 Jeffrey Heath, *Jewish and Muslim Dialects of Moroccan Arabic* (Routledge Curzon: University of Oxford, 2003), 10–13.

11 Joseph Chetrit, "Morpho-Phonetic Configurations in Judeo-Arabic of Meknes" in *Jewish Mother Communities: Studies on Fez and Meknes* (in Hebrew) (Haifa, 2006), 211–48.

12 Simon Levy, *Parlers arabes des Juifs de Maroc: particularités et emprunts* (Thèse d'état, Université de Paris VIII, 1990).

13 David Bunis, "Les langues juives du Moyen-Orient et d'Afrique du Nord" in *Le Monde sépharade* II, edité par Shmuel Trigano (Paris: Editions du Seuil, 2006), 537–64. Our subject is treated on pp. 546, 551 and see also the bibliography.

14 Maimonides. *Igeret Teman,* Halkin edition (New York, 1952), see note 16.

Arabs involved in the affair are called *lefsolim*,[15] i.e., "the illegitimate ones." This conforms with Maimonides' writings, who did not refer to the Muslim prophet by name, but called him, "the illegitimate one."[16] Similarly the term *leqonsil lmafsud* refers not only to the panel of judges who condemned Sol, but also is intended to equate the Islamic environment in its totality with negation, loss, and illegitimacy.

Indeed the *Qesāt Hanna Solika di blād Fass* from *Qesot ha-Arash* is transformed at two levels, in form and in content. The changes compromise the quality of the form of the *qesā*. This version retains neither the correct number of syllables in each row nor meter, cadence, or consonance (apart from the rhymes) and even rejects the grammatical matrix to be found in Elbaz's work as reproduced in the Fleischer edition. We have already demonstrated the far-reaching changes by citing two verses that reveal the addition of new content, such as the addition of the words *Mshyinn 'aliya* ("leave me") at the beginning of the first verse. In the case of the second verse, apart from the first word *ma* ("no") and the last word *sud*, there is no resemblance between the two versions. *The hada almaksud* ("this matter") is transformed into *ya had adin almafsud* ("this corrupt religion"). The original claim as to the unfairness of the trial has been transformed into a full-scale attack on Islam. This differs from the Fleischer edition. The changes in content demonstrate major revision by the compiler, reflecting his opinions about the serious incident in Fez, an opinion that expresses a scornful condemnation of Islam. Yosef Elbaz's approach was to restrict the terms of the quarrel between Sol and the Muslims to the boundaries and definitions appropriate to a Jew (*Dhimmi*) living under Muslim rule. Indeed his *qesā*, as it is reproduced in the Fleischer edition, does not argue against the restrictions applicable to Jews in Islamic countries. The *qesā* is extremely successful in instilling an identification with Sol and admiration for her desire to die as a martyr–but without any denigration of Islam. The Muslims portrayed in the poem are average people, not members of the legal and ruling classes. They endeavour to dissuade her from sacrificing her life. Their efforts include offers of presents, such as expensive clothes and precious stones, accompanied by what they believe to be persuasive arguments, such as a girl who is so young and beautiful is not allowed to perish since it would destroy her beauty. The Muslims speak reasonably since they want to preserve her life and also remain good neighbors with the Jews. In spite of the impossible situation in which Sol finds herself, we are not witnessing

---

15 For example, the *qesā* that is to be found in the manuscript at Bar-Ilan University (no. 142) opens with the sentence: "shim'u ya nash ma zra \ fimdinat Fes Lqahra" ("Hear gentlemen what happened in the despicable city Fez"). In line 16 we read: "Get up illegitimate witnesses and testify..." The poet is referring to Muslims, whom the Jews considered to be illegitimate. In general, the Jews of Morocco in each generation used this term (in Hebrew *pasul*) to refer to Muslims.

16 Maimonides, *Igeret Teman,* Halkin edition (New York, 1952), 28, 52.

the complete break-down of the relations between the two communities, Jewish and Muslim. The texture or the "strings" (to use the local idiom) of relationships between them, which is the product of hundreds of years of cohabitation, may include occasions when the strings are loose, i.e., a failure of communication. However, in the *qesā,* as it appears in Fleischer's edition, we do not encounter a situation in which the strings are cut and there is danger to the *Dhimmis* (Jews) in a Muslim country. In spite of the seriousness of the righteous Sol's case, the *qesā* does not try to make the matter more serious. The author prefers to preserve the delicate texture of life side by side without losing sight of the problems that had arisen (the loosening of the strings). The approach in the *Qesāt ha-Arash* is completely different.

b. *Din belkhyut maqbud* versus *Din bel'eqād ma'equd*

Sol responds to the Muslims who are trying to dissuade her, asserting that their faith must, indeed, be corrupt if they think that they can influence a Jewish girl with a materialistic approach; her attachment to her faith is not that weak (verse 23, lines 43–45)

קאלתהום יכפא ומא תנסדו עלייא
ואס אנא ענדי דין בלכיוט מקבוד

She said, "Enough! And even if you will pressure me,
do you think that my attachment to my religion is tied with string?"

In the Arabic, the poet uses the literary metaphor "tied with string," i.e. weakly attached, which is appropriate to the context. In the previous verse Sol had been offered expensive garments. The text informs the reader of the materialistic culture in Morocco in the first half of the nineteenth century, when there were two types of garments: one type attached lapels loosely with string, the other stronger, using loops and buttons. For Sol, the plan to seduce her with fine garments and make her agree to convert to Islam seems stupid and completely divorced from reality. The rhetorical question "Is my attachment to my religion with string?" shows that her faith is strongly rooted. The meaning of the figurative sentence and its relationship with the clothing industry in Morocco was not clear to Fleischer. He explained it as "religiosity fastened with strings" (durch fäden festgehaltene religiosität)[17] and added a further explanation in French: "une affaire bâclée" (a sloppy matter), i.e., the failure to devote enough attention.

The text uses *Din belkhyut maqbud* and not *Din belkhyut ma'equd,* faith that is attached with string. At this stage, we would like to comment on the source of the idiom in order to reveal the connection between the simile and its source. In Morocco, the hems of the coats and robes of both men and

17 See Heinrich Fleischer, "Judisch Arabisches aus Magreb" in *Zeitschrift der Deutschen Morgenlandischen Gesellschafts,* 1864, 332, note 5.

women were attached by *'aqda,* a button that was bound to one side of the garment opposite a loop on the other side. The button was made using silk embroidery thread. It should be noted that the trade in these buttons made of different colored silk in Meknes was another way of creating contacts between Jews and Muslims.[18] The manufacturers of the buttons (*l'eqād*) were mostly Jewish women. Muslims who worked in the textile industry were to be found in the streets of the Jewish quarter and were often invited into the houses in order to buy buttons from a Jewess. Many times, after completion of their work, the Jewesses went to the shops of the Muslims to sell their wares. One must remember that a Muslim who was faithful to his religion and to social custom would not enter a Muslim woman's house even for business reasons. It was, however, permissible to visit a Jewess. Thus this item was able to function as a motive for the formation of relationships between Muslims and Jews in Morocco, leading to the weakening of the barriers between them. Co-existence was facilitated by the fact that the Jewish house was not off-limits to the Muslim. However, the entry of Muslims into Jewish households had its dangers and sometimes even led to tragedy for Jewish families. The visits sometimes led to a romantic relationship between the Muslim guest and the Jewish daughter of the house that resulted in her leaving her home and moving into his house, an irrevocable action that eventually led to her conversion. If a Jewish woman accepted her Muslim suitor and left her house in order to hide with her Muslim bridegroom's family until her wedding, there was no way back. Regret and a desire to return to her parents' house were futile.

At this stage it is appropriate to demonstrate the nature of the *l'eqād,* in the tying up of the garment's hem. The process began by attaching a cloth marble to the end of a small, sharp, iron pole that was placed next to the chest in order to wrap a small marble in silk thread of the color that had been chosen until it was the size of a small button. The wrapping was done by placing the threads one within the other and crossing them until the marble was covered by a web of silk thread. At the end of the process they would detach the button from the rod leaving a small hole at the bottom of the button to use for sewing the button onto the garment. They would close the garment at the hem by threading the button through a loop on the opposite hem. Then the hem of garment was closed securely by a button and not attached with string. Sol, when talking to her tempters, indeed claims that her faith is secure. Her faith is securely bound like a button threaded through a loop (*Din bel'eqād ma'equd*) and not attached with strings (*Din*

---

[18] With regard to the buttons called, *'eqād*, I lived in the Jewish quarter in Meknes until 1962 and witnessed the Jewesses manufacturing the buttons and selling them. And I am familiar with the process of preparing the *akad* as described in this article, having collected considerable information about the way of life of Moroccan Jewry in Meknes and other towns.

belkhyut maqbud). The *qesā is* based on the difference and the modulation between two types of attachment using the literary metaphor from material culture in order to explain the types of attachment to religion and the difference between Sol, the Jewess, and the Muslims, her tempters.

However in Yosef Elbaz's *qesā* as it appears in the Fleischer edition there is no wish to make any statement that would undermine the current web of attachments. One should emphasize that the picture of the relationship between Jew and Muslim does not merely carry a semiotic charge. The semiotic charge within the text has implications for the genre of the *qesā* as a form of popular literature. The popular poem was preserved throughout centuries through a metric structure, using recurrent sounds and rhythms and themes repeated throughout the poem. The use of repetition, which is central to the popular verse, contributes to the preservation of the form and enables it to include variant forms without destroying the original. Popular narrative verse, such as this *qesā* written by Yosef Elbaz, has strict laws regarding the plot and the content and form, so essential to the poem. The content and form of the popular *qesā* are not "tied together with strings" but are "buttoned together" (*ma'equdin*) in order to form a strong system that cannot easily be dismantled. For us, the two figures of attachment act as a metonymy representing rootlessness vis-à-vis rootedness and we will discuss the grasp of reality and the popular existence of the *qesā* in the Fleischer version as opposed to the version to be found in *Qesot ha-Arash.*

II. *The Changes in the Genre of the Popular Qesā, and in the Relationship between Jews and Muslims*

In most cases, the variant readings that are used to fill in gaps of knowledge take into account the form and content of the original and try to adjust themselves to the existing framework. One might say that the laws of preservation of popular poetry are inherent in its forms, which embody the aim to preserve the existing framework and from within the framework the verse breaks out like a well from within the earth. As part of a reality from which it draws its sustenance, the popular verse is not interested in the instigation of revolutions. It wishes to remain connected with the framework as it would seem from our explanation of the figure *din belkhyut maqbud* contrasted with *din bel'eqād ma'equd.* This form of preservation is most noticeable in Elbaz's *qesā* in the Fleischer edition in the way in which he portrays the Muslim community. We are discussing Muslims whose authority and status are not defined and who agree to listen to Sol and hear all her claims–not the supreme judicial council of Fez (*majlis al-Ulama*). This is not the case in the variant that appears in *Qesāt Hanna Solika di blād Fass,* which describes both the religion and its judicial system as *adin almafsud* ("the corrupt religion"). Within this popular poem, we find a vituperative attack on the Islamic establishment. It would seem that *Qesāt Hanna Solika* had collected many variants, including those that undermined the legitimacy of the governmental and social structure in Morocco, as well as those that governed the Judeo-Arabic *qesā* in Morocco.

The vituperative attack on the council of the Ulamas of Fez in *Qesāt Hanna Solika* as it appears in the collection *Qesot ha-Arash,* which was first published in Algeria in 1892, informs us of the Jewish condition in Algeria at that time. It would seem that an effort had been made to adapt the *qesā* to the aims of the collection, i.e., recitation on the Ninth of Av and on Shabbat Hazon in the synagogue before women who did not know how to read or write in Hebrew. Yosef Elbaz's poem (in the Fleischer version) was adopted by the Algiers congregation and the historical, social and cultural distance facilitated the breakthrough from within the boundaries of popular writing into the liturgy.

As we have mentioned, the collection begins with the story of Hannah and Her Seven Sons and concludes with *Qesāt Hanna Solika di blād Fass.* In between, occur *qinot* over the destruction of the Temple that are read on the Ninth of Av throughout the diaspora, such as, for example, the *qina* for Job and that dealing with the Ten Martyrs. Thus Sol's *qesā* formed part of a collection that was based on a cultural memory that had survived hundreds of years, beginning with the story of Hannah and Her Seven Sons, whose historicity is questionable, and concludes with a story that is historically accurate and had occurred recently in a distant community. (At that time Algerian Jewry saw Fez as a distant city). Both the beginning and the conclusion are concerned with women who faced martyrdom. The second woman, Sol, was granted the name Hanna, that of the first martyr, as an additional name. The story of an historical figure whose biography was recounted orally from 1834 until the end of the nineteenth century was now to be published in a book to be used in the synagogue. Once published, the many variants in the *qesā* about Sol, as it appears in *Qesot ha-Arash,* seemed a social statement attacking the Moroccan authorities for their treatment of the Jews. Twenty years had elapsed since the Algerian Jews who had received French citizenship under the Crémieux Law and had lived under French rule ceased to be afraid of the Muslim environment. They were, therefore, enraged by the situation of Moroccan Jews, who were still *dhimmis*[19] as reflected in the story of Sol. We should mention that Tetua-

[19] The Moroccan Jews were defined as *dhimmis* or a "protected minority" by the Muslim authorities. The practice was common in the case of non-Muslims and included both Jews and Christians, who were described as the "People of the Book." They were allowed to live under Muslim rule as long as they accepted certain limitations embodied in the "Pact of Omar," which was named for their originator, Omar b. abd-El-Aziz, known as Omar II and were compiled in 717–720 C.E. (Muslim date, A.H. 78). These conditions were designed to ensure the supremacy of Islam over the other religions. One of the clauses relevant to our discussion is the prohibition against hindering anyone interested in converting to Islam. The *dhimmis* (including Jews) who obeyed these rules were guaranteed protection of their life and possessions and the freedom

nian Jews, who had escaped from the war between Spain and Morocco in 1860, had settled in Algeria and Oran. These Jews, who nurtured the remembrance of Sol, arranged for the performance[20] of the story by Romero[21] and the play by Calle,[22] Spanish artists who knew how to glorify the heroism of the "Jewish girl" and we may assume that the variants were intended to strengthen that tradition. In order to adapt the *qesā* about Sol to the spirit of the collection, the compiler added a long extract on the destruction of Jerusalem. The Fleischer version ends with Sol's reading of the *Shema'*. However, in the *ha-Arash* collection it was not sufficient to mention the destruction of the temple and a prayer for its restoration, as we find in other versions. Rather, here 14 verses are devoted to the subject. To Fleischer's version, which included 25 verses of two rows with ten syllables in each row, was added one verse together with 14 verses of two rows devoted to a dirge mourning the destruction of Jerusalem. Its final part differs considerably from the section that tells the story of the martyr, the change being the use of a higher lexical register. The reader is very much aware of the transition from the register of the first part to that of the second, as the change affects the rhythm and the assonance that are heavier than the free flow of Elbaz's original. In the *Qesot ha-Arash* version, the heaviness of the rhythm and the assonance is felt also in the narrative part, in which the rows are lengthened to more than ten syllables by the addition of idioms, etc. The part devoted to the destruction of Jerusalem demonstrates the scholarship of the compiler with regard to the geography of Eretz Israel, but disturbs the stylistic unity that is essential to the *qesā* genre. The expert in semiotics, Umberto Eco, calls the phenomenon: "saut des registres,"[23] i.e., changes in the semantic register. In his opinion, this is not necessarily dictated by a conscious decision on the part of the writer; the

---

to organize their religious and social life. The aim of the "Pact of Omar" was to separate Islam from other communities. This segregation has deepened over time, so that by the beginning of the nineteenth century there was very little communication between the Jewish community and the Muslim authorities, a situation that had been exacerbated by persecution. Jews could neither read not write Classical Arabic, since as *dhimmis* they were not allowed to study the Qur'ān. This explains the Jewish ignorance of complex legal matters such as the *Ridda,* under whose provisions Sol was sentenced to death. See Antoine Fattal, *Le Statut légal des non-musulmans en pays d'Islam* (Beirut, 1958), 61–63 and André Chouraqui, *La Condition juridique de l'Israélite marocain* (Paris, 1950), 21–25, 47–55.

20 With regard to the Sol heritage in Algeria, see Isidor Loeb, "Une martyre juive au Maroc" in *Archives israélites* 40 (1879), 343–44; vol. 41, 181–82, 187–88, 196–97, 207, 214

21 See note 1.

22 Antonio Calle, *El martiro de la joven Hachuel, o la heroina hebrea* (Seville, 1852).

23 Umberto Eco, *De la littérature* (Paris: Grasset, 2002), 402–3.

changes in register are also caused by the places in which the events occurred, which were not uniform from a cultural point of view. In the case of the *Qesāt Hanna Solika di blād Fass*, we witness the appropriation of a story that took place in Tangier and Fez, by the Algerian community, who made major changes in the content and form of the original version. The appropriation of the story occurred within the framework of changes in the status of the Jews in Algeria. At the end of the nineteenth century, the Jews in Algeria felt themselves separated from the Muslim population that had not been awarded French citizenship. The changes in their status improved their situation and their fear of Muslim neighbors was diminished. Using Eco's approach, we can say that the variants introduced into the version that appeared in *Qesot ha-Arash* represent a vituperative statement about the situation of the Jews in Morocco. In this version, we hear two different voices from a cultural point of view: the voice of the Algerian Jews, who were already partially emancipated, and the voice of the Moroccan Jews, who still suffered under the yoke of Muslim rule. The changes in register with regard to style may be attributed to a lack of cultural uniformity between the voices to be heard within the text. This phenomenon that is expressed through the changes in the text has repercussions for the conventions of the popular *qesā*. The additional second part distorts this version of *Qesāt Hanna Solika di blād Fass.* The lack of uniformity in style prevents retention of the *qesā*, its memorization by women who can neither read nor write and by men who perform and narrate oral poetry. The oral *qesā,* like other oral poetry, relies on uniformity of style at every level–verse, meter, division into verses–and recurring structures, phenomena that facilitate memorization. With regard to changes in genre, we would like to point out that in the Fleischer edition, at the end of the *qesā* are the name of the author (Yosef Elbaz), the name of the heroine, the name of her parents, and their city of origin. These are the only details written in Hebrew and not in Judeo-Arabic–the text itself is written in Judeo-Arabic:

[24]סוליקא בת שלמן חתויל מתושבי עיר טאנזיא בת שמחה

Solika the daughter of Shalman Hatwil of the city of Tangier, the daughter of Simha

In his book, Romero claims that Sol's father's name was Hayyim, which seems to be reliable since Romero spent some time in Tangier after the execution in order to record her story. His book was published in 1837 in Gibraltar, where the father was employed at the time of the case. The inscription at the end of the *qesā* does not appear in any of the other versions, including *Qesāt Hanna Solika di blād Fass*. The list of names had been completely forgotten, which included that of the author, who does

[24] Fleischer, *op. cit.*, 331.

not leave us an acrostic in the original version. This phenomenon of "forgetfulness" contributes to the strengthening of the tendency to turn the story into folklore and to the acceptance of the *qesā* by Elbaz as a popular work among many congregations in Morocco throughout the generations. This tendency to forget names is in accordance with the theories of Hippolyte Delahaye[25] on hagiographic writings. In his opinion, the disappearance of the names of saints and of their fathers is essential to hagiographic writing; the saint becomes more removed from daily life in order to turn him into a generalized legendary figure. The stripping of the *qesā* of the relevant names that appeared in the original version contributed to its development as a work of folklore to be sung by the Moroccan women, women who did not know how to read and write.[26] This is not the case for the version in *Qesot ha-Arash*, which includes elements of "de-folklorizing," even though the names, with the exception of the city of Fez, do not appear. However, the compiler did not know that Sol was born in Tangier though executed in Fez.

All the changes that we have discussed, both in content and in form, transform *Qesāt Hanna Solika di blād Fass,* which is no longer a popular work but rather a literary work one whose intentions was to engender change. If we adopt the theories of Jacobson and Bogatyrev regarding the differences between the popular act and the artistic act,[27] we can say that the transmitter and the compiler who wrote the *qesā* as it appears in *Qesot ha-Arash* betrayed their duty as preservers of popular writing and even assumed the rôle of author. This drastic change from preserver to adapter, in the opinion of Jacobson and Bogatyrev, suggests a lack of coordination between the compiler and publisher, on the one hand, and the society that created the text, on the other. The compiler of *Qesot ha-Arash* was almost certainly an inhabitant of Algeria and far removed from the cultural, social, and linguistic environment in which the *qesā* as it appears in the Fleischer edition was brought into being. The compiler's distance from the source of this *qesā* enabled him to intervene and to remodel the different versions

---

25 Delahaye, *Hippolyte. Les légendes hagiographiques* (Brussels, 1927), 196–97.

26 See André Elbaz, *Folktales of the Canadian Sephardim* (Toronto, 1982), 156–57 for his English translation of Yosef Elbaz's *qesā* from the Fleischer edition. There is a recording in Judeo-Arabic that was made in the 1970s by Mazal-Tov Amar née Hassine, who, though over eighty years old, sings the entire *qesā* from memory. Mazal-Tov is my great-aunt, a descendant of the *paytan* Rabbi David Hassine. She is well versed in Moroccan Jewry's popular heritage though unable to read or write and lives in Montreal, Canada.

27 Roman Jacobson and Petr Bogatyrev, "On the Boundaries between Studies of Folklore and Literature" in *Readings in Russian Poetics,* edited by L. Matjeka and K. Pomorska (Cambridge, M.I.T., 1971), 91–93. In this connection, see also Jacobson's article on Bogatyrev, "Petr Bogatyrev, Specialist of Transfiguration" in *Semiotics, Linguistics and Poetics* [Hebrew] (Tel-Aviv: Hakibbutz Hameuchad Press, 1986), 304–13.

then available. In his intervention he did not feel it necessary to take account of the social situation in which Yosef Elbaz's *qesā* was created, a *qesā* that was careful not to cause tension between the Jewish Dhimmis and the local Muslim authorities. The compiler did not feel the need to adopt the self-censorship that permeated the popular version. This is the appropriate place to cite Jacobson and Bogatyrev.

> The orientation of the creative personality in literary as compared with folklore life are different. A lack of correspondence between the demands of the social milieu and a literary work may be the result of the author's blunder, or it may be the premeditated intention of an author who has in mind a transformation of the demands of the milieu, that is, the literary reeducation of the environment. In the realm of folklore, the unconditional rule of preliminary censorship, condemning any conflict of a work to fruitlessness if censored, results in the formation of a special class of participants in poetic art; it imposes on the creative personality a prohibition against any attempt to overcome censorship.[28]

According to the theories of Jacobson and Bogatyrev, the existence of the popular work is dependent upon internal censorship. It develops into a literary work when the censorship is weakened or removed. If we accept this approach, the version in *Qesot ha-Arash* may be regarded as estranged from its origins and not as "bound to them by buttons (*ma'equda*)." The strong connection with the popular and communal roots, with all their complexity, allowed the Fleischer *qesā* to serve as the defender of the popular experience and oral tradition, a phenomenon that is attested to by the fact that up until the last generation several of the older women from Morocco who could neither read nor write remembered the *qesā* word for word and could sing it from the beginning through to the end. This was not the case for the version in *Qesot ha-Arash,* which was not accepted as a popular work among the Algerian Jews owing to the changes in style, which in turn led to a change in its purpose. The *qesā* from the Fleischer edition owed its strength to its preservative purpose, whereas the *qesā* from *Qesot ha-Arash* was intended to serve as an agent of change and to fight the sort of reality that led to Sol's martyrdom. The fact that it was included in a collection of *qinot* for the ninth of Av and Shabbat Hazon, to be read in the synagogue, transformed it into a literary work that exists independently of the person who reads it, unlike the popular work that is dependent upon its oral performer. The only way for a popular work to be accepted is the transfer from oral performer to oral performer. After the death of the performers, the traditions cannot exist for long. Thus Elbaz's *qesā* and its traditional tune, which had been preserved orally until the 1970s and was sung from its beginning to its end by the old women of Meknes, Fez, and Sefrou, was forgotten. The women emigrated from Morocco to North America with Sol

28 *Id.* 92.

treasured in their memories. We mention that the academic interest in the manuscripts and their variants has no relevance to the question of the survival of the popular *qesot* on Sol. In this context, we note that in 1979 the poet Erez Biton published a poem entitled "Qasidat Solika,"[29] which is included in a collection of his work, *Sefer ha-N'an'a.* In 2005, a play in three acts entitled *Solika* was published. Both works included various material from the popular heritage, but the absorption of popular material into the works of Erez Biton does not transform them into a popular work. In both the poem and the play, popular material is treated using the methods that are appropriate to modern verse. We are referring to literary productions with a social and cultural message, including criticism of Israeli society, and we summarize by saying that the assumptions of Jacobson and Bogatyrev with regard to variant texts, genres, and their connection to the preservation or change of society are validated by the changes in the heritage of the Sol Ha-Tsadiqa.

In this discussion, we attempted to prove the strong connection between historical situations and poetic situations. The latter are expressed through changes in both content and style, including changes in genre. The relationship between Jews and Muslims in Tangier and Fez, the capital at the time when Sol was executed, and their development are reflected in the variants of the *qesā* in manuscript form, which were transmitted orally for decades.

---

29 The changes in the genre of the classical *Qasida* in the poem *Qasidat Solika* by Erez Biton are examined in my "Diyyun be-Gilgula" and "The Martyrdom of Sol Hachuel" (see note 3 above).

Jews and Muslims in France in Light of France's Middle Eastern Policy 2000–2006

TSILLA HERSHCO

Since the outbreak of the Second "Intifada" at the end of September 2000, there has been a substantial increase in the acts of aggression perpetrated by young French Muslims of North African origin against members of the Jewish community and Jewish institutions. At the core of this essay is an examination and an analysis of three major dimensions of this complex and painful issue: the social, economic, and political factors within France; the rise of extreme Islamism in the global arena; and France's Middle Eastern policy.

It will be argued that France's Middle East policy, especially with regards to the Israeli-Palestinian conflict during the second Intifada and during other crises such as the war in Iraq in March 2003 and the Second Lebanon War in summer 2006, played a counter-productive role and reduced the effectiveness of multiple French measures intended to eliminate anti-Semitic acts of violence within France.

The Importance of the Issue

Before approaching the core of the subject, it would be worthwhile to briefly emphasize the reasons for which the issue discussed in this essay deserves special academic examination.

Firstly, most of the anti-Semitic acts of aggression in France are carried out by members of France's significant Muslim population, estimated between four to ten million, which is the greatest in Europe.[1]

Secondly, the French Jewish community, being the third-largest Jewish community in the world (about 600,000),[2] is subject to high incidence of

---

1 The French demographer Michele Tribalat (l'INED, Institut national d'études démographiques, National Institute of Demographic Studies) claims that these numbers are exaggerated and stipulates her assessment that there are 3.700.000 Muslims in France. See: *L'express*, 4.12.2003; Jonathan Laurence and Justin Vaisse, *Integrating Islam, Political and Religious Challenges in Contemporary France* (Washington, D.C.: Brookings Institution Press, 2006), 232. Hence: *Integrating Islam*. In 2004 and 2005 Arabs and Muslims in France committed respectively 34 and 41 percent of the anti-Semitic acts of violence, as compared to 7 and 10 percent for the extreme right, while 59 and 48 percent were either not attributed or were attributed to individuals without ties to either group (in 20 percent of cases).

2 There are other estimates. See, for example, Jean-Yves Camus, "The French Left and Political Islam: Secularism versus the Temptation of an Alliance," http://www.

anti-Semitic attacks since the outbreak of the second Intifada in September 2000.[3]

In addition, France holds a mixed historical image of its attitudes toward the Jews. On the one hand, France enjoys the moral image as the defender of human rights and the first country to grant civil rights to the Jews. Consequently, France manifests an extreme sensibility to cherish and preserve this image and is anxious that it should not be tarnished by the anti-Semitic acts of aggression. On the other hand, French history includes shameful anti-Semitic chapters, such as the Vichy regime in World War II. More than sixty years after the end of World War II, the memory of culpability and responsibility for the murder of about 76,000 Jews during the Holocaust still haunts the French public discourse. Subsequently, the French manifest almost obsessive attitudes toward the Shoah, especially in connection with the current acts of anti-Semitism in the country. Additionally, French statesmen in their public declarations often emphasize the importance of absorbing the lessons of the Holocaust so as to prevent the recurrence of similar crimes.[4]

France's special model of separation of state and religion (Laïcite), as well as its distinctive concept of integrating immigration, adds a unique perspective to the problem. It explains the initial French refusal to accept neither ethno-national nor ethno-religious divisions and tensions, identifying them with the pejorative term for tribal and communal loyalty (*communautarism*). Moreover, this model occasionally entails the normative and legislative taboo on registration of French citizens according to ethno-religious or ethno-national criteria,[5] thus reducing the prospects of obtaining authen-

---

tau.ac.il/Anti-Semitism/asw2005/camus.html#_ednref3. Camus speaks of 575,000 Jews in France and an estimated 3.7 to 6 million Muslims (about 10 percent of the French total population), with growing political power, including that of radical Islam.

3 See the annual country reports of the Stephan Roth Institute for the Study of Anti-Semitism and Racism in Tel Aviv University. http://www.tau.ac.il/Anti-Semitism/CR.htm.

4 See, for example, the Elysee internet site, hence: Elysee, President Jacques Chirac, 16.7.1995. www.elysee.fr/elysee/elysee.fr/francais/interventions/discours_et_declarations/; Prime Minister Jean-Pierre Raffarin, 27.1.2004, in a meeting of the French Inter-Ministerial Committee for the Struggle against Racism and Anti-Semitism. www.france.diplomatie.gouv.fr/actu/bulletin.asp?liste=20040128.html#Chapitre5. Tsilla Hershco, "The Jewish Resistance in France during World War II: The Gap between History and Memory," *Jewish Political Studies Review 19:1–2 (Spring 2007).* http://www.jcpa.org/JCPA/Templates/ShowPage.asp?DBID=1&TMID=111&LNGID=1&FID=388&PID=0&IID=1674; Henry Rousso, *Le Syndrome de Vichy: De 1944 à Nos Jours* (Paris: Le Seuil, 1990), 15–59. Rousso introduced the term "the Vichy syndrome" to describe the French obsession with the Holocaust.

5 CRIF's internet site, Conseil Représentatif des Organisations Juives de France, hence:

tic results in public opinion surveys on pertinent issues such as anti-Semitic aggressions.

Finally, intensive French diplomatic involvement in the Middle East has significant repercussions on the problem of anti-Semitic violence within France. It should be noted that the Middle East constitutes a pillar of high priority in French foreign policy. As a permanent member of the U.N. Security Council and as a prominent member of the European Union, France is highly involved in the international diplomatic scene and, in particular, in mediation in Middle East conflicts. Historical presence since the crusades, geographical proximity, colonial history and shared economic and strategic interests, as well as tight personal contacts between French leaders and Middle Eastern and Muslim leaders, led to the well-known French "Politique Arabe."[6] Additionally, France enjoys a relatively favorable image in Arab and Muslim countries because of its long-standing support for the Palestinian cause.

Furthermore, France attaches great importance to its role of "civilizing mission" *(la mission civilisatrice)* as a tool for promoting French influence in the region. Accordingly, France invests widely in its worldwide presence, spreading French culture, French language, and French values of human rights and democracy.

All the factors hereby mentioned confer special significance to the analysis of the complex and painful issue of Muslim violence against Jews in France in light of French Middle East Policy.

Social, Economic, and Political Factors within France

An enormous amount of academic publications and media coverage refer to the underlying social, economic, and political factors that triggered the violent acts by Muslims against French Jewry.[7] They point to the lack of integration of thousands of young Muslims into French society–including discrimination, unemployment, poor housing conditions, and inferior schooling and education–all of which resulted in growing feelings of bitterness, alienation, and frustration toward the French Republic.[8] The disruptive and

CRIF, 8.2.2007. http://www.crif.org/index.php?page=articles_display/detail&aid=8305&returnto=search&artyd=5.

6 See Eric Aeschimann and Chritophe Boltanski, *Chirac d'Arabie* (Paris: Grasset, 2006).

7 See, for example, Michel Wieviorka, *l'Antisémitism* (ParisL Ballard, Paris, 2004); Ezra Suleiman, "One and Divisible" November 2005, http://riotsfrance.ssrc.org/Suleiman; ibid., Olivier Roy, "The Nature of French Riots," November, 2005, http://riotsfrance.ssrc.org/Roy/.

8 Bénédicte Suzan and Jean-Marc Dreyfus, "Muslim and Jews in France: Communal Conflict in a Secular State" *The Brookings Institution*, March 2004. http://www.brookings.edu/fp/cusf/analysis/suzan20040229.pdf. The authors claim that the perception of a Jewish-Muslim communal conflict, as well as the dimensions of Muslims'

destructive reaction to these conditions was well evident during the riots in the suburbs of Paris in November 2005, when thousands of cars, public institutions, and property were set on fire followed by severe clashes with law enforcement units. In this context, the violence against the Jews was explained as resentment and outrage directed against the Jewish population, which is perceived as politically, economically, and socially well integrated into mainstream French society.[9]

Ignoring the Problem

Initially, following the outburst of anti-Semitic violence in September 2000, the French government did not seem to grasp, or preferred not to grasp, the magnitude of the problem, in spite of the frequent and numerous protests and warnings by Jewish community leaders. Shmuel Trigano interpreted French attitudes as stemming from an erroneous calculation that paying attention to the problem would only bring about its escalation, similar to adding fuel to a fire.[10] Robert Wistrich, in an address given in Vienna on June 19, 2003, to the Organization for Security and Cooperation in Europe (OSCE), asserted that anti-Semitism could not be fought where there was an "obstinate denial" that the phenomenon even existed. To illustrate his point he referred to French President Jacques Chirac's declaration according to which there was no anti-Semitism in France. Wistrich claimed that despite the tripling or quadrupling of the amount of acts of aggression perpetrated by Muslims against Jews in France since September 2000, despite the fact that synagogues and community centers were set on fire, and despite the fact that Jewish children and adults were attacked, the French authorities and media suppressed the magnitude of the alarming news. Wistrich further criticized the French authorities' attempt to parallel anti-Semitism and "Islamophobia," claiming that the Muslims attacked the Jews in France and not *vice versa*.[11]

---

lack of integration into French society, has been highly exaggerated, essentially by radical Muslim circles that wish to use the problem as a leverage to advance their influence among the Muslims.

9 Laurence and Vaisse, *Integrating Islam,* 232–33, 237.

10 Shmuel Trigano, "Les Juifs de France visés par l'Intifada?" *Observatoire du Monde Juif*, 1 (November 2001): 1–2; Raphaël Israéli, "Le conflit Moyen Oriental s'exporte vers les démocraties occidentales," *Observatoire du Monde Juif*, 1 (November 2001): 10–17.

11 Robert Wistrich, "Anti-Semitism in Europe Today," Address to the Organization for Security and Cooperation in Europe (OSCE), Vienna, 19.6.2003, http://sicsa.huji.ac.il; Robert Wistrich, "Waging war on Judeophobes Old and New," *Haaretz*, 1.8.2003. Robert S. Wistrich is head of the Vidal Sassoon International Center for the Study of anti-Semitism. As to the word "Islamophobia" (an irrational fear or prejudice toward Islam and Muslims), see: http://en.wikipedia.org/wiki/Islamophobia.

The French philosopher Alain Finkielkraut, one of France's leading intellectuals, proposes his interpretation of the perverted disregard of Muslims' aggression against Jews. He points an accusing finger at France's intellectual elite, which, driven by its culpability regarding "the devils of the past," namely the memory of the holocaust, perversely refrains from criticizing the Muslim perpetrators of aggression, fearing being regarded as racists. Furthermore, Finkielkraut claims that France's influential elite incorrectly perceives the Israeli-Palestinian conflict as a colonialist phenomenon, viewing Israel as a colonial and racist country.[12]

Fighting Anti-Semitic Violence

With the escalating anti-Semitic acts of violence, the French government gradually became aware of the strategic threat to law and order within the French Republic. In addition, there was a growing sense of embarrassment and concern for France's image in the world, especially in light of the severe criticism emanating from Jewish American Organizations, such as the American Jewish Committee (AJC).[13] Consequently, France changed its attitudes and gave impetus to the launching of its policy to prevent anti-Semitism with inter-ministerial cooperation as its focal point.

For instance, former President Jacques Chirac explicitly declared in November 2003 that anti-Semitic acts were perceived as acts against the French Republic and were in contradiction to its basic values and perceptions.[14] In addition, the governments of Jean-Pierre Raffarin (2002–2005) and Dominique de Villepin (2005–2007) advanced the educational instruction of the Holocaust,[15] decreed a law against the denial of the Holocaust,[16] promoted the imposition of more severe penalties and law enforcement

---

[12] Alain Finkielkraut, *Au Nom de l'Autre: Réflexions sur l'Antisémitisme Qui Vient*, (Paris: Editions Gallimard, 2003). See also Tsilla Hershco, "Are These Demons Old or New?" *Haaretz*, 16.6.2004. http://www.haaretz.com/hasen/pages/ShArt.jhtml?itemNo=437894&sw=france.

[13] See, for example, David A. Harris, "Anti-Semitism Virus Strikes in France," 4.12.2002. David A. Harris is executive director of the American Jewish Committee. http://www.ajc.org/site/apps/nl/content2.asp?c=ijITI2PHKoG&b=838493&ct=1152695.

[14] See: Elysee, Jacques Chirac, 17.11.2003. http://www.elysee.fr/elysee/elysee.fr/francais_archives/les_dossiers/lutte_contre_les_discriminations/2003/17-11-2003_extraits_des_propos_du_president_de_la_republique.21484.html.

[15] See, for example, the Internet site of French Foreign Ministry, hence: FFM, Michel Barnier, French foreign minister, 18.10 2004, Roglit, Israel. Roglit, near Beit Shemesh has a memorial site for the French Jews murdered in the Holocaust: www.diplomatie.gouv.fr/actu/bulletin.asp?liste=20041018.html#Chapitre7.

[16] A special legislation, the Gayssot Law, July 1990, prohibits Holocaust denial. http://www.legifrance.gouv.fr/affichTexte.do?cidTexte=JORFTEXT000000532990&dateTexte=. See also Valerie Igounet, *Histoire du Négationnisme en France* (Paris: Editions du Seuil, 2000).

against anti-Semitic assailants and implemented tightened security measures to protect the Jewish institutions. Another way of coping with the problem was to reinforce the 1905 republican law of "laïcité" (Laicism), meaning the absence of religious interference in government affairs, and *vice-versa*. A new law, passed in March 2004, banned the introduction of conspicuous religious symbols, such as the Jewish Magen David, Christian crosses, and Muslim head scarves in French public schools.[17]

Furthermore, in 2003 Nicolas Sarkozy, then the French Minister of Interior, initiated harsh measures to limit illegal immigration from North Africa.[18] In February 2004, Sarkozy expressed France's zero tolerance toward anti-Semitic aggressions: "The government shall not tolerate one single act of anti-Semitism on the French soil...All means will be used to find the culprits. One said that the means were not up to the task. This is not true any more. Today, the courts of justice show firmness."[19] Simultaneously, the French authorities promoted policies of positive discrimination designed to better integrate the Muslim population.[20]

French efforts to curb anti-Semitic violence bore fruit. And, indeed, at the annual dinner of CRIF in February of 2006, CRIF's president Roger Cukierman expressed his deep satisfaction at the reported sharp drop in the number of anti-Semitic acts. Cukierman nonetheless deplored the fact that the rate of anti-Semitic acts of violence still remained seven times higher than before September 2000.[21]

---

17 Elysee, Jacques Chirac, 17.12.2003. http://www.elysee.fr/rech/voir.php?SUJET=interdiction+des+signes+religieux+a+l%5C%27ecole&C5=&C1=C1&C2=C2&C3=C3. See also "Jonathan Laurence, Islam in France: A Contest between the Wind and the Sun," Brookings, November 2004. http://www.brookings.edu/articles/2004/11 france_laurence.aspx.

18 Maurice T. Maschino, *Le monde Diplomatique*, March, 2003. http://www.monde-diplomatique.fr/2003/03/MASCHINO/9967; See also: BBC News, "France to fingerprint tourist visa applicants," 30.4.2003. http://news.bbc.co.uk/1/hi/world/europe/2989637.stm.

19 CRIF, Sarkozy to CRIF delegation in Toulouse, 5.2.2004. http://www.crif.org/index.php?page=articles_display/detail&aid=2384&returnto=search/search&artyd=2.

20 Elysee, French President, Jacques Chirac, 14.7.2004. http://www.elysee.fr/cgi-bin/auracom/aurweb/search/file?aur_file=discours/2004/IT040714.html.

21 CRIF, Cukierman's speech at the annual CRIF dinner, 21.2.2006. http://www.crif.org/index.php?page=articles_display/detail&aid=6470&returnto=search/search&artyd=58; See also: The annual report of the Stephan Roth Institute for the Study of Anti-Semitism and Racism in Tel Aviv University, about the anti-Semitism rate in France in 2005: http://whttp://www.tau.ac.il/Anti-Semitism/asw2005/france.htmw. tau.ac.il/Anti-Semitism/asw2005/france.htm. According to this report the CRIF reported a total of 371 anti-Semitic incidents in 2006, compared to 300 in 2005, while the French Ministry of the Interior recorded 541 events compared to 506 in 2005.

The Murder of Ilan Halimi

In fact, one of the most shocking and traumatic acts of anti-Semitic aggression was committed in January/February 2006, when a gang of French Muslims kidnapped, tortured, and murdered 23-year-old Ilan Halimi.[22] The shocking murder of Ilan Halimi raised huge national protests and controversy over the extent of anti-Semitism in France, as well as the motivations of the brutal offenders, who for three weeks demanded ransom from the Halimi family while all the time torturing the young man to death.

CRIF's president, Cukierman, well expressed the atrociousness of the crime and the distressing image it reflected of French society:

> Two-thousand-year-old prejudices remain very strong (Jew=money=power) ....Some thirty people took part in this "operation," coming from different backgrounds, representing the social fabric of this new France. People of African, West Indian, North African, Portuguese and native French origin ...while a young man was being tortured for three long weeks, not one of these young people felt the need to do an act of civic duty and compassion by calling the police, even anonymously.[23]

Ruth Halimi painfully said that her son was murdered because he was a Jew. Indeed, the police found literature linking some suspects to Palestinian and fundamentalist Muslim causes. However, Nicolas Sarkozy, then Minister of Interior, warned against blaming the country's Muslims: "What we don't need now, in addition to this barbarity, is misunderstanding, intolerance and racism," minimizing the importance of the anti-Semitic aspect of the killing for fear of increasing tensions with Muslims.[24] The declaration attributed to Sarkozy, who is known for his determined struggle against anti-Semitic violence, demonstrates the dilemma of the French authorities, who sincerely wish to fight Muslim anti-Semitism in France but at the same time are anxious not to stigmatize the Muslim population and thus create further impediments to its integration. It goes without saying that this kind of ambiguous policy has potentially dire implications for French Jewry.

Whether the crime was motivated by criminal intent, plain racketeering of money, anti-Semitic stereotypes, Muslim religious radicalism, or by all these actors, it undoubtedly constituted a watershed in anti-Semitic violence in France and drew more focused attention to radical Islam in France.

---

22 See the annual reports of the Stephan Roth Institute for the Study of Anti-Semitism and Racism in Tel Aviv University. http://www.tau.ac.il/Anti-Semitism/asw2006/france.htm.

23 CRIF, Cukierman, anti-Zionism inevitably leads to anti-Semitism, 6.7.2006.

24 Arian Bernard and Craig S. Smith, "French Officials Now Say Killing of Jew Was in Part a Hate Crime," *New York Times*, 23.2.2006.

The Rise of Radical Islam

The rise in the global arena of extreme Islamism, which preaches a Jihad (Holy) war against the nonbelievers, is another dimension that explains anti-Semitic aggression in France, as well as the French difficulties in containing and eliminating them. It should be noted that due to the French law that separates state and religion, the current practice of the Muslim religion in France is largely funded by contributions from extremist Muslim elements and countries, such as Saudi Arabia, Pakistan, and Yemen. Thus, Muslims in France are often exposed to the preaching of extremist imams who incite hatred and even Jihad.[25]

Equally, Muslims in France, as elsewhere, are exposed to poisonous anti-Semitic incitement through multiple television channels and internet websites. French security authorities are fully aware of this menacing phenomenon, which eventually constituted a tangible security threat.[26] For instance, in 2004 French authorities reacted by banning the broadcasts of the Hezbollah TV network Al-Manar,[27] expelling radical imams from France,[28] and advancing laws for governmental financing to tighten the control of the practice of the Muslim religion.[29]

Meanwhile, French Jewish organizations have endorsed various initiatives of "rapprochement" between Jews and Muslims, essentially through Muslim representative organizations, such as the "Conseil Français du Culte Musulman" (French Council of the Muslim Faith), usually abbreviated to CFCM.[30] Apparently, these initiatives are mostly confined to the leadership level and do not really reach those who carry out the anti-Semitic attacks.

---

25 International Crisis group, *France and Its Muslims: Riots, Jihadism and Depoliticisation,* Europe Report no. 172, 9 March 2006, Brussels. http://www.crisisgroup.org/home/index.cfm?l=2&id=4014 See also: Laurence and Vaisse, *Integrating Islam*, 235–36. Anti-Semitism among practicing Muslims reaches 46 percent and declines with level of practicing.

26 Eric Pelletier, Jean-Marie Pontaut, Boris Thiolay, "Des étudiants sous surveillance," *L'Express*, 9.11.2006.

27 See, for example, CRIF, "Le Conseil d'Etat interdit Al Manar in France," 14.12.2004. http://www.crif.org/index.php?page=articles_display/detail&aid=3984&returnto=search/search&artyd=5; ibid., CRIF's President at the annual diner of CRIF, 17.2.2005. http://www.crif.orgindex.php?page=articles_displaydetail&aid=4296&returnto=search/search&artyd=2; See also: video, Pierre Lellouche–Fogiel debate about Al-Manar,29.5.2005.http://www.dailymotion.com/relevance/search/Pierre%2BLellouche%2Bfogiel/video/xkg97_fogiel-lellouche-sindignent-digneme_news.

28 *BBC News*," France to expel radical imams," 15.7.2005.

29 Denis Jeambar, "Sarkozy s'explique," *L'Express*, 1.11.2004; Nicolas Sarkozy, *La République, les religions, l'espérance*, Editions du Cerf, Paris, 2004; Claire Chartier, "L'Etat doit-il financer le culte musulman?" *L'Express*, 10.1.2005.

30 See, for example, CRIF, "Amitié Judéo-Musulmane de France: C'est reparti pour deux tours," 9.3.2006.

In this context, the report of an international crisis group, which deals with the issue of lack of integration of young Muslims in France, admits that France is worried about the prospects of radicalization of young Muslims resulting from exposure to radical preaching. The report recommends encouraging integration of these young people into existing political structures, since they do not identify with Muslim organizations, such as the Union of Islamic Organizations of France (UOIF), perceived as being co-opted by the government.[31] Yet, this recommendation might be impractical since the problems that cause the lack of economic and social integration of these young Muslims equally enhance their alienation from mainstream political life and intensify the prospects of radical Muslim influence.

Despite the enormous challenges and difficulties related to the repercussions that radical Islam has on anti-Semitic violence, optimistic assessments of eventual positive results are not to be dismissed, due to the French authorities' manifested determination to combat the influence of radical Islam within France.

France's Middle East Policy

While factors previously highlighted have been widely explored by academic research, the correlation between Muslim anti-Semitic violence in France and French Middle Eastern policy has not yet received the appropriate academic attention. Hence, the central part of this essay deals with France's Middle East policy as a factor in Jewish-Muslim relationship in France and focuses on French Foreign Ministry attitudes toward the Israeli-Palestinian conflict in the years 2000 to 2006. French attitudes on other significant Middle Eastern issues, such as the crises in Iraq and Lebanon, will be discussed briefly, as well as their ramifications on anti-Semitic aggression in France. It will be argued that France's Middle Eastern policy has often played a counterproductive role in its previously mentioned efforts to combat anti-Semitism in France.

France and the Israeli-Palestinian Conflict: Motivations and Considerations

The failure of the Oslo process, especially the failure of the Camp David meeting in July 2000 and the outbreak of the first acts of violence in September 2000, which marked the beginning of the second Intifada, led to tremendous disappointment and frustration among French leaders and diplomats. It should be noted that France has been struggling for more than twenty years to realize its vision of establishing a viable Palestinian state that lives peacefully alongside the state of Israel. Already in March 1982, former French President François Mitterrand, in his speech at the *Knesset*, called

31 See note 25.

Israel to recognize the Palestinians' right to a state of their own.[32] France occasionally expressed pride in its success in persuading the European Union, the United States, and even Israel to accept its vision of two states as the only solution to the Israeli-Palestinian conflict.[33]

France explained its attachment to the establishment of a Palestinian state as motivated by strategic and political considerations, as well as by moral ones.[34] France stressed that the Israeli-Palestinian conflict strategically endangered not only the stability of the region but also the stability of the entire world. Consequently, France demonstrated an immense sensitivity to what it regarded as the importation of the conflict to France. Additionally, France justified its striving for a Palestinian state in ideological and moral terms. France insisted that conflicts should be resolved through dialogue rather than by the unilateral use of military force. Accordingly, France stressed the central role of the United Nations in the settlement of conflicts and the importance of abiding by international law and agreements. Therefore, the French criticized Israel and repeatedly demanded the implementation of U.N. decisions 242 and 338, which, according to the French interpretation, called for Israeli withdrawal from all territories occupied in 1967. Thus, paradoxically, France fixed in advance the terms of the final agreement despite its claims that it should be done through dialogue.

Apart from the already cited rational considerations, France is also influenced by contradictory emotional motives in the formulating of her policy toward Israel and the Israeli-Palestinian conflict. On the one hand, French attitudes are characterized by nostalgic aspirations to renew its influence in the region. On the other hand, France is influenced by contradictory tendencies, as powerful as the first ones, of condemnation and repentance due to its colonial past and the projection of its historical experience in Algeria over the Israeli-Palestinian conflict. To these factors is added widespread French sympathy toward the Palestinians, who are considered to be the weaker side and the victims in the conflict.[35]

---

32 Eliezer Palmor, *François Mitterrand and the Israeli-Palestinian Conflict* (Jerusalem: The Leonard Davis Institute for International Relations, The Hebrew University of Jerusalem, 1999), 22–23 (in Hebrew).

33 See, for example, FFM, Vedrine, interviewed by "Temoignage Chretien," 4.1.2001.

34 Tsilla Hershco, "French-Israeli Relations in the Twenty-First Century" in: *Europe and the Middle East* (Ramat Gan: The Begin-Sadat Center for Strategic Studies, Bar-Ilan University, *BESA* Colloquia on Strategy and Diplomacy, no. 19, June 2006), 35–42. http://www.biu.ac.il/SOC/besa/coll19.pdf.

35 Ibid.; Tsilla Hershco, *French Policy regarding the Israeli-Palestinian Conflict during the Second Intifada: 2000–2005* (Mideast Security and Policy Studies, Begin-Sadat Center for Strategic Studies, Bar Ilan University, July 2006), 6–7 (in Hebrew). http://www.biu.ac.il/SOC/besa/MSPS68.pdf.

All the previously mentioned factors converged to create a distinctly one-sided pro-Palestinian attitude, which was manifest from the beginning of the second Intifada in September 2000.

France's One-sided Position

The French justified the Palestinians' riots, claiming that they stemmed from frustration that arose from the Israeli long occupation.[36] The French did not use their influence and popularity in the Palestinian Authority to exercise pressures on Arafat to stop the violence, even though they admitted that Israeli Prime Minister Ehud Barak offered the Palestinians the best peace package deal they had ever received.[37] In addition, Chirac advised Arafat to demand the establishment of an international committee for the investigation of "the violent Israeli reactions,"[38] thus either directly or indirectly encouraging him not to sign the cease-fire agreement at the crucial Paris conference on October 4–5, 2000. Furthermore, France automatically adopted the anti-Israeli Palestinian versions without previously checking their validity or accuracy. For instance, France formally adopted Palestinians' claims that Sharon's visit on the Temple Mount esplanade on September 28, 2000 was an intentional provocation motivated by internal political considerations, triggering the Second Intifada. Hubert Vedrine, France's foreign minister, reiterated his deep personal disappointment that numerous long-standing diplomatic efforts were destroyed as result of irrelevant considerations that caused tremendous damages.[39] France's irresponsible rapid adoption of the Palestinian version on the sensitive issue of the Temple Mount provoked further Muslim incitement against Israel and against the Jews in France and elsewhere. It is to be noted that after Sharon's election as Israel's prime minister on February 2001, Vedrine reneged on his accusations as to Sharon's intentional provocation, contending, nonetheless, that Sharon's visit was an erroneous decision.[40] Another example of biased French attitudes is evident in the French Ministry of Foreign Affairs' immediate adoption of false Palestinian claims about the alleged massacre in Jenin in April 2002 during the Israeli "Operation Defensive Shield," allegations that intensified anti-Semitic incitement in France and elsewhere.[41]

---

36 FFM, French Foreign Ministry spokesperson, 21.11.2000.

37 Ibid., Vedrine, interviewed by "RTL," 5.10.2000.

38 Ibid., Freddy Eitan, *La France, Israel et les Arabes: Le Double Jeu* (Paris: Picollec, Paris, 2005), 21–24.

39 FFM, Vedrine, interviewed by "France 2," 6.10.2000.

40 Ibid., Vedrine, interviewed by "RTL," 5.10.2000; ibid., Vedrine, interviewed by "France Inter," 7.2.2001.

41 Ibid., French Foreign Ministry spokesperson, 10.4.2002, 12.4.2002.

Additionally, the French vigorously criticized Israel for measures primarily intended to defend its own citizens from Palestinian suicide bombers, such as the erection of barriers, targeted killing of terrorists, military excursions into the Palestinian territories to arrest terrorists, and the security wall of separation. In its formal reactions to Israeli's military measures against the Palestinian terrorists, the Quai d'Orsay speaker expressed the French regret for the killing of Israeli innocent citizens, but at the same time demanded that the Israeli government refrain from military actions since it created a vicious "circle of violence." In these formal declarations, France created a dangerous analogy between the terrorists and those who were defending themselves against terror, consequently legitimizing further acts of aggressions on the part of the Palestinians.

Vedrine's criticism was that Israel's military reaction was counterproductive, asserting that it weakened Arafat as well as his security forces, consequently creating a vacuum that was exploited by radical Muslim organizations to increase their hold and influence in the Palestinian Authority.[42] Vedrine further criticized Israeli targeted killing of terrorists, as well as the casualties caused to Palestinian civilians as a result of Israeli military operations against terrorists, claiming that both represent a severe violation of international law.[43] In this context, it is worth noting that Vedrine's reply in March 2001 to a journalist who critically wondered why Israel should acquiesce in Palestinians' terrorist acts, which are intended to impose the Palestinians' political demands on Israel, a tactic in principle unacceptable to any other state. Vedrine, in his reply, compared Israeli's antiterrorist combat to a Sisyphean attempt to empty the ocean with a bottle, claiming that Israeli counter-attacks enlarged the vicious cycle of terror, while providing terrorists with justifications and motivation to continue their activities, thus increasing the number of adherents to terror organizations.[44] French condemnations of Israeli use of force against Palestinian terror continued as a constant formulated expression in French Foreign Ministry declarations in the following years, during the tenures of French Foreign Ministers, Dominique De Villepin (May 2002–March 2004), Michel Barnier (March 2004–June 2005), and Phillippe Douste Blazy (June 2005–May 2007), and continue up to present with Bernard Kouchner, now the head of the Quai d'Orsay, creating an immoral balance between the perpetrators of terror attacks on Israel and Israel's military measures to protect its citizens.

---

42 Ibid., Vedrine's declaration to the media, 3.6.2001; ibid., Vedrine, interviewed by "France Inter," 5.6.2001.

43 Ibid., Vedrine, interviewed by "RTL," 23.3.2001; ibid., French Foreign Ministry spokesperson, 6.4.2001; 17.4.2001.

44 Ibid., Vedrine, interviewed by the "BBC," 2.4.2002.

Besides the public condemnations of Israel, the French were active in the international arena, as well as within the European Union, in initiating anti-Israel decisions.[45] In doing so, they caused severe political damage to Israel's international position, undermined the legitimacy of Israel's attempts to combat Palestinian terror, and projected a message with a distinct double standard, implying that the Israeli struggle against Palestinian terror is not as legitimate as the struggle against Al Qaeda after the September 11, 2001, mega-terror attacks on the United States.[46] Shmuel Trigano maintains that this mind-set entails a refusal to acknowledge Jews' rights to political existence and their legitimate use of force.[47]

The French consistently supported Arafat, even when his implication in terrorist activities was proved beyond all doubt, as was the case of the capture by Israel of the Palestinian arms shipment aboard the "Karine A" in January 2002.[48] The French supported Yassir Arafat as the elected leader of the Palestinians, whom they saw as representing the legal aspirations of the Palestinians for an independent state. France's constant political and financial assistance to the Palestinian Authority granted France the incontestable image as the main defender of the Palestinian cause.[49] France could have probably exercised its influence upon Arafat and the Palestinian Authority to restrain the violence and the terror activities. Yet, France chose to disregard the fact that Arafat was a despotic leader who brought disaster upon his own people through his erroneous decisions, his support of terror, and his corrupt management of public funds and affairs.[50] Moreover, France ignored the anti-Semitic character of the Palestinian Authority. For instance, anti-Semitic incitement was propagated, *inter alia*, in Palestinian Authority

---

45 See, for example, ibid., French Foreign Ministry spokesperson, 23.4.2002, 2.5.2002, 14.5.2002; ibid., French Foreign Minister De Villepin and the minister in charge of European affairs, Reynaud Donnedieu de Varbes, 13.5.2002.

46 On the French distinction between the struggle against Al-Qaeda, on one hand, and against Palestinian terror, on the other, see, for example, ibid., Vedrine, the 56th UN General Assembly, 10.11.2001; ibid., Vedrine, interviewed by "France 2," 20.9.2001.

47 Manfred Gerstenfeld, an interview with Shmuel Trigano, "Europe's Distortion of the Meaning of the Shoah's Memory and Its Consequences for the Jews and Israel," *Post-Holocaust and Anti-Semitism*, 42, 1 March, 2006, www.jcpa.org/phas/phas-042-trigano.htm.

48 FFM, French Foreign Ministry spokesperson, 8.1.2002, 15.1.2002.

49 See, for example, French declaration after Arafat's death: Elysee, Chirac's communication to the media, 11.11.2004; FFM, French Foreign Minister Michel Barnier, 11.11.2004.

50 For Arafat see, Barry Rubin, Judith Colp Rubin, *Yasir Arafat, a Political Biography*, (Oxford: Oxford University Press); Efraim Karsh, *Arafat's War: The Man and His Battle for Israeli Conquest* (Grove Press, 2003).

school textbooks, ironically financed by the European Union.[51] Hence, it seems that France made a clear differentiation between the struggle against anti-Semitic acts within France, which became a declared target of a determined governmental policy, and the Palestinian Authority's evident anti-Semitism, which supposedly, could be ignored.

France's formal, biased attitude toward the Israeli-Palestinian conflict and its ruthless criticism of Israel was reflected in the French media.[52] Its distorted presentation of the news and its demonization of the Jewish State resulted in an increasing wave of hatred and anti-Semitic violence toward the Jews in France, who were perceived as supporters of the Jewish state.[53] These were manifested, *inter alia*, during Sharon's visit to France on July 6, 2001, when a demonstration against Sharon, followed by derogatory names in which he was called an assassin, turned into a violent outburst of further anti-Semitic violence.[54]

On August 30, 2001, in a very unfortunate remark, Vedrine even went as far as to criticize the United States for letting Israel hurt the Palestinians, comparing the United States to the Roman governor Pontius Pilate, who crucified Jesus Christ.[55]

---

51 FFM, Vedrine, 26.3.2001, a response to a question raised in the French Parliament on the issue of the European Union's assistance to the Palestinian education system; ibid., Vedrine, interviewed by "Europe 1," 20.4.2001. See also http://www.edume.org/research/pa/index.html, reports of the Institute of Monitoring Peace and Cultural Tolerance in School Education (CMIP). It should be noted that anti-Semitic references were found in French textbooks as well. See François Zimeray, a member of the European Parliament, press communicate, 12.11.2003. http://www.col.fr/article-359.html; Barbara Lefebre, "Comment on parle d'Israël dans le manuels scolaires: opinions, maladresses et sous-entendus," *L'Arch*, 553, 2004, 42–77; Daphne Burdman, "Hatred of the Jews as a Psychological Phenomenon in Palestinian Society, *Jewish Political Studies Review,* 18:3–4 (Fall 2006): 51–64.

52 Shmuel Trigano, "French Anti-Semitism: A Barometer for Gauging Society Perverseness," Jerusalem Center for Public Affairs, 1.11.2004. http://www.jcpa.org/phas/phas-26.htm; Paul Giniewski, "The Jews of France Tormented by the Intifada of the Suburbs," *Nativ online*, Vol. 5, August 2004. http://www.acpr.org.il/ENGLISH-NATIV/05-issue/giniewski-5.htm; Antoine Spire, *France-Israel, Les médias en question*, Editions le bord de l'Eau, Paris, 2005.

53 See CRIF, "Analysis" 1.12.2003; ibid., "France," 1.12.2003. http://www.crif.org/index.php?page=articles_display/detail&aid=2019&returnto=search/search&artyd=5; Paul Giniewski, *Antisionisme: Le nouvel antisémitisme*, Éditions Cheminements, Paris, 2005.

54 http://www.cephasministry.com/israel_in_july_2001.html. See also FFM, French Foreign Ministry spokesperson, 5.6.2001. A reply to a journalist who called Sharon "assassin."

55 FFM, Vedrine, interviewed by "Le Figaro," 38.8.2001. French diplomats used anti-Semitic expressions already in 1948. See: Tsilla Hershco, *Entre Paris et Jérusalem, La France, Le Sionisme et la Création de l'Etat d'Israël: 1945–1949* (Paris–Geneva: Editions Honoré Champion, 2003), 216.

Anti-Semitic Violence as a Political Issue

France's policy eventually caused a severe deterioration in French-Israeli relations, further complicated by the deteriorating situation of French Jews. Hence, the anti-Semitic attacks in France became a political issue in French-Israeli relations.

For instance, Prime Minister Sharon's call on July 2004 for French Jews to leave France and come to Israel because of anti-Semitic attacks triggered a wave of French protests demanding that Israeli leaders declare that France was not an anti-Semitic country. The CRIF, the representative Council of the Organizations of French Jewry–torn between its attachment to France and its solidarity with Israel, and wishing concurrently to avoid being accused of dual loyalty–declared that making "*Aliya*" was a personal decision that should not be introduced into the public sphere of Jewish affairs.[56] At the same time, the CRIF expressed its support for Israel during the difficult days of the second Intifada and later on during the second Lebanon war.[57] In addition, the CRIF called for a more balanced French attitude and tried to reconcile French and Israeli positions. It should be noted that ten days after his controversial statement, Sharon changed his tone. On July 28, 2004, at a welcoming ceremony for new immigrants from France, Sharon praised Chirac's and the French government's determined struggle against anti-Semitism in France. Sharon's statement was welcomed by the French foreign ministry, as well as by France's Jewish-community leadership.[58]

Upgrading Bilateral Relations with Israel

Toward the second half of 2002, France initiated a gradual process of improving bilateral relations with Israel in various fields, such as science, culture, and commerce and promoted a political and strategic dialogue between the two countries. The process started formally with the establishing of a high-ranking Franco-Israeli committee for the upgrading of the bilateral relations headed by Prof. David Khayat, De Villepin's personal friend, and Yehuda Lankri, former Israeli ambassador to Paris. The formal Franco-Israeli agreement regarding the upgrading of bilateral relations, in accordance with the committee's recommendations, was signed on September

[56] FFM, French Foreign Ministry spokesperson, 18.7.2004; *Le monde,* 19.7.2004, 20.7.2004; CRIF, "L'appel de Sharon aux Juifs de France," 9.7.2004. http://www.crif.org/index.php?page=articles_display/detail&aid=3345&returnto=search/search&artyd=5; ibid., "Diplomatic Incident Between France and Israel," 20.7.2004, http://www.crif.org/index.php?page=articles_display/detail&aid=3360&returnto= articles_display/detail_th_type&thid=15&artyd=58.

[57] See, for example, CRIF, "Solidarity Trip to Israel," 10.11.2003. http://www.crif.org/index.php?page=articles_display/detail&aid=1862&returnto=search/search&artyd =64.

[58] CRIF, "Sharon Defuses Tensions between France and Israel," 30.7.2004, http://www.crif.org/index.php?page=articles_display/detail&aid=3412&returnto=articles_display/detail_th_type&thid=15&artyd=58.

16, 2003.[59] This policy transformation stemmed essentially from France's gradual realization that its one-sided approach, even though often denied, was counterproductive to French objectives, undermining France's position as a potential mediator in the Israeli-Palestinian conflict.[60] Additionally, France was embarrassed by the Israeli, as well as Jewish, organizations' condemnation and accusations of France as an anti-Semitic country.[61]It was equally sensitive to France's moral image in the world and concerned that the Israeli-Palestinian conflict had been imported into France. Some political developments contributed to this process as well: the death of Arafat in November 2004, which removed one of the main causes for French-Israeli disagreements; the emergence of new common interests and objectives, such as opposition to Syrian presence in Lebanon following the murder of Hariri in February 2005; and the mutual opposition to the development of Iran's nuclear capabilities. Finally, France believed that a new window of opportunity was created by the disengagement plan of summer 2005, and that it should be fully exploited for the advancing of a solution to the Israeli-Palestinian conflict.

The implementation of the recommendations of the Khyat-Lankri committee led to the state visit (Visit d'Etat) of former president Moshe Katzav to Paris on February 2004. The visit marked an historic milestone in the process of the tightening of French-Israeli relations. President Katzav was warmly received by President Chirac, who stressed France's commitment to "the existence, legitimacy and security of the state of Israel."[62] A large delegation of distinguished Israeli businessmen, scientists, intellectuals, and journalists that joined the president launched a variety of joint projects in the fields of science, commerce, education, and culture, as well as the tightening of political and strategic dialogue. For French Jews it was a remarkable event of pride and hope, especially the impressive view of Israeli flags hanging all along the famous boulevard Champs Elysees. Another significant

---

[59] FFM, French Foreign Minister Dominique de Villepin, Press Conference in Paris with Shimon Peres, then Israel's foreign minister, 29.7.2002; ibid., press communication of French and Israeli foreign ministers, 17.9.2003; ibid., French Foreign Ministry spokesperson, 17.9.2003.

[60] See Elie Barnavi, Luc Rosenzweig, *La France et Israël, Une Affaire Passionnelle* (Paris: Perrin, 2002), 40–41. Elie Barnavi, Israel's former ambassador to France, reported in his book that Vedrine admitted that France's constant support of the Palestinians caused its distancing from the mediation. As for French denials, see, for example: FFM, Vedrine, interviewed by "Marianne," 20.11.2000; ibid.,Vedrine, interviewed by "RFI," 21.5.2001.

[61] FFM, French Foreign Ministry spokesperson, 9.7.2002.

[62] Ibid., President Chirac's at a joint press conference with President Moshe Katzav, 16.2.2008. http://www.ambafrance-uk.org/Statements-made-by-M-Jacques,4599.html?var_recherche=president%20katzav.

point, with implications for the issue of anti-Semitic aggressions in France, was related to a halt during the visit of the one-sided anti-Israeli pattern of media reportages, which in previous years were a significant factor in inflaming Muslim aggression. This change was reflected in the extensive positive coverage by the local media of the four-day visit.[63]

The anti-Semitic issue was a central point in Chirac's speech during the dinner, offered in honor of the Israeli president on February 16, 2004:

> I reiterated the government's unwavering determination to fight against all forms of racism and anti-Semitism. France is engaged in a relentless combat in this sphere and against these scourges. The results, moreover, demonstrate the effectiveness of our efforts. We are and we will remain unbending on this issue, which is why we will not countenance the unfounded accusations, that are sometimes made against us and which attack or violate the honor of France.[64]

President Katzav, in his speech at the dinner, nevertheless reiterated Israel's concern regarding anti-Semitic violence in France, while acknowledging French determination to fight anti-Semitic acts of aggression.[65] It seems that his French hosts were pleased with the statement, that France was not an anti-Semitic country, a statement that was later repeated as a diplomatic formula by other Israeli statesmen who visited France.[66]

Despite the gradual amelioration of French-Israeli bilateral relations, substantial political differences of opinion still play a dominant role in the relations between the two countries. For instance, France often criticizes Israeli settlements in Judea and Samaria, asserting that they constitute an obstacle to lasting peace. In addition, major differences of opinion exist, as in the past, regarding Israeli use of force against Palestinian terror. Thus, France condemns Israeli measures intended to prevent Palestinian acts of terror, such as the security wall of separation and the security barriers. Furthermore, in spite of France's unequivocal condemnation of the launching of rockets from Gaza, which started in 2001 and was intensified at the aftermath of the Israeli disengagement in summer 2005, France also expresses its opposition to Israeli military operations against these acts of terror, demanding Israeli restraint. That being the case, it seems that France persists

---

63 CRIF, "Série d'opinions publiés dans la presse française," 16.2.2004; See also note 53.

64 FFM, President Chirac's speech at a state dinner in honor of the president of Israel and Mrs. Moshe Katzav, 16.2.2004. http://www.ambafrance-uk.org/Speech-by-M-Jacques-Chirac,4598.html?var_recherche=president%20katzav.

65 Internet site of Israeli presidency, former president Katzav, 16.2.2004; see also President Katzav, interviewed by "Nouvel Observateur," 12.2.2004.

66 See, for example, the Internet site of the Israeli Foreign Ministry, "PM Sharon meets with French President Chirac," 27.7.2005. http://www.mfa.gov.il/MFA/Government/Communiques/2005/PM+Sharon+meets+with+French+President+Chirac+27Jul-2005. htm.

with its double standard of conducting a determined struggle against the anti-Semitic violence within France, on the one hand, and sending contradictory messages through its demands of Israeli restraint regarding Palestinian terror, which aspires to eliminate the Jewish state, on the other. Thus, French paradoxical attitudes are counterproductive both to its efforts to resolve the Israeli-Palestinian conflict as well as to its struggle against anti-Semitism.

The War in Iraq

French vocal opposition to the war in Iraq before the American military offensive in March 2003 and afterward raised French prestige in the Arab and Muslim world. The French claimed that the diplomatic process aimed at solving the crisis of international inspection of Iraqi nuclear projects was not sufficiently exhausted. They insisted that the invasion was a severe mistake that was not going to solve the problems but only aggravate them and create new ones. Later on, they argued that the raging terror in Iraq proved that their warnings were justified, especially in light of the fact that no weapons of mass destruction were found in Iraq. The Americans, and especially the American media, counterattacked the French, accusing them of ingratitude and cowardice. Condoleezza Rice, who was at that time the United States' national security adviser, famously declared: "Forgive Russia. Ignore Germany. Punish France." France exploited the transatlantic rift to promote its status in the Muslim world, nourished by hatred of the United States, which was perceived as a supporter of Israel. In their public declarations, French President and Foreign Minister Dominique de Villepin made provocative comparisons of France's opposition to the use of force in Iraq and the Israeli-Palestinian conflict. Chirac opined that the war in Iraq reinforced the feeling of injustice throughout the Arab world, which resulted from the unfair, severe, and unequal treatment of Iraq compared to the lenient attitudes toward Israel. Dominique de Villepin elaborated this theory, asserting that the feeling of injustice caused by the Israeli-Palestinian conflict strengthened the Muslim extremists, thereby creating instability and preventing economic, social, and democratic reforms in the region.[67] Consequently, De Villepin's rhetoric implied that the Israeli-Palestinian conflict–or Israel itself–was responsible for all the conflicts in the region and that as long as this central conflict was not resolved, other conflicts, such as the Iraqi crisis, would persist. These anti-Israeli declarations and the mass protests against the war that accompanied them increased anti-Semitic violence in France. Thus, the French position toward the Iraqi war probably enhanced its prestige in the Arab and Muslim world, but also caused a significant increase in Muslim anti-Semitic activity in France.[68]

---

[67] FFM, De Villepin, interviewed by "Politique Internationale," February, 2004.

[68] *BBC News*, "French Anti-Semitism Reports Surge," 27.3.2003.

The Second Lebanon War

Another illustration of France's counterproductive policy was its ambiguous attitudes toward the Hezbollah, especially during the Second Lebanon War in July–August 2006.

The Second Lebanon War broke out on July 12, 2006, following the terrorist kidnapping of two Israeli soldiers on Israeli territory, the killing of eight others, and the massive bombardment of northern Israel. France's reaction was to unequivocally condemn Hezbollah's terrorist act, while, at the same time, criticizing Israel severely for its reaction of massive bombardments, labeling it disproportional and firmly demanding that Israel end the hostilities.[69] The vigorous French condemnation of Israel was undoubtedly due to Chirac's personal ties with Lebanon's leaders, France's long historical presence in Lebanon, and, in particular, its deep frustration after the collapse of its efforts to rehabilitate Lebanon after the long civil war (1975–1990). France emphasized its uncompromising support of Lebanon's territorial integrity, sovereignty, and independence and expressed its solidarity with the suffering of the Lebanese. In August 2006, France, along with the United States, played a central role in formulating U.N. Security Council Resolution 1701 and in the establishment of the expanded UNIFIL force, in which France's 1600 soldiers played a prominent role.

The war in Lebanon did not change the basic French attitudes toward the Hezbollah. It should be noted that France opposes the inclusion of the Hezbollah on the list of terror organizations, claiming that Hezbollah constitutes an integral part of Lebanese political life. France's policy of placating Hezbollah and its refusal to include it in the list of terror organizations elicits harsh criticism in the light of Hezbollah's international terrorist activities against both military and civilian targets for almost three decades and its non-compliance with and even defiance of U.N. Security Council resolutions 1559 and 1701 to dismantle its military force and release the two abducted Israeli soldiers Eldad Regev and Ehud Goldvaser. Moreover, these French attitudes toward the Hezbollah have been counterproductive to France's policy of zero tolerance toward anti-Semitism in light of Hezbollah's overt anti-Semitic declarations as well as its avowed aspiration and incitation to annihilate the Jewish State, which resemble those of its Iranian sponsor.[70]

---

69 FFM, French Foreign Minister Philippe Douste-Blazy, interviewed by "Europe 1," 13.7.2006.

70 For Hezbollah's anti-Semitism, see: Esther Webman, "Anti-Semitic Motifs in the Ideology of the Hezbollah and the Hamas," *Anti-Semitic Motifs in the Ideology of Hizballah and Hamas* (Tel Aviv: Tel Aviv University Print Shop, 1994); Ely Karmon, "International Terror and Antisemitism: Two Modern Day Curses: Is There a Connection?" 2005, http://www.tau.ac.il/Anti-Semitism/asw2005/karmon.html.

Indeed, during July and August 2006 there was a major rise in anti-Semitic violence perpetrated by Muslims in France. A special study of the European Jewish Congress detailed the increase during the Second Lebanon War of anti-Semitic violence in European Union countries, including the increase in France. The extensive study demonstrated the correlation between the one-sided media coverage of the war, which emphasized the suffering inflicted by Israel upon the Lebanese, on one hand, and the anti-Semitic and anti-Israeli atmosphere, on the other hand.[71]

Anti-Zionism versus Anti-Semitism

Biased French criticism of Israel, detailed above, brings to light another sensitive aspect, which concerns the correlation between anti-Zionism and anti-Semitism. Pierre André Taguieff identified a new kind of anti-Semitism alongside the traditional anti-Semitism. Taguieff calls it "New Judeophobia," arguing that it is characterized by extreme anti-Zionism and targets the Jews as a reaction for the suffering of the Palestinians.[72] Nonna Mayer rejects the notion of "New Judeophobia," basing her arguments on public opinion surveys. She claims that "despite deterioration in Israel's image and despite the multiplication of acts of violence against Jewish French people...anti-Semitism in the classical sense of prejudice against Jews is not gaining ground but rather the contrary." Furthermore, she insists that "Judeophobia" is just the same as it was in the past, since it affects principally the extreme right, as well as socially and culturally disadvantaged circles.[73]

Laurence and Vaisse agree with Mayer's conclusion that the link between anti-Israeli opinions and anti-Jewish attitudes in France is difficult to assess. They argue that "It is safe to say that anti-Zionism is not replacing traditional anti-Semitism as the primary source of anti-Jewish attitudes." However, they also admit that since the French public identifies more and more with the Palestinians (18 percent of respondents declared themselves more sympathetic to the Palestinians in 2000, 30 percent in 2002, and 34 percent in 2004), the new "Judeophobia" could be reflected in the general French population's lack of concern for anti-Semitic violence. They equally admit that even though anti-Semitic acts of violence are committed mainly by "uprooted, marginalized petty criminal young Muslims," the violence in the Middle East provides them with a political pretext to justify their actions.[74]

---

71 EJC Report, "Anti-Semitic Incidents and Discourse in Europe during the Israel-Hezbollah War," 15.11.2006. http://www.eurojewcong.org/ejc/news.php?id_article=601.

72 Pierre André Taguieff, *La Nouvelle Judéophobie*, Fayard -Mille et Une Nuits, Paris, janvier 2002.

73 Nonna Mayer, "Transformations in French Anti-Semitism," in *International Journal of Conflict and Violence*, 1 (2007): 51-60.

74 Laurence and Vaisse, *Integrating Islam*, 232-35.

Nevertheless, there is an important element that seriously undermines the ability to draw conclusions regarding the correlation between anti-Semitism and anti-Zionism on the basis of such public opinion surveys. In today's French society it is not considered politically correct to express anti-Semitic views and opinions. People, who participate in such surveys might, therefore, disguise their anti-Semitism as anti-Israeli and anti-Zionist attitudes, which are considered legitimate and "politically correct." Indeed, France's constant unbalanced criticism of legitimate Israeli efforts to defend its citizens against radical, terrorist Islamist groups contributes to the anti-Semitic discourse, which often hides behind the anti-Zionist anti-Israeli discourse. This notion was validated by Jean-Christophe Rufin in an official report published in October 2004 by the French Ministry of the Interior that linked anti-Semitism with "radical anti-Zionism" (anti-Sionisme radical), and equated the denying of Israel's right to exist with anti-Semitism. Rufin, in presenting the report to the press, said:

> By justifying whatever kind of armed struggle of the Palestinians, even when it aims at innocent civilians, anti-Zionism offers a radical vision of the news justifying violent actions perpetrated in France itself. I consider (anti-Zionism) to be anti-Semitism by proxy. In the same way, accusations of racism, apartheid and of Nazism leveled at Israel have extremely important moral implications. By contagion, they may endanger the lives of our Jewish citizens. I suggest these outbursts should be punished.[75]

CONCLUSION

The painful issue of Muslim attacks on Jews in France cannot be regarded solely through the narrow, restricted prism of local affairs in France. Indeed, France's formal coercive, educational, and correctional measures combined with the French Jewish community's initiatives of "rapprochement" toward moderate Muslims in France, are all indispensable and should not be underestimated. Pressure on France by Israeli, as well as American Jewish organizations, is equally significant and noteworthy. Yet, the impact of these multi-dimensional measures is reduced by France's contradictory policies of appeasing Islamic anti-Semitic terrorist groups in the Arab-Muslim world.

Thus, on the backdrop of the Israeli-Palestinian conflict, the resurgence of anti-Semitic violence in France was fueled by one-sided French demonization of Israel's legitimate measures of self defense. In addition, France's distorted presentation of the Israeli-Palestinian conflict as a central theme in its criticism regarding the Iraq War in March 2003, even though Israel was not implicated in it, has been equally detrimental to France's struggle against

[75] CRIF, "French Official Report Links Anti-Zionism and Anti-Semitism," 8.11.2004. http://www.crif.org/index.php?page=articles_display/detail&aid=3811&returnto=search/search&artyd=2. See also: US Department of State, Report on Global Anti-Semitism, 5.1.2005. http://www.state.gov/g/rls/40258.

anti-Semitism. France's unbalanced critique of Israeli military intervention to stop Hezbollah's rocket attack on Israeli citizens during the Second Lebanon War was followed by a significant increase in anti-Semitic attacks in France.

In this context, it is worthwhile to cite the straightforward, sober observations made by Cukierman at the CRIF annual dinner in February 2005, which correspond to the arguments made in the present essay:

> At this point I must express the malaise that I feel. Malaise in the face of what appears to me to be an incompatibility between France's foreign policy and its internal struggle against anti-Semitism. We read in the Rufin Report, ordered by the Minister of Interior: "It is not conceivable today to fight effectively in France against anti-Semitism, with the new forms that it has taken on, without doing all that can be done to seek to bring a greater balance in the appreciation of the situation in the Middle East among the general public..." France's foreign policy is often perceived as identifying America with Israel, Zionism with imperialism, globalization with oppression. Whether it is deliberately sought by our diplomats or not, this confusion is very real in the mind of public opinion, and nourishes the simplistic lumping together of notions whose harmful effect is felt by the Jewish people....It is true that this case came to a "happy" conclusion, but it was for me a painful revelation. I realized the importance given to French foreign policy. To the point of running the risk of weakening France's resolve in fighting anti-Semitism.[76]

Indeed, French awareness of the gravity of anti-Semitic violence within France, as well as its ominous repercussions, caused France to change its policy from one of total denial of the very existence of the problem to a full-fledged, determined struggle against the appalling phenomenon. Similarly, French realization that its one-sided attitudes regarding the Israeli-Palestinian conflict at the beginning of the Intifada undermined France's influence as a mediator played a significant role in the launching of a more balanced stance toward Israel. Subsequent French-Israeli cooperation and dialogue may have contributed to the decrease in anti-Semitic acts of violence in 2005. Yet, despite the fruitful dialogue, significant differences of opinion regarding Israeli use of force against radical Islamist terror still persist as a central source of contention.

While France's arguments as to the legitimacy of criticizing Israeli policy regarding the Palestinian issue are fully acceptable, a distinction must be made between constructive and realistic criticism, on the one hand, and destructive unrealistic accusations, on the other. Criticizing Israel for defending its citizens against terror attacks and demanding Israeli restraint when reacting to radical Islamist terror groups encourages the ongoing anti-Semitic and anti-Zionist barrage against the Jewish state and confronts Israel with

---

[76] CRIF, Cukierman at the CRIF annual dinner, 17.2.2005. http://www.crif.org/index.php?page=articles_display/detail&aid=4296&returnto=search/search&artyd=2.

growing existential challenges. Furthermore, French demands for restraint might be detrimental to peace and stability in the Middle East as a whole, since radical Islam endangers not only the Jewish state but also the moderate Arabic states. In addition, France's demand for dialogue and compromise is unrealistic in light of the fact that radical Islamist groups, such as Hamas and Hezbollah, do not hide their fanatic uncompromising plans to kill Jews and destroy the Jewish State. At the same time, French authorities themselves do not negotiate with the perpetrators of anti-Semitic violence but impose French laws and punitive measures on them.

Consequently, France should be conscious of the damaging discrepancy between its own determined efforts to curb anti-Semitism within France in light of the principle of "zero tolerance" toward Anti-Semitism, on the one hand, and its traditionally appeasing attitude regarding the same issue in the Middle East, on the other. The adoption of a consistent, determined approach in the local, as well as the foreign, fronts of combating Muslim anti-Semitism is crucial for both moral and strategic considerations. Moreover, France can use its influence and prestige in the Middle East in order to promote its declared values of tolerance. France can equally use its "civilizing mission" as a "soft power" factor in pursuing the struggle against anti-Semitism in the Muslim-Arab world. In this respect a broad perception of the issue of Muslim anti-Semitic acts of violence, which includes the radical Islamist anti-Semitic attack on the Jewish state as well, combined with multi-dimensional measures and global cooperation, is imperative for the solution or at least the containment of the problem in France and elsewhere.

Jewish-Muslim Relations in Nineteenth-Century Morocco

MOHAMMED KENBIB

One must be circumspect when dealing with Muslim-Jewish relations in nineteenth-century Morocco. Attention to the general context and complexity of the multidimensional process that finally led to the fall of the country under French and Spanish rule in 1912 is essential. Any balanced approach must consider at least three fundamental issues:

1. the ways Moroccans reacted to European penetration and, in particular, the contradictions having characterized the reforms that the sultans unsuccessfully tried to implement;
2. the role played by the Jewish merchant elite, which acted previously within the so-called "toujjar sultan system," as well as by the new Jewish modern elite, educated in the schools of the Alliance Israelite Universelle;
3. the long-term implications of all these developments, their specific impact on Muslim-Jewish coexistence, and, ultimately, the mass emigration that started in 1948 and led, within less than three decades, to the drastic reduction of the deeply rooted Jewish presence in Morocco.

The weakening of the traditional foundations of Muslim Jewish relations was, in fact, part of the general process that the Moroccan economy, society, and state underwent between 1844 and 1912 and, in a second historical stage, between 1912 and 1956. The events of the nineteenth century appear to have been a decisive prelude to the changes that the country experienced during the Protectorate era.

In the pre-colonial era, the Muslims thought and felt that European penetration targeted not only their land but also their faith, customs, and way of life. Learned people opposing foreign influence rejected Western slogans heralding "progress," "civilization," and "improvement of the natives' standard of living." They considered that the colonial powers' ambitions, economic supremacy, territorial infringements, and "clientélization" of a substantial proportion of the native upper classes would result in nothing but "confusion," "division," and "disorder." In particular, the risk of *fitna* ("internal confrontation," "civil war") was central to their argument. This concept, largely borrowed from the Qur'ān and religious exegesis dealing with fundamental disagreements undermining the unity and cohesion of the "community of believers," became a sort of leitmotiv in the sultan's correspondence and in the fetwas of the ulemas during most of the nineteenth and early twentieth centuries.

The reactions of the scholar Mohamed Boujandar from Rabat (1845–1926) were significant in this respect. In his writings, he railed against the changes he had witnessed. He blamed the Makhzen for what he perceived to be negative innovations (*bid'aa*), for their being responsible for the emergence and spread of the governmental institutions. In his view, the appointment of merchants to official key positions was harmful to the country's interests and independence:

> These people have grown mighty... Their mismanagement was a fatal blow to the Moroccan State....The situation has become worse due to the injustice and abuses perpetrated by other Makhzen officials... Confusion spread everywhere.

Another witness, the well-known historian Ahmed Naciri (died in 1897), author of *Al-Istiqsa*, described, in striking terms, the effects of European penetration. He lamented that everything had radically changed in the country within less than one generation. He witnessed new forms of behavior in the Moroccan daily life, the depreciation of the currency, the rise in the cost of basic goods, and the invasion of the country's markets by manufactured imports. He held the "Christians" responsible for all these pernicious developments. Specifically, he spoke against the Western concept of freedom and blamed the Jews who adopted it and relied upon influential foreign coreligionists to get rid of their canonical obligations. According to him, Moses Montefiore's visit to Morocco (1864) and the misuse of the royal edict sealed at his request by the sultan Sidi Mohammed Ben Abderrahmane (1859–1873) had shattered any basis for inter-communal relations and pushed the Jews toward "rebellion."

Naciri's criticism arose out of a defense of the canonical order in the chaotic aftermath of the humiliating war lost by the Moroccans (1859–1860) after Spain had attacked them and occupied the city of Tetouan (1860–1862). His condemnation of Jewish activists who trespassed agreed limits should perhaps be understood in light of Muslim-Jewish relations in general, as expressed by Norman Stillman:

> There is no obsession with the Jews comparable to that found in medieval European literature. Most of the Moroccan stereotypes of Jews may be negative, but they are also peripheral. They are perceived primarily as dhimmis, humbled, but protected subjects. As long as the Jew conforms to his role, he arouses little interest.

Foreign consular and diplomatic reports are full of information and comments that shed additional light on the nineteenth-century context. For example, Boujandar's judgment on the "confusion" prevailing in the country can be seen as similar to the thoughts expressed in the early 1880s by the British Ambassador in Tangiers, John Hay Drummond Hay, or those of the

U.S General Consul, Felix Mathews. Fearing a brutal explosion and a sudden collapse of the Makhzen that could dangerously increase European rivalries and risks of military confrontation, Hay declared that he and his colleagues "were... living in this country (Morocco), as if it were, on the crater of a Volcano." Mathews, for his part, observed that "the Empire of Morocco (was) in a state of almost absolute disorganization."

Where did the Jews stand in this context ? A detailed report sent to the Foreign Office in July 1893 by one of the successors of J.H.D. Hay at the head of the British Legation, West Ridgeway, provides useful indications of their general condition during the last decade of the nineteenth century. Describing their situation, the Ambassador wrote to Earl of Rosebery that :

> The Jews of Morocco number about 300,000, but many are in the mountain districts absorbed in the general population, with whom they fare equally well. The position of the others is much improved for the better by the exertions of the Anglo-Jewish Association and the Alliance Israelite Universelle. Indeed, on the whole, the treatment of the Jew is better than that of the Moor. Most rich Jews enjoy (foreign) protection, and even the poor Jew, who is still a Moorish subject, is exempt from taxation... and military service.

In his report, Ridgeway did not neglect to mention the differences between the upper socio-economic categories (usually referred to as the "Jews of the first class") and the popular masses, particularly the small paddlers, artisans, and jobless, who lived (or survived) in crowded mellahs.

During their explorations into remote parts of the country, some European ethnographers noticed, more than two decades prior to 1893, that even in regions usually considered by foreigners as "wild" and being "lands of dissidence" (*bled siba*), the Jews lived in tranquillity amidst their Muslim neighbors. In 1871 a British geographer, J.D. Hooker, and his botanist partner, J. Ball, observed that "it does not appear that the condition of the Jews is practically as bad as that of the same people in Romania and some other so-called Christian states. In some respects, indeed, they are better of than their Mohammedan neighbors."

This broad picture should be nuanced. The merchants, indeed, took advantage of ever-increasing in imports and exports, but the Jewish masses still faced a hard life, especially during periods of natural calamity, such as the six consecutive years of drought that devastated the country between 1878 and 1884. Here and there, they too had to endure the cruelty and actions of tyrannical governors. However, thanks to the pressures and protests of the foreign powers and the European Jewish associations, they escaped corporal punishment (*bastinado*) from the mid-1860s onward.

In contrast, the Muslim *fellahin* (peasants) had little to rejoice over. They were continually extorted and were subject to flogging at the hands of the brutal caïds and governors. Also, they had to endure increased tax burdens and a relentless demand for military service (the so-called *harka*). Unlike the Jews, who could resort to influential coreligionists and to foreign legations, there was no remedy for the authorities' abuses but armed rebellion. As the general situation continued to deteriorate, some of the peasants sought to become *mokhalets* (agricultural associates) or *semsars* (commercial agents) of protected Jews or European residents in order to have access to the fiscal advantages of the "protégé" status. In the ulemas' perspective, such a move meant a total perversion and subversion of the canonical order insofar as "true believers" were deliberately putting themselves under the protection of "infidels." A *de facto* "inversion of the dhimma" was in the air. Although paradoxical at first sight, such a situation expressed the extent of the duality and complexity that prevailed in inter-communal relations during the second half of the nineteenth century.

Naturalized and protected Jews acted as efficient purveyors of cards of *mokhalet*s and *semsar*s for Muslim farmers who could afford such services. Along with foreign residents, both parties would declare their partnership "*sohba*" (an ambiguous term signifying, in this specific context, a sort of "business friendship") and register their mutual obligations in notarized documents. However, many notaries (*adul*s) were notoriously corrupt and most of these partnerships were fictitious. Many diplomatic and consular reports dealing with protégés and foreigners who drew revenues from these irregularities depict them as "the sleeping partners of the Moorish farmers."

These practices gave rise to all sorts of difficulties, especially when, in periods of drought, the farmers could not meet their obligations. Many of them were imprisoned and had their lands seized to the benefit of the "sleeping partners." Particularly significant in this respect was the response given by the British Prime Minister, Earl Granville, to a petition of the Board of Deputies of British Jews (1880) asking him to reject any claim of the sultan Moulay Hassan (1873–1894) restricting the protection system. Granville declared that "there are great abuses connected with these irregular privileges; they are bought and sold by fraud and exercised most unjustly. This practice does excite...a feeling of animosity against the Jews in Morocco."

The sultan, in a letter to his *naïb* [representative] in Tangier, stated that

> It is because of their...pride that the [tribes] (*ahl al Gharb*) uprise against their governors for the slightest abuse, massacre them, plunder their properties and burn their casbahs. Despite the severe repression inflicted on them by the Makhzen (troops), they do not refrain from rebelling whenever they feel they have unjustly been treated....If they act this way against their own Muslim brothers, how could you expect them to act toward the Jews in case they decide to...react to their provocations and assaults?

These episodic incidents in the country were limited in their occurrence, rather isolated, and involved only a few individuals. Jewish dignitaries tried to help avoid these sorts of incidents by issuing, from time to time, appeals to their brethren to behave with moderation and restraint. The Board of Deputies and the Anglo-Jewish Association joined these efforts.

Moses Montefiore exhorted his Moroccan coreligionists to avoid getting into conflict with the authorities and their fellow-countrymen. In one of his letters, read in the synagogues, he solemnly declared : "Let neither actions nor words from you induce your fellow-countrymen of the Mohammedan faith to suppose that you are in any way unmindful or regardless of your duties of subjects of His Imperial Majesty."

However, animosity and periodic incidents did not prevent an increasing number of well-to-do Muslims in the countryside from seeking foreign protection through Jews regardless of the religious implications of such status and the threats of ulemas who promised hell to all those who applied for the protection of the "infidels," Christian as well as Jewish.

Anti-protégé fetwas and sermons in the mosques did not stop the race for privileges. Sometimes, people trying to gain a sort of second-, if not third-, degree protection resorted to old religious practices when pleading with a protégé to provide assistance. A report sent to the State Department by a Moroccan Jew, Meyer Corcos, acting as American vice-consul in Essaouira, reveals part of this ritual linking of Moslem to Jew:

> As a custom in Morocco, it is wrong to turn out of the house people who bring such sign of refuge called *al'ar*. My late father has many times, and for many months, Moors lodging in the house....(He) he could not send (them) away until they chose to go themselves....Several times (he) settled amicably affairs pending between his lodgers and the governors of the surrounding districts.

Commenting on this state of affairs, Daniel Schroeter observed that "the powerful Jewish merchants of Essaouira were able to extend protection to Muslims, mirroring the marabouts of the south. Merchant houses became sanctuaries, just like the zaouias."

Although in the past prominent brotherhood figures symbolized "jihad" and a resistance to Christian threats, in the nineteenth century some agreed to serve the powers' political influence and did not disdain holding cards of foreign protégé. It was in this context that the head of the zaouia of Ouezzane, Haj Abdeslam Ouezzani, became a French protégé (1884) and his dealings with France caused serious tensions in Franco-Moroccan relations. Paris' legation in Tangiers had used its protégé's influence to enlarge French interests in the country. But ambassadors, such as Charles Féraud, did not conceal in their confidential reports to the Quai d'Orsay that they despised Ouezzani, his dissolute life, and the way he treated his British wife, Emily Keen, a spouse he finally divorced before taking as a sort of concubine, a young Tangerine Jewess supposedly converted to Islam ("supposedly" is quoted from a French diplomatic report).

It is almost impossible to know the exact figures of Jews and Moslems enjoying foreign protection. According to various diplomatic reports, some 15,000 to 20,000 Jews were holding regular–and irregular–cards of protégés and foreign passports. All the Jewish upper classes enjoyed such privileges and skillfully used them to remain competitive in the new commercial environment. Those who acted earlier as "toujjar sultan" and were entitled to royal decrees of Respect and Safeguard (*Tawqir wa Ihtiram*) had no choice after the signing of the Anglo-Moroccan Treaty of 1856 but to apply for foreign protection. Such status was needed to adjust to the abolition of the royal monopolies they had exploited in the name of the sultan. Their Muslim homologues followed the same path for the same reasons.

The extension of foreign protection and naturalizations to Jewish and Muslim upper socio-economic categories had all sorts of tax implications that resulted in serious losses for the Moroccan Treasury. It also had numerous political repercussions. The exemption of the Jewish merchants and other groups holding cards of protégés or foreign passports meant that all the rich refrained from paying the *jizya* (canonical poll tax). Therefore, they left no option to the Makhzen but *de facto* to renounce this income and to turn a blind eye on its religious significance. Because of the poverty and suffering of the Jewish popular masses, especially after the quasi-collapse in many mellahs of the communal institutions dedicated to assisting needy coreligionists, collecting the jizya became an impossible task.

Choosing *de facto* not to impose the payment of the jizya represented a blow to the sultan's legitimacy because, as Commander of the Faithful, he had the religious obligation to defend and implement all the Qur'ān's prescriptions, including, of course, the dhimma stipulations. However, this renunciation did not help improve the socio-economic condition of the Jewish masses. Their plight continued to deteriorate. Except for "alerting" the Board of Deputies and the Alliance Israelite in periods of famine, wealthy native coreligionists did almost nothing to help. It was precisely in such circumstances that Zionist activists started speaking out against the "selfishness" of opulent merchants in Essaouira and elsewhere and stressing the need for a quick "restoration of jewish values and ideals."

Unlike the overwhelming majority of the population living in the mellahs and, *a fortiori*, the Muslim fellah masses suffering an increasing tax burden, the Jewish merchants succeeded to preserve their opulent life-style and to maintain themselves as vital intermediaries for foreign firms. The combination of foreign protection, their in-depth knowledge of the country, and their close relations with senior Makhzen officials served their interests as did, in a more particular way, the European powers, whose strategy targeted the ethno-religious differences and the instrumentalization of minority-majority contradictions. The powers gave preference to the Jews, hoping to rely on them to enlarge their respective influences. Such a plan went along with a sort of routinization of a discourse praising the Jews' skills, their deeply rooted experience as middlemen, and their predispositions toward modernity. "*This ethnic element represents the sole native group that the West could rely upon to bring civilization and progress to Morocco*" became a leitmotiv in European propaganda.

However, during the last decades of nineteenth century, the slogans put forward in this respect started losing their relevance. This shift came as a result of both the spread of anti-Semitism in Europe (including in democratic countries such as France and Great Britain) and the exacerbation of colonial rivalries and ambitions aimed at the direct exploitation of Moroccan natural resources. European Chambers of Commerce (i.e., Manchester, Liverpool, Marseille) put forth claims and launched newspaper campaigns denouncing the *status quo* prevailing along the southern edge of the Straits of Gibraltar. In particular, they criticized what they considered as a *de facto* monopoly enjoyed by the Jews in the commercial sector and what they called "the exorbitant privileges granted to native Jews." Their chairs and influential members in London and elsewhere lobbied actively in order to convince their governments to drastically restrict the protection system. Some foreign ministers responded positively. They agreed to such a principle provided that the sultan accepted a new commercial treaty completely liberalizing maritime trade.

Reacting to these campaigns and the threat of restriction, or even abrogation, of privileges, foreign-protected Jews having access to the royal palace encouraged the sultan to reject further liberalization of the maritime trade. As the ulemas were backing this resistance, European ambassadors interpreted this common position as an obvious "collusion" between the Jews and the Muslims. Consequently, they abandoned their lenient apology of the pro-Western sympathies attributed to the Moroccan Jews and severely criticized what they called "Hebraic fanaticism," which they considered as being "equally inflexible in comparison with Muslim fanaticism." Insidious Jews, insisted some of them, actually conspired with the most reactionary clans within the Makhzen and maliciously stood behind "the Chinese inclinations of the Moorish Court." A French diplomat wrote in explicit terms that "the Jews affected pro-liberal attitudes as far as their own interests were not concerned but actually backed the fanatic clan and regarded Morocco as their own affair."

The prejudice and the anti-Semitic ideology lying behind such views and impressions blurred the objective reasons that dictated the strategy of wealthy Jewish merchants after 1856. All of them were aware of European economic supremacy and the implications of the inexorable integration of Morocco into the world market. Therefore, they voluntarily choose to take advantage of their knowledge of Moroccan realities and networks to impose themselves upon European firms. Given the circumstances, it was absolutely normal in their view to enjoy the immunities that the foreign powers agreed to grant to native merchants. Indeed, they started enjoying these immunities but without renouncing the old privileges they had enjoyed while "serving" the sultan, his viziers, and powerful governors. They perceived such a combination as being the most efficient means to successfully compete with foreign merchants established in Morocco, to preserve their traditional middlemen role, and to increase their fortune. Representatives of the foreign powers in Tangiers regarded high-profile Jewish merchants enjoying the advantages drawn from the two systems as playing "a shameful double jeu."[1]

At the end of the nineteenth century and early twentieth, the French, in particular, had other compelling reasons for this dissatisfaction. The smuggling, through Jews, of modern arms and ammunition to tribes in southwest

---

[1] Some of these figures deserve a comprehensive biographical study, putting under close scrutiny their motivations and strategies. Such studies would usefully parallel the illuminating "monography" devoted by D. Schroeter to Meir Macnin. It would illucidate the similarities and differences that existed between ancient toujjar sultan in the pre-1856 era and the ways the latter and other merchants adjusted to the new post-mid-nineteenth-century conditions. At least three significant "models" could easily be included in such a study:

(1) Ya'cob Ohana (1856–1899), a supplier of the royal palace in Meknès and French protégé who amassed considerable wealth. One of his European hosts, the French novelist Pierre Loti, described him as an "elegant vizir," enjoying the delights of "one thousand and one nights in his finely designed and richly furnished house." The privileges and facilities granted to him by Moulay Hassan and his grand-vizir Ba Ahmed (d. 1900) included farming taxes such as those collected on the transactions carried out in the markets (*mostafad*) and at the gates of Meknès, selling the crops of the royal domains, supplying the troops with tents and other commodities, and renting at low cost shops and warehouses belonging to the Treasury or to the Habous (Muslim religious endowment). However, his high-placed protection did not prevent the local authorities (especially the *Muhtassib* Mohamed Ajana, provost of the city in charge of the markets, the guilds, and overseer of public morality) from keeping a watchful eye on his violations of common rules and regulations. Even his own coreligionists frequently protested against his monopolistic practices, as well as his interference in the appointment of the head of the community and its *dayyanim* (judges).

(2) Ischua Corcos (d. 1929) was the well-known head of the Jewish community of Marrakech. In spite of his French protection, he had business relations and even a close friendship with Sultan Moulay Hassan, the Grand-Vizir Ba Ahmed, the grand caïds of the South, and even with Cheikh Ma el Ainine, leader of the resistance in the Sahara. Europeans portrayed him as "*the most important capitalist of the South*," "*Jacques Cœur du Haouz*," "*Père Goriot*" and "*Shylock*." Even more significant was the financial support he brought to the so-called "*sultan of jihad*," Moulay Hafid, one of the brothers of the reigning sultan Moulay Abdel-Aziz (1894–1907), who started conspiring against the latter in 1904 and finally overthrew him and obtained his own proclamation in Marrakech in 1907.

(3) Moses Aflalo, another "tajir sultan" resided in London and was considered by the British authorities as the *Unofficial Adviser of His Sharifian Majesty*. He acted as one of the most important informers of Moulay Hassan about British general policy and the move toward an Anglo-Franco-Russian alliance. In 1904 he published a book, *The Truth about Morocco*, to protest the "deal" agreed upon by France and Great Britain at the expense of Morocco and Egypt.

Algeria, as well as to Moroccan tribes, was a major source of their disillusionment. Indeed, tribesmen whom the French authorities regarded as "rebels" or "dissidents" bought modern Winchester and Mauser rifles to resist French and Spanish territorial encroachments. They disregarded the sultan's objection to their official proclamation of "jihad," sent delegates to make appropriate contacts with Jewish merchants–especially in Tangiers–who could supply them with European- or American-made rifles, and acted as "holy fighters." Criticism of these transactions sometimes had an explicit anti-Semitic tone. A French Ambassador depicted the Jews encouraging the Makhzen resistance as "cosmopolitains de mauvais aloi."

In the early twentieth-century prominent Jewish figures in Tangiers and elsewhere expressed their attachment to the *status quo* when they denied foreign allegations regarding the general condition of their coreligionists in Morocco. They contradicted the claims made by European and American Jewish associations. It was, for instance, at the request of the Union of American Hebrew Congregations (New York) and one of its influential members, the wealthy banker of Russian origin, Jacob Schiff, that the American president, Theodore Roosevelt, tried to include "religious freedom" in the agenda of the international conference gathered at Algesiras (1906). The grand-rabbi of Tangier, Mordekhay Bengio, in hius letter to President Roosevelt objected to this proposal:

> Apparently, the American government is under the impression that Moroccan Jews are badly treated and oppressed, but this is not the case at all....In justice to the Moroccan government, I declare that the Jews of Morocco are well treated...and that we have absolutely no reason of complaint.

In the same circumstances, a member of the American delegation to the Algesiras conference (1906), Lewis Einstein, dispatched to Morocco to inquire on the exact situation of the Jews and to assess the extent of the "oppression" and discriminatory measures they were subjected to, specified in his report to the State Department that:

> Many mellahs are overcrowded, but this is not the fault of the Muslim authorities....The British Minister in Tangier, Sir Arthur Nicolson, had persuaded the sultan to grant a parcel of land at Mogador to be used for enlarging the Jewish quarter....A few Jewish landlords, however, who owned the entire mellah, prevented their poor coreligionists from moving.

The "conservatism" of large segments of the Jewish "oligarchy" and the cautious attitude of Muslim notables also concerned about the preservation of traditional ties existing since time immemorial between Jews and Muslims helped both of parties to resist the dangers of strife resulting from the instability caused by colonial penetration and loss of control by the Makhzen. It was in this context of relentless unrest that periodic incidents occurred between Jews and Muslims. However, the clashes that sporadically broke out, especially during periods of drought, epidemics, or famine–such as the six consecutive years of natural calamities that devastated the country between 1878 and 1884–were generally limited to individuals. Indeed, they never deteriorated to the point where they caused major confrontations between the groups, as was occurring during the same period in Central and Eastern Europe and even in the Middle East.

In regard to the preservation of peaceful inter-communal relations, despite the deterioration of traditional institutions and the anachronism of many codes and behaviors, of particular symbolic significance was a fact recorded by a rabbi of Meknes, David Ovadia (b. 1913), relying on oral tradition and reporting what he had heard about Muslim-Jewish relations in Sefrou, a small city near Fès where the Jews were half the population. Talking in particular about a rabbi, Moshe Elbaz (1823–1897), he wrote that:

> During times of famine, the great one of the Muslims used to ask him to pray much....(Sometimes), when the Imam used to ascend the tower of their house of prayer at dawn to welcome the day with songs of prayer, the rabbi also used to respond to him (*oneb liqrato*) from the window of his home with hymns (*baqqashot*) in Arabic. The Imam (then) used to stay silent to hear him.

The Jewish notables and the popular masses attached to the *status quo* easily understood such affinities. This could hardly be the case of a substantial proportion of modern educated Jews. Largely influenced by what they had learned in the Alliance schools, they expected a quick move to a completely new situation and aspired to what they regarded as "emancipation." In their perspective, they would be better off if France succeeded in imposing her rule upon Morocco. Most of them had in mind the Cremieux Decree (1870) and the naturalization "en bloc" granted to their coreligionists in neighboring Algeria. Their profile, aspirations, and impatience created a sort of cultural gap within the Jewish communities. Conservative Jews disapproved of their disruptiveness and disdain for the traditional social order within the *kehilot*, as well as their lack of concern for Muslim-Jewish relations.

The gap between the so-called "évolués" and their Muslim neighbors was even greater. Having at least two generations of advanced, modern education, mainly in the Alliance schools, they considered the Muslims to be backward, bigoted, and totally impervious to modernity. As they preferred to speak French instead of Judeo-Arabic or Berber, adopted French or Spanish surnames, and started wearing Western-style pants, jackets, and hats, the "évolués" widened the cultural distance between them and their Muslim countrymen.

Only a small minority of the "évolués" remained skeptical of the potential benefits French rule could bring to their communities. Open to Zionist ideology, they did not share the pro-French enthusiastic expectations of their coreligionists. Of particular significance in this respect was the speech that a Moroccan Jew living in New York, Haim Toledano, delivered in Tangiers in 1913. Addressing the annual meeting of the AIU Alumni Association, Toledano said that:

> The new era that begins now for Morocco is pregnant of a new life. The traditional role of the Jew is destroyed in these circumstances....Except those who had built positions able to challenge any assault, native Israelite masses will soon feel the economic pressure of the new regime.

Toledano's prediction did not alter the expectations and optimism of the overwhelming majority of "évolués." It took three or four decades before they understood the truth of his message. Meanwhile, other internal and international developments continued to erode the traditional foundations of Muslim-Jewish relations in Morocco.

Events moved with such rapidity in the aftermath of World War II that many found it difficult to understand *a posteriori* what exactly had happened to them. It was as a response to this situation that the chronicler Victor Malka published *La mémoire brisée des Juifs marocains*. Similar preoccupations are to be found in Joseph Toledano's *Le temps des mellahs*. Based partly on their own personal experiences, Edmond Amran El Maleh's *Parcours immobile* (Paris, 1980) and *Mille ans, un jour* (Ed. La Pensée sauvage, 1986), and Bouganim Ami's *Récits du mellah* (JC Lattès, Paris, 1981) provide seminal material that could help reconstruct the historical context and avoid Manichean perceptions of the past.

Selected Bibliography

Ami, Bouganim. *Récits du mellah.* JC Lattès, Paris, 1981.

Deshen, Shlomo. *The Mellah Society. Jewish Community Life in Sherifian Morocco*. The University of Chicago Press, Chicago and London, 1989.

El Maleh, Edmond A. *Parcours immobile,* Paris, 1980.

———— *Mille ans, un jour,* La Pensée sauvage, 1986.

Hooker, J. D. and J. Ball, *Journal of a Tour in Morocco and the Great Atlas*, London, 1878, p. 168.

Kenbib, Mohammed. *Juifs et Musulmans au Maroc, 1859–1948. Contribution à l'histoire des relations inter-communautaires en terre d'Islam*. Publications de la Faculté des Lettres et des Sciences Humaines de Rabat, Rabat, 1994.

———— *Les protégés. Contribution à l'histoire contemporaine du Maroc*. Rabat, 1996.

Malka, Victor. *La mémoire brisée des Juifs marocains*. Ed. Entente, 1978.

Parsons, F. V. *The Origins of the Morocco Question 1800–1900*. London, Duckworth, 1976.

Rivet, Daniel. *Le Maroc de Lyautey à Mohammed V.* Casablanca, Ed. Porte d'Anfa, 2004.

Schroeter, Daniel J. *The Sultan's Jew. Morocco and the Sephardi World*. Stanford University Press, Stanford, 2002.

———— "The Politics of Reform in Morocco : The Writings of Yshaq Ben Yâ'ish Halewî in Hasfirah (1891)," in *Misgav Yerushalayim Studies in Jewish Literature*, ed. Ephraim Hazan. Misgav Yerushalayim, 1987, 73-84.

Toledano, Haim. *Le Maroc nouveau et les Israélites*. Tanger, Imprimeries Marocaines, 1913.

Toledano, Joseph. *Le temps des mellahs*. 1982.

Activity of Satmar Hassidim in Yemen in the 1980s and 1990s

YITZHAK MUALEM

The establishment of the State of Israel fundamentally changed the relations between Jews and Muslims. The introduction of the Zionist dimension brought about a fundamental change to the attitude of Muslims toward Jews in some of the Muslim countries. In some of these countries, the government's attitude toward Jews changed for the worse: Jews were deprived of the right to emigrate and their social privileges were curtailed.

The State of Israel, which was defined as an enemy state by the Arab states, could not intervene on their behalf. However, Jewish institutions, such as the Satmar Hassidic sect, were able to operate in these countries on behalf of Jews. One such example is its decades-long activity in Yemen, in the service of religious and communal needs.[1] This activity was accepted and even approved by Yemen's leaders, who found common interest with the activities of Satmar. The latter were striving to reach their Jewish goals in Yemen, while the government of Yemen saw these activities as a tool for achieving its own political objectives, in both domestic and foreign relations.

This case study discusses the cooperative relations between the Satmar Hassidic sect and the Yemenite government on activities conducted on behalf of Yemenite Jews during the 1980s, and their emigration from Yemen during the 1990s, seen against the activities of the government of Israel, the Jewish Agency, and the Jewish Lobby for Yemenite Jewry.[2] This study will examine the extent to which the negative stance held by Satmar toward the State of Israel was conducive to their activities in Yemen and in removing Jews from Yemen to the United States and to Britain.

This study discusses the role and influence of a religious organization in the international political arena. The Satmar Hassidic organization, while lacking any semblance of sovereignty and military capabilities, nevertheless

---

1 Daniel Elazar, "Israeli-United States Relations in the Context of the World Jewish Community," *Kivunim* 3 (June 1979): 93–116 [Hebrew]; Noah Klein, *The Loss of My Country* (N.Y.: Hadar Graphic, 1998) [Hebrew].

2 See Haim Tawil, *On Wings of Eagles: Operation Esther* (Jerusalem: Gur Aryeh, 2006) [Hebrew]; Yehiel Hivshush, *The Last of the Jews in Yemen* (Bnei Brak: Private family publication, 1990) [Hebrew].

endeavored to influence the policy of the government of Yemen on the status and future of the Jews of that country. The Satmar activity in Yemen began in the late 1970s with the arrival of the first Hassidim to Yemen and the commencement of their activities among the Jewish Yemenite community under the patronage of the radical Islamic government.

The objective of this study, as stated, is to examine the extent of Satmar's influence as a religious entity in the international political arena. The Satmar Hassidic sect is defined as a political non-governmental transnational entity, whose activities in Yemen influenced this sovereign government's policy vis-à-vis the fate of its Jews.[3] We will examine to what extent and how this non-state entity utilized the conflictual state of relations between Israel and Yemen in order to promote its ideological-political objectives in Yemen, on the basis of a political common denominator, namely, their negative stance toward the State of Israel.

Theoretical Framework

Satmar's activity and influence is examined from a unique political perspective, due to the singularity of this phenomenon in world politics. This study attempts to examine the connection between religion and politics in the international arena. This research area is problematic from a theoretical and empirical perspective: Hitherto-conducted studies in this area dealt with the connection between religion and politics in the domestic area,[4] while studies dealing with the linkage between religion and world politics focused on the tension found between these two phenomena, which facilitated the creation of conflicts in the world political arena.[5]

Sandler and Fox in their studies presented a theoretical perspective of the negative influence of such a connection on the world political system.[6] This current study, however, will attempt to provide a different perspective on the relations between religion and politics by examining the cooperation

---

3 On the history of the Jews of Yemen, see Shlomo Goitein, *The Yemenites: History, Social Order, and Spiritual Life* (Jerusalem: Ben-Zvi Institute, 1983) [Hebrew]; Bat-Zion Iraqi Klorman, *The Jews of Yemen: History, Society and Culture*, vol. B (Raanana: Open University, 2004), 339–80 [Hebrew]; Yosef Tobi, *The Jews of Yemen: Studies in Their History and Cultural* (Leiden: Brill, 1999); Isaac Hollander, *Jews and Muslims in Lower Yemen* (Leiden: Brill, 1999).

4 Mark Juergensmeyer, *The New Cold War? Religious Nationalism Confronts The Secular States* (Berkeley: University of California Press, 1993).

5 Regina S. Schwartz, *The Curse of Cain: The Violent Legacy of Monotheism* (Chicago: University of Chicago Press, 1997).

6 Shmuel Sandler and Jonathan Fox, eds., *Bringing Religion into International Relations* (New York: Palgrave Macmillan, 2004); Shmuel Sandler and Jonathan Fox, "The Question of Religion and World Politics," in *Religion in World Conflict*, eds. Shmuel Sandler and Jonathan Fox (London: Routledge, 2006), 1–10.

between the Jews, representatives of Satmar, and the Muslims, representing the Yemenite government. The cooperation between them was possible as long as both sides defined and based their relations according to a distinctly hierarchical manner, placing both the Yemenite Jews and Satmar's representatives as protégés of the Islamic government.[7] As will be seen below, this state of affairs enabled the Satmar Hassidim to conduct their activities in Yemen since the 1970s.

The examination of Satmar's activity and influence will be conducted within the theoretical framework of world politics, the Constructivist approach in international relations. This approach enables the examination of this religious-political activity within the framework of transnational relations,[8] which transcend the sovereign borders of the State, of Yemen.[9] This approach enables the study and analysis of non-governmental entities in world politics in a context that is not an existential, military one. Instead, the analysis of Satmar's activity and influence will focus on the socio-political area, examining those issues on its social, religious and political agenda.[10]

Studies of the influence of religious entities as autonomous actors in world politics were conducted already in the 1970s, with the study of the influence of the Catholic Church.[11] This actor's activity is characterized by its ability to create global communication systems that transcend sovereign

---

7 Moshe Zadok, "The Relations between Jews and Arabs in Yemen," in *The Jews of Yemen*, eds. Yisrael Yeshayahu and Josef Tobi (Jerusalem: Yad Yitzhak Ban Zvi, 1976), 147–63; Laurence O. Leob, "Jewish-Muslim Socio-Political Relations Twentieth Century in South Yemen," in *Judeo-Yemenite Studies*, eds. Ephraim Isaac and Yosef Tobi (Piscataway, N.J.: Institute of Semitic Studies, 1999), 71–99.

8 Joseph S. Jr. Nye and Robert O. Keohane, "Transnational Relations and World Politics: A Introduction," in *International Organization*, vol. 25, no. 3 (Summer 1971); 329–49; Jeffrey Checkel, "Constructivism and Foreign Policy," in *Foreign Policy Theories, Actors, Cases*, eds. Steve Smith, Aelia Hadfield and Tim Dunne (Oxford: Oxford University Press, 2008) 71–82; Dale C. Copeland, "The Constructivism Challenge to Structural Realism: A Review Assay," in *Constructivism and International Relations*, eds. Stefano Guzzini and Anna Leander (London and New York: Routledge, 2006), 1–20.

9 Robert O. Koehane and Joseph S. Jr. Nye, "Governance in Globalizing World," in *Power and Governance in A Partial Globalize World*, ed. Robert O. Koehane (New York: Routledge, 2002), 193–218; Richard Mansbach, Yale H. Ferguson, and Donald Lampart, *The Web of World Politics* (Englewood Cliffs, N.J.: Prentice-Hall, 1976).

10 Robert W. Cox "Social Forces, States and World Orders: Beyond International Theory," in *Neorialism and Its Critics*, ed. Robert O. Koehane (New York: Colombia University Press, 1986), 204–54.

11 Ivan Vallier, "The Roman Catholic Church: A Transnational Actor," in *International Organization*, vol. 25, no. 3 (1971): 479–502.

borders and create cross-country politics, governments, and parliaments.[12] The study of further cases only emphasized the need to continue the discussion of the function and influence of such autonomous actors who represent religious groups in the arena of world politics.[13]

Accordingly, the Satmar Hassidic sect is defined as an autonomous actor in the world political arena with unique objectives and influence. Its activity will be discussed in the social-humanitarian context that is influenced by the very definition of this actor as a religious entity.[14] Satmar, indeed, conducted activities in the area of material and spiritual assistance to Yemenite Jewry and others, however this activity was complex. Satmar acted on behalf of the Jews of Yemen within the framework of cooperation with the Yemenite government with the aim of realizing the basic objectives of its belief and ideology, but at the same time this also expressed its continued struggle against the Zionist entity, i.e., the State of Israel.

The function and influence of an actor in world politics is a function of the resources at its disposal and its ability to utilize them. The aforementioned theoretical approach assists us in examining the influence even of non-governmental entities by focusing specifically on a particular activity area that is defined according to its social, rather than the context of military force.[15] Therefore, we will examine the function, actions, and influence of Satmar as a non-governmental entity in world politics within the framework of the entirety of its resources and abilities to realize its objectives in the world political arena on the subject of the status and future of Yemenite Jewry.

Satmar's unique influence is examined here over two different time periods, which show the impact of this influence and the way in which Satmar conducted itself in Yemen. The first period covers the activity of Satmar in Yemen from the late 1970s until Yemen's reunification in the 1990s. During

12 Robert O. Koehane and Joseph S. Jr. Nye, *Power and Interdependence* (Boston: Little Brown and Company, 1977), 25–27; James N. Rosenau, *Turbulence in World Politics* (Princeton, N.J.: Princeton University Press, 1990), 243–97.

13 See publication by Bruce Maddy-Weitzman and Efraim Inbar on the influence of religious groups on world politics: Bruce Maddy-Weitzman and Efraim Inbar, *Religious Radicalism in the Greater Middle East* (London: Fank Cass, 1997).

14 See definitions and activity of non-governmental actors in world politics in Oran R. Young, "The Actors in World Politics," in *The Analysis of International Politics*, eds. James N. Rosenau, East Maurice Davis Vincent (New York: The Free Press, 1972); Walter Carlsnaes, "Actors, Structures and Foreign Policy Analysis," in *Foreign Policy Theories, Actors, Cases*, eds. Steve Smith, Aelia Hadfield and Tim Dunne (Oxford: Oxford University Press, 2007), 85–100.

15 Joseph S. Jr. Nye, "The Changing Nature of World Power," *Political Science Quarterly*, 105, no. 2 (1990: 177–92; M. Barnet and R. Duvall, "Power in International Politics," *International Organization*, 59, no. 1 (2005): 39–76.

that period, Satmar operated almost exclusively and was able to exert its influence over the Yemenite government, as will be shown below, while during the second period, following the unification of Yemen, Satmar competed with other dominant governmental entities, such as the State of Israel and the United States Administration, as well as other non-governmental organizations operating in this area, which compelled the former to exert its utmost efforts to influence the Yemenite government in its direction.

Satmar Ideology and Policy

Rabbi Yoel Teitelbaum (the Satmar Rebbe) was not only the founder of the Satmar Hassidic sect, but he also gave it content and its *raison d'etre* and uniqueness through its unrelenting anti-Zionist struggle against the existence of the State of Israel.[16] The origins of the ideological anti-Zionist dimension in the Satmar Rebbe's teachings lie in the traditional perceptions related to the issue of the continued existence of the Jewish people in the Diaspora and the struggle against the Zionist phenomenon as a secular movement.[17] According to the Satmar Rebbe's approach, the Zionist movement wholly denied the continued Jewish existence in the Diaspora, and acted to expedite the political redemption of the Jewish people by bringing them to the Land of Israel and establishing a sovereign state, going against religious decrees found in the scriptures.[18]

The Satmar Rebbe claimed that the Jewish people's *raison d'etre* is embedded in its universal mission of religious faith, the belief in the unity of God and of creation.[19] The Jewish people have a mission in the world, and its objective is to express God's revelation in this world by keeping his commandments. The significance of this idea is that all is determined and direct-

---

16 Zvi Jonathan Kaplan, "Rabbi Joel Teitelbaum, Zionism, and Hungarian Ultra-Orthodoxy," *Modern Judaism*, 24, no. 2 (2004): 163–78; Allan Nadler, "Piety and Politics: The Case of the Satmar Rebbe," *Judaism*, 31, no. 2 (Spring 1982): 135–52.

17 David Sorotzkin, "The Building of the Land Below and Destruction of the Land Above: The Satmar Rebbe and the Radical Orthodox System of Thought," in *The Land of Israel in Jewish Thought in the Twentieth Century*, ed. Aviezer Ravitzky (Jerusalem: Yad Ben Zvi Publishers, 2004), 139–59 [Hebrew]; Shalom Ratsabi, "Anti-Zionism and Messianic Tension in the Teachings of Rabbi Shalom Dov Ber," *HaZionut*, 20 (1996): 77–101 [Hebrew].

18 Yitzhak Kraus, "Judaism and Zionism - Two which Cannot Go Together: The Teachings of Rabbi Joel Teitelbaum - The Satmar Rebbe," *HaZionut*, 22 (2000): 37–60 [Hebrew]; Aviezer Ravitzky, *The Revealed End and the Jewish State* (Tel Aviv: Am Oved, 1993), 60–67 [Hebrew]. For a contrasting approach to that of messianic Zionism, see Moshe Yaakov Bergman, *The Jewish State* (Jerusalem: M. J. Bergman, 2003) [Hebrew].

19 Hanoch Ben Pazi, "On the Anti-Universalism of the "Zionist Idea" - The Satmar Perspective on Rabbi Joel Teitelbaum," *Education and Its Environment* 29 (Tel Aviv: Kibbutzim College of Education Publishers, 2007), 291–304 [Hebrew].

ed from Above. God's rule is the one that determines man's fate and, therefore, the Zionist movement and its activities are heresy, the denial of God's existence.[20] The redemption of the Jewish people will be miraculous and timely and not by the hands of the Zionist earthly, non-miraculous, and political action, which constitutes a rebellion against God's existence and unity.[21]

In his book, Vayoel Moshe, the Satmar Rebbe presents his followers with his anti-Zionist approach and his clear outlook on the issue of God's unity on the one hand and his negative approach to the State of Israel on the other.[22] This book was written in a period that witnessed significant changes in the Jewish and world political arena and thus served as a guidebook for Satmar Hassidism in its approach to Zionism and the State of Israel. He claimed that the continued existence of the Jewish people in the Diaspora should not be meddled with, not to begin with nor after the fact, just as the ways of the Torah have not changed with the changing realities.[23]

The Zionist enterprise and the establishment of the State of Israel, founded on the basis of immigration and land settlement, denies the messianic notion of the miraculous redemption of the Jewish people, prolongs the continued destruction of Jerusalem Above (a heavenly Jerusalem) and Jerusalem Below (the earthly Jerusalem),[24] and will delay the arrival of the Messiah.[25]

According to this approach, the members and followers of the Zionist organization are considered idol worshippers and impure, since their actions prove their disbelief in the existence of God.[26] The Satmar Rebbe advocated political passivity and objected to all the immigration waves that took place, basing his objection to the immigration act as defying God's will on a source in the Talmud, in Tractate *Ketubot*,[27] in which Rabbi Zeira enumerates three oaths, referring to the Jewish people's status in the Diaspora, their relations with non-Jews, and their continued sojourn in the Diaspora. The oaths state that the Jewish people will not rebel against the nations, and

20 Ibid., 291-300; Kraus, "Judaism and Zionism," 43–45.

21 Ravitzky, *The Revealed End*, 67–74; Kraus, "Judaism and Zionism," 67–74.

22 Joel Teitelbaum, *Vayoel Moshe* (Brooklyn, N.Y.: Jerusalem Publication, 2000) [Hebrew], first published in 1961; Yitzhak Kraus, *The Three Oaths as the Basis for the Anti-Zionist Teachings of Rabbi Yoel Teitelbaum,* MA Thesis (Jerusalem: The Hebrew University of Jerusalem-Baltimore, 1990) [Hebrew].

23 Kraus, "Judaism and Zionism," 39.

24 Sorotzkin, "The Building of the Land," 159–63; Ben-Pazi, "Anti-Universalism," 297–300.

25 Sorotzkin, "The Building of the Land," 161; Kraus, "Judaism and Zionism," 50–55.

26 Kraus, "Judaism and Zionism," 44–45.

27 Ravitzky, *The Revealed End*, 89–93; Kraus, "Judaism and Zionism," 40–43.

will abide by their rule; that they may not by their sins delay the redemption; and lastly, that they are not allowed to ascend to the Land of Israel by force[28]—consequently, they will not create a reality of redemption through non-believers. Any move that causes the breach of these oaths is heresy, which is why the policy of passivity should be enacted. Under these conditions, ascension to the Land of Israel is irrelevant and is a diabolical feat.[29]

Immigration into the Land of Israel, according to this, does not constitute the fulfillment of the religious commandment to settle the Land of Israel. Immigration during this period is a negative phenomenon that might hinder the arrival of the Messiah.[30] Therefore, everything must be done to stop immigration into the Land of Israel, on the one hand, and, on the other, to endeavor to strengthen the Jewish existence in the Diaspora, including those Jewish communities residing in Islamic countries.[31] In light of this, the Satmar rebbe claimed that one should act in cooperation with the local government to enable the continued Jewish existence in each place and to provide the Jews with the opportunity to continue maintaining a religious life while recognizing the Jews' position as protégés of that country and taking care not to harm the sovereignty and authority of the Islamic country.[32]

As a non-governmental religious entity, Satmar Hassidism is active in the world political arena and uses its political assets in its relations with the Islamic government in Yemen. Furthermore, in order to promote its ideological objectives concerning the Jews of Yemen it takes advantage of the absence of diplomatic relations between the governments of Israel and Yemen. And lastly, Satmar's limiting its activities to the social aspect, which constitutes no threat to Yemen's material-existential goals, facilitates the realization of the former's goals. This activity will be explained below according to the Constructivist approach in international relations, which emphasizes social issues in the world political system.

---

28 Ben-Pazi, "Anti-Universalism," 301–4; Ravitzky, *The Revealed End*, 277–305.

29 Sorotzkin, "The Building of the Land," 159–62.

30 Sorotzkin, "The Building of the Land," 162–65; Ratsabi, "Anti-Zionism and Messianic Tension," 80–85.

31 *The Tehran Children Accuse* (Jerusalem: Agudat Israel Executive Committee, 1947) [Hebrew].

32 On the condition of Jews in Yemen under Islamic rule, see Gershon Agronsky, "The Jews in Yemen and Aden During the Imam Yihya," in *The Jews of Yemen in the New Era* ed. Josef Tobi (Jerusalem: Zalman Shazar Center, 1984), 163–77 [Hebrew].

Satmar Activity in Yemen in the Late 1970s and in the 1980s

The exodus of Jews from Yemen to Israel, which began in 1949 with "Operation On Wings of Eagles," continued in changing volume and frequency until 1962, with the onset of the Yemen civil war.[33] The assessment of the Israeli government and the Jewish Agency in the late 1970s, as expressed by then Minister of Absorption Yaakov Zur, was that no Jews remained in Yemen after the Jewish community was wiped out in the early 1960s. Nevertheless, since the 1960s,[34] Jews in Israel never ceased to cry out and demand the intervention of the Israeli government on behalf of the Jewish survivors who still existed in Yemen, predominantly in North Yemen, under the Yemen Arab Republic.[35] However, the refrainment of the Israeli government to act on behalf of the Yemenite Jews created a vacuum into which stepped Satmar, who set out to act on their behalf as soon as the news about Jews still living in Yemen reached them.

Satmar's assistance to Diaspora Jews was guided by the Satmar Rebbe's approach, which he formed already in the 1950s, regarding the big wave of immigration from Morocco in those years. When the Satmar Rebbe saw what he perceived as the immigrants' spiritual corruption and destruction of Jewish souls by the Zionists, he decided to act for their spiritual redemption.[36] He preached to his followers in speeches and lectures on the need to establish organizations for the rescue of Jews in distress. He established the institute "Rav Tuv," whose aim was to assist Jewish communities in the Diaspora, particularly in Muslim countries such as Tunisia, Syria, Iran, and Yemen.[37]

In Yemen, the Satmar Hassidim used their non-governmental status to their advantage to impact on social and economic issues. They created an international network of ties that enabled them to act undisturbed within a Muslim country, such as their ties with PLO activists in New York.[38] Furthermore, Satmar's objection to the very existence of the State of Israel was sufficient for the Yemenite government to permit Satmar's representatives to operate in the rural and urban Jewish communities in Yemen. In the course of this period, central activists from Satmar arrived in Yemen, joined

---

33 Paul Dresch, *A History of Modern Yemen* (Cambridge: Cambridge University Press, 2000), 89–119; Reuben Ahroni, *Jewish Emigration from the Yemen 1951–98* (Richmond: Curzon, 2001), 83–103.

34 Nahum Moshe, *Between Two Cultures* (Jerusalem: M. Nahum, 1989), 150 [Hebrew].

35 Tawil, *On Wings of Eagles,* 65–68.

36 Klein, *The Loss of My Country*; Interview with Rabbi Shmuel Fefenheim, editor of the Satmar community's newspaper, 23 June 2006; interview prepared by Mr. Avi Yihya.

37 Elazar, "Israeli-United States Relations."

38 Tawil, *On Wings of Eagles*, 56; Amnon Kapliuk, "My Visit to the Remaining Jews of Yemen," *Yediot Aharonot*, Weekend Supplement, 16 Nov. 1984, 18.

by additional activists from Neturei Karta, who also accepted the Satmar Rebbe's anti-Zionist approach and authority in this context.[39] Among the prominent activists who arrived were delegates from the Committee for the Rescue of Yemenite Jews from New York, consisting of Rabbi Hirsch Yissachar, Rabbi Noah Klein, Rabbi Yitzhak Chaim Freund, and the central and dominant activist, Rabbi Yosef Bachar, from Neturai Karta, whose activity had great influence among Yemenite Jews in this period, during the late 1970s, the 1980s, and in the 1990s following the unification of Yemen.[40]

Satmar claims that all the activities it conducts within states that are hostile to Israel are not an act of defiance against Israel but rather have the saving of Jews in mind.[41] Nevertheless, the activity of the Satmar Hassidic sect cannot be understood without the related ideological-religious background. The negative approach of Satmar to Israel was compatible with North Yemen's policy at the time, as expressed by President Abdallah Salih.[42] He viewed the State of Israel as an imperialistic state that deported the Palestinians from their country. The intensification of their negative rhetoric against Israel opened the way for negotiations between Satmar and the representatives of the PLO in New York, who arranged their entry permits to Yemen.[43]

The most dominant and influential delegate who arrived in Yemen was Rabbi Yosef Bachar, whose political stance toward Israel was in agreement with that of the PLO and the Yemenite government. They saw the former as an advocate of their approach, whose principle was to implement policies detrimental to the very existence of the State of Israel. In practice, this would be implemented by preventing Jews from immigrating to Israel. Thus, Bachar placed on his social-political agenda to act, on one hand, to maintain Jewish existence in Yemen and, on the other, to prevent Jews from immigrating to Israel.[44] The government of North Yemen perceived Satmar's work as a positive factor. Their social-religious activity among the Jews did not pose any danger for the Islamic rule of the country, since both Satmar Hassidim and Yemenite Jews themselves encouraged the continuation of Jewish life in Yemen as protégés of the State.[45]

---

39 Menachem Friedman, *The Haredi Ultra-Orthodox Society: Sources, Trends and Processes* (The Jerusalem Institute for Israel Studies, Jerusalem, 1991), 88–103 [Hebrew]; Amnon Levi, *The Ultra-Orthodox* (Jerusalem: Keter Publishers, 1989), 191–203 [Hebrew].

40 Hivshush, *The last Jews of Yemen*, 59–61; idem, *In Siege and Distress* (Israel: private family publication, 1995), 90–91 [Hebrew].

41 Interview with Rabbi Shmuel Fefenheim.

42 Ahroni, *Jewish Emigration*, 87.

43 Hivshush, *The Last Jews of Yemen*, 59; Ahroni, *Jewish Emigration*, 87–98.

44 Hivshush, *In Siege and Distress*, 91; Tawil, *On Wings of Eagles*, 57.

45 Tawil, *On Wings of Eagles*, 56–57.

Satmar's contribution is questioned in relation to the nature and intentions of their activity vis-à-vis Yemenite Jewry in the 1980s. Indeed, Rabbi Bachar and his colleagues conducted activities both in spiritual and material areas by purchasing ritual articles, holy books, and funding the establishment of houses of Torah learning.[46] They also printed pamphlets and posters against the State of Israel.[47] Since they were the only Jewish activists acting for Jews in Yemen, they served as their new connection to the Jewish world. Satmar was in contact with the government in an endeavor also to improve the physical and material situation of the Jews. This activity was enabled solely through the close connections created between Satmar and PLO representatives in Yemen.

No obstacles were placed in front of Satmar in the cultural and humanitarian areas. They were able to act freely and implement the doctrine of the Satmar Rebbe among the Jews of Yemen. Some claim that while his anti-Zionist heritage was implemented, the Hassidim's spiritual and material assistance was lacking. They did not attempt to rehabilitate community life or to provide for the needs of the Jewish elderly, widows, and children, and particularly orphans.[48] Additionally, Rabbi Bachar ensured that the Jews of Yemen would become his followers. He enlisted the heads of prominent families in Yemen by providing them and their communities with financial aid.[49]

However, a general examination shows that the scope of activity does not seem significant, since it consisted mainly in providing prayer-books and other religious articles. The focus of activity was the realization of its anti-Zionist objective, the prevention of emigration, by continued anti-Israel exhortation, while providing misleading information on events in Israel.[50] This line of action continued throughout the period, even while the Jews' situation in Yemen became aggravated following the deportation of PLO activists from Lebanon in the wake of the Lebanon War.[51] These deportees lived in close vicinity to some Jewish neighborhoods near the capital, San'a, and the northern town of Sada. They physically harmed Jews, took over

[46] Amos Nevo, "The Black Net," *Yediot Aharonot*, 17 Dec. 1993, 47; Hivshush, *In Siege and Distress*, 85–89; "On the Backs of the Yemenites," *Panim Hadashot*, vol. 262, 23 July 1993, 12. See the letter of Rabbi Yosef Bachar to Rabbi Yaish son of Rabbi Yihya Levi, 7 June 1980, on the issue of contributions for setting up houses of learning in Yemen, from the private archive of Mr. Shlomo Jeraffi, Gadera, Israel.

[47] Hivshush, *In Siege and Distress*, 90.

[48] Ibid., 91.

[49] Amos Nevo, "The Black Net," 47; Hivshush, *In Siege and Distress*, 92.

[50] Aryeh Bender, "From Yemen to Israel," *Maariv* [Hebrew], 15 July 1993, 3; "On the Backs of the Yemenites," op. cit.

[51] Hivshush, *The Last Jews of Yemen*, 118; Tawil, *On Wings of Eagles*, 66.

Jewish property and even synagogues in revenge for their defeat in the war with Israel. Satmar, as a religious-social entity, had no ability to change this situation. Change came from another source, the Yemenite government, which brought the situation under control out of fear of sharing Lebanon's experience of civil war.[52]

With the free hand given to Satmar, it could be expected that the situation of the Jews during this period would have improved to no end, especially due to the wealth of resources of the Satmar community in America.[53] However, no significant improvement was made to the quality of life of the Jews of Yemen, which could also have had its effect on the spiritual aspect. Satmar's central aim was to implement the Satmar Rebbe's teachings and to keep the Jews in Yemen, where they could maintain their religious, traditional life. Satmar could continue its exclusive activity due to the state of relations between the two parts of Yemen, due to the Islamic nature of the government, and also due to the state of relations between North Yemen and the United States. However, in the 1990s, changes occurred that compelled Satmar to change its mode of action.

Satmar Activity in the 1990s

Toward the late 1980s, Satmar, as a social-religious entity, faced several challenges that curbed its activity in North Yemen. These challenges were systemic as well as related to United States-Yemen relations, and to the activity of the State of Israel in those years on this issue. However, the biggest and most direct threat to the continuation of Satmar's activity in North Yemen was the International Coalition for the Revival of the Jews of Yemen (ICROJOY),[54] which aimed at improving the conditions of the Jews in Yemen spiritually and materially, as well as enabling them to emigrate to Israel. This was a Jewish-American organization, officially recognized by the United States, established in December 1988 by American Jews of Yemenite origin. The organization's members had connections in the United States Congress and the Administration. They had ties with senators such as Alfonso D'Amato, Daniel Patrick Moynihan, and Robert Graham, and with congressmen Benjamin Gilman, Mel Levin, and James Scheuer. They had connections also with State Department personnel such as Richard Schifter, who was Assistant Secretary of State for Human Rights and Humanitarian Affairs.[55]

The ICROJOY's activities were successful. It began its activities in North Yemen with the aim of bringing about a change in official policy toward

52 Hivshush, *The Last Jews of Yemen*, 119.

53 Interview with Rabbi Shmuel Fefenheim.

54 Tawil, *On Wings of Eagles*, 87–100; Ahroni, *Jewish Emigration*, 105–8.

55 Ahroni, *Jewish Emigration*, 105.

Jews in Yemen and of influencing emigration policy regarding this population, which numbered approximately 1,500 people.[56] Thus, with the tightening of relations between the United States and Yemen, so did the ICROJOY increase its influence and scope of activity in Yemen. Its main activists, Hayim Tawil, Pierre Goloubinoff, Shlomo Jeraffi, Lester Smarka, and Saadia Shapiro, created positive reciprocal relations with North Yemen's political leadership. In their visits to Yemen in September 1989 and January 1990 they met with Abdul Karim Al Iryani, North Yemen's foreign minister.[57] These meetings facilitated the organization to bring about change in the government's policy toward the Jews, to the discontent of Satmar. The diplomatic steps by both countries compelled Satmar to radically change its mode of action.

A gradual, positive development in the relations of the two countries took place during the 1980s. In 1989, the Americans began an intensive endeavor to improve bilateral relations out of their interest in improving the United States position in this geographical area. During the course of the 1980s, the United States supplied North Yemen with aircraft, trained its military officers, and sent over technicians from Taiwan to maintain and operate the military equipment. In the economic sphere, the United States assisted in the transfer of tons of food. In the agricultural area it assisted in the development and cultivation of large areas of uncultivated land.[58] North Yemen's dire economic situation compelled it to take significant steps in order to bring about the warming of relations with the United States, since the United States suspended its aid program (PL-480) to Yemen until conditions of the Yemenite Jews were improved.[59]

During the visit by Ali Abdullah Saleh, President of the Yemen Arab Republic (North Yemen) to the United States in January 1990, several bilateral issues came up for discussion. One of the issues raised in the meetings between United States President George Bush and Yemen's President Saleh, together with Secretary of State James Baker, was the human rights status of the Jews of North Yemen.[60] These meetings had implications on the policymaking of North Yemen in this area. The Satmar Hassidim and Neturei Karta, who were apprehensive of a change in Yemenite policy, published an article in the Washington Post in which they congratulated the North Yemenite president on his visit to the United States and thanked him for the religious freedom enjoyed by the Jews in Yemen as citizens of the republic.

---

[56] Hivshush, *In Siege and Distress*, 11-12; Ahroni, *Jewish Emigration*, 107-8.

[57] Tawil, *On Wings of Eagles*, 149-73.

[58] Ibid., 108-9.

[59] Ibid., 171-73.

[60] Ahroni, *Jewish Emigration*, 111-12.

Satmar's aim in this publication was to request Ali Abdullah Saleh to stick to his current policy and not introduce any changes to it.[61]

Satmar found itself in a new political reality, one that differed from the previous one of exclusive activity encouraged by PLO in Yemen and Jewish-Muslim cooperation based on common interests consisting of a negative approach to the State of Israel. However, at this stage, as a social-religious entity, it ran into difficulties in acting and influencing decisions made and influenced by the inter-state dimension, a trend that became more pronounced over time. Therefore, Satmar decided to operate on three levels: (1) relating to the United States Administration in order to prevent any change to its human rights policy regarding the Jews of North Yemen; (2) changing the new policy of the Yemenite government; and (3) focusing on activity in Yemen within the Jewish community and beyond it in the endeavor to continue the Jewish existence in Yemen and within Satmar's communities in the United States and in Britain.

The unification of the two parts of Yemen in May 1990[62] and the support of united Yemen in the invasion of Iraq to Kuwait in August 1990 had a detrimental effect on Yemen's economy due to the deportation of about a million Yemenite workers and their families from Saudi Arabia.[63] The need for financial aid compelled the Yemenite government to turn to the United States government. The United States conditioned the provision of assistance on improvements in the area of the Jews' human rights in Yemen.[64] Yemen's president stated in an interview he gave on October that year that Jews could leave Yemen as tourists.[65] This statement became policy by the end of June 1991, when the Yemenite government gave official and legal permission to Jews to leave its boundaries as tourists.[66] Satmar, which was fully aware of the negative repercussions this policy would have on them, tried to have this policy rescinded.

First, Satmar tried to influence the domestic United States political arena. In July 1990, the Union of Orthodox Rabbis of the United States and Canada (UOR) addressed a letter to the United States president, in which it demanded the president's intervention in preventing the Jews' exit from Yemen.

---

61 Tawil, *On Wings of Eagles*, 180.

62 Josef Kostiner, *Yemen* (Beit Berl: HaHistadrut HaKlalit shel HaOvdim b'Eretz Yisrael, 1992), 25–26 [Hebrew]; Ahroni, *Jewish Emigration*, 112–15; Dresch, *A History of Modern Yemen*, 186–93.

63 Yossi Melman, "Haim and Pierre's Magic Carpet," *Haaretz* [Hebrew], 22 Aug. 1999, 3B; Lily Galilee, "The Exodus of the Jews Assists the Yemenite Government," *Panim Hadashot*, vol. 262, 13; Dresch, *A History of Modern Yemen*, 183–86.

64 Ahroni, *Jewish Emigration*, 111.

65 Ibid., 113.

66 Ibid., 115.

They claimed that the Administration was misled by ICROJOY regarding the alleged curtailment of the Jews' rights in Yemen. Yemen is an exemplary country for peaceful coexistence between Jews and Muslims, and for enjoying equal rights, as in the United States. The UOR requested that the American president prevent the ICROJOY from realizing its goals in this issue.[67]

Satmar's social and political influence is quite substantial in relation to its small numbers among the U.S. population. The Satmar Hassidic sect is known to be a wealthy one, with members who are considered to have political and financial clout among American Jewry, as well as among politicians in New York and Washington. Yaakov Israel Freund, who was one of the founders of the Committee for the Rescue of Yemenite Jews, lived in the town of Monroe in New York State, and was close to the United States Administration and to George Bush. He used these connections for the benefit of Satmar's activities in Yemen and to bring changes to the new policy decided upon in Yemen.[68]

After years of a wavering policy, Israel decided to implement an active policy for saving the Jews of Yemen. In 1990, Prime Minister Yitzhak Shamir ordered the setting up of a governmental committee headed by Avigdor Kahalani to bring Yemenite Jewry to Israel.[69] The change in Israeli policy brought about the increased pressure by the United States Administration on the Yemenite government to reach a comprehensive decision to provide exit permits to any Yemenite Jew interested in doing so. The government of Yemen feared that all the Jews under its jurisdiction would emigrate to Israel, where they would be granted entry under the Israeli law of Right of Return.[70] It did not wish to make a decision that would go against the policy of the Arab League, regarding the exit of Jews from Muslim countries. The Arab League's policy derived from the viewpoint that the Jews immigrating to Israel increased the number of soldiers in the Israeli army.[71]

Nevertheless, due to Yemen's deteriorating economic situation, it decided to demonstrate openness in its relations with the West and particularly

---

67 Ibid., 117.

68 Interview with Rabbi Shmuel Fefenheim.

69 Tawil, *On Wings of Eagles*, 188; Baruch Kimmerling, "The Yemenite Exodus," *Haaretz*, 6 Aug. 1999, 14B. See statement by Yitzhak Katabi, Council Head of Israeli town of Ekron in the 1980s, who was a member of the Committee for the Rescue of Yemenite Jews, according to whom, the committee pressed the State of Israel to act and addressed the United States Administration on this matter (interview on 21 May 2006, by Avi Yihya).

70 This approach is held by Yemen's Foreign Minister. See Tawil, *On Wings of Eagles*, 172.

71 Dafna Yulen, "The New Yemenite Immigrants Call Him the Messiah," *Arim* [Hebrew], 25 July 1997, 56.

with the United States, and in 1992 and 1993 it permitted the exit of the Jews, who left mainly for Israel.[72] In response to the criticism expressed by the media in Yemen and in the Arab countries, the Yemenite president stated that Jews had equal rights, same as in Syria, which allowed its Jews to be reunited with their families in the United States and South America.[73]

At this stage, Satmar endeavored to bring about a change to this decision by acting also in the domestic Yemenite arena. Rabbi Yosef Bachar met with Yemen's foreign minister and other high-ranking officials and demanded to bring the exit of Jews to a halt.[74] He protested their allowing Jews to leave their country for the Zionists' state. Satmar also attempted to mobilize Arab high-ranking officials to persuade the government of Yemen to halt the exit of the Jews, who were at risk of losing their religious faith in Israel.[75] Satmar also used propaganda. They exposed the covert activity of Israel in transporting Jews from Yemen to Israel.[76] Based on Satmar publications, the Arab newspaper Al-Sharq Al-Awsat researched the immigration of Yemenite Jews to Israel, with the aim of bringing the stream of immigration to a halt.[77] This newspaper praised the activity in Yemen of Satmar and Neturei Karta in their efforts to keep the Jews in Yemen.

Satmar Hassids, who were aware of the change in policy by the Yemenite government, decided to step up their activities also among the Yemenite Jews who were not immigrating to Israel. This type of activity was conducted throughout the first period, as mentioned above. However, it was intensified during the second period along with the policy changes. When Rabbi Yosef Bachar comprehended the new situation, he inquired of the Yemenite government to enable him and his counterparts to send young Jews to study in Britain and the United States in order that they return to Yemen at a later stage and be the pillars of the Jewish community in Yemen, and thus prevent them from immigrating to Israel.[78]

---

72 Ahroni, *Jewish Emigration*, 131.

73 Sheffy Gabai and Avraham Tirosh, "A Yemenite Leader: The Exodus of the Jews Is Not Causing Us Damage," *Maariv* [Hebrew], 15 July 1993, 4.

74 Zadok Yehezkely, "Eight Jews Left Yemen for London on a Journey against the Immigration to Israel," *Yediot Aharonot*, 20 July 1993, 15. According to Mr. Shlomo Jeraffi, a member of ICROJOY, Satmar's activity became more radical at this stage, with the success of the ICROJOY in the area of immigration (interview on 26 June 2006, by Avi Yihya).

75 "On the Backs of the Yemenites," op. cit.; on this issue see the article by Steve Gillon in *The Jewish Press Magazine*, 20 Aug 1993, 12.

76 Ahroni, *Jewish Emigration*, 129.

77 About this research see Sheffy Gabai, "Since July 1992 120 Jews left Yemen," *Maariv*, 30 March 1993, 16; Ahroni, *Jewish Emigration*, 129–32.

78 Zadok Yehezkely, "Eight Jews"; Yehudit Yehezkely, "How I Missed My Mother,"

Another method implemented by Satmar was the anti-Zionist propaganda used on the Yemenite Jews. They were told that Israel has no food, people die of hunger, children are kidnapped, and people are forced to give up their religion. Satmar activists called their counterparts in Israel to contact Jews in Yemen by phone and through letters and verify the tales of hardships in Israel, in order to turn the Jews of Yemen against Israel. They confiscated passports.[79] They sent Yemenite children to study in Satmar institutes in the United States as hostages in order to prevent the parents from immigrating to Israel. Satmar's activities did succeed to a certain extent in halting the immigration to Israel.[80]

These activities were not stopped by the Yemenite government, due to their long-standing reciprocal relations hailing from the 1980s. Satmar, as a social-religious entity, could influence this international arena as long as it shared common interests with the government of Yemen regarding the status of Jews in Yemen. However, with the changing international political circumstances and conditions, improvement in relations between the two states, Yemen and the United States, Satmar found it increasingly difficult to continue its influence in maintaining Jewish existence in Yemen. Despite Satmar's endeavor to act on three different levels: within the United States Administration, within the political system in Yemen, and among the Jews of Yemen, they were not particularly successful. Their religious ideological mission was left unrealized at this time.

Conclusion

The religious-social activity of the Satmar Hassidic sect in Yemen was discussed in this essay in the theoretical framework of world politics, the Institutionalist, Constructivist approach. This approach enables the examination and analysis of non-governmental entities whose activities transcend boundaries of nations, states, and governments. This approach emphasizes the international system's social aspect rather than its dimension of military force. The social and economic issues constitute an important part in the

---

Yediot Aharonot, 29 March 2005, 12–13; Natasha Mozgovia, "The Magic Carpet from Brooklyn," *Yediot Aharonot*, 3 June 2004, 3; Orr Heler, "I No Longer Fear the Satmars," *Maariv*, 25 Feb. 2001, 4–5.

79 Nevo, "The Black Net"; Aryeh Bender, "I thought Israel was a desert, with no roads or cars," *Panim Hadashot*, v. 262, 13. See letters sent by Satmar Hassidim to Jews in Yemen; e.g., the letter by Rabbi Yosef Bachar to Mr. Ibrahim Suleiman from 4 August 1994. Another example is the letter by Yisrael Matityahu Grossman from Beer Yaakov to Rabbi Eliezer in San'a, 3 Feb. 1994. See also the publication sent to Yemenite Jews by Neturei Karta, "Better Having Few Righteous Men than Many Wicked Ones" from 18 April 1994 (private archive of Shlomo Jeraffi, Gadera).

80 Nevo, "The Black Net"; Hivshush, *In Siege and Distress*, 3–94; Dana Luzon, "A Stolen Child," *Yediot America* [Hebrew], 7 April 2000, 5.

activity within the world political system, which is expressed in the framework of diplomatic negotiations.

Satmar used the existence of the social dimension in the international system to implement its anti-Zionist ideology on the issue of the status of the Jews of Yemen by negotiating both with the United States administration and with the Yemenite government, both of which enabled the former's activities in assisting Yemenite Jews as this was not perceived as jeopardizing any of their national objectives.

Satmar's activities are examined over the periods of the 1980s and 1990s. During the 1980s, Satmar could act exclusively among the Jews of Yemen. Its activities were conducted with the cooperation and endorsement of the Yemenite government, which perceived them as a beneficial activity whose sole purpose was to prevent immigration to Israel, which indeed Satmar was able to attain in this period. However, in the 1990s, due to systemic and regional changes following the Gulf War, there was a warming of relations between Yemen and the United States. United States aid to Yemen was conditioned on the extent of change in the area of human rights made to Yemen's policy. Improvement of conditions in this area resulted in the opening of Yemen's gates, which made it difficult for Satmar to operate in Yemen and in the United States. Satmar Hassidim, who had connections both in the United States Administration and in the Yemenite government, sought to negotiate a change of policy that the state entities saw no reason to curtail as Satmar's activities in this area were limited to the social-religious area.

Muslims and Jews in the Sephardic Ballad Tradition

HILARY POMEROY

For nearly five centuries, the Jews of the Ottoman Empire and North Africa have kept alive ballads composed by Christian minstrels in fifteenth-century Spain. These highly dramatic narrative poems were immensely popular throughout Spain and were enjoyed by the masses and court alike.[1] The Spanish Jews who went into exile after the 1492 Edict of Expulsion took the ballads with them, a token of Jewish integration into Spanish culture and an enduring reminder of their Spanish origin. I propose to look at the portrayal of the Muslim protagonists in the Sephardic Romancero and to demonstrate how, throughout the Sephardic tradition, whether within or outside Spain, the Moor continues to be represented from a Christian rather than a Jewish perspective. I will also discuss vestiges of the so-called *convivencia* between Christians, Muslims, and Jews as depicted in the Romancero.

Perhaps one of the most unexpected aspects of the Sephardic ballad tradition is that its protagonists are almost exclusively Muslim or Christian. Jews are glimpsed in less than a handful of the ballads and when they do appear it is in the context of the three religions of Medieval Spain and not as individuals in their own right. Nevertheless, Sephardic Jews have played an important role as guardians of the Spanish ballad tradition, keeping it alive well into the twentieth century in Morocco and in the former Ottoman Empire. In so doing they have maintained this venerable Hispanic repertoire with remarkable fidelity to the early texts that evolved during the final century of Jewish life in Spain.[2]

---

1 Spanish ballads have a formal structure of sixteen-syllable lines with a fixed assonance running the length of each poem.

2 Rina Benmayor, "Social Determinants in Poetic Transmission: The Sephardic Romancero," in *The Sepharadi and Oriental Jewish Heritage: Studies*, ed. Issachar Ben-Ami (Jerusalem: The Magnes Press, The Hebrew University, 1982), 254 convincingly argues that it was precisely because Jews, like other accepted religious minorities, were allowed religious and cultural independence that the Sephardic ballad flourished within Muslim lands: "It was a product of a social system and set of relations that allowed Jews to retain an identity distinct from that of the surrounding foreign context."

Muslims in the Sephardic Ballad

Many of the oldest Spanish ballads relate episodes of the country's early history, imparting news of the frontier battles and skirmishes between Muslims and Christians during the Christian Reconquest of Spain.[3] They were composed to publicize and make known events of the time, particularly the exploits of Christian nobles as they repelled their Muslim foes and won back territory that had formerly been Christian. "Ballads [...] were also consciously exploited to protect the future memory of events."[4] Not only do Spanish ballads record the sieges, battles, raids, and acts of military daring or rashness that characterize much of the fifteenth century, they also reflect the new Spain emerging from its medieval past. The background of the Spanish ballad and, consequently, that of the Sephardic tradition that preserved it, is a clearly Christian state. It is, therefore, to be expected that Sephardic ballads, consisting for the most part of pre-Expulsion texts, should abound in Christian terms and allusions to the church, bishops, friars, and saints' days are numerous. The references to the Jews in ballads such as *La buena hija* (*The Good Daughter*) and *Moriana y Galván* (*Moriana and Galván*) (infra) are exceptional.

When Spain was at last united in 1469 under one crown upon the marriage of Ferdinand of Aragon and Isabel of Castile, the Spanish monarchs could concentrate their energy on the final stages of winning back territory lost to Muslim rule.[5] The Jewish contribution to the Reconquest movement was unseen, for it took the part of supporting state finance. The focus of the ballads is on Christians and Muslims pitted against each other–the Jews are invisible. Nevertheless, these texts have been kept alive by the Jews of Muslim lands, certainly in the case of Morocco, living amongst descendants of those same Muslims, Moors or *moros* whose exploits the ballads recount.

Historical ballads, including the *romances fronterizos*, frequently comment upon the Moor's appearance.[6] The clothing of Christians is rarely alluded to and then only because it has been carefully selected to serve a

---

3 See Samuel G. Armistead, *El Romancero judeo-español en el Archivo Menéndez Pidal: catálogo-índice de romances y canciones*, with Selma Margaretten, Paloma Montero & Ana Valenciano, FERS, 1–3 (Madrid: CSMP, 1978).

4 Angus MacKay, "Religion, Culture, and Ideology on the Late Medieval Castilian-Granadan Frontier," in *Medieval Frontier Societies*, ed. Robert Bartlett and Angus MacKay (Oxford: Clarendon, 1989), 235.

5 Angus MacKay, *Spain in the Middle Ages: From Frontier to Empire, 1000–1500* (New York: Palgrave Macmillan, 1997), 197 has pointed out that "during the period 1350–1460 there were eighty-five years of peace and only twenty-five of 'official' war with the kingdom of Granada."

6 The Sephardic Romancero is divided into a number of distinct categories that range from the earliest subtypes, Epic, Carolongian, and Historical, A, B, and C, to Various Subjects, X (Armistead, *El Romancero*).

particular purpose, such as to seduce or to indicate power. In *Búcar sobre Valencia*, *Búcar at Valencia*, for example, the Cid urges his daughter to dress in her best festive clothes so as to seduce the Moor, Búcar. This will give the Cid the opportunity to kill Búcar: "quítate panos de siempre / y ponte los de la pascua."[7] The frequent references to the Moor's sumptuous clothing, however, emphasize the image of the Muslim as the Other, whose apparel is very different from that of the Christian. In *El moro de Antequera*, *The Moor of Antequera*, the Moor's costume is highly distinctive:

> la toca que él yevava, lavrada a la maravía;
> que se la lavró esta toca Xerifá, la su amiga;
> Xerifá que está en altas torres, las más altas que Turquía.[8]
>
> [The headdress that he wore was wonderfully embroidered;
> his beloved Xerifá had embroidered it for him;
> Xerifá who is in a high tower, the highest in Turkey.][9]

This reference to Turkey emphasizes both the exotic and the foreign in the Moor and his entourage. The Moors against whom the Spanish Christians were fighting in these frontier encounters were descendants of the early Muslim settlers. However, as demonstrated here, the term Turkish, to indicate a Muslim, was used also in both Sephardic and Peninsular ballads, for the enemy of the Spanish Christians was now the Turkish/Ottoman fleet against which the Spanish fought several battles in the sixteenth century.[10] For that reason the term "Turkish" could refer to someone from either Morocco or, possibly, the Ottoman Empire. The Moroccan sultan, Mostadí, of *El Mostadí*, is, therefore, referred to as *el Gran Turco*, the Great Turk.[11]

The description in Moshe Attias's reading from Salonica elaborates on the lavishness of the Moor of Antequera's turban and the awe it would inspire, for it is adorned with a sapphire that at night shines even more brightly than the midday sun:

---

7 Paul Bénichou, *Romancero Judeo-español de Marruecos* (Madrid: Castalia, 1968), 38, l. 15.

8 Samuel G. Armistead and Joseph H. Silverman, eds., "Dos romances fronterizos en la tradición sefardí oriental," in *Nueva Revista de Filología Hispánica*, 13, Armistead and Silverman (1959), 91–92, ll. 6–8. The town of Antequera in southern Andalucia was recaptured in 1410.

9 Unless otherwise stated, the translations are mine.

10 Paloma Díaz-Mas "La visión del otro en la literatura oral: judíos y musulmanes en el romancero hispánico," *Studi Ispanici*, 32 (2007): 26 comments as follows on the changing frontier: "La nueva lucha fronteriza estaba ahora en el Mediterráneo, con la expansión del imperio otomano y las frecuentes incursiones desde el imperio turco y sus provincias sobre los barcos de los reinos cristianos."

11 Armistead, *El Romancero*, I, 185–87.

Al cabo de la su toca tiene una pieḍra źafira,
qu'arelumbra en la noche más que el sol de mediodía.[12]

Spanish versions of our ballad depict the Moor setting out from Antequera on his mission to ask for reinforcements for the town: "De Antequera partió el moro / tres horas antes del día."[13] In Sephardic readings, however, (the ballad has been collected in Jerusalem and Rhodes) the geographical setting, Antequera, has disappeared. Instead, we are told that the Moor is setting out from Friday prayers: "De la yuma sale el moro, / de la yuma al mediodía,"[14] once again stressing the Moor's alien habits. The name of the distant Spanish town, Antequera, a place that no longer had any significance for the Sephardic interpreters of the song, has been replaced by the familiar concept for the Jews in Muslim lands of Friday prayers. This introduces into the original Spanish text a feature of Muslim life that was familiar to the Jews of Muslim lands and adds *couleur locale* to the Hispanic ballad.[15]

The vivid concise portraits of Moorish warriors are not restricted to their clothing but include references to the Moors' horses, emphasizing the close bond between horseman and steed, and the implied skill at handling the horses. The Arabian stallions are decorated with the same lavish textiles and decorations as their masters, melding them into one showy vigorous unit. Indeed, the Moor of Antequera's horse has such a sumptuous harness that it would enrich a hundred thousand poor men: "cien mil pobres riquecía."[16]

Not only did the Moors wear elaborate headdresses and richly embroidered clothing and adorn their thoroughbred horses with pennants and embroideries but they also decorated their faces and bodies with cosmetics. In yet another historical ballad, *Garcilaso de la Vega* (Garcilaso is the name of the Christian protagonist), a Moor rides up to challenge the besieged

12 Attias, Moshe, ed., *Romancero sefaradí: romanzas y cantes populares en judeo-español* (Jerusalem: Ben-Zvi Institute, 1961), 107, ll. 47–50. Rosaflorida's castle is equally lavish; its battlements are surmounted by a similarly extraordinary jewel (*Rosaflorida y Montesinos*): "entre almena y almena / esta una piedra safira.// tanto relumbra de noche / como el sol de al medio dia" (Pomeroy 2005: 171, ll. 3–4). Hilary S. Pomeroy, ed., *An Edition and Study of the Secular Ballads in the Sephardic Ballad Notebook of Halia Isaac Cohen* (Newark, Del.: Juan de la Cuesta, 2005). I have retained the spelling and punctuation of the notebook.

13 Armistead and Silverman, "Dos romances fronterizos," 96, ll.1–2, who quote, in full, the *Cancionero de romances impreso en Amberes sin año* text.

14 Armistead, *El Romancero*, I, 157–58. *Yuma* (Ar.) "Friday prayer assembly."

15 Samuel G. Armistead, *Tres calas en el romancero sefardí: Rodas, Jerusalén, Estados Unidos* (Madrid: Castalia, 1979), 44–45, 91–92, has studied both the Rhodes and Jerusalem texts.

16 Paloma Díaz-Mas, *Poesía oral sefardí* (Coruña: Esquío, 1994), 98, l. 5. This description recalls the Duke of Gandía's costly ring (*La muerte del duque de Gandía*): "Anillo lleva en el dedo, / cjen probes ricos s'hacían" (Attias, *Romancero*, 120 ll. 5–6).

Christians of Santa Fuente. The Moor's appearance is grotesquely menacing. He has a glass eye and his other eye is circled with the cosmetic kohl; his arms are dyed with henna:

> un ojo tiene de vidrio y el otro alcoholado, [...]
> el brazo blanco y peludo, la meatad de él alheñado.[17]

Such cosmetics, widely used throughout the Eastern Mediterranean and North Africa, had been introduced into Spain by the Moors. Indeed, Muhammad VI, king of fourteenth-century Granada, was known as the Red King because of his hennaed hair and beard.[18] The practice was documented in Sebastian de Covarrubias's 1611 dictionary of the Spanish language: "Con las raízes desta planta tiñen en Turquía y otras partes las colas y clines de los cavallos, y los moros y moras los cabellos y uñas."[19]

Once the reunification of Christian Spain had been achieved in 1469, after decades of internal political strife, the Reconquest of Muslim Spain resumed in earnest. On 28 February 1482, in a surprise attack, Christian forces recaptured Alhama, a Muslim stronghold in the kingdom of Granada, and a "new and final phase" in the Reconquest was set in motion.[20] Hernando Pulgar, the Catholic monarch's official historian, spoke of the "terrible destruction' the Christians wreaked upon the town."[21] News of Alhama's capture was given in two ballads, *La pérdida de Alhama*, *The Loss of Alhama*, and *El alcaide de Alhama*, *The Commander of Alhama*.[22] The latter text, *El alcaide de Alhama*, is related from the point of view of the town's Moorish commander and presents an imagined dialogue between the *alcaide*, the commander, and a messenger from the Muslim king of Granada. The messenger's opening words present the commander as a fierce soldier with the references to his beard stressing the commander's virility.[23]

17 Paloma Díaz-Mas, *Romancero* (Barcelona: Crítica, 1994), 404, ll. 10, 12. "Anillo lleva 'n su dedo, cien prove rico s'hazía." Rina Benmayor, *Romances judeo-españoles de Oriente*, FERS, 5 (Madrid: CSMP-Gedos, 1979), 31, 2a, l. 8.

18 "Muhammad VI est dénommé *Rey Bermejo* par les chroniqueurs castillans en raison de la couleur de ses cheveux et de sa barbe" Rachel Arié, *L'Espagne musulmane au temps des Nasrides, 1232–1492* (Paris: Boccard, 1973), 391.

19 Sebastián de Covarrubias Orozco, *Tesoro de la lengua castellana o española según la impression de 1611*, ed. Martin de Riquer (Barcelona: Horta, 1943), 89. Armistead and Silverman, "Dos romances fronterizos," 94; note the appearance of the Moorish leaders.

20 For more details, see L. P. Harvey, *Islamic Spain, 1250–1500* (Chicago: University of Chicago Press, 1990), 269.

21 Ibid., 271.

22 Jan Gilbert, "The Lamentable Loss of Alhama in Paseábase el rey moro," *Modern Languages Review* 100.4 (2005): 1000–14.

23 As Díaz-Mas, (*Romancero*), 201 n. 1, has commented "la barba es signo de honor viril."

The king berates the *alcaide* (who had, in fact, received royal permission to leave Alhama to attend a wedding) for letting the town fall to the Christians. He orders the *alcaide*'s arrest and execution, demanding that his decapitated head be displayed on a lance for all to see:

> moro alcalde moro alcalde el de la belluda barba
> el rey le mando prender por la perdida de alama
> que le corten la cabeza y se la enfilen en la lanza
> para sea el castigo y otros tambien de mirarla.[24]

Such drastic and brutal punishment was not unusual at this time nor was such activity confined to the Muslims. Contemporary accounts of the dual between the one-eyed hennaed Moor from Antequera and his Christian opponent, Garcia Laso de la Vega, (*Garcilaso de la Vega*), tell us that García Laso was equally bloodthirsty: "consigue derribar al infiel, al que corta la cabeza y quita la lanza y el caballo, que lleva como trofeo, entre los gritos de entusiasmo y aclamaciones del ejército cristiano."[25] Sadly, such beheadings may well have been familiar to the Sephardic singers who kept the ballad alive well into the twentieth century, for it was reputedly the unfortunate lot of Moroccan Jews to collect and salt the decapitated heads of prisoners.[26] However, those events so distant in time and place, the recapture of Antequera in 1410 and of Alhama in 1482, had little significance for the Sephardim of the Diaspora. In *El moro de Antequera*, the name Antequera has disappeared altogether and in most versions of *El alcaide de Alhama* the name Alhama is distorted. *El alcaide de Alhama* has survived, among the Sephardis in a truncated version of the longer Spanish text for its human, rather than its historical, interest.

The concluding lines of Sephardic versions of *El alcaide de Alhama* are succinct. The commander's reply is that while the Muslim king has indeed lost the town, the commander himself has suffered an even greater loss–his

---

24 Pomeroy 2005: 110, 1-4. Jan Gilbert's comment: "while the Christian protagonists are afforded some individuality in the ballad through their names, the Muslim characters remain unnamed, generic figures, as occurs in numerous *romances fronterizos*" applies here (2005: 1013).

25 Antonio Salazar, "García Laso de la Vega," in *Revista de Estudios Extremeños*, 19 (1963), 491. Angus MacKay, "Religion, Culture, and Ideology on the Late Medieval Castilian-Granada Frontier," in *Medieval Frontier Societies*, eds. Robert Bartlett and Angus MacKay (Oxford: Clarendon, 1989), 228-29, speaks of the "patterns of savage cruelty" exhibited by both sides and gives explicit examples.

26 According to the historian Howard Sachar, *Farewell España: The World of the Sephardim Remembered* (N.Y.: Vintage, 1994), 196, "Well into the nineteenth century, the government assigned Jews the degrading chore of personally gathering up the heads of executed criminals or rebels fallen in combat, then salting the remains and hanging them on city gates for public display. In smaller towns, the repugnant obligation continued into the twentieth century."

honorable name and his family. Despite the *alcaide*'s offer to pay a generous ransom, he has lost his most precious possession, his beloved daughter, who has converted to Christianity. The ballad of *El Alcaide de Alhama* has died out in the Peninsular oral tradition. It has been left to the Sephardic Jews living in Muslim lands to keep alive the memory of the sad events of Alhama and, in particular, to sympathize with the inconsolable Muslim and his bitter grief at his beloved daughter's conversion. One cannot help but wonder whether these Sephardic singers recalling that event felt any emotion at singing a song about forced conversion to Christianity, a fate their forefathers had chosen to avoid at such great cost.

In yet other ballads it is the Muslims whose aim is to convert the enemy to the true faith. The Muslim king of *El cautiverio de Guarinos*, *The Captivity of Guarinos*, seeks in vain to persuade his high-ranking Christian captive, Guarinos, to convert to Islam. He offers increasingly valuable enticements: vineyards, wealth, even his sister as a wife.[27] Guarinos resists all such temptations and the Moor reacts by inflicting horrific punishment:

> M*a*rlotes con gran enojo   en carceles lo manda echar
> con esposas alas manos   porque pierda el pelear
> el agua fasta la cinta   porque pierda el caualgar
> siete quintales de fierro   desde el hombro al cancañar.[28]
>
> In a great rage, Marlotes orders Guarinos thrown into the dungeon:
> with shackles on his hands so that he could no longer fight,
> water up to his waist so that he could no longer ride,
> and seven iron weights from his shoulders to his heels.]

The Judeo-Spanish Romancero has a specific ballad category devoted to prisoners and captives. It is interesting to note that although they are present also in the Eastern Mediterranean Sephardic tradition, such ballads form a particularly substantial part of the Moroccan repertoire, doubtless because so many Moroccan Sephardi Jews had experienced, or lived in the fear of experiencing, captivity at the hands of the Barbary corsairs who held sway over the Mediterranean.

> Throughout the twenty-year struggle for control of Granada, Barbary pirates and potentates—particularly those of Tlemcen and Morocco—supplied their Muslim allies by sea. [...] Actual expeditions were also launched from Africa. Christian lands were pillaged, villages were burnt, and captives carried off.[29]

---

27 Pomeroy 2009: 274, ll. 10–12.

28 Armistead and Silverman, *Judeo-Spanish Ballads from Oral Tradition, II: Carolingian Ballads, I: Roncesvalles*, with Israel J. Katz, Folk Literature of the Sephardic Jews, 3 (Berkeley: University of California Press, 1994), 91, ll. 20–23.

29 Jacques Heers, *The Barbary Corsairs: Warfare in the Mediterranean, 1480–1580*, trans. Jonathan North (London: Greenhill, 2003), 25.

In ballads of prisoners and captives, the captives are usually Christian, invariably royal or of high rank, and the kidnappers Muslim. The kidnapping usually takes place on Spanish soil as in *Las hermanas reina y cautiva*, *The Two Sisters: Queen and Captive*:

> la reina cherifa mora   la que moraen almeria
> dice que tiene deseo   de una cristiana cautiva.[30]
>
> [The noble Moorish queen, she who lives in Almeria,
> Says that she wants a Christian as a slave.]

And so, Count Flores's wife is duly abducted and forced to become housekeeper to the Muslim queen.

In yet other ballads, the kidnappers are not local Muslims living in Spain but the pirates or corsairs from Morocco who carry their human booty back to North Africa. Jews were not alone in fearing North African corsairs. For decades the inhabitants of Spain's Mediterranean coast lived in constant fear of Muslim marauders. Although Christian nobles were particularly welcome targets, for they would attract high ransoms, humble citizens were also abducted to be sold as slaves. In fifteenth-century Spanish versions of *El cautivo del renegado*, *The Renegade's Captive*, the setting is usually Andalucia. In some Peninsular and most Sephardic versions, the slave market to which the unfortunate captive is taken is in Vélez de la Gomera, a pirate's base situated between Melilla and Tetuán.[31] The Christian captive is treated with the cruelty associated with Muslim masters and his harsh treatment closely resembles that found in the accounts of European survivors. The starving slave lives on a frugal diet of stale bread and a little water. He is forced to wear a bit between his teeth to prevent him eating, in desperation, the raw grain that he mills for his master:

> el dia a majar esparto.   la noche a moler sidera.
> frenito en la mi boca   porque de ello no comiera.[32]

Jews in the Sephardic Ballad

As Paloma Díaz-Mas has pointed out, the fifteenth century was one when "sucedieron una serie de acontecimientos importantisimos en la historia de los judíos de la Peninsula Ibérica."[33] Nonetheless, "prácticamente nada de esto se refleja en el romancero, donde los judíos parecen estar totalments ausente, con unas pocas - y significativas - excepciones."[34] Despite this

30 Pomeroy 2005: 85, ll. 1–2.

31 For a study of the treatment of Spanish captives in Morocco, see Ellen G. Friedman. *Spanish Captives in North Africa in the Early Modern Age* (Madison, Wisc.: The University of Wisconsin Press, 1983).

32 Pomeroy 2005: 269, ll. 8–9.

33 Paloma Díaz-Mas, "'La visión del otro," 12.

34 Ibid.

almost complete absence of Jewish protagonists their presence is occasionally glimpsed. The earliest depiction of tri-religious Spain occurs in Peninsular versions of the Carolingian ballad *El cautiverio de Guarinosy.* Here, members of Spain's three faiths joyfully, and perhaps incongruously, celebrate together a Christian saint's day, that of St. John, 24 June, a sign of cultural symbiosis:

> van se dias vienen dias venido era el de sant juan
> donde christianos y moros hazen gran solenidad
> los christianos echan junça y los moros arayhan
> los judios echan eneas por la fiesta mas honrrar.[35]

> [Days went by, other days came, then came the Day of Saint John,
> which all the Moors and Christians celebrate with great pomp.
> The Christians throw down sedge and the Moors sweet basil
> and the Jews throw bulrushes to honor the feast even more.]

This mid-sixteenth-century depiction of Christians, Muslims, and Jews celebrating the same festive day has not lived on in Sephardic versions of the ballad. References to the three religions have, however, survived intact in Sephardic readings of the Spanish ballads *La buena hija*, *The Good Daughter*, and *Moriana y Galván*, *Moriana and Galván*. In each ballad, the question "Who has harmed you?" is asked in tripartite form. In *La buena hija*, the Cid weeps because he cannot provide a dowry for the eponymous daughter while in *Moriana y Galván*, Moriana weeps over her captivity:

> Si os han hecho mal los moros, los mandaré yo a matare;
> si os han hecho mal quistianos, los mandaré a cativare;
> so os han hecho mal judíos, los mandaré a desterrare.[36]

> [If the Moors have harmed you, I will have them killed;
> If the Christians have harmed you, I will have them taken captive;
> If the Jews have harmed you, I will order them exiled.]

In both Spanish ballads the answer to these questions is in the negative, for neither Christians, Moors, nor Jews have harmed the daughter. Sephardic versions frequently modify this answer, distinguishing Jews from the other two groups and defending them:

---

[35] Samuel G. Armistead, "The Memory of Tri-Religious Spain in the Sephardic *Romancero*," in *Encuentros* and *Desencuentros: Spanish Jewish Cultural Interaction throughout History*, ed. Carlos Carrete Parrondo et al. (Tel-Aviv: University Publishing Projects, 2000), 266. Armistead, whose translation I also reproduce, cites the version published in the *Cancionero de romances impreso en Amberes sin año* (ff. 100v.-103 r.). For more details of Muslim-Christian symbiosis, see Armistead and Silverman, "*La sanjuanada*: ¿huellas de una ḫarǧa mozárabe en la tradición actual?" *Nueva Revista de Filología Hispánica* 18 (1961): 436-43 and Armistead, "The Memory of Tri-Religious Spain," 282, n.13.

[36] Bénichou, *Romancero,* 180: ll. 4-6.

> Ni me han hecho mal los moros, ni los mandes a matare;
> ni me ha hecho mal quistianos, no los mandes a cativare.
> ni me han hecho mal judíos, gente es que mal no hazen.[37]
>
> [The Moors have done me no harm, do not have them killed;
> nor have the Christians harmed me, do not have them taken captive;
> nor have Jews caused me any harm, they are a people who do no ill.]

There is also a vague recollection of *convivencia*, in the Sephardic ballad, *La princess rescatada*, *The Rescued Princess*, set in the busy port of Tetuan. Here, once again, the three religions are present but, unusually, a fourth group, one intimately linked with Tetuan, appears: the *andalusis* or *moriscos*, Muslims from Spain who developed the town. This would suggest that the ballad was created after their expulsion from Spain in 1609.

> ganaron judios y moros los cristianos pierden mas
> ganaron los andalusos la jente de tetuan. [38]
>
> [The Jews and Moors profited, the Christians lost,
> The Andaluses, the people of Tetuan, profited, too.]

The opening lines of *La expulsión de los judíos de Portugal*, *The Expulsion of the Jews from Portugal*, another Sephardic creation, have various motifs characteristic of the traditional Spanish ballad.[39] There are three sisters, the youngest of whom, the main protagonist, is searching for a husband. Following this formulaic introduction the ballad recounts the Spanish princess's arrival in Portugal for her marriage to the king. Somehow or other the distant memory of Spain's three religions now resurfaces with a description of a ceremony practiced in medieval Spain. The scene closely recalls one in an anonymous mid-twelfth-century prose chronicle, the *Chronica Adefonsi imperatoris*, *The Chronicle of Emperor Alfonso*. It relates Alfonso VII's jubilant return to his capital, Toledo, following triumphant campaigns in Muslim territory. In accord with medieval custom, members of the three religious communities leave the city to welcome their sovereign:

> Post haec autem, Imperator disposuit venire Toletum. Sed cum omnis populus audisset quod imperator veniret Toletum, omnes principes christianorum et Sarracenorum et Iudaeorum, et tota plebs civitatis, longe a civitate exierunt obviam ei cum timpanis et citharis et psalteriis et omni genere musicorum.[40]

---

[37] Ibid., ll. 7-9.

[38] Pomeroy 2005: 79, ll. 4-5.

[39] The ballad is studied in Rosalie Guzofsky, "Mujeres heroicas en el romancero judeoespañol" (Ph.D. diss., University of Pennsylvania, 1990), 166-85. See also Armistead 2003: 267-69, Pomeroy 2005: 135-44, and Díaz-Mas, "La visión del otro," 13-14.

[40] *Chronica Adefonsi imperatoris*, ed. Luis Sánchez Belda (Madrid: CSIC, 1950) 379r-380v.

> [After these events, the Emperor decided to go to Toledo. But when the populace heard that he was coming to Toledo, all the Christian, Muslim and Jewish leaders and the commoners of the city went out to meet him with tambourines, lutes, psalteries and all sorts of musical instruments.]

Likewise, the ballad presents members of the three religions leaving the capital in order to greet the princess:

> y salieron me a encontrar   tres leyes a maravilla
> los cristianos con sus cruses.   los moros ala turquilla
> los judios con las sus leyes   por D. que bien parecia.[41]
>
> [Members of the three religions came out to meet me:
> Christians with their crosses, Muslim dressed Turkish style,
> Jews with their torah scrolls to please God.]

In this vivid image, each religion is linked to its most distinguishing visual feature: Christians carry their crosses, Muslims are clothed in their exotic "Turkish" dress, and Jews bring out their Torah scrolls.

An even closer link to the twelfth-century Chronicle's account has survived in a Moroccan reading. Here the Jews do not, as in other versions, parade the Torah scrolls, but, as in the *Chronica Adefonsi imperatoris*, they play medieval musical instruments: "los judíos con vihuelas / que la ciudad se estrujía" ["The Jews with their *vihuelas* that made the city resound"].[42] A version from Salonica, recorded by Armistead and Silverman in New York in 1959, adapts and transports the procession to its Ottoman counterpart. The Moors are now Turks attending their mosques and the Christians are Greek Orthodox going to church:

> Los turkos en las meskitas,   los gregos van a la klisa,
> los ǧidiós a la Ley Santa,   la ke la sivdá mos guadra.[43]

However appealing this image of religious harmony in Portugal might be, it is fictitious. Isabel had stipulated, as part of her marriage contract to Dom Manuel, that Portugal expel its Jews before her arrival. Yet, according to the Sephardic text, the princess is horrified to encounter Jews advancing to welcome her:

> en la siudad de mi padre no ubo judio ni judia
> y ahora si D. me ayuda lo mismo haré en las mias.[44]

---

41 Pomeroy 2005: 135, ll. 7–9.

42 Ramón, Menéndez Pidal, ed., "Catálogo del romancero judío-español," *Cultura Española*, 4 (1906): 1064, l. 9. The *vihuela* was an early form of the guitar.

43 Armistead and Silverman, *Tres calas*: 128, ll. 12–13.

44 Pomeroy 2005: 135, ll. 10–11.

She thereupon insists that the Jews be expelled forthwith:

> Ya sacan á los judíos, los sacan de la juderia,
> de ellos se iban por mar, de ellos por tierra se iban.
> La reina saliera á ver, á ver como ellos salían.[45]

La pérdida del rey don Sebastián, *The Death of King Sebastian* narrates the attempted Portuguese invasion of northern Morocco in 1578, thus maintaining the Hispanic tradition of disseminating contemporary events in ballad form. Only three versions, all oral, have been collected.[46] The events as related in the ballad correspond accurately to archival accounts, suggesting that the ballad was created shortly after the invasion, sometime in the late sixteenth century, while still fresh in the memory. In most Hispanic ballads the Muslims are the enemy, but here the roles are reversed. The enemy is now a Christian king, Dom Sebastian of Portugal. Sebastian proposed not only to expand his foothold in Morocco but, supported by the pope, to convert the local population, Muslim or Jewish, to Catholicism. So while in Peninsular ballads it is the Christians and Moors who confront each other and there is no mention of Jews, in this unique Sephardic creation the Portuguese Christians cross the Mediterranean to attack Muslim and Jewish inhabitants alike:

> Estábanse los cristianos en Portugal asentados:
> –Vamos a Berbería; traeremos muchos ducados;
> traeremos moros y moras y judíos cautivados.[47]

Funded to a great extent by the monies he had received from New Christians whom he had allowed to leave Portugal the previous year, Sebastian and his vast army set off across the Mediterranean Sea. Once again, the Sephardic Jews who had fled across the Mediterranean from Spain and Portugal in order to escape conversion were under threat. Fortunately for Jews and Muslims alike, after some initial success, Sebastian and his army suffered overwhelming defeat. The ballad concludes with a particularly gruesome scene. Sebastian attempts to escape by throwing himself into the sea. The Moors fish him out, flay him alive, and stuff his skin with bran.

The most recent Sephardic creation relates the tragic death, probably in 1834, of a young Jewess from Tangier, Sol Hachuel. Like the fifteenth-century Spanish historical ballads, *El moro de Antequera and El alcaide de Alhama*, works that disseminated news of outstanding events, Sol's martyrdom–for she was falsely accused of apostasy by her Muslim neighbors–has been

45 Menéndez Pidal, "Catálogo," 1064, ll. 13–15.

46 Manuel Manrique de Lara collected these versions in Tetuan in 1916 (Armistead, *El Romancero*, 182–83). They are kept in the Archivo Menéndez Pidal.

47 Paloma Díaz-Mas. "Temas comunes en el romancero Portugués y Sefardí," in *Os judeus sefarditas: Entre Portugal, España e Marrocos* (Lisbon: Colibri, 2004), 254: ll. 1–3.

kept alive in the common memory in *Sol la Saddika*, one of the most popular ballads among young Moroccan girls, well into the twentieth century.[48] A victim of Muslim treachery, unyielding to promises of reward and defying all threats, this *eshet hayil,* dies a martyr "Yo, señor, he nacido hebrea, / y hebrea tendré que morir."[49]

So what image of Muslims and Jews emerges in the Sephardic ballad? It is basically the one created in an essentially Christian genre. Flourishing in the fifteenth century, it mirrors the unfolding history of the emerging Spain. Portraits of each religious group are in accord with the Christian perception. Jews disappear, with no apparent role to play other than as part of the memory of that distant *convivencia*, Muslims defend their last remaining kingdom with courage and daring. A foreign alien presence whose exotic, oriental appearance sets him apart, a skilled warrior and a cruel, barbaric enemy whose aim is to convert the Christian foe to the law of Mohammed, such is the portrayal of the Moor. And where do the Sephardic Jews fit into this? Well, it is very much thanks to them that these poetic accounts of the frontier wars have survived and so faithful are the surviving Sephardic versions to the original Christian texts that there is only the very rare attempt at giving some defensive comment and always in the tri-religious context. With the Jews set apart, confined to their own communities, it is precisely because of Muslim law that the absorption of Jewish culture into the local one was prevented. As in the early Spanish texts with their terse dialogue, vivid dramatic action, Sephardic contributions to the genre maintain the traditional hostility between Islam and Christianity, leaving the Jews, as so often the case, set aside.

---

48 Messod Salama has written a detailed study of the ballad and its background in "'Yo, señor, he nacido hebrea / y hebrea tendré que morir': Forced Conversion, Religious Conflict, and Female Martyrdom in the Judeo-Spanish Ballad *Sol la Saddika,"* in *Proceedings of the Twelfth British Conference on Judeo-Spanish Studies (2001): Sephardic Language, Literature and History*, ed. Hilary Pomeroy and Michael Alpert (Leiden: Brill, 2004), 129–40. See also Sarah Leibovici, "Sol Hachuel la Tsaddikah ou la force de la Foi (1834)," *Pardes*, 4 (1986): 134–45.

49 Salama, "'Yo, señor," 129.

The Jews of al-Andalus
Factionalism in the Golden Age

JONATHAN RAY

For scholars of Judaic Studies, the subject of Andalusi Jewry usually brings to mind two distinct fields of inquiry: the intellectual and cultural symbiosis that helped to produce a Golden Age of Jewish literature, philosophy, and science, and the outbreaks of anti-Jewish violence and persecution that were, in large part, a reaction to the high degree of Jewish integration into Muslim society. As such, adaptation and exclusion have become opposite poles that have helped to define and measure the level of cultural accommodation of Andalusi Jewry, what some have referred to as "Arabization."[1] What has generally gone unnoticed is the degree to which the same exclusionary attitudes that threatened the stability of the Andalusi Jews from without were replicated within the community itself. Indeed, Jewish assimilation of Arabic social norms helped to produce a local Jewish community that was often beset by factionalism and intellectual and social discord. As the new center of Jewish civilization in al-Andalus rose to prominence during the tenth and eleventh centuries, it came to be characterized by a provincial nativism that privileged regional identity, as well as religious affiliation. This hostility to outsiders within the local Jewish community had a critical impact on the way in which the Jews in this region interacted with the older Jewish centers of the Near East, and must be viewed as an internalization of Andalusi Muslim society.

Efforts to sharpen our understanding of the correlation between Jewish and Islamic culture in the pre-modern world have been hampered by an inability to integrate the structures of intellectual and social history. The result has been an unnecessarily narrow definition of Arabization that fails to consider social divisions and political partisanship within the Jewish polity as a reflection of the dissonant nature of its host society. It may be helpful

1 Ross Brann, "The Arabized Jews," in *The Literature of al-Andalus*, ed. María Rosa Menocal, Raymond Scheindlin, and Michael Sells (Cambridge, 2000), 435–54. For other efforts to define the character of Andalusi Jewry in light of the influence of its host society, see Esperanza Alfonso, "La construcción de la identidad judía en al-Andalus en la Edad Media," *El Olivo* 49 (1999): 5–24; and Yom Tov Assis, "'Sefarad:' A Definition in the Context of a Cultural Encounter, in *Encuentros and Desencuentros: Spanish Jewish Cultural Interaction Throughout History*, ed. Carlos Carrete Parrondo (Tel Aviv, 2000), 29–37.

to bear in mind that, despite the presence of a string of rabbinic luminaries whose diverse intellectual output gave rise to the term "Golden Age," Jewish communal power in al-Andalus remained in the hands of a merchant oligarchy that was routinely divided into competing factions.[2] Though such internal strife was by no means unique, several aspects of local Jewish and local Muslim society helped to shape the direction and intensity of these socio-political divides. The lack of long-standing institutions such as the Exilarchate and the Gaonate also meant that Andalusi Jewry did not have any clear, formally recognized leader, a situation that was no doubt exacerbated during the fragmentation of Muslim political power during the Taifa period (ca. eleventh century). This lack of an institutional framework and clear process of succession in Jewish communal government would have important implications for the formation of Sephardic political and intellectual leadership.

An exploration of Andalusi Jewish attitudes toward themselves and others should probably begin with the great foundation myth of Sephardic Judaism popularized by Abraham Ibn Daud in his twelfth-century chronicle, *Sefer ha-Qabbalah*. According to Ibn Daud, the Jewish community of Cordoba effected the transfer of religious authority from East to West by appointing the rabbinic immigrant Moses ben Hanokh as their leader and judge, and using his considerable knowledge as the basis of a new, independent Jewish center.[3] The story goes on to note that the Jews of Cordoba officially recognized R. Moses' authority by allotting him a large stipend and other trappings of communal leadership, a gesture that was approved by the local Muslim king 'Abd al-Rahman III (r. 912–961). Ibn Daud then explains that once word of R. Moses' instillation as head of Cordoban Jewry spread among the Jews of Spain and North Africa, the latter promptly switched their allegiance and financial support from the old academies of Baghdad to those of al-Andalus. This last passage echoes the story's opening lines and would seem to bring to a close the account of Sephardic succession of the Baghdadi center. At this point, however, Ibn Daud includes an aside that gives some insight into the nature of Sephardic leadership, or at least Sephardic self-perception. He notes that both R. Moses and his son and successor R. Hanokh married into a local family called Ibn Falija, which the chronicler characterizes as the leading Jewish clan in Cordoba. Later, we are told, R. Hanokh's daughter also was married to a man from this same family,

---

[2] A letter from Baghdad to Spain shows that the practice of interrupting prayers was used in Spain as a means of communal governance. The geonic response to the Andalusi practice was one of surprise that they did not have a judge, and that they allowed such matters to be decided by the community. Michael Walzer et al., eds., *The Jewish Political Tradition*, vol. 1 (New Haven, 2000), 398.

[3] Gerson D. Cohen, *Sefer Ha-Qabbalah, The Book of Tradition by Abraham Ibn Daud* (Philadelphia, 1967), 68.

ending the distinct Eastern (i.e. "foreign") lineage of the great sage. Thus, it is only after assimilating into the pre-existing oligarchy of the local community that the transfer of power is complete.

This legendary account of Andalusi Jewry's independence resonates with the actual historical problems caused by its evolution into a leading Jewish center. Moses ben Hanokh was a real figure and one of a wave of Jewish immigrants drawn to Spain by the wealthy and charismatic tenth-century *nasi* of Cordoba, Hasday ibn Shaprut. Of the sweeping effects of Hasday's tenure as leader of Cordoban Jewry, the Muslim chronicler Sa'id al-Andalusi notes:

> He was the first to open for Andalusi Jewry the gates of their science of jurisprudence, chronology, and other subjects. Previously, they had recourse to the Jews of Baghdad, in order to learn the law of their faith and in order to adjust the calendar and determine the dates of their holidays.[4]

As noted in this passage, Hasday followed the lead of the Andalusi Umayyad Caliphate and gathered about him leading scholars from throughout the Jewish world who came to Cordoba seeking his teaching and patronage.[5] It was only with the *nasi*'s backing that Moses was able to attain the position of leading rabbi and judge in Spain. As much as this development prompted concern within the older Jewish centers of the East, it created an even greater problem for the families of the native Sephardic oligarchy, who now found their status and authority challenged by a wave of new immigrants. During his long reign, Ibn Shaprut was able to keep this nativist faction at bay by the sheer weight of his own power and connections to the Muslim court. Upon his death and the death of his disciple R. Moses, however, the struggle for power over the religious and civil leadership of the community was brought into the open. The two leading claimants for the rabbinic seat at Cordoba were R. Moses' son, Hanokh, and Moses' other protégé, Joseph Ibn Abitur.

Born in the Andalusi town of Merida from an old Sephardic family, Ibn Abitur represents the epitome of the complex relationship between the nascent Sephardic community and the older centers of the East. Historians have long recognized that his halakhic decisions reflect a continued influence of the Baghdadi academies, closely adhering to geonic practice and viewing their legislation as binding. What has not been emphasized is that these intellectual ties to the eastern institutions also have important socio-political corollaries.[6] For generations, families like those of Ibn Abitur had

---

4 Cited in Norman Stillman, "Aspects of Jewish Culture in the Middle Ages," in *Aspects of Jewish Culture in the Middle Ages*, ed. Paul E. Szarmach (Albany, 1979), 60.

5 Al-Harizi writes: "He gathered around him every rabbi and gaon, from Islam and Christendom, from East to West." *Sefer Tahkemoni* (Tel Aviv, 1952), 184.

6 On Ibn Abitur see Eliyahu Ashtor, *Jews of Moslem Spain*, 3 vols. (Philadelphia, 1973), vol. 1, 356–69; and Judit M. Targarona Borrás, "Breves notas sobre Yosef Ibn Abitur,"

gained local prestige and power through their contacts with the East and their ability to act as local arbiters of the increasingly universal geonic legal tradition. The gradual move toward autonomy from Baghdad thus threatened to undermine a key element of their social status and political clout.

Faced with a challenge to his position of prominence among Andalusi Jews, Ibn Abitur's first recourse was to seek the backing of Ibn Shaprut's successor at court. This was Jacob Ibn Jau, a local silk merchant who had won (or, perhaps more accurately, purchased) the royal appointment as the titular head of Cordoban Jewry. In contrast to his famous predecessor, however, Ibn Jau's tenure as *nasi* would be a short one, and Ibn Abitur's political fortunes declined when his patron was removed from office by the Muslim viceroy, al-Mansur. When his promotion of his native heritage and carefully cultivated relationship with the ruling Umayyad's failed to win him the seat of power in Cordoba, Ibn Abitur quickly turned to outsiders for support. The *geonim*, who were desperately attempting to prevent the fragmentation of Jewish legal and political authority, happily continued to grant Ibn Abitur their attention and respect, even after his excommunication and exile from Spain. Such support was to little avail, however, and Ibn Abitur was forced to cede his leadership of Andalusi Jewry to his foreign-born rival, R. Hanokh. Though he was able to successfully establish himself prominently among the Jews of Palestine and Egypt, Ibn Abitur never abandoned his claim as rightful leader of the Cordoban community, carrying on a protracted struggle against the persistent attacks of his Andalusi rivals.[7] Hanokh's victory was ultimately marked by his successful integration into the Sephardic oligarchy through intermarriage into the Ibn Falija clan. It is also proof of the enduring legacy of Ibn Shaprut, for there is strong evidence that R. Hanokh followed the *nasi*'s policy of developing an independent rabbinic center in al-Andalus, breaking with geonic authority. A letter from the Cairo Geniza collection written by the Baghdadi Gaon, Hai, testifies to his vexation over R. Hanokh's decision to ignore the correspondence sent by Hai's father, Sherira.[8]

Throughout the medieval Mediterranean world, Jewish communal leadership was highly unstable and plagued by factionalism of all sorts. Commu-

---

Miscelanéa de estudios Árabes y Hebraicos 33 (1982): 53–85. For the best account of the social and political framework of Sephardic independence, see Gerson D. Cohen, "The Story of the Four Captives," *Proceedings of the American Academy for Jewish Research* 29 (1960–61): 118–21, and *passim*.

7 See Jacob Mann, *The Jews in Egypt and in Palestine under the Fatimid Caliphs*, 2 vols. (Oxford, 1920), vol. 2, 67–70, and the sources listed in Cohen, "Four Captives," 72, n. 72.

8 The letter was sent to R. Jacob ben Nissim of Qayrawan, and can be found in Jacob Mann, *Texts and Studies in Jewish History and Literature*, 2 vols. (New York, 1972), vol. 1, 121.

nities often became divided with regard to class and ethnicity, as well as intellectual or religious orientation, and though scholarly disagreements on points of philology or philosophy held little interest for the average Jew, the fallout from such disputes could result in social and political fragmentation that would affect whole communities. A letter from this period found in the Cairo Genizah laments that the "bickering among scholars is the delight of the common people."[9] Indeed, in this highly volatile climate, disputes over literary or religious philosophy became the fodder for power struggles by which political fortunes could be won or lost. Even the most abstract or theoretical debate might easily have repercussions that extended beyond the circles of the intellectual elite.

As we have seen in the case of R. Moses, a powerful *nasi* such as Ibn Shaprut was able to shift power away from native Sephardim by granting his patronage to one of the newcomers to the region. Another prominent example of such social restructuring was Ibn Shaprut's transference of his support from the Andalusi-born scholar Menahem Ibn Saruq, to the North African émigré Dunash Ibn Labrat.[10]

The struggle between Menahem and Dunash over the establishment of Hebrew literary norms within Sephardic society of the ninth century has received a great deal of scholarly attention. While this conflict is usually discussed in terms of Jewish acculturation and religious identity, it also affords us the opportunity to view the nexus of Andalusi social and literary development, demonstrating that, in the medieval world, fields of intellectual inquiry had the potential to become battlegrounds that overlapped with local political and social tensions.[11]

Menahem, a native of Tortosa, became a client of Ibn Shaprut in the mid-tenth century and achieved fame as the author of the first comprehensive Hebrew grammar and dictionary. He and his students saw Hebrew as distinct from, and superior to, all other languages, and were opposed to adapting it to Arabic grammatical forms. Dunash, a student of the great Baghdadi Gaon, Saadia, arrived in Cordoba at the height of Menahem's fame and immediately challenged the latter's rejection of Arabic grammatical models. He championed the Baghdadi intellectual curriculum of Saadia and disparaged Menahem's ideas as those of a provincial upstart. The thinly veiled

9 Shlomo Dov Goitein, *A Mediterranean Society: The Jewish Communities of the Arab World as Portrayed in the Cairo Genizah*, 6 vols. (Berkeley, 1967), vol. 2, 65.

10 Ashtor, *The Jews of Moslem Spain*, 160–70.

11 The best introduction to this subject is the work of Ángel Sáenz-Badillos, most notably his introduction to his Spanish edition of Menahem's *mahberet* (Salamanca, 1986); and his article "Menahem and Dunash in search of the Foundations of Hebrew Language," *Studia Orientalia* 95 (2003): 177–90. See also the bibliography assembled by Santiaga Benavente Robles in her critical edition of the polemical *Teshubot* of Menahem's students against Dunash (Granada, 1986).

charges of Karaism leveled at Menahem's faction must be seen in this context. Furthermore, Dunash viewed the assertion of Andalusi intellectual autonomy as an affront on geonic hegemony.[12] Whether or not one can find traces of philo-Karaitic attitudes in Menahem's writings, the accusations of his rivals appear to be a general calumny against those who exhibited intellectual independence from Baghdad. Similarly, with his claim of having stamped out Karaism in the peninsula, Samuel ha-Nagid attempted to disentangle Sephardic independence from perceived religious innovation.[13]

The seemingly innocuous academic dispute that arose between Dunash and Menahem would have important social consequences. In order to establish himself as the arbiter of Hebrew linguistic and literary style, Dunash aggressively pursued and won Ibn Shaprut's patronage, in part by slandering his rival and causing him to be physically beaten and imprisoned. Nor did the dispute end there. The disciples of each scholar formed competing factions that issued defenses of their teacher's positions that were dedicated to the great *nasi*, Ibn Shaprut, most likely in the hopes of winning his endorsement. But even the support of Cordoba's most influential courtier could not guarantee the allegiance of all elements within the community. The faction formed by Menahem's students and their families viewed Dunash's arrival onto the Andalusi intellectual scene as that of a foreign interloper, just as they did his introduction of Arabic grammatical style as foreign to Judaism.[14] The greatest of all Menahem's disciples, Isaac ibn Chiquitilla, was a native of the great rabbinic center of Lucena, and another of his chief defenders, Isaac Ibn Capron, appears to have come from an old Cordoban family.[15] Their open letter to Dunash is as much a nativist defense of the "Sages of Sepharad" as it is an exposition of their interpretation of Hebrew grammar. As the following illustrative passage from this work makes clear, they have taken Dunash's critique of the *mahberet* as an affront to their "national" honor, declaring:

> And do not think that what I have discussed thus far was meant as a defense of Menahem and his interpretation. Rather, it was a response to the foolish-

---

12 See, for instance, Dunash's defense of Saadia Gaon in *Teshubot de Dunash ben Labrat: edición crítica y traducción española*, ed. Ángel Sáenz-Badillos, 5–6.

13 Ángel Sáenz-Badillos and Judit Targarona, eds. *Gramáticos hebréos de al-Andalus* (Córdoba, 1988), 25. On the polemical relationship between Rabbanites and Karaites during this period, see Haggai Ben-Shammai, "Major Trends in Karaite Philosophy and Polemics in the Tenth and Eleventh Centuries," in *Karaite Judaism: A Guide to its History and its Sources*, ed. Meira Polliack (Leiden, 2003), 339–62.

14 Esperanza Alfonso, "*Los límites del saber. Reacción de intelectuales judíos a la cultura de procedencia islámica*," in *Judíos y musulmanes en al-Andalus y el Magreb*, ed. Maria Isabel Fierro (Madrid, 2002), 62–63.

15 Another, Yehudah ibn Dud, was also from an old Iberian family that had lived among Christians and perhaps was forced to convert at some point.

ness planted in your heart, and the ignorance of your writings, and because you have made your heart conceited and opened your mouth, imagining that the sages and scholars of Sepharad are without judgment and devoid of wisdom, acting as if they did not exist, paying them no attention, and saying that 'there are none among them who can understand my words and answer me,' and comparing them to the Philistines who saw that their champion was dead, and fled, thinking that in slaying Menahem the teachings of the rest of the scholars of Sepharad would be reduced to fragments, and they would run and hide. Thus I have filled myself with words, for you have inflamed the spirit within me to nullify your thoughts so that you might recognize that there are in Sepharad those who have attained wisdom, and men of erudition."[16]

The North African contingent responded to this defiant assertion of Sephardic prowess by maintaining that such local pride was little more than base provincialism. In his counter-defense of his master's position, Dunash's student, Yehudi Ibn Sheshet, depicted his Iberian rivals as crude heathens, unworthy of participation in serious scholarly debate.[17] In the end, the native Sephardic faction would prevail, but not before many of the core ideas introduced by the "foreigner," Dunash, had become integral parts of the Sephardic curriculum. Intellectually, these disparate grammatical and stylistic approaches would come to form a synthesis and, by the twelfth century, most elites within both the Jewish and Muslim communities adhered to a form of Andalusi "nationalism" that zealously championed their distinct philosophical worldview and literary heritage.[18] Conversely, though the Andalusi Jewish elite retained much of their ethnocentric pride, they divorced themselves from the intellectual legacy championed by Menahem and his school. While they made extensive use of Menahem's *mahberet*, the great Andalusi Jewish philologists of the eleventh century make no mention of its author. In an odd twist of fate, his fame would be revived only outside the Sephardic sphere, by Ashkenazi scholars such as Rashi and his grandson, Rabbenu Tam.[19]

The central issue of the controversy was, therefore, less a question of linguistic and cultural competition between Hebrew and Arabic as much as it was a product of local and immigrant cliques that were vying for power in

16 *Teshubot de los Discípulos de Menahem contra Dunash ben Labrat*, Santiaga Benavente Robles, ed. and trans. (Granada, 1986), 15–16, Hebrew section.

17 *Teshubot de Yehudi ben Sheshet*, ed. and trans. María Encarnación Varela Moreno (Granada, 1981).

18 See Steven M. Wasserstrom, "Jewish-Muslim Relations in the Context of Andalusian Emigration," in *Christians, Muslims and Jews in Medieval and Early Modern Spain*, ed. Mark Meyerson and Edward English (Notre Dame, Ind., 2000), 69–87.

19 Ángel Sáenz-Badillos and Judit Targarona, eds. *Gramáticos hebréos de al-Andalus* (Córdoba, 1988), 38.

the burgeoning center. As with Ibn Daud's account of the "Sephardization" of R. Moses and his dynasty, the resolution of this matter was brought about by subsuming the foreign intellectual elements into the Andalusi curriculum without altering that society's sense of uniqueness and superiority. This synthesis is reflected also in the career of Jonah Ibn Janah (ca. 990–1050), perhaps the leading Jewish philologist of the Middle Ages and a vociferous champion of Sephardic linguistic supremacy, who would glorify his native Sephardic genealogy while also castigating his fellow Sephardim for not engaging in the science of grammar, as did the Arabs.[20] Interest in genealogy and the ability to trace one's family back to the Arabian Peninsula was widespread in the medieval Muslim world, but particularly acute among Andalusi Muslim intellectuals, many of whom were descended from Berber converts. The use of genealogies to prove legitimacy and authority was shared also by their Jewish counterparts, such as the great courtier-poet Samuel ha-Nagid, who made frequent reference to his ancient priestly lineage.[21]

This description of the slow, contentious development of Andalusi Jewry stands in stark contrast to the general portrait of Jewish political organization and intellectual development in the Middle Ages presented by modern scholarship, which has tended to stress communal cohesion. In his classic discussion of the nature of Jewish leadership in medieval Muslim lands, Salo Baron emphasized solidarity among the intellectual elite over factionalism and socio-political rivalries, writing that "Despite occasional rivalries, even minor manifestations of xenophobia, foreign Jewish scholars were assured brotherly reception in most communities." Yet such an approach unnecessarily divorces the Jewish experience from that of its social and cultural milieu. In Muslim Spain, as in much of the medieval Islamic world, clan and kinship ties were of paramount importance, and subsequently found expression in terms of tribalism and political strife.[22] Similarly, in addition to the general factionalism that plagued Jewish society throughout the medieval Islamic world, reactionary opposition to foreign interlopers was a central theme of Andalusi society and politics in the tenth and eleventh cen-

---

20 Norman Roth, "Jewish Reactions to 'Arabiyya and the Renaissance of Hebrew in Spain," *Journal of Jewish Studies* 28 (1983): 80.

21 James T. Monroe, *The Shu'ubiyya in Al-Andalus* (Berkeley, 1970), 99. On ha-Nagid, see Norman Roth, "Jewish Reactions to 'Arabiyya," 71.

22 Salo Baron, *A Social and Religious History of the Jews*, 20 vols. (Philadelphia, 1952–93), vol. 5, 53. Generally, see Yitzhak Baer, "The Foundations and Beginnings of the Jewish Community Structure in the Middle Ages," *Zion* 15 (1950): 1–41 [Hebrew]; Shlomo Albeck, "Sources for the Authority of the Kehillot in Spain until R. Meir Abulafia," *Zion* 25 (1960): 85–121 [Hebrew]; and Gerald Blidstein "Individual and Community in the Middle Ages: Halakhic Theory," in *Kinship and Consent*, ed. Daniel Elazar (Washington, D.C., 1983), 215–56. For factionalism in Andalusi society, see Thomas Glick, *Islamic and Christian Spain in the Early Middle Ages* (Princeton, 1979), 137–46.

turies, and Jewish communal rivalries must also be viewed within this context. The nativist-immigrant tensions reflected in the disputes that led to the downfall of Joseph Ibn Abitur and Menahem ben Saruq echoed similar discord in the broader Hispano-Muslim society, where shifts in the political and demographic landscape of the ninth to eleventh centuries produced an ongoing debate concerning the inclusion and rank of certain groups within the social order.

These fissures within Jewish society did not take place in a vacuum. As part of his program to centralize political authority around his caliphal seat at Cordoba, 'Abd al-Rahman III had also sought to forge a new Andalusi identity that would transcend the ethnic and social boundaries between those Muslims who boasted Arab lineage and those descended from Berbers, Slavs, and converts from Christianity and Judaism.[23] Yet despite great advances in the social integration of disparate neo-Muslim groups under the caliphate, there persisted a strong resentment of these "outsiders" among the Arab aristocracy and the intellectual elite they supported. Civil servants who were drawn from the urban middle classes and who attained power by dint of their abilities rather than their lineage began to challenge the social dominance of the old guard. The latter could do relatively little to resist the threat of these upstarts other than composing poetry that lamented the inversion of their social hierarchy. A manifestation of continuing social tensions can be seen in the development of a distinctively Andalusi form of *shu'ubism*—the Arab discourse on the value of ethnicity—in which neo-Muslims asserted their rights to social equality among Andalusi Arabs. An eleventh-century Andalusi of Slavic heritage, Abu 'Amir Ibn Gharsiyah, wrote a treatise championing the virtues of his ethnic heritage, sentiments that were echoed by a contemporary work entitled *Clear and Victorious Arguments against Those who Deny the Excellencies of the Sclavonians*.[24] In the case of Andalusi Jewry, the dialectic between insider and outsider appears to have been the reverse of that which developed among the Andalusi Muslim community. That is to say, the older, native, elite faction within the Jewish community was the one that initially resisted the incursion of Arabic grammatical and literary forms, whereas their Muslim counterparts, the Andalusi Arab elite, sought to promote and defend the "purity" of Arabic

---

[23] Hugh Kennedy, *Muslim Spain and Portugal: A Political History of al-Andalus* (London, 1996), 82–94. For the problem of Arab ethnicity and the formation of a distinct Andalusi identity, see Pierre Guichard, *Al-Andalus: Estructura antropológica de una sociedad islámica en occidente* (Granada, 1995), and David Wasserstein, *Rise and Fall of the Party Kings: Politics and Society in Islamic Spain 1002–1086* (Princeton, 1986), ch. 6.

[24] On Ibn Gharsiyah, see the introduction to Monroe, *The Shu'ubiyya in Al-Andalus*, 1–10; Göran Larson, *Ibn García's Shu'ubiyya Letter: ethnic and theological tensions in medieval al-Andalus* (Leiden, 2003); and Wasserstein, *Party Kings*, 169–73.

culture against outsiders. Nonetheless, in both instances, local factions reacted sharply to the idea of having to share control over the cultural norms of their society with new arrivals whom they viewed as foreign and threatening.

Moreover, the international dimension of Sephardic political strife was, like the factionalism itself, a characteristic that Andalusi Jewry shared with the broader Iberian society. In medieval Spain, the extension and maintenance of political power was never a purely "local" affair. On the contrary, in the long struggle for peninsular domination between the eighth and thirteenth centuries, both Andalusi and Hispano-Christian princes continuously sought alliances with military forces from Europe, North Africa, and the Middle East.[25] I would like to suggest that a similar situation existed for Iberian Jews. As various factions within the Sephardic world fought for control of their rapidly growing community, they frequently turned to their coreligionists in North Africa and the Middle East in an attempt to enlist their support. One of the principal reasons for the continued importance of political ties to the East was the persistence throughout the tenth and into the eleventh century of a strong conservative element within Andalusi Jewry that was greatly troubled by those scholars and courtiers attempting to arrogate central authority to themselves, and that sought to retain close bonds with the Baghdadi academies as a means of strengthening their own local political power.

To the eyes of modern scholars, the emergence of self-sufficient provincial centers within the medieval Judeo-Arabic world came as a response to the decline of the previously dominant Jewish institutions of Baghdad.[26] Yet if the rise of Andalusi Jewry appears to have been a natural and, perhaps, inevitable phenomenon, its leaders retained a noticeable measure of apprehension regarding their newfound autonomy. Indeed, even during the zenith of their creative productivity and prominence, the Sephardic intellectual elite and their supporters were careful to emphasize the legitimacy of their emergence as a politically and scholarly autonomous Jewish center. [27]

---

25 See Thomas Glick, *Islamic and Christian Spain in the Early Middle Ages* (Princeton, 1979), 19–42; Ann Christys, "Crossing the Frontier in 9th-c. Hispania," in *Medieval Frontiers: Concepts and Practices*, ed. David Abulafia and Nora Berend (Cambridge, 2002), 35–53; Eduardo Manzano Moreno, "Christian-Muslim Frontier in al-Andalus: Idea and Reality," in *The Arab Influence in Medieval Europe*, ed. Dionisius A. Agius and R. Hitchcock (Reading, 1994), 83–99; and Ron Barkai, *Cristianos y musulmanes en la España medieval: el enemigo en el espejo* (Madrid, 1984), 72–98.

26 On the decline of the Babylonian Gaonate and Exilarchate, see Henry Malter, "Saadia's Controversy with Ben Meir," in idem, *Saadia Gaon* (Philadelphia, 1942), 69–88; and Ellis Rivkin, "The Saadia-Ben Zakkai Controversy: A Structural Analysis" in M. Ben-Horin et al. eds. *Studies and Essays Presented in Honor of Abraham Neuman* (Philadelphia, 1962), 388–423.

27 See the defensive claims of Sephardic legitimacy made by Samuel ha-Nagid, *Hilkhot Ha-Nagid*, ed. Mordechai Margoliot (Jerusalem, 1962), 92–93.

Their need to continually make the case for their authority reflects two important concerns. The first appears to have been an interest in promoting themselves to the Jews beyond the Iberian Peninsula as a new option for the patronage that had heretofore been given to Baghdad and Jerusalem.[28] Secondly and, perhaps, more interestingly, it seems that such claims of legitimacy were made for the benefit of local, Andalusi audiences, including both potential Jewish supporters as well as the Muslim rulers who would ultimately validate their authority.

Efforts to delineate the unique character and identity of the medieval Sephardim will naturally, and correctly, continue to do so against that of their host society. Yet, what I have suggested here is that the Arabization of Andalusi Jewry need not be viewed solely in terms of intellectual accomplishments and the adaptation of more laudable cultural norms. Rather, the factionalism and social conflict that characterized Sephardic society throughout much of the so-called Golden Age must also be seen as an illustration of cultural borrowing and of the complex relationship between Jews and Muslims. Much like their Muslim neighbors, the native-born Jews of al-Andalus reacted sharply and defensively against challenges to their authority and social control.

Despite the neat transferal of Jewish authority from East to West presented by Ibn Daud, the much celebrated rise of Andalusi Jewry was a long and gradual process. Throughout the tenth and eleventh centuries, those who would claim political and spiritual leadership of an autonomous Sephardic community would still need to contend with the counter-claims of the Baghdadi institutions and, in many instances, the latter's Andalusi supporters. For Andalusi Jews of this period, political rivalries and intra-communal factionalism were key factors and motivating forces both in the construction of their distinct cultural identity and in their rise to prominence among the Jewish communities of the medieval Mediterranean world. This form of Sephardic nativism and the social and political backlash it provoked must be understood as part of a broader Andalusi milieu. Current studies that seek to lionize the degree to which Jews adopted elements of Arabic culture should take into account that the rise of regional Jewish cultural identities and the subsequent factionalism they produced were as much an example of medieval "convivencia" as poetry, philosophy, and science.

28 Shlomo Dov Goitein, "The Qayrawan United Appeal for the Babylonian Yeshivot and the Emergence of the Nagid," *Zion* 27 (1962): 156–65 [Hebrew]; and Menahem Ben-Sasson, "Inter-communal Relations in the Geonic Period," in Daniel Frank, ed. *The Jews of Medieval Islam: Society, Community and Identity* (Leiden, 1995), 22, n. 17; and Menahem Ben-Sasson, *The Emergence of the Local Jewish Community in the Muslim World: Qayrawan, 800–1057* (Jerusalem, 1996), 74–109 [Hebrew].

Revisiting Jihad
Current Muslim Perspectives of Peace with Israel

YITZHAK REITER

The classical doctrine of war and peace in Islam maintains that all people in the world are supposed to embrace Islam or submit to its protection. Islam is in a perpetual state of expansion and, hence, it cannot grant legitimacy to co-existence with non-Muslim communities unless they submit to its protection (in the case of the people of the book: Christians and Jews; Zoroastrians and Sabaeans where added to this category) and agree to act within its political and legal framework.[1] Applying this doctrine to present-day relations with Jews and with the Jewish State has become more complicated and even more extreme because of Israel. Israel is generally perceived by Arabs and Muslims as an alien and illegitimate creature in the Middle East. They see Israel as an entity that usurped Islamic holy land, seized the third-holiest shrine of Islam (Al-Haram al-Sharif/Al-Aqsa mosque), expelled Palestinians, and controls the life of Muslims, as well as committing atrocities against Palestinians.[2]

---

1 On the classical doctrine see Majid Khadduri, *War and Peace in the Law of Islam* (Baltimore and London: Johns Hopkins University Press, 1955); Rudolph Peters, *Jihad in Mediaeval and Modern Islam* (Leiden: E.J. Brill, 1977); David Cook, *Understanding Jihad.* (Berkeley, Los Angeles and London: University of California Press, 2005); Muhammad Hamidulla,. *The Muslim Conduct of State* (Lahore, 1973); Ann Elizabeth Mayer. "War and Peace in the Islamic Tradition and International Law", in John Kelsay and James Turner Johnson (eds.) *Just War and Jihad: Historical and Theoretical Perspectives on War and Peace in Western and Islamic Traditions* (Westport: Greenwood Press, 1991); "Djihad" in *The Encyclopaedia of Islam*; Alfred Morabia, *Le Gihâd dans l'Islâm médiéval. "Le combat sacré" des origines au XIIe siècle* (Paris: Albin Michel, 1993); Andrew G. Bostom, ed., *The Legacy of Jihad: Islamic Holy War and the Fate of Non-Muslims* (Prometheus Books, 2005); Reuven Firestone: *Jihad. The Origin of Holy War in Islam* (Oxford University Press, 2002); Hadia Dajani-Shakeel and Ronald Messier, *The Jihad and Its Times* (Center for Near Eastern and North African Studies of the University of Michigan, 1991); Bernard Lewis, *The Political Language of Islam* (University of Chicago Press, 1991); S.K. Malik, *The Quranic Concept of War* (Himalayan Books, 1986).

2 Yehoshafat Harkabi, *Arab Attitudes toward Israel* (New York: Hart, 1972); Bernard Lewis, *The Crisis of Islam, Holy War and Unholy Terror* (Random House, 2003), 116; See as an example al-Qaradawi's *fatwa* discussed below as well as the Hamas Charter.

If this is the general perception, why are some Muslim states, some of which rely on Islamic law—the *shari'a*—as their main source of legislation (such as Saudi Arabia), willing to deviate from this Islamic tenet and sign a permanent peace accord with Israel, an accord that includes recognition of a Jewish state that controls a geographic area they previously considered to be Muslim territory (*dar al-Islam*)? On March 28, 2002, the summit of Arab foreign ministers, which assembled in Beirut as the fourteenth session of the Arab League, approved the "Arab Peace Initiative," which was known in its previous incarnation as the "Saudi Peace Initiative."[3] This initiative included a proposal to establish normal relations between the Arab states and Israel, and a readiness to declare an end to the Arab-Israeli conflict in exchange for an Israeli withdrawal to the June 4, 1967 borders, the establishment of a Palestinian state with its capital in East Jerusalem, and a just and agreed upon solution to the Palestinian refugee issue, in accordance with UN Resolution 194. Regardless of the different interpretations of the initiative it is clear from the text that the Arab League and prominent Muslim states granted Israel legitimacy (though conditional).

In March 2007, the Arab League summit that convened in Riyadh, Saudi Arabia ratified the Arab Peace Initiative, which stated, among other things, that the Arab states reaffirm that "a just and comprehensive peace in the Middle East is the strategic option of the Arab countries, to be achieved in accordance with international legality."[4] This choice ostensibly contradicts the rules of Islamic law, which stipulate that Islam must persistently act, via *jihad*, to expand the control of Islam in the world and that a cessation in fighting is permissible only for short periods of time in order to build up strength.

This essay seeks to revisit the jihad doctrine in a historical perspective in order to review the changing interpretations of jihad from warfare in the seventh century to a concept that is compatible with modern international relations in the twentieth century and, in some cases, even approves peace with Israel with some stipulations.

The Classic Doctrine of Jihad and Accords with Non-Muslims

The term "jihad" is derived from the Arabic root *j-h-d* meaning "exerted effort." The term originally connoted a struggle or striving toward a goal. However, it also has the connotation of warfare: a holy war against those

---

[3] For the text of the Initiative see http://www.al-bab.com/arab/docs/league/peace02.htm. See also Elie Podeh, *From Fahd to 'Abdallah: The Origins of the Saudi Peace Initiatives and Their Impact on the Arab System and Israel* (Gitelson Peace Publications 24; Jerusalem: The Harry S. Truman Research Institute for the Advancement of Peace, July 2003).

[4] "2007 Riyadh Arab Summit Resolutions." Arabic Summit 1428–2007. The Jewish Virtual Library website (A Division of the American-Israeli Cooperative Enterprise).

who do not accept Islam. Among the 36 verses in the Qur'ān in which the term "jihad" appears, only ten verses connote warfare. In other cases, the Muslim exegetes of the Qur'ān suggest several other meanings: (1) the personal struggle against one's urges and weaknesses; (2) persistence in fulfilling a religious commandment; (3) the quest for religious knowledge; (4) adherence to Muslim tradition; (5) obedience to God and the recruitment of believers. Over time, the understanding of the term in the sense of warfare has overshadowed the non-belligerent interpretations.[5]

The objective of jihad as a theological-political outlook is to impose the word of Allah upon the world.[6] This doctrine maintains that any human collective that is unwilling to accept Islam or to submit and accept the protection of Islam, that is, to become *dhimmis*, is doomed to die by the sword. Yet, Qur'ān 2:256 states: "no compulsion in Islam." This ambivalence leaves wide latitude for interpretation.

In medieval times Islam refused to see the non-Muslim nations as equal in status because Islam considered itself "the best human group (*ummah*) on the face of the earth." Even when armistice agreements were signed with them, the Muslims tried not to express recognition of non-Muslim peoples. Classical Muslim jurists and thinkers regarded the notion that Islam is the only true religion as self-evident. Consequently, it is legitimate to wage war against other religions because their doctrines are erroneous.[7]

During the period of Islam's expansion, the non-Muslim world was defined by Muslim jurists as "the domain of war" (*dar al-harb*). It is a region where the Muslims, who belong to "the domain of Islam" (*dar al-Islam*), are supposed to bring others under the rule of Islam by peaceably calling for the unbelievers to convert, but, if they refuse, to use non-peaceful means. Thus, war is an ongoing instrument that can be postponed or halted, only temporarily, in order to build up forces and to continue fighting when this becomes possible. Consequently the Muslim entity, à priori, cannot enter into a permanent peace treaty but only into a non-belligerence pact for a limited period of time and only when facing an inferior balance of power vis-à-vis the rival camp. These circumstances justify signing a treaty with the enemy under two conditions: (1) extreme necessity (*darura qușwa*), such as severe Muslim inferiority on the battlefield; and (2) benefit (*maslaha*) for the Muslims, such as the rival's readiness to pay a ransom or tax.[8]

---

5 Reuven Firestone, *Jihad: The Origin of Holy War in Islam* (Oxford University Press, 1999); Ela Landau-Tasseron, "Jihad," *The Encyclopedia of the Quran*, vol. 3, 35–42.

6 Khadduri, *War and Peace*, 55.

7 Raja Bahlul, *From Jihad to Peaceful Co-existence: The Development of Islamic Views on Politics and International Relations* (Birzeit: Birzeit University, 2003), 19.

8 For example: Al-Qalqashandi, *Subh al-A'sha fi Sina'at al-Insha'* (Cairo: Muhammd 'Abd al-Rasul Ibrahim, 1913–20) XIV 8–9.

As noted, a cease-fire was originally supposed to be limited in time (as opposed to a permanent accord), but the military and political reality was not amenable to the doctrine formulated in the seventh century. The conquerors were stymied during the Umayyad period in the Taurus Mountains (in eastern Turkey of today) and Armenia, and the Byzantine Empire continued to exist in Constantinople. After Islam was blocked at the gates of the Byzantine Empire, the Umayyad caliphs (661–750) and their Abbasid successors entered into treaties of limited duration that were extended from time to time and lasted longer than the period of time stipulated in the precedents from the days of the Prophet and his immediate successors.[9] During these long periods of armistice, active cooperation in many areas existed between Byzantium and the Umayyad rulers.[10]

Political Realism as a Driver of Changing Interpretation of War and Peace

The military and political reality during the halt of Islamic conquest is what apparently led Muslim jurists to adopt the idea of a *hudna* (truce) or *sulh* (truce or peace), which was not limited in duration. But, in order to avoid deviating from the doctrine of jihad, they stipulated that the *hudna* could be revoked when circumstances changed. One of the examples of this is the *hudna* treaty signed in the year 637 between the Muslims and Byzantine Egypt. The treaty enabled the Muslims to focus on the war in Mesopotamia. But when the military situation improved for the Muslims, they waged war against Egypt prior to the expiration of the treaty.[11]

The formulators of the classical doctrine of law, who defined the territory of the unbelievers as "the domain of war" (*dar al-harb*) as opposed to the domain of Islam (*dar al-Islam*), generally ignored the precedents of agreements the Prophet Muhammad and his successors forged with various groups of non-Muslim peoples. These agreements often granted non-Muslims the right to continue ruling their own territory–and sometimes without even paying a poll tax to Muslims–in exchange for recognition of the legal and political authority of Islam over their territory and their citizens. These precedents led the Jurist al-Shafi'i (d. 815), who established one of the four schools of Islamic jurisprudence, to add a third political domain to

---

9 Khadduri, *War and Peace in the Law of Islam*, p. 216; D. R. Hill *The Termination of Hostilities in the Early Arab Conquests* (London: Luzak, 1971); W.B. Bishai, "Negotiations and Peace Agreements between Muslims and non-Muslims in Islamic History" in Sami.A. Hanna (ed.) *Medieval and Middle Eastern Studies in Honor of Aziz Suryal Atiya* (Leiden: E.J. Brill, 1972), 50–61.

10 Claude Cahen, *L'Islam : des origines au debut de l'Empire Ottoman* (Paris: Bordas, 1970), 42.

11 Patrick Sookhdeo, *Understanding Islamic Terrorism: The Islamic Doctrine of War.* (Pewsey U.K.: Issac, 2004), 92–93.

the two domains previous depicted: *dar 'ahd,* "the domain of pact."[12] Al-Shafi'i explained that there are regions with which Islam has reached an accord that is not limited in duration (and that should not be violated unless hostile actions were taken by the inhabitants). On the one hand, these regions were no longer part of the "domain of war," but, on the other hand, they still were not part of the "domain of Islam." This was because the Muslims enabled certain groups to maintain their laws without coming under the protection of Islamic law. These two or three domains were coined by jurists and, therefore, are debated by contemporary interpreters as holding only historical meaning.

The change in Islamic law since the days of the Prophet Muhammad has been the product of continuing adaptation to the shifting political reality. The technique for bridging the gap between legal theory and political action was generally the signing of agreements for a period of ten years (in line with the precedent of Hudaybiyya). This agreement of non-combat was conducted between the Prophet Muhammad and his enemies, the tribe of Quraysh, in Mecca in the year 628, when the Prophet's camp was weaker than his enemies and when Muhammad needed this pact in order to turn against the Jews of Haybar without fearing that their strong allies of Quraysh would open another front against him. The agreement was designed to last ten years but was violated after just two, and, ever since, there has been debate as to who was responsible for breaking the pact. Pacts based on this precedent were renewed and extended for additional periods of similar length. Such were the treaties the Mamlukes conducted with the neighboring Christian rulers.[13] During medieval times, jihad was not viewed as a religious mission, but rather as "dormant war" in the shadow of temporary accords with non-Muslim rulers.[14] There were also treaties signed as a result of military inferiority of Islamic political entities, and these were usually not limited in duration (for example, the surrender of the Muslims at Granada in the fifteenth century and the Ottoman Empire's treaties with the European powers, starting in the seventeenth century).

The wars of the Muslims against the Christians in Spain created complex political situations of war and peace. Near the end of the *Reconquista* of Spain by the Christians, the Muslim ruler Abu al-Walid ibn al-Ahmar was forced to pay a tribute to the Christians. The last Muslim caliphate in Granada was finally defeated in 1492 by the united armies of Ferdinand, the king of Aragon, and Isabella, the queen of Castile. The Granada treaty of surren-

---

12 Al-Shafi'I, *Kitab al-Umm* (Second ed. Beirut: Dar al-Fikr, 1983), IV 103.

13 P.M. Holt, *Early Mamluk Diplomacy (1260–1290): Treaties of Baybars and Qalawun with Christian Rulers* (Leiden, New York and Koln: E.J. Brill, 1995).

14 Majid Khadduri, *The Islamic Conception of Justice.* (Baltimore and London: Johns Hopkins University Press, 1984), 167.

der included 67 articles that stipulated, inter alia, that the lives and property of the Muslims would be protected; that they could remain in their homes, observe their religion and be judged according to *shari'a* law; that the mosques and Islamic waqfs would remain intact; that it would be prohibited for a Christian or Jew to impose any laws on the Muslims; that Muslim prisoners would be released; that anyone requesting to immigrate to Morocco would be allowed to do so; and that a Muslim who killed a Christian during the period of war would not be punished.[15]

During Ottoman rule the treaties signed by the sultans were far-reaching from the perspective of classical Islamic law. Most of the peace treaties from the seventeenth century onward were, in fact, treaties of surrender, with the European powers defeating the Ottomans on the battlefield time after time. The sultans had no alternative but to accept the dictates and legal norms of the European powers with which they signed the treaties. They abandoned the classical strategy of jihad allowing only temporary truce and learned the rules of the politics of survival and the rules of the new era of diplomacy developed in Europe.[16] The treaties could be justified according to the two main Islamic legal principles of *darura* (duress) and *maslaha* (utility for Muslims).

International law began to develop in Europe in 1648 in the "Peace of Westphalia," which ended the Thirty Years War. This treaty, which was an internal European one (without the Ottomans), created recognition of the principle of the sovereignty of states over their territory and led to the stability of the states in Europe for about 130 years, until the French Revolution and the wars of Napoleon in the late eighteenth century and early nineteenth century. These wars were resolved in the Congress of Vienna (1814–15), in which all of the states of Europe participated and which restored the political situation to the status quo ante.

Following their defeat of the Ottomans, the European powers imposed a series of humiliating peace treaties on the sultans. These treaties included the concession of territory previously under the control of the Ottomans (and thus belonged to *dar al-Islam*). Sometime they were even forced to pay compensation for the damage they had inflicted on their rivals. For example, in the wake of the Ottoman defeat in the war of 1768–1774 against Russia, the Treaty of Küçük Kaynarca, signed in Bulgaria (July 21, 1774),[17] granted Russia direct access to the Black Sea and freedom of navigation in the Dardanelles Straits. In addition, the Ottoman Empire was

---

15 Muhammad Kheir Heikal, *Al-Jihad wal-Qital fil-Siyasa al-Shar'iyya* (Damascus: Dar Ibn Hazm, 1996), 59.

16 Shireen T. Hunter, *The Future of Islam and the West: Clash of Civilizations or Peaceful Coexistence?* (Washington D.C.: CSIR, Praeger, 1998), 286.

17 Farid Muhammad Bey, *Ta'rikh al-Dawla al-'Aliyya al-'Uthmaniyya* (6th ed.; Beirut: Dar al-Nafas, 1988), 342–58.

forced to cede the territories of the Tartars (who won independence), lands in Serbia, and other land in the East. It was agreed that the czar of Russian would be referred to in official documents by the title "padisha," which means emperor of all of the lands of Russia, and that Russia would extend its protection to the Christian subjects of the Ottoman Empire, who would be represented by the Russian ambassador in their country. The treaty also stated that Russian pilgrimage to Jerusalem and the Holy Land would be free and exempt from any taxes and that a new church would be built in Istanbul and operate under the patronage of the Russian ambassador. It also stipulated that the Ottoman Empire would pay a monetary "war tax" to Russia.[18] The treaty was not limited in duration and was called in Arabic a *sulh wa-masalaha* that puts an end to hostile relations.

The treaties signed between the Ottomans and the European powers in the mid-nineteenth century already explicitly cited the rules of "international law" and the principle of "resolving conflicts through peaceful means," concepts foreign to the *shari'a*. The most prominent document in this regard was the Treaty of Paris (March 30, 1856), which ended the Crimean War and effectively brought the sultan into the concert of Europe. The Ottoman Empire, thereby, became part of the family of nations and the newly emerging world order accepted by the powers of Europe, adopting the European concept of international relations. Articles 8 and 27 of the treaty stipulated the principle of conflict resolution through peaceful means. In Article 14, which deals with navigation rights on the Danube River, the sides also promised to act in accordance with "international maritime law" as defined in the Vienna treaty in regard to navigation along the rivers that traversed a number of states.[19]

There were also peace treaties signed between Muslim rulers and non-Muslim states that were backed by a *fatwa* (legal opinion) issued by a mufti. One of the interesting examples of this involves Algeria. In the 1830s, a local Muslim ruler, 'Abd al-Qader, entered into agreements with the French colonial government, which had conquered northern Algeria. A *fatwa* of the senior *ulema* (Muslim sages) from Morocco supported these initiatives.[20] From the perspective of Islamic law, in Algeria France was an occupying power.[21] Islamic territory had been seized by non-believers; an obligatory war, *jihad*, was therefore waged against them, and peace accords were ulti-

---

18 Ibid., 513–24; Khadduri, *War and Peace*, 216; D.R. Hill, *The Termination of Hostilities in the Early Arab Conquests* (London: Luzak, 1971); Bishai, "Negotiations," 50–61.

19 David Cook, *Understanding Jihad* (Berkeley, Los Angeles and London: University of California Press, 2005), 93.

20 Hunter, *The Future of Islam*, 286.

21 Raphael Danziger, *Abd Al-Qadir and the Algerians: Resistance to the French and Internal Consolidation* (New York and London: Holmes & Meier, 1977).

mately signed with them. In the case of Algeria, the importance of agreements between the Muslims and the French is greater because they were signed on the Muslim side by a leader of local religious stature, who made sure to receive a *fatwa* from the top *ulema* of Fez (Morocco) in all matters related to the enforcement of a jihad against the French.

The historical development described above was accompanied by an interpretative effort by Muslim sages to adapt Islam to the reality of modern international relations. After Islamic states freed themselves from European colonialism, they tended not to adopt the doctrine of classic *jihad*. Instead, they accepted the authority of international law, decided to join the United Nations. thereby committing to live in peace with other states and to resolve conflicts through peaceful means. It could be argued that the very act of signing the Charter of the United Nations constitutes an ostensible violation of the Islamic *shari'a* as it had been interpreted since the seventh century. This signing was equivalent to a permanent peace treaty with all the states that had been defined by important Muslim jurists since the early Middle Ages as "the domain of war." This reality is what motivated contemporary *shari'a* sages to write *fatwa*s stating that peace treaties between an Islamic state and a non-Islamic state are valid treaties and do not contradict the *shari'a*. The new Islamic interpretation, which could be described as "adaptive" or "pragmatic," was designed to accord legitimacy to the modern reality of international relations and to accept the principles of international law governing relations between states.[22] The examples in the following section elaborate on how this new interpretation was justified in Islamic legal terms.

Fatwas Addressing Peace with Israel

As noted above, as part of a treaty process the Algerian leader of the 1830s sought a *fatwa* from the prominent sages of North Africa. A *fatwa* is a legal opinion, a response to a question, written by a scholar called a *mufti*. It is not a binding legal document and its authority derives from the stature of its author. *Fatwas* are the primary tool for the development of Muslim law and its adaptation to the changing circumstances of society in accordance with the spirit of the time and place. In the twentieth century, the muftis began to compose political *fatwa*s (for example, *fatawa mu'asira*–"Contemporary *Fatwa*s" by Sheikh Dr. Yusuf al-Qaradawi).[23] These *fatwa*s are an integral part of the political and ideological discourse on the questions of domestic and foreign policy that occupy the attention of the Arab and Muslim world. In addition to the *fatwa*'s role in providing a response to a legal

[22] See chapter 10 of Yitzhak Reiter, *War, Peace and International Relations in Islam: Muslim Scholars on Peace Accords with Israel* (Jerusalem: Jerusalem Institute for Israel Studies, 2009).

[23] Yusuf Al-Qaradawi, *Al-Fatawi al-Mu'asira* (Al-Mansura, Egypt: Dar al-Wafa', 1996).

question, it is sometimes used as a means to disseminate political views and to achieve political influence.

In many cases, because of the muftis' religious authority and popularity, their *fatwas* influence public opinion. Contributing to this development is the mass media revolution that enables the rapid and massive dissemination of opinions by authoritative muftis. Today, one can find hundreds of new *fatwas* published frequently on dozens of Internet sites that offer an "online *fatwa*." There are prominent muftis who have their own Internet sites, as well as other, more general sites where muftis work on a rotational basis or where a council of muftis formulates responses to questions of social importance.A *fatwa* that addresses a political issue is designed to imbue the regime's actions with legitimacy (by the official muftis) or to deny such legitimacy (by Muslim sages affiliated with opposition groups).[24]

When studying *fatwas* that address whether it is permissible according to *shari'a* to sign a peace treaty with Israel–it being a Jewish state on historical Islamic soil–I found two main streams of thought among muftis and Muslim religious thinkers: a radical one that strongly rejects any treaty with Israel and a pragmatic stream that legitimizes peace accords with Israel.The radical school is more vocal and is more prominent in the media.

There is a *fatwa* issued by today's most-prominent Islamic scholar, Sheikh Yusuf al-Qaradawi. Al-Qaradawi (b. 1926) is a graduate of Al-Azhar University, where he received a doctorate in 1973. He was an activist in the Muslim Brotherhood in Egypt and was arrested during the Nasser period. Later, he was "lent" by Egypt (in 1961) to Qatar to serve as the head of the Institute for Islamic Studies. His sermons at the main mosque in Qatar are broadcast live on television and he appears on a popular weekly television program on the Al-Jazeera channel that deals with practical questions regarding the *shari'a*. Al-Qaradawi ruled that peace cannot be made with those who steal Islamic land and then ask for peace. He maintains that the Prophet Muhammad did not sign the Hudaybiyya agreement because his camp was inferior in strength to the Quraysh camp, but rather for other reasons. This historical pact was no more than a temporary cease-fire agreement with an enemy that is not granted recognition, and the requisite strength must be mobilized in order to defeat this enemy in the future. With this interpretation, al-Qaradawi tries to rebut those pragmatists in the Arab world who favor peace agreements with Israel, on the basis of Israel's military superiority and the inability of the Arabs to overcome it.[25] Another

24 On *fatwa* and Egyptian *fatwas*, see Jacob Skovgaard-Petersen, *Defining Islam for the Egyptian State: Muftis and Fatwas of the Dar al-Ifta* (Leiden: Brill, 1997); idem, "A Typology of State Muftis,", in *Islamic Law and the Challenge of Modernity*, eds. Yvonne Yazbeck Haddad and Barbara Freyer Stowasser (Lanham, Md.: AltaMira Press, 2004), 81-97.

25 http://www.qaradawi.net/site/topics/printArticle.asp?cu_no=2&item_no=4534

example is a *fatwa* written by Sheikh Muhammad Husayn Fadlallah, a Hezbullah affiliate from Lebanon. Fadlallah ruled that "the Jews are occupiers of a Muslim territory and hence there is no legal justification to any treaty that legitimates the Jews' political presence on this Islamic soil. The same applies to the Jews' control of Palestine after they have deported its [Muslim] inhabitants in a way that one people will occupy the place of another people."[26]

Those *fatwa*s supporting peace with Israel, issued by moderate muftis, mostly the chief muftis of their countries, are featured less in the media. I cite three examples. The first one is a *fatwa* from January 1956, written by the grand mufti of Egypt, Hasan Ma'mun, (d. 1973).[27] Ma'mun began his *fatwa* by stating that the birth of the State of Israel in the 1948 was an act of aggression, an invasion of the territory of Islam and theft of Muslim land. Therefore, from this perspective, it is impossible to recognize Israel and to make peace with it since such an agreement would mean granting legitimacy to a non-Muslim entity that had stolen Muslim land. However, he goes on to state that it is permitted to sign an agreement with the enemy aimed at restoring stolen land to its owners, but not in order to grant legitimacy to the aggressor. The Egyptian mufti adds that an agreement with Israel may be signed "under conditions that will ensure benefit for the Muslims." Interestingly, the mufti of Egypt ruled that the Jews in Palestine have a special status by virtue of the *hudna* (the cease-fire) agreements signed with them by Arab states in 1949 "under pressure of the superpowers." Moreover, these Arab-Muslim governments regard a *hudna* as a temporary agreement [despite the fact that no time period is stipulated] "until a just solution is found for the problem." Here, Ma'mun states that Israel actually received both Islamic and international legitimacy. However, he states that since Israel violated the *hudna,* it is permissible to launch hostile acts against it. Hasan Ma'mun's *fatwa* is quite surprising in light of the belligerent tension that prevailed at the time it was written and the pan-Arab nationalist stance of Gamal Abdel Nasser against Israel. It is also surprising in that it leaves a broad opening for interpretation that would allow for a peace agreement with Israel in the future under certain conditions. The Fatwa Committee of the Al-Azhar institution, headed by the former grand mufti, Sheikh Hasanayn Makhluf, was not happy with Ma'mun's opinion. The committee issued a

---

&version=1&template_id=256&parent_id=12; http://www.qaradawi.net/site/topics/article.asp?cu_no=2&item_no=2187&version=1&template_id=105&parent_id=16; http://www.qaradawi.net/site/topics/article.asp?cu_no=2&item_no=4988&version=1&template_id=187&parent_id=18.

26 http://www.islamonline.net/livefatwa/arabic/Browse.asp?hGuestID=R2p33W.

27 The *fatwa* of 8 January 1956 was published in *Al-Fatawa al-Islamiyya of Dar al-Ifta' al-Misriyya* (Cairo, 1983). VII 2647-2643 and is available at http://www.lahdah.com/vb/archive/index.php?t-15218.html.

counter-*fatwa* ruling that, from a *shari'a* perspective, there is no place for a peace agreement with Israel.[28]

The second fatwa supporting peace with Israel, which is the most important document that represents the pragmatic approach, was written by the mufti of Egypt, Jad al-Haqq 'Ali Jad al-Haqq, who lent support to the peace agreement between Egypt and Israel in March 1979. The importance of his *fatwa* emanates from the great authority he wielded both as an outstanding and learned man in the field of religious law (the head of the most prestigious institute for accreditation in the Islamic world–al-Azhar in Cairo) and as the religious leader of Egypt at that time. In addition, the *fatwa* of Jad al-Haqq[29] is important in that it is a document of great breadth, based on the Qur'ān and the Sunna (the Prophet's tradition), that cannot easily be dismissed. Furthermore, in the context of the controversy between authorities that are not extremist and radical Islam, the document poses a challenge to the latter. Jad al-Haqq presented the treaties the Prophet Muhammad made with non-Muslims as precedents that underlined the principle that a peace accord with non-Muslims must bring benefit to the Muslims. He also used positively the Hudaybiyya pact as a precedent for peace accords with non-believers. Jad al-Haqq stressed that Islam commands that agreements be honored and stipulated that the violation of an agreement is equivalent to the severest transgression of abandoning Islam. He seized upon the duty to restore conquered Islamic land (here, the Sinai peninsula), including its Muslim residents, to the heart of *Dar al-Islam*. Restoring territory via a peace accord, he wrote, is preferable to restoring it via war. Jad al-Haqq wrote in his long *fatwa* that the peace treaty between Egypt and Israel did not legitimate Israel's occupation of Islamic territory; on the contrary, he argued, it liberated land that was conquered. He added that the international situation was such that it was preferable for the Muslims to sign a peace accord with Israel. And, in this case, the Muslim ruler [Sadat] was obliged to act for the benefit of the Muslims. Jad al-Haqq criticized the Arab states and their policy of "no peace and no war," which imposed a significant burden on the citizens of these states. According to al-Haqq, the Arab states missed an opportunity to "climb aboard the wagon of peace" and to derive benefit from the treaty that was signed. He emphasized that Egypt had not set a new precedent when it signed a peace treaty with Israel in March 1979. Like Ma'mun in 1956, he noted the initial agreements, armistice accords, between the Arab states and Israel, signed in the wake of the 1948 war. Herein lays another revolutionary approach in Jad al-Haqq's interpretation: recognition of Israel as an established fact and not as part of the Dar al-Islam

28 *Majallat al-Azhar* XXVII (1375/January 1956), 686–82.

29 Fatwa dated 29 November 1979: *Al-Fatawa al-Islamiyya* (Cairo: Dar al-Ifta' al-Misriyya, 1983), X 3621–36; available also at http://www.lahdah.com/vb/archive/index.php?t-15218.html.

that was subject to occupation and colonial settlement, which is the prevalent narrative in the Arab world. Another point the Egyptian mufti made in his arguments was that the peace treaty between Egypt and Israel involves the Jews, who have a special status in Islam as "people of the book" (*ahl al-kitab*) as opposed to idolaters, against whom an uncompromising war must be waged until they convert to Islam. Jad al-Haqq quoted verses from the Qur'ān that permit befriending Jews and Christians, even granting permission to marry them and eat their foods.[30] From this it is possible to deduce that there is nothing to prevent conducting relations of peace with them. However, here Jad al-Haqq completely ignored the Islamic sources stipulating that, in peace accords with people of the book, the latter must accept the patronage of Islam and pay a poll tax.

A third *fatwa* supporting peace with Israel was issued to support PLO's chairman Yasser Arafat, who signed a peace agreement with Israel known as the Oslo Accords. The Oslo Accords constituted an initial breakthrough in the Israeli-Palestinian conflict and naturally stirred a severe internal dispute among the parties to the conflict. On the Palestinian and inter-Arab side, there were those who opposed the Oslo Accords for a number of reasons: it was a separate agreement; it did not resolve the refugee problem; it gave Israel what it wanted most, acceptance of the 1949 borders, before securing the PLO demand for an independent and viable Palestinian state within the 1967 borders, etc.; and Israel retained the power to delay implementation of the agreement or to refrain from fulfilling parts of it. The grand-mufti of Saudi Arabia, Sheikh 'Abd al-'Aziz Ibn Baz, in September 1995, gave Islamic legal backing to the PLO peace-making with Israel under the broad justification of "benefit for the Muslims.[31] His principled position was that the inability to overcome the enemy justified engaging in a peace accord that will bring benefit to the Muslims (the return of territories). Ibn Baz ruled that it is possible to conduct full normalization with Israel, but the ruler of each Muslim state must separately evaluate whether this would bring benefit to his state and his countrymen. Thus, Ibn Baz provides *shari'a* approval for the independence of the Arab and Muslim territorial nation states, for the division of the Islamic nation into particularistic political units, and for modern international relations between states. As the two above-mentioned Egyptian muftis did before him, he too cited the Hudaybiyya precedent, emphasizing that although the Quraysh tribe, like Israel,

[30] On the status of Jews see chapter 6 of Yochanan Friedmann, *Tolerance and Coercion in Islam: Interfaith Relations in the Muslim Tradition* (New York: Cambridge University Press, 2003).

[31] For the *fatwa* see http://www.binbaz.org.sa/index.php?pg=mat&type=article&id=568. See also http://www.binbaz.org.sa/index.php?pg=mat&type=article&id=730 and http://www.binbaz.org.sa/index.php?pg=mat&type=fatawa&id=1943. Accessed 7 May, 2009.

had stolen land from the Muslims (the Prophet's followers), the Prophet still concluded an agreement with them. Here, Ibn baz stated that the Hudaybiyya Pact was based on a realistic assessment by the Prophet that he would not be strong enough to vanquish the enemy. Thus, the agreement was a necessity of the hour (*darura*). In this grounding Ibn Baz differed from the two Egyptian muftis mentioned above. Unlike Ma'mun and Jad al-Haqq, he also noted that even a *hudna* that is not limited in time can be terminated when no longer needed.

Conclusion

A reading of legal opinions issued by Muslim jurists and sages shows that Islam has not rested on its laurels, neither during the Middle Ages nor during the modern era. True, the fundamentalist radicals continued to preserve the classical doctrine of *jihad*, including violence, as a mean to impose religion. However, in a world in which Islam was in decline vis-à-vis the power of the West, the pragmatists had no alternative but to create a new doctrine that would provide a response to the demands of the time. Accommodation of the rules of *jihad* to new circumstances grounded in the legal principles of *maslaha* and *darura* began early in the seventh century. Then, in the wake of military defeats, beginning in the seventeenth century, Islam changed its perception of non-Muslims from exclusivist and non-recognition to an acceptance that the other must be recognized as an equal party to an agreement.

Important muftis accorded Islamic legitimacy to the signing of peace accords between Muslim Arab entities and Israel. The major justification was the realization of Israel's strategic and military superiority. They reasoned that if it was not possible to overcome Israel militarily, it would still benefit all Muslims if peaceful means were used to force Israel to return Muslim territory taken in war, that is: "Land for Peace," in other words: withdrawal from all territory conquered by Israel in 1967, a condition that underlies all the proposals for a *hudna*. Additional justifications provided by the muftis for permitting the signing of a peace agreement with Israel include: (1) the era of jihad in its classical sense of a war against non-believers is over; (2) benefit for the Muslims: since they are unable to overpower Israel, they will derive benefit from the return of territories (and their inhabitants) to Muslim sovereignty in exchange for a peace agreement; there is no longer any point or benefit to be gained from the principle of "all or nothing"; (3) the necessity of the hour; (4) precedents: agreements the Prophet Muhammad signed with his opponents and the Hudaybiyya agreement in particular; and (5) an agreement with Israel would ultimately bring the Arabs part of Jerusalem.

Lastly, why do Muslim leaders need a non-binding ruling on Islamic law, a *fatwa*, to authorize their policy if legitimate sovereign institutions have approved this policy? The president of Egypt, Anwar Sadat, King Hussein of Jordan, and Yasser Arafat, all of whom signed peace accords with Israel, initiated a diplomatic move that received the approval of their political institutions. Formal backing via a *fatwa* by Islamic sages was not required from a constitutional perspective. Nonetheless, precisely because of opposition from radical Islamic elements, an Islamic ruling in support of the ruler's actions has great importance. Islamic law is an accepted cultural code in Muslim Arab societies. Therefore, in order to contend with the radical element, the ruler needs "to speak their language," the language of religious law. In this context, the propaganda value of a *fatwa* in support of the government's stance, endorsing its policy, is great; it softens and limits public opposition.

The rulings of Islamic law cited in this article are likely to serve as a textual and intellectual basis for the public discourse on peace between Israel and the Palestinians and Arab states. Based on past experience, if and when Israel signs peace accords with the Palestinians or additional Arab states, it can be assumed that these agreements will receive the backing of *fatwa*s that grant *shari'a* legitimacy to the political decision.

Judeo-Islamic Sacred Soundscapes

The "Maqamization" of Eastern Sephardic Jewish Liturgy

EDWIN SEROUSSI

Most contemporary performances of liturgical services by Eastern Mediterranean, Near Eastern, and some North African Sephardic Jews (henceforth I will refer to them simply as Sephardic Jews) abide to a set of musical rules that are conceptualized by its practitioners (*ḥazzanim*) as *maqam/makam* (Arabic/Turkish respectively; pl. *maqamat/makamlar*).[1] Maqamization, the setting of the Jewish liturgy according to musical modes, genres, and melodies from the Arab and Ottoman urban cultures, is a neologism that I coined to describe this major phenomenon in the performance practice of the Sephardic liturgy. A crucial component of the Jewish soundscape under Islam, liturgical maqamization is a persistent sonic dimension (due to its weekly performance) of the millenary Islamic-Jewish entanglement heard nowadays in spaces that are physically, mentally, and politically removed from each other by conflict and despairing narratives.

Researching this shared sonic space between Islam and Judaism from an historical perspective requires the reading of a wide variety of documents whose relationship is not readily apparent, as well as tackling an array of theoretical questions. Ethnographic presentism has dominated the study of Sephardic musical repertoires, avoiding crucial questions about the context under which the Jewish liturgy was "musicalized" by practitioners at particular coordinates of time and place through a modal system that developed mostly outside of Jewish musical practices.[2] Also pushed to the side are questions regarding the motivations behind such a process of liturgical musicalization, the nature of power relations between Muslim majorities and their tolerated religious minorities in the musical sphere, and how the constitution of a distinctive Jewish self under Islam accommodated the sharing of Muslim musical repertoires.

The preparation of this research was facilitated by a grant from the Israel Science Foundation (grant no. 1103/05).

[1] This article employs both spellings alternatively, depending on the Arabic or Turkish context of the discussion.

[2] Throughout this article, the word "system" and the phrases "modal system" and "*maqam/makam* system" refer to the integral whole of scales, melody types, rhythmic cycles, musical genres, performance practices. and reception comprising a *maqam/makam* tradition.

The secondary diasporic condition of the absolute majority of the Jews of Islam after their immigration, voluntary or forced, from their lands of origin to Western Europe, the Americas, and Israel since the late nineteenth and throughout the twentieth centuries further complicates this study. One may inquire as to the social and emotional mechanisms that maintain liturgical performances based on a musical system whose aesthetics are twice removed from present cultural contexts, once for being Jewish and a second time for being Islamic (or referred to by the more restricted and essentialized term "Arabic"). In sum, understanding the maqamization of the Jewish liturgies of the Eastern Mediterranean (generically known as "Oriental") can illuminate processes, whereas a certain brand of modern Jewish identity is displayed through religious music. It also may inform new readings of what constitutes a Jew in pre-modern and modern settings that challenge the Eurocentric perspective still prevailing in the literature about Jewish musical cultures.

The concept of "musicalization" that we employ to characterize maqamization needs some refinement here. Jewish liturgies (there are several variants) consist of a compilation of texts that was accumulated over the centuries starting in the Second Temple period (5th century B.C.E. to 1st century C.E.). Biblical passages or selections of verses were combined with ancient formulaic blessings, talmudic texts, and, later on, liturgical poetry. Medieval canonizations (around the 10th century) settled on a specific selection of texts comprising a normative order (Heb. *siddur*) that was accepted by most Jewish communities until the advent of the Reform Movement of Judaism in Germany (early 19th century). To this canonic order of daily, Sabbath, and holiday prayers abide all Sephardic communities, albeit in their specific variants.

The order of prayers can be performed in public (if a quorum of ten adult men is present) or individually. Public performances take place (although not necessarily) in synagogues and are guided by a knowledgeable individual called *sheliaḥ tzibbur* (Heb. "envoy of the congregation") or *ḥazzan* ("cantor" in the Anglo-Saxon tradition), if he is trained, acts on a permanent capacity, and is remunerated by the congregation.

A deeply embedded misconception of the Jewish liturgy informed by the exposure of the public to modern performances is that of a musical event. However, most historical and ethnographic evidence points to rather unmusical soundscapes. The "sound" of the synagogue was always distinctive, usually demarcating a space that was closed to others, and was seldom musical, certainly not in its totality. The ongoing process of musicalization started on the wings of the introduction of new liturgical poetry in the late Byzantine Middle East around the sixth century C.E., and developed in each geographical center at a different pace and always through a dialogue with or resistance to the music of the surrounding non-Jewish society. These sonic innovations are related also to the fixation of the Jewish liturgical canon. Once the normative liturgical text was sealed, musicalization developed more forcefully. Yet, even in the most musicalized traditional (i.e. pre-Reform) Jewish liturgies, large sections continued to be performed with sound patterns that were not conceptualized by the practitioners under the category of "music," such as biblical cantillation, diverse psalmodic formulae, or improvised prayer recitations without clear beat. It is in this historical context of musicalization that maqamization should be explored.

The Study of Maqamization

Since the publication of Abraham Zvi Idelsohn's (1882–1938) landmark article "Die makamen in der hebräischen Poesie der orientalischen Jüden" in 1913, maqamization was sparingly addressed in the musicological literature.[3] Idelsohn reported two phenomena that he found among the Syrian Jews whom he met in Jerusalem a few years after their immigration to the city in the first decade of the twentieth century.[4] One phenomenon was the organization of compilations of religious Hebrew poetry in chapters, each one corresponding to one Arabic *maqam*. The second one was the "*maqam* calendar," i.e., a list of *maqamat* according to the Jewish calendar, one *maqam* per Shabbat around the yearly cycle defined by the weekly *parashah* (biblical readings). It is worth noting at this point that Idelsohn's study of the Arabic *maqam* was a pioneering work not only in its Jewish context but in the general Islamic one as well. His article includes the first comprehensive description of this modal music system by a modern Western musicologist based on field research, not just on written treatises. Since Idelsohn's ground-breaking study, several scholars have explored maqamization as a paradigm of the integration of Jewish musicians and Jewish musical culture in the soundscape of the lands of Islam. Research from recent years provides overwhelming evidence and detailed analyses of this phenomenon in the present-day practices of Sephardic Jews in Israel and the United Sates.[5]

It is customary to describe *maqam* as the modal system underlying Turkish and Arabic music genres described by the Western concepts of "art," "learned" or "classic." The literature about *maqam*-based music usually dis-

---

3 Abraham Zvi Idelsohn, "Die makamen in der hebräischen Poesie der orientalischen Juden," *Monatschrift für Geschichte und Wissenschaft des Judentums* 57 (1913): 314–25.

4 Syrian Jews emigrated to Israel, Western Europe, and the Americas. See: Joseph A. D. Sutton, *Magic Carpet: Aleppo-in-Flatbush: The Story of a Unique Ethnic Jewish Community* (New York: Thayer-Jacoby, 1979); Walter Paul Zenner, *A Global Community: The Jews from Aleppo, Syria* (Detroit: Wayne State University Press, 2000); idem, "The Descendants of Aleppo Jews in Jerusalem," *Israel Affairs* 3/2 (1996): 95–110.

5 See Mark Kligman, *Maqam and Liturgy: Ritual, Music, and Aesthetics of Syrian Jews in Brooklyn* (Detroit, Wayne State University Press, 2008); Essica Marks, *Music and Society in the "Aboab" Synagogue in Safed* (Ph.D. Diss., Bar-Ilan University, 2002) [Hebrew]; Komiko Yayama, *The Baqqashot Music of the Jews of Aleppo in Jerusalem: Modal System and Cantorial Style* (Ph.D. Diss., Hebrew University, Jerusalem, 2003) [in Hebrew].

tinguishes between improvised genres without clear beat (vocal or instrumental) and fixed forms accompanied by percussion instruments marking a rhythmic cycle that runs throughout the piece. *Maqam* genres developed in secular and religious urban contexts (especially in the courts of rulers and in Sufi confraternities) since approximately the sixteenth century. These modes, whose contemporary practice is informed by earlier ones (which I shall refrain from defining them by using the Eurocentric historiographical concept of "medieval") determine the tonal framework of musical pieces at various structural levels, in both improvised and fixed vocal and instrumental genres. The *maqam* of a piece regulates the selection pitches and their hierarchy, cadential patterns, melodic formulae, melodic contour, and the overall directionality of entire compositions (called in Turkish music theory *seyir*, "path" or "route").

Although the application of the *maqam* system by Jews in liturgical and paraliturgical (i.e., non-normative or voluntary religious devotions) rituals is the clearest sonic dimension of Muslim-Jewish interactions for at least the past five centuries, I would like to stress some idiosyncrasies of Jewish maqamic practices. This paper is an incursion into the uniqueness of the "Jewish *maqam*," based on historical observations that are related to processes and contexts generally ignored by previous research. These observations shed new light onto the Jewish liturgical *maqam* system as both an expression of a trans-cultural, trans-religious, and trans-national musical exchange and a marker of a separate Jewish sonic sphere under Islam and, more recently, in the diasporas of the Jews of Islam. It also stresses the role of the Ottoman Turkish, rather than Arabic, *makam* system, at the genesis of the maqamization process, thus subverting the hegemony of the Arab *maqam* (as practiced in modern Egypt, Syria, and Lebanon), which dominates present-day "Oriental" Jewish musical narratives, practices, and scholarship.

Rabbi Israel Najara

The first, dramatic appearance of a fully developed *maqam* system in Sephardic Jewish music occurred in 1587, when the collection of *piyyutim* (religious poems) *Zemirot Israel* by Rabbi Israel Najara (ca. 1550–1625) was published (in the first of its three editions) at the new Hebrew press in the city of Safed in upper Galilee. Heir to immigrants from Spain, Najara stands out as one of the most engaging Jewish artists of early modernity.[6] A rabbinical scholar, preacher, poet, composer, singer, sculptor, and scribe, Najara's poetical output is still an object of admiration by Sephardic performers who sing his songs (with newer music of course) to this day.

6 For the most complete biography of Najara to date, see Meir Benayahu, "Rabbi Israel Najara," *Assufot* 4 (1990): 203–84 [in Hebrew]. Najara's copious poetic output still awaits a comprehensive evaluation. Meanwhile, see Tova Beeri, "The Hispanic Foundations of Rabbi Israel Najara's Poetry," *Pe'amim* 49 (1992): 54–67 [in Hebrew]; idem, "*'Olat ha-*

Precedents of the use of *maqam*-related techniques among Eastern Mediterranean Jews prior to Najara exist, but tangible evidence about them is meager. In spite of the residuals of Arabic culture in their lore, the Jewish immigrants from Spain who settled in the Ottoman Empire (as did Najara's family) were no experts on the complexities of the *maqam* system, having lived in Iberia for almost three centuries under Christian rule. If at all, one should look for such antecedents in the musical culture of the local Byzantine Jews of Turkey and Greece, who were exposed to the early Ottoman culture (and to its Persian musical pedigree) since its beginnings. For example, the superscription "*leniggum yishma'eli*" ("[sung to] a Muslim tune") appearing above several poems by the Ottoman Romaniote (Greek-speaking) poet Rabbi Shlomo Mazal Tov (d. ca. 1540) in his posthumous collection titled *Shirim uzemirot vetushbaḥot* (Constantinople, 1545) is not enough data to argue for the presence of a fully developed modal system in the work of this poet.[7]

The first mention of *makam* terminology in a Hebrew songster occurs in *Pizmonim ubaqqashot* by the kabbalist, poet, and preacher Rabbi Menahem de Lonzano (ca. 1550 - after 1624). This work published in Constantinople in 1573/4 (together with other works by him) shows the author's immersion in Turkish and Arabic song. De Lonzano is the first early-modern Hebrew poet to include the first lines of Turkish and Arabic songs in Hebrew characters as melodic clues.[8] This background further enhances our suggestion that Najara's work was unprecedented in its scope, a genuine innovation resulting from the new cultural spaces opened to Sephardic Jews in the Ottoman Empire in the generations immediately subsequent to their expulsion from the Iberian Peninsula in the late fifteenth century.

Which musical and religious drives led Najara to arrange his collection according to the relatively novel system of the Ottoman *makamlar*? Emerg-

---

Ḥodesh by Rabbi Israel Najara - Topics and Contents," *Assufot* 4 (1990): 311-24 [in Hebrew]; Aharon Mirsky, "Ge'ulah Songs by Rabbi Israel Najara." *Sefunot* 5 (1961): 207-34 [in Hebrew]; Yosef Yahalom, "Rabbi Israel Najara and the Renewal of Hebrew Poetry in the East," *Pe'amim* 13 (1982): 92-124 [in Hebrew]. For Najara in the framework of his Islamic context, see Paul B. Fenton, "Israël Najâra, un poète hébreu au carrefour de la mystique musulmane," *Dédale*, 11-12 (2000): 638-44; Yosef Yahalom, "Mystic Hebrew Poetry and Its Turkish Background," *Tarbiz* 60 (1991): 225-48 [in Hebrew]. For Najara as a musician, see Edwin Seroussi, "Rabbi Israel Najara: Moulder of Sacred Singing after the Expulsion from Spain," *Assufot* 4 (1990): 285-310 [in Hebrew]. The literature about Najara in English is practically nonexistent.

[7] Tova Beeri, "Shelomo Mazal Tov and the Beginnings of Turkish Influence on Hebrew Poetry," *Pe'amim* 59 (1994): 65-76 [in Hebrew].

[8] Moshe Geshuri, "Haniggun vehafiyyut befi Rabbi Menahem de Lonzano," *Bizaron* 22 (1950/1): 178-87 (Melody and Song according to Rabbi Menahem de Lonzano); Edwin Seroussi, "The Ethnomusicologist Rabbi Menahem de Lonzano," Memorial Book in Honor of Meir Benayahu (in press) [in Hebrew].

ing since the mid-fifteenth century at the courts of the sultans in Edirne and later in Constantinople, as well as in Sufi lodges, especially of the Mevlevi order, the Ottoman *makam* became the normative modal system for all learned music of most religious denominations in the major urban centers of the empire.[9] Therefore, the Ottoman *makam* system, not the Arabic *maqamat* one that predominates today in the Eastern Sephardic liturgy, is the point of departure for the study of maqamization of the Jewish liturgy.

Theories of cultural "influence" of the surrounding culture of the Muslim majority over a Jewish minority were, of course, the first recourse in trying to explain maqamization. Indeed, in my first incursions into this subject, I interpreted the adoption of the *makam* system by Najara as a symptom of acculturation of the Jews from Spain in their new Ottoman space.[10] Yet, such a deterministic hypothesis denies the possibility of more profound and subtle cultural processes, as well as the agency of the Jewish minority.

A more complex approach to the question of how maqamization evolved is to assume that a musical exchange between ethnic and religious minorities was taking place in the Ottoman Empire at Najara's time. This exchange encompassed repertoire, music theory, and ideologies about the transformative powers of listening to and performing music. Najara capitalized on his exposure to diverse Ottoman musical circles within the Arabic spaces in which he resided (he spent most of his life as a preacher in the Damascus district and later on as a rabbi in Gaza). For example, he may have had access to the quarters and cafés of the Janissaries in Damascus.[11] Najara's knowledge of songs by Pir Abdal Sultan (d. 1445), a major Sufi poet who was favored by the Alawite Bektasi Sufi order to which many in the Janissary corps adhered, points to such a connection. Najara mentions the first lines (incipit) of Abdal's songs as melodic cues for the singing of some of his *piyyutim* included in *Zemirot Israel*.[12]

---

9 Walter Feldman, *Music of the Ottoman Court: Makam, Composition and the Early Ottoman Instrumental Repertoire* (Intercultural Music Studies 10; Berlin: VWB-Verlag für Wissenschaft und Bildung 1996). For the musical repertoires of the major Ottoman Sufi orders, see idem, "Musical Genres and Zikir of the Sunni Tarikats of Istanbul," in *The Dervish Lodge: Architecture, Art and Sufism in Ottoman Turkey*, ed. R. Lifchez (Berkeley: University of California Press, 1992), 187–202. The modern Turkish *makam* system is expounded (in English) in the still indispensable monograph by Karl L. Signell, *Makam: Modal Practice in Turkish Art Music* (Seattle, Wash.: Asian Music Publications, 1977). For a Turkish version of the system in the early twentieth century, see the classic entry by Rauf Yekta Bey, "La musique turque," in Albert Lavignac and Lionel de La Laurencie (eds.), *Encyclopédie de la Musique et Dictionnaire du Conservatoire*, vol. 5 (1921): 2945–3064.

10 Edwin Seroussi, "The Turkish *Makam* in the Musical Culture of the Ottoman Jews, Sources and Examples," *Israel Studies in Musicology* 5 (1990): 43–68.

11 This hypothesis was advanced in the liner notes by Walter Feldman, "Minority Composers," in *Lalezar – Music of the Sultans, Sufis & Seraglio. Volume III: Minority Composers*. (Traditional Crossroads, CD 4303, 2001).

12 Andreas Tietze and Joseph Yahalom, *Ottoman Melodies, Hebrew Hymns. A 16th*

In addition, during his sojourns to Safed in the Upper Galilee (his father's city and where he probably resided for a certain period too) or around Damascus, Najara may have had access to local Sufi sites and to the rituals taking place in them, as did other Galilean *talmidei ḥakhamin* (learned sages) of the sixteenth century.[13] In his mystical diary *Maggid mesharim*, the major early modern codifier of the Jewish law Rabbi Joseph Caro (1488–1575) recounts how he and other devout Jewish mystics, on their way home from the synagogue, stopped by a neighboring Sufi lodge (the event occurred probably in Adrianople [Edirne, Turkey] or Nicopolis [Nikopol, Bulgaria]).[14] The erotic gaze that Caro experienced during that visit, which probably could be accompanied by music, caused a reprimand by the *maggid* (the heavenly voice that guided Caro in his reveries). The seduction of the sound of the Muslim Other and its repression index a dialectic pendulum of attraction and resistance that characterize maqamization well into the modern period.

Another phenomenon behind Najara's musical and poetical oeuvre was the development of new forms of Jewish devotion at the time and space in which he acted. As Haviva Pedaya points out, a diversification in Jewish mystical devotions occurred in the sixteenth century, moving from more individual and meditative forms inherited from the medieval period into ecstatic and group (*ḥavurah*) gatherings that boosted the role of a more developed musical component (including instrumental genres).[15] In this context, Pedaya interprets the work of Najara as an innovation related to the development of Jewish communal mystical practices. One may add that the ascent of the Muslim *'ulema*, especially of the Mevlevi Sufi order, to political prominence in the Ottoman court and among the elites may have been

---

Century Cross-Cultural Adventure (Budapest: Akadémiai Kaidó, 1995). See also Fenton, "Israël Najâra" (note 6 above).

13 Paul Fenton, "Sufi influences on the Kabbalah of Safed," *Maḥanayyim* 6 (1993): 170–79 [in Hebrew]; idem, "Solitary Meditation in Jewish and Islamic Mysticism in the Light of a Recent Archeological Discovery," *Medieval Encounters* 1/2 (1995), 271–96. The extent of the exposure of members of the kabbalistic circles of Safed to Sufism (as opposed to medieval Spain) advanced also by Moshe Idel has been lately contested by Yoni Garb, "The Cult of the Saints in Lurianic Kabbalah," *Jewish Quarterly Review* 98/2 (2008), 203–29.

14 R. J. Zwi Werblowski, *Rabbi Joseph Karo: Layer and Mystic*. (2nd ed. Philadelphia, 1980), 138–39.

15 Haviva Pedaya, "Merḥav ha-layla: Bitzu'a ha-teqst ke-ritual galut muziqali ha-mamḥish et hadarat ha-shenah," *Music and the Jewish Experience*, ed. Eitan Avitsur, Marina Ritsarev and Edwin Seroussi. (Ramat Gan: Bar-Ilan University Press, in press) ("The nightly space: the performance of the text as a musical ritual of exile materializing the postponement of sleep"). One of the most prominent practitioners of private devotions in medieval Spain was Rabbi Abraham Abulafia. See Moshe Idel, *The Mystical Experience in Abraham Abulafia* (New York: State University of New York Press, 1988).

another source of inspiration for the prominence of mystical orders within the Jewish community, whose social life and institutions were regulated by religious authority.

Maqamat, the Ten Sefirot, and Hebrew Poetry

No study of maqamization of the Jewish liturgy can be detached from the extra-musical associations of Arabic/Turkish musical modes appearing in writings about music from the early period in the history of the Ottoman/Turkish *makam* as a derivation of older Persian and Central Asian speculative doctrines.[16] From the fifteenth century on, such associations circulate in the Ottoman Empire in treatises such as *Al-Risâla Fâtihiyah* (Epistle of Victory) by Muhammad Ibn 'Abd al-Hamid al-Ladhiqi (ca. 1430–1495). Al-Ladhiqi, who served in later life at the court in Constantinople under Sultan Beyezid II, states that "the oldest musicians...had observed certain ideal relationships between the maqam-s, Zodiac constellations and the elements, between avaz-s, the planets and the elements, and the shu'ba-s and the [four] elements."[17] Ideas in this vein about the cosmic reverberations of musical modes probably reached sixteenth-century Jewish mystics and musicians as Najara.[18]

Following his possible exposure to ideas about the extra-musical signification of musical modes, Najara designed an ambitious plan for his poetical opus. Instead of grouping his poems according to their literary content or context of performance as his predecessors from Spain and the Ottoman Empire had done, he designed one of the three sections of *Zemirot Israel* as a poetical edifice that would symbolically reflect the ten *sefirot* (Emana-

---

16 For a thorough descriptive catalogue of tractates discussing this issues, see Amnon Shiloah, *The Theory of Music in Arabic Writings (c. 900–1900): Descriptive Catalogue of Manuscripts in Libraries of Europe and the U.S.A.* (München: G. Henle Verlag, 1979); idem, *The Theory of Music in Arabic Writings (c. 900–1900): Descriptive Catalogue of Manuscripts in Libraries of Egypt, Israel, Morocco, Russia, Tunisia, Uzbekistan, and Supplement to B X.* (München: G. Henle Verlag, 2003). For a succinct study of the extra-musical associations of *maqamat*, see Amnon Shiloah, "The Arabic Concept of Mode," *Journal of the American Musicological Society* 34/1 (1981): 19–42.

17 Jozef Pacholczyk, "Music and Astronomy in the Muslim World," *Leonardo* 29/2 (1996): 148.

18 Similar ideas about the transformative powers of music circulated among Italian Jews in the fifteenth and sixteenth centuries. See Moshe Idel, "The Magical and Theurgical Interpretation of Music in Jewish Sources from the Renaissance to Hassidism," *Yuval* 4 (1982): 33–62 (Hebrew section). To what extent these musical speculations reached the shores of the Eastern Mediterranean via the Italian Jewish route is difficult to assess, although it is clear that strong connections existed between both prominent Jewish centers at various levels, such as the assiduous printing of works by Middle Eastern Jewish sages (including Najara) in Venice.

tions, Radiances, Eluminices, or Powers of the Divine) of Kabbalah.[19] He achieved this goal by classifying the section, including the poems for the nightly vigils (titled *'olat ha-tamid*, lit. "perpetual sacrifice") of the first edition of *Zemirot Israel*, according to ten out of the twelve basic Ottoman *makamlar*, apparently intending each *makam* to connote one of the ten emanations.

Since the extent of Najara's associations with the diverse circles of kabbalists in Safed and Damascus is unknown, we cannot ascertain to which of the kabbalistic systems circulating in that city he adhered.[20] However, there is no doubt that he was a major and controversial figure known for his ties to the Muslim community. According to one legend, Rabbi Isaac Luria Ashkenazi (1534–1572) said of Najara that he was a "spark of King David." However, considering the very short sojourn of Luria in the Upper Galilee in the last two years of his life, when Najara was still a young man, it is doubtful whether he actually pronounced such a far-reaching statement. According to Benayahu, this legend was part of a much later attempt (stemming from Sabbatean circles) to rehabilitate Najara following the harsh reprimands of the poet's behavior cast, among others, by Luria's self-appointed chief disciple and carrier of his heritage, Rabbi Haim Vital (1543–1620).[21] Vital, who lived in close proximity to Najara in Damascus, chastised the poet in his *Sefer ha-Ḥezyonot* (Book of Visions) for his careless religious and moral behavior. Vital himself did not disclose the mesmerizing details of his accusations against the poet/musician. These bold accusations (drunkenness, filthy mouth, singing loudly while sharing the table with non-Jews, drinking and eating in periods of mourning, sodomy, wife abusing) were rather exposed to the public during the exorcism of a young Jewish woman in Damascus whose soul was possessed by a spirit.[22] Exposing the high tensions over Jewish religious authority in early-seventeenth-century Syria, one subtext of this dramatic episode relevant to our study is that Najara's "performing" persona was probably charismatic. His singing, informed by his

19 The relations between music, kabbalah, and other types of Jewish mysticism are complex and manifold. For a useful introduction to this subject, see Moshe Idel, "Conceptualizations of Music in Jewish Mysticism," in *Enchanting Powers*, Laurence E. Sullivan ed. (Cambridge: Harvard University Press, 1997), 159–88.

20 See the introduction of Joseph Yahalom to Tietze and Yahalom, *Ottoman Melodies and Hebrew Hymns* (note 12 above).

21 Benayahu, "Rabbi Israel Najara," 227–31.

22 Spirit possession is thoroughly analyzed by Jeffrey Howard Chajes, *Between Worlds: Dybbuks, Exorcists, and Early Modern Judaism* (Philadelphia: University of Pennsylvania Press, 2003), esp. 111–13. For Vital's testimony, see Hayim ben Yosef Vital, *Sefer ha-ḥezyonot: yomano shel R. Ḥayim Vital*, ed. Moshe M. Faierstein (Jerusalem: Ben Zvi Institute, 2005). (*Sefer ha-ḥezyonot: The Diary of R. Hayim Vital*).

musical connections outside of the Jewish community, had attracted the attention of various segments of the Jewish population and had become a kind of subversive behavior that challenged established authority.

Contemporary evidence appears to confirm the new poetic and musical dimensions that the ten divine emanations acquired during the late sixteenth and early seventeenth centuries. It is conceivable that some poems of ten stanzas, in which the poet dedicates each strophe to a *sefira*, were intended to be sung in ten different musical modes of sixteenth-century Ottoman music. Such may be at least the case of the famous song *El mistater be-shafrir ḥeviyon* ("Almighty well hidden beyond reason's edge in soft realms") by Rabbi Abraham Maimin (apparently a disciple of Rabbi Moses Cordovero).[23] The same may have applied to the poem for the reception of the Sabbath, *Lekha dodi* by Rabbi Shlomo Alkabetz (c. 1500–1580), which, as Kimmelman has shown, is impregnated with the notion of the *sefirot*.[24] This theme, in turn, probably marked some of the musical practices associated with this poem that are sung up to the present day, following the practices of the kabbalists of Safed, on the eve of the Sabbath. Pedaya notices that members of the Bratslav Hassidic dynasty (followers of Rabbi Nachman of Breslav, 1772–1810, grandson of Rabbi Israel Baal Shem Tov, initiator of the Hassidic movement in Eastern Europe) sing *Lekha dodi* to ten different melodies.[25]

The memory of this possible extra-musical agenda underlying the makamic organization of *Zemirot Israel* by Najara vanished in the course of time, although it has left clear literary and musical traces in the liturgical and paraliturgical practices of Sephardic Jews. Najara's original approach made room for a more systematic practice of the *makam*, reflecting, once again, current intellectual trends in Ottoman music from the seventeenth century onward. In the third, expanded edition of *Zemirot Israel* by Najara (Venice, 1599/1600), the number of the *makamlar* is not ten but twelve, following the standard organization of modes in contemporary musical theory, as well as in Ottoman collections of poems designed to be sung.[26] In Najara's still unpublished later collection *She'erit Israel* (early seventeenth century), his

---

23 This is the interpretative English translation by Prof. Rabbi Zalman Schachter-Shalomi published in the blog *The Rab Zalman Legacy Project* (http://www.rzlp.org, accessed September 26, 2010). The constant performance of this *piyyut* in several circles of Jewish mystics to this day attests to its status as one of the main poetic expositions of the ten *sefirot*.

24 Reuven Kimelman, *The Mystical Meaning of Lekhah Dodi and Kabbalat Shabbat* (Los Angeles and Jerusalem: Cherub Press, 2003) [in Hebrew].

25 Pedaya, "Merḥav ha-layla" (note 15 above).

26 Owen Wright, *Words without Songs: A Musicological Study of an Early Ottoman Anthology and Its Precursors* (London: SOAS, University of London, 1992).

proficiency in contemporary Ottoman music is more evident and the number of *makamlar* still higher.[27]

Moreover, the Ottoman followers of Najara in Turkey, Syria, Greece, and Palestine adhered to the *makam* system as the musical framework for their Hebrew religious poetry. A school of Ottoman Hebrew poets/musicians from the seventeenth to the early twentieth centuries continued to develop and perform nightly vigils on Sabbaths and other special occasions on the basis of *makam*. Numerous "musical" manuscripts from this period, i.e., compilations of Hebrew poems arranged according to the Ottoman *makamlar* and with superscriptions pointing to the Turkish counterpart poem whose melody ought to be adapted to the Hebrew text, attest to the central role that *makam* music played in certain circles of the Ottoman Jewish communities. At the same time, Jewish composers and instrumentalists appear in the rosters of the Sublime Porte during the seventeenth and eighteenth centuries, sometimes achieving the highest ranks in the music personnel of the Seraglio.[28] That the names of compositions by such an illustrious figure in the history of Ottoman art music as the Moldavian Prince Demetrie Cantemir (1673–1723, known in Turkish sources as Kantemiroglu) appear in Hebrew characters in manuscript collections of religious Hebrew poetry further demonstrates the link between the repertoire of the sultan's palace and that of the Ottoman synagogues.[29]

In addition, the proficiency of the Ottoman Jews in Turkish *makam* theory that was triggered by Najara's work continued with even more impetus among his followers in Turkey and Syria. An unpublished manuscript fragment that I would like to mention here for the first time confirms this profi-

27 This development of Najara's proficiency in Ottoman music is treated in detail in Seroussi, "Rabbi Israel Najara."

28 Edwin Seroussi, "From Court and *Tarikat* to Synagogue: Ottoman Art Music and Hebrew Sacred Songs," in *Sufism, Music, and Society in the Middle East*, ed. Anders Hammarlund, Tord Olsson and Elisabeth Özdalga. Transactions, vol. 10 (Istanbul: Curzon Press, 2001), 81–96.

29 For example, Ms. 1214 of the Jewish Theological Seminary of America in New York includes two Hebrew poems set to two compositions attributed to Cantemir in the *pesrev* form, a classical Ottoman multi-sectional instrumental genre that serves as overture to the secular compound suite (*fasıl*) and to the Mevlevi ritual cycle (*ayin*). The pieces are in *makam* Bestenigar, usul Berefsan (fol. 170a) and *makam* Sulatni Irak, usul Devri kebir (p. 335a) respectively. Ottoman Jews set pieces of instrumental genres, such as the *pesrev*, to texts in order to facilitate their performance on the Sabbath, when the playing of musical instruments was banned by religious legislation. See Edwin Seroussi, "The *pesrev* as a Vocal Genre in Ottoman Hebrew Sources," *Turkish Music Quarterly* 4/3 (1991), 1–9. For Cantemir as musician (he also was an historian, philologist, translator, and politician), see Eugenia Popescu-Judetz, *Prince Dimitrie Cantemir, Theorist and Composer of Turkish Music* (Istanbul: Pan Yayıncılık, 1999) and the magnificent edition of his compositions by Owen Wright, *Demetrius Cantemir: The Collection of Notations.* Volume I: *Text*, Volume 2: *Commentary*. SOAS Musicology Series (Aldershot: Ashgate, 2000).

ciency. Searching the astounding number of manuscript collections of Hebrew poems organized according to musical modes, we found in an eighteenth-century collection of *piyyutim* a small fragment of a unique music manual.[30] Addressed in first person by a master to his disciple in Ladino (Judeo-Spanish), this text, probably a fragment from a larger, now lost, document, explains the basic principles of the *makam* system in a pedagogical manner. It also lists the rhythmic cycles (*usul*, pl. *usular*) of Ottoman court music. This document shows close similarities to contemporary Ottoman musical treatises compiled by Armenian and Greek Ottoman music scholars, such as the *Musîkî Edvâri* by Kücük Arutin Tamburi (active 1730-1754).[31] In spite of its extreme fragmentary nature, this Ladino document shows that by the eighteenth-century no expressed extra-musical meanings were attached to the *makamlar*, as they were perhaps during Najara's period.

However, a later document testifies that associations between *makamlar* and the *sefirot* persisted as a type of esoteric knowledge among Ottoman Sephardic poets. A poem consisting of stanzas pairing the *makamlar* (whose names are phonetically imitated by Hebrew words) with the *sefirot* and their corresponding biblical figures appears in the introduction to the important printed collection of *piyyutim* arranged according to the Turkish *makamlar*, *Shirei Israel be-Eretz Haqedem* (Istanbul 1921/2). Attributed to the notable seventeenth-century kabbalist Rabbi Moshe Zacuto (ca. 1625-1697) from Venice, the origins of this poem are still unknown.[32] Below is the introductory text to that poem by Rabbi Haim Becerano (1846-1931), then chief rabbi of Turkey and himself a musician, as it appears in *Shirei Israel be-Eretz Haqedem* followed by the poem itself:

> [Among the poets], there were kabbalists who strived with all their might to create connections between the *niggunim* and [their respective] *makams* with the names of our holy fathers and with the *sefirot* and the Holy Names; and all this to honor and praise, and to serve [God] through them with awe and fear, and they shall be sung with majestic holiness and respect for his Highness. And I will present, as an example, one such song, unique of its kind, and it seems that it is composed by Rabbi Moshe Zacuto of blessed memory....

30 Jewish Theological Seminary of America, Ms. 4538, fols. 203b and 242-243b. See, Edwin Seroussi, "A Textbook on Classical Ottoman Music in an 18th -century Ladino Manuscript," *Hikrei Ma'arav U-Mizrah: Studies in Language, Literature and History Presented to Joseph Chetrit*, ed. Yosef Tobi and Dennis Kurzon (Haifa: Matanel, University of Haifa and Carmel Press, 2011), 491-503 [in Hebrew].

31 Eugenia Popescu-Judetz (ed.), *Tanburi Küçük Artin, A Musical Treatise of the Eighteenth Century* (Istanbul: Pan Yayıncılık, 2002).

32 Edwin Seroussi, "The Musical World of Rabbi Moses Zacuto in Light of his Sacred Poetry," *Pe'amim* 96 (2004): 53-70 [in Hebrew].

הושיעני [Hüsseyni] מפי אריה / בזכות אברהם
חסדך אל אקו איה / כמו איש נדהם
מהר שלח הדור אהיה / שמך אהיה אותך קויתי

רצוני [Rast] דרך מצוותיך / אלהי יצחק
אמלל גבורתך / יושב בשחק בלתי הוחק
שבתי לאמונתך / ולא תעיתי

מהור [Mahur] אני לעבדך / אביר יעקב
ואם לבי מפחדך / אנוש ועקוב
יהוה גדל חסדך / לשוני יקוב
על תפארת אודך / כי בך חפצתי

נגרש [Nikris] כים אחי מצר / ובתורת משה
נצח אהגה במקום צר / מבור לי המשה
יה נצח ישראל / האר בנותי

אוזאל [Uzzal] שבח זהב אופיר / ד'הול אהרון
שסל צבאות כי הפיר / עצת נוי וחרון
ומחשבות עמים החפיר / שומרי רעתי

שח-נס [Şehnaz] גוג עמו / מלפני חי עלמין
יסוד בית המקדש שלמה / לקץ הימין
יבנה שדי ממרומו / כי הוא עזרתי

זבולי [Zembule] חבלי / במלכות דוד
יהוה אדני חילי / נזר ורביד
שם מלכותו זבד / טוב דיזבי
כתר שם טוב ישפיע לי / דעת חכמתי

גער יה [Gerâh] חית בין / עדת אבירים
טורפת יקר ראובן / אורם מטורים
שימה למרגמן אבן / מדרך לישירים
חכמי הימן הדוש מתבן / מכל עתדי

העגם [Acem] נפש קמים אויבים / על מטה שמעון
מחצצים בין משאבים / בתוך בית מעון
קדשך על מדין שביסיו / בנוב [=בינה?] וגדעון
פטדה הם מתנדבים / לבית תפארתי

At the end of the poem, Bejerano adds:

> Up to here I found utterly written and the rest is missing, and each reader can observe in the words printed with big characters the names of the *makamlar* (*niggunim*) as homonyms [of Hebrew words]... and also the names of the Fathers, the *Sefirot* and the Holy Names [of God] will shine in the eyes [of the reader]. And pay attention to the book *Sha'arei ora*.[33]

The idea of composing a poem with the names of musical modes inserted into its lines may have its roots in the Ottoman musical genre called *kâr-i natik*, a complex piece in which each strophe is sung in a different *makam* whose name is embedded into the text by alliteration.[34] *Shirei Israel be-Eretz Haqedem* includes one poem in this genre (pp. 204–5) attributed to the Ottoman Hebrew poet Aharon Hamon (d. 1721; the acrostic reads only "Aharon"). This composition includes the names of the *makamlar* embedded into the Hebrew text ("*haseg yad*" ["stop" or "end"] for *makam* Segâh; "*lehoshi'eni*" ["to redeem me"] for Hüsseyni) but not associations to the *sefirot*.

Maqam/Makam and Hebrew Liturgy

The use of the *maqam* in Ottoman Sephardic circles was first restricted to the singing of paraliturgical poetry (*piyyutim* or *pizmonim*) on special nightly vigils of the type still known today as *baqqashot* (seeking or supplications).[35] From these performative contexts, the *maqamat* slowly "invaded" the normative Sephardic liturgy that was otherwise performed by a combination of non-maqamic genres of recitation and simple strophic melodies. Maqamization of the liturgy is then a later development that would be hard to conceive in earlier times, especially among kabbalistic circles, where any intrusion in the flowing performance of the normative services impinged on the *kavvanot* (hidden mystical intentions) of the prayer (*tefillah*). Maqamization implied musical elaborations that lead cantors to incur in the repetition of words or in their "disintegration" by long melismas. To the eyes of rabbis and kabbalists these phenomena disrupted the integrity of the liturgical text and hence their resistance to maqamization.

---

33 Becerano seems to be hinting at the relation of the *sefirot* to the days of the week in the book *Sha'are ora* by the Spanish kabbalist Joseph ben Abraham Gikatilla (1248–c.1310), ed. Yosef Ben Shlomo (Jerusalem: Mossad Bialik, 1971), vol. 2, p. 46. For a thorough discussion of *piyyutim* based on the *sefirot*, see Moshe Halamish, *Kabbalah: In Liturgy, Halakhah and Customs* (Ramat Gan: Bar Ilan University, 2000), 251 [in Hebrew].

34 Walter Feldman, "Ottoman Sources concerning the Development of Taksim," *Yearbook for Traditional Music* 25 (1993), 20.

35 Paul Fenton, "Les baqqasot d'orient et d'occident," *Revue des Études Juives* 134 (1975): 101–21.

A key document in the historical documentation of the maqamization process is a manuscript by Moshe Hacohen, titled *Sefer ne'im zemirot* (British Library, Ms. Add. 26967).[36] Dated in Venice, post-1702, this is a collection of *piyyutim* arranged according of the Ottoman *makamlar*, the tradition of this cantor from Sarajevo who served in the Levantine synagogue of Venice, the western-most outpost of the Jewish *makam* practice. In the index to this volume, Moshe Hacohen, or one of his direct descendants who owned and expanded this manuscript, added in small letters what I call a "*makam* program." Simply put, the cantor designated which melody was to be used for the performance of the texts of the holiday or Sabbath liturgy that I defined as the "musical stations" of the traditional Sephardic liturgy because their performance departs from the predominant recitation without clear beat and moves into a fixed piece with clear beat and meter. Among these texts are several sections of the *zemirot* (or *pesuqei dezimra*, opening section of the morning liturgy), such as "*nishmat kol ḥay*," "*shava'at aniyim*," and "*smeḥim be-tzetam*," as well as the *qaddish* before *barekhu*.[37]

All the melodies for each holiday selected by the cantor who prepared the indices of the *Sefer ne'im zemirot* shared the same *makam*, clear evidence that during the eighteenth century, if not before, the liturgy for special Sabbaths and holidays was regulated by one *makam*. In the course of time, the sections that used to be recited without clear pitch also became "*maqamized*" by performing them with the motifs characteristic of the *makam* selected for the service (e.g., opening melodic gestures, recitation tones, preparation of cadences, and cadences). Moreover, certain *maqamat* were linked, at least in Syria, to specific holidays and Sabbaths, as Idelsohn already showed in his article of 1913.

The design of "*makam* programs" found in the Venetian manuscript became a common practice in Sephardic synagogues, continuing until the present. Contemporary Sephardic *ḥazzanim* in the Middle East who are fully immersed in the modern (Egyptian-oriented) world of *maqam* use *pinkasim* (notebooks), in which they write down several combinations of melodies arranged by *maqamat*, as an *aide de memoire*. Cantor Abraham Abughanim (1908–2002), who officiated for many years at the *Yegea' kapayim* synagogue in the Maḥaneh Yehudah quarter of Jerusalem, a stronghold of the Sephardic *maqam* tradition in the city since the early twentieth-cen-

36 Meir Benayahu, "Rabbi Moshe be-Rabbi Mikhael Hacohen u-sifro 'et la-sofer: makor nekhbad le-qorot shvuyyei belgrad," *Assufot* 8 (1994): 297–342 ("Rabbi Moshe son of Rabbi Mikhael Hacohen and his book *'Et la-sofer*: A notable source for the history of the captives from Belgrade").

37 The practice of singing these sections of the liturgy with distinctive melodies in Istanbul in the second half of the sixteenth century is already attested by Rabbi Menahem de Lonzano. See, Seroussi, "The Ethnomusicologist Rabbi Menahem de Lonzano" (note 8 above).

tury, used to bring to our recording sessions a bundle of papers that were attached to his *siddur* (prayer book). In these scattered handwritten notes, he listed the names of melodies for the "musical stations" of the Sabbath morning liturgy, arranged according to the Arabic *maqamat*. Many of these melodies, by the way, belonged to songs in Judeo-Spanish, whose tonal organization was appropriate for the *maqam* system, just as Rabbi Israel Najara had done in some of his *piyyutim* more than four hundred years ago.

Modern Local Maqam *Hebrew Repertoires*

Considering the diverse regional practices of maqamization in existence throughout the Ottoman Empire and the wide reservoir of melodies available in each geographical area, many different Jewish *maqam* traditions developed and were transmitted by specific lineages of cantors. Some of these lineages have survived via oral tradition; others have disappeared without a trace. Three surviving lineages with several ramifications are clearly identifiable: the Ottoman-Turkish, the Aleppo, and the Jerusalem-Sephardic (in their chronological order of development).

The Turkish lineage had, in the past, branches in the main cities of Jewish settlement in the Ottoman Empire: Salonika, Edirne, Istanbul, Bursa, and Izmir.[38] The most prominent of these centers was the one in Edirne, located in western Thrace (close to the Turkish border with Bulgaria and Greece). A local myth circulating until the beginning of the twentieth century at the main center of Jewish religious musical activities in Edirne, the "Portugal" synagogue, recounted the appearances by Rabbi Israel Najara in dreams to the sexton of the synagogue in order to teach him the different *makamlar*.[39] Although probably apocryphal, this folktale conveys a narrative of continuity in the chain of transmission from Najara, the founder of the *makam* tradition, to his heirs in Edirne.

Abraham Danon (1857–1925), a distinguished modern Ottoman Jewish scholar who grew up in close association with the musical circles of his native city of Edirne, offered in his introduction (in Hebrew) to the compendium *Shirei Israel be-Eretz Haqedem* the following hypothesis to justify the centrality of his city to the Hebrew *makam* tradition:

---

38 Edwin Seroussi, "Maftirim olgusuna tarihsel genel bir bakis / Towards an Historical Overview of the Maftirim Phenomenon/ Un egzamen istoriko del fenomeno de Maftirim," in *Maftirim: Türk-Sefarad Sinagog Ilahileri/Turkish Sephardic Synagogue Hymns* ed. Karen Gerson-Sarhon (Istanbul: Gözlem Gazetcilik Basin ve Yayin, Ottoman-Turkish Sephardic Culture Research Center, 2009), 54–78.

39 Menahem Azuz, "On the History of the Jews in Adrianopolis," *Ḥemdat yamim: kovets le-zikhro shel ge'on yisrael maran Ḥayim Ḥizkyahu Medini (ha-H"M) meḥaber sifre Sede ḥemed ve-'od, le-milet arba'im shanah le-fetirato kislev 665-kislev 705*, ed. Abraham Elmaleh (Jerusalem: Bet ha-ḥolim ha-kelali Misgav La-dakh, 1945/46), 157–68.

> Why did [Edirne have] the exclusive privilege [of being a center of music and poetry] unlike any other city? Because for a long time the whirling dervishes (monks) were found there, the disciples of the mystic (Sufi) Mevlana Celaleddin Rumi who dance every Friday to the sound of musical instruments in their sanctuary called by them *tekke*....And the persecuted [Jewish] refugees who came [to Edirne] from Spain and Portugal, exhausted and fatigued from their journey, found a tradition ready for them [to adopt] and they too established a choir of musicians in the format of the Muslims in order to forget their sorrowfulness.

This association between the Ottoman Jews and the Mevlevi Sufi order anchors the development of the Sephardic *makam* tradition to or in dialogue with the main spiritual center of Ottoman Muslim religiosity. It is difficult, however, to support Danon's hypothesis with convincing historical data, because of the discontinuities in the Jewish presence in Edirne since the time of the expulsion of the Jews from Spain. A capital of the Ottoman capital until the conquest of Constantinople (1453), Edirne fell from prominence in the sixteenth century, returning to notoriety only in the mid-seventeenth century under Sultan Mehmed IV (1649–1687), who established his court in that city to escape the intrigues of Istanbul. Joining the sultan, and with his encouragement, was a reinvigorated Jewish community that resettled in Edirne and flourished there until the Balkan Wars (1912–1913) decimated this community forever. Thus, Danon's musical narrative resounds as a chapter of the lachrymose variety of Jewish history that dominated Jewish historical discourses in Europe at the outset of the twentieth century. An apologetic subtext characteristic of late Ottomanism can also account for Danon's stressing of the historical Judeo-Mevlevi connection.

Political turmoil caused by the violent downfall of the Ottoman Empire and the emergence of new nation-states from the imperial ashes marked the end to the Ottoman Jewish musical ecumene. Experts of local Jewish *makam* traditions from Edirne, Izmir, and Salonika slowly converged in Istanbul, now the capital of the new Turkish Republic, in the 1920s or emigrated to other lands seeking greener pastures. The metropolis offered manifold opportunities to Jewish musicians, such as recording studios, numerous musical cafés and theaters catering to a plethora of immigrants and refugees from the European wars and the Bolshevik Revolution.

It was in this period that the compendium *Shirei Israel be-Eretz Haqedem* appeared, a work that culminates the long history of the Ottoman Hebrew *makam* tradition. Immigrant musicians from Edirne were the catalyst in this process of canonization. Promoted among others by Rabbi Haim Becerano, the aforementioned first chief rabbi of the Turkish Republic (and the last one for several decades) and expert of the Hebrew *makam* repertoire, this publication summarizes that history in a project that combines the scholarly discipline of the secular *Wissenschaft des Judenthums* (including an endorsement by the "national" Hebrew poet Haim Nachman Bialik) with the long-standing chain of "musical" manuscripts used for synagogue performances.[40]

Weakened by emigration, by secularization within the Jewish community, and by the cultural policies of President Kemal Atatürk promoting ethnic Turks at all levels of the state apparatus that controlled the major musical institutions of the country at the expense of minorities, the activities of Ottoman Jewish *makam* experts in Istanbul was reduced.[41] A few experts of the Hebrew *makam* of the last generations remained in Istanbul and tenaciously kept the memory of this repertoire alive in the Sephardic synagogues still operating in the city. One should mention in this context three cantors who in the late 1980s recorded what remained in their memory from the *makam* repertoire canonized in the compendium *Shirei Israel be-Eretz Haqedem*: David Behar (b. 1920), Izak Maçoro (or Machorro, 1918–2008), and their disciple David Sevi (b. 1953), presently active as cantor of the Şişli synagogue in Istanbul. Behar, who studied the Hebrew *makam* from the immigrants from Edirne, as well as at the Municipal Conservatory of Istanbul, maintained an active Jewish choir that served also as a school for younger cantors.

A chain of Ottoman *makam* transmission continued among the Turkish Jewish immigrants in Palestine/Israel, especially after the immigration to Tel Aviv of Isaac Eliyahu Navon (1859-1952), poet, singer, and editor of *Shirei Israel be-Eretz Haqedem*, in 1929, and the great composer Moshe (Moiz) Cordova (1881-1967) in 1936. One of Cordova's main disciples in Tel Aviv was Refael Elnadav (b.1921). Born of Yemenite and Sephardic parents and educated in Jerusalem in the local (i.e., Syrian-oriented) *maqam* synagogue repertoire and in Western classical music (he was the first non-European student of the new Jerusalem Conservatory in the late 1930s), Elnadav carried the Ottoman Hebrew *makam* torch in his own path of immigration to Cuba (mid-1950s) and later on to Brooklyn (1960). However, Elnadav's high proficiency in the Ottoman *makam* repertoire was mostly disregarded in Brooklyn, where the Arabic *maqam* practice from Aleppo/Jerusalem dominated. Another branch of the Ottoman tradition continued in Seattle with the Reverend Samuel Benaroya (1908–2003). Born in Edirne and educated in Istanbul, Benaroya's path of immigration, first to Geneva (early 1930s) and after World War II to the northwestern coast of the United Sates, is another typical transcontinental and trans-cultural diasporic route of Ottoman/Turkish Jewish *makam* masters in the twentieth century.[42]

---

40 On Bialik's text see Edwin Seroussi, "Bialik's Prophecy on Oriental Music in the New Hebrew Culture," *Pe'amim* 119 (2009): 173–80 [in Hebrew].

41 Maureen Jackson, "Crossing Musical Worlds: Jews Making Ottoman and Turkish Classical Music," *Turkish Studies Association Journal* 31/1-2 (2007/2009).

42 Edwin Seroussi, *Ottoman Hebrew Sacred Songs Performed by Samuel Benaroya*,

The Aleppo Hebrew *maqam* tradition developed around the circles of Rabbi Mordechai ben Yaacov Abadi (d. 1883) in the second half of the nineteenth century. Abadi, a leader of the local kabbalistic circles, was the editor of the first Syrian printed anthologies of Hebrew poetry for singing with *maqam* music.[43] The Aleppo tradition reflects the transition from older Ottoman-oriented musical practices to the local and venerated Arabic *muwashshaḥ* tradition. This "new" tradition was revitalized by Abu Khalil al-Qabbani (1832/5–1904), 'Ali al-Darwish (1872–1952), and Umar al-Batsh (1885–1950) as an expression of Syrian-Arab national autonomy from Ottoman colonial power and continued throughout the twentieth century, especially in the local Sufi lodges.[44] Songs were performed in "suites" of several pieces called *waslah*. A *waslah* from Aleppo included up to eight *muwaş-şaḥat* linked by improvised sections and preceded by an instrumental introduction (*sama'i* or *bashraf*) in a compound form that recalls the strings of *piyyutim* performed in the synagogues of Aleppo (and later on Jerusalem).[45]

The Aleppo Jewish tradition is unique in maintaining some of the extra-musical associations of the *maqamat*. It systematized the use of *maqamat* according to the *parashah* (weekly biblical portion) read on each Shabbat, a feature that was already mentioned in relation to Idelsohn's study.[46] Cantors of Aleppo abided by the authority of this *maqam* table, unlike the practice of contemporary Jerusalem-Sephardic cantors in which the selection of the *maqam* is mostly left to the discretion or the ability of each cantor (except for holidays and other special occasions).

Beginning in the early twentieth century, the practitioners of the Aleppo *maqam* tradition relocated to Jerusalem, the New York City area, and Latin America (especially Mexico City, Buenos Aires, Sao Paolo and Panama City).[47] While the American Aleppo tradition remained relatively faithful to

---

Anthology of Music Traditions in Israel 12 (AMTI 9803) (Jerusalem: Jewish Music Research Centre, 1998).

43 An earlier Hebrew *maqam* anthology related to the Aleppo tradition, *Yitzḥaq yeranen*, was published by Refael Isaac Altaras (an immigrant from Aleppo) in Jerusalem in 1856/7. See, Edwin Seroussi, "On the Beginnings of the Singing of *Bakkashot* in 19th-Century Jerusalem," *Pe'amim* 56 (1993): 106–24 [in Hebrew].

44 Jonathan Holt Shannon, *Among the Jasmine Trees: Music and Modernity in Contemporary Syria* (Middleton, Conn.: Wesleyan University Press, 2006).

45 Habib Hassan Touma, *The Music of the Arabs*, trans. Laurie Schwartz (Portland, Or.: Amadeus Press, 1996), 83.

46 See also, Mark Kligman, "The Bible, Prayer, and *Maqam*: Extra-Musical Associations of Syrian Jews," *Ethnomusicology* 45/3 (2001): 443–79.

47 For a detailed account of the Aleppo Jewish musical diaspora, see Kay Kaufman Shelemay, *Let Jasmine Rain Down: Song and Remembrance among Syrian Jews* (Chicago: Chicago University Press, 1998).

its sources, the Jerusalem derivative, later to become the "Jerusalem Sephardic" *maqam* tradition, gradually adjusted to the multi-cultural social circumstances of the city lead by composers and singers from Aleppo, such as Raphael Antebi (aka "Tabush," 1873–1919), and kabbalists, such as Rabbi Yaacov Ades (1857–1925). Antebi was considered the most prominent of the poet/musicians of Aleppo with four hundred *piyyutim* to his credit set mostly to Arabic melodies.

In spite of its strong canonic status in the contemporary Sephardic liturgy, maqamization was not always a welcome phenomenon in rabbinical circles, as we already noted in relation to the kabbalists of the sixteenth century. The focused attention of the congregants on the *maqamic* musical performance by the cantor was perceived as detrimental to the pious concentration on the text. As an example, we quote the opinion of Rabbi Haim ben Yaacov Palache from Izmir, a most respected Sephardic rabbinical authority of the nineteenth century who, in his *Kaf ha-ḥayyim* (Saloniki 1859/1860, chapter 13, 6), says: "Who will allow and warn poets and singers (*payytanim ve-meshorerim*) that they should not sing the *qaddish* and the *qeddushah* in the manner of the gentiles with *makam* [because] it is known that [singing with *makam*] leads [the singer] to evil contemplations." This is yet another chapter in the perennial struggle between text and music in ritual spaces (and between religious authority and music practitioners) that has been shared by Islam and Judaism throughout the ages.[48]

The Jerusalem maqam *as a Global Sephardic Liturgical Music System*

Two factors marked the Jerusalem Hebrew *maqam* style and repertoire and slowly distinguished it from its original Aleppo sources. A multi-ethnic Sephardic community in Jerusalem that included Jews from "non-*maqamic*" cultures such as Yemen, Persia, Bukhara, and Kurdistan led to the incorporation into the repertoire of melodies from diverse geographical origins that were fit to the different *maqamat*, as Israel Najara did in the late sixteenth-century.[49] A second source of inspiration for the Jerusalem reper-

---

48 One of most engaging contemporary rabbinical figures to address this issue is Rabbi Ovadiyah Yossef, former Chief Sephardic Rabbi of the State of Israel and uncontested spiritual leader of the powerful Sha"s political party. Rabbi Yossef, originally from Baghdad and partially educated in Egypt, is a well-known aficionado of the maqamized Jewish liturgy. For an examination of his positions in light of previous Sephardic rabbinical discourses about the relations between music and text in ritual prayer see, Amnon Shiloah, "Mi-Hay Gaon 'ad Ovadiyah Yossef," in *Meḥqarim be-qorot yehude Bavel uve-tarbutam: divre ha-Kongres ha-benle'umi ha-sheni le-ḥeqer Yahadut Bavel (Yuni 1998)* eds. Yitshak Avishur and Zvi Yehuda (Or Yehuda: Merkaz Moreshet Yahadut Bavel, 2002), 119–28 ("From Hay Gaon to Ovadiyah Yossef"). For a more general discussion of this issue, see idem, "The Attitude towards Music of Jewish Religious Authorities," *The Dimension of Music in Islamic and Jewish Culture* (Aldershot: Ashgate, 1993), article no. XII, 1–11.

49 Essica Marks, "The Music in a Sephardi Synagogue in Israel: A Case Study," *Pacific*

toire was the modern Egyptian music industry, which, since the late 1920s, has swept the entire Arab world, the "Oriental" Jews in Palestine included, via the electronic media, first through commercial records, later on by radio stations, and finally the cinema. The aesthetics of this modern hegemonic repertoire, associated with the great artists of the Egyptian stage and cinema such as Muhammad Abd al-Wahab, Farid al-Atrash, and Umm Kulthum, spread into the soundscapes of the Sephardic synagogues in Jerusalem and elsewhere like wildfire.[50]

The spread and eventual canonization and globalization of the Jerusalem-Sephardic maqamization of the liturgy was the result of the prestige of the holy city, the growing prominence of Jerusalem as a center of Sephardic learning, and the immigration of distinguished cantors from Jerusalem that started already in the early twentieth century. One of the most influential figures in the constitution of the Jerusalemite *maqam* tradition was Haim Shaul Abud. A disciple of Raphael Antebi, Abud was born in Aleppo in 1906 and immigrated in his youth to Argentina, where he taught the Aleppo *maqam* tradition. Upon his return to Palestine in the early 1930s, he edited the compendium *Sefer Shirei Zimra haShalem veSefer haBaqqashot le-Shabbat*, which, in its several editions since its first publication in 1931, has become the text for the Aleppo/Jerusalem *maqam* performance on a global scale.[51] A well-known poet and teacher, Abud, who died in 1977, was one of the undisputed leaders of the "Jerusalem-Sephardic" school of *maqam* singers.

Another exceptional and well-documented case of the geographical distribution of maqamization in the Jerusalem-Sephardic vein is the city of Tunis, where the renowned Jerusalemite cantor and composer Asher Mizrahi (1890–1967) resided, first from 1914 to 1918 and then from 1927 to 1967. Mizrahi brought to that city the maqamized style of the Jerusalem liturgy and implanted it among young local cantors who shifted their style from the local liturgical traditions to the most prestigious and cosmopolitan repertoire coming from the Holy Land and tinted with the latest fashions in

Review in Ethnomusicology 12 (2006); www.ethnomusic.ucla.edu/pre/Vol12 (accessed 4 September 2007).

50 The influence of modern Egyptian music on the music of the repertoire of the Aleppo Jews in New York is thoroughly discussed in Kaufman Shelemay, *Let Jasmine Rain Down*. For the impact of new technologies on Middle Eastern repertoires and aesthetics, see Ali J. Racy, "Record Industry and Egyptian Traditional Music, 1904–1932," *Ethnomusicology* 20 (1976), 23–48; idem, "Musical Aesthetics in Present Day Cairo," *Ethnomusicology* 26 (1982), 391–406. Indispensable in this context is Virginia Danielson, *The Voice of Egypt: Umm Kulthum, Arabic Song, and Egyptian Society in the Twentieth Century* (Chicago: University of Chicago Press, 1997).

51 *The Complete Book of Songs and Book of Supplications for the Sabbath* (Jerusalem: The author, 1931).

Arabic music. One of Mizrahi's students, David Riahi, who lives in Netanya, Israel, became a distinguished scion of this tradition upon his immigration to Israel. In the 1980s, Riahi himself produced a series of non-commercial learning cassettes titled *The World of the Maqam*.

Riahi's production is not a curiosity. The modern hegemony of the Arabic *maqam* practice in Sephardic synagogues within and outside Israel has generated a plethora of instruction manuals, institutions of learning, recordings, and, most recently, websites. One of the main Israeli centers dedicated to the dissemination of the *maqamized* liturgy since the 1980s is Renanot, the Institute of Jewish Music in Jerusalem. Under the long tenure of the distinguished Jerusalemite cantor and Jewish *maqam* expert Ezra Barnea as director, Renanot has published several series of recordings designed to instruct young cantors on the mastery of applying the *maqam* system to the Jewish liturgy.

The normative status of maqamization in the Jerusalem/Aleppo style as the central feature of contemporary Sephardic liturgical practices is expressed also in cyberspace. The website www.pizmonim.org, dedicated to the Aleppo tradition, includes a section entitled "The Weekly Maqam of the Aleppo tradition," including the melodies of "model" *pizmonim* for each *parashah*. This website celebrates the lore of Ḥazzan Gabriel A. Shrem (1916–1986), describing him as

> a man who valued his heritage greatly and safeguarded every aspect of it thoroughly when he immigrated to America in 1932. His voice, as heard on the many tape recordings that he made, continues to inspire and teach people throughout the world. As the editor of the Jewish Syrian (i.e. Aleppo) community's *pizmonim* book, *Shir u-shvaḥah halel ve-zimra*, he assembled songs from many different traditions of Middle Eastern Jewry.[52]

In addition to the common associations of *maqamat* with moods, this website includes some novelties. For example, *maqam* Sabah is found appropriate for any *parashah* that mentions the army or anything related to it, simply because in Hebrew "*tzavah*" (pronounced "sabah" by Judeo-Arabic speakers) means "army"! Such extra-musical associations of *maqamat* persist also in the modern Arab world, for example, among Sufi sects in Egypt.[53]

Final Remarks

Knowledge of the liturgical application of the *maqam* system has become the global yardstick against which Sephardic cantors are judged. However, the depth and style of maqamization varies from cantor to cantor. Some nominally pray based on *maqamat*, but their knowledge is limited to two

52 Quoted from www.pizmonim.org.

53 Michael Frishkopf, "Tarab in the Mystic Sufi Chant of Egypt," in *Colors of Enchantment*, ed. S. Zuhur (Cairo: American University in Cairo Press, 2001), 233–69.

or three basic species, usually Rast, Bayat, and Hijaz. Virtuosos, on the other hand, demonstrate their vast knowledge and vocal skills by modulating from *maqam* to *maqam* within a short prayer.[54] On a learning tape in my possession recorded in Israel in the 1980s, the distinguished Jerusalem-Sephardic cantor Rafi Barazani modulates to a different *maqam* in almost each sentence of the Sabbath morning prayer *Nishmat kol ḥay*.

To illustrate the uniqueness of each cantor's career, repertoire, and style, we shall conclude with the analysis of one case. On the website of the Sephardic Bikur Holim Synagogue of Seattle we learn about the career of its ḥazzan, Rabbi Frank Varon (www.sbhseattle.org/Bio-F-Varon).[55] Born and raised in Seattle, he served as ḥazzan at the Sephardic Jewish Center of Canarsie in Brooklyn and the Sephardic Congregation of Adath Yeshurun" in Kew Gardens (Queens, New York City). Ḥazzan Varon "was trained in the Sephardic musical mode, or maqam, under the instruction of the Turkish-born Ḥazzan, Rev. Samuel Benaroya." We noted that Samuel Benaroya continued the Ottoman Jewish *makam* practice in America beginning in the early 1950s. His lore, however, was circumscribed to Seattle, where other cantors, most notable Ḥazzan Isaac Azose, inherited his style and repertoire. But Ḥazzan Varon was exposed to the Jerusalem-Sephardic practice too as "he subsequently received Rabbinical Ordination from Medrash Sephardic [sic] in Jerusalem, Israel." Another distinctive aspect of the musical career of Rabbi Varon, one that derives from his upbringing in the Ladino-speaking community of Seattle, is his release of *Mi Alma*, a CD of "popular Ladino Romanzas." As the website reports, these are "moving renditions of Sephardic folklore tunes that preserve the music's rich tradition and at the same time appeal to listeners of today. Rabbi Varon has engineered several original adaptations from the Ladino music into the liturgy of the synagogue as an enhancement for public prayer." We see here a young contemporary Sephardic cantor who assimilates the Ottoman *makam*, is also exposed to the Arabic-based *maqam* predominant in Jerusalem and beyond, and incorporates into the liturgy melodies of westernized songs in Ladino.

Cybernetic reincarnations of the Jewish *maqam* system that emanate from outside the Sephardic communities link it to "Jewish exoticism" as well as to New-Age spirituality. The Introductory Notes to the CD *Tuning the Soul: Worlds of Jewish Sacred Music* (http://www.kaplanmusic.com/Writings) is one case of such contemporary perceptions:

---

54 Successful modulations between *maqamat* are at the core of artistry in *maqam* culture, especially in the improvised genres. See, Scott Marcus, "Modulation in Arabic Music: Documenting Oral Concepts, Performance Rules and Strategies," *Ethnomusicology* 36/2 (1992), 171–96.

55 www.sbhseattle.org/Bio-F-Varon, accessed September 27, 2010.

> We have placed a special emphasis on Mizrachi ["Oriental" ES] music, whose tonalities often sound "out of tune" to the Western ear, but whose subtle inflections of intonation and melody can become captivating when one grants them open-eared listening. This is the world of *makam*, an Arabic word that means "a place from which to rise." It is related to the Hebrew word *makom*, meaning "place." *Makam* is a system of tonal organization, similar to others found in Asia and the Middle East, such as the Indian *raga*, (meaning "emotional coloration"). More than just the series of pitches that make up its "scale," a *makam* has a "musical personality," with its peculiarities of movement, hierarchy of tones, ornamentations, and psycho-spiritual aspects. Some common *makamat* (plural) are *Hijaz, Rast, Bayati, Nahawand, and Ajam*. In Mizrachi and Sephardic communities, different *makamat* are used each week to chant the Sabbath prayers, giving tremendous musical variety to their services.

Reviving the "psycho-spiritual aspects" of the *maqamat* represents a new turn in the history of the maqamization of the Jewish liturgy exposed in this article. The massive circulation of information about venerable musical practices, including from scholarly sources such as the present text, generates a renewed interest in the "ancient" powers attributed to musical constellations by religious sages of the past. In an era when the search for musical "roots" (including in virtual reality) comprises one vital component in the constitution of self, Jewish or otherwise, the appeal of the Hebrew *maqam* system and its universal cosmic reverberations is expected. Add to it the contemporary political potential of a shared Islamic-Jewish sonic space that, in an era dominated by the constant collision between these two religions (and their respective national incarnations), offers a symbolic hope for tolerance and sharing. The question of whether this perception can be translated into tangible and effective action remains an open one.

Medical Relationships between Jews and Non-Jews in the Ottoman Empire in Pre-Modern Times according to Rabbinic Literature

Halakhah and Reality

ABRAHAM OFIR SHEMESH

The patient-doctor relationship is the basis of all medical systems and it is inherent in all stable human societies. Such interpersonal relations are socially significant as well, as they create an essential point of convergence between people who belong to diverse faiths and cultures, which are sometimes even rival and hostile. Various studies have dealt with the issue of interaction between Jews and non-Jews in the medical field, however this topic requires further inquiry.[1] The existing studies focused mainly on the degree to which members of one faith required and requested medical services provided by the other. However, the research reflects the historical reality without sufficient attention to the attitude of Jewish sages to such interactions. This religious-halakhic issue has present-day implications and it is discussed in studies and articles by halakhic authorities. However, it has not been researched from a historical-scientific perspective.

The current article deals with the religious, social, and historical aspects of medical relationships between Jews and Muslims in Islamic countries in pre-modern times as reflected in rabbinic literature from Turkey, Greece, and Land of Israel from the fifteenth to eighteenth centuries. This study addresses the following three questions:

Which halakhic problems were identified by the rabbis in regard to medical relationships with non-Jews in the Ottoman period?

How did Jewish sages in Islamic countries relate to medical relationships with non-Jews? And does this attitude differ from that reflected in earlier documents?

---

[1] On the treatment or the transfer of knowledge between Jewish and Christian neighbors, midwives, and doctors in Spain, Provence, Germany, and northern France, see, for example, S. Shachar, *Medieval Childhood* (Tel Aviv, 1990), 85 [Hebrew]; J. Shatzmiller, *Jews, Medicine and Medieval Society* (Berkeley-Los Angeles-London, 1994), 119–39; E. Baumgarten, "'Thus Say the Wise Midwives': Midwives and Midwifery in 13th-Century Ashkenaz," *Zion* 65 (2000): 56–57 [Hebrew]; idem in more detail in her book *Mothers and Children: Jewish Family Life in Medieval Ashkenaz* (Jerusalem, 2005), 80–85, 208–216 [Hebrew]. On relations between healers of different faiths in eighteenth-century Eastern Europe, see N. M. Gelber, "History of Jewish Physicians in Eighteenth-Century Poland," in *Tribute to Yeshaayahu*, ed. Y. Tirosh (Tel Aviv, 1957), 347–48 [Hebrew]; M. Rosman, *Founder of Hasidim: A Quest for the Historical Ba'al Shem Tov* (University of California Press, 1996), 57.

Are the views of contemporary rabbis compatible or inconsistent with actual medical relationships at the time?

Before turning to the period under discussion, we will begin with a short review of the position of early Jewish halakhic sources on the topic of medical relationships of Jews and non-Jews.

Early Jewish Halakhah

The Bible voices no injunction against medical relationships with non-Jews. The story of Elisha the Prophet, who cured Naaman, the Aramaic captain of the guard who suffered from leprosy, may indicate that there was no such restriction.[2] The first signs of medical constraints evolved and crystallized in the rabbinic period. The rabbis basically imposed a double restriction: First of all, they prohibited the provision of medical services to non-Jews: treating them, circumcising them, or delivering their babies,[3] officially based on the injunction against assisting and supporting pagan societies that contradict the foundations of monotheistic Jewish faith.[4]

At the same time, receiving services from non-Jewish physicians and healers was limited for fear of harassment or murder disguised as a medical failure.[5] It was forbidden to receive medical treatment from non-Jews or to buy medicine that might be lethal, such as opium extracted from the Opium Poppy (*Papaver Somniferum*)[6] and Theriac,[7] of which inexact doses may

2 2Kings 5: 1–14. The story was clearly intended to reinforce the status of the prophet as miracle-maker. On this trend in the Elisha stories, see A. Rofe, *The Prophetical Stories: The Narratives about the Prophets in the Hebrew Bible, Their Literary Types and History* (Jerusalem, 1983), 42–64 [Hebrew]; U. Simon, *Literary Reading of the Bible: Stories of the Prophets* (Jerusalem and Ramat Gan, 1997), 279–324 [Hebrew].

3 Bavli, *Avoda Zara*, 26b. For the injunction against assisting non-Jewish women in labor, see Mishna, *Avoda Zara*, 2:1.

4 Medical prohibitions constitute just one of several lists of rabbinic restrictions on relationships between Jews and non-Jews, based on the concern of idol worship or the that non-Jews would harm Jews, for example, by selling products during idolatrous festivals, receiving haircuts from non-Jewish barbers, or walking together for fear of attack. See Mishna, *Avoda Zara*, 1:1–2; 2:2; Bavli, ibid., 25b.

5 Mishna, *Avoda Zara*, 2:2; *Tosefta Hulin*, 2:21 (Zuckermandel ed.; Jerusalem, 1975).

6 Yerushalmi *Avoda Zara*, 2:2, 40:4. Opium is a narcotic obtained from the milky sap of the seed capsules of the Opium Poppy. Opium contains approximately 30 alkaloids with psycho-active properties; it is addictive, and large doses can be lethal. The best known of these are morphine, codeine, thebaine, narcotine, and papaverine. Medical usage of opium is known since ancient times. On its use in antiquity and in medieval times, see E. Lev, *Medicinal Substances of the Medieval Levant* (Tel Aviv, 2002), 218–19 [Hebrew].

7 Yerushalmi, ibid. Theriac is a serum used for treating snake bites that contained a variety of medical substances, some of them dangerous, such as snake and scorpion venom. On theriac and its components, see Z. Amar, "The Export of Theriac from the

be lethal. Another concern was the use of idolatrous elements contradicting the patient's Jewish faith as part of the medical treatment, or negative religious influence of the non-Jewish physician on the Jewish patient.[8] Rabbis permitted Jews to receive medical treatment from non-Jews with a number of restrictions: If the patient is an important and prominent person, or if the physician is an expert with a well-known reputation, such that he would be prevented from any harmful intentions toward Jews,[9] or if the patient is at death's door, as in such case the treatment could only be beneficial.[10]

The restrictions and prohibitions mentioned above display an atmosphere of distrust and social hostility between Jews and their non-Jewish environment. These religious restrictions might have aggravated the friction between the faiths and created severe social conflicts, particularly in circumstances that entailed a mixed society utilizing joint systems (economy, trade). As a result, as early as the talmudic age we see rabbinic reservations in regard to the all-inclusive prohibition of medical relationships. Accordingly, the risk of inter-faith tension served as grounds for permitting medical treatment of non-Jews and assisting in the labor of non-Jewish women, for a fee.[11]

In dealing with pre-modern times we shall refer to three aspects of medical relationships between Jews and Muslims: (1) treating Muslim patients; (2) receiving medical services from non-Jewish physicians and employing the services of Muslim circumcisers to circumcise Jewish babies; and (3) delivering Muslim babies. We will begin with two important methodical-literary notes related to the Responsa on this topic:

- Rabbinic texts often do not identify the patient's faith, mentioning only that the patient is non-Jewish ("*goy*," "*nokhri*"). The basic premise is that texts by sages operating in Islamic countries usually refer to Muslim patients, who comprised most of the population. Sometimes there is a reference to the patient's faith, e.g., "Ishmaelite patient," "Arab patient," "Togarmi," or "Turk."
- Some halakhic authorities do not distinguish between Muslims and Christians, as they make no distinction between the two faiths in regard to restrictions or dispensations to maintain medical relationships.

Land of Israel and Its Uses in the Middle Ages," *Korot*, 12 (1996–1997):17ff. [Hebrew]; Lev, *Medicinal*, 279–80; N.G. Siraisi, *Medieval and Early Renaissance Medicine: An Introduction to Knowledge and Practice* (Chicago and London: The University of Chicago Press, 1990), 119.

8 Bavli, *Avoda Zara*, 27b.

9 Ibid., 28a.

10 Ibid., 27a.

11 *Avoda Zara*, 26b.

We will first describe the reality in the Ottoman Empire and examine whether this indeed reflects contemporary halakhic views.

A. Providing Medical Services to Non-Jewish Patients

Dealing with the Early Prohibition against Treating Non-Jews

Despite rabbinic restrictions on medical relationships between Jews and non-Jews, rabbis in the Ottoman Empire permitted providing medical services to non-Jews. Two major factors may have facilitated this dispensation: (1) the identification of Islam as a non-idolatrous faith; and (2) the inferior status of Jews and the fear of animosity by Muslim society.

Recognizing Muslims as non-idolaters: Rabbi Joseph Karo (Israel sixteenth century) in his commentary "Kesef Mishne" claimed that the Rambam believed that the rabbinic prohibition against treating non-Jews refers only to those idolaters who existed when the injunction was decreed.[12] Rabbi Karo stated this principle in general without specifically mentioning Muslims. However, we may assume that this was his intention.[13] In his halakhic tome "Mishne Torah," the Rambam (1138–1204) objected to treating non-Jews,[14] although in practice he served as the personal physician and court physician of the Egyptian Ayoubi ruler El Fadil, vizier of Salah a-Din Ayoubi. Perhaps he agreed to serve the Muslim ruler based on the belief that Muslims are not idolaters and therefore they may be treated.[15]

One of the rabbis who supported medical care of Muslims was the Turkish rabbi Chaim Benveniste, who lived and operated in seventeenth-century Izmir. When asked by a Jewish midwife whether it is permitted to deliver a

12 *Kesef Mishne* on Mishne Torah, *Hilkhot Avodat Kokhavim*, 10:2. This claim was voiced in previous centuries by other sages, for example, Rabbi Menachem Hame'iri in his commentary Beit Habehira (Provence thirteenth century), *Avoda Zara* 26a.

13 Halakhic authorities deliberated whether Muslims should be defined as idolaters. Two major views were presented on the matter. Some claimed that Muslims are not idolaters since they do not worship idols (for example, see Rambam, *Hilkhot Ma'achalot Asurot* 11:7; Rambam Responsa [Freiman ed.; Jerusalem, 1938], 369). In contrast, others claimed that the Muslim faith is complete idolatry. For example, see Radbaz Responsa (Warsaw, 1892), 1123 (IV, 92). For other opinions on this controversy, see A. Steinberg, *Encyclopedia of Jewish Medical Ethics*, vol. A (Jerusalem, 1988) 125 [Hebrew].

14 The Rambam objects a number of times to treating non-Jews in his "Mishne Torah." Based on Bavli, *Avoda Zara* 26b, he permits the circumcision of non-Jews in order to fulfill the commandment of circumcision, although not when it has medical purposes (*Hilkhot Mila* 3:7). He forbids assisting non-Jews even in the case of a landslide that occurs on the Sabbath (see *Hilkhot Shabbat* 2:20–21).

15 On Jewish court physicians and doctors in Muslims hospitals in the eleventh to thirteenth centuries according to the Geniza documents, see S. D. Goitein, *A Mediterranean Society* (Tel Aviv, 2005) 134–35, 192 [Hebrew].

"Togarmi woman" (=Muslim of Turkish origin) on the Sabbath, he claimed in his book "Knesset Hagedolah" that the prohibition to deliver and treat non-Jewish patients refers to idolaters, and since Muslims believe in God they are, therefore, not included.[16] On this basis, Benveniste granted the Jewish midwife dispensation to assist the Muslim woman in labor on the Sabbath, with the provision that she will not perform operations involving desecration of the Sabbath. It follows that on weekdays there is no reason not to provide regular medical care to non-Jews. Rabbi Benveniste does not claim that concessions on this matter were made as a result of the fear of animosity by Muslim society, and this reinforces the conclusion that he believed that there was never any problem with medical care of Muslims. As he understood the matter, the Rambam forbade treatment or delivery of non-Jews and even of members of monotheistic faiths, such as Muslims, but as stated, others claim that the Rambam permitted treating members of faiths that professed their belief in God.[17]

The status of Jews in Muslim society: The inferior personal status of Jews as protected people (dhimmis) excluded the option to avoid medical treatment of non-Jews. As claimed by Amnon Cohen, the Jewish minority's treatment of Muslim majority patients was a very sensitive issue. Thus, cases of complication or failed medical treatment might have resulted in undesirable actions against the Jewish physician or even the entire Jewish community.[18] In such circumstances it was only natural that halakhic authorities operating in Christian and Islamic countries[19] gave their consent to providing medical services to non-Jews, based on the rabbinic dispensation stated above.[20]

16 *Knesset Hagedolah* (Jerusalem, 1966), *Orach Chaim*, 330, 187. Rabbi Benveniste discusses treating non-Jews in other places in his books (see Dina Dehaya [Constantinople 1742], Lavin 45, 41:4; *Knesset Hagedolah, Yoreh De'ah*, 154:6).

17 Compare this to the claim by the Italian rabbi Ishmael Hacohen Modena (1724–1811) that the dispensation to assist non-Jewish women in labor for reasons of animosity was based on the concern of insult, as refraining from treating them would have created the impression that Jews consider non-Jews to be "animals" and thus might justifiably cause them insult and arouse their anger (Responsa Zera Emet [Livorno, 1833], III, *Orah Chaim* 32 (on *Hilkhot Shabbat* 301), 40:1.

18 A. Cohen, *Jews under the Rule of Islam, the Jerusalem Community in the Early Ottoman Period* (Jerusalem, 1982) 189 [Hebrew]; A. Cohen, E. Simon-Pikali, and O. Salama, *Jews in the Moslem Religious Court (in the Eighteenth Century)* (Jerusalem, 1996), 323 [Hebrew].

19 For example, compared to the responsum by Rabbi Shlomo ben Aderet (Rashba 1235–1310), who lived and operated in the city of Barcelona in Christian Spain, regarding a Jewish physician's treatment of a non-Jewish (probably Christian) woman suffering from infertility, where he permits treating her, particularly when the physician provides medical services to the general population, for fear of arousing animosity. He states that his rabbi, the Ramban, acted similarly and consulted a woman who suffered from a similar problem (Rashba Responsa, I [Bnei Brak, 1958], 120).

The Historical Reality

The historical reality is certainly compatible with the widespread dispensation to treat non-Jews. There is abundant historical evidence indicating that Jewish physicians provided medical services to Muslims in the Ottoman period. Such evidence is immersed in various literary genres: rabbinic literature, historical chronicles, and archives of the Muslim courts. The Responsa literature includes a fairly wide range of discussions dealing with halakhic questions submitted to rabbis by Jewish physicians concerning caring for non-Jews.[21] Interestingly, in these discussions the rabbis refer to the treatment of non-Jews as self-evident and do not refer to or comment upon the prohibition to treat non-Jews, a fact that indicates the prevalence of the dispensation to treat non-Jews.

Jewish physicians treated both Muslim and Christian patients, and we may assume that, at least for some of these physicians, the medical occupation was perceived as a way to attain a prominent position in the courts of kings and rulers.[22] The Ottoman sultans not only allowed the Jewish and Marrano immigrants to profess their religion but, unlike many Christian rulers in Europe, also permitted the physicians among them to treat non-Jewish patients. Moreover, the sultans asked them to be court doctors. The most famous Jewish physician in the second half of the fifteenth century was Jacob of Gaeta, known as ḥekim Yakūb, the private physician to Sultan Meḥemmed II, the conqueror of Constantinople (1451–1481).[23] The most famous physicians at the Ottoman court in the first half of the sixteenth century were members of the Hamon family. Josef Hamon, a native of Granada and probably a relative of Isaac Hamon, physician to one of the last Muslim rulers there became court physician under Bāyezid II, the ruling sultan. His son, Moses Hamon (1490–1554), also became physician at the Ottoman court

---

20 The extent to which this dispensation was utilized in the Ottoman period will be addressed below.

21 See, for example, Moharikash, Erech Lechem, Rabbi Yaakov Castro (Egypt, sixteenth century) (Constantinople, 1728), *Yoreh De'ah* 112, 28:1; Responsa Mabit by Rabbi Moshe of Trani (Israel, sixteenth century) (Jerusalem, 1974; originally printed in Lamberg, 1861), II, 169; Responsa Darkhei Noam by Rabbi Mordechai Halevy (Egypt seventeenth century) (Jerusalem, 1970; originally printed in Venice, 1707), XIV, 26; Responsa Rav Pe'alim by Rabbi Yoseph Chaim Ben Eliyahu (Iraq, nineteenth century) (Jerusalem, 1970; originally printed in Jerusalem 1901–1913), III - Orach Chaim 1.

22 Examples of physicians who treated Christians include Rabbi David de-Silva (1684–1740), a native of Jerusalem of Portuguese ancestry who treated a woman from the Armenian Convent in Jerusalem, and Rabbi Tuvia the physician (1652–1729), who treated a monk at the Franciscan Hospital. See Z. Amar, "Comrades in Medicine: Medicine as a Bridge between Franciscans and Jews in Ottoman Jerusalem," *Et-Mol* 29 (172, Heshvan 5764, 2003): 22–23 [Hebrew].

23 See B. Lewis, "The Privilege Granted by Meḥemmed II to His Physician," *BSOAS,* 14 (1952): 550–63.

in the reign of Sultan Süleymān the Magnificent (1520-1566).[24] Another Jewish physician at the Ottoman court in Istanbul in the sixteenth century was Doctor Abraham Ibn Shanjis.[25]

One physician who treated Muslims was a chief rabbi of Israel, Rabbi Yosef Mordechai Meyuhas, whose medical expertise was greatly valued by the Muslims.[26] Others in the Land of Israel were Ibrahim Ben Shomali,[27] Rabbi Yaakov Tzemach, who served as personal physician to the governor of Safed,[28] as well as the physicians Rabbi Mordechai Harofeh (=the physician), Rabbi Salmon Harofeh (=the physician), and Salmon Hamenate'ach (=the surgeon), mentioned in cases involving Muslims treated with unfavorable results.[29] Protocols from the archives of the Muslim court that operated in Jerusalem in the eighteenth-century report, among other things, on a Jewish physician who treated Muslims and enjoyed the support of the sultan, an eye healer who treated Muslim patients, and a Jewish surgeon who operated on Muslims.[30]

Some physicians, such as Rabbi Chaim Vital (Safed 1543 - Damascus 1620) took a more rigid stance toward medical interactions with non-Jews. However, the impression is that they were a minority. In his account of prescribed treatments in time of epidemic, Vital describes a protective talisman and notes that its secret should not be revealed to non-Jews.[31] We do not know whether he also refrained from treating non-Jews and why he objected to revealing the secret of the medical prescription to non-Jews, whether from fear of religious hostility or his desire to keep the prescription secret. In any case, he himself did not hesitate to benefit from non-Jewish medical services (see below).

---

24 On Moses Hamon and his son Josef Hamon, see: U. Heyd, "Moses Hamon, Chief Jewish Physician to Sultan Süleymān the Magnificent," *Oriens,* 16 (1963): 152–70; S.W. Baron, *A Social and Religious History of the Jews*, 18 (1983), 74–77; M. Rozen, *A History of the Jewish Community in Istanbul: The Formative Years, 1453–1566* (Leiden: Brill, 2002) 208–9.

25 M. M. Weinstein, "The Correspondence of Dr. Abraham Ibn Sanchi," *Studies in Bibliography and Booklore*, 20 (1998): 145–76.

26 Z. Amar, "Jewish Physicians of Jerusalem in the 16th–18th Centuries," in *Medicine in Jerusalem throughout the Ages*, eds. E. Lev et al. (Tel Aviv, 1999) 94, no. 46 [Hebrew].

27 Mentioned in a document from 1542 in regard to treatment of a Muslim patient. See Cohen, *Jews under the Rule of Islam,* 189.

28 Amar, "Jewish Physicians," 93, no. 24.

29 Ibid., 93–94, nos. 32, 33, 44.

30 See Cohen et al., *Eighteenth Century*, document 280, p. 326; document 282, p. 327; document 286, p. 328; document 287, p. 329.

31 Manuscript in the Musayof collection, no. 228, Yad Itzchak Ben Zvi, tape no. 2675. For his medical techniques, see Y. Buchman and Z. Amar, *Practical Medicine of Rabbi Chayyim Vital* (Jerusalem, 2007), 9–29 [Hebrew].

An extreme position on the healing of Gentiles appears in a response sent by Abraham Baruch ha-Rofe to Rabbi Chaim Benveniste in 1665. Doctor Baruch inquired whether Jewish physicians attending Gentiles are permitted to kill them by administering poison drugs or to cause their death indirectly by withholding medical treatment:

> Query: May our Rabbi teach us whether doctors who treat Gentiles, Ishmaelites [=Muslims], 'Arelim' [=uncircumcised, Christians] and Amalekites[32] are permitted to give them counter-medicines so that they die [medical compounds containing toxins that were used to cure snake bites and the like but could also cause death] or to at least withhold treatment so that they die, or is all of this prohibited.[33]

This seemingly general question by Abraham Baruch raises the real possibility of a doctor misusing his medical authority in order to harm innocent people under the guise of failed medical treatment. The questions that arise are: who was this doctor Abraham Baruch, what was the background to his question, and does it imply a real intention to harm Gentiles?

Gershom Scholem surmised that Abraham Baruch was a well-known doctor from Izmir who was a follower of Shabbetai Zvi. This is apparently the same man as mentioned by the name Doctor Barut in a book by the Dutch priest Thomas Künen published in 1669, in which he was described as a doctor whose medical services were used by many Christians. Abraham Baruch, who was appointed by Shabbetai Zvi as king of Portugal, was descended from Portuguese crypto-Jews, and some of his family still lived as crypto-Jews in France.[34] Assuming that this is the same person, David Tamar proposed that his hatred for Gentiles, in general, and for Christians, in particular, was caused by his own life experience and by his messianic zeal. It is not surprising that such a man, who believed that the Messiah had arrived and would redeem Israel and avenge its enemies, wanted to be an active participant in that process.[35]

In his lengthy answer, Rabbi Chaim Benveniste quoted multiple sources from talmudic and rabbinic literature that deal with the different situations in which it is permitted or forbidden to cause the death of Gentiles, such as when they are not at war with Jews or when Jews are in a weakened position. In his summary, Rabbi Benveniste presents three different opinions

---

32 The meaning of "Amalekites" in this case is unclear.

33 Rabbi Chaim Benveniste, *Responsa Baye Haye* (Jerusalem, 1970), *Yoreh De'ah*, 178, 129b.

34 G. Scholem, *Shabbetai Zvi and the Shabbetaien Movement during His Period* (Tel Aviv, 1957), 111, 351 n. 2 and 615 [Hebrew]. On Shabbetean doctors, see Y. Barnai, "The Marranos of Portugal in Izmir in the Seventeenth Century" in *Nation and Its History*, vol. II, ed. S. Etinger (Jerusalem, 1984) 291–92 [Hebrew].

35 D. Tamar, *Researches in the Jews' History in Eretz Israel and in Eastern Lands* (Jerusalem, 1981), 143–44 [Hebrew].

current among halakhic authorities: (a) According to Rabbi Joseph Caro and others, it is not only permissible to withhold treatment from a Gentile, but even to cause his death by giving him counter-medicines, although this is optional, not a religious duty; (b) According to Rabbi Joel Cirkis, a seventeenth-century Polish rabbinical authority and author of the well-known book "Bayit Hadash," in any case it is not permitted to cause the death of a non-Jew, even by inaction; and (c) According to Rabbi David Ha-Levi, also from seventeenth-century Poland and author of "Turei Zahav," it is forbidden to cause the death of a Gentile directly, such as by the administration of poison, but it is permitted to allow him to die through inaction or by withholding treatment that could save his life.[36]

In practice, Rabbi Benveniste recommends a moderate course, but not in all cases. If the Gentile is a person who harms Jews, it is permitted to harm him, even directly, in the guise of medical treatment. On the other hand, if the Gentile is not harmful to Jews, there is no obligation to harm him and it is better not to do so, even indirectly. Even though Rabbi Benveniste does conclude with a ruling, the feeling is that he considered the discussion to be mainly theoretical and philosophical. He treats the different halakhic opinions technically, without considering the practical consequences for the relations between Jews and Gentiles, such as attacks by non-Jews. Even more strangely, he does not consider the halakhic prohibition against causing enmity.

Halakhic Conflicts that Resulted from Treating Non-Jewish Patients

The basic dispensation to treat Muslims did not solve all the problems that arose from the encounter between the two faiths. Providing medical treatment to non-Jews aroused various halakhic problems that presented the rabbis with new and varied challenges.[37] One of the questions was whether it is permitted to deliver or treat non-Jews on the Sabbath, as the treatment requires labors forbidden by Jewish law.

Some halakhic authorities permitted the treatment of non-Jews in principle but prohibited the provision of medical services on the Sabbath. Rabbi Benveniste, the Turkish rabbi mentioned above, permitted the treatment of Muslims, but claimed that the fact that they are not idolaters does not sanction their treatment on the Sabbath if this requires any halakhic transgres-

36 *Baye Haye*, 130b.

37 Physicians working in public hospitals or in the courts of rulers encountered halakhic problems related to kashrut, such as wine or mead manufactured by non-Jews and added to medicines. One example is a question referred to Rabbi Nissim Chaim Mizrachi, rabbi of Jerusalem in the eighteenth century: "The custom of Israeli doctors serving in the homes of rulers, who prepare concoctions and for these concoctions use wine of non-Jews or honey of non-Jews and other prohibited substances" (*Responsa Admat Qodesh* [Constantinople, 1752], II, 12).

sion, even if only of a rabbinical commandment.[38] Rabbi Benveniste did not refer to the possibility that refraining from treating Muslim patients on the Sabbath could lead to antagonism by Muslim society. Perhaps he was aware that if a Jewish physician refrained from providing treatment due to a religious law or necessity the Muslims would treat this with respect. It is interesting that a number of European halakhic authorities over the last few centuries have permitted the treatment of non-Jews on the Sabbath even when involving labors forbidden by the Torah due to the fear of inter-faith antagonism or since non-Jewish physicians might refrain from treating Jews in protest.[39]

B. Benefiting from the Medical Services of Non-Jewish Physicians

Evading medical treatment of Muslims risked, as stated, animosity or antagonism by the non-Jewish environment. However when Jews were in need of medical assistance the situation was completely different. It was generally possible to seek the services of Jewish physicians. However, they were not always available, and sometimes there was the need for someone more professional and proficient, who happened to be non-Jewish. What did the rabbis decide in regard to medical treatment provided by non-Jewish physicians in Ottoman-occupied countries?

Texts by halakhic authorities from pre-modern times continue to cite strict classical rabbinic restrictions regarding medical services received from non-Jews.[40] However, as we will see below, some of the restrictions were modified in accordance with the reality prevalent under Ottoman rule.

Receiving Medical Services from an Observant Non-Jewish Physician

Receiving medical care from non-Jewish medical staff was discussed in a letter sent to Rabbi Binyamin Ben Matitya, who lived and operated in the first half of the sixteenth century. Rabbi Binyamin served as a judge in the court of Arta (northwestern Greece) and his answers include information about Jewish life in Greece and Asia Minor. The inquirer was interested to know in principle if it was permitted to receive medical care from a non-Jewish physician or only from a Jewish physician.[41] Conspicuously absent from the arguments on both sides is the fear that the physician might harm the patient, as mentioned in the Talmud. In this era there was probably no rea-

---

38 *Knesset Hagedolah*, *Hilkhot Shabbat*, 330, p. 187; *Shyarei Knesset Hagedolah* (Salonica, 1767), *Yoreh De'ah* 154, *Hagahot Bet Yosef*, 10.

39 See, for example, *Responsa Divrei Chaim* by R. Chaim Halberstam from Sanz (Bilgoria, 1929), II, *Orah Chaim*, 25. For additional sources, see Steinberg, *Encyclopedia*, 126–27.

40 On medieval rabbinic halakhah, see Rambam, *Hilkhot Rotzeach Ushmirat Hanefesh*, 12:9; Shulhan Arukh, *Yoreh De'ah*, 155:1.

41 *Responsa Binyamin Ze'ev* (Jerusalem, 1959), 408.

son for such fears, as Ottoman authorities took it upon themselves to protect their foreign subjects, who could even file cases in Muslim courts (about this aspect see further below).

In his response, Rabbi Binyamin discusses medical care provided by a non-Jewish physician without identifying him as Christian or Muslim. Rabbi Binyamin operated in a Christian environment. However, this is not conclusive as he answered questions referred also by Jews under Ottoman rule, and we do not know who asked the question. In any case, Rabbi Binyamin makes an essential distinction between observant and non-observant physicians. He believes that it is forbidden to use the services of a strictly observant physician, even an expert, as forbidden spells might be employed as part of the treatment. If so, it seems that Rabbi Binyamin believed that the healer's faith is insignificant, unless the medical care provided integrates religious elements that contradict Jewish faith.[42]

Rabbi Binyamin concludes that although it is permissible to use the medical services of a non-Jew who does not use non-Jewish elements in his practice, it is undesirable. He does not state his reasons, however. Perhaps he was still concerned that non-Jewish elements might inadvertently be used or that the physician might exert a bad influence on the patient.

Circumcision of Jewish Babies by Muslim Physicians

Circumcision of babies is customary both in Jewish and Muslim law. This is basically a religious ceremony. However, the surgical intervention is truly a medical operation, requiring the medical skill of a circumciser. Early halakhic sources discuss the issue as to whether a Jewish circumciser may circumcise non-Jews,[43] and vice versa: when no Jewish circumciser is available the permissibility of a physician from another faith to circumcise a Jewish baby.[44] In this article we will focus on the latter aspect.

The Babylonian Talmud discusses whether physicians of different faiths may circumcise Jews, for example, a Kuti (Samaritan), a person who has not been circumcised (e.g., Christian), etc.[45] One of the primary reasons to forbid the services of a non-Jewish circumciser was the fear that the child or

---

42 A similar halakhic principle was presented by medieval Ashkenazi authorities who permitted the use of medical services of non-Jewish doctors. For example, see Mahzor Vitri, Rabbi Simcha of Vitri (R.S. Horowitz ed.; Nuremberg, 1923), *Hilkhot Shchita Misefer Ha'Truma,* 755–82, 98.

43 *Rambam Responsa* (Jerusalem, 1934), 124, and in the additions at the end of the book (p. 370).

44 Bavli, *Avoda Zara* 26b–27a. In light of the discussion in the Bavli, the Rambam and later Rabbi Yosef Karo decided that non-Jews may not circumcise Jewish babies, even if the circumciser has been circumcised. See Rambam, *Hilkhot Mila*, 2:1; *Shulchan Arukh*, *Yoreh De'ah*, 264:1.

45 *Avoda Zara*, ibid.

his sexual organ would be harmed (and he would be castrated). A discussion on the issue of Muslim circumcisers is found in the book "Medical Works" by Rabbi Rafael Mordechai Malki, who served as physician in the Jewish community of Jerusalem in the seventeenth century. This text includes information about the medical services that existed in Jerusalem during the Ottoman period, as well as Malki's references to halakhic aspects related to medicine. He writes:

> When there is a city that has no Israelite circumciser and that has an idolatrous non-Jewish physician proficient in circumcision and also a Kuti who knows how to circumcise, it is preferable that the non-Jew circumcise than the Kuti, since the idolatrous non-Jew does not intend to fulfill the commandment of circumcision, unlike the Kuti who does intend fulfill the commandment of circumcision but does so in honor of Mt. Grizim. So too the Ishmaelites[46] who circumcise in honor of their prophet Muhammad.[47]

Rabbi Rafael Malki refers to three types of physician-circumcisers: the idolater, the Kuti (Samaritan), and the Muslim. Malki prefers an idolatrous physician (maybe he means a Christian) since circumcising males is not part of his faith and thus there is no risk that he will integrate forbidden spells into the ceremony. In contrast, a Samaritan circumciser and a Muslim circumciser, who are accustomed to circumcising their sons, should not circumcise Jewish babies, as Samaritans mention Mt. Grizim, their holy site, as part of the ceremony, while Muslims mention Muhammad, their prophet.[48] Malki feared the inclusion of Islamic elements in the circumcision ceremony, but he does not mention the opinions of the rabbis (Rambam and Rabbi Joseph Karo) who disqualify non-Jews from circumcising Jews in any circumstance, even when not involving the use of spells contra-indicated by Jewish faith.

Using the Medical Services of Non-Jews: Historical Reality

We have seen that rabbinic texts express reservations concerning medical services received from non-Jewish physicians. The question is: What actually happened? Did Jews, in fact, refrain from using these services? Historical

[46] *Yad Ne'eman* by Rabbi Chaim Abraham ben Shmuel of Miranda, a famed rabbi and commentator from the city of Salonica who had Rafael Malki's commentary on the Book of Genesis, has the version: "So too the Ishmaelites and so too the Turks who are circumcisers etc." (*Yad Ne'eman*, 35:3). On this text see Rafael Mordecai Malki, *Medical Works of Rabbi Rafael Mordecai Malki* (M. Benayahu ed.; Jerusalem, 1985), 13 [Hebrew].

[47] Malki, *Medical Works*, 129 [Hebrew].

[48] Such concerns existed also among Medieval European Jews. They were reluctant to use Christian midwives for fear of appeals to the Virgin and to other Christian figures. See E. Baumgarten, *Mothers and Children: Jewish Family Life in Medieval Ashkenaz* (Jerusalem, 2005), 80 [Hebrew]. Baumgarten also mentioned the Jewish fear that Christian midwives would baptize the babies they delivered (ibid., p. 84).

sources indicate that in times of need Jews turned to non-Jewish physicians, and rabbis and scholars were no exception. Here are some examples. In 1604, when in Damascus, Rabbi Chaim Vital (Safed 1543–Damascus 1620) contracted a serious disease that impaired his vision. A year later, seeking a cure, he visited a "sorcerer" *(mechashef)*, probably a Muslim, who, he attests, was "proficient in curing those afflicted by demons." He stated that the purpose of his visit was to "examine his wisdom and also to ask about my vision problems."[49] Vital's son, Rabbi Shmuel Vital, did not hesitate to receive medical care from non-Jewish clerics as well.[50]

Discussion

The current study shows that pre-modern halakhic authorities permitted the medical treatment of Muslims as a matter of principle. This dispensation was related to the inferior personal and social status of the Jews and to the risk of being harmed by non-Jewish society. This was particularly true of physicians, whose status was even more sensitive. Knowing that Jewish physicians treated both Muslims and Christians, we may assume that the rabbis' halakhic decisions had a part in shaping reality. However, we cannot exclude the possibility that people's actual conduct stemmed from lack of choice and existential needs and was not necessarily a direct derivative of rabbinic decisions.

One of the issues arising from our study is the degree to which Jews and non-Jews in the Ottoman Empire interacted for medical purposes, and, as a result, the degree to which it was necessary to permit medical relationships between members of the two faiths. Jewish and Muslim medical interactions depended to a great degree on the type of medical institution in which they existed. Three major types of medical facilities were extant in the Ottoman Empire: (1) general-public hospitals, which served people of all faiths and socioeconomic status; (2) ethnic-community medical services for Jews or Christians who preferred independent facilities; and (3) private clinics.[51] Studies dealing with the medical establishment during the Ottoman period indicate that although imperial hospitals were intended for the entire population, in reality they served only single, poor, or mentally ill Muslims.[52] The

49 Rabbi Chaim Vital, *Sefer Hahezyonot* (A.Z. Eshkoli ed.; Jerusalem: Mosad Harav Kuk, 1954), 12–13, 18 [Hebrew]. See also Y. Buchman, "Medical works of Rabbi Chaim Vital," *Korot*, 17 (2004): 24 [Hebrew].

50 See "Story of a Spirit" printed at the end of *Sha'ar Hagilgulim*, Rabbi Chaim Vital (Jerusalem, 1988), 186:1.

51 Cohen, *Jews under the Rule of Islam*, 191; Z. Amar and E. Lev, *Physicians, Drugs, and Remedies in Jerusalem from the 10th to the 18th Century* (Tel Aviv, 2000), 74–76 [Hebrew].

52 M. Shefer, "Hospitals in Three Ottoman Capitals (Bursa, Edirne, and Istanbul) in the Sixteenth and Seventeenth Centuries" (Ph.D. thesis, Tel-Aviv University, Tel-Aviv 2001), 54–56 [Hebrew].

reason was that members of Ottoman society preferred to receive medical aid from their family members, and in more severe cases they turned to private healers or to clerics who used traditional medical techniques.[53]

Physicians from various faiths could all serve in public hospitals and some were appointed by the central authorities in Istanbul. Such hospitals saw an intermingling of physicians from different religious and national groups, and these included Jewish physicians, such as Yihye the Physician, whose letter of appointment (from October 19, 1564) stated that he preferred to be a physician in Jerusalem.[54] Jews who served in public hospitals and saw Muslim patients clearly relied on the halakhic permit to treat Muslims, and it seems that this was true also of physicians who worked in private clinics, sought by people of all faiths.

In community hospitals the situation was slightly different. In Jerusalem the Jewish congregation established autonomous-community hospitals (Sephardic and Ashkenazi),[55] which operated according to Jewish norms and rules in regard to the laws of kashrut, Sabbath, etc., and they employed Jewish physicians.[56] In these facilities physicians treated only Jews, so there was no need for permission to treat non-Jews. However, we must remember that a not insignificant number of non-Jewish patients requested the services of these physicians when the latter were not busy at the Jewish hospital, so the permission to treat non-Jews was relevant in these cases as well.

The findings presented in the current study concerning halakhic problems that arose as a result of medical relationships support the views of

53 Abraham Marcus, *The Middle East on the Eve of Modernity: Aleppo in the Eighteenth Century* (New York: Columbia University Press 1989), 265–66; R. Murphy, "Ottoman Medicine and Transculturalism from the Sixteenth through the Eighteenth Century," *Bulletin of the History of Medicine*, 66 (1992): 376–403; L. I. Conrad, "The Arab-Islamic Medical Tradition," in *The Western Medical Tradition 800 BC to 1800 AD*, eds. L. I. Conrad et al. (Cambridge: Cambridge University Press, 1995), 93–138.

54 Cohen et al., *Jews in the Moslem Religious Court*, document no. 303, p. 269 [Hebrew]. On physicians in Jerusalem during the Ottoman period,see U. Heyd, "The Jews of Israel in the Late Seventeenth Century," *Jerusalem, Studies of Israel, dedicated to Yesha'ayahu Peres*, 4 (1953), 179–80 [Hebrew]; Cohen, *Jews under the Rule of Islam*, 188; M. Rozen, *The Jewish Community of Jerusalem in the Seventeenth Century* (Tel Aviv, 1985), 232-33 [Hebrew]; Amar, "Jewish Physicians," 79–98 [Hebrew].

55 On the hospital (*albimarstan*) that functioned in Jerusalem during the sixteenth and eighteenth centuries and served members of the Ashkenazi and Sephardic congregations, see Amar and Lev, *Physicians, Drugs*, 76–78.

56 Two types of physicians operated in Jerusalem. There were physicians authorized by the authorities who had acquired their medical education at European universities or at the medical schools in the center of major Ottoman cities or who had received their medical accreditation based on experience and practice in the hospitals. However, there were also unqualified physicians who had no licensed medical training and were not registered by the authorities. See Amar and Lev, *Physicians, Drugs*, 72.

Amar and Lev, who claim that establishing a special hospital for Jews solved some of the problems and received the approval of the Ottoman authorities, who recognized the special needs professed by Jews and the halakhic problems that they might encounter in public hospitals and in interactions with physicians of other faiths.[57]

A review of Responsa that state grounds for permitting desecration of the Sabbath in order to help non-Jewish patients indicates that the issue occupied halakhic authorities operating mainly in Christian countries (Europe) but relatively few in Muslim countries.[58] This fact leads to the question as to whether the concern of animosity from non-Jewish sources was more relevant and tangible in Christian countries, whereas people in Muslim countries demonstrated understanding and tolerance toward physicians' religious limitations? Maybe so. However, this must be examined in a separate discussion.

Rabbis were afraid that non-Jewish doctors might harm Jewish patients. The case of Abraham Baruch shows that also Jewish doctors could misuse their medical authority in order to harm innocent Gentiles under the guise of failed medical treatment. It would seem that the harmful intentions of Abraham Baruch against Gentiles were the exception to the rule, and were motivated by his personal mind-set, and they cannot be seen as part of a wider phenomenon. In any case, we see that not only could the ruling majority harm the minority, but that the opposite was also possible.

Using Muslim Medical Services: The Relevance of Rabbinic Prohibitions in the Ottoman Period

Following the hospital typology presented above, we presume that throughout the empire, when the community did not arrange to care for its ill, they were more dependent on non-Jewish physicians and, therefore, there must have been more of a halakhic conflict concerning whether to permit treatment by non-Jews.Various halakhic authorities expressed reservations about the use of non-Jewish medical services. Did Christian and Muslim religious authorities hold similar views? Reservations about medical relationships were not characteristic only of Jewish authorities, rather also of Christian clerics, who occasionally renewed their instructions to avoid

57 Amar and Lev, *Physicians, Drugs*, 75–76.

58 See, for example, the new Bach (*Bait Hadash*) Responsa by Rabbi Yoel Sirkis (Poland seventeenth century) (Jerusalem, 1959), 2; *Tiferet Yisrael* by Rabbi Israel Lifschitz (Danzig, nineteenth century), Mishnah *Avoda Zara*, 2:6; *Responsa Chatam Sofer*, II - *Yoreh De'ah*, 131; *Responsa Divrei Chaim*, II, *Orah Chaim*, 25. We reached this insight among others through Rabbi Ovadia Yosef's reference to the issue, which is still relevant today. All the sources mentioned in the answer given by Rabbi Yosef, who is recognized as a halakhic authority who often quotes other Responsa, are of European rabbis. See *Responsa Yabia Omer*, VIII *Orah Chaim*, 38.

initiating medical contact with Jews.[59] In contrast, we have no knowledge of Muslim regulations prohibiting the use of Jewish medical services.

Rabbis expressed reservations about using non-Jewish medical services, although in the Ottoman period deliberate harm to Jewish patients by non-Jewish physicians was a relatively far-fetched concern. The reason was that authorized physicians licensed to practice medicine were supervised by the authorities or by the "head physician" in charge of the medical guild.[60] Documents of the Muslim court archives from the sixteenth to eighteenth centuries bear testimony of cases filed against physicians and healers who neglected their duty and caused damage to patients under their care. We have found cases filed by Muslims against Jewish physicians and healers, but not vice versa.[61] It is natural for medical treatment to occasionally culminate in undesirable results and for this reason it would not be logical to assume that in no instance were Jews harmed by their non-Jewish physicians. The lack of findings is inconclusive. However, it gives rise to a number of questions: Did Jews have the option to sue Muslim physicians? If so, does the absence of lawsuits stem from their concern? Does this indicate distrust of the Muslim legal system? We have no conclusive answers to these questions.

In light of our premise that there was no room for any concern of deliberate harm to Jewish patients, why did the rabbis disapprove of non-Jewish medical services? We believe that during the Ottoman period the main concern was of the use of spells or medicines contradicting Jewish law or the fear of bad religious influences resulting from the physician-patient relationship.

While in regard to treating non-Jewish patients the dispensations awarded by the rabbis are compatible with reality, the situation is different in regard to using the medical services of non-Jewish physicians. The impression is one of incompatibility between the rabbis and the lower social strata. Some rabbis did not approve of using non-Jewish medical services, albeit it

---

59 On the objection of Christian clerics to medical relationships between Jews and Christians, as, for example, in the hiring of Jewish wet-nurses or receiving medications from Jews, see: S. Grayzel, *The Church and the Jews in the Thirteenth Century* (New York, 1966), 306–7; N. Shor, "The Jewish Population of Jerusalem in the 16th–18th Centuries according to Franciscan Chronicles and Catholic and Protestant Traveler Journals," in *Chapters in the History of Jerusalem at the Beginning of the Ottoman Period*, ed. A. Cohen (Jerusalem, 1979), 434–43 [Hebrew].

60 On the appointment of the head physician and his role in supervising physicians, see Amar and Lev, *Physicians, Drugs*, p. 72.

61 See Cohen et al., *Eighteenth Century*, 323–30. However, it is important to state that if Jews were physically harmed by Muslims, even inadvertently, they did not hesitate to bring this to the attention of the Kadi (Cohen et al., *Jews in the Moslem Religious Court*, 152 [Hebrew]). However, this is not an indication of cases in which Muslim physicians harmed patients under their care.

was customary among the general public. The objecting rabbis expressed the classical Jewish approach derived from the sources, which maintains avoidance of such relationships, although the public assumed a more practical view.

Despite the rabbis' disapproval of turning to conventional non-Jewish physicians, in times of need the public turned to non-Jewish healers and this conduct was embraced by religious authorities as well. Rabbis, such as Chaim Vital and his son Shmuel, were not reluctant to approach even popular healers who used sorcery, despite the biblical warnings against associating with such people. The question is whether the association with non-Jewish sorcerers was perceived as permissible only by rabbis in the Ottoman empire, or whether Ashkenazi halakhic authorities employed such mitigations as well?

In principal, European Jews (in Spain, Provence, Germany, and northern France) also used non-Jewish medical services. Shatzmiller and Baumgarten showed that in medieval times the employment of non-Jewish physicians and midwives was perceived as routine within Jewish society and that the rabbis were not conspicuously opposed to this phenomenon.[62] A similar medical reality was customary among Jews in Muslim countries in the Ottoman period as well. Regarding the use of sorcerers, Yosef Hayut has shown that also rabbis in Christian Europe permitted the use of non-Jewish sorcerers. Examples are Rabbi Shlomo Luria (Maharshal), who lived and operated in Poland in the sixteenth century,[63] and Rabbi Shlomo Ganzfried, author of the *Qitzur Shulhan Arukh*, who lived in Hungary in the nineteenth century.[64] These two rabbis permitted consultation of non-Jewish sorcerers in cases of lethal illnesses or diseases caused by sorcery or evil spirits.[65]

Hayut suggested two possible reasons for this medical practice, which may also reflect the halakhic views of rabbis in the Ottoman empire: First of all, there is a rich and long-standing Jewish occult tradition, adhered to by renown rabbis, proving that occult activities are legitimate. The second reason is based on Moshe Idel's definition that the structure of Judaism as a performance-based religion facilitates its conception as an occult faith as well.[66]

---

62 Shatzmiller, *Jews, Medicine and Medieval Society*, 119–39; Baumgarten, *Mothers and Children*, 82–85. Baumgarten's study focuses on the period from the ninth to the mid-fourteenth century, but it seems that this norm continued later as well.

63 Rabbi Shlomo Luria, *Responsa Maharshal* (Jerusalem, 1969), 3.

64 *Qitzur Shulhan Arukh* (Jerusalem: Mosad Harav Kuk, 1975), 166:5, p. 319.

65 Y. Hayut, "Rabbi Moshe Zacuto Banisher of Spirits: Kabbalah, Witchcraft, and Medicine in Early Modern Times," *Pe'amim* 96 (2003): 138–39 [Hebrew].

66 M. Idel, *Kabbalah: New Perspectives* (Jerusalem, 1993), 280–81 [Hebrew].

Conclusion

The patient-doctor relationship is the foundation of a healthy society. These relationships hold social significance as well. History indicates that when people are sick they are usually more tolerant toward strangers and others. In such instances "the walls come down," as do religious-social divisions between sects, ethnic groups, and faiths, and the level of assistance and consideration rises.

Jewish law, as reflected in rabbinic literature, took a strict approach to medical relationships between Jews and non-Jews. In principle (aside from certain circumstances) a double ban existed: the rabbis forbade Jews to provide non-Jews with medical services: to treat them, circumcise them, or deliver their babies, in order to refrain from helping pagan-idolatrous society. Jews were also forbidden to use non-Jewish medical services (medical treatments or the purchasing of certain medications) for fear of harassment or murder disguised as the failure of medical treatment.

We have pointed out that circumstances did not enable the public to fulfill these instructions to the letter and, therefore, many halakhic authorities in the post-talmudic period dispensed with the prohibition of medical relationships almost completely; some even permitted the treating of non-Jews on the Sabbath, even though it might involve its desecration. Stricter views were voiced concerning the treatment of Christians, but the dispensation to treat Muslims and deliver their babies was clearer. Halakhic authorities claimed that the original prohibition involved idolaters, whereas Muslims do not engage in idolatry. Another major claim supporting the concession was the concern of animosity and harassment by the non-Jewish environment.

The historical sources indicate that in practice Jewish physicians, some of them rabbis and scholars, did treat non-Jews, both Muslims and Christians. The sources also indicate that Jews sought the services of non-Jewish physicians, so we see that in practice the medical relationships between Jews and Muslims persevered.

Islam and Sabbateanism in the Chronicle Sefer Divrei Yosef

SHIMON SHTOBER

The seventeenth-century historian, Joseph Sambari, was a witness to the great messianic eruption of his day, i.e., the Sabbatean movement, which emerged in the second half of the seventeenth century. Sambari was on the scene, having met Shabbatai Ṣevi in Cairo more than once. Unfortunately, the pages that contained his report on Sabbatianism were ripped out of his chronicle, a mystery that we shall explore below.

Sambari: A Biographical Sketch

Joseph Sambari was born in Cairo, probably in the 1630s, where he spent his entire life as a member of the Musta'ribī congregation of the Jewish community (autochthonous Eastern Jews, assimilated into the Arabic culture). Aside from his name, that of his father, Isaac, and his toponymic nickname, Qatāya, there is almost nothing we know about Sambari. He studied in Cairo at the *yeshiva* headed by Rabbi Abraham Scandarī, whose extensive library not only aroused in the young student an intense curiosity in history, but also provided him with a considerable number of sources he later used in his works. Sambari seems to have been one of the few Cairene scholars of his time whose research went beyond history proper and included the history of biblical texts as well, especially in the field of *Masora*. He also had a keen interest in the topography of Egypt, especially that of its capital, Cairo.[1]

The only available information about the later years of Sambari pertains to his professional life. In the 1670s, he functioned as a clerk in the service of Raphael Yosef,[2] the *ṣarraf-bashi* (the treasurer) of Qaraqash 'Alī, then the Ottoman governor of Egypt. The generous support of his patron, the above-mentioned treasurer, enabled Sambari to indulge in historical research and writing. Although he complained bitterly about the hard times

---

[1] On Sambari, see Shimon Shtober, *Sefer Divrei Yosef: Eleven Hundred Years of Jewish History under Muslim Rule* (Jerusalem, 1994) [henceforth: Shtober, *SDY*], 13–16, 18, 54–55. He himself supplied most of the autobiographical data. Cf. *Sefer Divrei Yosef*, 79, l. 47–81, l. 83.

[2] For the role that Rafael Yosef played in the history of Sabbateanism, see below near notes 22, 25.

that befell him after the assassination of his benefactor in 1669, the historian managed to complete his main historical work five years later.[3]

The Historical Work of Sambari: Sefer Divrei Yosef

In the introduction to the second part of his main work, Sambari delineated the structure and the scope of his historical project, which consisted of two consecutive Hebrew chronicles, spanning a chronology of 1100 years. The first one, *Sefer Divrei Ḥakhamim* (The Book Containing the Sayings of the Sages), is an historical account from Adam to *Rabbanan Savorai* (Babylonian sages of the seventh century), which is no longer extant. The second one is *Sefer Divrei Yosef* (The Book of Yosef's Sayings)[4] [henceforth: *SDY*], which was completed on 23 January 1673.

The historical material in the *SDY* was cast into a structure resembling concentric circles. The outermost circle gives a concise description of the politico-religious history of Islam written in florid, biblical language. Here Sambari chose to begin with a short description of the birth of Islam in the first decades of the seventh century. Then he portrays succinctly the biographies of Islamic rulers, beginning with the first four caliphs, called by Islamic tradition *rāshidûn* (632–661), and followed by the next six dynasties: Umayyads, Abbasids, Fatimids, Ayyubids, Mamluks and Ottomans, which ruled in the East up to his time, in the seventeenth century.

The second circle is a history of the Jews written against this Islamic backdrop, telling the life-stories and activities of Jewish leaders and sages who lived around the Mediterranean from the tenth to the close of the seventeenth centuries. In addition, Sambari elaborates on the variegated manifestations of the messianic phenomenon in the Middle Ages and the beginnings of the new era.

The story of the Jewish community in Egypt, and particularly that of Cairo, makes up the third circle, which is a more detailed continuation of the preceding circle, discussing topographical and demographic data, relations between Jews and Muslims, communal institutions, and the intellectual achievements of outstanding personages who lived in Egypt (e.g., Maimonides and his pedigree). It is within this third circle that Sambari documented *inter alia* various calamities, especially episodes of persecution that befell the Jews of Egypt, and interspersed the scanty autobiographical particulars that have reached us.[5]

---

[3] Ibid., 17–18, 315–16.

[4] The name Yosef alludes to the author's name.

[5] See Shtober, *SDY* 19–45. The following quantitative data will illustrate the centrality of Egypt and its Jewish community to Sambari's chronicle: The author devoted 77 of the 228 chapters in the book to the history of Muslim Egypt. The history of the Jewish community in Egypt is covered in 56 chapters.

Why Did Sambari Set up an Islamic Backdrop to the SDY?

There is no doubt that Sambari made up his mind that he was going to write the history of his nation and set it within the framework of the world of Muslim kingdoms. He already planned this structure at an early stage, while he was collecting the raw historical materials for his chronicle. Hence, we find throughout the *SDY*, that its author intentionally created an overlapping of the internal Jewish sphere and the external-universal-Muslim sphere. This overlapping is represented in the chronicle by a brief outline of the history of each Muslim dynasty, preceding the lengthy chapters telling the story of the Jews who lived in the days of that ruling dynasty, be it a caliphate or a sultanate.

Sambari expressed his intention to integrate both Jewish and Islamic histories not only in the way in which he structured his work, but by stating this intention explicitly in the introduction to his book. There, he declared that he is using Islamic history as the backdrop for his writings, viewing history from theological and political perspectives, as seen in the opening sentences to *SDY*:

I. These are the kings who reigned in the land of Babylon (='Iraq), Egypt and Constantinople, after sovereignty (מלכות) had ceased among the sons of Israel. It was long after the destruction of our glory, the temple. Should the Hebrew servant ask:[6] What does it matter to us to know the reckonings of the Ishmaelite kings, whether they ruled or not? Then go and tell him what our sages of blessed memory said about the Chronologies of the Kings of Media and Persia: "You did not want to reckon your own accounts [of years], so you will count those of others, as it is written: 'In the second year of Darius (Hag 1:1); in the second year of Nebuchadnezzar (Dan 2:1), etc. You did not want to submit to the rule of Heaven, so you had to submit to the rule of the Arab peoples (גוים ערביים). And truly these 'Abbāsid Caliphs, who reigned in Babylon, are the descendants of their prophet (i.e., Muhammad), who is a son of the Arabs.[7]

II. When we[8] will find the gem, we will throw away the pebbles,[9] just as our sages of blessed memory said about the verse: "These are the kings who reigned in the land of Edom" (Gen 36:31). You find written in the

---

6 The phrase concerning the Hebrew slave alludes to Exod 21:5.

7 See Shtober, *SDY*, 77, ll. 1–9. In the last two sentences Sambari offers a slightly abridged quotation from Mekhilta, *Ba-ḥodesh*; cf. *Mekhilta de-Rabbi Yishma'el*, eds. H. S. Horovitz, I. A. Rabin (Frankfurt a. Main, 1931), 203 ll.7–9, 15–16.

8 I.e., Sambari. He also uses the plural form in the next sentences.

9 The gem = chapters of Jewish history, particularly those dealing with eminent sages. The pebbles = Muslim history. The metaphors were taken from *Midrash Tanḥuma*, (Venice, 1545), fol. 44b.

> ten generations from Adam to Noaḥ "X begot Y."[10] However, as the Torah reached Noaḥ it was talking about him at length. The same [formula] is applied to the ten generations from Noaḥ to Abraham.... Thus, we will enumerate some of the Ishmaelite kings, but we deal with them in short. Contrariwise, when we come to Maimonides of blessed memory and to similar personages, we will talk about them at length.[11]

Sambari believed that the method he had chosen for presenting historical material in his book was a novel one and, therefore, he felt the need to justify and explain it in these introductory sentences. He also hints (in paragraph I.) at one of the major themes of *SDY*: the social marginalization and the humiliation of his brethren, "the Hebrew slaves" under Muslim rule.[12] From Sambari's point of view, the inferior social status of the Jews was one of the factors that paved the way for the Sabbatean redemptive tiding affecting the hearts of so many Jewish people. However, the question arises: Was this politico-religious status of his brethren the only motive that urged Sambari to create the unique integrative structure to his work? Why was Islam chosen as the sole framework within which to portray the Jewish material of *SDY*?

Another factor may have motivated Sambari to use this model for his writing. Like many others, he experienced a deep feeling of disillusionment after the debacle of the Sabbatean movement, which followed the unexpected apostasy of the messiah. Most of the Jews who lived in Europe, North Africa, and Asia were shocked by this act of treachery, perpetrated by the person they believed to have been on a messianic mission. Sambari injected this agony into his writing.

Sabbateanism as a Factor in the Composition of SDY

Sabbateanism derived its name from Shabbatai Ṣevi, who was born in the important Anatolian seaport of Smyrna in 1626. Shabbatai, who was a devotee of the *Kabbalah*, had been experiencing repeated mystical and messianic visions.[13] In 1652, the rabbis of Smyrna expelled him from the town owing to his religiously offensive behavior, which included, among other things, pronouncing out loud the Tetragrammaton, the ineffable four-letter

10 Cf. Gen 5:6, 9, 12 and so on. This formulation recurs in the "generations" enumerated in the first two portions of Genesis.

11 See Shtober, *SDY*, 78, ll. 20–27.

12 See the detailed analysis of this excerpt of the introduction in M. Jacobs, "An Ex-Sabbatean's Remorse? Sambari's Polemics against Islam" *JQR*, 97 (2007): 356–59.

13 The main source for Shabbatai Ṣevi's biography and the Sabbatean movement during his lifetime is Gershom Scholem's magisterial work *Sabbatai Ṣevi – The Mystical Messiah 1626–1676* (Princeton: Princeton University Press, 1973). See there the beginnings of Shabbatai Ṣevi: pp. 98–103.

name of God.[14] Thereafter, he wandered and lived in different provinces of the Balkans and the Middle East. Upon his arrival at Gaza in the spring of 1665—Shabbatai was then on his way to Jerusalem—he met the famous mystic, Abraham Nathan Ashkenazi, who, the previous February, had made a startling announcement: he had learned in a prophetic vision that Shabbatai Ṣevi would be the Messiah.[15] During lengthy meetings between the two kabbalists, Nathan worked hard to convince Shabbatai that he was destined to be the Redeemer of Israel. Thereupon, rumors about the appearance of the messiah spread very quickly, generating waves of excitement throughout the entire Jewish Diaspora. In the course of the next sixteen months (June 1, 1665—September 16, 1666), the messiah (Shabbatai Ṣevi) and his prophet (Nathan), with the help of a small band of ardent believers, infused the masses in the Jewish world with the hope of redemption. The geographical range of the Sabbatian movement at its peak was astounding, reaching from Yemen to England, from Poland to Italy, and from Persia to Morocco.[16] The decline of this short-lived movement began with the messiah's apostasy, under the pressure of the Ottoman sultan, in 1666.

The ultimate act of this "messiah," his conversion to Islam—and the psychological crisis that ensued—led the historian to re-examine the relationship between the Jewish nation and the Islamic world. He observed the profound disappointment of the people, the despair that followed the shock of Shabbatai's apostasy. Sabbateanism had engendered great hopes of life in a "world of *Tiqqun*" (a world in which harmony has been restored). That (unrealized) hope for freedom from the yoke of the Gentiles was suddenly shattered, vanished, the moment the messiah stumbled and fell into the Islamic "abyss." Thus, the believers found themselves in the midst of a crisis, one that exposed with utter clarity the bitter reality of their enslavement to the Ishmaelites (their Muslim [rulers]; in the East, the Ottoman sultans).[17]

Sambari had to have been sobered by this unnerving experience, as were tens of thousands of his disillusioned fellow Jews. As the messianic intoxication vanished, he experienced a deep distress that motivated him to document the history of his people, including the harsh events that had befallen them. Furthermore, he viewed the significance of those critical

14 Later, when Shabbatai was already recognized as the messiah designate, he intensified the "strange actions," such as eating forbidden foods, changing prayer services, or annulling fast days. Cf. Scholem, *Sabbatai Ṣevi*, 142–46, 413–14, 508–9, 533–35, 615–33, 731–32 etc.

15 On the prophecies of Nathan of Gaza, see M. Goldish, *The Sabbatean Prophets* (Cambridge, Mass., 2004), 56–88 and the notes to pp. 191–99.

16 The full story of the swift expansion of the Sabbatean movement and its repercussions in the Jewish communities is told in Scholem, *Sabbatai Ṣevi*, 327–820.

17 Cf. the discussion of the introductory notes to *SDY*, above in chapter: "Why did Sambari set up an Islamic backdrop..."

events within the context of the theological doctrine of retribution, according to which the relationship between God and his people is one of "measure for measure." He expressed this view clearly in the introduction to his work, where he quoted the *midrash*: "You did not want to submit to the rule of Heaven, so you had to submit to the rule of the Arab peoples (גוים ערביים)."[18] The materialization of this principle was made profoundly clear to him during the years following the Sabbatean crisis.

Sambari Writes about Shabbatai Ṣevi

From the scanty data known about Sambari's life, it appears that the effects of the aftermath of this messianic movement did not escape him. He was an eyewitness to its entire vicissitudes, from its dizzying ascent, to the messiah's apostasy, to its decline. No wonder that we find various references to Shabbatai interspersed within *SDY*. The following references shed light on the historian's attitude as far as it is concerned with Shabbatai and the movement he created.

(1)

In chapter 153 of the chronicle, dealing with the Ottoman governors sent to Egypt, Sambari notes the date of Shabbatai Ṣevi's appearance in Egypt. He alludes to this date in the annalistic lists of those Ottoman governors, as follows: "In 1073 A.H. 'Omar came to power, and in his day the *Qeren ha-Ṣevi*[19] emerged (אלף וע"ג עומאר, כי בימיו צמח קרן הצבי)."[20] The metaphor *Qeren ha-Ṣevi* is an allusion to the messianic pretensions of Sabbatai Ṣevi.[21] The year 1073 of the hijra corresponds to 1662, the year of his arrival in Cairo.

(2)

The capital of Egypt, Cairo, was one of the main stations on his way from Smyrna to Jerusalem. During his sojourn in Egypt, Sabbatai Ṣevi befriended the tax farmer and treasurer Raphael Joseph.[22] Apparently, it was then that Sambari, a member of Raphael Joseph's entourage, met him.[23] Two years

---

18 See above.

19 The literal meaning of the idiom *qeren ha-ṣevi* is "antler of the deer". It is an ironic/comic pun based on Shabbatai's second name, *ṣevi*, as the Hebrew idiom has a pejorative connotation. It means to be someone reckless or to act unreasonably.

20 See Shtober, *SDY*, 315, ll. 28–29.

21 Cf. below.

22 On Rafael Yosef, see above, in the section "Sambari: A Biographical Sketch," between notes 1–2; M. Benayahu, *Rabbi Ḥayyim Yosef David Azolay* (Jerusalem, 1959), 295–98; J. Barnai, *Sabbateanism- Social Perspectives* (Jerusalem, 2000), 175–78 and Shtober, *SDY*, 17–18, 315, l. 32, 316, l. 51.

23 In *SDY* (315–16), Sambari praises his benefactor after his assassination in 1669 and tells

later, Sambari again met Shabbatai Ṣevi, when the latter returned to Egypt in 1664 as an emissary of the Jewish community in Jerusalem to collect money for its needs. On this occasion, he remained in Egypt for more than half a year. From there he journeyed to Gaza in May 1665 for the decisive meeting with the kabbalist Abraham Nathan Ashkenazi, who revealed the secret of the root of his soul to him–the soul of the messiah.[24]

Raphael Joseph was one of the first enthusiasts of this new messianic movement. He maintained a frequent and lively correspondence with Sabbatai Ṣevi and Nathan with regard to the theology of Sabbateanism. Moreover, he did much to spread Sabbatean teachings and generously supported the messiah's followers.[25]

(3)

Like his patron, Sambari was an adherent of the Sabbatean movement during its heyday. He wrote a first-hand history of the movement, perhaps even recording impressions and details of his acquaintanceship with the person who was to become the messiah. I adduce the indices Sambari prepared for his book. Among the sections in which he grouped the subject matters of the chronicle was a section entitled "The deeds of the villain prophets, who go astray after their delusions and their messiahs that God did not send."[26] The Sabbatean affair itself was entitled in this section "The story of Nathan of Gaza, who prophesied about his messiah, Shabbatai Ṣevi, and the deeds which he had done" (סיפור נתן העזתי אשר נבא על שבתי צבי משיחו ואת מעשיו אשר עשה). The story about those "deeds" should have been identical to chapters 147 to 149 of the chronicle, but, alas, almost all of it is gone. Here, we encounter one of the ill-fated vicissitudes of Jewish historiography, as the precious pages of the manuscripts that had contained this intriguing historical material were deliberately ripped out of the two extant manuscripts of *SDY*.[27] Undoubtedly, someone tore out folio numbers 89–96 from the Bodleian manuscript, leading the copyist of the chronicle to add

about his own work as a scribe (?), who was serving Rafael Yosef, in a necrology. Here are some excerpts of this personal text: "He [Rafael Yosef] raised the standard of the Law to observe and keep it, and there was no king like him before him who turned to the Lord with all his heart and with all his soul and with all his might... and I the unworthy author [of *SDY*] was one of his servants; I ate his fruit and drank his water and enjoyed the sitting in his shadow."

24 See Scholem, *Sabbatai Ṣevi*, 177–78, (Shabbatai's first stay in Egypt), 191–98 (second visit in Egypt).

25 Ibid., 213–14, 245, 330–31, 336, 430, 641 etc.

26 See Shtober, *SDY*, 87, ll. 234–35 (the Sabbatean chapters in the indices).

27 The two manuscripts were described in Shtober, *SDY*, 63. In the Bodleian Library the shelf mark of the ms. is Opp. Add. 834. The shelf mark of the Parisian ms. (conserved in the library of the Alliance Israèlite Universelle) is H130A.

on folio 88a the remark: "And here was written the story of Shabbatai Ṣevi, and it was removed from the book."[28] In the Parisian manuscript, which is the earlier of the two and from which the folios containing the Sabbatean story were originally torn out, there is no such comment.[29] However, we learn about the removal of the pages, since the introductory lines of the Sabbatian story survived in this manuscript at the end of folio 92b. There it states: "And now we shall begin to report matters of controversy, strife and discord, with spears and swords, which befell in the market places and streets" (עתה נתחיל לכתוב דברי ריבות מלחמות וקרבות ברמחים ובחרבות בשוקים אשר [נפלו]).[30] This remark apparently reflects the high tension that led to a violent outburst in a certain Mediterranean community during the Sabbatean surge.

In the opinion of Gershom Scholem, the doyen of the research into Sabbateanism, the folios that disappeared from the manuscript had fallen victim to the censorship of later anti-Sabbatian zealots. Scholem's conjecture regarding censorship is supported by a comment accompanying the mention of the story of Sabbatai Ṣevi in the original indices of *SDY*. As stated above, Sambari summarized the Sabbatean chapters as follows: "The story of Nathan of Gaza, who prophesied about Shabbatai Ṣevi, his Messiah, and the deeds that he had done." As well as in the chronicle itself,[31] here (in the indices) too, some copyist added the next remark to the Bodleian manuscript: "and this story is missing from the book. It is the glory of God to conceal a thing" (והסיפור הזה חסר מן הספר, משום כבוד אלקים הסתר דבר).[32]

Scholem interprets the biblical verse "it is the glory of God to conceal a thing" (Prov 25:2), which was inserted into this prosaic sentence, as an expression of admiration for Shabbatai Ṣevi on the part of the person writing the comment, as various Sabbatian believers deified their messiah.[33] I must stress once more that this remark is a later gloss, made by someone else, not by Sambari. Even if the historian had been a follower of the Sabbatean movement, there is no doubt that after the apostasy he turned his back on it, as did most of those whom Shabbatai Ṣevi had disappointed.

28 See Shtober, *SDY*, 312 (= the note about alternative version to line 26).

29 It is self-evident that the earlier and maybe even the holograph of the author will not contain such a remark.

30 Cf. Shtober, *SDY*, 312, ll. 27–28. Chronologically, Sambari set the story of the Sabbatean movement just after a vivid report about the fire that devoured Constantinople in the year 1660.

31 See above.

32 Cf. Shtober, *SDY*, 87. See the note to l. 235 (the indices).

33 As for "the glory of God" etc. see G. Scholem, *Sabbatai Ṣevi and the Sabbatean Movement of His Times* (Tel-Aviv, 1957), vol. I, 144 [Hebrew]. For evidence of the deification of Shabbatai Ṣevi, ibid., 835–36, 870–72, 915–16.

(4)

After discussing in detail the case of the missing pages, we will now turn to several other allusions to Shabbatai Ṣevi, which substantiate my assumption that in the wake of the messiah's apostasy, Sambari underwent an extreme emotional conversion. Consequently, at the time when he wrote the story of this false messiah, he was no longer a supporter of the Sabbatean movement.

- Sambari wrote at the end of the story of a different messianic arousal, the 1530s Re'uvenī-Molcho movement,[34] as follows: "And they still believe in him (=in Molcho's resurrection after he was burnt at the stake in Mantua) as occurred in our time that there are some fools who believe in *Qeren ha-Ṣevi*" (ועדין מאמינים בו כמו שאירע בזמננו זה שיש כמה שוטים מאמינים בקרן הצבי).[35]
- The mocking epithet "*Qeren ha-Ṣevi*," which alludes to Shabbatai Ṣevi, appears three more times: it is found, as mentioned above, in the lists of the Turkish governors of Egypt, and it is also incorporated into the poems about *Qeren ha-Ṣevi*, which Sambari included in his work.[36] Incidentally, these poems, as well, were ripped out of the *S.D.Y.* manuscript, as, without doubt, they were satirical, anti-Sabbatian poems.[37]
- In another chapter of *SDY*, in which Sambari describes the suffering of the Jews following a fire that devoured Constantinople in 1660, he summarizes the description as follows: "And they (the Jews) shall remain expelled from their comfortable homes until the time that God shall gaze and see from the heavens and will send us the true Messiah, the son of David, speedily, in our days. Amen." (ונשארו גרושים מבית תענוגיהם עד ישקיף וירא ה' משמים וישלח לנו משיח האמיתי בן דוד במהרה בימינו אמן).[38]

This chapter was juxtaposed with the story of Shabbatai Ṣevi, which was removed from the manuscript. There is no doubt that here, too, the intention of the historian was to compare the true messiah [=the son of David] with the false messiah, namely Shabbatai Ṣevi.

---

[34] For this messianic movement, see A. Z. Eshkoli, *The Story of Ha-Re'uvenī* (Jerusalem, 1940) [Hebrew]. Molcho, a former Portuguese *conversos* who returned to his paternal religion, became a celebrated Kabbalist and was deeply involved in the messianic movement that erupted in Italy in the 1530s.

[35] See Shtober, *SDY*, 302, ll. 185–86 and note 63 there.

[36] Ibid., 89, ll. 282–83; 315, l. 29. See also notes 19–20 above.

[37] The poems were evidently included in the chronicle, since they are registered in the indices in the section Sambari set apart for poems. Cf. Shtober, *SDY*, 88–89, ll. 271–84.

[38] Ibid., 312, ll. 24–25 and cf. above note 30.

Once More Sabbateanism and Islam in the SDY

I have argued that in the wake of the messiah's apostasy, Sambari became an anti-Sabbatean.[39] Yet, if I go back to the heyday of the movement, there arises the question as to whether *SDY* contains any indications of the author's attitude to Sabbatianism before the apostasy?

I assume that there is some evidence to his attitude in a number of focal chapters that unequivocally connect Islam and the Sabbatean movement. At the very beginning of the chronicle, Sambari chose to form a cluster of five chapters that deal with the inception of Islam as a religion and as a political community, and its relations with the Jews. I suggest that here the historian disguised his early links to the great messianic movement, when he was still a believer in the mission of Shabbatai Ṣevi. In that cluster of five chapters, he explains how the Muslim religion and polity were created and, strangely enough, divests some of the founding fathers of the new religion of their Arabic origin and invents a Jewish origin for them. The most outstanding of these founding fathers were Abu Bakr, the father-in-law of Muḥammad, and ʻAlī ibn Abī Ṭālib, his cousin and son-in-law.[40] Both are presented as originally being Jewish sages who had felt an urgent need to go to Muḥammad, to join him by converting to Islam, all this being done for "nationalistic" reasons. Their intention was to save their people from conspiracies by Muḥammad's friends to destroy them.[41] Sambari writes about Abu Bakr as follows:

> After these things, Baḥira, the Christian,[42] advised Muḥammad to destroy, to kill, and to exterminate all the seed of the Jews. When one of the sages of Israel saw all the troubles that befell Israel [due to the evil designs of Baḥira], he went and made a pact with Muḥammad, and became his soldier-hero and changed his name to Abu Bakr.[43]

---

39 See above "Sambari writes about Shabbatai Ṣevi," in the end of section three and the beginning of section 4.

40 In addition to the familial relations between Muḥammad and the two persons here mentioned, Abu Bakr was the first caliph (632–34) and ʻAlī was the fourth caliph (656–61) in the history of Islam. On Abu Bakr, see W. Montgomery Watt, "Abu Bakr" in *Encyclopaedia of Islam*, vol. 1, eds. H. A. R. Gibb et al. (Leiden: E. J. Brill, 1960), 109–11; On ʻAlī b. Abī Tālib see H. A. R. Gibb, "ʻAlī b. Abī Tālib," ibid., 381–86.

41 Cf. my article: "Present at the Dawn of Islam: Polemic and Reality in the Medieval Story of Muhammad's Jewish Companions" in Michael M. Laskier and Yaacov Lev (eds.), *The Convergence of Judaism and Islam, Religious, Scientific, and Cultural Dimensions.* (University Press of Florida, 2011), 64–88, in the text between notes 50–55.

42 On Baḥīrā and his links with Muḥammad, see my article "The Monk Baḥīrā the Counselor of Muḥammad, and the Jews: Between Polemic and Historiography," *Proceedings of the Tenth World Congress of Jewish Studies*, vol. I (Jerusalem, 1990), 69-78 and Moshe Gil."The Story of Baḥīrā and Its Jewish Versions" in *Hebrew and Arabic Studies in Honor of Joshua Blau*, ed. H. Ben-Shammay (Tel-Aviv and Jerusalem, 1993), 193–210 [Hebrew].

43 Shtober, *SDY*, 93, ll. 52–57.

'Alī, who was described earlier as "a wise man among the sages of Israel, and he changed his name to al-Imam 'Alī," joined Abu Bakr in order to foil the conspiracy to destroy the Jews.[44]

This motif of self-sacrifice and willingness to go as far as to surrender their individual identity and convert to Islam in order to save their people is attributed here to Jewish sages, who became the first and most senior members of the emerging Muslim community.[45] Surprisingly, this same motif appears also as an explanation for Shabbatai Ṣevi's conversion to Islam. The existence of this motif (or a similar one) is found in various forms in the writings of Sabbatean believers and in the evidence supplied by non-Jewish observers. All these sources offer the explanation that Shabbatai converted to Islam in order to save the Jewish people from complete annihilation.

I have already pointed out that Shabbatai Ṣevi generated enormous excitement during those two years of intense messianic activity (1665-66).[46] There was mounting hope among the masses that he would renew the Kingdom of Israel, especially after his return to Anatolia and his stay in Smyrna in 1666.[47] The unrest did not subside even after he was banished to Gallipoli and imprisoned there in a castle nicknamed by Shabbatai's devotees *Migdal Oz* ("Tower of Strength"). This unrest was cause for great concern among the Ottoman viziers, for they regarded the messianic turmoil as a Jewish revolt against the sultanate. Thus, because of these circumstances, the decision was made in September 1666 to dissolve the "court" of Shabbatai Ṣevi in Gallipoli and to bring him to justice before the sultan Meḥmet VI. There he was given the choice of being executed or of converting to Islam, and the choice of the pseudo-messiah is well known.[48]

However, even before Shabbatai Ṣevi decided in favor of Islam, which was forced upon him, the decision had already been made to take revenge on the Nation of Israel for its answering the messianic call. Because of this act of rebellion, harsh measures were decreed against the Jews of the major communities of Adrianople and Constantinople, or at least against their leaders.[49] This was Shabbatai Ṣevi's opportunity and, in the opinion of his followers, this could partially explain his terrible deed, the conversion to Islam. Since the time for redemption was not yet at hand and he lacked the

---

44 'Alī: ibid., 91, lines 15-16, p.93, ll. 58-59.

45 Cf. note 40.

46 See near note 16 in the section "Sabbateanism as a factor in the composition of *SDY*."

47 Scholem wrote extensively about the enthusiastic atmosphere that swept masses of adherents to the Sabbatean movement in the years 1665-66. See his *Sabbatai Ṣevi,* 327-602.

48 The removal of Shabbatai Ṣevi to Gallipoli: ibid. 444-56. The apostasy of the messiah: ibid., 672-86. Shabbatai's apostasy took place on September 16 in 1666.

49 For the grave threat of destruction to the Turkish Jewry and Shabbatai Ṣevi's share in the averting the disaster, see ibid. 683-84, 699-702.

power to perform a miracle, he wanted, at least, to save his nation. Accordingly, he was willing to suffer and convert to Islam, so that they would be left alone. As an example of the way the believers described these critical events, I will present the words of Baruch of Arezzo:[50]

> And when it became known among the Turks [that is, Muslims] and the uncircumcised [that is, Christians] in Adrianople that the sultan had sent for Our Lord,[51] they assumed that they would behead him immediately and kill all the Jews, as it was known that the sultan had ordered all the Jews in the city to be killed. Couriers had also been sent with instructions to do likewise in Constantinople, and they sharpened their swords and waited for the day when they could do with the Jews as they pleased.
>
> However, Our Lord reached the city two days later than expected and, as he arrived in the evening, it was too late to go to him [the sultan]. In the morning, he appeared before the sultan, who said to him: "Peace is with thee." He [Shabbatai] replied in Turkish, "Upon thee peace." Thereupon a royal attendant came to him bringing a robe that the sultan had worn and another attendant with one of the sultan's turbans, and they clothed him with these and called him Meḥmet, in the name of the sultan. Thus, the rumor got about that he had apostatized, and *there was a great deliverance to the Jews.*[52] *Our Lord made request before the sultan for the Jews* to reverse the letters of wrath and anger that he had written to destroy all the Jews in Constantinople...and no Jew *suffered any harm because of this.*[53]

In addition to the narrative of the believers in the false messiah, there is also testimony by non-Jewish observers, including local Armenians and several Europeans who were present at the time of the decisive events, both in Smyrna in Anatolia, and in Istanbul, the capital of the empire.[54] Even though their accounts do not coincide with everything that was written by the believers, they all have something in common, i.e., that there had been an edict signed by the sultan that was revoked. For instance, there are reports by Thomas Coenen, who officiated in the years 1662–71 as the Protestant chaplain of the Dutch congregation in Smyrna.[55] Scholem appreciated that he was one of the shrewdest observers of the developments in the Sabbate-

---

50 Baruch ben Gershon of Arezzo, an ardent believer, wrote the story of Shabbatai Ṣevi. He named his book *Zikkaron li-Benei Yisrael* ("A Memorial unto the Children of Israel"). It was printed by A. Freimann, in his Sabbatean anthology *Inyenei Shabbatai Ṣevi* (Berlin, 1913), 43–68.

51 This was the customary honorific nickname of Shabbatai Ṣevi in the Sabbatean literature.

52 The emphasis on the last two sentences is mine.

53 Baruch, *Zikkaron,* 58 (= it was cited in Scholem *Sabbatai Ṣevi*, 683).

54 Cf. Scholem, *Sabbatai Ṣevi*, 668–82.

55 Th. Coenen, *Ydele verwachtinge der Joden getoont in den Persoon van Sabethai Zevi* (Amsterdam, 1669), 86–88. On Coenen, see the introduction of Y. Kaplan to the Hebrew translation of Th. Coenen's book (Jerusalem, 1998), 7–21.

an movement in Anatolia and he was sufficiently interested in "the madness of the Jews" not to miss any of its manifestations.[56] His reports are among the more reliable and comprehensive testimonies regarding the Sabbatean affair. According to Coenen, at the time of the apostasy the sultan gave orders to arrest a number of the leading believers (twelve in the capital, and a similar number in Smyrna) and to bring them to Adrianople, where, presumably, they were to be put to death. The couriers were dispatched with lists of persons responsible for the messianic propaganda who were to be brought to trial. Coenen reported that some arrests had already been made before counter-orders were issued. The edict was canceled, the rabbis were given only a reprimand, and the Jews were pardoned. Moreover, the Dutch minister presents two accounts with regard to the identity of the very influential person who had interceded on behalf of the Jews. According to one account, it was the mother of the sultan. But according to another account, "they also tell here [in Smyrna] that it was the false messiah himself who influenced the sultan and made him change his mind" by accepting full responsibility for everything that had happened and pleading that the innocent people should not be punished for having been misled by him, as he alone was guilty.[57]

Even if these sources did not reach Sambari, rumors no doubt abounded throughout the Jewish world with regard to the deliverance of the Jews. Undoubtedly, they very quickly reached Egypt—a very important crossroads in the believers' information distribution system—and were, thus, in a very sophisticated manner, worked into the *S.D.Y.* account of the emergence of Islam.

Summary

It would seem obvious that an event as stormy and traumatic as the Sabbatean messianic outburst, which sparked the imaginations of many and kindled so much hope among the Jews, could not vanish without leaving an impression on a historian such as Sambari. He was present as an eyewitness at the first stages of the emergence of the movement. He was then physically at the heart of the drama, in Cairo. Evidently, Sambari, like so many of his brethren, was swept by the storm of enthusiasm and apocalyptic hopes created by the messianic movement and became a believer in the messiah, in Shabbatai Ṣevi. That phase of elation in the history of Sabbateanism turned out to be short-lived, at least as far as it concerns the actual redemptive aspect. Nevertheless, the short period that was full of elation and charged with messianic expectations gave expression in the opening chapters of his chronicle.

---

56 Scholem, *Sabbatai Ṣevi*, 372.

57 Coenen, *Ydele*, 87. Cf. the sentences I have stressed in the excerpt of Baruch, *Zikkaron*, 58. See above, near note 53.

In those chapters, Sambari describes the inception of Islam as a religion and a political community. Among the founding fathers of the new religion there were, according to his narrative, Jewish sages who had converted to Islam, joined Muḥammad, and did their utmost to foil the conspiracies to destroy their former brethren, the Jews. The analogy between the motives of those early Jewish converts and the motives that urged Shabbatai Ṣevi to apostatize is quite apparent. In my opinion, the historian disguised in the story of the beginnings of Islam his early links to the great messianic movement of his day, when he was still a believer in the mission of Shabbatai Ṣevi.

In other references to the false messiah, Sambari levels sharp criticism of Sabbateanism. Here, he explicitly expresses his negative attitude toward the messiah who had failed. Both stances, the positive statement concerning the messianic movement and the contrary one, lead us to conclude that the intense messianic drama largely shaped *Sefer Divrei Yosef*, by confronting the author with the centrality of Islam as one of the main factors that formed the historical framework and lent insight into his whole historical *opus magnum*. This is, in consequence, the explanation of the powerful connection between Islam and the Sabbatean movement that is found in *Sefer Divrei Yosef*.

The Muslim in the Folk Literature of the Jews of Libya

RACHEL SIMON

Beliefs, customs, attitudes, and social conventions of ethnic groups are often expressed in their folk literature. Variants of numerous motifs do occur in the folklore of several groups, but each society adds its unique flavor. Consequently, much cultural and social information can be drawn from Jewish folk literature, which derives from a combination of Jewish tradition and outside influences, be they of indigenous gentile population or foreigners, including Jews from other regions.

The Jews of Libya (ca. 35,000 in the late 1940s) consisted of a veteran group augmented by immigrants from other Jewish diasporas, mainly of Sephardi origin. Most of the Jews lived in urban centers on the Mediterranean coast in Tripolitania (western Libya), with a substantial number residing in Cyrenaica (eastern Libya) and in the hinterland in small towns and villages. The society at large was composed mainly of Muslim Arabs and Berbers, ruled by Ottoman Turks (1551-1911), followed by Italy (1911-1943), British Military Administration (1943-1951), and independent Arab rule. This historical, social, economic, and geographic background is reflected in the folklore.

One way to better understand how a group views itself is to examine how it regards the "other." It is quite possible that opinions and attitudes that could not freely be expressed in an overt way by a minority group that was looked down upon by an autocratic regime and a conceited majority were disclosed in its folk literature that was transmitted orally, exclusively within the group in its own dialect. The current study examines the way the Muslim "other" is portrayed in the folk literature of Libyan Jews, based on published folk tales that were selected mainly from the Israeli Archive of Jewish Folk Tales.[1] Some tales have the appearance of legends, whereas others are portrayed as a true description of events, at times even as personal testimonies, referring to specific places and identifiable characters, either Jewish or Muslim. Most of the events take place in Libya and several stories provide a detailed social and economic background. When examining these published tales it should be remembered that they were told in Israel by

[1] Most of the tales were published in Dov Noy, *Jewish Folktales from Libya* (Jerusalem: Bi-Tefutsot ha-Golah, 1967) [Hebrew].

Jews who emigrated from Libya some twenty years earlier, and the new environment might have shaped the telling of the tale as well as some characteristics of the proponents. Included are legends with or without salient Jewish characteristics, stories with traditional Jewish background, and tales with specific Libyan context.

The Muslim "other" appears in many tales: about a third of the tales in the collection refer to relations between Jews and Arabs or Turks. These stories are clearly told from the point of view of the Jewish community, which is viewed as the primary circle of identification, while the Muslims are positioned in separate, though sometimes tangent, frameworks. In most stories the relations between Jews and Muslims are peaceful and cordial, although cases of maltreatment, attacks, and persecution of Jews do occur. Overall, even when Jews suffer in the hands of Muslims, they are saved through miracles, the intervention of saints, or their wisdom; no case ends with the Jew having the lower hand or being the loser.

Daily Life

Jews and Muslims in Libya interacted on a social, economic, and cultural basis despite the existence of clear boundaries between them. These contacts could be positive, reflecting understanding and cooperation, or negative, showing deceit, rivalry and persecution. A wide range of relations is in the background of several stories, even though the purpose of the narrator was to teach a moral rather than to describe daily life.

Occasionally economic rivalry shaped the relations between Jews and Muslims as is demonstrated in the testimony of a Jewish fisherman telling about his relations with Arab fishermen in the 1940s.[2] Not many Jews were fishermen, but some who lived near areas rich in fish took that profession, as did Jews of the eastern Tripolitanian coastal town of Misurata. Arab fishermen, in contrast to most Jewish ones, had often used explosives in their fishing, although it was illegal at the time. The Arabs were angry that the law-abiding Jews refrained from using this method and thus were not bothered by the authorities. The Jewish fisherman Hlafo Dabush, who like other Jews did not use explosives, was famous for his expertise in fishing and locating rich fishing grounds, but was poor and did not own a boat. Arab fishermen, who wanted to benefit from his expertise and at the same time get rid of his competition, asked him to join them in their boat in order to locate new fishing areas. He agreed on condition that they split the revenues equally. When the boat was about two miles off the coast, Hlafo detected a large shoal of high-quality fish and the fishermen spread their large net. Meanwhile, Hlafo dived and while under water saw a huge fish distancing quickly. Hlafo started to chase the fish, not noticing that he had

---

[2] Noy, *Jewish Folktales*, 52–53.

left the boat far behind. He managed to catch the fish, but when he surfaced he realized that the boat had disappeared and he could not see the coast. He was in the middle of the stormy sea and swam for about an hour and a half. The great effort of diving and swimming had weakened him when all of a sudden he remembered the "Song of the Sea," which he had heard in the synagogue. Although he did not understand the meaning of the song,[3] he knew that it served as a remedy (*segulah*) against drowning and so began to recite it, all the while struggling with the huge waves. Suddenly he felt that he had landed on a rock and then fainted. Luckily, a British officer detected Hlafo through his binoculars and called a patrol boat to rescue him. Later on, the Arab owners of the boat were sued for abandoning Hlafo in the midst of the stormy sea and leaving him to die. The judges decreed that the Arab fishermen be imprisoned and pay a large sum to Hlafo, who from then on severed his ties with Arab fishermen and with the help of the Jewish community acquired his own fishing boat.

The aim of this story was to show the power of the "Song of the Sea," but it also presents attitudes toward the "other" and one's own community. Jews are shown as obeying the law, trustful and ready to help one of their own as well as members of other communities: Hlafo agreed to collaborate, for an appropriate compensation, with Arab fishermen, and the Jewish community as a group joined forces to help one of their own, Hlafo, buy a boat and become independent. In this case, the protagonist survived death and reached economic independence and prosperity through divine intervention, decent behavior of the gentile (British) authorities, and cooperation of his community. The attitude toward gentiles is mixed: Arabs are depicted as disobeying the law by using illegal, destructive, and dangerous fishing methods. Moreover, they were ready to lure an innocent economic rival into collaboration in order to steal economic secrets and then liquidate their Jewish competitor. The result, however, was not as the Arabs had anticipated and they were imprisoned and had to pay a heavy fine. The British authorities, on the other hand, are depicted as just, as in the case of the coast guards and the judges: they were the instrument of divine intervention.

Economic deceit and contempt for sacred beliefs are at the heart of another story.[4] Yehuda Luzon, a Jewish Tripolitan carpenter, was respected for his craftsmanship and his honesty by both Jews and Arabs who placed

3 Although most Libyan Jewish men received basic formal Jewish education and could recite portions of the Hebrew Holy Scriptures and prayers, they often did not understand the meaning of the Hebrew (or Aramaic) text they were reading, because their spoken language was Judeo-Arabic, and later Italian, but not Hebrew. Hlafo's story reflects this.

4 Noy, *Jewish Folktales*, 61–62; Frigia Zuaretz et al. eds., *Libyan Jewry* (Tel-Aviv: Council of Libyan Communities in Israel, 1982), 417–18 [Hebrew], according to which it occurred in 1924.

orders with him. Once, an Arab grocer, Elfezani, who was infamous for his wickedness, had ordered some work from Luzon at the agreed sum of 300 Italian lire. Luzon started the job and, as it progressed, Elfezani paid him 200 lire on account. When Luzon had finished the work, Elfezani denied that he still owed 100 lire, claiming that the agreement was for only 200 lire. Policemen who heard the quarrel sent them to the judge, who asked Elfezani to swear that the agreement was for only 200 lire. The judge told Luzon that he could not require Elfezani to more than an oath, because there were no witnesses to their oral agreement. Luzon, who could decide where Elfezani would take the oath, asked that this be performed in the presence of R. Shim'on Guetta, the director of the Jewish home for the aged. The judge, wanting to avoid the possibility of a false oath, tried to reach a compromise with the sum of 250 lire; but Elfezani refused. Elfezani then swore on the Bible, even after Rabbi Guetta warned him of the dire consequences of swearing falsely. On the following day, Friday, Elfezani boasted how he had triumphed over the Jewish carpenter and mocked the oath-taking ceremony. But on Saturday morning he was found dead in bed, this despite his being known as a healthy and strong individual. Jews and Arabs alike interpreted Elfezani's death as divine punishment for exploiting the carpenter and swearing a false oath.

The purpose of this story is to show the consequences of perjury, and it does so by describing economic and social relations between Jews and Arabs. Many in the Jewish community were petty craftsmen and the society as a whole, Jews and Muslims alike, depended on their services. The relationship between craftsmen and their customers, regardless of religious affiliation, was based on mutual trust, although there were always those individuals who took advantage of a trust based on an oral agreement. The court of law, when lacking evidence or witnesses, could not pass judgment and, therefore, required the taking of oaths, albeit quite likely that whichever party had violated the agreement would not shrink from perjury. In this story, the oath took place in a doubly sacred environment: over the Bible, which is holy to both Jews and Muslims, and in front of a pious man who was respected by both communities. The Arab's evil character is demonstrated once again when he fearlessly boasted how he had tricked the helpless Jew. The immediacy of the Arab's death—and maybe also the fact that it took place on the Sabbath—was proof enough for Jews and Arabs that he died because he had cheated and given a false oath. Although the main character is an evil Arab, his group of origin is not tainted by his actions. And while the Jewish carpenter did not receive his full payment, the Arab was severely punished for his deeds.

One reason for contacts between Jews and Muslims was the division of labor based on communal background, when certain professions were held almost exclusively by members of one group. Money-lenders and peddlers were usually Jews and their modes of operation are referred to in a story concerning Barah, the janitor of the Tripolitan rabbi Shalom Agib (d. 1869).[5] In order to improve his economic circumstances, the janitor used to lend small sums of money to local policemen for short periods of time, until they received their salary. At the time, Ottoman government employees in Tripoli had often suffered delays in receiving their salaries and this caused a great demand for loans, which were usually provided by Jews. Once, a policeman wanted a larger loan in order to celebrate the circumcision of his son. Barah refused, because, being a prudent lender, he was reluctant to provide large loans. In order to entice him into giving the loan, the policeman disclosed confidential economic information to Barah, namely, that the authorities planned to cancel a certain coin within a few days and if Barah would get rid of these specific coins that had been in his possession, he would benefit nicely. This reflects the Ottoman practice of debasing its currency in times of economic distress by calling in certain coins in circulation. New coins would be minted with a different composition: a decrease in the proportion of an expensive metal, such as gold or silver, and an increase in a cheaper metal, such as copper. Following this economic tip-off, Barah gave the policeman the requested loan and bought with his coins all the wheat and oil available in the marketplace. With nothing left for regular customers, the people rushed to the governor to complain. The governor then supplied the population with wheat and oil from his military stores–it was common practice in Muslim and Ottoman towns for the authorities to ensure the availability of certain basic commodities whose price was under government control in order to prevent public rioting. Subsequently the governor investigated the cause of the shortage and, as a result, imprisoned Barah. The following day Barah stood trial before the governor, who accused him of attempting to starve the population and thereby incite public unrest. Barah was sentenced to be hung opposite the central synagogue, a warning to anyone who might contemplate taking advantage of the economic situation to harm the population and cause public disturbances.

Among those in the Jewish community who tried to intervene in favor of Barah was a female peddler who had access to local Arab dignitaries, Turkish officers, and the governor's household.[6] The peddler implored the governor's mother to intervene on Barah's behalf and she, in turn, asked her son, when he came to receive her blessing before going to pray in the

---

5 Noy, *Jewish Folktales*, 57–58. On R. 'Agib, see Zuaretz, *Libyan Jewry*, pp. 70–71.

6 At the time, peddlers in Libya were mainly Jews, who often interacted with Muslim women. Although it was not common for a woman to work outside the home, a few did, especially older women, mostly widows, and it seems that female peddlers developed especially close contacts with Muslim women. On peddlers in Libya, see Rachel Simon, "Jewish Itinerant Peddlers in Ottoman Libya: Economic, Social, and Cultural Aspects," in *Decision Making and Change in the Ottoman Empire*, ed. C.E Farah (Kirksville: Thomas Jefferson University Press, 1993), 293–304.

mosque, to grant amnesty to Barah. But the governor refused. In this tale the Jew suffers not because he is a Jew, but because he is seen as causing a public disturbance that the authorities regarded as dangerous.[7] While the Muslim policeman is described as ready to leak state economic secrets for private financial gain, the Muslim governor is depicted as strictly fulfilling the responsibilities of his office and his mother as a compassionate woman, friendly to Jews.

Another story refers to other professions held by Jews in the early nineteenth century that provided for contacts with the Muslim population.[8] During that period, the only cosmeticians in Tripoli were three Jewish women, who attended all the brides, regardless of religious affiliation. During the investigation of a brutal murder, these three cosmeticians were interrogated and one identified the amputated head of a young Muslim woman she had worked on. The cosmetician knew the woman, when and whom she had married, and when her make-up had been last applied. The story mentions the two heads (*emin*) of the guilds of the goldsmiths and embroiders, who were Jews, as were most of the craftsmen in these professions. When interrogated, the *emins* could identify who made the jewelry and the embroidered sash of the murdered woman, and the Jewish craftsmen could tell who ordered the items, how much was paid, and when the purchase was made.[9] The story shows that Jews could know a great deal about the lives of their Muslim customers.

Jews, in turn, were at times dependent on services provided by Muslim professionals. Such was the case of R. Yitshak Vaturi (d. 1911), who was blind for some thirty three years until a Moroccan Arab physician restored his eyesight. Although the story emphasizes that the rabbi was cured with God's help, since it is God who cures all humans,[10] nonetheless, it depicts trust and respect between members of the two religious groups, enabling members of one community to benefit from the expertise of specialists of the other.

Some stories encouraged Jews to act in order to prevent injusticc, even when the victim was unknown and a Gentile, with no immediate gain in sight. Two stories, based on a typical social and economic background, demonstrate how good deeds performed by Jews on behalf of Muslim strangers in distress later benefited the Jews, and even saved their lives. The stories do recognize, though, that some Muslims were wicked, just as some Jews behaved improperly.

---

7 For the end of this story, see Noy, *Jewish Folktales*, 58–59.

8 The story refers to a Karamanli ruler named Tahir. An Ottoman governor named Tahir Paşa governed Tripoli in 1836–1837, but the Karamanli dynasty did not have a ruler named Tahir.

9 Noy, *Jewish Folktales*, 107–14, especially 109 and 111–12.

10 Ibid., 75. On R. Vaturi, see Zuaretz, *Libyan Jewry*, 79.

The first story is set during the Ottoman period and deals with a poor Tripolitan Jewish peddler who used to travel the countryside, trading with the villagers. Security on the highways was poor and travelers were often robbed. Once, during his stay in town, the peddler saw a stranger being molested by some unruly Jewish youths. The peddler took pity on the stranger, invited him to his house, fed him, and let him spend the night there. When the stranger departed the next day, he thanked the Jew, adding that they would meet again on a "black day." The peddler was quite annoyed that, after taking care of the stranger, this was the latter's response, which the peddler interpreted to be a threat. Over time the Jew forgot all about it. Many years later, when travelling in the desert, the peddler was accosted by armed robbers who demanded his donkey and his merchandise; otherwise they would kill him. The peddler had no choice but to comply. He then began the slow walk home, when suddenly he was approached by a horseman who demanded to know what had happened. The Jew told the stranger about the robbery. The stranger became angry and took the Jew to the house where the robbers were staying, whereupon the horseman demanded that they return the stolen goods to the Jew. The stranger then asked the Jew if he recognized him and when the Jew answered in the negative, the Arab said that it was he who had been molested by the Jewish thugs, saved by the Jew, and, when departing, had promised that they would meet on a "black day," as indeed, they now did. The Arab, who accompanied the Jew to the outskirts of town, identified himself as Mansur bin Salim, the most notorious robber in the Libyan desert, and gave the peddler many presents as a reward for the favor he had shown him in the past, stressing that good deeds are not forgotten.[11]

A similar story dealt with a rich Tripolitan Jewish goldsmith, Yitshak 'Amirah, who once paid the expenses of an Arab stranger who could not pay for his own meal. When departing, the Arab said that they would meet on a "black day" with no sun. 'Amirah, too, was furious with this response, but over time forgot it. Years later he was travelling with much jewelry from Tripoli to Zliten to attend market day. However, his caravan was attacked by robbers who brought everyone, including an Italian and three Ottoman officers, to a cave, where the robbers relieved them of their goods. When the thieves realized that there were Jews in the caravan, they wanted to kill them. While the Jews were pleading for their lives, the leader of the robbers arrived and ordered his men to kill the officers immediately. He then asked the Jews for their names, and told them that their turn would come the following day, but in the mean time they should eat some bread. The other robbers began mocking the Jews, saying that this way they would arrive in heaven with full bellies. The following day, the leader of the robbers approached 'Amirah, saying that he seemed to be the most important among

[11] Noy, *Jewish Folktales*, 55–57.

these Jews, and asked him if he had ever done a favor to someone he did not know. 'Amirah replied that he did many favors, but at that moment could not recall any of them. The Arab then reminded 'Amirah of how he had once paid for his meal, following which he had promised that they would meet on a "black day." Thus, 'Amirah's good deed saved him and his fellow Jews, who were allowed to leave safely.[12]

These two stories show that while there are many evil Muslims, some—even the leaders of robbers—remember favors done to them and are grateful to those who helped them.

Folk literature sometimes tried to explain miraculous deliverance from natural disasters. One story deals with the big flood of 1903, when water gushing from the mountains toward the sea near Tripoli did no harm to the Jewish cemetery. According to the story, the Arab guard of the cemetery at midnight witnessed two old men directing the floodwaters to bypass the cemetery, though numerous near-by houses were destroyed. The guard was very impressed and announced in the streets of Tripoli: *"La din illa din al-Yahud"* [There is no religion except the religion of the Jews]. This angered his coreligionists who wanted to kill him, but the police saved his life by putting him in prison where he safely stayed until the Italian occupation.[13] According to the story-teller, quite a few Tripolitan Jews remembered this Arab and often heard him tell this story.[14] The explanation that the cemetery was saved thanks to the two old men who directed the flood water is part of a legend. Still, the fact remains that the Jewish cemetery had been saved, and the Arab guard had regarded it as a miracle that demonstrated the power of the Jewish religion. He had risked his life by declaring this in public, angering his fellow Arabs, though they had no other explanation for the miracle.

It may be of no surprise that story-tellers view members of their own group as being smarter than outsiders. One story tells about three travelling friends, a Muslim, a Christian, and a Jew, who, because of their poverty, could buy only a small amount of food, which was not sufficient for all three. Before they went to sleep, they agreed that whoever's dream was the nicest would get all the food. The Jew could not fall asleep due to his hunger and ate all the food while the other two slept. In the morning, the Muslim told he dreamt of meeting Muhammad with whom he entered heaven and the Christian told about meeting Jesus and entering heaven with him. When it was the Jew's turn to tell his dream, he said that he had been unable to sleep and had looked desperately for his friends, but could not find them; now he understood where they had gone. Since he was afraid that the food would

12 Ibid., 85-87.

13 Ibid., 60.

14 Ibid., 187.

get spoiled, he ate it all.[15] While this story has no specific relation to Libya, it indicates that Jews regarded themselves as smarter than the gentiles and did not hesitate to use cunning in their dealings with them.

The Authorities and the Jews

Deterioration in the relations between the authorities and the Jews due to an economic crisis are reflected in a story about the Karamanli dynasty (1711–1835). Under this dynasty the Jews of Libya enjoyed full rights and their rabbis even served as advisors to the rulers. The situation changed, however, under Yusuf Paşa (1795–1835), who was remembered by the Jews as a cruel ruler who mistreated their merchants. His treasury was often depleted and so his soldiers frequently did not receive their salaries on time. Consequently Yusuf was frequently obliged to take loans from the Jews, but would contrive how to avoid repaying them. Once, when the unpaid soldiers started to rebel, Yusuf Paşa had initially levied a huge tax on the Jewish community. But the tax was rescinded and a story was told as to the reason. According to the tale, Yusuf Paşa and two of his secretaries had gone out walking one evening in the Jewish quarter to see what the Jews were up to. They found them in the synagogues, praying for deliverance from their trouble, which was a common response. Yusuf Paşa then went outside the city walls, where he saw a Jewish shepherd praying. When the shepherd did not interrupt his prayer to respond to the ruler's greetings, Yusuf Paşa became angry and asked the shepherd if he did not recognize him. The shepherd answered calmly that he did know who he was, but could not stop his talk with someone more senior than even the ruler (namely, God). He then added that, in fact, the positions of ruler and shepherd were quite similar: just as a ruler guards the townspeople, punishes robbers, and ensures that his policemen, judges, and clerks perform their jobs properly, so a shepherd guards the sheep entrusted to him. The Jew added that the ruler might have oppressed the people had he not feared that God might eventually punish him. Yusuf Paşa was so impressed by what the shepherd had said, that he decided to cancel the tax on the Jews, hoping that God would help him find other means for getting the needed money.[16] In this story, even a lowly Jewish shepherd was able to maintain his dignity before a powerful ruler and thereby induce the Muslim to change his mind.

The relationship between Jews and the authorities was also the subject of a story about a rich Jew who had tried to cheat the community. Jews were well rooted in the region and enjoyed neighborly relations with Muslims, in whose midst Jewish peddlers traded in safety. The story focuses on a stingy Jewish peddler and his son, who, being stingy like his father, tried to evade paying communal dues and burial expenses for his father by pretend-

15 Ibid., 91.

16 Ibid., 102–3.

ing that a poor Jewish porter was to be buried, not the older peddler. A scandal ensued and the Turkish officials became aware of the situation. The son of the miser tried to excuse himself with false explanations to the governor, who stopped him and informed him that he was fully aware of the behavior of his miser father toward the Jewish community in the past. The governor threatened that if the son did not compensate the porter who was supposedly buried, the state authorities would confiscate his father's property and distribute it among those who suffered as a result of his actions. Consequently, the peddler's son told the true course of events, and the governor ordered him to pay a large sum to the burial society and to compensate the porter generously.[17] The story provides the names of several Jewish individuals, but the location and period are not mentioned except for the fact that it took place during the Ottoman period in a large village, apparently in Tripolitania. The tale purports to show that the Ottoman authorities were often aware of internal affairs within the Jewish community. as well as the character of certain individuals. The authorities, here, are depicted as protectors of the public order and of the weak, taking a tough stand toward those who tried to cheat the community, even when those individuals were among the wealthiest in the community and could easily bribe the authorities.

Many stories combine legendary characters with historical figures, including Muslim rulers whose activities were almost legendary. Such is a story that takes place outside of Libya and involves the caliph Harun al-Rashid (766–809) and a Jewish craftsman. The caliph, his advisor, and a slave were walking incognito at night in Baghdad in order to find out the activities and thoughts of the population. They entered the home of Abu Nisim,[18] who, after eating a sumptuous meal, told them that he lived on miracles and worked as a carpenter. The following day the caliph ordered all carpenter shops to be closed. But soon after, the caliph found out that Abu Nisim had become a middleman in the marketplace and thus could afford to continue his nocturnal feasts. When, the next day, the caliph closed all the markets, Abu Nisim then served as a mediator for a husband and a wife, and, after convincing them not to divorce, was handsomely compensated by them and so could once more rejoice at night. The following day Abu Nisim was summoned to the palace, where the caliph told him that, since he was a master of all crafts, he wanted him to serve in his court. When the caliph offered him the position of guardsman, Abu Nisim replied that he was ready to fulfill the caliph's order, but since he was short, he could not serve with the tall guardsmen. Moreover, being a Jew, he could not eat the non-kosher food served in the palace. As a result, the caliph appointed him to be a state-salaried hangman. Abu Nisim prepared a sword made of bull hide and paint-

[17] Ibid., 103–7.

[18] "The father of Nisim," which can also mean "the father of miracles."

ed the blade with silver. After a while, a thief was condemned to death, and the decapitation was to take place in the central square, in view of the entire population, including the caliph and his entourage. Whispering into the condemned man's ear, Abu Nisim asked him if he admitted his guilt. The man began to weep and it was clear that the thief regretted his deed. Abu Nisim declared that his sword would judge the fate of the man and so, when he brought the blade down forcefully upon the man's neck, the latter's head was not cut off. Abu Nisim then bowed before the caliph, saying that he would perform any other job, but asked the caliph to discharge him from the position of a hangman because the Ten Commandments demanded: "Thou shalt not kill." Moreover, he asked that the thief be pardoned, because he had repented of his evil deeds. As a result, the caliph made Abu Nisim a senior advisor and the thief was pardoned.[19]

This story depicts the caliph in a positive light, as a ruler who took pains to learn about his subjects. Once the caliph was impressed with the ingenuity of the Jewish craftsman, he wanted to benefit from his services. The Jew, on the other hand, was not ready to break Jewish law, and refused to hold a position that would have required him to eat non-kosher food. The Jew could not refuse to accept a position offered him by the caliph, but he managed to avoid one job, that of guardsman, due to physical limitations. But he could not refuse to become a hangman. Abu Nisim schemed how to rid himself also of this position without alienating the ruler, and eventually became the caliph's advisor. The attitude to the Muslims, high and low, is positive in this story, and the Jew managed to get his way and improve his position thanks to his wisdom without jeopardizing his principles. While this story has clear legendary features, it does offer insights into Jewish-Muslim relations. It is known that some Jews had become advisors to Muslim rulers, including professionals, such as physicians, who were close to the rulers and advised them privately in matters of state. And it is well known that Jews often served Muslim rulers as hangmen, which made them dependent on the ruler and hated by the population.

The involvement of Jews in state affairs is reflected in a story about R. Shalom Tito (1788–1878), who was a member of the supreme court (*majlis*) of Tripoli, which was headed by the Ottoman governor with representatives of the majority and minority groups. Rabbi Tito had once convinced his fellow members not to rush to judgment on an Arab indicted for murder. It was subsequently discovered that witnesses had lied, and so the man was released. Later on, the freed Arab kissed Tito's feet, praised the justice and wisdom of Jewish rabbis, and gave Tito presents, which the latter distributed among the poor. Thus, Tito's wisdom, modesty, and piety became well known among Jews and Muslims alike.[20]

19 Noy, *Jewish Folktales*, 92–94.

20 Ibid., 158–59, 231. On Tito, see Zuaretz, *Libyan Jewry*, 71–72.

Religious Contiguity

Jews and Muslims in Libya often worshipped the same saints, tombs, and holy objects. It was usually agreed who "owned" what, but there were also attempts by the Muslims to seize control of Jewish sacred places and objects, by taking advantage of their sheer numbers and being under Muslim rule. A major case in point is the tomb of R. Simon Lavi, a sixteenth-century Sephardi rabbi and mystic who revived Jewish communal life in Tripoli.[21] Lavi's tomb was sacred to both groups, and stories of its miracles continued to be told in the twentieth century. One tale deals with R. Khmus Yamin (1850–1930), the rabbi of 'Amrus, near Tripoli, who, when once traveling to Tripoli, was attacked by robbers. The rabbi ran to Lavi's tomb, which was nearby, and, grasping the two iron rings on the door, implored Rabbi Lavi to rescue him. When the robbers reached the tomb, Rabbi Khmus realized that, thanks to Lavi's sanctity, he had become invisible. The robbers eventually left and, when day broke, Rabbi Khmus safely arrived in Tripoli.[22] Although it is not clear what actually happened at the tomb, the tale's message is that whoever respects its sanctity is rewarded; even members of the stronger Muslim majority are powerless in its wake.

Sometime after Rabbi Lavi's death, Arabs took control of his tomb, referring to him as "Ibn al-imam." They built a dome above the tomb and prevented Jews from approaching it. The Jews, nonetheless, continued to hope that one day the tomb would be restored to them. Following the Italian occupation of Libya (1911) and the deterioration in Italian-Arab relations due to the Arab rebellion against Italian rule, the Italian authorities granted the Jews permission to transfer Lavi's bones to the Jewish cemetery. Thousands of Jews participated in the funeral, but the leaders of the community allowed only a few to enter the cemetery. The exact location of Lavi's internment remains a secret in order to prevent the Arabs from stealing his bones. According to another version, despite the permission granted by the authorities, the Jewish leaders told the Arabs that they had decided to return the bones to their former tomb. Consequently, no one knows for sure where Lavi is buried.[23] In this episode, the Jews had a major grievance against the Muslims, but did not want to have the relations deteriorate further, even if that meant foregoing what was theirs by law, because they feared that the Italian authorities, at some point, would be unable to protect them against Muslim hostility.

Sacred objects also were a source of contention between Jews and Arabs. One of the most famous cases involves a tiny Torah scroll, known as the Zgheyr, which was kept at the synagogue of Dernah. Jews from all over

---

21 On R. Lavi, see Zuaretz, *Libyan Jewry*, 66.

22 Zuaretz, *Libyan Jewry,* 404 and on R. Khmus Yamin, see p. 89.

23 Noy, *Jewish Folktales*, 57, 185–86; Zuaretz, *Libyan Jewry,* 66, 403–4.

Libya used to seek assistance from the Zgheyr, especially for remedies for the sick. In view of its sacredness and the miracles attributed to it, many people gave the Zgheyr expensive gifts, which were kept at the synagogue. Several stories tell of attempts by Muslims to steal the Zgheyr and the gifts. But each time the perpetrator was struck by blindness or paralysis until the objects were returned.[24] According to one version, one night Muslim thieves tried to steal the presents donated to the Zgheyr. They entered the synagogue and took the jewelry from the Holy Ark. But when they tried to leave and got close to the windows, they were struck with a blinding light and the beadle [*shamash*] pounded their fingers with a hammer. They thereupon returned the jewelry to its place, found the door, and left empty-handed. Upon returning home they became paralyzed and recovered only after their families donated large sums to the Zgheyr's synagogue.[25] According to another story, a Muslim entered the synagogue at night aiming to steal the Zgheyr in order to sell it in another town. Once he managed to open the Holy Ark and take the Zgheyr, he became blind and could not find his way out. He regained his eyesight and left only after returning the Zgheyr to its place. In order to seek forgiveness, he brought a jug of oil to light the synagogue.[26] Another Muslim thief who tried to steal the Zgheyr at night became paralyzed when he touched the Holy Ark, and recovered only when he swore that he would never steal again.[27] It is difficult to tell what indeed happened in the synagogue during these nights, but the fact remains that the Zgheyr was not stolen, and it seems that there was no noticeable decrease in the gifts kept in the synagogue.

Just as tombs and Torah scrolls were venerated by Jews and Muslims alike, so were several rabbis, even if in some cases the Muslims were slow to recognize the sanctity of these individuals. Some stories refer to the mistreatment, directly or indirectly, of revered rabbis and how these saintly men were saved from harm. In all these cases, the Muslim authorities and the public eventually come to realize the sanctity of the rabbi. One story is about a dream that convinced the ruler of Tripoli to exempt a saintly poor rabbi from a special tax and to deduct this sum from the total amount levied on the community. The story describes how a Muslim ruler of Tripoli, Yusuf Karamanli (1795–1835), came to recognize the greatness of R. Yehuda Lavi

[24] Interestingly enough, when rich American Jews tried to acquire the Zgheyr illegally, they or their local collaborators were not punished for the attempted theft, contrary to when Muslims tried to get hold of the scroll (Noy, *Jewish Folktales*, 99). The Jews of Derna took the Zgheyr with them when they emigrated to Israel.

[25] Noy, *Jewish Folktales*, 98–99 and for more stories about the miracles of the Zgheyr, see pp. 97–98, 194–95.

[26] Ibid., 195, which tells also about an attempted theft by a Jewish peddler who wanted protection for his travels in the desert.

[27] Ibid., 100.

(d. 1833), a blind kabbalist and miracle-worker.[28] The ruler demanded a huge sum of money from the Tripolitan Jewish community, whose leadership apportioned the levy among all family heads, including Lavi, who was very poor. Lavi understood the pressure the community was under, but he lacked the means to pay. One night he dreamt of an old man who told him that the decree would be canceled and that no one would bother him. And indeed, the following day Lavi was informed that the ruler dreamt that an old man had warned him not to harm Lavi, who should be exempted from any tax. Yusuf Karamanli summoned the leaders of the Tripolitan Jewish community and told them to exempt Lavi and to deduct the sum that was levied on him from the total amount required from the community. It is difficult to tell what made the ruler change his mind. It is possible that stories about the holiness of the rabbi and his supernatural powers convinced the ruler that he had better not make the rabbi cast the evil eye on him, especially since the ruler was at the time under difficult economic and political stress. In any case, Tripolitan Jews felt that a stern Muslim ruler had come to recognize the sanctity of a rabbi.

Another story tells about the release from jail of the janitor of a renowned rabbi whose forgiveness was requested following mysterious beatings that the governor of Tripoli had suffered while asleep. In this case, the janitor of R. Shalom Agib of Tripoli was arrested for his economic activities.[29] After relatives of the janitor had exhausted their efforts at freeing him, they asked Rabbi Agib to intervene. The rabbi assured them that by Friday night the janitor would be free to return home. That night, the governor of Tripoli believed that he was being severely beaten while asleep, but he saw no one. When he asked the unseen attackers who they were and what they wanted, they replied that they were R. Shim'on bar Yohai and his son R. El'azar, whose writings were studied by Rabbi Agib, and if the governor did not release Agib's janitor at once, the governor would suffer gravely. As a result, he immediately freed the janitor and returned him to Agib's home, asking for Agib's forgiveness, while the janitor went home to celebrate the Sabbath.[30] It is difficult to tell what made the governor change his mind, but it might be that stories about the sanctity of Agib and the dangers resulting from harming saints had frightened the governor to the degree that he decided to free the janitor. It is hardly likely that the governor knew about the specific Jewish elements that were mentioned in the story (e.g., the names of renowned rabbis and sacred Jewish books studied by Agib); these might have been added by the local Jews in order to explain the decision of the governor, who previously had refused to listen to any request to free the

28 Ibid., 157 and on Lavi, see p. 226.

29 For the beginning of this story, see *ibid.*, 57–58.

30 Noy, *Jewish Folktales*, 58–59.

janitor. In this case, even a Turkish governor who had slighted a revered rabbi came to recognize his reputation.

Tense relations between Jews and Arabs are reflected in a story about an Arab molesting a righteous Jew. At times, relations between the communities deteriorated to the degree that Jews could not walk in an Arab neighborhood and vice versa.[31] Thus, once, when R. Abraham Habib (1850–1923)[32] had passed through an Arab street in Tripoli, a young Arab teased him and pulled his beard and robe. Upon hearing this, some Jewish strongmen proceeded to the Arab neighborhood in order to punish the molester. The rabbi, whom they met on their way, prevented them from attacking the Arab, saying that everything would be settled satisfactorily without their intervention. Four days later, that Arab was found in the street brutally murdered, his killer unknown. Jews and Arabs alike interpreted this as divine punishment for harassing a righteous man.[33]

The story reveals a number of customary behavior patterns in Jewish-Arab relations in Libya. There were instances when the cordial relations between members of the two communities were tense, and they tried to keep out of each other's way, though at times passing through "enemy territory" was inevitable. On such occasions, it could happen that Jews, including renowned rabbis, who were usually respected by both communities, would be mistreated. In order to protect Jews from being harassed, there were groups of Jewish toughs who took it upon themselves to defend individuals and the community at large. Earlier in the Ottoman period, such Tripolitan groups were well organized, and their members used to conduct weekly training. With the improvement of public safety in Tripoli during the late Ottoman period, this organization gradually dissolved.[34] Nonetheless, there were still times when Jewish self-defense was required and some individual Jews took it upon themselves to respond in a less-organized manner to defend the Jewish community against Arab attack. While it is not clear why Habib passed through the Arab neighborhood, it is known that one of the ways to the Jewish cemetery passed through Arab sections of Tripoli.

---

31 Although the latter case was much less common, there are descriptions of Jews, mostly unruly youths, harassing individual Arabs; see, for example, Noy, *Jewish Folktales*, 55.

32 R. Abraham Habib (1850–1923) was the head of the Jewish court in Tripoli. According to the story-teller, the event took place two years before Habib's death (see Noy, *Jewish Folktales*, 187).

33 Noy, *Jewish Folktales*, 60–61. See also Zuaretz, *Libyan Jewry,* 417, where the Arab is identified by name as Grisi'ah.

34 Rachel Simon, "Jewish Defense in Libya," *Jewish Political Studies Review* 13 (2001): 109–10; Harvey E. Goldberg, *Jewish Life in Muslim Libya* (Chicago and London: University of Chicago Press, 1990), 29–34.

Libyan Jewish folk literature recognizes the existence of anti-Semite gentiles, but the tales show how these gentiles ultimately realize the smartness of the Jews, who get the upper hand. While not explicitly talking about Muslims, Jews in Libya were surrounded almost exclusively by Muslims, and when they referred to gentiles, it essentially meant Muslims. One story describes a contest between gentiles and Jews imposed by an anti-Semitic gentile. When walking near a Jewish religious seminary in Tripoli he heard the saying: "The least of you will become a thousand, and the smallest a mighty nation" (Isa 60:22), and asked the rabbi for an explanation.[35] After the rabbi described the glorious future of Israel, the gentile told the king that the Jews intended to overthrow the government and seek revenge. When the angry king asked the gentile what to do, the latter suggested a public contest in which he would ask the rabbi theological questions. If the rabbi could not answer correctly, he would be condemned to death and, even if he could answer, the Jews would be frightened and would not dare to rebel. The king agreed, and the rabbi was informed about the contest, and was told that he could send a substitute. The community gathered to pray and fast for divine guidance. Just before the day of the contest a Jewish peddler arrived in town and, upon hearing of the contest, volunteered to participate in it, assuring the townsmen that his profession taught him to compete with anyone. Besides, if he did lose, they could say that an ignorant Jew was the loser. If, on the other hand, he won, everyone would say that a simple Jewish peddler overcame a learned gentile. During the contest, the gentile made various physical gestures that the peddler answered with his own, whereupon the gentile declared the Jew the winner. The gentile went on to explain the religious meaning of each of his gestures and how the peddler had refuted each religious point with a gesture of his own. Later on the peddler revealed to his fellow Jews the real meaning of his gestures, which were not theological at all, but simply normal, down-to-earth gestures and that the gentile, thankfully, had assigned them a level of meaning never intended. As a result of the contest, the anti-Jewish persecution was canceled, the gentile was put to death because he incited against the clever Jews who brought prosperity to Libya, and the day was commemorated annually.[36] This story presents a simple Jewish peddler as being smarter than a learned gentile. While there were similar stories throughout the Diaspora, this story shows that in Libya, too, the notion existed of the simple but smart Jew overcoming the wicked anti-Semite. The ruler is depicted as doing his duty, trying to get to the bottom of the problem, and, when it is resolved, acting justly against one of his own and in favor of the Jews.

Folk literature also tried to explain why there were so few conversions from Judaism to Islam in Libya. One story tells of a Jewish merchant who

---

35 There is no explanation in the story as to how the Arab understood the Hebrew phrase.

36 Noy, *Jewish Folktales*, 66–68.

had a shop opposite a big mosque and who was renown by Jews and Muslims for his generosity. Because of their great respect for him, Muslim religious dignitaries thought he should convert to Islam. The Jew hesitated as to how to respond; if he refused, he and his family would suffer. In response, he told them about a dream he had dreamt in which a Muslim, a Christian, and a Jew entered paradise without any problem, but a converted Jew could not enter, because a person is born into a specific religion. Moreover, the convert and all those who had influenced him into converting would be consigned to hell. The listeners decided that the meaning of the dream was quite clear: the merchant should remain in the religion to which he was born, Judaism. Since then, so the story goes, it is forbidden for Arabs to convert Jews to Islam and for Jews to convert to Islam.[37]

The story was designed to explain the small number of conversions by Jews, both to Islam and Christianity, in Libya, all the while showing how a Jew cleverly managed to defuse a dangerous situation. When this story was retold in the 1960s, it was dated "some thirty years ago," which would supposedly place it in the Italian period. It is highly unlikely that the event took place when the state authority was not Muslim, because Muslims in Tripoli were unlikely to cause much fear among Tripolitan Jews during the Italian period. On the other hand it is known that during the November 1945 riots in Tripolitania, the Jews of Mislata were forced to temporarily convert to Islam in order to save their lives[38] and occasionally Jewish women were kidnapped by Muslim men and were forced to marry the latter and convert to Islam.

Conclusion

The Jewish community of Libya was involved in the majority's political, social, and cultural life only to a very limited extent. Jewish-Muslim economic interdependence and commonly held mystic beliefs were major areas of intersection between Jew and Muslim, as can be discerned in folk tales. Most stories portray the Jewish protagonist as an outsider, as belonging to a lower political and socioeconomic stratum. Yet the overall perception is that although Muslims might seem to have the upper hand, the Jewish "circle of identity" is often more competent and, through ingenuity, self-help, the assistance of people of good will, and divine intervention, the Jewish community could safeguard its position and even improve it. Although most Muslims seem to occupy a higher rank than do the Jews, the latter are usually not harmed, often improve their status, and even outsmart and outmaneuver those supposedly superior to them. The folk tales reflect a world

37 Ibid., 81–85.

38 Irit Abramski-Bligh, ed., *Pinkas hakehilot: Libya, Tunisia* (Jerusalem: Yad Vashem, 1997), 171–72 [Hebrew].

in which weak and strong may be only a matter of outward appearance, for those perceived to be of a lower rank are, in fact, equal and should be respected and not mistreated.

Medieval Jewish Culture in Spain

Between Islam and Christianity

YOSEF TOBI

In terms of culture, Jewish existence in medieval Spain was unique in Jewish history. No other Jewish community might be compared to it, neither the Alexandrian with Philo in antiquity nor the Western, especially the American, in modern times. The medieval Spanish community reflected the most successful embodiment of what in the modern expression may be called a multi-culture. Spanish Jewry in the Muslim, rather than the Christian, milieu was deeply immersed in the canonic culture of the Gentile environment, yet it never abandoned its Hebrew-Jewish cultural possessions or its national identity. Of course, one should not ignore individual cases of Jews who converted to Islam during the Muslim epoch in Spain; in any case, there were no episodes of mass conversion as happened during the Christian era.[1] By contrast, the Hellenistic community of Alexandria lost its knowledge of Hebrew and modern Western Jewish communities are more or less in the same position.[2]

Let us briefly draw the chronological framework of the Jewish existence in medieval Spain. I shall omit the Jewish community under the rule of the Visigoth kingdom in early medieval times, as for many reasons this is an entirely different story.[3] By and large, our concern is with two main periods: that under Muslim rule, which began in 711 CE, when the Muslim army

---

1 On conversion of Jews to Islam and Christianity, see Norman Roth, *Jews, Visigoths, and Muslims in Medieval Spain: Cooperation and Conflict* (Leiden, 1994), especially the Index, p. 351, "Conversion," "Conversos"; also idem *Conversos, Inquisition, and the Expulsion of the Jews from Spain* (Madison, Wisc., 1995). On Hebrew in medieval Spain, see idem "Jewish Reactions to the 'Arabiyya and the Renaissance of Hebrew in Spain," *Journal of Semitic Studies* 28 (1983): 63–84.

2 On Hellenistic Jewry, see Erich S. Gruen, *Heritage and Hellenism: The Reinvention of Jewish Tradition* (Berkeley, Calif., 1988) and James Barr, "Hebrew, Aramaic and Greek in the Hellenistic Age," in *The Cambridge History of Judaism* II (1989), 79-114; on Hebrew in modern American Jewry, see Naftali Ruthenberg, "The Hebrew Language as Guarantor of the Continuity of American Jewry," *HaDoar*, 29.1 (1993) and Hezi Brosh, "Hebrew Language Diffusion through Schools and Universities in America," *Journal of Jewish Education* 62 (1996): 1-20.

3 On the Jews in Visigoth Spain, see Alfredo Mordekhai Rabello, *The Jews in Spain before the Arab Conquest as Reflected in Legislation* (Jerusalem, 1983) [Hebrew]; also Roth, *Jews, Visigoths, and Muslims*, ch. 1, 7-40.

crossed what was later called the Straits of Gibraltar separating Europe from Africa;[4] and that under Christian rule, which started in 1145, when the first period ended and another Muslim army, this time consisting of a body of extreme zealots, the Almohads (*al-Muwaḥḥidūn*), made the same crossing from North Africa to Andalusia. This army conquered the country and in diverse ways destroyed the Jewish communities. Most Jews made their way to the northern part of the peninsula (though some left for Italy, North Africa, or the East) as refugees under Christian rule,[5] which in the political process known as *Reconquista* expanded southward to reduce the Muslim domain. Thus, Toledo was taken back by the Christians earlier, in 1085; and in the heart of Muslim Spain, Cordova was reclaimed in 1236 and Seville in 1248. Thereafter, only small, insignificant Jewish communities existed within the Muslim kingdom of Granada. The second period of Jewish existence in medieval Spain completely terminated with the famous event of the Expulsion from Spain in 1492 and from Portugal in 1496.[6]

Jews under Muslim Regime

The new Muslim rulers at the beginning of the eighth century were at least warmly accepted by the Jews, who had until then been fiercely oppressed by the Christian Visigoths. The information we possess about the Jews during the time following the Muslim conquest and up to the middle of the tenth century is relatively scarce.[7] This contrasts sharply with the situation thereafter, when a wealth of various kinds of information, mostly from Jewish sources, allows a detailed depiction of the different aspects of Jewish life in Spain. The Jews had now become a very active, significant, and welcome element of the population.[8] This period was crucial for Jewish existence in Spain owing to the combination of two complementary factors. The first one was the resolve of ʿAbd al-Raḥmān III (912-961), the new king, now called caliph, of the western Umayyī Muslim kingdom to build up his realm

---

4 For a comprehensive depiction of Jewish life under Muslim rule in Spain, see Eliyahu Ashtor, *The Jews of Moslem Spain*; trans. from the Hebrew by Aaron Klein and Jenny Machlowitz Klein, with introduction by David J. Wasserstein, 3 vols. (Philadelphia, Pa., 1973); on the Jews in the Taifa States (1002–1086), see David J. Wasserstein, *The Rise and Fall of the Party-Kings: Politics and Society in Islamic Spain, 1002–1086* (Princeton, N.J., 1985), 190–223.

5 On the tragic results of the *Muwaḥḥidī* conquest of Southern Spain for the Jews, see Roth, *Jews, Visigoths, and Muslims*, 116–29.

6 For a general depiction of Jewish life in medieval Spanish Christendom, see Isaac Baer, *A History of the Jews in Christian Spain*; trans. Louis Schoffman (Philadelphia, 1996); Roth, *Conversos, Inquisition, and the Expulsion.*

7 Rabello, *The Jews in Spain.*

8 Ashtor, *The Jews of Moslem Spain*, 264–90; on the Jewish viziers in the Taifa States, see Wasserstein, *The Rise and Fall of the Party-Kings*, 209–17.

to rival the 'Abbāsī Caliphate, centered in Baghdad, and to challenge its supremacy in the Muslim world. To this end, 'Abd al-Raḥmān did not hesitate to utilize every national and religious element in his country, including the Jews, and to expressly ignore the strict religious Muslim prohibition against the appointment of any Jew (or Christian, for that matter) to a position in government.

The Jews in Muslim Spain were recognized as a "protected minority" (*ahl al-dhimma*), theoretically the same status that their co-religionists enjoyed in the eastern Muslim regimes, but they did not suffer from the new anti-Jewish regulations that had been established in the 'Abbāsī and Fāṭimi kingdoms.[9] It should be noted that the Arabs themselves were a minority in Spain and could rely on the Jewish minority, which had helped them in their conquest of the country, since the Jews had desperately been looking for another regime after having been severely persecuted by the Visigoths.[10] In any event, the convenient political status of the Jews in Muslim Spain started to deteriorate, first after the North African fanatical Berber tribes known as al-*Murābiṭūn* gained control of the country in 1090, and later, when the al-*Muwaḥḥidūn*, also from North Africa, took over in 1146. Thus, for example, there was an attempt to compel Islam on the flourishing Jewish community of Lucena in 1107.

Adaptation of Arab Culture by the Jews of Spain

The second factor essential to Jewish existence in Spain was the readiness of the Jewish community and its leadership to play their part in the Muslim-Jewish partnership by becoming a positive, normal component of the population through adopting the culture of the dominant stratum of society. On its face it was an Arab-Muslim culture, but actually it was fused with many local Iberian elements, which eased its acceptance by the Jews.[11] In addition, Muslim culture was the highest in the Western world of the time, far above the prevailing culture of European Christendom. The Jews were quite proud to be fluent in Arabic language and literature, as well as in Arab philosophy and science. That tendency had already been approved by Saadia Gaon (882-942), the ultimate spiritual-religious authority in Baghdad, the center of Jewish learning, who opened the gates of Judaism to Arabic and

---

9 On the legal status of the Jews in Muslim Spain as *dhimmīs*, see Norman Roth, "Dhimma: Jews and Muslims in the Early Medieval Period," *Studies in Honour of Clifford Edmund Bosworth*, ed. Richard Netton (Leiden, 2000), 238–66.

10 On the Muslim expansion in Spain during the reign of 'Abd al-Raḥmān III and his policy toward religious minorities, see Ashtor, *The Jews of Moslem Spain*, 157–59; Maribel Fierro, *Abd-al-Rahman III of Cordoba* (London, 2005).

11 On ethnic relations in early Middle Ages Spain, see Thomas F. Glick, *Islamic and Christian Spain in the Early Middle Ages* (Leiden, 2005), 184–219.

Arab culture.[12] On the other hand, Jews were not required to forgo their religious and national legacy, namely to convert to Islam, in order to be acknowledged as legal citizens of the country. They could hold even the highest positions in the government. An example is Ḥisday ben Saprut, leader of Andalusian Jewry, who functioned as vizier, the second most powerful figure after the suzerain, in the court of ʿAbd al-Raḥmān III in Cordova. Ḥisday administered his sovereign's foreign as well as internal policy.[13] But he was not the only high-ranking Jew in the administration of this Muslim kingdom In essence, nothing in Islam was contradictory to the Jewish faith, as the belief in unity of God and the moral commandments are identical. This fact was later approved by Maimonides, the highest authority in regard to the Jewish religious code in the Middle Ages, who ruled that Islam was not a kind of idol worship, in contrast to Christianity. Nevertheless, Maimonides also declared that there had never been a foreign power more cruel to Jews than Islam.[14] Thus, on the one hand, the Jews were extremely anxious to retain their religious legacy, to observe the commandments, to develop learning of the Torah in the religious academies (*yeshiva*s), to retain their ties with other Jewish centers, and to continue to wait for the Messiah. On the other hand, as a result of their involvement in administration and economy, not a few Jews belonged to the court circles and were dignified personalities. Some even acquired positions of great influence in courts of their own, in which there were poets, scholars, and scientists, whom they supported financially.[15]

By now, the Jews spoke Arabic and their scholars wrote a variety of books in that language, as well as in Judeo-Arabic (Arabic language in Hebrew script), including translations and commentaries to the Bible and halakhic studies. Naturally, all works in new genres, such as philosophy, gram-

[12] On Saadia's crucial role in the openness of Jewish communities to Arabic and Arabic culture, see Yosef Tobi, *Proximity and Distance: Medieval Hebrew and Arabic Poetry*; trans. Murray Rosovsky (Leiden, 2004), 65–175.

[13] On his significant contribution to the remarkable cultural status of the Jews in Spain, see Maria R. Menocal, *The Ornament of the World: How Muslims, Jews, and Christians Created a Culture of Tolerance in Medieval Spain* (Boston, 2002), 79–90.

[14] Maimonides reveals his attitude toward Islam and Muslims in his *Iggeret Ha-Šemad*. For a scholarly edition, see Yitzḥaq Shilat, *Maimonides' Epistles,* 2 vols. (Jerusalem, 1995), I, 25–59 [Hebrew]; Eliezer Schlossberg, "The Attitude of R. Maimon, the Father of Maimonides, to Islam and Muslim Persecution," *Sefunot* 20 (1991): 95–107 [Hebrew].

[15] On Hebrew poets in Jewish courts, see Haim Schirmann, "The Function of the Hebrew Poet in Medieval Spain," *Jewish Social Studies* 16 (1954): 235–52; H. Schirmann and E. Fleischer, *The History of Hebrew Poetry in Muslim Spain*, edited, supplemented and annotated by Ezra Fleischer (Jerusalem, 1996) I, 27–28, n. 69 [Hebrew]; Ann Brener, *Isaac Ibn Khalfun: A Wandering Hebrew Poet of the Eleventh Century* (Leiden, 2003).

mar and lexicography, medicine, astronomy, and mathematics, were written in Judeo-Arabic. This was not just by chance, since from the time of the controversy over the new school of poetry, which Dunas ben Labrat had brought from the East to Cordova in the middle of the tenth century (see below), until Abraham bar Ḥiyya (c. 1065-1136/1145), who lived in Barcelona, the capital of Catalonia and far away from Muslim Spain, there had been no Jewish scholar in Spain who penned works, save poetry, in Hebrew. Even bar Ḥiyya wrote his books–some of them translations from Arabic–not for the Jewish communities of Andalusia, but for those in France (Provence), who did not know Arabic.[16] Another scholar, a younger contemporary of Bar Ḥiyya, was Abraham ibn Ezra (1092-1167), who left Spain for Italy and other countries in Western Europe, acted in the same way: translating Arabic scientific books into Hebrew or composing original works in Hebrew for Jewish communities that were not familiar with Arabic. It is estimated that in the course of some 250 years (or from 1150-1400), more than one thousand Arabic and Judeo-Arabic books were translated into Hebrew by 160 scholars.[17] Some of the Hebrew treatises, original or translations from the Arabic, were later translated into Latin by Jewish scholars who collaborated with their Christian counterparts (see below). Especially numerous are Ibn Ezra's astrological tracts in Latin translation;[18] however, the most important Judeo-Arabic essays that were translated into Latin are Ibn Gabirol's *Fons Vitae* and Maimonides' *Guide of the Perplexed*.[19] Both these works became an integral part of Christian scholarship in Western Europe.

All these scholarly fields, it should be noted, were completely new to Jewish learning, borrowed from Muslim scholarship or from other sources through Arabic translations, compilations, and commentaries. The immense impact of Arabic studies on Jewish studies started in the East and in North Africa, but reached its culmination in Andalusia, where Judeo-Arabic literature flourished throughout the so-called "Golden Age" (950-1140).[20] Yet

---

[16] Hanokh Gamliel, "The Language of R. Abraham bar Ḥiyya," *Lešonenu* 60 (1997): 277–95 [Hebrew]. On Provence as a center of translations from Arabic, see Daniel Lasker, "Christianity, Philosophy, and Polemics in Jewish Provence," *Zion* 68 (2003):316–19 [Hebrew].

[17] Chaim Rabin, *The Principles of the Hebrew Language History* (Jerusalem, 1973), 41 [Hebrew].

[18] Lynn Thorndike, "The Latin Translations of the Astrological Tracts of Abraham Abenezra," *Isis* 35 (1944): 293–302; Shlomo Sela, *Abraham Ibn Ezra and the Rise of Medieval Hebrew Science* (Leiden, 2003).

[19] The Judeo-Arabic original of *Fons Vitae* has not been preserved, but is known in its Hebrew translation as *Meqor Ḥayyim*.

[20] On Judeo-Arabic literature in Spain, see Moritz Steinschneider, *Die Arabische Literatur der Juden* (Hildesheim, 1964), 115–75.

we should bear in mind that both Jewish and Muslim science and philosophy were not genuine Arab wisdom. They were acquired in the East from Classical Greek wisdom of the fifth century BCE through translations into Arabic made by local Christians and Jews who knew both languages.[21] Still, Jewish scholarship took possession of and expanded many new fields as mentioned. The Muslim and Jewish schools were Neo-platonic in outlook, a philosophy that was most suitable and accommodating for monotheist religions.[22] Among the known names in Jewish scholarship of that time may be noted the aforementioned vizier, the physician Ḥisday ben Saprut; poet and grammarian Dunas ben Labrat; the grammarian and lexicographer Yona ibn Janāḥ; the vizier and poet Šemuel Hanagid, who served two kings in Granada; the philosopher and poet Šelomo ibn Gabirol; the halakhic jurist and poet Yiṣḥaq ibn Ghiyāth; the moralist philosopher Baḥye ibn Paquda; the poet and scholar of poetics Mose ibn Ezra; and the poet and philosopher Yehuda Halevy. All of them won everlasting renown through their written works.[23]

Hebrew Poetry on the Track of Arabic Poetry

We may add a word about Jewish poets and their poetry. As mentioned above, Jewish scholars wrote their books in Arabic, although all these writers were masters of Hebrew. Poetry was an exception, being composed only in Hebrew. Some modern scholars tend to explain this fact by the supposition that the Jewish poets were not adequately skilled in Arabic to meet the high demands of its poetry.[24] Another explanation that has been advanced is that the Jewish poets limited their writing of Arabic-language poems because the Muslims refused to read Jewish religious material written in Arabic.[25] Both theories are untenable, for we know that the Jewish

---

21 On how Greek scholarship and science entered Arabic culture, see De Lacy O'Leary, *How Greek Science Passed to the Arabs* (London, 1949); 'Abd al-Raḥmān Badawī, *La Transmission de la philosophi grecque au Monde Arabe* (Paris, 1968); Franz Rosenthal, *The Classical heritage in Islam*; trans. E. and J. Marmorstein (London, 1975).

22 About Neo-platonism in Islam and Judaism, see Ian Richard Netton, *Muslim Neoplatonists: An Introduction to the Thought of the Brethren of Purity (Ikhwan al-Safa').* (London, 1982); Majid Fakhri, *Al-Farābā, Founder of Islamic Neoplatonism: His Life, Works and Influence* (Rockport, Mass., 2002); Sarah Pessin, "Jewish Neoplatonism: Being above Being and Divine Emanation in Solomon Ibn Gabirol and Isaac Israeli," in *Cambridge Companion to Medieval Jewish Philosophy*, eds. Daniel Frank and Oliver Leaman (Cambridge, 2003), 91–110.

23 For all them, see Schirmann and Fleischer, *Poetry in Muslim Spain*, 99–480.

24 Joshua Blau, *The Emergence and Linguistic Background of Judeo-Arabic: A Study of the Origins of Middle Arabic* (Jerusalem, 1981), 22–25.

25 Yehuda Ratzaby, "Arabic Poetry Written by Andalusian Jews," in *Israel Levin Jubilede Volume*, I, eds. Reuven Tsur and Tova Rosen (Tel Aviv, 1994), 332 [Hebrew].

poets wrote Hebrew poetry only for Jews who knew Hebrew; when obliged to write poems for non-Jewish personalities, even though this was not the usual reason for writing poetry, they did so perfectly well in Arabic. Their work, in fact, rivaled Arabic poetry written by Muslims.[26]

The Jewish poets admired Arabic poetry. The first who wrote under its explicit conscious impact was Dunas ben Labrat. Around 950, he left Baghdad, where he had studied with Saadia, and went to the New World of the time, namely Andalusia or more precisely its capital, Cordova.[27] There he was well received at the court under the viziership of Ḥisday ben Saprut and was allowed to produce his new style of poetry, as well as to teach it to the poets of his time and to bequeath it to the generations to come. In Spain, Dunas was considered the foremost of the poets who employed in Hebrew poetry the Arabic poetical models with all their components, and gained legitimacy for this use. In the words of Mose ibn Ezra in his poetics: "Once we decided to adopt Arabic models, we cannot select part of them and reject others."[28] Because of the style of his Judeo-Arabic scholarly books and his use of Arabic rhetoric in his Hebrew poetry, Ibn Ezra, who was as well the historian of Hebrew poetry in Spain and its literary critic, is recognized as the most "Arab" of the Jewish writers.[29] Furthermore, at least one modern researcher considers him to be a supporter of the *'arabiyya* versus the *šu'ūbiyya*; that is, the school of Muslim intellectuals who opined that the Arab spiritual and literary culture excelled any other, including the original local one.[30] In general, the Jews in Spain tried hard to side with the Arabs in the spiritual dispute between *'arabiyya* and *su'ūbiyya*, while the non-Arab element, even if Muslim, rejected this claim.[31] Ibn Ezra did not refer to bib-

26 Abraham Shalom Yahuda, *Hebrews and Arabs: A Collection of Studies and Articles, Arab Poetry, Memoirs and Impressions* (New York, 1946),105–18 [Hebrew]; Ratzaby, "Arabic Poetry"; Joseph Sadan, "R. Yehuda Alḥarizi as a Cultural Juncture," *Pe'amim* 68 (1996):16–67; 'Abd al-Raḥmān Amīn Mar'ī, *Al-Adab al-'ibrī fi al-andalus bayn al-taqlīd wa-al-tajdīd*. Kafr Qari' (Israel, 2008), 200–63 [Arabic].

27 Schirmann and Fleischer, *Poetry in Muslim Spain*, 129–43.

28 Moshe ben Ya'akov ibn Ezra, Kitāb al-Muḥaḍara wal-Mudhākara: *Liber Discussionis et Commemorationis (Poetica Hebraica)*, ed. and trans. A. S. Halkin (Jerusalem, 1975), 223.

29 Neḥemya Allony, "The Reaction of Moshe ibn Ezra to the *'Arabiyya'* ," *Tarbiz* 42 (1973): 97–112; idem, "A Study of *Kitāb al-muḥāḍara wa-l-mudhākara* by Moses ibn Ezra," in *Studia Orientalia: Memoriae D.H. Baneth Dedicata*, eds. J. Blau, S. Pines, M. J. Kister and S. Shaked (Jerusalem, 1979), 41–65.

30 Allony, "The Reaction of Moshe ibn Ezra."

31 James T. Monroe, *The Shi'ūbiyya in al-Andalus: The Risāla of Ibn Garcia and Five Refutations* (Berkeley, Calif., 1970); Goran Larsson, *Ibn Garcia's Shu'ūbiyya Letter: Ethnic and Theological Tensions in Medieval Al-Andalus (The Medieval & Early Modern Iberian World)* (Leiden, 2003).

lical Hebrew poetry as real poetry on account of its lack of scanning and rhyming, which according to contemporary medieval poetics were critical to any literary piece called poetry.[32] Beyond all the literary obligations that Ibn Ezra voluntarily adopted from Arabic poetry, however, his final and real view was that biblical Hebrew poetry was superior to Arabic poetry in terms of historical precedence, rhetoric, and morality.[33]

Some critics found nothing different in Hebrew poetry from Arabic except the language or believe that nothing special characterizes the secular Hebrew poetry of Spain. Thus, several of the central figures of the Jewish Enlightenment movement (*Haskala*) in Europe in the nineteenth and first decades of the twentieth century, such as Jacob Goldenthal, who wrote the first instructional book in Hebrew for Arabic (*Ha-Maspiq*, Wien 1857), and the poet Saul Tchernichovski, believed that medieval Hebrew poetry was nothing more than a pale, unimpressive imitation of Arabic poetry.[34] In this vein, S.I. Is Horowitz, for instance, wrote in 1909 about most of the poetry of Yehuda Halevy, the most admired medieval Hebrew poet (translated from the Hebrew):[35]

> They are just rhyming of the common kind, a poetry that was ordinary in Middle Ages, grinding a ground flour, repetition ten times over of the same matter in different words about everything that is tasteless and nonsense. [...] Even the poems he penned in his youth about life and love are imitation of the contemporary Arabic poems more than his own creativity.

This judgment is absolutely mistaken, however, as it refers solely to the external features of Hebrew poetry in Spain, such as rhyme, meter, and motifs. A more serious investigation of this poetry, based on a profound and skillful comparison with Arabic poetry, will show at once that the Jewish poets, at least the best of them, could write under the influence of Arabic,

---

32 Ibn Ezra, Kitāb al-Muḥaḍara, 47.

33 Yosef Tobi, *Kitāb al-Muḥāḍara wa-al-mudhākara* by Moshe ibn Ezra Compared to *kitāb al-Badī' by* Ibn al-Mu'tazz," in *A Message upon the Garden: Studies in Medieval Jewish Poetry*, eds. Alessandro Guetta and Masha Itzhaki (Leiden, 2008).

34 For Goldenthal's view on medieval Hebrew poetry versus Arabic poetry, see his response in a letter sent to S.D. Luzatto, in Yitzḥaq ben Immanuel di Lattes, *Responsa* (Vienna, 1860), 161–68; for Tchernichovski, see his correspondence with A. Sh. Yahuda, Tobi, *Proximity and Distance*, 12–15.

35 Sh.I. Ish Horovitz, "Rabbi Yehuda Halevy," in his *From Where and to Where: An Anthology of Studies about Jews and Judaism* (Berlin, 1914), 173–74 [Hebrew]. On how Yehuda Halevy was perceived by the Enlightenment movement, see Shemuel Verses, "Yehuda Halevy Reflected in the Nineteenth Century," in *Aharon Mirsky Jubilee Volume: Essays on Jewish Culture*, ed. Zvi Malachi (Lod, 1986), 247–86 [Hebrew]; Aviva Doron, "Basic Trends in the Criticism of Yehuda Halevy's Poetry: Rationalism, Romantics, Myth," in *Peles: Studies in the Hebrew Literature Criticism, An Anthology in Memory of Sh. I. Penu'eli*, ed. Nurit Guvrin (Tel Aviv, 1980), 297–308; idem, *Yehuda Halevy: Selected Critical Articles on His Poetry* (Tel Aviv, 1988) [Hebrew].

yet still sustain originality in their poetry as a whole and individually. Thus, we have Hebrew poetry that is no less artistic and aesthetic or excellent than Arabic poetry. I would even dare say that, generally speaking, Hebrew medieval poetry reached higher peaks than its Arabic contemporary.[36]

The Move from the Domain of Arab Culture to Christian Culture

Having a clear idea of the place of Arab culture within Jewish culture in medieval Spain, one may wonder about the place of Christian culture. The answer is simple: there was hardly any. In fact, until the twelfth century, Latin Europe was completely disconnected from Muslim culture and erudition, which were the spiritual heirs of Classical Greece. Moreover, there was nothing challenging in local Christian culture in Spain, for either Muslims or Jews, since it was solely based on the religion and folklore of the subject Christian population. For Muslims and Jews, Christians in the Muslim kingdoms in the south or in the Christian kingdoms in the north were regarded as barbarians, an ignorant and uncultured people. We may illustrate this attitude by the personality of the Jewish poet Mose ibn Ezra. He was born in Granada (1055), the most important–politically and culturally–of the petty Muslim kingdoms, and was raised on both Jewish and Arabic cultures. He particularly excelled in Arabic poetics and, as mentioned, is considered to have adopted Arab poetic values more than any other Jewish poet. In 1090, he was forced to leave his birthplace, the cultural center of Islam in the West, and for almost fifty years he wandered in what was for him "a spiritual desert," the northern Christian areas.[37] Ibn Ezra articulated his strong feeling and longing for Granada and its Judeo-Arabic culture in his secular poetry. He was the only Hebrew poet who wrote in the Arabic poetic genre of *ḥanīn*, that is to say, poems written by Muslim poets about their yearnings for their hometowns taken by the Christians in the framework of the *Reconquista*.[38] Ibn Ezra's clinging, and that of the Jewish intelligentsia in Spain as a whole, to Arabic culture is betrayed by the fact that, except for

---

36 Yosef Tobi, "The Religious Element in the War Poems of Šemuel Ha-Nagid and in the Arabic Panegyrics in Andalusia," in his *Between Hebrew and Arabic Poetry: Studies in Spanish Medieval Hebrew Poetry* (Leiden, 2010), 93–115; idem, "Love in Hebrew Secular Poetry in the Setting of Medieval Arabic Poetry," op. cit., 116–47; idem, "The Chase as an Allegory for the Wrong and Suffering in the World as Found in Taḥkemoni by Yehuda Alḥarizi against the Background of Arabic Poetry," op. cit., 190–226.

37 Schirmann and Fleischer, *Poetry in Muslim Spain,* 398–403; Dan Pagis, *Secular Poetry and Poetic Theory: Moses ibn Ezra and His Contemporaries* (Jerusalem, 1970), 292–307 [Hebrew].

38 On the Arabic *ḥanīn* poems, see ʻAbd Allah Muḥammad al-Zayyāt, *Rithā' al-mudun fi al-shi'r al-Andalus.* (Benghazi, Libya, 1990); on the Hebrew poems, see Ross Brann, "Constructions of the Exile in Hispano-Hebrew and Hispano-Arabic Elegies," in *Israel Levin Jubilede Volume*, I, 45–61; Aviva Doron, "Towns in Spanish Hebrew Poetry," in *Israel Levin Jubilede Volume*, I, 69–78.

Semuel Hanagid and Yehuda Halevy, none felt it appropriate to include the national-religious motif of longing for the Land of Israel in their secular poetic work, which was assigned to their social life, but only in their liturgical work, meant for religious assemblies in the synagogues.[39]

However, we may think of one literary phenomenon deriving from the local Romance culture, namely the *muwassaḥ*.[40] This strophic poetic model, unknown in original Arabic poetry, was adopted from Romanic (the ancient Spanish) folk poetry by Muslim Spanish poets just after the middle of the tenth century. About a generation later, that poetic model was warmly received in Spanish Hebrew poetry, but even then it was by way of Arabic poetry.[41] As noted, we do not have a large number of Arabic poems written by Jewish poets in the framework of Jewish-Arab ties, as opposed to internal Jewish needs. To the best of my knowledge, not a single verse was written by Jews in Romanic. However, we may refer at this point to the important role played by Jewish musicians in the courts of Christian kingdoms in Spain, which was probably due to their high-quality acquaintance with Arab music.[42]

The prevailing orientation toward Arabic culture by Spanish Jewry, and the ignoring of Christian culture in its entirety, became modified during the twelfth century for different reasons. First, large Jewish communities developed within Spanish Christendom in consequence of the *Reconquista*, as the Christians took over ever more areas from the Saracens. Secondly, Jewish communities in the south were almost all destroyed as a result of the *Muwaḥḥidī* invasion from North Africa. The Jews then fled to the Christian north, where they were welcomed not only by their brethren but also by the Christian rulers. However, the major factor in opening a gap between Arabic culture and the Jews at that time was probably their disappointment as their world became ruined by followers of the great aesthetic culture they had so admired, especially its poetry and Neo-platonic philosophy. Thirdly, although there were circles of high-ranking Jewish personalities

---

39 Yosef Tobi, "Eretz-Yisrael and the National Subject Matter in the Hebrew Poetry from Sa'adia Gaon to Shemu'el Ha-Nagid," in his *Between Hebrew and Arabic Poetry*, 53–92.

40 On the different opinions on the origin of the *muwaššaḥ*, see Otto Zwartjes, *Love Songs from al-Andalus: History, Structure, and Meaning of the Kharja* (Leiden, 1997), 23–124.

41 On the Hebrew *muwaššaḥ*, see Tova Rosen-Moked, *The Hebrew Girdle Poem (Muwashshaḥ) in the Middle Ages* (Haifa, 1985) [Hebrew]; Ezra Fleischer, "Stages in the Development of the Hebrew 'Muwaššaḥ' (from Spain to Yemen)," in *Studies in Hebrew Literature and Yemenite Culture: Jubilee Volume Presented to Yehuda Ratzaby* (Ramat Gan, 1991), 111–59 [Hebrew]; Yosef Tobi, "Yemeni Jewish and Muslim Muwaššḥāt," in *Hebrew Strophic Poetry and Its Romance Parallels, School of Oriental & African Studies, London, 8–10 October 2003* (London, 2006) 319–27.

42 Higinio Anglès, " La musique juive dans l'Espagne médiévale," *Yuval* 1 (1968): 52–60.

close to Christian regimes, those Jews could not completely identify with the *culture* of the Christian regimes because of its strong religious nature. Thus it is not surprising that conversion to Christianity became a dominant phenomenon among Jewish communities in Christian Spain, far beyond the relatively limited number of occurrences of conversion to Islam in Muslim Spain. We cannot speak, then, about Judeo-Christian culture, or even about Judeo-Spanish culture, since Hebrew–and not Spanish–took the place of Arabic in Christian Spain. At any rate, all Judeo-Arabic culture and the intellectual and literary values of openness to other cultures entirely collapsed. The disappointed Jews lost all their naivete regarding the benefit they could gain from their close relationship with the external Arabo-Muslim culture and began to seek another cultural-spiritual environment in which to settle as proud and secure Jews, and where they could develop their potential.

One of the most amazing results of the deep change that Jewish culture passed through from the Muslim sphere to the Christian sphere is connected with poetry. This field of literary creativity was almost totally disappeared in Spain, either in Christian or Muslim domain, after the death of Mose ibn Ezra (c. 1138) and the departure of Yehuda Halevy and Yiṣḥaq ibn Ezra to the East (1140) and that of Abraham ibn Ezra, Yiṣḥaq's father, to Italy (1140). Hebrew poetry re-appeared, in Christian Spain and in Provence, during the 1230s, but ignoring for methodical reasons Todros Abul'āfia's poetry, which will be discussed below, the Jewish poets in those countries established, in fact, a new school of poetry, of which we will deal only with one aspect. Two of the main features of Hebrew poetry in Muslim Spain were the "secular" motifs of Love and of Nature, although the latter consisted of the picturesque and stylized gardens around houses in cities and towns. These two motifs did not exist *per se* in Hebrew poetry in Christian Spain and Provence, certainly owing to their "secular" character. What is surprising is that the poets of Provence, who lived within a much more impressive landscape than Andalusia, wrapped as it was with brilliant, evergreen foliage on its hills and rich with rivers and streams, did not chant about that natural beauty. This abstention was in clear contradiction to the theme of nature, especially that of spring awakening, which was intertwined with the troubadours' lyric love poetry, such as Cercamon and Jaufre Rudel (twelfth century) of the "Gascon School,"[43] or was featured in the two forms of poetry–the Pastorelles (usually a dialogue between a troubadour and a shepherd) and the Aubades (dawn).[44]

43 George Wolf and Roy Rosenstein, *The Poetry of Cercamon and Jaufre Rudel* (New York, 1983).

44 John Frederick Rowbotham, *The Troubadours and Courts of Love* (New York, 1895), 87–89, 227–29. On the influence of the troubadours' poetry on Hebrew Provençal poetry, see H. Schirmann and E. Fleischer, *The History of Hebrew Poetry in Christian Spain and Southern France*, edited, supplemented and annotated by Ezra Fleischer (Jerusalem, 1997), 482ff. [Hebrew]. See also n. 70 below.

Fortunately for the Jews, another influential process emerged in Latin Christendom at exactly that time, namely the twelfth-century Renaissance. In contrast to the onset of the political and cultural deterioration of the Saracens in the south, Christian Spain began to flourish, and here the Jews played a notable role. The twelfth-century Renaissance was a combination of two processes. One was the re-studying of the Latin literature of Rome from the first century BCE to the third century CE in poetry, grammar, law, and historical writings. This was fairly straightforward, because Latin had not lost its status as a literary and scholarly language in Latin Christendom (Italy, Germany, France, England, and Spain) prior to the twelfth century; only then did the vernaculars start to dislodge its place in popular literature and wisdom. This was not the case with the second process, the renaissance of Classical Greek erudition, since, except for a small center in the Norman Kingdom in southern Italy and Sicily, Greek was unknown in central and western Europe.[45] The renaissance of Greek philosophy and sciences, however, could not have materialized without the Arabic and Hebrew languages, into which an impressive amount of Greek classics had been rendered in the East beginning from the eighth century. It should be noted that these Arabic and Hebrew renditions, although in general slavishly literal, were not faithful presentations of the Greek sources, as they contained inaccuracies. In addition, most of the Greek Classical legacy in Arabic or Hebrew clothing was colored by Eastern monotheistic interpretation; sometimes that legacy existed only in commentaries written by Muslim or Jewish scholars (see below). However, if the Latin renaissance made its way from beyond the Pyrenees southward from France, the Greek renaissance took the other route, from Spain northward to France, England, Germany, and Italy.

The general attitude toward Jews in Spain's Christian kingdoms was not hostile in the period from 1150 to 1350. Many Jews held high positions in the administrations of these kingdoms, and the Jewish communities were economically strong and well organized. Here we observe the same phenomenon as occurred in Andalusia, with Jews being involved in these societies politically, economically, socially, and culturally.[46] Sometimes Jews were authors or translators, as in the case of Pedro de Alfonso (Huesca 1062-c. 1140), a converted Jew (1106) who is known in Jewish sources as Mose Ha-Sefaradi. His famous work, *Disciplina Clericalis* (the Priest's Directives), is a compilation of 39 conversations (*Dialogues*) between a father

---

45 Charles Homer Haskins, *The Renaissance of the Twelfth Century* (Cleveland and New York, 1957), 280. On the twelfth-century Renaissance, see ibid. and Robert L.Benson et al., eds., *Renaissance and Renewal in the Twelfth Century* (Cambridge, Mass., 1982).

46 Haim Beinart, "The Image of the Jewish Courtiers in Spain," in his *Spain Chapters*, I (Jerusalem, 1998), 51-62 [Hebrew].

and his son, in which many oriental stories were included for the first time in Latin rendition. What is more significant for the issue under discussion is that Pedro de Alfonso devoted one of the *Dialogues* to a polemic against Islam. That work, "which is outstanding for the accuracy of its information about Islam,"[47] was written by a scholar who knew Arabic, lived among Muslims, and was acquainted with their tenets and practices. Pedro de Alfonso, however, dwelled polemically on the hedonistic delights of the Islamic garden of paradise, and his very popular account became "the standard mediaeval version of the Quran's promised paradise, that is, a garden of delights, the flowing waters, [...] and beautiful virgins, 'untouched by men or demons.'"[48]

The Role of Jewish Scholars in the Translation of Greek and Arabic Scholarship into Latin

The contribution of Jews in the Spanish Christian kingdoms as translators of Greek science into Arabic renditions and commentaries and of Muslim scholarship into European languages was much greater than their contribution in the preceding era to the culture of Muslim kingdoms in the south. Although, as stated, Jews wrote all their works in Arabic, except for poetry, Muslim scholars essentially ignored them, as they did everything non-Muslim. Jews are seldom referred to in Muslim writings, and if they are it is usually not for their cultural importance but for their political positions or in connection with their status as *dhimmīs* (non-Muslim protected subjects).[49] Admittedly, script presented a serious obstacle for Muslim scholars, as the Arabic literature of the Jews was written entirely in Hebrew characters, a luxury that Muslim scholars did not allow themselves or made any attempt to acquire. As a result, they did not have direct access to Jewish sources,

47 W. Montgomery Watt, *The Influence of Islam on Medieval Europe* (Edinburgh, 1972), 73.

48 Norman Daniel, *Islam and the West* (Edinburgh, 1960), 148. See, also, R.W. Southern, *Western Views of Islam in the Middle Ages* (Cambridge, Mass., 1962). For additional information on Pedro de Alfonso, see Ḥen Merḥavia, *The Talmud as Reflected in Christianity* (Jerusalem, 1970), 93–127 [Hebrew]; Schirmann and Fleischer, *Poetry in Christian Spain*, 96–97, n. 15; Yona David, "Petrus Alfonsi and His *Disciplina Clericalis*," in *Israel Levin Jubilede Volume*, I, 63–68.

49 Thus, for example, regarding the information about Šemuel Hanagid as vizier of the Zīrī county of Granada (Moshe Perlmann, "Eleventh-Century Andalusian Authors on the Jews of Granada," *Proceedings of the American Academy for Jewish Research,* 18 (1949): 269–90; Ross Brann, "Arabic Representations of Samuel the Nagid," in *Ancient Near Eastern, Biblical and Judaic Studies in Honor of Baruch A. Levine*, eds. R. Chazan, B. Hallo, and L. Schiffman (Winona Lake, Ind., 1999), 443–65 or regarding the Jewish poets who penned Arabic verse (Ratzaby, "Arabic Poetry"; Marʿī, *Al-Adab al-ʾibrī,* 204–221). For the Jews of Yemen, see, also, Yosef Tobi, "The Jews of Yemen in Arabic Yemeni Works," *Pe'amim* 64 (1995): 68–102 [Hebrew].

whether in Hebrew or Judeo-Arabic, and as a rule had to be helped to this end by Jewish scholars.[50]

Naturally, the literary contribution of the Jews in Christendom was not only in the current languages, Latin and Spanish vernacular, but in Latin script as well, since the translations were specifically produced for Christians. The special role of the Jews in the twelfth-century "translation movement" derives from the fact that Christian scholars were not interested in the literature of Classical antiquity, mostly Greek, because of its pagan origin, but sought new scientific, philosophical, and, to a lesser extent, religious texts.[51] The last concern was reflected in a renewed interest in translations of the Greek Church Fathers into Latin, a concern with translating Jewish teachings from Hebrew, and most significantly an interest in the Qur'ān and other Islamic religious texts. Jewish scholars could not translate from Greek, an unfamiliar language for them, but they could from Arabic, Judeo-Arabic, or Hebrew treatises. The main center of the translation movement was Toledo, which, despite having been taken by the Christians (1085), retained many Muslims and Arabic-speaking Jews.

The current view is that most translations were produced by two scholars working together: one was a Christian, who chose the work to be translated and gave the Latin text its final form, while the collaborator rendered the sense of the Arabic into Latin. In other words, it is apparent that the interpretation of Jewish scholars frequently took the form of translation from Arabic into the current Spanish idiom, which the Christian translator then turned into Latin. It should be noted that a large number of translations from Arabic into Hebrew were later rendered into Latin, as attested by Steinschneider's great volume on Hebrew translations.[52] For instance, one of the earliest Jewish translators in Toledo was Avendauth (Abraham ibn Daud, who had become a Christian), who in cooperation with Domingo Gundisalvo, Archdeacon of Segovia, translated Avicenna's encyclopedia, *Kitāb al-Shifā* (*The Book of Healing*) into Latin, and scientific works in arithmetic, astronomy, astrology, medicine, and philosophy into spoken Castellan.[53]

---

50 Thus, for example, Ibn Ḥazm (Spain 994–1064) in some of his writings. See Moshe Zucker, "Elucidations in the History of the Religious Debates between Judaism and Islam," in *Aharon Kaminka Jubilee Volume in His Seventieth Year* (Vienna, 1937), 38.

51 J.L. Teicher, "The Latin-Hebrew School of Translators in Spain in the Twelfth Century," in *Homenaje a Millás Vallicrosa,* II (Barcelona, 1956), 403–44. On Jews as translators, see also Moritz Steinschneider, *Die hebräischen Übersetzungen des Mittelalters und die Juden als Dolmetscher* (Graz, 1956), 971–87.

52 Steinschneider, *Die hebräischen Übersetzungen*. On medieval European translations from Arabic, see idem, *Die europäischen Übersetzungen aus dem Arabischen bis Mitte des 17.Jahrhunderts* (Graz, 1956).

53 Some scholars, such as Moritz Steinschneider, identified Avendauth with John of Seville, also a twelfth-century translator from Arabic to Latin, but this identification is

The most productive of the Toledo translators was Gerard of Cremona (d. 1187), who came from Italy and translated 87 books, including Isaac Israeli ben Solomon's medical treatises, *De elementis* and *De definitionibus*.[54]

Another translation center was Barcelona, in the northeastern part of Iberia, where the aforesaid Abraham bar Ḥiyya translated works on geometry and astronomy from both Hebrew and Arabic with Plato of Tivoli, another Italian scholar. One of their joint works is *Liber embadorum*. Another notable example of collaboration between Jewish and Christian scholars occurred when Simon de Cordo of Genoa, who was physician to Pope Nicholas IV (1288-1292), and the Jew Abraham of Tortosa (northern Spain) translated a book by Ibn Sarābī (Syria, c. 1070), who was known in Europe as Serapion Junior. It is probable that Ibn Sarābī's book—based of the writings of Dioscorides and Galen—was translated into Latin from the Hebrew. It was first published, as *Liber Aggregatus*, in Milan in 1473.[55]

Again, one may wonder how Jews living in a Christian domain could carry out the task of transferring the Greek legacy from Arabic to Latin and the vernacular. There is no question that the Greek legacy was written in Arabic; however, even after moving from the Muslim to the Christian domain, the Jews tended not to detach themselves from Arab scholarship.[56] After all, this scholarship retained its supremacy over Latin Christian scholarship, and the stream of scholarly information flowed only in one direction, from Muslims to Christians. Thus, even three generations after leaving the Muslim domain. Jews are found to be educated in Arabic language and literature, in addition to being naturally fluent in the Spanish vernacular and steeped in Latin Christian erudition. Some Jews, such as Jacob ben El'azar, who lived in Toledo (1170?-1233), even wrote in Judeo-Arabic, such as his work *Kitāb al-Kāmil* on Hebrew grammar,[57] as had Ibn Janāḥ and Šemuel Hanagid in Muslim Andalusia two centuries earlier. In addition, a sizable

quite doubtful. See Lynn Thorndike, "John of Seville," *Speculum* 34 (2003): 20-38; M. Robinson, "The History and Myths surrounding Johannes Hispalensis," *Bulletin of Hispanic Studies*, 80 (2003): 443-70.

54 Watt, *The Influence of Islam*, 60. Isaac Israeli was born in Egypt (832?) and died in Qairawān, Tunisia (932?). Some of his medical works were translated into Latin as early as 1087 by Constantine of Carthage, who used them as textbooks at the University of Salerno, the earliest university in Western Europe.

55 Edward Grant, *A Source Book in Medieval Science* (Cambridge, Mass., 1974), 734, n. 22; Donald Campbell, *Arabian Medicine and Its Influence on the Middle Ages* (Amsterdam, 2001), 100.

56 On maintaining the tradition of Judeo-Arabic among the Jews in Christian Spain, see Yom Tov Assis, "The Judeo-Arabic Tradition in Christian Spain," in *The Jews of Medieval Islam: Community, Society, and Identity*, ed. Daniel Frank (Leiden, 1995), 111-24.

57 Ya'aqov ben El'azar, *Kitāb al-Kāmil*, ed. Neḥemya Allony (Jerusalem, 1977).

Muslim population, the *Mudejar*, still existed within the Christian domain. This term, a corruption of the Arabic word *mudajjan*, designated the local Muslim component of the population that stayed in Muslim areas conquered by the Christian kings.[58]

The famous Alfonso X (1252-1284), known as *el Sabio* (the Wise), was a patron to Jews (including Kabbalists), Christians, and Moslems alike, not a few of whom were courtiers in his inner circle. From the beginning of his reign, Alfonso X encouraged the tendency to retain the Muslim legacy and employed at his court Jewish, Christian, and Muslim scholars to translate books from Arabic into the vernacular (Old Spanish). Thus it was that much Greek philosophy, science, and mathematics, preserved in Arabic, was translated into Latin and found its way back into Western Europe through France and Arabic Sicily to Italy. We know of at least five Jewish scholars who served as translators, all of whom collaborated with Christian scholars: (1) Alfonso's physician, Yehuda ben Mose Cohen (Mosca el Menor); (2) Isaac Ibn Cid (Rabiçag), the cantor of Toledo and a wealthy capitalist who supported Alfonso financially; (3) Abraham Alfaqui de Toledo, physician to Alfonso and his son, Sancho; (4) Semuel Halevy Abul'āfia; and (5) Xosse Alfaqui.[59] Indeed, the total production of this collaboration between Jewish and Christian scholars is very impressive, with dozens of scientific treatises in all fields. It should be borne in mind, though, that in spite of this highly important contribution by Jewish translators to Western scholarship, its impact on Jewish medieval wisdom was next to zero, as Jews were not the learned clientele to whom those translations were directed. Moreover, none of the Jewish translators took his place in Jewish history for this kind of activity, but for other pursuits. For the Jewish scholarly public in Spain and in Provence, who were more familiar with Hebrew, only a few of the works translated into Latin were rendered into Hebrew.

Jews or converted Jews served as teachers of Arabic for the Christian scholars who came to Spain from beyond the Pyrenees to be acquainted with Greek classics. The Spanish tide also flowed in the other direction, over the Pyrenees into southern France, to centers such as Narbonne, Béziers, Toulouse, Montpellier, and Marseilles, where the new astronomy

---

58 On the *Mudejar* and their contribution to the culture of medieval Spain and Western Europe as a whole, see Menocal, *The Ornament of the World*; Richard Rubenstein, *Aristotle's Children: How Christians, Muslims, and Jews Rediscovered Ancient Wisdom and Illuminated the Middle Ages* (Orlando, Fl., 2003).

59 On Jewish collaborators on Alfonso's scientific work, see Norman Roth, "Jewish Translators at the Court of Alfonso X," *Thought*, 60 (1985): 439–55; idem, "Jewish Collaborators in Alfonso's Scientific Work," in *Emperor of Culture: Alfonso X the Learned of Castile and His Thirteenth-Century Renaissance Culture*, ed. Robert I. Burns (Philadelphia, 1990), 59–71, 223–30; Fernando Diaz Esteban, "The Spanish Literary Work of the Jews," in *The Legacy of Sefarad*, ed. Haim Beinart (Jerusalem, 1992), 332–43.

appeared as early as 1139. Traces can be found also of the astrology, philosophy, and medicine of the Arabs into the fourteenth century. Here the share of Jewish translators was large, perhaps even relatively larger than in Spain; and many of the versions came by way of the Hebrew. A significant role in this regard should be ascribed to Spanish Jewish and Arabic physicians, whose works were so important for the development of medicine in Europe and whose personal services were requested by Christians. Jews, then, played an important role as transmitters of Greek and Arab science and philosophy, since they were often in close touch with the Christian scholars of Western Europe.[60]

The aforementioned Pedro de Alfonso is a good example. A converted Jew, he served as court physician to Alfonso I of Aragon and later went to live in England, where he was summoned by King Henry I to be his physician. Pedro de Alfonso had great influence on the astronomers of the Christian calendar, especially in France and England. He was also the source of knowledge of astronomy for the Englishman Walcher of Malvern in 1120. Walcher and Adelard of Bath, the first English scientist and Arabist (c.1080-c.1152), who may have come also under the influence of Pedro de Alfonso, helped to form a scientific tradition that reached its apex in Robert Grosseteste (d. 1253), who was for a time chancellor of the Oxford University.[61] Another important medieval Christian scholar who learned Arabic and was assisted by converted Jews in his translations was Michael Scot (c.1170-c.1236). Scot visited Toledo in 1217 and was later invited by the Roman king of Sicily, Frederick II, to his court, where he produced a Latin translation of Maimonides' *Guide for the Perplexed* (using the Hebrew translation from Judeo-Arabic) with the help of Jewish and Muslim scholars.[62] One of these Jewish scholars was Jacob Anatoli (1194-1256), who refers many times to Michael Scot in his book *Malmad Ha-Talmidim* as "the sage I befriended."[63] Roger Bacon claimed that another such scholar was a former

60 Watt, *The Influence of Islam*, 63.

61 Ibid., 64-65. On Adelard of Bath, see Charles Burnett, *Adelard of Bath: An English Scientist and Arabist of the Early twelfth Century* (London, 1989).

62 On Michael Scot, see Haskins, *Studies in the History of Mediaeval Science* (New York, 1967), 272-98; Thorndike, *Michael Scot* (London, 1965). Concerning his relation to the development of Jewish Law in the fourteenth century, see Judah D. Galinsky and James T. Robinson, "Rabbi Jeruham b. Meshullam, Michael Scot, and the Development of Jewish law in Fourteenth-Century," *Harvard Theological Review* 100 (2007): 489-504. The first Spanish translation *of Guide for the Perplexed* was done during the years 1416-1432 by Pedro de Toledo, whose Jewish father, Juan, was a converso (Itzhak Bar-Lewaw, "Pedro de Toledo, el Primer Traductor Español del *More Nebujim*," in *Homenaje a Rodríguez-Moñino: Estudios de Erudición que le Ofrecen sus Amigos o Discípulos Hispanistas Norteamericanos*, I (Madrid, 1966), 57-64.

63 Colette Sirat, "Les traducteurs juifs a la cour des rois de Sicile et de Naples," in *Traduc-*

Jew, Master Andrew, canon of Palencia (Castile), whom the pope praised in 1225 for his knowledge of Arabic, Hebrew, Chaldee, and Latin, as well as of the seven liberal arts.[64]

Notwithstanding all the aforementioned, it should be underscored that after the decisive victory of the Christian kingdoms over the Muslim Muwahhidi power in Las Navas de Tolosa in 1212, Christianity gained supremacy in all of Spain, and the political and cultural importance of the Jewish communities as mediators with the world of Islam started to decline. There were more and more attacks on the Jewish religion and its followers as a result of the penetration of Christian religious intolerance from beyond the Pyrenees into the Iberian Peninsula.

The Hebrew Maqāma and Prose Writings in Light of Christian Culture

The unique situation of Spanish Jews between Islamic culture and Christian culture may be illustrated through the literary genre of the *maqāma*. This genre has special features, most notably a narrative written in rhymed prose. Undoubtedly, it was created in the Muslim East by two famous Muslim poets, al-Hamadhānī (d. ca. 965) and al-Ḥarīrī (d. 1122). Nothing should seem surprising in the fact that Jewish poets in Spain imitated this new and very respectable genre and composed Hebrew *maqāma*s. In fact, the Spanish Jewish poet Alḥarīzī (1165-1225) even left a Hebrew rendition of al-Ḥarīrī's *maqāma*, which he entitled *Maḥberot Iti'el*.[65] All but one of the Spanish Hebrew *maqāma*s were written within the Christian realm, the exception being *Taḥkemoni*, Alḥarīzī's original Hebrew *maqāma*,[66] which was written in Aleppo, Syria, where he settled after long travels throughout the Jewish world.[67] It seems, however, that the imitation of the *maqāma* genre by Jewish poets was only partial: they took the form but used it for a completely different purpose. While Eastern Muslim poets used this genre to produce entertaining literary works to be read in order to pass the time in good spirits, Jewish poets considered it an instrument for very serious goals,

tion et traducteurs au moyen âge: actes du colloque internationale du CNRS, organisé à Paris, ed. Geneviève Contamine (Paris, 1989), 69-191.

64 Gad Freudenthal, "Maimonides' Guide of the Perplexed and the Transmission of the Mathematical Tract 'On Two Asymptotic Lines' in the Arabic, Latin and Hebrew Translation," in *Maimonides and the Sciences*, eds. Robert S. Cohen and Hillel Levine (Dordrecht, 2000), 35-56, 54, n. 25.

65 Abraham Lavi, "Why and How Did Alḥarizi Judaicized in *Maḥberot Iti'el* the Proper Names in *Maqāmāt al-Ḥarīrī,*" *Bar-Ilan* 20/21 (1983): 172-81 [Hebrew]; 1984; Schirmann and Fleischer, *Poetry in Christian Spain,* 177-84.

66 Not exactly, as at least eight are translations or Jewish-Hebrew adaptations of Arabic *maqāma*s. On the influence of al-Hamadhānī and al-Ḥarīrī on Alḥarīzī, see Mar'ī, *Al-Adab al-'ibrī*, 328-55.

67 Sadan, "R. Yehuda Alḥarizi."

such as education, improving Jewish society, and glorifying philosophy rather than poetry.[68] Furthermore, the Hebrew *maqāma* gradually lost the genre's formal specifications as its essential use as an educational tool diminished. Moreover, some works in the *maqāma* genre, such as Ben El'azar's *Sefer Ha-Mešalim*, Falaqera's *Ha-Mevaqqeš*, and Kalonymos' *Even Boḥan*, served as satire and criticism of Andalusian poetry and its literary values (see more on this below).[69]

The *maqāma* genre is seemingly the best tool, although not the only one, with which to study the influence of contemporary Christian culture on Hebrew belles-lettres. The impact of Christian poetry, specifically its religious poetry, is very limited and restricted to one Hebrew poet, Todros Abul'āfia (1247-1299+), who was in the entourage of Alfonso X. Abul'āfia wrote a wonderful series of short poems in imitation of his king and other contemporary Christian poets.[70] This is, certainly, in clear contrast to the extent of the influence of Arabic religious poetry on Hebrew poets in Andalusia, as poets in both these languages and convictions actually shared in principle the same philosophical-moral values.[71] For a better understanding of the essence of the Hebrew *maqāma*, we should bear in mind that something happened in Latin Christendom in the twelfth century, during which this genre was employed within the Christian domain, and in the following century, namely the medieval Renaissance. That era, of which the Jews of Spain were an integral part, saw the expansion of learning, reflected in part in the founding of the first universities in Western Europe.[72] The

68 The real literary qualities of the Hebrew *maqāma* versus the Arabic *maqāma* have not been deeply studied. On the Hebrew *maqāma* as a keen satire of medieval Jewish society, see Ayelet Oettinger-Salama, "The Aspect of the Satirical Modus in Yehuda Alḥarizi's *Taḥkemoni*" (Ph.D. diss., The University of Haifa, 2003) [Hebrew].

69 Haim Schirmannn, "A Story about a Hypocrite Old Man," in his *Hebrew Poetry and Drama*, I (Jerusalem, 1979), 388-75; Schirmann and Fleischer *Poetry in Christian Spain*, 335-41, 529-40; Yosef Tobi, "Šem Ṭov Ibn Falaqera's Critique of Poetry," in his *Between Hebrew and Arabic Poetry*, 467-82.

70 Aviva Doron, *Todros Ha-Levi Abulafia: A Hebrew Poet in Christina Spain* (Tel Aviv, 1990) [Hebrew]; Tova Rosen-Moked, "Literary Mannerism as an Aspect of Cultural Archaism: Lines of the Cultural Image of Todros Abulafia," *Sadan* I (1994): 49-76 [Hebrew]; Schirmann and Fleischer, *Poetry in Christian Spain*, 408-14. Another feature of Todros' verse, which might be explained by the impact of Christian poets, especially the troubadours, is the rude language used in the series of invective debate poems between him and another poet, Pinḥas Hacohen. See Angel Sáenz Badillos, "Maimonides y la Poesia," in *Sobre le Vida y Obra de Maimonides, I Congreso Internacional (Córdoba, 1985)*, ed. Jesus Pelaez del Rosal (Córdoba, 1996), 483-95.

71 Yehuda Ratzaby, "Borrowed Motifs from Arabic Poetry and Philosophy in Yehuda Halevy's Liturgy," *Molad* 245/246 (1978): 165-75 [Hebrew]; idem, *From the Treasures of Ancient Verse* (Jerusalem, 1991), 337-91 [Hebrew].

72 On medieval universities and other schools, see Hastings Rashdall, *The Universities of*

new philosophy, grounded in Aristotle, was hostile to poetry, which was deemed useless (see below). Hence, the content of Hebrew *maqāma* was not borrowed from Arabic *maqāma* together with its form, but expressed the real spiritual-cultural aspects of contemporary Jewish life, which in many respects was identical to that of the Christian environment. For that reason, although one of the early Hebrew works in *maqāma*-style, *Sefer Ša'ašu'im* by Yosef ibn Zabāra of Barcelona (ca. 1140-1200), presents a Hebrew adaptation of an Arabic work, *Risālat Da'wa al-Aṭibbā'a* (The Physicians' Dinner Party) by the Christian physician Ibn Buṭlān (Baghdad, d. 1066),[73] the book as whole is a treasury of proverbs, folktales, and medical information (Ibn Zabāra was a doctor) that was intended to educate and to provide scientific and philosophical information.[74] As a whole, the Hebrew rhymed-prose literature, a significant proportion of which was translated into European languages, was a very important channel for the transmission and diffusion of scientific and philosophical materials from the East to the West.[75] A more distinctive liaison between a *maqāma*-style Hebrew work and Christian literature (not religious!) is Ben El'azar's *Sefer Ha-Mešalim*, which betrays the unquestionable impact of European *Romance* literature.[76]

Special mention should be made of *Mešal Ha-Qadmoni* by Yiṣḥaq ibn Sahula (Guadaljara, Castile, 1244-after 1284).[77] Apart from the general influ-

---

Europe in the Middle Ages; new edition ed. P.N. Powicke and A.B. Emden (Oxford, 1936).

73 A fragment of this work was found in the Geniza (Cambridge, T-S Ar.19.8). See Colin Baker, "Medical Examination at the Dinner Table," *Genizah Fragments* (The Newsletter of Cambridge University's Taylor-Schechter Genizah Research Unit at Cambridge University Library, no. 20). See, also, Arie Schippers, "Ibn Zabara's *Book of Delight* (Barcelona, 1170) and the Transmission of Wisdom from East to West," *Frankfurter Judaistische Beiträge*, 26 (1999): 159-60.

74 For Zabāra's role in the transmission of wisdom from East to West, see Schippers, "Ibn Zabara's *Book of Delight*"; Joseph Ben Meir Ibn Zabara, *Sepher Sha'ashuim: A Book of Medieval Lore*, ed. Israel Davidson (New York, 1914); Judith Dishon, *The Book of Delight Composed by Joseph ben Meir Zabara* (Jerusalem, 1985) [Hebrew].

75 Schirmann and Fleischer, *Poetry in Christian Spain*, 330-65.

76 Haim Schirmann, "Les contes rimés de Jacob ben Eléazar de Tolěde," in *Études d'orientalisme dédiées à la memoire de Levi-Provençal* (Paris 1962), I, 285-97; Raymond Scheindlin, "Love Tales of Ya'aqov ben El'azar: Between Arabic Literature and Romance," *Proceedings of the 11th World Congress of Judaic Studies*, 3 (Jerusalem, 1994), 16-20 [Hebrew]; Yona David's Introduction to *The Love Stories of Jacob Ben Eleazar (1170 -1233?)* (Tel Aviv, 1993).

77 For a scholarly edition with an English translation and a comprehensive introduction by Raphael Loewe, see Isaac Ibn Sahula, *Meshal Haqadmoni: Fables from the Distant Past*. A parallel Hebrew-English Text. ed. and trans. Raphael Loewe. 2 vols. (Oxford, 2004).

ence of Christian fables literature on his work, this influence is clearly seen in the illustrations integrated by the author himself into the fables, to which he refers in his Introduction:[78]

> Likewise, methinks, the pictures which conjoint I place with texts they illustrate, should point the moral, and retain the interest of children, while for those that are oppressed by cares, providing light relief through art; thus peradventure they shall find their heart drawn to essentials of my goad, and lay aside their Homer, and will put away what heretics and what free-thinkers say.

Ibn Sahula, then, uses literary and other cultural sources of Christian provenance, but he did it implicitly to remove his coreligionists from Christian influence. That was the kind of compromise that Saadia implemented when he used the Arabic language and Muslim sources to present Jewish tradition.[79]

The affinity of Hebrew belles-lettres—although not necessarily only in Spain, but in France and England as well—to European literature in Western Europe is proved by works like *King Artus*, a Hebrew translation of Arthurian *Romance* that was produced from the Italian by an anonymous Italian Jew in 1279.[80] The witty and juicy love stories that comprise an essential component of Hebrew *maqāma* literature much more than in Arabic *maqāma* probably originated in the fabliaux literature that flourished in France in the thirteenth century, some of which had been incorporated into *Le Roman de Renart* and Chaucer's *Canterbury Tales*.[81] On the other hand, we find in the famous *Libro de Buen Amor* by Juan Ruiz (1283-1350) some parallels to Hebrew *maqamas* of the twelfth and thirteenth centuries.[82] However, there was no original Jewish work of this kind during the time when Jews lived in Spain. We know of several Spanish playwrights in the fifteenth century who were born to Christian parents but were of Jewish origin.[83] The best known of them is Fernando de Rojas (1470-1541), who penned (in Spanish) *The Tragi-Comedy of Calisto and Melibea*, better known as *La Celestina* (first printed in Burgos 1499 or Toledo 1500) after the name of its main character. This play of lust, greed, deception, and the

78 Ibid., I, pp. 14–16; for an in-depth discussion of the illustrations from the cultural aspect, see Ayelet Oettinger, "The Relation between the Literal Art and the Visual Art in Yitzḥaq ibn Sahūla's *Mešal Ha-Qadmoni*," *Dappim* 13 (2003): 229–56.

79 Yosef Tobi, *Proximity and Distance*, 65–175.

80 See Curt Leviant, *King Artus: A Hebrew Arthurian Romance of 1279* (New York, 1969).

81 On the *Fabliaux*, see Holly A. Crocker, ed., *Comic Provocations: Exposing the Corpus of Old French Fabliaux* (New York, 2006).

82 Maria Rosa Lida de Malkiel, *Two Spanish Masterpieces:* The Book of good love, and The Celestina (Urbana. Ill., 1961) 21–24, 31–32, 49.

83 Diaz Esteban, "The Spanish Literary Work of the Jews," 358–60.

perversion of innocence in fifteenth-century Spain imbibes from late-West European-medieval literature.[84] We may conclude at this point with the words of F. Diaz Esteban (translated from Hebrew): "The contribution of the Jews and the conversos to the Spanish literature is enormous, and in some cases even crucial."[85]

It seems that the relationship between Spanish literature and Hebrew literature in Spain did not cease with the expulsion of the Jews in 1492/6. We find that a very interesting paragraph about harmful foods in Cervantes' (1547-1616) *Don Quixote* has a parallel in Zabāra's *Sefer Ša'ašu'im*.[86] We also know that some Indian and Arabic *maqama*-like works found their way into European languages through their Hebrew translation. Thus, for example, the Indian work *Kalila wa-Dimna* was translated around 1260 into Latin from the Hebrew version by the converted Jew John of Capua (Southern Italy). This Latin translation was used for producing the European versions.[87] Another book whose Hebrew version is thought to serve as the basis for European translations is *Misle Sendebar*.[88]

However, original works written by Jews in Spanish were quite limited. One of them is *Proverbios morales* by Sem Ṭov ibn Arduṭi'el, who is also known by his Spanish name, Santob de Carrión.[89] We should bear in mind that this unique work, in terms of its literary genre and contents, which is beyond our discussion here, was not intended for the Jewish public, as it was written in Latin characters and addressed and dedicated to the Christian king of Castile.[90] This would not have been the case during the Muslim peri-

[84] For an English translation, see Fernando de Rojas, *The Celestina: A Fifteenth-Century Novel in Dialogue*; trans. Lesley Byrd Simpson (Berkeley, 2006). A sixteenth-century Italian Jew, Samuel Sarfati, wrote an introductory poem to his now-lost Hebrew translation of *Celestina*. See D.W. McPheeters, "Una Traducción Hebrea de *La Celestina* en el Siglo XVI," in *Homenaje a Antonio Rodríguez-Moñino: Estudios de Erudición que le Ofrecen sus Amigos o Discípulos Hispanistas Norteamericanos*, I (Madrid, 1966) 399–411. On *Celestina* and Hebrew Spanish literature, see Lida de Malkiel, *Two Spanish Masterpieces*.

[85] Diaz Esteban, "The Spanish Literary Work of the Jews," 364.

[86] Haim Schirmann, "The Harmful Foods: A Curious Parallel between Cervantes and Joseph Zabara," in *Romanica et Occidentalia: Etudes dédiées à la mèmoire de Hiram Peri (Pflaum)* (Jerusalem, 1963), 140–42.

[87] Joseph Derenbourg, *Johannis de Capua Directorium Vitae Humanae: version latine de livre de Kalilah et Dimnah* (Paris, 1887).

[88] Morris Epstein, *Tales of Sendebar: An edition and translation of the Hebrew version of the seven sages based on unpublished manuscripts* (Philadelphia, 1967).

[89] Sanford Shephard, *Shem Tov: His World and His Words* (Miami, Fl., 1978); Theodore Anthony Perry, *The Moral Proverbs of Santob de Carrión: Jewish Wisdom in Christian Spain* (Princeton, N.J., 1987); Diaz Esteban, "The Spanish Literary Work of the Jews," 346–48.

[90] Perry, *Moral Proverbs*, 4, 58.

od, when Jewish writers penned their literary essays in Arabic, though in Hebrew characters, since they were addressed to the Jewish public. In contrast, then, to Américo Castro's conclusion, it seems that *Proverbios morales* is not a unique testimony to the coexistence of two religions and ethnic communities, "but rather an interchange of different points of view."[91]

Another work, this one in Hebrew, that is closely connected to medieval Western European literature is *Amadis de Gaula*, which was translated by Ya'aqov di Algaba, a physician to the Ottoman sultan who probably had been exiled from Spain in 1492 and had brought the manuscript from that country (the Hebrew work first printed in Constantinople in 1541). The book, as its title implies, belongs to the "knights' literature." Although it is not an original work but a translation of a famous medieval *romance* in Castilian (first printed in 1519?) by Garcia Ordoflez de Montalvo (d. 1504), and done already within the framework of the Jewish community in Constantinople, it had been part of the Jewish literary legacy in Spain before the Expulsion in 1492[92] in the same way that Ladino love songs known as *romances* and *romaceros* originated in the Iberian Peninsula[93] and were maintained in the folklore of the Sephardic Diaspora in the Balkans and the East until the twenty-first century.[94] Most likely, *Amadis de Gaula* was not the only Spanish *romance* work read by Jews; for example, the famous Spanish play *Tragedia Josefina* by Michael de Carvajal (possibly a Jewish Marrano) was originally printed in Hebrew characters.[95]

Criticism of Poetry in the Maqāma

One may not be surprised to learn that Maimonides, the twelfth-century jurist, physician, and philosopher (1138-1204), disliked poetry for religious as well as for philosophical reasons.[96] But to reveal that the literary genre of

---

91 Américo Castro, *The Structure of Spanish History*; trans. Edmund King (Princeton, N.J., 1954), 551-88; Perry, *Moral Proverbs*, 4.

92 For a new edition of the Hebrew with an introduction by Zvi Malachi, see *Amadis de Gaula: Hebrew Translation by the Physician Jacob di Algaba* (Tel Aviv, 1991); for an English translation, see Zvi Malachi, *The Loving Knight: The Romance Amadis de Gaula and Its Hebrew Adaptation*, Turkey, c.1541. trans. Phyllis Hackett (Lod, Israel, 1982).

93 Diaz Esteban, "The Spanish Literary Work of the Jews," 343-58.

94 See, for example, Moshe Attias, *Romancero sefaradi; romanzos y cantes populares en judeo-espanol, tr. al hebreo, con una introduccio´n, anotaciones y un glosario* (Jerusalem, 1972) [Hebrew]; William Samelson, "Romances and Songs of the Sephardim," in *The Sephardi Heritage: Essays on the History and Cultural Contribution of the Jews of Spain and Portugal*, I, ed. R.D. Barnett (London, 1971), 527-51. See, also, Anglès, " La musique," 63-64.

95 A fragment of this publication was preserved in the Geniza (Malachi, *Amadis de Gaula*, 51).

96 Sáenz-Badillos, "Maimonides y la Poesia"; Schirmann and Fleischer, *Poetry in Chris-*

the *maqāma* was the contemporary means of attacking poetry and of lauding philosophy is really astonishing. The second chapter of Jacob ben El'azar's *maqāmas* is a public contest between prose, representing philosophy, and poetry. After having to struggle for its right to exist, to apologize, and to repel all the severe attacks on it, poetry eventually emerges as the winner. Nevertheless, the only argument poetry employs to justify its existence is not something that arises from itself as a literary work but the service it renders philosophy and science in the ease it affords for memorizing informative or ethical texts.[97] Another *maqāma*-style work is Šem Tov ibn Falaqera's mid-thirteenth-century *Ha-Mevaqqeš* (The Seeker). In this work, the protagonist, a young man who goes from one professional to another to find the right pursuit to engage in, is disappointed by all of them, save the philosopher, with whom he eventually finds repose. It is not unintentional that the most attacked and criticized occupation is that of the poet. And the vehicle for all this is a poetical work,[98] a fictitious adventure reminiscent of the real adventures of John of Salisbury (ca. 1115-1180), one of the most prominent figures of the twelfth-century Renaissance, that he himself related about his wandering from one mentor to another in northern France from 1136 to 1148.[99] Actually, the entire frame story of students and curious individuals wandering from one place to another to acquire wisdom is typical of contemporary Western Europe. This is the idea behind *terra aliena* (exile), which was the prerequisite for advanced study or, as John of Salisbury counted it, one of "the keys of the wisdom."[100] But what is no less important is John's judgment on poetry, which is not far from that of Maimonides' disciples, as all of whom came from the field of philosophy. According to John in his *Metalogicon*, "poetry belongs to grammar, which is the mother and source of its study." It is the cradle of philosophy, but this

tian Spain, 279–86; Yosef Tobi, "Maimonides' Attitude towards Secular Poetry, Secular Arab and Hebrew Literature, Liturgical Poetry, and towards Their Cultural Environment," in his *Between Hebrew and Arabic Poetry*, 423–66.

97 Ben El'azar 1993, 23–27; Schirmann and Fleischer, *Poetry in Christian Spain*, 252–53.

98 Tobi, "The Criticism of R. ŠemṬov."

99 Christopher Brooke, *The Twelfth Century Renaissance* (Norwich, 1969), 60. On the "international" character of twelfth-century universities and the wandering of students, as well as teachers, from one school to another all over Western Europe, see Helen Waddell, *The Wandering Scholars* (London, 1944); Haskins, *The Renaissance*, 368–96.

100 Compare Theresa Gross-Diaz, *The Psalms Commentary of Gilbert of Potiers: From* Lection Divina *to* Lecture Room (Leiden, 1966), p. 5: "Having exhausted the fund of wisdom in their local schools, the would-be great scholars of the twelfth century sought out the rare master whose reputation had reached across geographic and political boundaries."

may mean that it is the easiest study to undertake before the pupil can approach more difficult texts.[101]

Maqāma as Satire in the Style of European Literature

The most valuable aspect of the *maqāma* is its satirical distinctiveness.[102] In this regard, and in contrast to secular poetry, the *maqāma*s might serve as a true mirror of twelfth to fourteenth-century Spanish Jewish society. Secular Hebrew poems written in accordance with Arabic poetics do not reflect relevant Jewish life in Spain; they are more of a literary creation somehow disconnected from reality.[103] Thus, for example, the Arabic genre of love poems adopted by Hebrew poets in Spain mainly assumed the quality of an allegory for different subjects.[104] The luxury of having secular poetry mirroring hedonistic society was impossible to retain in the generations after the disappointment with Arabic poetry following the Muwaṣṣidī conquest and in the light of the philosophical perception of the twelfth century. Furthermore, the positive attitude toward secular poetry, so admired and cherished by all previous Muslim regimes in Spain, had greatly waned during the Muwaṣṣidī regime (1145-1223).[105] In addition, the *maqāma* served, in addition to its educational aspect, as satire for the betterment of Jewish society. It is not unreasonable to suggest that Latin satires such as those of Persius and Lucan, and especially those of Juvenal, were in the mind of Hebrew *maqāma* writers.

As is known, the Church did not reject Juvenal as it did other Latin works. After the revival of learning under Charlemagne, Juvenal became popular and was one of the most widely read Latin authors in medieval and Renaissance schools.[106] His *Satires* survived, then, in many manuscript cop-

---

101 On John's views on grammar and poetry, see chapters 17–25 in his *Metalogicon*, Book I, (John of Salisbury, *The Metalogicon: A Twelfth-Century Defense of the Verbal and Logical Arts of the Trivium*. trans. with an introduction and notes by Daniel D. McGarry [Berkeley, Calif., 1962], 51–72).

102 On the satirical qualities of the Hebrew *maqāma*, see Dan Almagor, "Social Satire in the Hebrew *Maqāma* Literature," *Alei Siyah* 7/8 (1980): 132–58 [Hebrew]; Oettinger, "The Aspect of the Satirical Modus."

103 Ephraim Hazan, "Were There Really Court Poets and Court Poetry?" *Criticism and Interpretation* 39 (2007) [Hebrew]: 9–15; Yosef Tobi, "Secular Hebrew Poetry in Spain as Courtly Poetry: Is It Indeed?" in his *Between Hebrew and Arabic Poetry*, 3–24.

104 Tobi, "Love in Hebrew Secular Poetry."

105 For an English translation of Juvenal's *Satires*, see Juvenal, *Thirteen Satires*, with a commentary by J.E.B. Mayor and a new introduction and bibliography by John Henderson (Bristol, 2003); for a Hebrew translation with a useful introduction and notes, see Decimus Iunius Iuvenalis, *Saturae*, trans. Rachel Birnbaum (Jerusalem, 2003) [Hebrew].

106 On Juvenal's presence in West European culture and literature in the Middle Ages,

ies. To the medieval reader, Juvenal was primarily an ethical writer, whose moral indignation was respected and admired. Thus, Alexander Neckam (1157-1217), monk of St. Albans and abbot of Cirencester, England, advises the student to keep "the moral precepts of Juvenal in his innermost heart."[107] Chaucer, among others, refers to Juvenal, whose harsh criticism of the Roman Empire helped ensure the survival of his work throughout the Middle Ages, as Christian scholars were pleased to find flaws in the daunting pagan legacy of the Romans. From the beast fables, fabliaux, and Chaucerian caricatures, the satirical tradition flourished from the Middle Ages to the Renaissance, culminating in the golden age of satire in the late seventeenth and early eighteenth centuries.[108]

One of the main elements of Hebrew *maqāmas* or *maqāma*-style works, from Šelomo ibn Ṣaqbel's *Ne'um Asher Ben Yehuda* (second quarter of the twelfth century) to Jacob Frances' *Ma'ase Ševu'el ve-Na'ama* (Mantuba, Italy, 1615-1667), is the almost permanent presence of the character of the woman, usually in the frame of a discussion of pro and con and heavily colored with misogyny and misogamy. This literature has been widely discussed by modern scholars, who have also sought its probable ideological sources.[109] There is no question that the social status of the woman in both Jewish and Muslim societies, whether in the East or in Spain and Western Europe, was not high. However, that status reflected no ideological-philosophical significance. Thus, Arabic poetry and the Hebrew poetry that came

especially in the twelfth and thirteenth centuries, see Katharina M. Wilson and Elizabeth M. Makowski, *Wykked Wyves and the Woes of Marriage: Misogamous Literature from Juvenal to Chaucer* (Albany, N.Y., 1990), according to the Index, 202–203, "Juvenal"; Wolf and Rosenstein, *The Poetry of Cercamon*, 11.

107 Haskins, *The Renaissance*, 109.

108 For medieval commentaries on Juvenal's satires and other Classical Greek and Latin works, see Robert E. Kaske, *Medieval Christian Literary Imagery: A guide to interpretation*, in collaboration with Arthur Groos and Michael W. Twomey (Toronto, 1988), 116–31.

109 Israel Davidson, *Parody in Jewish Literature* (New York, 1966), 7–15; Davidson in Ibn Zabāra, *Sepher Sha'ashuim*, xlix–lix; Judith Dishon, "The Sources of Yehuda ibn Shabbetay's *Minḥat Yehuda* and Its Impact on Yehuda Alharizi's *The Wedding Maqāma*," *Otzar Yehude Sefarad* 11/12 (1970): 57–73 [Hebrew]; Dishon, *The Book of Delight*, 53–92, 195–96; Norman Roth, "The 'Wiles of Women' Motif in the Medieval Hebrew Literature of Spain," *Hebrew Annual Review* 2 (1978): 145–65; T. Fishman, "A Medieval Parody of Misogyny: Judah ibn Shabbetai's 'Minhat Yehudah Sone Hanashim'," *Prooftexts* 8 (1988): 89–111; Matti Huss, "Minḥat Yehuda, 'Ezrat Ha-Našim *and* 'En Mišpaṭ: Critical Editions with an Introduction, Sources, and Commentaries" (Ph.D. diss., The Hebrew University, Jerusalem, 1992); Schirmann and Fleischer, *Poetry in Christian Spain*, 129–44; Oettinger, "The Aspect of the Satirical Modus," 80–107; Tova Rosen, *Unveiling Eve: Reading Gender in Medieval Hebrew Literature* (Philadelphia, 2003), 103–23.

in its track do not betray any special anti-feminist inclinations even if one of the anthologies of Arabic poetry presents a small collection of verses in denouncement of women[110] or there is an extremely negative and crude depiction of a woman in al-Ḥarīrī's forty-first *maqāma (al-tabrīziyya)*. That *maqāma* was adapted by Alḥarizi in his fortieth *maḥberet*, but he enhanced the ugly mutual defamations of the husband and his wife to the level of a fundamental dialogue regarding a philosophical issue: Who is more important for the continuance of the World: Man or Woman?

The negative manner of dealing with women, however, is an innovation that we cannot trace in Arabic tradition or Muslim culture. It was precisely "Western" culture that advocated this tendency, first by the Classical Greek writers such as Simonides (556-468 BCE), who wrote a poem in defamation of women; then in Plato's contrasting the image of the woman for matter versus the image of man for spirit; followed by medieval Christianity, which adapted this approach and associated women with deceptions and trickeries connected with sexual deeds;[111] the escalating disparaging discussion of women derived from twelfth-century Christian reality, the increasing literature about Maria, on the one hand, and the almost pornographic poems about sensual love by the Goliards.[112] It is exactly here that Juvenal's *Satires*, especially *Satire* 6, fit in with his anti-feminist line, which is conspicuously misogamous. He warns against sexual relationships, because women's resourcefulness and resilience give them an unbeatable advantage in their encounters with men.[113] Juvenal's influence was strongly felt in the third book of the famous work *De Amore* by Andreas Capellanus, as well as on other High Middle Ages writers, such as Walter of Chantillon and Bernard of Cluny, who wrote about the vices of contemporary women.[114] It is only against the background of that literary reality, and not that of Arabic poetry and *maqāmas*, that we can explain the appearance of anti-feminist Hebrew works, starting with Zabāra's *Sefer Ša'ašu'im* in the second half of

110 Abū Tammām, *Dīwān al-ḥamāsa bi-ru'yat abī manṣūr al-jūlīqī* (Beirut, 1997), 396–403.

111 Gadi Elgazi, "Abelar, Aloise and Astrolab: A Footnote on the Babies' Cry and the Learnts' Tranquility," in *Women, Old Men and Small Children: An Anthology in Honor of Shulamit Shaḥar*, eds. Miri Eliav-Paldon and Yitzhak Ḥen (Jerusalem, 2001), 85–98 [Hebrew].

112 George F. Whicher, *The Goliard Poets: Medieval Latin Songs and Satires*, with verse translations (New York, 1965).

113 Wilson and Makowski, *Wykked Wyves*. Horace shared the same negative approach toward women and marriage; see Warren S. Smith, "Advice on Sex by the Self-Defeating Satirists: Horace *Sermones* 1.2, Juvenal *Satire* 6, and Roman Satiric Writings," in *Satiric Advice on Women and Marriage: From Plautus to Chaucer*, ed. Warren S. Smith (Ann Arbor, Mich., 2005), 111–28.

114 P. G. Walsh, "Antifeminism in High Middle Ages," in Smith, *Satiric Advice*, 222–42.

the twelfth century[115] and then–more artfully–Yehuda ibn Šabbetay's *Minḥat Yehuda*. The latter, an anti-feminist novella perhaps influenced by the anti-Catholic movement of the Cathars (Albigensians), which flourished in Provence in the thirteenth century, even disapproves, as a literary motif, of the holy, traditional Jewish institution of marriage.[116] Finally, it should be pointed out that from the twelfth to the fifteenth century, an anti-feminist satirical literature flourished in Christian Provence as noted by Alfred Jeanroy:

> S'il est un thème agaçant par l'absurde parti pris qui s'y étale, c'est la satire contre les femmes. Ce theme qui, du xiie au xve siècle, a défrayé une si abondante et monotone littérature en latin et en françaíse, a été noins souvent, et parfois plus heureusement, traité par les toubadours.[117]

Another typical feature of the Hebrew *maqāmah*, criticism of the hypocritical religious and temporal leaderships, seems to be borrowed as well from Christian literature, although the character of the shameless, greedy, and lustful clergyman in the mosque (*qāḍī*, *khaṭīb*) appears in Arabic *maqāmas* and is reflected in the character of the synagogue *ḥazzan* (cantor or beadle) in the Hebrew *maḥbarot*.[118] However, the social range of the figures criticized in Alḥarīzi's *Taḥkemoni* is much wider than in the Arabic *maqāmas*, just as it is in at least four *maqāma*-style Hebrew works from Christian Western Europe: Binyamin min Ha'anavim's *Massa Gue Hizzayon* (Italy, thirteenth century); the eighth chapter of Ben El'azar's *Sefer Ha-Mešalim*; Falaqera's *Ha-Mevaqqeš*; and Kalonymos' *Even Boḥan*.[119] These works follow West European literature in criticizing the different social strata and professionals.[120]

Juvenal's *Satires* may be compared with the *maqāma* in regard to another point, the exaggerated treatment of food. Juvenal's criticism in this regard

---

115 Judith Dishon, "Was Joseph ibn Zabara a Misogynist?" *Bitzaron* 7 (27/28) (1985):46-52 [Hebrew].

116 In contrast to the current view of most scholars of medieval Hebrew literature, it was recently claimed that Ibn Sabbetay adopted the anti-feminist and anti-marriage views of the Cathars not just as a literary motif (Denis Sobolev, unpublished paper).

117 Alfred Jeanroy, *La Poésie lyrique des Troubadours* (Toulouse-Paris, 1934), II, 192; cf. C.C. Fauriel, *History of Provneçal Poetry* (New York, 1860), 462-96.

118 On the character of the *ḥazzan* in Hebrew *maḥbarot*, see Judith Dishon, "The Cantor in the Spanish Hebrew *Maqāma*," *Sinai* 74 (1974): 242-51; Dishon, *The Book of Delight*, 174-79; Oettinger, "The Aspect of the Satirical Modus," 54-57.

119 For *Massa Gue Ḥizzayon*, see David's Introduction to Binyamin 1967; for the eighth chapter of *Sefer Ha-Mešalim*, see Schirmann, Hypocrite Old Man"; for *Ha-Mevaqqeš*–Tobi, "The Criticism of R. ŠemṬov"; and for *Even Boḥan*, see Schirmann and Fleischer, *Poetry in Christian Spain*, 529-40.

120 For an in-depth discussion of that issue, mainly based on Alḥarīzi's *Taḥkemoni*, see Oettinger, "The Aspect of the Satirical Modus," 5-15.

was part of his censure of Roman society of his time; this is opposed to classical Arabic poetry, as well as Andalusian Hebrew poetry, which is devoid of this irreverent topic. The boasting of being rich and having no restrictions on preparing an elaborate meal consisting of innumerable courses is well documented in al-Hamadhānī's tenth *maqāma (al-maḍiriyya)*,[121] which Alḥarīzī imitated in his thirty-fourth *maḥberet,* about the merchant who wanted to impress his guests with his wealth and the variety of his enormous gastronomic abilities.[122] Gluttony was a frequent subject in Hebrew *maqāmas*; this did not reflect a simple literary influence of Arabic literature, but emerged in the framework of the general trend in the Christian West, of which the Jews of Spain were part, to learn more about science from Arabic books. Thus, for instance, Ibn Zabāra, a professional doctor, devotes significant sections of his *Sefer Ša'ašu'im* to the subject of food and the preferred and undesirable habits of eating. It should be noted that *Taqwīm al-Ṣiḥḥa*, a medical essay by the aforementioned Ibn Buṭlān, was translated at that time into Latin for the benefit of students of medicine in Christian Europe.[123]

In point of fact, the motif of the host who wants to impress his guests with his aggrandizement and the detailed depiction of the meal's many courses and of the host's house were highlighted in "Trimalchio's Dinner," the only long-preserved passage of the *Satyricon*, the satirical work of the Roman writer Petronius (c. 27-c. 66 CE). This story, which was known to John of Salisbury,[124] depicts the dinner party given by a vulgar freedman in a small Italian town that was attended by the work's three protagonists and an assortment of low-born but successful men. The story is delightful not only for its picture of vulgar ostentation and the ignorant aping of good society but also for its keen psychology, with the refined but decadent and worthless protagonists played off against the boorish but vital and human local citizens.[125] Because of its scandalous earthiness, including the main characters' homosexual affection for one another, this work was copied and circulated only hand to hand throughout the Middle Ages and remained

121 For a comprehensive discussion of that *maqāma*, see Monroe, *The Shi'ūbiyya in al-Andalus*.

122 See Judah Alharizi, *The Book of Tahkemoni: Jewish Tales from Medieval Spain*; translated, explicated, and annotated by David S. Segal (Oxford, 2001), 276–78, 578–84.

123 The Latin translation, *Tacuinum Sanitatis in Medicina,* was first printed in Strasburg in 1531.

124 Brooke, *The Twelfth Century Renaissance*, 61: "He [John of Salisbury] was the only scholar between the fall of Rome and Petrarch to show any knowledge of Petronius' *Dream of Trimalchio*."

125 See T. Wade Richardson, "Problems in the Text-History of Petronius in Antiquity and the Middle Ages," *The American Journal of Philology*, 96 (1975): 290–305. It is generally believed that *Satyricon* was the first recognizable novel in the West and that the original manuscript may have been 400,000 words long, stretched across 20 volumes.

unprinted until 1664. However, we know that "Trimalchio's Dinner" was not the only section of Petronius' *Satyricon* that was circulated in medieval Hebrew works. A story cited by John of Salisbury, "The Widow of Ephesus" (*Satyricon* 110.6-113.4),[126] is alluded to in the Babylonian Talmud (Tract. *Qiddušin*, fol. 80b) and was adapted by three Jewish writers in the Middle Ages: (1) R. Ḥanan'el ben Ḥuši'el (Qayrawān, c. 965-1055) in his commentary on Tractate *Qiddušin* 81b; (2) Ibn Zabāra in *Sefer Ša'ašu'im*; (3) Berekhia Ha-Neqdan in *Mišle Šu'alim*.[127] There is no doubt that the Jewish authors had access to this story through Eastern sources, as well as through Western Christian sources.

A short comment should be added here concerning the Kabbalistic school of Judaism. It first flourished on Christian soil, influenced by Christian wisdom and beliefs, in the far north of Spain during the thirteenth century.[128] Thus, Ramon Lull (ca. 1232-1315), the central figure of Spanish mysticism, had close relations with Jewish philosophers, from whom he learned the fundamentals of Kabbalah.[129] However, from there it spread to all Jewish communities.

Conclusion

Despite Judaism's considerable achievements under continuous contact with Latin Christianity in the kingdoms of Castile, Aragon, Navarra, and Portugal, especially during the twelfth-century Renaissance,[130] and in spite of the important role played by Jews in the long process of transplanting Greek and Arabic scholarship and culture into Christendom and Western

126 Wilson-Makowski, *Wykked Wyves*, 85; for a general study of the "Widow of Ephesus," see Thomas Wray Milnes, *The Widow of Ephesus: The Delectable Tale from the Satyricon of Titus Petronius Arbiter Done into a Play with Designs by Albert Wainwright* (Leeds, 1925).

127 Davidson in his Introduction to Ibn Zabāra, *Sepher Sha'ashuim*, pp. lii–liii; Dishon, *The Book of Delight*, 73–77; "The Aspect of the Satirical Modus," 125–26. A version of that story existed in Tunisian folk literature at least until the end of the nineteenth century, when it was recorded by Hans Stumme, *Tunisische Märchen und Gedichte. Band I: Transcribierte Texte nebst Einleitung* (Leipzig, 1893), 50–51 [Arabic]; 78–80 [German].

128 On Christian influences in the Zohar, see Yehuda Liebes, "Christian Influences in the Zohar," *Immanuel* 17 (1983/4): 43-67.

129 Moshe Idel, "Ramon Lull and Ecstatic Kabbalah: A Preliminary Observation," *Journal of the Warburg Courtould Institute*, 51 (1988): 170–75; Harvey J. Hames, *The Art of Conversion: Christianity and Kabbalah in the Thirteenth Century* (Leiden, 2000).

130 For a stimulating study on historical consciousness and the challenging Christian culture among the Jews of Spain and Provence, see Ram Ben-Shalom, *In Front of Christian Culture: Historic Consciousness and Past Images among the Jews of Spain and Provence in the Middle Ages* (Jerusalem, 2007) [Hebrew]; see, also, Bernard Septimus, *Hispano-Jewish Culture in Transition (*Cambridge, Mass., 1982).

languages, the Golden Age of Jewish scholarship was undoubtedly the era in which Jews maintained a special relationship with Arabic-Muslim culture. Almost none of the Jewish scholars of the second epoch—except for Hisday Crescas (c. 1340-1410), who probably influenced such later thinkers as Spinoza, Newton, and Kant[131]—was comparable with the outstanding polymaths of the first. No Hebrew poet or prose writer on Christian soil could rise to the highest stages of literature as did Hebrew poets on Muslim soil; indeed, these poets challenged the marvelous Arabic poetry of Spain. The greatest of the Jewish intellectuals whose roots lie firmly in the Jewish arena of Muslim Spain was indisputably Maimonides, who, like the Muslim Averros (Ibn Rusd, 1126-1198) and the Christians—the Italian Thomas Aquinas (1227-1274), the Englishman Roger Bacon (1214-1294), and Siger de Brabant (c.1240-1280) from the southern Low Countries—tried hard to reconcile the science of Aristotle with his faith and to practice religion illuminated with reason or intelligence elucidated by belief.[132]

Another significant disparity between Jewish culture in Muslim Spain and in Christian Spain concerns language. Jewish intellectuals in the first epoch were completely immersed in the general cultural milieu, using Judeo-Arabic for all fields of literary creation and Hebrew, almost exclusively, for their verse. In contrast, the Jewish scholars of Christian Spain penned their literary works for the most part only in Hebrew—poetry and rhymed prose, as well as scholarly writings. As a result, the affinity of their spiritual production to Christian literature was much more limited in comparison to that of writers in the Muslim area. Indeed, Jewish literature in Christian Spain was much more Judaic, more limited in terms of openness toward the surrounding culture and society and dealing more with genuine traditional, religious subjects. It is not for nothing, then, that the term "Golden Age" refers to the "Muslim" epoch, not the "Christian."

A highly significant difference between the two periods of Jewish existence in Spain is the main direction of mutual cultural transference, from the Jewish communities to the surrounding majority inhabitants and vice-versa. In the Muslim period, cultural values flowed almost totally from the Muslims to the Jews, who adjusted themselves to Muslim culture, first of all by

---

131 See Harry Austryn Wolfson, *Crescas' Critique of Aristotle* (Cambridge, Mass., 1929).

132 See, for instance, Jeremiah Hackett, *Roger Bacon and the Sciences: Commemorative Essays* (Leiden, 1997) (Bacon); Colloque de Cordoue, *Ibn Rochd, Maïmonide, saint Thomas ou la filiation entre foi et raison: le colloque de Cordoue, 8, 9 et 10 mai 1992* (Castelnau-le-Lez, France, 1994) (Ibn Rusd, Thomas Aquinas); David B. Burrell, "Aquinas and Islamic and Jewish Thinkers," in *The Cambridge Companion to Aquinas*, eds. Norman Kretzmann and Eleonore Stump (Cambridge, 1993), 61-84; Pierre Mandonnet, *Siger de Brabant et l'averroïsme latin au XIIIe siècle: étude critique et documents inédits* (Genève, 1976) (Siger de Brabant). On Thomas Aquinas in medieval Jewish literature, see Adolf Jellinek, *Thomas von Aquino in der jüdischen Literature* (Leipzig, 1853).

using its language, Arabic, although in Hebrew characters. As a result, Jews could be—and indeed were—wholly exposed to Arabic writings and absorbed whatever they liked of them. On the other hand, Muslim scholars could not read Hebrew or Hebrew characters, a crucial cultural flaw that made Jewish writings entirely inaccessible to them except with the assistance of Jewish scholars.[133] This was not the case with the Jews in the Christian kingdoms. Latin, the main language of written Christian scholarship, was not part of the erudition of Jewish scholars, save for a very limited number of them, who then had access to Latin literature. Therefore, Jews were not the *translators* of scientific material from Arabic, Judeo-Arabic, or Hebrew to Latin, but functioned as *collaborators* of the Christian scholars who mastered Latin. In addition, and in extreme contradiction to Muslim scholars, there were schools of Christian Hebraists who studied Hebrew, and even Aramaic, in order to better understand the Jewish Bible in its original Hebrew rendition. Not a few Hebrew-Latin or Hebrew-other language dictionaries, based *inter alia* on genuine rabbinical sources, such as Rashi's commentary to the Bible and the Talmud, were prepared to that end, even in pre-expulsion England.[134] There were, in addition, Jewish scholars who converted to Christianity and enriched Christian scholarship with Hebrew and Jewish wisdom. We also know that Jewish and Christian scholars exchanged books.[135] We may conclude, then, that the main direction of the cultural stream and the transferring of erudition flowed from the Jewish circles to the Christian.

---

133 See n. 50 above.

134 For a very useful and informative study on this subject, see Judith Olszowy-Schlanger, "A School of Christian Hebraists in Thirteenth-Century England: A Unique Hebrew-Latin-French and English Dictionary and Its Sources," *European Journal of Jewish Studies* 1 (2008): 249–77. The Jews were expelled from England in 1291. On the use of Christian scholars of Jewish Hebrew classical sources, although for anti-Jewish polemical purposes, see Ḥen Merḥavia, *The Talmud*; idem, "*Pugio Fidei*: Index of Its Citations," in *Exile after Exile: Studies in the History of the Jewish People, Presented to Prof. Haim Beinart in his Seventieth Year*, eds. Aharon Mirsky, Abraham Grossmann and Joseph Kaplan (Jerusalem, 1988)), 203–34 [Hebrew].

135 Colette Sirat, "Notes sur la circulation des livres entre Juifs et Chrétiens au Moyen Âge," in *Du copiste au collectionneur. Mélanges d'histoire des textes et des bibliothèques en l'honneur d'André Vernet* (=*Bibliologia* 18), eds. Donatella Nebbiai-Dalla Guarda and Jean-François Genest (Brepols, 1999), dir., 383–403.

Studies and Texts in Jewish History and Culture

The Joseph and Rebecca Meyerhoff Center for Jewish Studies
University of Maryland

General Editor: Bernard D. Cooperman

Vol. 1. *Religion and Politics in the Ancient Near East*
edited by Adele Berlin
ISBN: 1883053242; vi + 150 pp.; 1996.

Vol. 2. *Freedom and Moral Responsibility: General and Jewish Perspectives*
edited by Charles H. Manekin and Menachem M. Kellner.
ISBN: 1883053293; viii + 273 pp.; 1997.

Vol. 3. *Land and Community: Geography in Jewish Studies*
edited by Harold Brodsky
ISBN: 1883053307; x + 418 pp.; 1997.

Vol. 4. *A Life in Jewish Education: Essays in Honor of Louis L. Kaplan*
edited by Jack Fruchtman, Jr.
ISBN: 1883053383; 291 pp. 1997.

Vol. 5. *Religious and Ethnic Communities in Later Roman Palestine*
edited by Hayim Lapin
ISBN: 1883053315; xii + 298 pp.; 1998.

Vol. 6. *Hitting Back: An Austrian Jew in the French Résistance*
Dolly Steindling
ISBN: 1883053536; xxvi + 239 pp.; 2000.

Vol. 7. *The Jews of Italy: Memory and Identity*
edited by Barbara Garvin and Bernard D. Cooperman
ISBN: 9781883053369 (hard.); 9781934309162 (soft.); 462 pp.; 2000.

Vol. 8. *The Six-Day War and World Jewry*
edited by Eli Lederhendler
ISBN: 1883053595; x + 340 pp.; 2000.

Vol. 9. *Rememberings: The World of a Russian-Jewish Woman in the Nineteenth Century*
Pauline Wengeroff; translated by Henny Wenkart, edited with afterword by Bernard D. Cooperman
ISBN: 1883053-587 (hard.), ISBN: 1883053617 (soft.); xvi + 306 pp.; 2000.

Vol. 10. *Biblical Translation in Context*
edited by Frederick W. Knobloch
ISBN: 1883053404; xiii + 221 pp.; 2002.

Vol. 11. *Argentina, Israel, and the Jews: Peron, The Eichmann Capture and After*
Raanan Rein
ISBN: 1883053722; xxii + 275 pp.; 2003.

Vol. 12. *Jews, Antiquity, and the Nineteenth-Century Imagination*
edited by Hayim Lapin
ISBN: 1883053781; viii + 157 pp.; 2003.

Vol. 13. *Early Judaism: Religious Worlds of the First Judaic Millennium*
Martin S. Jaffee. ISBN: 9781883053932; x + 277 pp.; 2006.

Vol. 14. *Hebrew, Gender, and Modernity: Critical Responses to Dvora Baron's Fiction*
edited by Sheila E. Jelen and Shachar Pinsker
ISBN: 9781883053956; x + 291 pp.; 2007.

Vol. 15. *Jewish Literature and History: An Interdisciplinary Conversation*
edited by Eliyana R. Adler and Sheila E. Jelen
ISBN: 9781934309131; x + 248 pp.; 2008.

Vol. 16. *Manual of Judeo-Spanish: Language and Culture*
Marie-Christine Varol
ISBN: 9781934309193; 331 pp.; 2008.

Vol. 17. *Philosophers and the Jewish Bible*
edited by Charles H. Manekin and Robert Eisen
ISBN: 9781934309209; 256 pp.; 2008.

Vol. 18. *Issues in the Acquisition and Teaching of Hebrew*
edited by Avital Feuer, Sharon Armon-Lotem, and Bernard Dov Cooperman
ISBN: 9781934309216; 184 pp.; 2009.

Vol. 19. *Pleasant Are Their Names: Jewish Names in the Sephardi Diaspora*
edited by Aaron Demsky
ISBN: 9781934309247; 338 pp.; 2010.

Vol. 20. *Shaping the Middle East: Jews, Christians, and Muslims in an Age of Transition 400–800* C.E.
edited by Kenneth G. Holum and Hayim Lapin
ISBN: 9781934309315; 274 pp.; 2011.

Vol. 21. *Jews and Muslims in the Islamic World*
edited by Dov Cooperman and Zvi Zohar
ISBN: 9781934309322; 274 pp.398; 2013.